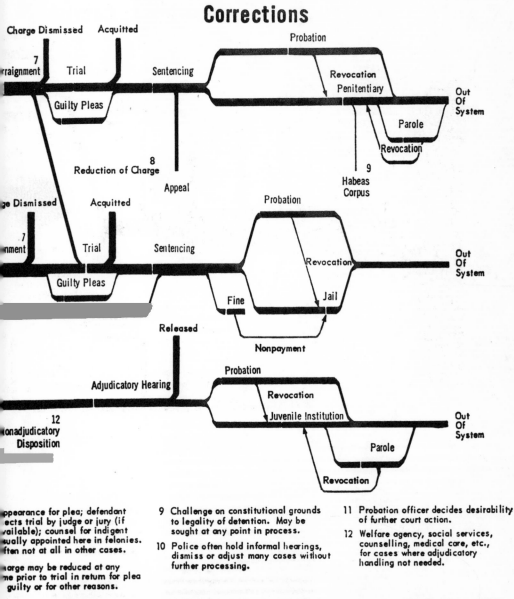

Corrections

Charge Dismissed   Acquitted   Probation

7
rraignment   Trial   Sentencing   Revocation
                                                             Penitentiary   Out
                                                                                 Of
        Guilty Pleas   System

                                                                        Parole

                                                                     Revocation

            8
    Reduction of Charge
                Appeal   9
                                                    Habeas
                                                    Corpus

ge Dismissed   Acquitted   Probation

7
nment   Trial   Sentencing   Revocation   Out
                                                                          Of
        Guilty Pleas   System

                                        Fine   Jail

            Released

                                        Nonpayment

                            Probation

    Adjudicatory Hearing   Revocation

                                Juvenile Institution   Out
12   Of
onadjudicatory   System
Disposition
                                            Parole

                                    Revocation

ppearance for plea; defendant   9 Challenge on constitutional grounds   11 Probation officer decides desirability
ects trial by judge or jury (if   to legality of detention. May be   of further court action.
ailable); counsel for indigent   sought at any point in process.
ually appointed here in felonies.   12 Welfare agency, social services,
ften not at all in other cases.   10 Police often hold informal hearings,   counselling, medical care, etc.,
                                        dismiss or adjust many cases without   for cases where adjudicatory
arge may be reduced at any   further processing.   handling not needed.
me prior to trial in return for plea
guilty or for other reasons.

  * Reprinted from The President's Commission on Law Enforcement and the Administration of Justice: THE
    CHALLENGE OF CRIME IN A FREE SOCIETY. Washington, D.C., Government Printing Office. February,
    1967, pp. 8–9, (Catalog No. Pr 36.8: L41/C86).

INTRODUCTION TO LAW ENFORCEMENT
AND CRIMINAL JUSTICE

Introduction To Law Enforcement And Criminal Justice

Twenty-third Printing,
Based on the Revised Nineteenth Printing

By

A. C. GERMANN, B.S., M.S. in P.A., D.P.A.

Professor of Criminal Justice
Department of Criminal Justice
California State University, Long Beach, California
Formerly, School of Criminal Justice
Michigan State University and Los Angeles Police Department

FRANK D. DAY, B.S., J.D.

Professor Emeritus of Criminal Justice
School of Criminal Justice
Michigan State University, East Lansing, Michigan
Formerly, Southern Police Institute
University of Louisville and New York Police Department

ROBERT R. J. GALLATI, B.S., LL.B., LL.M., S.J.D.

Director, New York State Identification and Intelligence System
On Leave, Police Department, City of New York, Assistant Chief Inspector—Chief of Planning
Formerly, Assistant Dean for Police Studies, The City University of New York

CHARLES C THOMAS · PUBLISHER
Springfield · Illinois · U.S.A.

Published and Distributed Throughout the World by
CHARLES C THOMAS • PUBLISHER
BANNERSTONE HOUSE
301-327 East Lawrence Avenue, Springfield, Illinois, U.S.A.

© 1962, 1966, 1968, 1969, 1970, and 1973 by CHARLES C THOMAS • PUBLISHER

ISBN 0-398-02647-5

Library of Congress Catalog Card Number: 72-92167

First Printing, 1962, 5000 copies
Second Printing, 1963, 3000 copies
Third Printing, 1964, 3000 copies
Revised Fourth Printing, 1966, 7000 copies
Fifth Printing, 1967, 5000 copies
Revised Sixth Printing, 1968, 5000 copies
Seventh Printing, 1968, 5000 copies
Eighth Printing, 1968, 3000 copies
Revised Ninth Printing, 1969, 8500 copies
Tenth Printing, 1969, 5000 copies
Eleventh Printing, 1970, 5000 copies
Revised Twelfth Printing, 1970, 10,000 copies
Thirteenth Printing, 1970, 10,000 copies
Fourteenth Printing, 1971, 10,000 copies
Fifteenth Printing, 1971, 10,000 copies
Sixteenth Printing, 1972, 10,000 copies
Seventeenth Printing, 1972, 10,000 copies
Eighteenth Printing, 1972, 10,000 copies
Revised Nineteenth Printing, 1973, 15,000 copies
Twentieth Printing, 1973, based on the Revised Nineteenth Printing, 10,000 copies
Twenty-first Printing, 1974, based on the Revised Nineteenth Printing, 10,000 copies
Twenty-second Printing, 1974, based on the Revised Nineteenth Printing, 15,000 copies
Twenty-third Printing, 1975, based on the Revised Nineteenth Printing, 10,000 copies

Printed in the United States of America
P-4

Dedicated to the young men and women of the United States who aspire to professional criminal justice careers, and by whose capacity, character, and dedication the future of the American criminal justice services as competent instruments of government and edifying guardians of the common good, will, pray God, be guaranteed . . .

PREFACE

From infancy to interment the entire population is directly affected by criminal justice. As child, adult, and senior citizen, life and property often depend upon the able operation of protective services; peaceful existence depends upon the maintenance of order; and the continuity of government depends upon a consistent and equitable achievement of the common good.

Criminal justice units throughout the world, regardless of the political structure under which they operate, are responsible for assuring tranquility. In a totalitarian state, the unrestrained and direct execution of centralized policy and rigid law results in an enforcement program which is often arbitrary and cruel and which often disregards the dignity of the citizenry as it acts with ruthless efficiency. In a democracy worthy of its title, compliance with governmental policy and law is effected by enforcement which is reasonable, and which is dedicated to the protection and service of each individual citizen, though perhaps it is of lesser efficiency due to the restraints imposed by a constitutional form of government.

In general, people receive the quality of criminal justice service that they deserve. If they are apathetic, vegetative, insensitive and ignorant, their criminal justice services will probably be instruments of power, rather than instruments of protection; and instruments of selfishness, rather than instruments of service.

In general, a criminal justice agency is an accurate barometer in gauging the moral tone of the community. If graft, corruption, simony, nepotism, and violence are accepted phenomena throughout the governmental, educational, industrial, commercial, religious, and social groupings, then so, too, throughout the criminal justice structure.

In general, the criminal justice service progresses according to the quality of public administration in any locale. If trained, carefully selected, conscientious public servants are the general rule, and not the exception, then, too, will such personnel be found in the criminal justice service.

The materials that are presented in this work will serve to sharpen the thinking of those who would unrealistically demand a quality of criminal justice incompatible with community norms, broaden the thinking of those who would myopically assert the sufficiency of current criminal justice operations, and organize the thinking of those who would confusedly expect a panacea for crime from the criminal justice vocation.

The authors desire to extend their appreciation to the many criminal justice administrators and academicians who have enthusiastically received, endorsed, and adopted this book.

A. C. G.
F. D. D.
R. R. J. G.

INTRODUCTION

Basic to any society, primitive or modern, is the necessity for compliance with authority, the necessity for disciplined behavior, and the necessity for community tranquility. Essential to any stable public order is some reliable and effective system of criminal justice.

Law enforcement may be achieved by raw military might, or by some form of police activity. Police activity, in turn, may be a simple and crude application of physical force, capable of inspiring fear, acting with ruthless efficiency, and completely disdainful of the dignity of the individual citizen—or, police activity may be a democratically oriented function achieving compliance with the least force, supported by the public, and mindful of the dignity of every citizen. There are no other alternatives: either the police perform effectively through public cooperation with minimum force, or the police perform effectively without public cooperation through brutal force.

Thus it can be seen why many of the law enforcement services in the United States are highly interested in the respect and goodwill of the public: without the respect and goodwill of the public, police prestige and status are low; with low status and prestige go low pay and difficulties in recruiting high-quality manpower; with low pay and insufficient personnel go overreliance on mechanization and overconcentration on detection; with overreliance on mechanization and overconcentration on detection go gross neglect of crime prevention; with gross neglect of crime prevention go increased crime rates and feelings of frustration; with increased crime rates and feelings of frustration go disregard for civil liberties and use of excessive force; and with disregard for civil liberties and use of excessive force go further losses of the respect and goodwill of the public—in a downward spiral difficult to reverse.

Although some law enforcement services in the United States are truly interested in the respect and goodwill of the public, there is, on the part of the public, a great lack of understanding of the police. Some public disdain, apathy, and indifference may be explained by references to odious examples of police deficiencies, by references to failures of the police to communicate openly with the public, and by reference to the intrusion of partisan politics into police administration. But, it must be said, a large segment of poor public attitude is explainable only by pointing to indications of general public ignorance of the role of law enforcement in a democratic society, and to general public ignorance of its responsibility toward the law enforcement function.

It is the purpose of this book to delineate the role of law enforcement with sufficient clarity so that both the law enforcement practitioner and citizen can understand their responsibilities one to the other, so that the young man or woman who contemplates a professional criminal justice career can receive an objective perspective, and so that interested students from other disciplines can appraise and evaluate criminal justice operations according to more logical criteria.

The presentation that follows is not "value free." Although the authors may present much substantive factual material which can be said to fall within the intellectual orientation usually called "positivistic" or "scientific," they will also present for consideration certain ideas and theories which are based on a philosophy that includes a positive belief in the existence of God, the freedom of the human will, and the immortality of the human soul.

PLAN OF THE BOOK

The book is divided into six parts.

Part I, *Philosophical Background to Criminal Justice,* will provide an orderly rationale of man and the state, justice and law, law enforcement and punishment, so that the reader may order, correlate, and subordinate the principles which delineate the ends and purposes of law enforcement activities and which serve as measuring rods for the propriety of means used.

Part II, *History of Criminal Justice,* will give a brief but complete résumé of the development of law enforcement through its ancient and feudal backgrounds, English precedents, and current development in the United States so that the reader may more readily understand present-day activities, and better appreciate anachronisms.

Part III, *Constitutional Limitations of Criminal Justice,* will discuss law enforcement and personal liberties, the Bill of Rights and major enforcement problems, and constitutional law enforcement—the extremely sensitive problem of conducting responsible, and responsive, law enforcement operations within our democratic federal republic.

Part IV, *Agencies of Criminal Justice,* will list the major local, private, state, and federal units involved, together with a statement of their primary duties and responsibilities. Part IV will also attempt to show the various interrelated organizations which affect law enforcement operations.

Part V, *Processes of Criminal Justice,* will give the reader a general understanding of the actual administration of criminal justice in the United States, delineating the pre-trial, trial, and post-trial processes in current usage, and the relationship of modern technology to the criminal justice system.

Part VI, *Evaluating Criminal Justice Today*, will discuss organized crime and corruption, human relations, efficiency, morality, legality, compassion, research areas, current trends and in addition, attempts to give some orientation relative to vocational careers.

No attempt has been made to be all-inclusive; all that has been attempted is the "rough sketch" from which the interested reader can pursue individual research desires. A compact selected bibliography has been included to give the reader a list of a few directly pertinent sources.

BASIC PRINCIPLES

The following twelve basic principles [1] *can* be applied to the American law enforcement service, *should* be acceptable to every American law enforcement agency, and are presented by the authors as a right and proper introduction to law enforcement:

I

The American law enforcement service has the responsibility to *prevent* crime and disorder, as an *alternative* to *repression* by regular police forces, military forces, or tyrannical police agencies.

II

The American law enforcement service has the responsibility to recognize that the authority and power to fulfill its function is dependent upon public approval of its existence, goals, and actions, and on its ability to secure and maintain public support and cooperation.

III

The American law enforcement service has the responsibility to recognize that to secure and maintain the approval, support, and cooperation of the public means also the securing of the willing assistance of the public in the task of securing observance of law; law enforcement has a duty to interpret to the community, with truth and objectivity, those conditions that create both law enforcement and community problems.

IV

The American law enforcement service has the responsibility to recognize that the extent to which the public cooperates and assists diminishes,

---

[1] Adapted from the Nine Principles of British Police collected and tabulated by Reith, Charles (1956). *A New Study of Police History*, pp. 287-288. Oliver and Boyd, Edinburgh.

proportionately, the need for the use of physical force and compulsion in achieving law enforcement objectives.

V

The American law enforcement service has the responsibility to seek and preserve public favor, not by pandering to public opinion, but by constantly demonstrating absolutely impartial service to Law, in complete independence of politics, and without regard to the justice or injustice of the substance of individual law; by ready offering of individual service and friendship to all members of the public without regard to their wealth, social standing, race, creed, or color; by ready exercise of courtesy and friendly good humor; and by ready offering of individual sacrifice.

VI

The American law enforcement service has the responsibility to use physical force only when the exercise of persuasion, advice, and warning is found to be insufficient to obtain public cooperation to an extent necessary to secure observance of law or to restore order; and to use only the minimum degree of physical force which is necessary on any particular occasion for achieving law enforcement objectives.

VII

The American law enforcement service has the responsibility to maintain, at all times, a relationship with the public that gives reality to the historic tradition that law enforcement is the public and that the public is law enforcement; law enforcement officers being only members of the public who are paid to give full-time attention to duties which are incumbent on every citizen, in the interests of the Common Good.

VIII

The American law enforcement service has the responsibility to recognize the need for strict adherence to the executive function and to refrain from even seeming to usurp the powers and authority of the judiciary in avenging individuals or the State, and in authoritatively judging guilt and punishing the guilty.

IX

The American law enforcement service has the responsibility to recognize that the test of law enforcement efficiency is the absence of crime and disorder, not the visible evidence of law enforcement action in dealing with them.

X

The American law enforcement service has the responsibility to recognize that the test of law enforcement integrity is the presence of personal moral responsibility exemplified by virtuous behavior on the part of each law enforcement officer, not the absence of public scandal.

XI

The American law enforcement service has the responsibility to recognize that the achievement of a professional level of service depends primarily upon the continued development of law enforcement education and training, planning, and research.

XII

The American law enforcement service has the responsibility to recognize that the stability of the republic and the continuity and vitality of democratic ideals depend upon a law enforcement service that is constantly aware of the sensitive balance between individual freedom and collective security, that is ever-alert to the dangers of extralegal or immoral procedures, and that is never willing to sacrifice principle by utilizing evil means to secure good ends.

TOPICS FOR DISCUSSION

1. What is the alternative to the "downward spiral?"
2. What do the authors mean by the statement, "The presentation that follows is not 'value free' "?
3. Of the twelve basic principles, which, if fully implemented, would have the greatest impact in this locale?

CONTENTS

UP TO PAGE → 73

Contents

PART V

PROCESSES OF CRIMINAL JUSTICE

PART VI

EVALUATING CRIMINAL JUSTICE TODAY

INTRODUCTION TO LAW ENFORCEMENT
AND CRIMINAL JUSTICE

PART I
PHILOSOPHICAL BACKGROUND TO CRIMINAL JUSTICE

Chapter I

MAN AND THE STATE

Because criminal justice activities focus upon men, the fundamental question in any study of criminal justice is *"What is man?"* Not until we develop some basic, open-ended answers and convictions about the nature of man, and thence the nature of the state, can we begin to understand, begin to develop the integrity, the competence, and the maturity of vision and action absolutely imperative in a criminal justice official.

MAN

Cultural Foundation. The student must consider the underlying philosophy of man in a nation whose culture is Western and, therefore, whose philosophical-religious-sociological patterns are Judaeo-Christian. This does *not* presume that *every* American is Jewish or Christian, nor that *every* American derives his origins from our planet's Western countries. This *does* note that the *fundamentum* of America's existence, as expressed in her Declaration of Independence and in her Constitution, is rooted in belief in the *God* who makes man in his image, and in belief in *each man* who is meant to develop his godliness in the world.

America's roots in the culture of Western nations are not merely evident in a love of Italian spaghetti, German beer, St. Patrick's Day parades, or Christian celebrations; nor are we culturally Western because the history we study as "our history" is that of Western Europe—that of Pepin and Charlemagne, the Crusades, the Renaissance, the Reformation, French and American and Russian Revolutions. Beyond these recognitions we see that America grounds her way of living by particularizing the philosophical-religious principles of her Judaeo-Christian culture (which, of its nature, allows the liberty of pluralism).

Dualistic Philosophies. Ironically, much of the philosophy in the two thousand years since Jesus is *anti*-biblical philosophy. Christians, in an attempt to explain the "good news," (i.e. gospel) of Jesus, expressed his message in the thought systems of their respective ages. In the twenty centuries since Christ's historical existence, the basic tone of Western philosophy has been *dualistic*. Dualism sees man composed of two distinct warring parts: matter and spirit, or body and soul, rather than as a whole, as one unified integral being.

5

Dualism devalues, negates, derogates and suspects matter (or body, or flesh). All that is material is regarded as evil and doomed to destruction. (The depreciation of man's sexuality, describing human sexual acts as merely "bodily pleasure" or "needs of the body," is a case in point.) Man's life is seen as a continuously exploding battleground in the warfare between his body and his soul. Man is urged not to be involved deeply with this *material* earth for he might impair his *spiritual* development. Consequently, dualism provides the anti-incarnational [1] philosophical framework which justifies noninvolvement in social issues, accepts the poverty and pain which "disciplines the body" and is "good for the soul." To be bawdy and low-class and crude is to be "earthy"; to be a perfect man is to be "angelic."

Ladder of Being. Logically, in dualistic thought, beings increase in value as they decrease in matter or in association with the bodily. Even the bastion of Aristotelian-Thomistic philosophy presumed to accept a "ladder of beings" going from the chemical, to the vegetable, on to the animal, thence to man—followed by a big jump to angels and a god beyond the ladder. While there is truth in the increasing capacity for complex activity in beings, this "ladder" or hierarchy does not adequately explain man's dignity.

Biblical Concept of Man. Psalm 8, characterizing Judaeo-Christian tradition, says of man:

> Yet you have made him little less than a god,
> You have crowned him with glory and splendor,
> Made him lord over the works of your hands,
> Set all things under his feet . . . .

To see man as "link #4" in the "great chain or ladder of being" depreciates his *divinization* which is central to the Scriptures of Jewish and Christian thought. The Scriptures (in the scholarship of which all other valid theological teaching is rooted) stress God's loving initiative in calling man into intimate relationship (covenant) with him. To accept the gift of one's love is somehow to accept being developed or further caused by that love. Consequently, in the Judaeo-Christian revelation of Western culture, man's *free* acceptance of God's *self*-gift opens man to sharing divine life, frees and opens man for *divinization*. This revelation reaches its peak in Christ's disclosure that *God* is to be—quite astoundingly—the *Father*

---

[1] Incarnation—literally "enfleshed" or "to be made flesh". The crux of the Christian message is that *God becomes man*; God enfleshes, involves, himself in the material evolving world of human history, and thereby reveals the greatness which man, in his *totality*, is called to.

of each man. The government, the laws, and the criminal justice system in a Western nation grounded in the beliefs of Judaeo-Christianity should, therefore, logically reflect and deepen man's realization of his dignity that he is the *son* of the Transcendent God. Such a belief relates sensitively to law enforcement, for man understands himself not so much by what he is told about himself, but by how he experiences himself.

Central, also, to the biblical notion of man, is man's responsible lordship over the universe. "God said, let us make man in our own image, in the likeness of ourselves, and let them be masters of the fish of the sea, the birds of the heaven, the cattle, all wild beasts and all the reptiles that crawl upon the earth . . ." (Genesis 1:26). Precisely does man image or reflect God in man's freedom to determine the particulars of what the world shall be. Rather than segregating man from the material world, or disconnecting him from other creatures via a conceptual chain or ladder, the Scriptural evidence calls for man's responsible authority over the world: the universe is what man makes of it. Human history is but the story of man's decision-making in his universe.

In past ages, a fragmented picture of man indicated that he was the image of God in his two uniquely human faculties: intellect and will. Often, these two "parts" of man were dangerously conceptualized as distinct from the *whole man* in his *environment*. Somehow—no matter what a person's life experience or upbringing—he should *know* better, he has an *intellect*. Somehow—no matter what a person's cultural conditioning or value system—he is *totally free* to change, he has a *free will*. Free will was seen as a muscle that gets stronger with repeated exercise; its interfusion with man in his totality, including his life situation, was not recognized.

The Hebrew mentality evident in Scripture and evident in Christ does *not* see man in a dualistic or fragmented fashion.[2] *To be man is to be unified within your Self and to be unified within the universe.*

Contemporary Philosophies. Our age is unique in history: not only do scholars for the first time have the tools of research to study the Judaeo-Christian Scriptures on which our country's principles are based, but also, for the first time in history, there are philosophical thought processes compatible with biblical themes. These key insights of existentialist thinking also provide the catalyst for thought-revolution interaction in other fields: sociology, history, law, politics, criminology, psychology, and art.

---

[2] We tend to understand things from our own frame of reference. Consequently, men have often superimposed their own thought categories onto Scripture—reading into Scripture definitions and ideas which are not there—e.g., reading St. Paul's "flesh vs. spirit" controversy in dualistic terms.

Pertaining to *man*, the primary existentialist-biblical ideas are appealing:

1. Man experiences his Self (himself) as a oneness, as a complex totality.
2. Each man alone expresses his own "I"—no one else can speak his "I" (his subjectivity) for him.
3. The ecstasy and anguish of human existence is rooted in being a non-transferable *self*, whose core is human freedom, and experienced as the radical apartness of being a person in whom abides the awesome power of decisions to love or hate, decide or withdraw, vegetate and stagnate or become more alive and creative in society.
4. Each man is an *open system onto existence*—man's very nature is his capacity to enter into union with life (people, ideas, objects, places, etc.) by taking this life into his Self.
5. Insofar as man is true to his nature and to his capacity to open onto the world does he increasingly grow rich in life, does he unfold his inner potential to be who he can be, and does he, *with each decision*, determine irrevocably—from all the immense possibilities—the *who* that he becomes.
6. Each man's greatness is in his unique particularization of humanity; this is his Person (the ground of his humanity) which is divinized.
7. Man profoundly experiences his own incommunicable existence. To some existentialist thinkers, this awareness is isolating, alienating, immobilizing. To the Christian existentialist, the personal weight of individual existence is man's own personal challenge to act and change and move history forward.
8. Man is not a static being—he is always in process of becoming more himself. Man evolves in response to his existential situation.

Extension of the preceding material could fill several volumes, and so, too, could conflicting theories of the nature of man. Suffice it to note that any serious student of criminal justice can well cogitate on the nature of man, for how a criminal justice practitioner regards himself, and his fellow-man, often determines his course of action be it mechanical or humane, legalistic or compassionate, alienated or unified.

THE STATE

How one answers the question, "What is the State?" is important to one interested in law enforcement for much of what is considered good or bad in law enforcement is judged so in terms of the nature of the State.

In considering the question, "What is the State?" depending upon one's intellectual orientation, answers will tend to imply that "the State is supreme, and man is a creature of the State," or that "the State is a set of institutions ordered to the service of man."

Theoretically, America chooses the latter definition as the logical follow-up to our cultural concept of man. The United States has always prided herself on being an adventure in government: "Government of the people, by the people, for the people."

Students must be ever conscious that America is only true to her own historico-cultural heritage and to her own founding principles when she, on the operative as well as the theoretical level, operates as a state where every man is recognized in his individual greatness, and where every man is allowed (and stimulated) to develop his human-beingness. The state, then, is not the master, but the servant of its people; it exists for the maintenance of life and development of all citizens.

If the state provides the creative and free environment for all of its people to develop as men, the state itself will be in process of development. This is not to say "chaos," but productive, ongoing change. To accept the fact that mankind, collectively and individually, develops or evolves, is to accept the reality that its cultural and institutional expressions change. Thus, only insofar as the state can maintain its integrity with what is of human value in its own history and its own principles, and only insofar as the state can grasp its intrinsically evolutionary nature, can she keep herself free to move forward toward a positive noble future. Thus will the state be most servant, for she serves her citizens in providing the climate in which they can be decisive, creative, and responsible.

Like domestic society (the family), or religious society (the Church), the civil society (State) must be constantly vigilant lest it dehumanize its members through overprotectiveness, anonymity, self-righteousness, authoritarianism, and bureaucracy. Any society best serves its members by creating the atmosphere in which they can fully mature as human beings.

Common to all forms of society are the requisites of authority and power. *Authority* is the right to direct and command. *Power* is the force by means of which others can be obliged to obey. Power without authority is tyrannical; authority without order is meaningless. Without authority and power no society could secure coordination of effort or permanency of cooperation—and there can never be any serious and successful cooperative effort without authoritative guidance and the potential use of sanctions.

The state is concerned with the maintenance of law, the promotion of the common welfare and public order, and the administration of public affairs. The state is, in our conception, an agency authorized by the people to use power, and is made up of experts or specialists in public order and welfare, and should be considered an instrument in the service of man. It must be stated, however, that in the conception of others, the state is an end in itself, with absolute authority and power, and with man existing for, and at the service of, the state.

Sovereignty—the possession of and right to supreme power—is either considered a natural and inalienable right of the state, separate from and above its people, or, is considered as a natural and inalienable right of the people, invested by them in the state. Our Declaration of Independence is quite clear on this point, stating that "governments derive their just powers from the consent of the governed."

The relationship between the people and the state in terms of authority and power is of critical importance to law enforcement, and makes clear the differences between law enforcement in a democratic and in a totalitarian state.

In a totalitarian state, authority and power are separate from and above the people, residing absolutely in the state—hence law enforcement officers are representatives of the state, deputies of the state, in the service of the state.

In a democratic state, authority and power are inherent in the people, invested by them in their government—hence law enforcement officers are representatives of the people, deputies of the people, in the service of the people.

Republic or Democracy. A republic is defined as "a state in which the sovereign power resides in a certain body of the people (the electorate)." A democracy is defined as "a government in which the supreme power is retained by the people and exercised either directly (absolute or pure democracy) or indirectly (representative democracy) through a system of representation."

Some would point out that there is no essential difference between a representative democracy and a republic. Others would indicate that, while a democracy may be a republic, a republic is not necessarily a democracy. The Union of Soviet Socialist Republics, for example, is a constitutional republic because under the U.S.S.R. constitution, the sovereign power resides in a certain body of the people—the Communist Party—but it is not a democracy because the power does not reside in all the people. In this kind of republic, legislative power rests in the hands of representatives selected by the "elite" rather than by the "masses," or "mob."

Our founding fathers did not think of this type of republic; the Preamble of the United States Constitution begins with the words "We, *the people*," and Article I states, "The House of Representatives shall be composed of members chosen every second year by *the people* of the several States." (Italics added.) They rejected the idea of a "ruling elite" and of an "electing elite."

Capitalism or Socialism. The distinctions between capitalism and socialism tend to blur. Spokesmen for both systems reject tyrannical and authoritarian rule, whether by totalitarian king, czar, or dictator, and favor an administrative and political system that functions as a servant of society, with freedom of information and communication, political pluralism, a variety of forms of social ownership, respect for truthfulness, efficiency, and the common good, freedom to work, freedom from arbitrary arrest by political police, and a system of criminal justice whose purpose is to protect society against antisocial behavior rather than make all citizens feel like criminals so that they may be more readily intimidated. But they differ markedly in terms of economic philosophy. Spokesmen for capitalism favor a free-enterprise economic system, with minimal government control over business and commerce, allowing the pressures of supply and demand to determine the policies of production and consumption. Spokesmen for socialism favor a sovereign national government which, in the interests of society, controls the use and development of the means of production and the distribution of the national product.

Government. Whereas the state can be considered as a set of institutions, *government* can be considered as the organized relationship between the people and their administrators. It is possible for the state to maintain its identity while undergoing changes in its form of government.

The fundamental authority and power of the state have been classically enumerated in the functions of government called legislative, judicial, and executive. Governments are either absolute and despotic—wherein all authority and power are in the hands of one man, or one group, *or* constitutional and limited—wherein there is a practical separation and restriction of authority and power.

Constitution. A constitution is the basic law which creates and regulates government; it is the principle of organization which defines and relates the various political offices, and which limits their authority and power. It is important for the law enforcement student to realize that the constitution is the law which creates and regulates government, *not* the law which a government creates in order to regulate the conduct of the people.

Some ask, "Is it not axiomatic that in a democracy the majority rules?" And if the majority wants prayers in its schools, Communists in prison, police allowed to work "unshackled" by court decisions, why cannot the majority have its way? Certainly, the will of the majority should be considered by all government officials, but the Constitution deliberately protects basic rights and liberties that cannot be nonchalantly changed by majority whim. Amendment, purposely, is difficult to achieve (Art. V.).

The Constitution is the source of governmental laws, for it provides for the methods of lawmaking, but it is more, for it establishes the legal standards by which subsequent laws of the government are measured. Hence, any law which violates the letter and spirit of the Constitution is judged unconstitutional. Hence, it is said that ours is a government of law, rather than a government of men—for our Constitution posits the supremacy of law over arbitrary decision. And hence, it is said that ours is a government "of the people, by the people, and for the people," for our Constitution provides that no man is above the law, and provides that all authority and power are derived through, and limited by, the Constitution which is of popular origin and cannot be changed except by the people as a whole.

It might be well noted that some peoples are but subjects of an absolute and despotic government, whereas other peoples are citizens of a limited and constitutional government, the difference corresponding to the status, freedom, rights and privileges of the people administered.

Our American political institutions are founded on the premises that man, as man, has a right to political liberty and equality, and that his natural rights are antecedent to the state. We see this philosophy reflected in the words of our Declaration of Independence: "to *secure* (hold fast, make safe) these rights, governments are instituted by men." The words "to grant" or "to give," are not used, for what the government is authorized and empowered to grant, it may be authorized and empowered to remove —and the natural rights of man are beyond the power of the state.

Nonetheless, certain rights and privileges are often formalized—such as the extension of universal suffrage, or the presence of a "Bill of Rights." The right of free speech and free assembly, immunity from unwarranted searches and seizures, due process, trial by jury, and the like, are not idle or sterile parts of our American ideology, but vital safeguards of the health of our democracy. Every conscientious student of law enforcement must be able to realize that any citizen of our country who can be coerced, intimidated, frightened, or bullied by any law enforcement officer differs only in name from the subject of an absolute despot, and only in name from the state slave of the totalitarian regime. And every conscientious student of law enforcement must be able to realize that any law enforcement officer who coerces, intimidates, frightens, or bullies any citizen differs only in name from the cruel agent of the brutal dictator.

ENDS OF MAN AND THE STATE

How one considers the nature of man will determine his conclusions relative to the propriety of human acts and the purpose of human existence; how one considers the nature of the state will determine his conclusions relative to the propriety of governmental actions and the purpose of civil society.

End of Man. If man is held to be but mere matter or but mere brute animal, his acts will be deemed to be determined, not free; his final purpose will be posited as material or animalistic, so many ergs of energy for the industrial machine, or so many pleasurable sense experiences.

If man is held to be a complex totality, unified within himself (his

Self) and unified within the universe, his decisions to act and change and move history forward harmonize with his destiny as an open system onto existence, and with his capacity to enter into union with life.

As one concludes to the end of man, one will judge the applicability of this or that plan of organization, the reasonableness of this or that method or technique, the goodness or badness of this or that act of a criminal justice agent or agency.

End of the State. If the state is held to be an absolute entity, and the repository and first source of all authority, power, right and privilege, its acts will be deemed to be above judgment; its final purpose will be posited as its own selfish interest—as race was for German nazism, as nation was for Italian fascism, and as economic community is for Russian communism.

If the state is held to be an instrument in the service of man, invested with authority and power by the people, and a safeguard of the rights of its people, its acts may be judged in accordance with law; and its final purpose will be posited as the good of the people—the common good.

As one concludes to the end of the state, one will judge the applicability, reasonableness, goodness or badness of this or that governmental activity.

TOPICS FOR DISCUSSION

1. What difference does it make, in terms of practical police work, how we regard "man"?
2. What difference does it make, in terms of practical police work, how we regard "the State"?
3. What is meant by the phrase, "ours is a government of law, rather than a government of men"?
4. What difference does it make, in terms of practical police work, how we regard the end (goal) of man, or the end (goal) of the state?

Chapter II

JUSTICE AND LAW

For man to live in community with his fellowmen implies interaction, or interpersonal living. Man's equality with his brothers is rooted in man's nature as a divinized human agent, an "I" who participates in the spirituality, and therefore the freedom, of God. Community or societal living demands that each man's dignity is recognized and therefore his actions, and the actions of his brothers toward him, are evaluated in reference to man's nature. In this chapter we consider the subjects of justice and law, for such evaluations are directly keyed to our understanding of individual or group responsibility. However, one distinction needs first be made.

Custom. When we stop to consider the behavior of the individual or the social group, we very often use the terms "custom" or "convention." What a *habit* is in terms of individual behavior, a *custom* is in terms of group behavior. The fact that individuals and groups can accept or reject, abide by or transgress, maintain or change habits or customs would tend to show that they are voluntary. Yet, accepted and established habits or customs resist change, as we all know. This can be "good" insofar as they may conserve the best of the past, or "bad" insofar as they impede progress.

Customs differ from time to time, and from place to place, yet this does not mean that no uniformity exists in reference to the actions of men, for natural or instinctive behavior is common to all members of the human race. The fact that there is a variety of customs, and that they change from time to time, merely indicates that they are voluntary and man-made.

Yet, some affirm that custom is the *only* measure of human behavior. This position rejects natural law and universal moral standards and substitutes the arbitrary for the rational, averages for norms. Others affirm that custom is the *only* measure of human judgments. These positions dispossess reason and make opinion—which prevails by weight of numbers—supreme as the criterion for morality and truth.

If custom is to be the ultimate standard for conduct, and the only criterion for moral judgment, then we cannot question the "goodness" or "badness" of a particular custom, or customary act. The customs of one group cannot then be impartially judged by another group, for judgment must be in accordance with custom—hence the custom has validity only for the group in which it is formed.

14

Thus, the descriptive sciences would tend to replace the normative. The study of morality would be a study of customs. Answers to the "goodness" or "badness" of human behavior could only be answered by pointing to the data of how men *have* behaved, not to whether or not they *should have* behaved so.

The issue is important to any consideration of justice and law, for just as some hold that the goodness or badness of man's behavior must be judged in accordance with his nature, so too is held the view that justice and law are to be evaluated not only in terms of the customary, but also in terms of the universal natural law: *Do good, avoid evil, and render to each his due.*

The issue is important to considerations of justice and law, for one must either hold that morality stems from nature and reason, or, that morality stems from custom or convention. Ultimately, one must hold that there are standards independent of custom, by which customs can be judged, or, one must hold that custom is the measure of human acts and human judgment and above any criticism.

JUSTICE

Justice, the measure of men and states, has been the subject of discussion over the centuries because of its universal scope.

To define justice properly, one must consider the actions of man as they affect the well-being of others. We would suggest that justice can properly be defined as *the process by which each receives what is due him.* To give to others what is their due is the essence of justice—and involves the concepts of duty or obligation.

Any discussion of justice seems to evolve into a conflict between the exponents of *might*—those who think that power makes right and that justice is expediency; and the exponents of *right*—those who think that power can be wrongly exercised and that justice is a universally applicable principle.

One will tend to take the position that what is just or unjust is completely relative to, dependent upon, and consequent to the state, its constitution, and its laws, or, that what is just or unjust is determined by some principle completely independent of and antecedent to the state, its constitution, and its laws.

If one takes the first position and holds that there is no justice apart from the state, its constitution, and its laws, one denies natural justice—justice apart from man-made institutions. The state, its constitution, and its laws cannot be judged just or unjust, for if *they* determine what *is* just and unjust, they *cannot* be so judged.

If one takes the second position and holds that what is just and unjust is determined by some principle completely independent of and antecedent to, the state, its constitution, and its laws, one posits natural justice, justice holding for all men, at all times, everywhere. The state, its constitution, and its laws then can be called just or unjust.

To the student of law enforcement, justice is an oft-used term, and often confused with what is customarily expected, or with what is legislatively ordained. Yet, in all truth, justice is often a chimerical quest by law enforcement agent, prosecution, defense, and judge. It is no small wonder that the concept is so often abused or misunderstood. To some, justice is a selfish concept, and to them what is just or unjust is related to personal needs; to others, justice is merely the application of community opinion and to them the just or unjust is related to customary practices; and yet, to others, justice is formulated in the universally applicable natural law: *Do good to others, injure no one, and render to every man his own.*

Civil Rights and Civil Liberties. The late President John F. Kennedy made a clear distinction between *civil rights* and *civil liberties:*[1]

> By civil rights we mean those *claims* which the citizen has to the affirmative assistance of government. In an age which insistently and properly demands that government secure the weak from needless dread and needless misery, the catalog of civil rights is never closed. The obligation of government in the area of civil rights is never wholly discharged.
>
> By civil liberties, I mean an individual's *immunity* from governmental oppression. A society which respects civil liberty realizes that the freedom of its people is built, in large part, upon their privacy. The Bill of Rights, in the eyes of its framers, was a catalog of immunities, not a schedule of claims. It was, in other words, a Bill of Liberties. The immunities defined in this Bill of Liberties were set forth in order that the promise of individual freedom might be made explicit. The framers dreamed that if their hope were codified, man's energies of mind and spirit might be released from fear.
>
> When civil rights are seen as claims and civil liberties as immunities, the government's differing responsibilities become clear. For the security of *rights,* the *energy* of government is essential. For the security of *liberty, restraint* is indispensable.

LAW

Law is often defined as *an ordinance of reason, directed to the common good,* or, as a *rule which should be obeyed and which can be disobeyed.*

When the natural scientist uses the word "law," his concept does not include that of "can be disobeyed," for his laws are inviolable (i.e., gravitation).

When the artist uses the word "law," his concept is flexible, for his laws are the expression of custom (i.e., grammar).

When the moralist, be he philosopher, attorney, police officer, or house-

---

[1] Quoted in Williams, Edward Bennett (1962). *One Man's Freedom,* pp. 298-299. Atheneum, New York.

wife, uses the word "law," applied to the sphere of human behavior, the reference is to essentially violable rules.

It might be helpful to distinguish the various types of law which direct human conduct.

First, the distinction between Natural Law and Human Law. Natural Law is that law discovered by examining man's nature, the law that reflects God's Eternal Law. Human Law is that law which is officially instituted by man, and which often reflects Natural Law. Natural Law and Human Law are alike insofar as they are directions of reason for the Common Good. Natural Law and Human Law differ in that Natural Law is unchanging and forbids all vices and sins; and Human Law is undergoing constant change, and forbids *those offenses which disturb society.*

Second, the distinctions between types of Human Law. Different terminologies have been used from time to time, making analysis and classification difficult, but the major categories are as follows: *Written Law* —usually refers to that law which has been formalized and codified; *Unwritten Law*—usually refers to customary law, and most often to *Common Law*, our traditional law; *Positive Law*—usually refers to law which has been posited by a law-giver; *Statutory Law*—usually refers to that law effected by legislative enactment (statutes, codes, ordinances); *Constitutional Law*—refers to the fundamental law which creates and regulates government by popular consent; *Contract Law*—usually refers to that portion of *Civil Law* which deals with the transactions between private entities; *Tort Law*—usually refers to that portion of *Civil Law* which deals with redress of grievances of a personal nature; *Criminal Law*—usually refers to those laws regulating conduct for the health, welfare, safety and protection of citizenry; *Administrative Law*—usually refers to those rules and regulations and procedures which delineate processes within an institution or organization; and *Canon Law*—usually refers to the codes of doctrine or discipline within an ecclesiastical organization.

It is generally recognized that a rule of human positive law cannot be made by any man, but only by him who has legislative authority.

It is generally recognized that *law enforcement officers*, for execution and enforcement; *attorneys*, for interpretation and representation; and *judges*, for inquiry, application of laws, and imposition of sanctions—are indispensable, and that laws would be meaningless without legal machinery—legal movement—litigation. The adversary system—"*The State of Alaska v. Jones*," "*Smith v. Brown*,"—is clearly a battleground where the issues are distinguished, processed, and eventually settled, rarely to the satisfaction of all persons involved.

In order that justice might prevail, the strict letter of the law is not always satisfactory; often *equity* must be considered, and legal justice corrected or supplemented by reference to the spirit of the law rather than to the *letter* of the law.

If laws do not have some measure by which they can be judged, no law could ever be resisted, no matter how unjust or injurious. Hence, the distinction between Hobbes, who states:

> . . . all laws, written and unwritten, have their authority and force from the will of the Commonwealth, . . . nothing the sovereign representative can do to a subject on whatever pretense can properly be called injustice or injury. (Leviathan, Part II, Chapter 26.)

and Aquinas, who states:

> . . . every human law has just so much of the character of law as it has derived from the law of nature. But if in any point it differs from the law of nature, it is no longer a law but a corruption of law. (Summa Theologica, Part I of Second Part, Q. 95, Art. 2.)

Thus, the legislators, in deciding whether to make a law, or courts, in interpreting a law, do not primarily base their decisions on what is of local or popular opinion, the attitude of those in power, community mores, but, instead, on universal standards of reason, right, and justice. So goes the theory. The practice often involves aggressive lobbying by pressure groups.

Today, there is public controversy relative to the use of "civil disobedience" as a method of public protest. Often, we note that clergymen and well-known civic leaders are involved in a mass refusal to obey the law and its agents.

Many would state, in rebuttal to this kind of action, that we are a nation of laws, not of men; that respect for the law is necessary for community and individual well-being; that if we can pick and choose among the laws—accepting or rejecting, at will, this or that statute, court order, official command—we are heading for anarchy; that no man can put himself above the law; and that any person who does so is an enemy of justice, for our system depends on seeking redress of grievances through the regular legal processes. Even though this argument might be made by a person who was more interested in maintaining the *status quo* than in expressing a philosophy of justice (*viz.*, the racist), civil disobedience presents a real problem. If obtaining redress of grievances through the regular legal process is blocked, civil disobedience often appears to be the only lever open to the citizen (*viz.*, violation of a segregation ordinance).

The law itself can be misused, and it can happen that no legal remedies are available and timely. The law is not the word of God, but the agreement between men, arbitrary, and a form of compromise. The law does not impose moral sanctions, but physical sanctions—fines, imprisonments, execution; pain to the pocket-book, to the body, or to the mind if freedom is restricted.

A free society has always put limits on the authority and power of civil law; our Bill of Rights indicates that our Founding Fathers knew of limits to the law. Centuries ago, Christian moralists gave recognition to the right of armed rebellion in certain instances. Our revolutionary war was an example of violent resistance to the force of unjust laws.

Today, we note that unjust laws are resisted, not by the violence of rebellion, but by massive public appeals to the conscience of the nation. Such appeals have had effect, for they go beyond impassioned pleas—when a citizen puts his body on the line, he uses a language that all can understand.

Who is it that decides that a law is unjust and deserves to be disobeyed because there are no available or timely legal processes? Each citizen must decide for himself—but the result is not always anarchy and lawlessness. The anti-social offender who violates the law does so *for his own selfish ends,* and *intends to escape the penalties of the law.* The citizen who protests by nonviolent civil disobedience acts for a different end, and in a different way. He violates the law *publicly,* and *openly,* to give point to his action, *to make people pass judgment on injustice,* to rouse indignation —and *he accepts the penalties.*

Certainly, civil disobedience is open to grave abuse. To understand when its use is proper and prudent calls for knowledge, wisdom, and high motivation; to make it effective calls for great skill and timing. Fanatics, fools, and ignorant citizens do great harm in the name of civil disobedience —but let us remember, cowards, conformists, and lazy citizens do great harm also by making existing law an absolute. As the former Chief Justice of the United States puts it, "The opposite of dissent is conformity, and nothing could be more deadly than to have conformity for the sake of conformity." [2]

There are degrading forms of legalized injustice that exist in our nation, and many citizens have been giving tacit approval by their silence and inaction. But not all citizens. Some have refused to do so, and have accepted the risks of civil disobedience. It may be that their efforts help us look at the reality of things, rather than outward appearances, and to place justice above legality. (Hitler's Reich had a formal legal foundation.)

The authors are put in mind of an ancient proverb: "Do what you want to do, but be prepared to pay the price!" They are of the opinion that civil disobedience is a serious business, and any person who contemplates its usage should search his mind and heart with care, should explore all

[2] Warren, Earl (1972). A Republic, If You Can Keep It, p. 104. Quadrangle, New York.

alternative routes, and should be aware of all possible consequences. The authors are opposed to any form of civil disobedience whenever there are adequate, available, and timely legal remedies with which to right a wrong.

As citizens, in observing the law, we must realize that the objective of our constitutional democracy is to require us to learn together how to cooperate for the common good—not to learn how to isolate ourselves in selfish individualism. As citizens, we are more than statistical units, objects of propaganda, or consumers, and we must learn our responsibilities in order to enjoy liberty under law. Our freedom as individuals must be protected, true enough, but we must grow in responsibility and knowledge of the true *meaning* of law.

Laws are necessary to control the conduct of men, not because men agree, but because they disagree. Hence, laws are a form of *compromise— they do not satisfy everyone.*[3]

The laws of man are not perfect for all persons at all times, but represent an attempt to solve a societal problem. Hence, laws are *arbitrary— they could be otherwise.*[4]

To the student of law enforcement, the facts that human laws are a form of compromise and are arbitrary are important. The fact that the law, like human nature, is not perfect, is a matter for serious meditation. The fact that the law is subject to judgment, criticism, and revision is an important consideration for those who are apt to become granite-jawed custodians of "the word" to the detriment of good sense, human compassion, and professional law enforcement.

To the student of law enforcement, the fact that the law is not merely coercion, command of a sovereign, an expression of power, or merely minimum sanction to prevent chaos, is important. The fact that the law stands for such moral universals as can be supported by the authority of the government must be understood. The fact that the law is essential and a necessary support to the formation of a more perfect union, establishment of justice, insurance of domestic tranquility, promotion of the general wel-

---

[3] The word "compromise" as used here, simply means that any man-made law, when proposed, has controversial features which are settled by adjustment or concession. *Viz.,* some may wish maximum speed limits to be 60 m.p.h.; others may desire a 90 m.p.h. limit. If 75 m.p.h. is established by the legislators, some persons will feel that it is too restrictive; others that it is dangerously high. The established legal limit then, obviously, will not satisfy everyone.

[4] The word "arbitrary" as used here, does not mean capricious or unreasonable, but only indicates that any man-made law could be written with different elements comprising the offense, and with different penalties attached. *Viz.,* Grand Theft or Grand Larceny may consist of thefts over $100 (Michigan), or may consist of thefts over $200 (California), or whatever is determined by the legislators. Either the Michigan or California criteria for Grand Theft or Grand Larceny could be otherwise.

fare, and securance of the blessings of liberty is an important consideration for those who are apt to forget its beneficent nature.

TOPICS FOR DISCUSSION

1. How does the interrelation of "custom" and "opinion" affect one's positions on choice of a vocation, importance of education, police professionalization, etc.?
2. What "yardstick" or measuring device can be used to determine what is "just" or "unjust"?
3. Is there any alternative to the "adversary system" for implementation of legal processes?
4. How does a thoroughly considered and conscientiously undertaken act of "civil disobedience" differ from the anti-social act of a lawless criminal?

Chapter III

LAW ENFORCEMENT AND PUNISHMENT

THE legislators frame and construct the law; attorneys study, interpret, and present the law; and judges make final interpretations and applications of the law and impose sanctions. *But,* the law enforcement officer applies the law immediately, gives it effectiveness, and executes the law in a direct personal fashion; his role, therefore, is one of extreme sensitivity.

As we look about us we observe the conduct of our fellowman and judge that it is good or bad as it promotes or is contrary to the end of man and the goals of society.

Bad conduct which is contrary to the laws of God we term *sin*; bad conduct which is contrary to the laws of man we term *crime*. Thus, a sin may or may not be a crime—for sinful bad conduct such as rudeness, gossiping, sloth, is not necessarily illegal or criminal. And, not all crimes could be considered sinful in themselves—for illegal conduct such as driving with an expired operator's license, walking one's dog into a restaurant, throwing a scrap of paper from an automobile, is not necessarily sinful or immoral. Bad conduct, sin or crime, which tends to become habitual, and which habituation tends to corrupt the physical, mental, and moral health of the people, we term *vice*.

When the student of law enforcement looks about him, he notes that some people violate laws and that some people obey laws—all in varying degree.

Why do people commit crime? Answers pour forth: They are ignorant of the law; they are greedy for money or power or fame; they are indifferent to society; they wish to show-off; they feel that laws are unnecessary restrictions on their freedom; they desire a "thrill"; they act instinctively as determined by their genetical antecedents; they are insane or mentally deficient; they come from social environments where the mores, economics, religion, family, government, school, and cultural pressures fashion their acts; they are physically handicapped; they are subject to concupiscence as a result of original sin . . . .

Why do people obey the law? They understand the law; they have a "good background"; they wish to set good example; the standards of the community agree with their own; they are fearful of punishment; they desire the approval of society; they are emotionally stable and mature; they accept the assistance of Divine Grace . . . .

The actual behavior of people in obeying or transgressing the law is the subject matter of ethics and criminology, and it is highly recommended that law enforcement students obtain perspectives in these areas. Suffice it to say that the authors of this book are in agreement that people commit crime or obey the law for many reasons, often due to the pressures of an individual or social nature, but, in the final analysis, always due to a free choice on their part. In fact, whenever a person is found to be insane, coerced, or otherwise unable to exercise freedom of choice, he is not held criminally liable.

LAW ENFORCEMENT

In order to make the law effective, it *must* be enforced. While it is true that the ruthless enforcement of the law can be tyrannical, it is also just as true that apathetic or indifferent enforcement of the law can make the law sterile and meaningless.

One hears the terms, "police authority," "police power," "police goals," "police methods," and "police role." These are not identical concepts, although often used interchangeably.

Police Authority means the right of the state to act relative to the general health, safety, and welfare.

Police Power means the force which is utilized by the state in acting relative to the general health, safety, and welfare.

Police Goals refer to two major objectives:

1. The prevention of crime and disorder and the preservation of the peace (for community security).

2. The protection of life and property and personal liberty (for individual security).

(A quarter-century ago, most working policemen would have decribed the police goals as "protecting life and property and keeping the peace." The professional policeman of today realizes the importance of *preventing crime and disorder* and his genuine duty to secure *personal liberty* for all citizens.)

These goals are achieved by five major *methods*:

1. *Crime Prevention*—by working with juveniles; by cooperating with probation and parole personnel; by educating the public; and by providing visible evidence of police ability and availability.

2. *Crime Repression*—by investigating crime; by identifying and apprehending offenders; by recovering stolen property and by assisting in the prosecution and conviction of those who violate the law. (A quarter-century ago, most working policemen would have regarded this method

as the *entirety* of the police task. As the officer has increased his perspective, he has come to see himself as a *part* of the administration of criminal justice, working with prosecutors, courts, probation, correctional, and parole personnel, and has enlarged his methods and emphasis. He now regards crime repression as necessary and proper, but not the sole reason for his existence; he also accepts crime prevention and protection of personal liberty as equally necessary and proper methods to achieve his goals.)

3. *Regulation of Noncriminal Conduct*—by controlling the noncriminal citizen in such areas as traffic (vehicles, parking, pedestrians), public events (crowd control), and social relations (domestic disputes), in order to maintain community tranquility.

4. *Provision of Services*—by rendering information, directions, advice, and general assistance, by counseling and referral, and through special services such as licensing and registration.

5. *Protection of Personal Liberty*—by protecting the individual citizen against unwarranted interference on the part of the state; and by instructing the citizenry in terms of their duties, obligations, rights, and privileges in reference to the law.

The authority, power, goals and methods of the police are parallel to all criminal justice activities which promote individual liberty, secure public safety, and emphasize social justice.

The modern, *professional* police *role* involves, not only sensitive and humane attitudes, but also a variety of activities:

1. The *community service* activities which care for the lost, confused, sick, distressed, and destitute, and which deliver such persons to a safe and helpful person or agency.

2. The *community education* activities which assist the community to understand the various enclaves and sub-groups, and which help the community to identify those factors which detract from community liberty, safety, and social justice.

3. The *peace-keeping* activities which manage emergencies and conflict in a fashion that always protects citizens' individual rights, that always observes due process, and that assists citizens to solve problems that are beyond their ability to cope with.

4. The *crime control* activities which promote security by wise and prudent enforcement of the criminal law. (At one time, in the history of American police, this activity was seen as the *total* of the police role, and some superannuated criminal justice personnel retain such a myopic concept even today.)

LEGAL SOURCES OF POLICE AUTHORITY AND POWER. The federal nature of the United States government makes it impossible to look to any one legislative enactment or judicial interpretation to determine the legal sources of, or restrictions on, police authority, power, policy, procedure, administration, organization, and operations. It is necessary to look to federal and state constitutions, to federal, state, and local laws, and to federal and state court decisions.

The Ninth Amendment to the U.S. Constitution provides that "the enumeration in the Constitution, of certain rights, shall not be construed to deny or disparage others retained by the people." The Tenth Amendment provides that "The powers not delegated to the United States by the Constitution, nor prohibited by it to the states, are reserved to the states respectively, or to the people." There are no specific provisions in the federal constitution relating to the police.

Federal courts have been able to restrict the activities of police in the various states through the use of: (1) the doctrine of "dual citizenship" expressed in the Fourteenth Amendment: "All persons born or naturalized in the United States, and subject to the jurisdiction thereof, are citizens of the United States and of the State wherein they reside", and through the use of (2) the "due process" clause of the same amendment: "No State shall make or enforce any law which shall abridge the privileges or immunities of citizens of the United States; nor shall any State deprive any person of life, liberty, or property, without due process of law; nor deny to any person within its jurisdiction the equal protection of the laws . . ."

Federal Police Agencies: The Constitution of the United States does not specifically provide for federal police forces, but the constitutionality of such forces rests heavily upon the doctrine of implied powers. No federal police agency has general police power; their specific authority and jurisdiction is delineated in the federal statute creating the agency.

State Police Agencies: Within the limits of the state constitutions, state legislatures have determined the authority and power of all officers operating within the state (except federal officers). As creatures of statute, state officers can exercise only the authority and duties specified by legislation.

County, Municipal, Borough, Township, Village Police Agencies: Police operating under the aegis of counties, cities, boroughs, townships and villages are considered "state" officers, and are limited by state statutes.

Philosophical Problems. As we look at the problems of law enforcement in these United States, several problems of a basic philosophical nature present themselves.

Depending upon the experimental and intellectual orientation of the student, upon his philosophy of life, upon his understanding of the nature of this democratic republic, and above all, upon his value system, will he resolve the following questions:

1. Are constitutional guarantees consistent or inconsistent with law enforcement of maximum efficiency?
2. Can law enforcement afford to be completely open with the general public in revealing data relative to its operations?
3. Can the law be enforced exactly as on the books, or is toleration to be allowed?
4. Can each antisocial member of society be said to surrender his civil rights at the moment he offends?
5. Can the law enforcement officer, in order to effectively perform his mission, violate the law?

The reader, before progressing further, might find it profitable to meditate a few moments and attempt to formulate an honest personal answer.

We shall now briefly consider each of the questions:

1. *Are constitutional guarantees consistent or inconsistent with law enforcement of maximum efficiency?* It would seem that the law enforcement of a totalitarian state would always be more efficient than the law enforcement of a democratic society. Without the constraints imposed by a Bill of Rights, enforcement activity can be direct, immediate, energetic, and highly effective. Yet individual freedom can be severely curtailed in the process. With the limitations of a Bill of Rights, enforcement activity is indirect, often delayed, plodding, and of lesser efficiency. Yet individual liberty is maintained in the process.

To balance individual freedom against collective security is the delicate task of law enforcement in a democratic society. It is well for all of us to realize that the constitutional guarantees which protect us against unwarranted searches and seizures, against illegal arrests, confinements, and detentions, against coerced or improperly obtained admissions and confessions, and those which guarantee us the right to counsel, to trial by jury, and to due process, are indeed obstructions to a ruthlessly efficient law enforcement that is neither democratic nor American—but also are indeed a treasured heritage of American democratic law enforcement.

Preservation of the social order and the maintenance of domestic tranquility do not only mean freedom from fear of bodily injury and loss or destruction of property, but also freedom from fear of unwarranted harassment by the state. In other words, some considerable attention needs be paid to the protection of individual freedom. Students of law enforcement must realize that *some* social order must be sacrificed if individual freedom is to be maintained. Students of law enforcement must early realize that **the law enforcement agency *cannot*** have a perfect record of crime solution and *still* operate within the legal restraints imposed by the Bill of Rights.

Part of the price that is paid for individual freedom is in terms of collective security, and, as yet, our citizenry has not seen fit to restrict our civil rights, and pray God, they will not. It is far better that an occasional miscreant escape justice—and our people retain freedom—than that all offenders be brought to task at the forfeit of our liberty.

But, it must be said, there are two strongly voiced views relative to this matter. One view suggests that some constitutional safeguards are being construed by some courts in a way that is inconsistent with the history and philosophy behind them. A few extremists go so far to proclaim that constitutional protections are outdated and unwelcome obstructions to effective law enforcement. People taking this position see nothing improper in the reduction of personal liberty in order to achieve community security.

Those who take this position note the silence of civil libertarians relative to crime and habitual anti-social activities, relative to the victims of the criminal, relative to the necessity for restrictions on conduct, relative to the danger of unlimited freedom, relative to disrespect for authority, and relative to civic duties. They note, instead, extreme stress on legal technicalities, overemphasis on criminal rights, maledictions against police, and they regard such stress, overemphasis, and vehemence as unwise, even though the result of zeal rather than malice.

Those who hold this attitude feel that many citizens do not realize the threat to the nation in terms of the crime rate, rising continuously. They feel that some people seem to side with the criminal, withholding information and assistance from the police. They feel that some citizens are indifferent to crime and disorder. They feel that moral decay is weakening the country, and that unless substantial discretion is allowed the police, the criminals will become more bold and contemptuous of the law.

Another view, just as strongly held, suggests that constitutional protections are to be rigorously followed, even if law enforcement is less effective. Those who take this position are willing to give up some social order in order to preserve personal liberty.

Those who take this position note the silence of police leadership relative to the rule of law, the importance of civil liberties, the necessity for police legality, and the need for edifying public example. They note, instead, some exaggerated stress on efficiency and performance, some overemphasis on crime rates, snarling remarks about the courts, and they regard such exaggeration, overemphasis and vehemence as unwise, even though the result of zeal rather than malice.

Those who hold this attitude feel that some police overconcentrate on a part of their duty, securing community safety, but ignore the equally important duty of protecting personal liberty. They hold that some police are losing public respect and support, and that this is due to police attitudes that are disdainful of human dignity. They indicate that some police treat suspect, offender, and good citizen with the same rudeness, suspicion, contempt, arrogance, and mechanical forced courtesy, and act as if they were far beyond the power of any human agency to control them.

Many police executives are frustrated today because of the heavy pressures brought to bear upon them, and their agencies, to eliminate crime and delinquency hazards and to successfully solve cases. Particularly is this true with reference to individual activities that are in extreme public disfavor, such as are exemplified by the narcotic addict, homosexual, alcoholic, vagrant, criminal syndicate member, and subversive. Instead of pressuring legislative representatives for changes in the law, many citizens pressure their chief of police. And much such pressure is without knowledge of the law and its limitations, its restrictive interpretations by the courts, and its scope.

Unfortunately, sometimes, frustrated police executives and officers accept and implement policies and procedures that are technically illegal, in order to placate public opinion, and "get the job done". The ultimate result is never constructive.

2. *Can law enforcement afford to be completely open with the general public in revealing data relative to its operations?* Much of law enforcement success lies in creating a mass state of mind in order to gain public compliance with law—hence the admonitions "Crime does not pay!" "Drunk drivers go to jail!" "Speed laws enforced by radar!"—in order to create the impression and belief that bad conduct will result in enforcement action. This would seem to be a well-founded rationale as most people act according to their beliefs. Yet, what are the chances of being observed, identified, apprehended? In most cases, the chances of being arrested are not nearly as great as the public believes, and relatively few offenders who commit major crime are found guilty in court.

We must realize that law enforcement is largely a preventive and deterrent activity aimed at achieving as high a degree of public compliance as is possible. This is accomplished by patrolling to supervise conduct, by investigating to identify offenders and to recover property, by warning, citing, and arresting those guilty of criminal behavior, and by assisting in the prosecution and trial which may result in penalizing. Thus is established a *belief* in the probability of detection, a *belief* in the certainty of enforcement action, and a *belief* in the adequacy of penalty.

Thus, certain data relative to police operations are not universally disseminated. It might be harmful (in terms of creating a psychological state of mind) to unduly publicize the numbers of cases which, for one reason or another, do not culminate in the identification and arrest of the offender.

On the other hand, police agencies cannot afford to be overly secretive, unnecessarily aloof, mysteriously uncommunicative, nor in a continuous hypersensitive sulk, if public support is to be engendered and maintained. As the late O. W. Wilson, former Superintendent of the Chicago Police Department put it:

> In many communities, police agencies have assumed the burden and responsibility for all that is criminal. It is high time that we in the law enforcement field get off the defensive. Crime is a community problem and stands today as one of the most serious challenges of our generation. Our citizens must be forced to recognize their responsibilities in its suppression. Law enforcement agencies are obligated to keep local citizens informed as to the magnitude of the crime problem, to point out weaknesses in the system for the administration of criminal justice, and to advocate those changes in state laws which will facilitate law enforcement without interference with the rights of individuals. A community which is well informed on the problems and which is unwilling to tolerate crime will succeed in its efforts to reduce it. Community intolerance of crime can best be reflected in the form of support—material and spiritual—for its local law enforcement agencies. The agency, in turn, must earn this support.[1]

Thus, all information (which will not compromise legitimate agency objectives, nor interfere with sensitive and privileged operations) should be made public and every effort extended to inform the community of police needs and opportunities for citizen cooperation.

This, of course, is required by the free press guarantee of the First Amendment, which, as the courts have interpreted it, is almost an absolute right. The right of a defendant to a fair trial, on the other hand, is guaranteed by the Sixth Amendment. The clash between these competing rights has produced some very difficult problems. Both bar and publishers associations have appointed special committees to try to find a mutually acceptable solution to the Constitutional issue.

The federal policy is to restrict the disclosure of evidence, prior to trial —such as confessions, alibis, or other statements of a defendant, identity of witnesses, and results of fingerprint, lie detector, ballistic or other tests. The federal policy permits the release of the following information before a trial:

1. The defendant's name, age, residence, employment, marital status, and similar background information.
2. The substance or text of the charge.

---

[1] Wilson, O. W. (1961). Address to the Annual Meeting of the International Association of Chiefs of Police, Montreal, Canada, October 3rd.

3. The identity of the investigating and arresting agency and the length of the investigation.
4. The circumstances immediately surrounding the arrest, including the time and place of arrest, resistance, pursuit, possession and use of weapons, and description of items seized at time of arrest.
5. A defendant's criminal record, but involving only federal crimes, and only *convictions*.
6. Photographs of defendants, but only where a "law enforcement function is served thereby".

It would not be at all surprising to see such federal policy adopted by state and local law enforcement agencies, with the full cooperation of the news media.

3. *Can the law be enforced exactly as on the books, or is discretion to be allowed?* Here we deal with exemption from the force of law and preferential treatment.

Which of the following should have special privilege? Relatives of the officer? Fellow officer? Mayor? Councilmen? Supervisors? Governor? Assemblymen? Congressmen? Clergymen? Doctors? Lawyers? Judges? Prosecutors? Prison officials? With reference to minor infractions only, or both major and minor violations?

Which of the following should be answered negatively? Should *one* mile per hour over the speed limit result in citation? Should *any* inebriation away from home mean incarceration? Should *any* gambling violation result in arrest?

If *no* exemption from the force of law, and *no* preferential treatment were allowed, doctors would be detained and cited en route to dying patients; police officers would write their wives traffic citations; the vice officer would arrest his father participating in a family penny-ante poker game; the patrolman would cite the newlywed whose automobile clattered too loudly; and the juvenile officer would arrest the chief's son for violation of the curfew laws.

The law enforcement officer must at all times perform his sworn duty and he has no right to ignore any violation of law. However, the most effective law enforcement officer is one who concentrates on those areas which pose the greatest problem or danger to the social structure. The professional law enforcement officer keeps in mind at all times the spirit of the law as well as the letter of the law. He realizes that he does not have the type of authority which is vested in the public prosecutor who may, in his discretion, avoid prosecuting in certain cases.

The officer must learn to decide issues with the best interests of the community *and* the best interests of the individual citizen as his criteria. A summons, citation, or arrest should never be merely a question of adding to the weekly or monthly production record of the officer. The law enforcement officer must learn to decide issues with prudence and with a sense of compassion—but never as an unfeeling, cold, mechanical instrument of government. A few examples will suffice to illustrate the point:

> It is 3:30 A.M. A vehicle fails to come to a complete stop at an intersection controlled by boulevard stop signs. The area is uninhabited, there is no other traffic on the roads, visibility is clear for several hundred yards in all directions, and the driver slowed down and looked about before starting through the intersection.

One type of officer would pull the car over, ask for operator's license, indicate that the stop was for failure to stop at a boulevard stop sign, write out a summons or citation, and release the driver. The officer has done nothing illegal or immoral. He has acted efficiently, going "by the book," and has written a citation or summons which will stand up in court, and which will count toward his production record.

Another type of officer would pull the car over, ask for operator's license, indicate that the stop was for failure to stop at a boulevard stop sign, discuss the matter of good driving habits, indicate that even though traffic was light and visibility good, citizens must condition themselves to careful attention to traffic control devices, warn the driver and release him. The officer has done nothing illegal or immoral. But, he has utilized prudence and discretion, accomplished a traffic mission, and, no doubt, given the citizen both food for thought and pride in his police.

Which type of officer does the best police work for the community? For the individual involved?

Another example:

> It is 6:00 A.M. and two men driving down a rain-slick freeway observe the scene of an accident. A car had struck an abutment and the driver had been thrown clear. Two other motorists who had stopped had moved him to the side and put out flares. Another motorist who had gone on said he would call police. The flares were about to go out and one of our two citizens lighted two more and was placing them on the freeway when an officer arrived.

One type of officer would say, "What do you think you're doing, playing cop?" and write a summons or citation for "stopping on the freeway."

Another type of officer would commend the citizens for their civic responsibility, even while warning of the hazards of stopping on a rain-swept freeway.

One more example:

> It is 11:00 P.M. and a driver is observed pulling away from the curb, lights out, moving slowly but erratically. There is no traffic, nor any parked cars, on a deserted residential street. Officer has stopped car, noted that driver is under the influence of alcohol, when a resident runs out of his house to the scene, stating that he wants to talk to officer "about that man in the car."

One type of officer would state, "This is none of your business, mister, return to your house right now or I'll arrest you for interference." Such officer would then impound the vehicle, arrest and book driver for drunk driving. The officer has done nothing illegal or immoral, has acted with dispatch and efficiency, and has scored another arrest for the production record.

Another type of officer would allow a statement to be made. Upon hearing that the driver had visited resident, was despondent because his wife had just died on the operating table, had been given whiskey by the resident in order to quiet his nerves, had five children in his house just three doors down the street, and was attempting to drive but 50 yards to his home, the officer would check out the story. If it were verified, officer would see that children were cared for, that driver was placed with friends or relatives, that vehicle was parked and locked, and the officer would then return to patrol.

Which officer made the more prudent decision?

Where serious crimes are involved, where police hazards are significant, where individual or community safety is jeopardized, the policeman does *not* have wide latitude in his decisions. But, nonetheless, there are many occasions where the spirit of the law can be considered, and the strict letter of the law left untarnished.

The wise and prudent officer does not allow himself to overlook violations, nor does he become an automatic machine, cold and insensitive.

(The authors do not here consider the matter of *self-serving* discretion —gross failure to enforce the law for selfish ends—such as occur in those cases where policemen, friends and relatives of policemen, government officials, holders of "courtesy cards" and "honorary membership" cards in police associations, or anyone who can do favors for police, are granted immunity from the enforcement of minor traffic laws, codes and ordinances. These practices cannot be considered as "discretion," but only as totally inexcusable acts of non-feasance, and as a reprehensible form of police incompetence.)

To attempt to enforce *all* the *law, all* the *time,* with respect to *all* citizens would result in utter chaos; to ignore *all* offenses, *all* the time, with respect to *all* citizens would result in immediate grave harm to the individual and society. The goals of law enforcement are to prevent crime and disorder, preserve the peace, and protect life, property, and individual freedom; hence, those offenses which *most gravely* threaten the health, welfare, safety, and stability of the community are given enforcement priority at the *time* they are most rampant, with respect to the *most troublesome* offenders. It is the responsibility of the Chief of Police or other top law enforcement administrator to set the enforcement policy for his jurisdiction, acting with the advice and counsel of the legislative body, governmental executive officers, prosecutors, and courts. It is the responsibility of the individual law enforcement officer to implement that policy with wisdom and objectivity.

4. *Can each anti-social member of society be said to surrender his civil rights at the moment he offends?* This is a *most* delicate point, and controversial. Currently, there are two strong positions held by people both within, and outside the police service.

Some would hold that when any person commits a crime, he forfeits any claims he might have to constitutional safeguards. They maintain that his choice of conduct, be he burglar, sex pervert, subversive, addict, or thief automatically deprives him of the privileges of community membership and citizenship. They hold that the person who commits such acts is beyond the pale of sympathy and courtesy, and should be treated as an enemy of society—as an enemy alien would be treated during a shooting war. They indicate that the safety of the community abrogates his claims to civil rights, and that any and all methods should be used to halt his insidious and malicious attacks upon the health, safety and welfare of the community and nation.

Some of those who hold this attitude feel that recent court decisions and recent legislation are "handcuffing the police," and that the guilty offender is slipping from justice due to a narrow and legalistic emphasis.

They would quote statements of American police leaders, such as— "either (the policeman) abides by the prescribed rules and renders ineffective service, or he violates or circumvents the rules and performs the service required of him," or, ". . . in severely limiting the powers of police it is anticipated that the police will ignore these legal limitations when the immediate public welfare appears to demand police lawlessness."

Some of those who hold this position do not demand that police attitudes and actions be perfect; do not require that police be more precise than other members of the community. They indicate that if "perfection" is required of police, the police will be immobilized, put in a "straitjacket."

Some of those who hold this attitude would quote the courts, as in *Kepner,* "there is more danger that criminals will escape justice than that they will be subjected to tyranny"; *Garsson,* "Our dangers do not lie in too little tenderness to the accused . . . what we need to fear is the archaic formalism and the watery sentiment that obstructs, delays, and defeats the prosecution of crime"; and the dissent in *Mapp,* "Our voice becomes only a voice of power, not of reason."

Others who hold this attitude feel that we cannot approach the criminal with some kind of "Marquis of Queensbury" etiquette. They hold that the criminal abides by no rules of fair play, and therefore a "free hand" is necessary to cope with those who would seek to damage and destroy our people and our communities. They feel that if more latitude is not allowed, we will fail in the responsibility of protecting our people. They hold, in essence, that "gentlemen cops don't catch crooks!"

They despise the civil libertarian who, with cunning, might attempt to exploit basic human desires for liberty and justice and place such desires in the service of anarchy or worse by convincing a jeopardized nation to overlook the need for order and control in the name of the Constitution.

Some who have this attitude often become emotional and irrational, and tag opposing concepts as the "teary-eyed blubbering of sob-sisters," the "delicate tenderness of the bleeding-hearts," the "myopic softness of the pseudo-liberal," the "fuzzy-minded dogma of egghead radicals," the "undermining of pinkos," the "inane chatter of theoreticians," and the "nonsense of starry-eyed idealists." Such labels are only the result of emotional frustrations and rational simplicism.

But others hold an equally strong position. They believe that all persons, innocent or guilty, are entitled to the fullest protection of the Constitution. They feel that all persons should be treated as innocent until proved guilty, and that the past record of the offender, or the heinousness of his offense, or the attitudes of the community, have no bearing on his right to all privileges of citizenship. They indicate that constitutional guarantees should be respected by every government official, and they call upon police to protect alike the rights of those who break the law as well as those who obey it.

Some of those who have this attitude feel that police thinking lags far behind that of the courts, which have the duty of enforcing the Constitution, and that some police stress the expedient at the expense of the lawful, missing the real meaning of the police role in a democracy. They would regard any policeman who knowingly and willfully ignored, violated, or circumvented the law as a dangerous subversive, undermining the edifice of justice, weakening the rule of law, and, by example, teaching the foul doctrine that "might makes right."

They would quote statements of American police leaders, such as— "The greatest evidence that law enforcement can offer to the community as proof that it has come of age as a profession is a rock-ribbed, unwavering preoccupation with, and regard for, personal rights and liberties," or, "Unless we abide by the very highest standards among ourselves, we have no business enforcing the law upon others."

Some of those who hold this attitude believe that it is never proper for police to assert that they must violate, ignore, or circumvent the law in order to be effective—never right to say, in effect, that the end justifies the means. They state that if expediency is the yardstick for police action, the police service will, in effect, demonstrate that "it takes one to catch one."

They would quote the courts, such as in *Cahan*, "history has demonstrated all too clearly how short the step is from lawless though efficient enforcement of the law to the stamping out of human rights"; *Boyd*, "It is the duty of the courts to be watchful for the constitutional rights of the citizen and against any stealthy encroachment thereon," and *Mapp*, "nothing can destroy a government more quickly than its failure to observe its own laws, or worse, its disregard of the charter of its own existence."

Others who hold this attitude feel that we cannot confront Communism if we practice its foolish disregard for the God-given rights, freedom and dignity of every human person. They feel that we must make the promises of our Constitution bold realities for the whole world to see. They feel that if we do not do this, we don't deserve either the leadership of the free world, or God's help in victory over the inhuman philosophy of Communism. They hold, in essence, that "democratic cops are gentlemen cops!"

They despise the police leader who, with cunning, might attempt to exploit basic human desires for community safety and place such desires in the service of the police state by convincing free men to overlook tyranny in the name of security.

Some who have this attitude often become emotional and irrational, and tag opposing concepts as the utterances of "incipient fascists," "badge-happy sadists," "steel-brained avengers," "compassionate robots," and "lovers of terror." Such labels are only the result of emotional frustration and rational simplicism.

Thus, we see two attitudes, each accepted with varying degrees of intellectuality and emotion by citizens both in and out of the police service.

One attitude suggests that there are very grave threats to the safety and security of our nation, and that, as a practical here-and-now matter, restrictions which hamper the most effective means of dealing with crime and disorder can justifiably be overlooked.

The other attitude holds that the rule of law is a cornerstone of our society, and that, as a practical here-and-now matter, constitutional protections must be observed at all times by all those entrusted with governmental authority and power.

As we reason, so we act. According to our positions do we praise or fault police. And according to his positions does the policeman do his work.

The authors recommend serious attention to this question of position, and urge commitment to the second position as one most reflective of American ideals and a proud democratic heritage. But, regardless of position, the authors would respectfully recommend a prudent reticence to engage in any categorical labeling of those who might challenge strongly held views.

5. *Can the law enforcement officer, in order to effectively perform his*

mission, violate the law? Does the *good* end, protection of the individual and society, justify *any* means used? Even trespass, illegal wire-tapping, excessive force, perjury, or illegal arrest?

It can be said that a certain amount of law enforcement activity lies in a *positive zone*—where actions are legal and moral, and would stand a penetrating evaluation of judge, scholar, minister, lawyer, and citizen. (Arrests made for crimes committed in an officer's presence; confessions and admissions freely given; searches and seizures conducted with a proper warrant. . . .)

It can be said that a small portion of law enforcement activity lies in a *negative zone*—where actions are legally or morally reprehensible, or could not be justified by the most agile casuistry. (Illegal arrests as a form of attitude punishment for minority group members; illegal arrests in order to satisfy departmental production demands; illegal arrests in order to abate a community hazard; illegal arrests in order to justify an overly pro-longed detention; illegal violence or unnecessary force; confessions and admissions obtained by duress, coercion, force, threat, or promise; searches of persons or places without reasonable cause; untruthful testimony in court for the purpose of justifying an otherwise bad arrest. . . .)

And it can be said that another portion of law enforcement activity lies in an *unclear zone*—where some illegal or immoral activities are somehow tolerated and rationalized by both public and police. (Harassment of un-desirables such as vagrants, or criminal syndicate members, subversives, homosexuals, alcoholics; illegal entry to secure evidence or information on which to base an investigation or arrest; the grant of immunity to an offender who informs; the trading down to lesser charges in return for cooperation; deceit in obtaining confessions and admissions; extralegal use of wiretap and microphone; violating, circumventing, or ignoring legal limi-tations for the sake of results. . . .)

The authors recommend firm commitment to the *positive zone*, unde-viating rejection of the *negative zone,* and willful avoidance of the *unclear zone,* to all who would wish professional recognition or stature.

These are controversial areas of discussion. The authors do not pretend to have the final word, particularly because experts—moral theologians as well as judicial scholars—are not in total agreement. Nonetheless, the authors feel that young men or women of high standards should realize that their entry into law enforcement is not likely to be without severe trials of conscience and judgment, and that there exists the risk that, with the passage of time, their consciences may become calloused, and their judgment conveniently blind. That is one reason why professional law en-forcement administrators welcome candidates possessed of absolute and unswerving personal integrity.

PUNISHMENT

People will sometimes ask for an opinion of punishment in general, or some punishment in particular. Punishment is usually defined as the infliction of pain or penalty. It goes into the judicial sentence after a plea or verdict of guilty.

More closely defined, *punishment* inflicts pain as a retribution for a misdeed, whereas *correction* is punishment with the idea of bringing about improvement or reform. *Discipline* carries the idea of punishment which educates or establishes useful habits.

Punishment can be *corporal*, inflicting bodily pain; or *spiritual* and environmental, the pain of loss of freedom; or *economic*, the pain of loss of money or property. Punishment tends to become fiendish or ferocious, especially corporal punishment that is habitual and unchecked.

Corporal punishment is still widespread throughout the world. It can be mild, such as simple cuffing; stocks, or pillory; infliction of monotonous food, or even prohibition of smoking. It can be of increased severity, such as forced hard labor, paddling, beating, whipping, branding, mutilation, or amputation—in other words, deliberate physical torture by various devices. Such devices are matters of current record in military and civilian prisons throughout most of the civilized world. In Scandinavian countries and in our own, however, there is less formal emphasis on corporal punishment than in an earlier day.

The maximum corporal punishment is capital punishment—the death penalty. This has been accomplished historically by torture limited only by the human imagination—boiling in oil or lead, impalement, burial alive, burning alive, exposure to wild beasts or to insects, or by simple exposure to the elements. Official infliction of death by execution in the world today is largely limited to hanging, the firing squad, asphyxiation by cyanide gas, by shock through electricity, by strangulation with garrote or by beheading (guillotine). There has been a sharp drop in death by capital punishment in the United States in recent years. Hundreds of prisoners are held in death rows in capital punishment states while legal delays occur and changes in the law are contemplated in the Federal system.

Spiritual punishment can be mild, such as a sentence of probation. It can be more severe, depending upon the individual, through ostracism or exile, banishment or deportation; or still more severe, through incarceration in a jail, reformatory or penitentiary. These punishments can also be combined. A person may be banished to an island and kept there in a prison. Any confinement in a prison is a painful process even under the most favorable conditions because of ego, sex, family and work deprivations.

Economic punishment may take the form of monetary fines, property confiscation, or damage or restitution payments. Other forms are available to a judge, such as a forced change of employment, or special restrictions, such as limitation or revocation of a driver's license.

There is general agreement that whoever has the authority to make the law has the authority to penalize. Thus, the legislature may specify penalties or may enact laws which allow discretion to the sentencing authority. That authority which implements the penalties enacted by the legislators is usually a judge.

There is also general agreement that *moral responsibility* on the part of the lawbreaker is a vital condition of a fair and just penalty in serious offenses. The offensive act must have been intentional. The degree of deliberation is a factor in the degree of punishment. The offender must have been aware of the nature of his act, must have known it was wrong, and must have been able to avoid committing it. Otherwise, questions arise as to the sanity of the wrongdoer.

Today there is increasing controversy in our society over the accomplishments of punishment in achieving the social goals claimed for it. The ancient code of the *lex talionis*—a life for a life, an eye for an eye, a tooth for a tooth—is largely discarded in the world today, except in highly visible and unusual crimes of great public reaction, such as assassination or treason. The tendency today is to think of punishment as including the *reform* of the transgressor. Other elements include deterrence of other transgressors; the requirement for justice; the necessity for proportion between penalty and offense; and the apparent need to have wrongdoers punished to make the average citizen feel rewarded and secure in his own avoidance of crime. The current trend is to regard punishment as largely incapable of accomplishing what is expected of it.

There is a reason that this *Introduction to Law Enforcement and Criminal Justice* begins with such general discussion. Very often, law enforcement officers, supervisors, and top-level executives are involved in public discussions on the purposes of law enforcement, the means which it utilizes to achieve its goals, and the legality, morality, efficiency and compassion of its operations. Very often, law enforcement people are involved in peripheral debates on prosecution processes, judicial activity, correctional processes, and probation and parole functions.

Such discussion and debate must, if it is to be productive of good for public and police, be based on reasonable foundations. Students of law enforcement must not only be prepared to master the skills and techniques of the vocation, but must also be thoroughly prepared to present and defend its proper goals and methods. Students of law enforcement must not only look forward to participating in traditional and customary police practices, but also to preserving and maintaining the good and wholesome, and to rejecting and eliminating the bad and reprehensible. Such a responsibility is awesome and sacred, demanding the utmost dedication, capacity, and character.

Further, social, economic, and geographic determinants which influence the gap between theory and practice must be studied. Dehumanizing influences such as racism, pollution, unemployment, disease, ignorance, violence, corruption, intimidation, brutality, and indifference may become so powerful that effective crime control is impossible.

The authors would *not* be satisfied to have law enforcement students enter the law enforcement vocation only to be classed as *"starry-eyed promoters of the premature."* Nor would they be satisfied to see them become tabbed as *"die-hard defenders of the obsolete."*

They would be deeply gratified to see the graduate careerist become a *"prudent advocate of the possible."* They would be gratified to see the graduate careerist become a *wise and learned professional practitioner of the art and science of democratic law enforcement.*

That is the challenge and opportunity awaiting the graduate of capacity and integrity. That is the key to an honorable and productive future for the vocation, its members, and the citizens they represent. That is the theme of this text.

TOPICS FOR DISCUSSION

1. Which of the five philosophical problems presents the largest arena of conflict in the administration of criminal justice?
2. Is it possible for law enforcement activity to avoid the "unclear zone"?
3. Which forms of punishment have the greatest deterrent effect?
4. Is "severe" punishment more or less effective than punishment that is "swift and certain"?
5. Authors call for "wise and learned professional practitioner(s) of the art and science of democratic law enforcement." What is the distinction between "wisdom" and "learning"; between an "art" and a "science"?

PART II
HISTORY OF CRIMINAL JUSTICE

Chapter IV

ANCIENT AND FEUDAL BACKGROUNDS

THE BEGINNINGS OF FORMAL LAW ENFORCEMENT activities are clouded within a historical mist. The ancient social order was of a patriarchal nature, with small family groups affiliating with tribes or clans. Tribal customs developed, and informal codes of conduct in conformity with the customs, but laws, as such, did not follow until written records were commonplace.

In early tribal and clan life, the people were the police, and the chief of the tribe or clan exercised executive, legislative, and judicial powers. Often he would appoint members of the tribe or clan to special duties—enforcing his edicts, or acting as his bodyguard—but they were primarily members of the community rather than a selected police body.

Crimes against a member of the tribe or clan were handled by the person injured, if he was able, or by his family. Crimes against the group were handled by the group—by the entire tribe or clan. Thus developed the idea of "kin police," wherein the family, tribe, or clan assumed some responsibility for obtaining justice. The philosophy of early justice and punishment was primarily retaliatory, and often crude. Branding or multilation of offenders was not uncommon, the first use of the "criminal record" for identification. Flaying, impalation, exposure to wild beasts, burning, stoning, and crucifixion were applied to serious offenses. It was during these early days of justice that the "blood feud" developed, which bound the victim's family, clan or tribe to vengeance, and led to prolonged and bloody warfare. As a method of mitigating and shortening these affairs, the practice of settling disputes with property evolved, the first evidences of *civil restitution* or *damages*.

Around 2100 B.C., the culture of centuries resulted in the codification of customs in the *Laws of Hammurabi*, King of Babylon. They dealt with the responsibilities of the individual to the group, private dealings between individuals, and contained penalties of the retributive type. *Messengers* are mentioned as carrying out the commands of the law.

Nineveh, the ancient center of the Assyrian empire, is said to have had tribunals (courts) which dealt with murder, theft, and adultery.

About 1500 B.C., Egypt had a system of judges and courts, and even more sophisticated laws, as for bribery and corruption. About 1400 B.C.,

Amenhotep, King of Egypt, developed a marine patrol on the coast of Egypt near the Delta, and set up custom houses.

In Persia, in the Sixth Century B.C., under Cyrus, there existed a road and postal system which points to the probability of institutional police; under Darius, the empire was divided into provinces for the purposes of administration with satraps placed in authority and given the authority to levy and collect taxes. The early Greek city states witnessed some development from tribal or clan policing to community (city) policing. Pisistratus, who was ruler of Athens, established a guard system to protect the tower, highways, and his own person. Sparta developed a ruler-appointed police, and as the regime was authoritarian, this body is often referred to as the first "secret police" system.

Solon, the ancient law-giver of Athens (638-559 B.C.) was asked to name the essential ingredient of the ideal community. His answer could be memorized by every law enforcement professional: "When those who have not been injured become as indignant as those who have!"

It might be noted that Plato, the Greek philosopher, who lived circa 427-347 B.C., involved himself in many discussions relative to the nature of society, the State, law, justice, and punishment. He indicated, as an example of his interest, that the proper end of punishment was not merely to render the guilty their due (retribution), but, at the same time, to make them better. Thus, he regarded punishment not only as retaliative or retributive, but also as a tool of reform or rehabilitation.

Early commentaries on ancient Rome indicate that order was primarily maintained by the military legions of the rulers. The magistrates of that ancient city utilized *Quaestores* (inquirers) to judge in certain criminal cases, and it is said that their method of arrest was to go to the house of the accused and blow a trumpet or horn as an indication of arrest. Augustus, first emperor of Rome (27 B.C.), created the *Praetorian Guard* by placing members of his legions at the palace with the specific duty of protecting the life and property of the emperor, and therein, the *urban cohorts* (500-600 men; one-tenth of a legion) to keep the peace of the city. The *praefectus urbi* (prefect of the city) had authority to impose rules about public order, fire risks, religious observances, meetings, activities of prostitutes, beggars, and foreigners, and had at his disposal magistrates known as *curatores urbis*, each responsible for a section of the city. They were aided by *stationarii*, the residents of a city block, and by *vigiles* and *lictores* who patrolled the streets and acted as enforcement officers. These men, whose duties were to keep the peace and fight fires, numbered several thousand, and formed a nonmilitary unit (although armed with staves and traditional shortsword) deployed in geographical precincts. Some commentators, noting their fire-fighting responsibility along with their police duty, have referred to them as the first instance of "integrated police-fire services." This Roman system was reflected, to some degree, in all cities of the empire.

Juvenal (A.D. 60?), Roman satirist, is remembered for his ever-pertinent question: *Sed quis custodiet ipsos custodes?* ("But who is to guard the guards themselves?")

Seneca, a Roman statesman and first-citizen (4 B.C.-A.D. 65) observed that "punishment is designed to protect society by removing the offender, to reform its subjects, and to render others more obedient." Thus, he added to the ancient philosophy of retaliation, which was modified by Plato to include reformation, the concepts of protecting the general welfare and deterrence of potential offenders.

Law enforcement among the ancient Jews had been administered by kings, high priests, and elders of the tribe. This process was maintained even under Roman rule. Matthew (XXVI, 47) notes that Christ was arrested in the garden by those who came from the "chief priests and elders of the people." Acts (XXII, 4) indicates that Paul bore letters from the high priests and elders granting him the right to arrest, bind, and commit to prison both men and women.

Police mythology is replete with its own stories of technique. It is alleged that ancient Oriental investigations utilized tests for deception which are based on scientific principles. In one, the suspects were given rice to chew, and when one of them was unable to spit it out, in a masticated, salivated mass, he was deemed guilty of deception. Such test is said to be based on the phenomenon that fear inhibits the secretion of saliva in some people. In another alleged test, the suspects were brought before a darkened room and told that the room contained a sacred donkey which would infallibly bray when the guilty party pulled its tail. Suspects were then sent, one by one, through the darkened room and told to pull the tail of the donkey. Upon exposure to light, the hands of the suspects were checked for cleanliness, because the tail of the donkey had been secretly sooted, and hence, the guilty party would ordinarily have been afraid to pull the tail and thus have clean hands. Such a test is said to be based on suggestibility, and quite sound psychologically.

Other than the development of the Praefectura Urbis in Rome and Constantinople, as the primary local government agency, the history of law enforcement and its practices is quite blank for the first five centuries, A.D., for after the fall of the Roman empire in A.D. 395, Europe was in a state of strife and turmoil, with warring nations engaging in brutal invasion and plunder.

Around A.D. 450-650, the Romano-Celtic people of England were invaded by Germanic tribes from the continent referred to as "Anglo-Saxons."

There, in England, developed small geographical groupings of people known as *tuns* (from which our word "town" is derived). In these tuns, a form of individual and group responsibility for policing evolved.

In China, about this time, under the T'Ang dynasty, the use of fingerprints as a means of identification was developed.

In France, the *Capitularies of Charlemagne* were issued in A.D. 785, and were a complicated set of laws dealing with weights and measures, tolls, sales, burial of the dead, emergency procedures for famine and pestilence, and crime. The enforcement of the law was through the feudal lord, for France had been divided into geographical areas known as *Contes* (counties), each under a *conte* (count), who acted as a representative of the king.

About this same time, in France, developed the earliest seeds of the jury system. Frankish kings developed the *inquisitio* (from which has developed our word "inquest") which was a method of deriving a just opinion. Leading persons were placed under oath and asked to render their opinion; as they were sworn, they were known as *jurata* (those sworn), and their statement to the king was known as a *veredictum* (true saying). Hence our words "jury," and "verdict." Originally they were confined to deciding issues relating to royal lands in dispute, but later gave opinions relative to taxation and the state of public order.

In A.D. 875, the Marshals of France, responsible to the king for the maintenance of security, developed a body of armed men known as "maréchaussée." A military force for protecting the highways was formed under Francis I (1494-1547), composed of mounted archers, and commanded by the *prevots de marechaux*. From these bodies developed the modern *gendarmerie* which police France today. No mention of French police history should fail to mention that architect of police power, Fouche, Duc d'Otranto, Minister of Police to Napoleon, 1759-1820.

ANGLO-SAXON ENGLAND

At this point we turn to Anglo-Saxon England to note the developments which took place between A.D. 700 and 900. The tuns, small villages, leaned heavily toward local self-government, yet there was a pressing need for greater organization, not only in terms of local justice, but also in terms of local defense.

The system of community and individual responsibility became more sophisticated. *Trial by ordeal,* as a method of determining guilt, subjected the suspect to a proof of innocence by surviving tests utilizing boiling water or a hot bed of coals. If he could plunge his arm into the water, or walk across the coals, without becoming horribly burned, this was deemed to be a sign of his innocence. *Trial by combat,* as a means of determining guilt, resolved the issue by battle, and the victor was deemed innocent. Parties to disputes, eventually, were able to have someone represent them on the field of battle. *Compurgation,* as a means of determining guilt, involved the taking of a serious oath by the disputants, and later involved the use of *Compurgators,* those who were willing to swear to the innocence of the accused.

Capital punishment was not often a part of Anglo-Saxon local community judicial process, but branding was utilized for the more heinous crimes such as murder and rape. Punishment was graduated to fit the crime, and an elaborate system of fines was installed. Restitution to the victim, to his family, or to his tun was common, and if an offender was unable to make restitution he was placed into the service of the victim, his family, or tun, for a period of time, or even for life in some cases. Penalties were enforced by the community, and if an offender escaped to another tun, he was turned back to his own village when apprehended; if the offender was not found, his family or tun would be required to make restitution. Thus we can see the legal beginnings of the *fine, restitution, involuntary servitude,* and *rendition.*

TITHING

The *Frank-Pledge* system, developed in France in the seventh century, also called *plegium liberale* and mentioned in the Leges Henrici of the 12th century, was a method of establishing the responsibility of each man for his neighbor, and of the group for each man. It resulted in the development of the English *borh* and *tithing system* which was utilized to ensure local justice and to protect the community from raiding tribes. (Saxon, borh; Norman, tithing).

Freemen were required to group themselves into a *tithing,* or group of ten families, for the purpose of maintaining the peace and sharing the duty of protecting the community. Each member of the tithing was responsible for the good behavior of his neighbor, and the tithing was responsible for the conduct of its members. If an errant member escaped, the tithing itself could be required to make restitution. Generally, a landed proprietor (thane) was responsible for all his dependents, and his whole group constituted a tithing; a landless freeman not attached to a thane had to combine with nine others like himself to form a tithing. Every freeman above twelve years of age was required to be enrolled in some tithing.

A "headborough" or "borsholder" or *tithingman* was elected from the group and was given the responsibility for raising the hue and cry and meting out punishment. (The *hue and cry* was a process whereby every able bodied man had to join in the common chase for offenders. Such activity was the origin of our current process of *citizen's arrest.*) The *tithing-*

man is mentioned as a peace official in the laws of Edgar (A.D. 959-975).

Ten tithings were called a *hundred*. The head-man of a hundred was called a *reeve*. These hundreds eventually began to meet every month, and some commentators have called this the earliest beginning of the town-meeting.

The *constable* (from the French institution *comes stabuli*, "master of horse"; the Constables of France had the duty of raising and maintaining the armies) was given the duty of supervising the weapons and equipment of the hundred. Later, High Constables were appointed over hundreds, and petty constables for towns and parishes within the hundred. Originally a military figure, the constable later emerged as a peace officer.

Several hundreds formed a *shire*, a geographical area equivalent to a county. The headman of the shire was called a *shire-reeve* (from which word "sheriff" was derived), and became a powerful military and judicial official appointed by noblemen, or by the king in areas not owned by noblemen. Shire-Reeves held the power of *posse comitatus* (power of the county) by which they could call upon all able-bodied men in the shire for assistance. Even today, in these United States, the County Sheriffs of most counties have a general power such as that.

Several shires made up an *earldom*, and the headman of the earldom was called an *earldom-man*.

This system came into existence between the seventh and ninth centuries. Alfred the Great, who made one nation of England in the latter part of the ninth century, found the system of great benefit in unifying the nation. Later, William the Conqueror refined the system to a great degree.

The system, however, had serious flaws. It was applicable to emergency situations, and worked well in an agrarian community where people were content to live in one place. When urban society began to develop, and people began to move about, the tithing system was difficult to keep intact. It also had a very serious defect in that it tended to encourage the concealment of crime and perjury in order that individual members of a tithing, or the tithing itself, might not have to make restitution for the acts of a tithing member.

Courts. Courts began to develop, such as the courts of *pied poudre* (dusty feet) which were set up in the county market area to deal with minor matters, and the *hundred courts*, or *courts of the shire* where the earldom-man presided, and sat with the local Bishop, Shire-Reeves, and Thanes.

Early Anglo-Saxon law held that children under seven years of age were not responsible in criminal matters, but offenders from seven to fourteen were examined, and if found responsible, were treated just as adults. The practice of *suspending sentence*, or withholding penalty on condition that the offender make restitution or reform his habits, developed, and, as well, the practice of *release on recognizance*, whereby people who were well-known were given freedom pending their trial.

TOPICS FOR DISCUSSION

1. What is the full meaning of the quote from Solon, ancient law-giver of Athens?
2. Could a tithing system for securing the peace work in the 20th Century?

Chapter V

ENGLISH PRECEDENTS

In 1066, William, Duke of Normandy, invaded and conquered England. The kind of philosophy of law enforcement brought with him was that of a highly repressive police system. Collective security was deemed far more important than individual freedom, so William proceeded to militarize the existing civil arrangements of the Anglo-Saxons. He divided England into fifty-five separate military areas and placed an officer of his own selection into each shire to take charge. In this way the *State* assumed the responsibility for keeping the peace, and set the stage for a *diminution of community responsibility* as had been required by the tithing system. Martial law was in effect.

King William decided that the shire-reeve should no longer try cases, and therefore selected his own judges to travel about the realm. They were called *vice comites* and represented a division of responsibility between law enforcement and judicial processes, for the shire-reeve heretofore had been authorized to perform both duties. The vice comes was an unpopular public officer, for the public believed that his purpose was to collect as many fines as possible. These travelling judges were the forerunners of the *circuit judge* of modern times.

In 1116, Henry I, son of William the Conqueror, issued the *Leges Henrici*, from which act Henry received the title "Law Giver." These laws divided England into thirty judicial districts, and are of particular import for the following statement: ". . . there will be certain offenses *against the king's peace,* arson, robbery, murder, false coinage, and crimes of violence." Thus comes into being the idea of *disturbance of the peace,* the concept that men were to be punished *by the State,* rather than by the individual or group that was injured.

A clear distinction of offense was made in the Leges Henrici. Serious crimes, such as murder, false coinage, arson, and crimes of violence, said the king, "we deem to be *felonious.*" (At this time, the word "felon" referred to a person of the lowest degree.) Other offenses were termed "*misdemeanors*" (meaning bad behavior) and included the lesser violations.

Henry II provided for the formulation, in each county, of juries consisting of twelve men of the hundred and four from each township to present felonies and accuse persons on a common report. In 1166, the first use was made of the jury system by a private person accused of crime at the *Assize of Clarendon*. (*Assize*: a court sitting, or session.) The Normans had brought the seeds of the system from France, where it had been used as an inquisition to determine rights. In its later French development, it operated by compelling those summoned before a royal representative to tell what they knew of anyone accused of committing an offense. At least twelve had to agree to the accuracy of the report in order to obtain royal action. In that type of operation, it acted as a jury of accusation, and as the forerunner of our *grand jury*.

The English development of the jury system resulted in a transformation, in that it heard witnesses and founded its decisions primarily upon that evidence. At first, witnesses were allowed only for the prosecution, but later development provided that witnesses for the defense could also be heard. During this evolution, rules of evidence were constructed, the rights to challenge jurymen were installed, and improved methods for impaneling the jury were inaugurated.

Thus, one can see the evolution of the jury from an instrument of royal absolutism to a safeguard of freedom. In its early use the authorities were more interested in repressing offenses against the king's peace than in abstract justice, and there was a tendency to treat the accused as guilty and begrudge him any means to prove his innocence. In the earlier days of jury process, it was regarded more as a privilege than as a right.

In his *Assize of Northampton* Henry II divided the country into six circuits and assigned three itinerant justices to each circuit to hold the "pleas of the crown"—that is, to determine which cases should go before the King's judges rather than before the county or manorial courts.

In his *Assize of Arms*, Henry II required every freeman to provide himself with arms to defend the realm and keep the peace.

The practice of recording judicial decisions begins in this era, and the English Common Law, or Customary Law, dates from this period. The division of Criminal Law and Tort Law, wherein the State prosecutes and punishes violations of the laws of the land, and requires restitution for private injuries, begins at this time.

The accused sometimes had a choice of trial by ordeal, trial by combat, or trial by jury. It was not much of a choice, for if the accused elected jury trial in its earlier days, and was found guilty, his property was seized along with that of his relatives.

Benefit of clergy exempted clergy from trial or punishment except through a church court; *sanctuary* was a custom that provided a fugitive from justice with immunity from arrest if he were in a church; the *liberties* consisted of various privileges and immunities granted by the King to both persons and communities.

Torture became a widely used tool to obtain confessions, and was often used for punishment after conviction. Punishment was varied, and crude.

The *Newgate Prison* was established about this time and contained prisoners accused of criminal, political, and religious offenses.

Capital punishment was primarily of two types: *beheading* (which was regarded as a noble form of dying), and *hanging* (which carried a definite stigma). *Strangulation, burying alive, boiling in oil or lead,* and *impaling* were occasionally utilized.

Lesser punishments consisted of the *pillory* (a device with holes for the head, hands, and feet, and to which a person was locked for a period of time so that he might undergo public ridicule); *scourging* or *whipping*; the *rack* (a machine which slowly stretched the offender); the *wheel* (a circular frame upon which the offender's bones were bent and broken); the *bastinado* (a beating of the offender's feet); the *strappado* (in which the offender had his hands tied behind him, a long rope attached and thrown over a high beam, and was then alternately lifted up and dropped down); and various forms of *mutilation.* There seemed to be no end of gruesome and savage processes for punishment.

In 1194, King Richard I assigned *coroners* to the counties. Not much is known of their duties. (Later, in 1275, under Edward I, the Coroner was given the specific duty to keep records and make inquiries concerning sudden and unnatural deaths. He also was given the responsibility for handling forfeitures to the crown, lost or abandoned property, wandering animals, and salvage.)

In 1195, Richard I appointed knights to see that all males over the age of fifteen were "sworn to the king"—the first formal example of the *loyalty oath.* (William the Conqueror is said to have required an oath of allegiance on the plains of Salisbury—but the Salisbury Oath was primarily one taken by the vanquished to the victor.) (By 1253 these knights became known as *peace wardens* or *conservators of the peace.* As time passed, and the importance of the shire-reeve's office waned, they were invested with judicial powers.)

During the twelfth century, the Norman system of game preservation was applied in England with great severity. The people were forbidden any liberty in the forests, and scores of officers were appointed to each forest to preserve the game. Special laws, law enforcement units, and courts were developed for the prevention and punishment of illegal hunting. *Verderers* were the judicial officers; *agisters* supervised the grazing land of the deer; *regarders* were responsible for the registration and declawing of dogs; and *foresters* and *rangers* were sworn to preserve the game and forests by enforcement of the law. Forest courts—*Woodmote Court, Court of Regard, Court of Suranimote,* and *Court of Justice Seat*—made inquiries, judged, and convicted. The people resented the harsh laws and broke them repeatedly. Their resentment was made particularly sharp due to the fact that the king and feudal nobles were excluded from the laws and could plunder the forests at will. This was the era of the "Robin Hood" band.

King John, brutal ruler of England, who took the throne in 1199 after the death of his brother, Richard I, was thoroughly despised by both people and nobles, and on the plain at *Runnymede,* June 15, 1215, he was forced to sign the *Magna Carta* (great charter) which guaranteed basic civil and political liberties to both people and nobles.

Two sections of the Magna Carta are of particular interest to law enforcement people:

Article 13 states, ". . . *and the City of London shall have all its ancient liberties and free customs. Moreover, we will grant that all other cities and villages shall have all their liberties and free customs.*" Thus was *local control* restored to the communities of England, and thus was established a clear separation between national and local government.

Article 39 states, "*No freeman may be taken or imprisoned or disseized or outlawed or banished or in any way destroyed . . . except by the lawful judgment of his peers, or by the law of the land. To none will we sell or deny or delay right or justice. We will not make men justicaries, constables, sheriffs, or bailiffs, unless they understand the law of the land, and are well disposed to observe it.*" Thus were *trial by jury* and *due process* installed as the right of a free people. (The student may note, here, the application of our Fifth and Sixth Amendments: ". . . *nor be deprived of life, liberty, or property without due process of laws;*" and, ". . . *the accused shall enjoy the right to a speedy and public trial, by an impartial jury. . . .*")

About 1250, the tithing system was fatally watered down in efficiency, and about all that remained was the obligation of rendering individual service when called upon to do so.

In 1252, Henry III issued a *writ* (legal order in writing) ordering that all men should be duly sworn to arms (enrolled in the national militia) before the local official. In townships or villages without such officials, a Constable was appointed for the purpose. A Head Constable, responsible for keeping the peace within the hundred, was also appointed. In London, the *watch* was inaugurated, utilizing householders in the area (*ward*) appointed in rotation from a roster. These people were unpaid, and their duties were unpopular. They were permitted to hire substitutes, but the substitutes were carelessly chosen, and were often the dregs of the community. In 1253, a standing watch under a constable was instituted, but the watch members were aged, crippled, sick, or of thieving habit.

The *Statute of Winchester,* issued by King Edward I in 1285, was a genuine effort to establish a systematic police system. It dealt with the system of watch and ward, both in and out of London.

It confirmed the ancient responsibility of the hundred for offenses committed within its boundaries and held it to be answerable. It ordained that "cries shall be made in all counties, markets, hundreds, fairs, so that none shall excuse himself by ignorance." It required every town to supplement its forces by deploying men at each gate to watch continually all night "from sun setting unto sun rising."

It provided that the gates of walled towns were to be shut between sunset and daybreak, and it forbade men to live in the suburbs except under the guarantee of a responsible householder. Thus, we see the development of the *curfew* idea.

It provided that every city, from May 26th to September 29th, should station a guard of six people at each gate; that every borough was to have a watch of twelve persons, and smaller cities from four to six. This watch was to be supervised by constables, and used during summer and autumn when it was impossible for the farmers to work the fields and protect their homes at the same time.

The watch and ward was manned by each householder in turn; refusal meant being sent to the pillory.

A local act specified the watch and ward for the City of London: gates were to be shut at night; twenty-four wards were to be established, with six watchmen in each; a marching watch was to be formed; and one alderman was to be responsible for arresting wrongdoers.

The act also provided that "There shall be established *bailiffs* and these bailiffs shall make an inquiry of all persons and lodgers and shall observe them at night." Thus, we note an early use of the bailiff who is, today, an officer of the court.

The Bailiff was required to check on all strangers every fifteen days. Thus, were sown the seeds of police identification bureaus. To assist him in his work, the Bailiff utilized *sergeants.*

There were several other interesting developments in law enforcement during this period. The *police des mouers* (police of the pouters) was established to regulate prostitution. A register was maintained, and no prostitutes were permitted except in certain parts of the city. Thus, the origin of the *red light district.*

On some watches, for the purpose of safety, the watchmen grouped themselves together and formed a *marching watch.* This may have been the germ of police *patrol activity.*

Edward III, in 1352, issued the *statutes of treason*, which provided that "Whoever shall give aid and comfort to the enemies of the land shall be guilty of *treason*, and shall forfeit his life." And these statutes also provided that "Whoever shall counterfeit the money of England knowing the money to be false, shall be guilty of treason." Thus, we note attention to *security violations* and *counterfeiting*.

In 1361, Edward III revived the peace wardens, or conservators of the peace, of Edward I. He issued an act relating to the *Justice of the Peace*. The act combined, in that office, the function of police and the function of judge, a combination that had been dead since William the Conqueror appointed the vice comites and restricted the functions of the shire-reeve.

These Justices of the Peace were country gentlemen, given authority by the crown for the preservation of the peace and for exercising judicial functions. They heard all felonies and trespasses, cared for prisoners, regulated prices and wages, administered the poor laws, saw that people went to church, and acted as the eyes and ears of the king. They were to be *learned in the law*, and could pursue, arrest, chastise, and imprison. Their charge was clear: "to restrain offenders, rioters and other barrators, and to pursue, to arrest, to take and to chastise them according to their offense." Later statutes increased their powers to include suppression of riots, punishment of unlawful hunters, and control of weight standards. The origin of *bail* is seen here, for part of their charge read: ". . . to take of all of them that be not of good fame, where they shall be found, sufficient surety for their good behavior."

There began, about this time, a struggle between the king and the people relative to the power of the king, with great machinations by the nobility.

In 1434, Henry VI, in order to encourage the identification of his detractors, created the position of *state informer*. Anyone who would discover and expose those engaging in seditious activities would be considered eligible for the position and would be given a monetary reward.

England was very much engaged, around 1500, in world trade. America had been discovered, and commercial activity was expanding. Wool was in short supply, and England had a great wool industry. Large landowners began to utilize more and more of their land for the grazing of sheep, and less and less for farming. Thus developed the *enclosure system* whereby more and more farmers were shoved away from their homes as the landowners converted the area to sheep-pasture. This resulted in a huge movement to the cities of England of poor and dispossessed and bitter people. *Crime began to rise.*

In 1585, Queen Elizabeth I issued a police act to improve government in the city of Westminster. Power was given to the Dean and High Steward of Westminster to punish "all matters of incontinencies, common scolds, common annoyances, and to commit to prison all who offend against the peace." The act was unenforceable and fell into disuse.

The merchants of England were very much dissatisfied with the protection offered to them. The middle class were rebelling against compulsory watch service and insisting upon the privilege of paying deputies to take their places. These hired deputies were not doing the job of protection that needed to be done. Therefore, the merchants began to hire their own *private police* to guard their establishments, to investigate crimes against them, and to recover property stolen from them. Thus developed the *Merchant Police* of England.

The cities were divided into parishes, and the people were becoming ever more upset over rising crime. They formed *Parochial Police*, at first requiring every member of the parish to serve in rotation, but later using paid parish constables.

The *Court of Star Chamber* (so called because the room in the palace where it met was so designated) was being used with vigor. It consisted of Councilors appointed by royal authority, met in secret session without a jury, used torture to force confessions, and handed down arbitrary judgments that were extremely severe. In essence, the Court of Star Chamber was a form of *legalized third degree*. It was finally abolished in 1641 by Charles I.

Civil war broke out in England and ended with a General, Oliver Cromwell, in power. From 1655 to 1657 the country was under Military Police. Cromwell divided the country into twelve districts and appointed a *Provost Marshal* to rule each district and act as judge. His rule was supported by some six thousand mounted troops under a major general. These troops had control of civilians as well as military personnel.

In 1663, King Charles II instituted a new system of night watch for London. The act provided for 1,000 watchmen or "bellmen" to be on duty from sunset to sunrise. They were ineffective and bore the brunt of English humor, being called *"Charlies"* and the *"shiver and shake watch."*

In 1688, the *Glorious Revolution* resulted in deposing James II, and in 1689 Parliament passed an act calculated to prevent a restoration of royal absolutism. This *bill of rights* provided guarantees of *freedom of speech*, and *protection against self-incrimination*. From the legalized third-degree of the Court of Star Chamber, England now moved to the position that no man was required to say anything that would incriminate him and that any man could speak his mind without fear of royal reprisal.

In 1692, crime was steadily increasing, so a system of *monetary reward* was instituted to encourage the population to assist in apprehending thieves and bandits. The result was disappointing, for it led only to a great deal of blackmail and false accusations.

In 1737, George II enlarged the Elizabethan Act of 1585 to allow for council of the city to levy taxes to pay for the night watch. As yet, the only paid watchmen were those paid by merchants, parishioners, and householders, and this was the first instance of *taxation for police protection.*

The 1745 Parliament set up a committee to inquire into the subject of maintenance of order—for crime was steadily rising.

In 1748, *Henry Fielding* was appointed magistrate for Middlesex and Westminster. He conceived the idea of *preventing crime by police action.* In 1751, he wrote *An Enquiry into the Cause of the Late Increase in Robberies* and suggested therein that *policing was a municipal function,* that there was a *need for well-paid men,* that some form of *mobile patrol was needed to protect the highways,* that separate *"runners" were needed to move swiftly to the scene of a crime,* and that a *separate police court* should be instituted. This was, indeed, the *first police survey.*

John Fielding assisted in the organization of the Bow Street station between 1754 and 1780. Three sections were developed: a foot-patrol to operate in the inner areas; a horse-patrol to operate in the outer areas as far as fifteen miles (these wore red waistcoats and were known as "Redbreasts"); and the *Bow Street Runners* or *"Thief Takers"* who were selected personnel who moved swiftly to the crime scene to begin immediate investigation. These runners never wore any kind of uniform. Because they were primarily concerned with investigation of crime, many observers have referred to the *Bow Street Runners* as the first *detective unit.*

In 1777, George III improved upon the 1737 Act of George II relative to watchmen. His new act prescribed wages, arms (staves), equipment (rattles, lanterns), duties, how they were to proclaim the time of night ("as loudly and audibly as he can"), how they were to see that all doors were safe and well secured (the first *door shakers* by royal edict), and how they were to apprehend all loose, idle, or disorderly persons.

In 1796, Dr. Colquhoun, Middlesex magistrate, wrote "On the Police of the Metropolis" and therein recommended a *register of offenders, communication improvement* between city and rural magistrates, and the creation of a *centralized, trained, vigilant and active police body.*

In 1798, under the auspices of the West India Merchants, Patrick Colquhoun and Sir John Harriott started the Marine Police Establishment to protect the docks and shipping on the Thames. In 1800 it became the Thames River Police.

Yet, with all of this police activity, crime continued to rise, unchecked.

From the cauldron seething so mightily worse was yet to come. And better too, in the person of Sir Robert Peel.

TOPICS FOR DISCUSSION

1. Early punishments were often grisly and bloody. Has modern civilized society in the 20th Century completely put aside such techniques or are variations still to be found?
2. It is said that "local control" was guaranteed by the Magna Carta. How important is "local control" or "local autonomy"? What are its strengths and weaknesses?

Chapter VI

THE PEELIAN REFORM

THE INDUSTRIAL REVOLUTION began in England around 1760 and brought great changes in social and economic organization. Hand tools were replaced by machine and power tools, and large-scale industrial production was made possible by factory processes.

Weaving and knitting machines, the steam engine, and new methods of steel production resulted in great industrial progress—but, at the same time, in great human suffering and poverty among the masses of people.

The cities began to develop great slum areas. The men, women, and children became virtual slaves of the factory, working up to sixteen hours per day, and after years of such virtual slavery, were unemployable wretches, broken physically and spiritually. The novels of Charles Dickens clearly point up the societal disorganization of this era.

Crime grew to alarming proportions. Gang activity increased, and the *fence* (one who deals in stolen property) came into being in large number, one estimate indicating at least 6,000 in London. Counterfeiting became so prevalent some commentaries indicate that, at one time, there was more bad money in circulation than good, and that over fifty false mints were operating in London.

Highwaymen infested the roads, footpads lurked about the urban areas, and bank robberies rose astronomically, numbering in the hundreds per years in larger cities such as London and Liverpool. Women and children were starving and turning to crime. One estimate indicates that at least 25,000 prostitutes were active in London. Children were trained as thieves by the fences, and for the first time, *juvenile delinquency* became a sore problem.

Attempts were made to combat the wide-spread lawlessness. *Vigilante groups* were formed to protect life and property and apprehend culprits. *Rewards* were offered for the arrest of highwaymen, horse-thieves, common thieves, and vagabonds. Householders began to place *wolf traps* within their homes to catch burglars, and many citizens found it necessary to carry arms regularly.

The courts utilized *long-term prison sentences* with increasing regularity, and the jails and prisons rapidly filled. *Transportation* (banishment

or deportation to another area) was applied with vigor, and many offenders were transported to America or Australia.

Punishments became increasingly severe, and at one time, there were
160 crimes *punishable by death*. Even stealing a loaf of bread was a hanging offense. For one month, over forty persons per day were executed. The
severity of penalty did not eliminate crime. It is said that at the same
moment that pick-pockets were being hanged, other pick-pockets were
operating among the crowds attending the execution.

Many eminent commentators were speaking with conviction. *Jeremy
Bentham* urged amendment of the criminal code, improvements of the
poor laws, abolition of transportation, sanitary and prison reform, and the
use of public prosecutors.

The Home Secretary at this time was *Sir Robert Peel*. In 1829, he introduced into Parliament *"An Act for Improving the Police In and Near
the Metropolis"*—the Metropolitan Police Act.

Sir Robert Peel was a farsighted man. He was familiar with the reforms
suggested by Fielding, Colquhoun, and Bentham, and came to the determination that a protective body of well-selected and trained men would be
necessary to prevent crime and to control the chaotic situation.

But Peel realized that police can never be effective or just if the laws
they are required to enforce are so wide in scope and heavy in penalty
that they do not receive public support. He knew that police could never
function well unless the laws were simple, clear, and respected by the
public. His first step was reform of the criminal law by limiting its scope
and reducing penalties drastically. (For example, he abolished the death
penalty for over a hundred offenses, and removed numerous criminal penalties entirely). There were many varieties of "police" at this time (see
Chapter V) and police responsibility was divided.

Sir Robert Peel noted that the poor quality of policing was a contribu-
tory factor to the social disorder. His recommendations were accepted by
Parliament, and he was placed in charge of the new organization. Formal
operation began September 29, 1829, with 1,000 men in six divisions. During the next ten years there was a complete and total revolution in law
enforcement. Modern policing, as we know it today, was born.

Many fundamental principles of the *Peelian Reform* are as applicable
today as they were in 1829. Peel held that:

1. The police must be stable, efficient, and organized along military
   lines.
2. The police must be under governmental control.
3. The absence of crime will best prove the efficiency of police.
4. The distribution of crime news is essential.

5. The deployment of police strength both by time and area is essential.
6. No quality is more indispensable to a policeman than a perfect command of temper; a quiet, determined manner has more effect than violent action.
7. Good appearance commands respect.
8. The securing and training of proper persons is at the root of efficiency.
9. Public security demands that every police officer be given a number.
10. Police headquarters should be centrally located and easily accessible to the people.
11. Policemen should be hired on a probationary basis.
12. Police records are necessary to the correct distribution of police strength.

The task of administering the "New" police was put into the hands of Colonel Charles Rowan and Richard Mayne who were appointed as commissioners and given headquarters at the home office. Later, they moved to 4 Whitehall Place, the back of which opened on to a courtyard which had been the site of a residence used by the Kings of Scotland, and which was called "Scotland Yard" by the merchants who used it as a place to display and sell goods. The back of 4 Whitehall Place was used as a police station. Because it was entered from this courtyard, the headquarters of the "New" police became known as "Scotland Yard."

A general order, issued to the new police in 1829 by Commissioner Charles Rowan, seems as timely for the seventies as when it was issued:

> It should be understood, at the outset, that the principal object to be obtained is the prevention of crime. To this great end, every effort of the police is to be directed. The security of person and property, the preservation of the public tranquility and all other objects of a police establishment would thus be better effected than by the detention and punishment of the offender after he has succeeded in committing the crime.

The police force of the City of London did not come into the Metropolitan Police, and to this day, the City of London, a one-mile square in the heart of London, has a separate police force.

The screening of manpower was begun. Men were offered jobs for life if they would produce in accordance with the new standards. Out of 12,000 candidates, 1,000 were immediately screened and placed into six divisions. Concentration was applied first to the high crime-rate areas, by taking out all existing police and placing the new men into the area.

By the end of 1830, the first major reorganization was complete. The metropolitan area was divided into 17 divisions, with about 80,000 population in each division, and a superintendent was placed over each. Each division was divided into eight patrol sections, and each patrol section was divided into eight beats. The total force now numbered 3,314, with 17 superintendents, 68 inspectors, 323 sergeants, and 2,906 constables. Each constable and sergeant wore a number, and, as well, the letter of his division. A day and night rotating shift was established with two-thirds of the force on night duty for an eight-month period, and one-third of the force on day duty for a four-month period.

The use of the probationary period was a forceful indication of the serious intention of Sir Robert Peel. During the first three years of the operation, there were 5,000 dismissals and 6,000 required resignations—the largest police turnover rate in history.

During the first few years of the Peelian reform, much strong opposition was encountered. Peel was denounced as a potential dictator making an insidious attempt to enslave the people by arbitrary and tyrannical methods. The *London Times* urged revolt, and a national secret body was organized to combat the police. The constables were derisively called *"Blue Devils,"* and *"Raw Lobsters."*

Within ten years, however, Sir Robert Peel became a national hero, and his men were affectionately called "Peelers," or "Bobbies"—the name "Bobby" still being carried by the English Constable.

The standardization of municipal policing in England was effected by the *Municipal Corporations* Act of 1835 which established police forces in the cities and towns of England.

The *Bow Street Runners* and the *Marine Police* were amalgamated within the Metropolitan Police.

In 1839, a *permissive* "County Police Act" led to the establishment of county constabularies, and between 1840 and 1848, about half of the counties of England and Wales created county forces.

In 1842, the first formal detective squad was inaugurated within the Metropolitan Police, the forerunner of today's Criminal Investigation Division (C.I.D.).

In 1856, the *County and Borough Police Act* made it compulsory for each county to establish paid police forces.

In 1878, the C.I.D. was placed under the direction of Howard Vincent, a lawyer who was brought in as chief, and given the title of Director. He chose 250 officers for detective duties, and within six years had developed the C.I.D. to a force of 800.

In 1882, the *Municipal Corporations Act* stated that no borough with a population under 20,000 could maintain an independent police force.

In 1888, the *Local Government Act* invested authority over county police forces in a standing joint committee made up of Justices and Councilors from each county.

In 1890, a *Police Pensions Act* granted retirement benefits to the members of the police service.

In 1901, Sir Edward Henry introduced *fingerprint* technology as a method of identification. Sir Francis Galton created the system of fingerprint classification.

In 1914, female constables in uniform were first utilized, and by 1918, the Woman Police Service was an integrated part of the Metropolitan Police.

Attempts to unionize the Metropolitan Police were made in 1917 and 1918, and during the latter year the London police went on strike. The strike was quickly settled by the government, and the union was replaced by a *Police Federation* authorized in 1919, with every police constable as a member.

In 1934, a scientific police laboratory was established for the Metropolitan Police.

The organization of the Metropolitan Police is basically the same today. The office of the Commissioner at New Scotland Yard is primarily the central office for the general administration and control of the force. There are now 20,000 personnel, servicing 742 square miles, and the force is divided into four main sub-areas or districts, and these are again subdivided into 23 divisions.

There are some 50 separate police forces in England and Wales, and some 21 in Scotland, representing County Police, Borough Police, Combined Police, London Metropolitan Police, and City of London Police.

The initial training of police is given in several police training centers, while the National Police College provides training for the middle and higher ranks.

Minimum standards are maintained by national inspections. Part of the cost of policing is from the national treasury, by a system of subventions to cities, counties and boroughs; in order to qualify for such financial assistance, each police force must meet national standards.

One source states,

> Underlying all police training in Britain is this theme—the job of a police force is not simply to prevent crime and catch wrongdoers, but to help the complex machinery of modern life to run more smoothly.
>
> The British police recruiting system has always looked for character in choosing police officers. The policeman is not a State policeman. He is an independent holder of a public office, exercising powers by virtue of his office and on his own responsibility except when acting on a magistrate's warrant. He must stand firmly on his own common sense and knowledge of the law,

and if he makes a mistaken action or makes a wrongful arrest he can be sued in the courts by the aggrieved citizen.

This emphasis on character and the "answerability" of the policeman for his actions goes a long way to explain the good relations between police and public. The policeman must have no political affiliations, belong to no trade union, have no business interests. He is not armed. Even the baton he carries is scarcely ever used. He must use the minimum of force in effecting an arrest.

The Peelian reform has led to an increased status and prestige for all those who have entered a career in public safety. Every American citizen, every American policeman, and every American police student should be able to recognize and appreciate the great contribution of Sir Robert Peel.

TOPICS FOR DISCUSSION

1. Which principles of the Peelian reform are of primary importance to modern American law enforcement?
2. England, Scotland and Wales have some 71 separate police units; there are over 46,000 separate units in the United States. What are the advantages and disadvantages of many or few units?
3. Great Britain maintains minimum standards by national inspections and by national subventions (grants-in-aid) contingent upon meeting national standards. Would such a system be possible in the United States?

Chapter VII

DEVELOPMENT IN THE UNITED STATES

ENGLISH COLONISTS AND DEPORTEES coming to America settled along the Atlantic Coast. In the New England area, in the northern colonies, the land was barren and the people depended upon commerce and industry for their livelihood. Thus, they had a tendency to settle in towns and villages. They were familiar with the watch system of their homeland, and tended to this form of protection. Those who settled in the southern colonies found good land, and developed a rural-agricultural community. Thus, they had a tendency to develop the county form of civil government, and just as in England, developed the office of sheriff to keep the peace. Thus, in the North, the Constable of the watch was developed, and in the South, the sheriff of the county.

Later, when the middle-west and far-west opened up, these people had a tendency to utilize both the constable and sheriff for police functions. Early constitutions of the various states sometimes provided for both sheriff and constable. Because many Americans were suspicious of central authority, they often made these offices elective and for short periods of time. For this reason, these offices have developed in a sickly fashion, and even today the sheriff and constable are rarely competitively selected, appointed, well-trained, career-oriented people.

One can sympathize with the colonists, for prior to 1800, over 90 per cent of the people were from England, and perhaps a third had been transported. They resented the abuses of royal authority in the old country, and were determined to prevent these evils from developing in the new land.

MUNICIPAL POLICE

The development of municipal policing in the new world was slow, due to the fact that the nation was essentially of a rural character. It was not until 1790 that there were six cities with a population over 8,000.

In 1636, a *night watch* was formed in Boston; in 1658, in New York, a *rattle watch* was formed, so called because the watch carried rattles with which to communicate their presence and signal each other; and, in 1700, Philadelphia appointed a night watch.

These early watchmen, like their counterparts in England at the time, were very lazy and inept. Minor offenders were sometimes *sentenced to serve on the watch* as punishment. Often called *leather heads*, these guards were so dull that the towns sometimes had to formalize even the most simple duties. New Haven, in 1722, had a regulation that "no watchman will have the liberty to sleep"; and a 1750 Boston rule stipulated that "watchmen will walk their rounds slowly and now and then stand and listen." These were not true police departments, but mostly volunteer groups, yet, up to 1800, these night patrols of "vigilantes" were the only law enforcement in the towns.

In some towns, all able-bodied males over sixteen years were required to serve without pay, and there were many refusals to accept watch duty. When cities began to pay night watchmen, there were attempts made to secure jobs through political influence so that one could work during the day and sleep during the watch.

In 1833, we see the advent of *daytime, paid police*. In that year, a Philadelphia ordinance provided for 23 policemen to serve by day, and 120 by night, all under one Captain *appointed* by the Mayor. In 1848, Philadelphia changed to 34 day policemen, and reestablished the old separate night watch. In 1854, the force was again consolidated under a Marshal *elected* for a two-year term. Later, the position of Marshal was abolished, and the office of Chief of Police created, appointed by the Mayor.

In 1838, Boston established a day force of six men. By 1846, there were thirty men, with eight of them on night duty, but separate from the old night watch; in 1850, the day and night watches were consolidated.

In 1844, New York State legislated funds for day and night police forces throughout the state, and empowered communities to organize police forces. In 1845, the New York city forces were consolidated, the old night watch abolished, and day and night shifts organized. The force was placed under a Superintendent appointed by the Mayor with consent of Council. New York's formation of a city force was followed by Chicago in 1851, by New Orleans and Cincinnati in 1852, Baltimore and Newark in 1857, Providence in 1864—and modern policing in the United States was under way.

These were difficult years for policing in the United States, for it was the *spoils era,* in which the motto "to the victor go the spoils" meant gross political interference. The winning party felt that its members should be immune from arrest, given special privileges in naming favorites for promotion, and assisted in vendettas against their political opponents.

Many police forces were experimental and notoriously inefficient, yet, at the same time, a political power and a political football. In some cities, all police were appointed year by year by nomination of councilmen or aldermen. Discipline could not be enforced; drunkenness, assault of superior officers, release of prisoners, and extortion were frequent occurrences. Some cities tried electing every policeman to office, but this did not stop political control; instead, it increased it.

The police uniform was looked upon as a badge of degradation and servitude and men refused to wear it. By 1855, some city forces wore regulation hats or caps, but there were no completely uniformed police in the United States. Members of the New York city force were required, by ordinance of 1855, to "wear a medal inside his clothes, suspended round his neck, both day and night when on duty, and shall expose the same when about restoring peace, or on making an arrest, or when performing any duty of that kind." In 1856, the New York city police adopted full police uniform; however, each ward of the city adopted its own style. In Philadelphia, an effort to have the police wear their badges outside their clothing was bitterly opposed. It wasn't until 1860 that they adopted complete uniforms.

Efforts to reduce the effects of political manipulation continued. Police boards or commissions began to appear in cities, in order to disengage policing from the hands of ward politicians. In 1857, the state of New York experimented with a state board, but it proved to be unsuccessful. Such experimentation took place in other states, and there are still several cities in the United States where the head of the police department or commission is appointed by the governor of the state.

In 1881, President Garfield was assassinated by a disappointed office seeker, and a wave of public revulsion followed, leading to the establishment, in 1883, of the _Pendleton Act,_ which provided for civil service in the federal government. The spoils era, which existed from 1829 to 1883, met the device that was to chase gross political interference from governmental operations. Slowly, civil service processes were introduced throughout state and local governments. From a small 10 per cent of federal employees in 1883, civil service has grown to cover over 95 per cent of all governmental employees at federal, state, and local levels. Today there are over 12 million persons in civil service positions, 3 million at the federal level and almost 10 million at the state and local level.

Civil service did not completely solve the problems of policing, nor did it ever completely remove graft and corruption from the service, but it supplied the impetus to the elimination of very serious political interference, and enhanced the concept of merit employment.

STATE POLICE

As the United States increased in population, and as the cities and counties multiplied, police problems multiplied. Very often, there existed communities where graft and corruption and crime flourished, and consequently, a demand for action by the people of the state. Very often, the office of sheriff or constable had elected incumbents who were inept or dishonest, and who allowed or tolerated grave violations of state statutes. Very often, criminals operated throughout a state, and local units found themselves unable to cope with the criminal who struck now at this town, then at another far across the state.

The *Texas Rangers,* organized in 1835, were the first form of state police, and dealt with cattle rustlers, outlaws, Indians, and marauding Mexican nationals who were protesting land seizures.

Massachusetts, in 1865, organized a force of state constables who were charged with the suppression of vice. The state of Connecticut, in 1902, formed a special squad of investigators to enforce the laws of the state in vice-infested areas.

Around 1905, during the civil unrest caused by state-wide coal strikes, the *Pennsylvania State Police* came into being. It was accused promptly of strike-breaking and partiality. This reputation was long in disappearing.

The greatest development of state police units occurred, however, after World War I, and today, all states have some form of state law enforcement. Some state police agencies are restricted to enforcement of the vehicular laws and protection of life and property on the highways. Others have been given general law enforcement authority, and have jurisdiction in criminal and traffic matters throughout the state. Very often, independent law enforcement units are found at the state level, such as investigation units, identification bureaus, narcotic units, and liquor control bureaus.

FEDERAL POLICE

The development of federal policing activity has been slow, primarily due to the responsibility of the state and local authorities to administer governmental functions. Authority for federal police action is derived from construction placed upon the implied powers of Art. I, Section 8, Clause 18 of the Federal Constitution which deals with common defense and promotion of the general welfare of the people. Interpretations of the Supreme Court are the basis for certain police authority and power, and legislative acts of Congress are the basis for additional authority and power.

Control over interstate commerce, the coinage of money, standards of weights and measures, and postal services led to the need for federal investigatory and protective units.

In 1789, a Revenue Cutter Service was inaugurated to prevent smuggling. In 1829, the Post Office Inspection system was begun to prevent mail fraud, and in 1836, Congress authorized the Postmaster General to pay agents who investigated postal matters.

In 1861, Congress appropriated money to the U.S. Attorney General for the investigation of crimes against the United States; and between 1842 and 1865, counterfeiting laws brought the establishment of the United States Secret Service.

In 1868, 25 detectives were authorized for the Internal Revenue Service, and between 1882 and 1886, problems of immigration and smuggling led to the establishment of the Border Patrol under the Customs Service. In 1870, due to the large problems of reconstruction following the Civil War, the Department of Justice was brought into being.

In 1895, federal attention was focused on lotteries being sent through the mails. In 1906, pure food and drug regulations were established. In 1909, narcotics control was inaugurated along with controls over interstate transportation of diseased fruits, vegetables, and plants.

In 1910, the White Slave Act, to prevent interestate transport of females for immoral purposes, and the Motor Vehicle Theft Act, covering interstate movement of vehicles, were adopted.

In 1913, federal controls over the manufacture of liquor were adopted. In 1915, narcotic control was placed as a section of the Internal Revenue Service. In 1918, the national prohibition laws were enacted.

In 1924, the Federal Bureau of Investigation was organized in the Department of Justice by J. Edgar Hoover.

In 1934, the National Kidnapping Act, Banking Act, Racketeering Act, and the Interstate Compact Act were passed by Congress.

With this interest of the federal government in law enforcement, agencies to deal with such matters were established, such as the United States Secret Service, Internal Revenue Service, Bureau of Narcotics, Immigration and Naturalization Service, and the F.B.I. The only large body of federal law enforcement which is associated with the military (and then, only in time of war) is the United States Coast Guard.

THE LAST HUNDRED YEARS

The last hundred years of American policing present a most interesting panorama, with operations that have ranged from the most sordid to the most splendid, and with practitioners whose capacity and character have spanned a continuum from the most incompetent and corrupt to the most brilliant and edifying.

Negative Aspects. *Detractors* of the American police service often limit themselves to a consideration of police failings:

1. *Inept Watches*—manned by lazy volunteers or indifferent mercenaries (1636-1829).

2. *Spoils Era Operations*—wherein political interference and manipulation, graft, and corruption were commonplace (1829-1883).

3. *Ugly Early Customs*—such as the third-degree, curbstone court for

vagrants, and extra-judicial punishment of offenders. (Often, the general public was apathetic to police operations directed toward the anti-social elements of the community, and, as long as those anti-social elements were kept under control, did not bother to scrutinize or evaluate police methods.)

4. *Prohibition Habits*—formed during the days of prohibition, when the general public did not observe the liquor control laws, and was not sympathetic to liquor control law enforcement. Some policemen learned to look the other way, to accept the gratuity offered for temporary blindness, and, at times, engaged in extortion. Certain current problems of police and public had their genesis during this period (1918-1932).

5. *Damages Due to World War II Manpower Shortages*—when the scarcity of qualified manpower resulted in the admission to police ranks of individuals of lesser abilities and motivations. Some communities protected their service by permitting only emergency, temporary, or provisional status during this time, but other agencies accepted the scrapings of the manpower barrel and gave poorly qualified individuals civil service tenure. This period was a difficult time for police recruitment, and we still live with some of the personnel decisions made then (1941-1945).

6. *Bad Housekeeping*—due to inadequate facilities and equipment often resulted in physically dirty, noisy, crowded, shoddy buildings, and antiquated, shabby, inadequate, grotesque uniforms and equipment.

7. *Inadequate Education and Training*—resulted in police services without advanced knowledges and techniques. Some agencies continue to operate a quarter-century behind the times, with outdated attitudes and habits, with inept policies and procedures, and with supervisory and administrative patterns that were replaced decades ago by progressive and viable agencies (prior to 1947).

8. *Incompetent and Immoral Personnel*—who fail to keep informed, to care properly for equipment, to patrol efficiently, to investigate properly, to advise correctly, to report adequately, to interview and interrogate properly, to search and seize legally; and who engage in mooching, chiseling, theft, perjury, extortion, favoritism, prejudice, illegal violence, and lechery.

9. *Overemphasis on Street Crime and Victimless Crime*—results in inadequate attention to the areas of Organized Crime and White-Collar Crime.

10. *Obstinate Refusal to Change Attitudes and Habits*—mar the 60's as rigid and mechanical police Neanderthals of all ages and ranks seek to solve all criminal justice problems with tons of hardware and immediate massive applications of force.

But, those are the murky hues of the panorama; the lively and bright colors deserve even greater attention, for they offer greater satisfaction, and are heartening indeed.

Positive Aspects. Any objective appraisal of the American police service must include a consideration of police successes:

1. *Peelian Reform*—had an impact on American policing (1830-1850).

2. *Civil Service Merit System Processes*—have aided greatly in combating the evil aspects of spoils era operations, by positing merit and ability as an alternative to political sponsorship, and by providing disciplinary machinery with which to deal with the problem of graft and corruption (1883 to date).

3. *Traffic Enforcement Responsibilities*—have brought the police into frequent contact with the law-abiding members of the community. These contacts have resulted in a public interest in police method, for when police attitudes and habits usually extended to the anti-social members of the community were extended to the law-abiding, the outcry was loud and clear. The resulting attention paid to selection and training had a great effect in eliminating many ugly early practices (after 1900).

4. *Depression Recruitment*—was salutary for the police service, for hundreds of thousands of unemployed were seeking work, many of them of excellent physique, health, education, character, and motivation. Turning toward the police service, many were able to enter the service and accept an honorable career—fine men who might otherwise have been lost to the vocation. For the most part, these fine people were able to withstand temptations of prohibition habits (1929-1941).

5. *World War II Veterans*—by the hundreds, mature, seasoned, used to uniform and discipline, entered the police service. These good people brought new life and vigor to a vocation greatly enervated by heavy wartime exertion and thinned ranks due to manpower shortages (1945-1947).

6. *New Equipment and Facilities*—for there has been an ever-increasing sophistication relative to the material needs of the police service during the past one hundred years.

Police buildings and facilities, in thoughtful communities, are spacious, well-planned for their purposes, and conducive to high morale and good public relations.

Police equipment, in thoughtful communities, is up-to-date, well-maintained, and sufficient for the assigned tasks. Crime laboratories, communication systems, records and identification equipment, transportation, armaments, and personal gear are improved each year.

This is not to say that *all* American communities have the equipment and facilities that are necessary to an effective and edifying police operation, but that the past one hundred years has seen sweeping and forceful change in the area of police materiél.

7. *Expanded Education and Training*—marks the current scene, with over 300 colleges and universities offering Associate and Bachelor degrees in law enforcement, and with scores of police academy programs providing for a wide variety of in-service training. No longer is the educated person an anomaly in the police agency; more and more agencies are requiring collegiate work as a primary qualification for employment, and as a prerequisite to promotional candidacy. The authors have no doubts but that very soon, in all professional police operations, advancement to and beyond the rank of Lieutenant will demand possession of the Baccalaureate degree (1947 to date).

8. *Personnel of Ability and Character*—for there has been an ever-increasing attention given to the selection, payment, development, regulation, and motivation of police manpower during the past one hundred years.

9. *Changes in Priorities*—as serious attention begins to focus upon Organized Crime and White-Collar Crime.

10. *Changes in Role Perception*—mark the 70's as sensitive and aware police professionals of all ages and ranks begin to reject the repressive orientation of the past ("hired guns of the haves") and openly welcome the people-oriented humane vision of the future ("ombudsmen of the have nots").

In thoughtful communities, hundreds and thousands of men have been carefully screened, adequately compensated, well-trained, effectively controlled and skillfully directed by inspired leadership.

Many of these people have been willing to accept the vision of a professional mode of police operation. Many of these fine men have been willing to follow departmental policy and procedure as taught to them in their recruit training, even though they may have found some of their colleagues, accustomed to the "old ways," lacking in sympathy for the "new way." Many of these fine men have flatly refused to accept or follow bad police tradition; instead, they have bought their coffee and meals; they have remained alert and energetic during the early morning hours; they have written scrupulously correct reports and records of their activities; they have given testimony with great respect for the facts; they have investigated assigned crime with skill and care; they have kept themselves well-informed; they have protected the physical health and property of suspects and offenders from harm; they have arrested offenders consistently in an impartial, objective, neutral, and wise fashion; they have guarded the status and dignity of the police badge by remaining proper in their conduct off-duty, as well as on-duty; they have improved their competence by attending college or university; and they have maintained their integrity by being sensitively and continuously aware of personal and departmental honor.

Many of these fine people are to be found in the smallest of departments, as well as the largest. And many of these fine people have decades of police experience, or little; high rank, as well as low.

These are the men who are molding the standards, setting the pace, and elevating the vocation by truly professional example. These are the men who will be giving productive leadership to the police student of today.

This is not to say that all American communities have the personnel and personnel policies that are necessary to an effective and edifying operation, but that the past one hundred years have witnessed a revolution in police manpower quality—a revolution that is benign and impressive.

The current of opinion within the American police service, at this time, is enthusiastically oriented toward improvement. What the future will bring will depend upon the wisdom, learning, energy, enthusiasm, capacity and character of every member of the vocation.

The writers do not wish to appear overly sanguine, yet it would seem that the American police service is about to enter its golden years—for our attention is focused far more sharply upon the individual police officer than ever before. No longer do we look upon buildings, facilities, equipment, gadgetry, technology, and science as the solution to our problems. We depend upon them, we desire to develop them, and we will continue to use them—but we are convinced that without the continued addition of motivated personnel, without the regular improvement of current personnel, and without the shared vision of a truly competent and edifying service, the vocation will not, and can not, rise.

The history of the American police service is less impressive when compared with its future potential.

(Before reading the next section, "Constitutional Limitations of Criminal Justice," the reader is advised to carefully peruse the materials in Appendix A and B.)

TOPICS FOR DISCUSSION

1. What are the advantages and disadvantages of a "Civil Service System"?
2. Which "negative aspects" of the "last hundred years" have most greatly hampered the development of a professional police service?
3. Which "positive aspects" of the "last hundred years" have most greatly enhanced the movement towards a professional police service?

PART III
CONSTITUTIONAL LIMITATIONS OF CRIMINAL JUSTICE

Chapter VIII

LAW ENFORCEMENT AND PERSONAL LIBERTIES

IT MAY BE REASONABLY ASSUMED that the most important task of any law enforcement service in America is the fulfillment of its function as the protector of the people. The people engaged in law enforcement must be ever-mindful of Daniel Defoe's admonition, "I hear much of people's calling out to 'Punish the Guilty!' But very few are concerned to 'Clear the Innocent.' "[1] The Bill of Rights of the United States Constitution stands like a beacon to guide law enforcement personnel in protecting personal rights, and in so doing, helps preserve democratic values.

There is evidence to indicate that only a small fraction of American citizens have any knowledge of the Bill of Rights—their constitutional freedoms, or why they are so important—particularly in these times.[2] This should not be the case with law enforcement officers. They should be much better informed about them than the average person. Whether this is so might be open to inquiry.

If a deduction can be made on the basis of surveys which have been conducted (bearing in mind fallacies which may affect any survey), seemingly, the answer is in the negative.[3] Law enforcement administrators have

---

[1] Defoe, Daniel (1903). *Later Stuart Tracts, Printed for J. Baker, at the Black Boy, in Paternoster Row, London, 1715*, p. 69. Archibald Constable Company, Ltd., Westminster, England.

[2] How little the average American knows about the most important documents of American history (if not world history) is shown in the Report of the President's Committee on Civil Rights, *To Secure These Rights*, United States Government Printing Office, 1947.

"In October, 1946, the National Opinion Research Center at the University of Denver, asked a cross-section of our adult population a series of questions about the Bill of Rights. Only one out of five Americans had a reasonably accurate knowledge of what is in the first Ten Amendments to the Constitution. Completely confused and inaccurate descriptions were offered by 12%. More than a third had heard of the Bill of Rights but could not identify it in any way. Another third had not even heard of it." The National Opinion Research Center report stated further, "even among the best informed people, however, the more privileged, educationally, economically, and occupationally—less than a majority can satisfactorily identify the Bill of Rights."

The same lack of knowledge is shown in a survey by the *American Institute of Public Opinion*, New Orleans States, May 3, 1947.

[3] Tresolini, Rocco, Taylor, Richard W., and Barnett, Elliott B. (1955). "Arrest Without Warrant: Extent and Social Implications." *The Journal of Criminal Law, Criminology and Police Science*, 46:187-198.

a far-reaching obligation to correct the condition if such a weakness does in fact exist.

There would be little serious argument, probably, in inferring that most people are less informed about the Constitution of the United States than they are about the Bill of Rights. Yet, the 4,373 words of the Constitution spell out the fundamental positive law of the land. The document sets up the national government and basically assumes the existence and continuance of the states, with the distribution of powers between states and nation. Although the national government is one of "limited powers," such powers are the paramount authority of the land.

Mr. Justice Holmes, referring to the Constitution, states its provisions "are not mathematical formulas having their essence in their form; they are organized living institutions transplanted from English soil. Their significance is vital and formal; it is to be gathered not simply by taking the words of a dictionary but by considering their origin and the line of their growth."

The Constitution also enumerates and guarantees personal rights, which are restraints on the national government and state governments. The limitation on the suspension of *habeas corpus* and the prohibition of Bills of Attainder are examples of personal liberties protected in the Constitution. Such rights are as fundamental as the ones guaranteed in the Bill of Rights. But, for the present, in considering personal rights, attention will be focused on the freedoms guaranteed in the Bill of Rights. The Bill of Rights has been defined as a declaration of individual rights reserved in the charter of government to safeguard the welfare of the free people. It is the heart, the vital part, of the Constitution. From the American viewpoint it embraces the wisdom of the ages as divined from man's struggle for freedom throughout civilization. It is as important in its way to our form of government as the teachings of the Bible are to Christianity.

This historic document contains only 462 words and can be read in only a few minutes. These 462 words were never more important. Every American should read and ponder them well. It is not enough merely to read the words. The meaning behind the words should be understood. (Please refer to Appendix A.)

Mr. Justice Frankfurter, in his historic dissents in the Harris[4] and Rabinowitz[5] cases, reviewing the search and seizure provision of the Bill of Rights, stated that the words of the Fourth Amendment "are not just a literary composition . . . to be read as they might be read by a man who knows English but has no knowledge of the history that gave rise to the words"; that the "founders of this country subordinated police action to

---

[4] *Harris v. United States*, 331 U.S. 145 (1947).
[5] *United States v. Rabinowitz*, 339 U.S. 56 (1950).

legal restraints not in order to convenience the guilty but to protect the innocent"; that "the knock at the door under the guise of a warrant of arrest for a venial or spurious offense was not unknown to our founders"; and "we have had grim reminders in our day of their experience"; that "arrest under a warrant for a minor or trumped up charge has been familiar practice in the past, is a commonplace in the police state of today, and too well-known in this country"; and that "the progress is too easy from police action unscrutinized by judicial authorization to the police state."

The verbal picture painted in those words should at once indicate to law enforcement officers the course they should follow. They cannot be satisfied with reading 462 words. They must prepare themselves, so that in their day-to-day duties of regulating human conduct, their actions will conform with constitutional standards.

We cannot be for the Bill of Rights "for ourselves and for our friends." The application of constitutional protection does not fluctuate according to our political, social, economic, and religious preferences. It is all or nothing. No man's rights are safe unless all men's rights are respected.

This means that the Black Muslim and the Jehovah Witness have the *same* equal rights under the law as do the Presbyterian and the Jew. It means that the Communist who confines his activity to the soapbox and printing press is under the *same* protections as is the racist politican. It means that the weakest pacifist is entitled to the *same* guarantees of liberty as the most powerful police official. It means that the most energetic civil rights demonstrator is entitled to the *same* constitutional safeguards as the most wealthy military industrialist. It means that all government officials, from the President of the United States to the Constable of the smallest village, are subject to the *same* constitutional controls relative to their treatment of the United States citizen.

It might be argued that "good" law enforcement is hampered by constitutional guarantees. Some observers may believe that there are a number of highly respected law enforcement administrators who, at first blush, sometimes appear to accept that philosophy. More likely, these administrators are the staunchest supporters of "the Blessings of Liberty," referred to in the Preamble to the United States Constitution. But, they must also be concerned with giving to the people security of person against a vicious criminal element which represents a small proportion of the population.

There are some police administrators who, from time to time, undoubtedly feel a more reasonable construction might be applied by the courts in interpreting constitutional guarantees. Their criticism of certain decisions is not leveled at constitutional safeguards. They do give protest to archaic and ill-advised laws. They show indignation when highly technical rulings free vicious criminals to return to society to prey on the society that law enforcement is sworn to protect. What they seek, therefore, is revision in penal laws and criminal procedures to bring them into harmony with the society of the twentieth century.

By way of illustration, arrest laws of today are substantially as written in the sixteenth century. What may have been reasonable restraints on law enforcement in that era have become unreasonable today. This is reflected in arrest laws which fail to provide for a temporary detention of a suspect, for at least two hours, for investigation; and, in the right the law confers on a private person to resist some kinds of arrests. There are many other instances which might be cited, not only in arrest laws, but in substantive and procedural laws as well.[6]

Our present-day methods of transportation, rapid-firing weapons, and highly developed communication systems, were unknown when most such laws were adopted. Though these social gains have added to comfort and welfare, at the same time, they have impaired the effectiveness of laws of by-gone days. The watch and ward of the early English police system, constable, and sheriff, faced very different problems from those that confront law enforcement agencies today.

In spite of the difficulties of today's problems little justification can be found for law enforcement which chips away the liberties of the individual. That is the very thing that law enforcement must seek to avoid. A forward step can be taken by placing more emphasis on adequate instruction for those who are charged with enforcing the laws. Law must not only be a basic tool in theory, in carrying out law enforcement duties, it must be a basic tool in practice. Put another way, law enforcement officers must know the law.

Both the letter and the spirit of the laws reveal that it is impossible to convert a neophyte into a law enforcement officer, in the true sense of the term, by the simple expedient of investing him with authority and a firearm. Poets may be born, but officers of the law must be made.

The men and women engaged in enforcing laws cannot afford to be numbered among those of little knowledge about the Constitution and the Bill of Rights.

LAW ENFORCEMENT AND GOVERNMENT

Our government was established in its present form to avoid the abuses of arbitrary authority that led to the Declaration of Independence and the Revolutionary War. Inscribed over the entrance to the United States Supreme Court building in Washington is the motto: "EQUAL JUSTICE

---

[6] For a discussion of law enforcement problems which involve inadequate laws, see "Are the Courts Handcuffing the Police? A Symposium on Law and Police Practices." (1957). *Northwestern University Law Review*, 52:1-76.

UNDER LAW." *Whether this ideal is real or illusory depends very much on the way laws are enforced.*

Because of that, Americans should have a better understanding of the relationship of law enforcement to their government. They should know more about the role it can play as a force for good or evil in their communities. No one can properly afford to take law enforcement for granted. It is too important to them and to their way of life to be regarded casually. Unfortunately, many Americans give little thought to it and fail to realize that, more than any other public service, law enforcement affects most of them in some way, almost every day.

Law enforcement is a unit of the executive branch of government. The relationship is the same at all levels of government—federal, state, county, and local. It is the agency that executes the legal mandates of the president, governor, chief executive of the county, or local mayor. As a function, under the executive, law enforcement is a potent force in any government. Textbooks, in summarizing principles of government, put it in this manner: "The legislator makes the law, the executive enforces it, and the judiciary determines violations."

When law enforcement is the servant *of the state,* rather than *of the people,* the individuals of the state may live as free people, or in virtual serfdom, depending upon the will of the one in power, or of a corrupt oligarchy. The police systems of many European and Far Eastern nations are of that nature.

Turn back the pages of history to the 1930s and 1940s. There can be found more than enough evidence to convince the most skeptical person that law enforcement can be a devastating force of evil. Many people of this generation lived in countries where freedom was muffled by law enforcement at the direction of the executive branch of government. The people who lived under the German Gestapo of Hitler, the Italian OVRA of Mussolini, and the Russian NKVD of Stalin, can tell the story for the asking—a story of tyranny which was possible only because law enforcement was the obedient servant of the state.

The name which identifies the secret police changes from time to time. Like the chameleon, which may be one color today, and another tomorrow, its purpose remains the same. And so it goes in many countries of the world today.

One of the most prominent distinctions between law enforcement in a democratic society and that of a totalitarian society is the sharp demarcation of the police role, as distinguished from the role of the court. The law enforcement job in this country is the enforcement of the laws. To the courts is left the job of interpreting the law and meting out punishment. On the other hand, the police system of a totalitarian state is the chief instrument of political domination, answerable to no one and to no institution except the will of the leader or oligarchy.

Chapman warns us about the possibilities and probabilities of the modern police state:

> The first stage . . . is the centralization of all police services . . . .
> The second state is when the . . . interests and procedures of the uniformed and criminal police services become subordinated to the special needs, functions and operational requirements of the political police.
> Finally, the police apparat detaches from its dependence on the army for armed force, and . . . a riot police section is reinforced with armoured vehicles . . . . When the police apparatus is immune to control by the civil service, the judiciary and the army, and is an independent leading state institution in its own right, a modern police state has been formed.[7]

Even though the reader has not had personal experience in a national police state, some citizens of the United States, in some areas, have had ugly experiences with federal, state, county, and local law enforcement agencies or agents operating with police state attitudes and with police state methods. Fortunately, as time goes by, and as our democratic institutions mature, edifying attitudes and proper methods are more and more uniformly in evidence. The elimination of any use of police state tactics (roughshod treatment; arrogant, brutal, and insensitive attitudes; intimidation; unnecessary psychological pressure or physical violence; illegal or immoral methods of arrest, search, seizure, detention, confinement, interrogation; ignoring, violating, or circumventing legal restrictions; unequal or warped application of the law) by American agencies or agents is the clear duty of the law enforcement vocation, of the courts, of the legislature, of the government, and—so important—the clear duty of each and every citizen.

In a police state, law enforcement is organized as a national police force operating on the formula that no private life is permitted. This centralization of authority is another characteristic of a national police force. The organizational structure of the national police force vests authority and power in a single person. The force has nationwide jurisdiction.

The chief of the national police force is accountable only to the chief executive, or top oligarchy, of the national government. Therefore, edicts good or bad, of the ruling power, are executed by the police chief.

One concept, in particular, should be kept in mind. A dictatorship can never exist unless the police system of the country is under the absolute control of the dictator. There is no other way to uphold a dictatorship except by terror, and the instrument of this total terror is the secret police,

---

[7] Chapman, Brian (1970). *Police State*, pp. 118-119. Praeger, New York.

whatever its name. *In every country where freedom has been lost, law enforcement has been a dominant instrument in destroying it.*

Many authorities familiar with the organization and direction of law enforcement services agree that a national police system is more efficient than many independent agencies. Our people, particularly law enforcement officers, must be alert, however, to the dangers inherent when law enforcement is vested in too few hands. They must be ever vigilant to combat attempts to bring this about cloaked in the persuasive arguments of greater efficiency. The danger far outweighs any resultant increases in efficiency. (This does not mean, however, that efforts to eliminate overlapping and duplication of effort and facilities should not continue. Certain staff and auxiliary services can be mutually shared by law enforcement agencies without the abdication of their jurisdiction.)

A firm adherence to the values of policing at the community level is the safest path to follow in order to contain any move toward a dictatorial state.[8] Our decentralized police system is not a product of chance. Its origin is firmly imbedded in the history of Anglo-American law enforcement. A change from the system, perhaps if only at a state level, could be the first step toward troublesome times. (This does not mean, however, that efforts to establish standards, or to assist in the support of smaller local units, should not continue. Just as in England, certain standards and assistance can be possible, without abdication of local jurisdiction.)

People, as a whole, in this country, firmly believe in the rule of law and are unwilling that any would-be demagogue disregard that rule. Mr. Justice Sutherland has said, "Liberty and order are the most precious possessions of man, and the essence of the problem of government is reconciliation of the two." What few people realize is that the problem is the same in law enforcement. On the one hand, protection of society is the task of law enforcement; on the other, safeguarding individual personal liberties is also the task of law enforcement. This can be done only when laws are enforced impartially. Those enforcing the laws must leave personal feelings and prejudices at home when on duty. Only when law enforcement discharges its function within the framework of constitutional guarantees, can a reasonable balance be maintained between the conflicting interests of society and the individual.

---

[8] If there is serious doubt as to whether a "strong man" might try to bring it about, just go back to the fall of 1957 to a typical midwestern city. Recall what did happen. One man, in defiance of a mandate of the United States Supreme Court, did set himself above the law. President Eisenhower, ordering United States military personnel to enforce a Supreme Court ruling, took for granted that the solemn judgment of the court is "the supreme law of the land." Federal troops and then National Guardsmen had to stand guard to preserve law and order.

The most effective way to assure that kind of enforcement is to provide adequate training for all, not a possible majority, of those who engage in such work. Such training reduces misunderstanding as to the relationship of law enforcement to government. And training makes it rather unlikely that law enforcement personnel will be numbered with the group of public employees who, in 1954, attracted national attention to themselves when the Honorable Earl Warren, Chief Justice of the United States, visited their city to deliver an address on the Bill of Rights.

Shortly before his address, a group of state employees, charged with the responsibility of determining what announcements could be posted on the state employees bulletin board, refused to permit the Bill of Rights to be posted because it was a "controversial" document. The dispute was resolved, but not until the Governor of the state gave them assurances in writing that the Bill of Rights could not be considered as being of a controversial nature.

The *New York Times* of December 16, 1954, reported that the Chief Justice, in commenting upon the incident, stated "And this happened in the United States of America on the 15th day of December, 1954, the 163rd Anniversary of our Bill of Rights, declared by proclamation of President Eisenhower to be Bill of Rights Day. It is straws in the wind like this which cause some thoughtful people to ask the question whether ratification of the Bill of Rights could be obtained today if we were faced squarely with the issue." It may be assumed that some of those employees had read the 462 words in the Bill of Rights. Few people would question their lack of understanding of them.

The Bill of Rights is inseparable from government and law enforcement in this country. Other classes of public employees may be able to carry out their tasks though confused about the Bill of Rights, and still meet acceptable performance standards. The same cannot be said of law enforcement officers. They work with human beings. Whether people enjoy the "Blessings of Liberty" depends, in no small measure, on the manner in which law enforcement officers fulfill their trust. They cannot properly discharge that trust unless they recognize the part they play in government. In the words of Sir Frederick Pollock, "The law cannot make all men equal, but they are equal before the law in the sense that their rights are equally the subject of protection and the duties of enforcement."

THE CONSTITUTION AND THE BILL OF RIGHTS

An understanding of a few of the problems which led to the adoption of the United States Constitution and Bill of Rights explains our government today, and illustrates some of the dangers against which our governments protect people. The problems which these documents helped to solve can be considered advantageously, and in the process, more than likely, a common fund of knowledge gathered, which can be related to many current law enforcement problems. In many respects, the same rationale that motivated the country's founders to find solutions to pressing problems of their time is applicable to unravelling some of today's law enforcement dilemmas. A law enforcement service, aware of restraints etched into the Constitution and Bill of Rights, can use such knowledge as guideposts for keeping operations well within those limitations, thus making law enforcement a real force in preserving democratic procedures and in winning the support of the public that is essential to success.

For a decade or more, before the Declaration of Independence, different incidents had brought about strained relations between the colonies and the British government. The events resulted in the growth of a feeling of common interest among the thirteen colonies which was the basis for the birth of national unity.

The American Revolution did not start with gunfire. It began with a document containing a theory—the *Declaration of Rights and Grievances*—drawn up in Philadelphia in 1765. This theory was a new expression of man's quest for dignity and held that man's rights are an extension of God's authority simply because God is God, man is man, and freedom is the way of man's existence. (The reader may recognize the philosophy of Aquinas, Bellarmine, Suarez, and Locke in this expression of rights.)

The First Continental Congress, a meeting of representatives of the various colonies, met in Philadelphia during September, 1774. The representatives initiated different measures hoping to secure freedom as British subjects. Their conciliatory efforts were of little avail. But, British policy continued unaltered. In April, 1775, fighting broke out between colonial militia and the British at Concord and Lexington, in the colony of Massachusetts. By the spring of 1776, the pretense of not waging war, but remaining loyal subjects of King George III was scarcely tenable. The Continental Congress adopted a formal Declaration of Independence on July 4, 1776. Accompanying this Declaration, was a resolution to the effect that steps be taken for the formation of a confederation of states.

More than a year passed before main points of difference were resolved with regard to a confederation of colonies. In the meantime, the war was prosecuted by the Continental Congress. On November 15, 1777, the Congress adopted the *Articles of Confederation*. Not till March 1, 1781 were the Articles (first American Constitution) ratified by all the states.

The Articles of Confederation created a loose federation of states. The confederation plan worked badly during the war. While it bound the thirteen colonies together to wage a war for independence, it was an unlikely basis for a continuous national unity. The lack of a strong national (central) government resulted in conditions which General Washington referred to as being "no better than anarchy." Among the many weaknesses in the Articles, the underlying one, the loose confederation of states, proved fatally defective. So the federation had to correct that defect when the war ended in order to enable the country to survive as a sovereign power among the nations of the world.

Because Britain was unable to enforce imperial control over the colonies, and because the loose confederation did not satisfy the fears of its leaders, the Continental Congress called together a convention to "revise the Articles of Confederation." Revision was dropped within five days when the convention adopted Randolph's resolution that "a national government ought to be established consisting of a supreme legislative, executive, and judiciary." The convention met in secret sessions (far different from present day methods of conducting important business?) and, after many compromises, a Constitution was finished.

The Draft Constitution was submitted to the several colonies for ratification. There was a struggle everywhere over its adoption. The chief source of hostility was the belief that a strong federal government would destroy both the rights of the states and the liberties of the individual citizens. There were those who insisted that these rights and liberties were adequately protected in the proposed Constitution, while others staunchly denied that claim. In the face of strong opposition, state conventions ratified the Constitution in the required number of states. However, feeling was very bitter, and in some states, notably New York, Virginia, and New Hampshire, the majorities were dangerously narrow.

Thomas Jefferson took part in objecting to the absence of a bill of rights in the new Constitution. While abroad, as American Minister to France, Jefferson wrote James Madison on December 20, 1787, saying "Let me add that a Bill of Rights is what the people are entitled to against every government on earth, general or particular, and what no government should refuse, or rest on inference." [9] Partly as a result of Jefferson's insistence, Madison pressed for the adoption of a Bill of Rights. Of 11 states originally ratifying, 5 had conditional ratifications dependent upon a Bill of Rights. Such people as Patrick Henry would have led a rebellion had not a Bill of Rights been assured.

On March 4, 1789, the Constitution of the United States became the law of the land. Thus was created the *first* modern government consisting of a national government *and* state governments. Seemingly, by it, a long debated problem was solved: how the powers to govern could be divided between the whole and its parts. The purpose of the Constitution was clear:

---

[9] Jefferson Papers, *Library of Congress*, 5F, 371-372.

Government must be restrained or it becomes tyrannical.

In general, the United States Constitution stands for:

1. Government by the *people*—that is, a republic with popular sovereignty rather than a dictatorship or government by the state (see President Lincoln's Gettysburg Address).
2. A *limited* government—that is, the only powers the government has are those given by the people; the rest remain with the states or with the people (see the Tenth Amendment).
3. A *federal* government—that is, both state and national governments have powers in different spheres.
4. A *separation* of powers—that is, between executive, legislative and judicial. Often criticized because it is confusing and may encourage lack of responsibility, it nonetheless helps prevent too much power in anyone's hands.
5. Supremacy of *federal* over state governments—that is, states cannot prevent the federal government from exercising powers given it by the Constitution; the Supreme Court has the final word in all disputes.

The first ten amendments to the Constitution, adopted December 15, 1791, constitute, and are called the Bill of Rights. These amendments were the price of ratification of the Constitution. Very few people would argue seriously today against the foresight of our ancestors who insisted that this basic catalogue of human rights be added to the Constitution. (All states have substantially the same provisions as part of their Constitutions. Readers should obtain a copy of their State Constitution and compare the parallel construction of their state Bill of Rights with the federal Bill of Rights.)

The Bill of Rights had no application to the states at the time of their adoption in 1791. This was the way the country's founders wanted it. That this was their position was made quite clear by Chief Justice John Marshall in *Barron v. Baltimore*, 7 Peters 243 (1833) when he declared that the first eight amendments "contain no expression indicating an intention to apply them to State governments. This Court cannot so apply them." (This view was not to withstand the test of time, however, as our discussion, hereafter, will bring out.)

Only the first eight amendments safeguard personal rights. The Ninth and Tenth Amendments are general rules of interpretation of the relation between the state and national governments—all powers not delegated by the Constitution to the United States, nor prohibited to the states, being reserved to the states and the people. The first eight amendments are actually a bill of "Don'ts." In other words, they are not a theoretical enumeration of rights, but a series of prohibitions that protect certain rights.

Many of the rights spelled out in the Bill of Rights are well-known as well as protected by "specific" constitutional guarantees. Other claims are not as fortunate. But consideration has been given, albeit limited, to a constitutional amendment to provide for them. The court also considered how to obtain recognition for them as long ago as 1819. Chief Justice John Marshall, in *McCulloch v. Maryland,* 17 U.S. (*Wheat*) 316, reasoned that an implied power did not have to be directly traceable to a particular express power: "Its existence may be deduced fairly from more than one of the substantive powers expressly defined, or from them all combined," he declared.

Recent advocates on behalf of unenumerated rights have occasionally relied on the Ninth Amendment, usually in connection with the Tenth. In 1965 in *Griswold v. Connecticut,* 381 U.S. 479, the Court "discovered" the Ninth Amendment, and in a very real sense used the amendment as a basis for a new constitutional "right of privacy," to invalidate Connecticut's *Comstock* law that regulated the sale and use of birth control devices of all kinds.[10] Mr. Justice Goldberg, in his concurring opinion, urged that the Ninth Amendment be used to protect all kinds of rights of privacy, as to which, Mr. Justice Black, in his dissenting opinion, disagreed vehemently.

But even if one agrees with using the Ninth Amendment in such a way, and even if one accepts the fact that the Court as a final arbiter has a molding as well as a judicial function, one should not carry the approach too far. To do this would mean that the Court no longer would be engaged in construing the Constitution by applying it to new situations: The Court will be engaged in amending the Constitution.[11]

The Court's power to move in this direction—apart from references to implied and express power—had its seed sown when the Fourteenth Amendment was adopted in 1868. Thereafter, it was suggested that the dual citizenship recognized by its first sentence secured for citizens federal protection for their elemental privileges and immunities of state citizenship. This view was rejected until the turn of the nineteenth century. The Court in this period, however, began to find power in the Amendment's due process clause to invalidate state action in the area of economic regulation.

This philosophy was carried over to the protection of human rights in *Gitlow v. New York,* 268 U.S. 652 (1925), when, for the first time, the court held that freedom of speech could be protected against arbitrary-

---

[10] Bartholomew, Paul G. (1968). "The Gitlow Doctrine Down to Date, II." *American Bar Association Journal,* 54:787.

[11] Rogge, O. John (1960). *The First and the Fifth,* pp. 279-305, especially at p. 304. Thomas Nelson and Sons, New York.

state action under the Fourteenth Amendment's due process clause. This constitutional-based philosophy, with its humble beginning in the 1890's, reached thundering climaxes in *Brown v. Board of Education*, 347 U.S. 438 (1954)—in human rights in school segregation—and, in *Baker v. Carr*, 369 U.S. 186 (1962)—in political rights in voter apportionment. The decisions represented a sharp break with Anglo-American legal tradition.

Courts, prior to 1950, had adhered rather assiduously to what lawyers call judicial restraint—a principle of law, a precedent, is overruled only rarely by a court. Under this doctrine, the justices reviewed each petition, or appeal, from a state court raising a federal-law issue that alleged a denial of due process, on a case-to-case basis. A judgment was made upon the whole course of the proceedings that were before the Court to ascertain whether they offended those canons of decency and fairness which expressed the notions of justice.[12] This application of the Fourteenth Amendment came to an end, however with changes in the Court.

In the 1950's the Court moved, and with an ever-increasing pace, away from the doctrine of judicial restraint. The early 1960's saw a majority mustered on the Court to enable it to shift from an *ad hoc* concept of due process to a position that the Fourteenth Amendment incorporates, absorbs whole, on a step-by-step basis, certain provisions of the Bill of Rights. As a result, by the end of the 1960's major guarantees of the Bill of Rights had been made applicable to the states through different clauses of the first section of the Fourteenth Amendment. (It would not be at all surprising to see all of the "specifics" of the Bill of Rights incorporated in the near future with the result that federal law will be the measuring-rod that will gauge the rightness or wrongness of state action. Some members of the Court, like Mr. Justice Black, have argued rather persuasively, over the years, that this was what the people wanted when the Fourteenth Amendment was added to the Constitution in 1868.)

A private person, so far, is not bound by the Bill of Rights as, historically, its prohibitions have been held to be a restraint only upon officers and agents of the Government. This interpretation was reaffirmed in unmistakable language in the Court's landmark decision of *Burdeau v. McDowell*, 256 U.S. 465 (1921). It may well be, however, that this doctrine's days are numbered as in the late 1960's, a few state courts, for example, in *Williams v. Williams* (Court of Common Pleas, Ohio, Clermont County) 8 Ohio Misc. 156, 221 N.E. 2d 622 (1966)—a divorce action —the court held that a private person is subject to the limitations in the Bill of Rights.

Another fact that should be kept in mind is that when a government

---

[12] An excellent analysis is made of due process' historical origin and evolution in *Adamson v. California*, 332 U.S. 46 (1947), by Mr. Justice Frankfurter, in particular, in his concurring opinion.

agent from a federal agency appears as a prosecution witness in a state court, he appears as a private person with no official standing. The State Bill of Rights in this situation, does not apply to him.

The same rationale did apply with respect to an agent of a state government as a witness in a federal court. The federal Bill of Rights did not apply to him. But, in *Elkins v. United States,* 364 U.S. 206 (1960), the Supreme Court of the United States in the exercise of its inherent supervisory power over federal courts, held that a federal court must exclude evidence that is proffered by a witness, who is an agent of state government, when the evidence was obtained during an *unreasonable* search.

That rule is not applicable to a federal agent as a witness in a state court, under like circumstances, as the Court has no supervisory power over state courts. The Court, however, may ultimately find a constitutional ground to foreclose the use of such evidence by a state court or, as some decisions indicate, for example, *Cleary v. Bolger,* 371 U.S. 392 (1963), the Court may enjoin (forbid) a federal agent to appear in a state court for the purpose of introducing tainted evidence.

All of these things are important in law enforcement for reasons other than providing information about historical and current facts. Law enforcement officers should be as conscious of the dangers of a strong central government as were the founders of this country. What happened in early days clearly shows that people feared giving too much power to any person or body politic. The same sentiment finds expression today. Current feeling can be discerned from views expressed by many congressmen. Fear of strong armed forces came to the forefront in 1958, when the Second Session of the 85th Congress by a large majority, rejected President Eisenhower's program for reorganization of the defense department. In accord with historic tradition, Congress is insistent on civilian control of the armed forces, which means, in effect, congressional control. On Capitol Hill there is a deep and real fear of granting too much leeway and power to a chief executive in respect to control over the armed forces.

Law enforcement officers, frequently and rather understandably, feel that restrictions set forth in the Constitution and Bill of Rights hamper efficient law enforcement. It would be naïve to deny that there are situations when such results occur. However, even though the Bill of Rights at times may cloak the criminal, it is the "hair shirt" that law enforcement must wear. And law enforcement officers of the largest and smallest agencies must wear it in good spirit, mindful of the fact that order is dependent on law, and law is dependent on enforcement, within limits set down in the Constitution and Bill of Rights.

The job will be much easier for law enforcement when more people share in the task. That task goes hand in hand with the rights that citizenship gives to the people. Everyone can do a great deal to aid law enforcement in safeguarding personal rights. Law enforcement is not a task for a few people, but a task for many people.

In the words of a justice of one of the state supreme courts, "Lofty abstractions about individual liberty and justice do not enforce themselves. These things must be reforged in men's hearts every day. And they are reforged by the law, for every jury trial in the land is a small daily miracle of democracy in action." [13] Public support can contribute much to law in action whether in the jury room or at the scene of a crime.

BI-SOVEREIGNTY AND DUAL CITIZENSHIP

Often the question may come up in the minds of law enforcement personnel, "*How can the national government, through the United States Supreme Court, void a conviction in a state court which was affirmed by the highest appellate court of the state, with the result that weeks or months of investigative and prosecutive effort are expended in vain?*" This, naturally, may raise another question: "*How can the United States Supreme Court bring about the release of notorious criminals, who, from all the evidence, were guilty as charged?*" These questions deserve an answer.

In order to answer them, it is necessary as a first step, to turn to the Tenth Amendment in the Bill of Rights which provides that "The powers not delegated to the United States by the Constitution, nor prohibited by it to the states, are reserved to the states respectively, or to the people." As a consequence of this "grant" and "reservation" *two* distinct and separate fields of government are established. Each government is supreme in its respective field. A great many problems concerning law enforcement can be resolved if that principle is clearly understood.

Second, consideration also must be given to *citizenship* in finding answers to the questions. It should be recognized that another result of national *and* state governments (bi-sovereignty) is *dual citizenship*. This result was not achieved, however, until the Fourteenth Amendment was adopted in 1868. Neither the Constitution nor act of Congress had defined citizenship or distinguished between United States citizenship and state citizenship before the Fourteenth Amendment. By the terms of that amendment, a person acquires United States citizenship by birth or naturalization in the United States (and is subject to its jurisdiction), but to acquire state citizenship, a person must, further, be a resident of the state concerned. The vast majority of the people in the United States, therefore, have dual citizenship—as citizens of the United States, and as citizens of the state in which they reside. (Aliens, though not citizens, have those rights which are reserved to them by treaties and the United States Constitution.)

---

[13] Travers, Robert (1958). *Anatomy of Murder,* p. 63. St. Martin's Press, New York.

It should be fairly evident that the national government has an obligation to protect personal liberties of its citizens from *state* action which unreasonably interferes with their rights *as citizens of the United States.* Only when the Fourteenth Amendment was adopted did it become possible for the United States and Congress to put an end to *state* action which encroached upon the human rights of citizens of the *United States.* This is brought about by a clause in Section 1, Fourteenth Amendment, which provides, "nor shall any state deprive any person of life, liberty or property without due process of law." *This clause is the source of the authority, generally exercised, in restraining unreasonable action by a state or local law enforcement officer.*

It seems neither necessary nor desirable, in mapping out a few landmarks on government and citizenship, to discuss due process of law in detail. A few comments, by way of definition, or for lack of one, may be of value in understanding this concept which has its origin, according to many legal historians, in the English Magna Carta of 1215.

One fact is clear: The United States Supreme Court has consistently refused to define due process in explicit terms. It is often referred to as "the law of the land," and in a context of "fundamental fairness." (See the 39th Article of Magna Carta in Chapter VI.) Another oft quoted definition of due process states it to mean that "a person shall not be arbitrarily deprived of life, liberty, or property."

A discussion of the implications of due process in a concurring opinion by Mr. Justice Frankfurter of the United States Supreme Court rather effectively effaces any pretense that its meaning can be conveniently simplified. He sets forth his view that " 'due process' cannot be imprisoned within the treacherous limits of any formula. Representing a profound attitude of fairness between man and man, and more particularly, between the individual and government, 'due process' is compounded of history, reason, the past course of decisions, and stout confidence in the strength of the democratic faith which we profess. Due process is not a mechanical instrument. It is not a yardstick. It is a process. It is a delicate process of adjustment inescapably involving the exercise of judgment by those whom the Constitution entrusted with the unfolding of the process." [14]

Herbert Hoover, when President of the United States, in speaking of the Constitution, said, "There must never be confusion in the Bill of Rights, the balance of power, local government, and a government of laws, not of men." Along the same line of reasoning, it might be suggested that law enforcement officers should ever recall that *"The Constitution of the United States is a law for rulers and people, equally in war and in peace, and covers*

---

[14] *Joint Anti-Fascist Refugee Committee v. McGrath*, 341 U.S. 123 (1951).

with the shield of its protection all classes of men, at all times, and under all circumstances." [15]

Our Constitution and Bill of Rights will give only paper protection if our people are more concerned with prosecutions that are overturned than with fundamental principles that are upheld.

TOPICS FOR DISCUSSION

1. What is the relationship of the Tenth Amendment of the Constitution to the question of bi-sovereignty?
2. What is the relationship of the Fourteenth Amendment to the Constitution to the question of dual-citizenship? Due Process?
3. What are the specific provisions in the constitution of this State that parallel the provisions of the Bill of Rights in the Federal Constitution?

---

[15] *Ex Parte Milligan*, 4 Wall 2 (1866).

Chapter IX

THE BILL OF RIGHTS AND MAJOR ENFORCEMENT PROBLEMS

Obviously, the Bill of Rights requires intelligent law enforcement, if law enforcement is to function as a public service in preserving an acceptable balance between law and order and the welfare of the individual. Only trained specialists can maintain order and preserve democratic values. Furthermore, being informed on important rules of law, in and of itself, is not enough. Good law enforcement demands a high sense of moral responsibility and a disciplined agency for impartial, competent enforcement under the rule of law. While the rights of individuals to be protected from unwarranted enforcement practices must be carefully safeguarded, the rights of the public to community security must also be considered.

There are some provisions in the Bill of Rights that create more acute enforcement problems than others. Very difficult tasks confront law enforcement officers every day in such areas because there is some doubt regarding the law in many situations. This uncertainty exists because the highest court of the land, while rightly fostering enforcement within the Constitution, frequently complicates tasks by failing to spell out adequate standards, as guides for law enforcement, in terms of rights and obligations.

The United States Supreme Court has an obligation and clear duty to make the Constitution a viable and continuously applicable instrument, for the Constitution is not only the basic law which *creates* our form of government, but also the basic law which *regulates* our governmental activities. We live in a country in which there are patriotic organizations that devote money, time, and effort to promoting respect for the Constitution. They sponsor essay and oratory contests in our public schools but some of them also attack the courts with varying degrees of vigor, apparently not accepting the concept that without the interpretation of the court, the Constitution has very little meaning. Any document, no matter how wisely conceived, is not self-administering. And no document, no matter how detailed, means the same thing to all people, at all times. Courts are necessary to interpret and apply the laws—and that also applies to the basic law of our Nation, the Constitution.

By an analysis of law enforcement functions in relation to key provisions of the Bill of Rights, some insight can be gained of the wider problem involved with the interrelation of security and liberty.

FIRST AMENDMENT RIGHTS

Freedom of Speech. Any experienced law enforcement officer appreciates the troublesome issues which are presented in controlling public meetings ranging from the street-corner soap-box orator to the speaker addressing a large religious rally. The enforcement problems involving the exercise of free speech, protected under the First Amendment, are infrequent as compared with everyday law enforcement work. But, when the issue is faced, it is one of paramount importance. Law enforcement officers must be prepared to handle each problem at the time and place of occurrence, and under conditions of pressure and tension, without the aid of textbooks and legal research. And, in performing such duties, they must do so in such a way as to merit a stamp of approval if subjected to later court review. A difficult task indeed. A task that is most difficult when reduced to concrete situations. It would be impractical to make an extensive inquiry into the overall problem because, first, the law itself is far from settled, and second, it would serve little useful purpose to attack this area of indefinite extension.

The right to speak freely and to promote a diversity of ideas and programs is one of the chief differences that sets our government apart from totalitarian regimes. Accordingly, a function of speech, under our system of government, is to encourage dispute, even though it might prove controversial and challenging. This does not mean, however, that speech is an inalienable right. There are occasions when limits can be placed on speakers. But, law enforcement officers, in the exercise of their authority, must use extreme caution in taking any action which deprives a person of his right to speak. Yet, law enforcement administrators must meet such problems in the day-to-day situations that involve speech and public order.

The United States Supreme Court does not deny localities power to devise a licensing system for the regulation of speech. A statute which requires a permit must, however, contain standards which leave little discretion in the issuing officer as to the issuance of a permit. Legislation which seems to meet "standards" does not exactly ease the burden of law enforcement administrators. Mr. Justice Jackson, dissenting in the *Kunz* case, indicates the reason why standards are not too meaningful by noting, "It seems hypercritical to strike down local laws on their faces for want of standards when we have no standards." [1]

A bare outline has been provided by the United States Supreme Court,

---

[1] *Kunz v. New York*, 340 U.S. 290 (1951).

confined to the enunciation of broad policies, to help law enforcement officers reach decisions when a speaker passes the bounds of free speech. Because of the very nature of the problem, that is about all that any court, federal or state, can do. Law enforcement officers, administrators, in particular, should be familiar with the standards. Such knowledge can be most helpful in establishing enforcement policies and planning strategy to control situations where speech becomes an issue.

An analysis of various decisions of the United States Supreme Court, involving freedom of speech, furnishes a framework of reference which can be followed within reasonable limitations in regulating speech. They are the standards. The standards should be followed when possible. For law enforcement officers to deviate too far from the standards (even conceding a lack of all-inclusiveness) is to gamble between good and questionable enforcement in this important area of human rights.

The decisions, with few exceptions, emphasize the duty of law enforcement administrators to have enough manpower available (not necessarily in view) at public gatherings to protect the speakers and cope with any incident that might arise. The ordinary murmurings and objections of a hostile audience cannot be allowed as grounds for silencing a speaker. But, any one in the audience who persists in unduly interfering with, and heckling a speaker who is voicing his beliefs, can, and should, be removed from the vicinity.[2]

It is very important, when freedom of speech is involved, that every effort be made to avoid arrest of the speaker. An arrest should not be made unless it is certain that what is said violates a criminal law. The law is fairly settled that a physical arrest on a permit violation should not be made—that is, when a speaker addresses a meeting without having secured the required permit to conduct the meeting—rather, proceed by complaint and warrant.

In addition to the aforementioned general rules, there are a few specific principles which can be drawn from decisions of the United States Supreme Court, and utilized as enforcement standards:

---

[2] The *Los Angeles Times*, November 8, 1963, news item, in part: "Three John Birch Society officers sentenced Thursday for breaking up a civil rights meeting were given a tongue lashing by a Torrance judge. . . ." The judge "suspended 10-day sentences, placed them on probation for two years and fined each of them $225." "Guilty pleas had been entered . . . They admitted being John Birch Society leaders in the South Bay area . . . Hecklers shouted down speakers and the meeting finally broke up in a cacophony of boos, hissing, clapping, shouting, and coughing . . . Some of the hecklers demanded to know if any Communists were connected with the sponsoring organization." "Judge Keene castigated the trio for 'taking what they thought to be the law into their own hands' and 'in their infinite wisdom determining what public forums should be permitted.'" "Judge Keene said such conduct 'violates every basic precept of freedom of speech' and is nothing more than 'adult delinquency.'"

1. Arrest when there is direct incitement to commit a definite crime; e.g., riot.
2. Arrest when plainly obscene language is used.
3. Arrest if there is a man-to-man insult in terms of common fighting words.
4. Arrest on a breach of the peace charge, in some jurisdictions, when the speaker causes a crowd to collect in a public street which interferes with the primary purposes of the street for pedestrian and vehicular traffic—after the speaker ignores two or three courteous requests (with explanation) to terminate his talk. (As a matter of practice, however, more often than not, it might be better policy to detour traffic and allow the speaker to continue.)

But, short of such situations, unmistakably shown, the law enforcement job is to maintain order and protect the speaker in the exercise of his constitutional rights.[3]

The peace bond has been a long-time favorite to curb the hate-monger and rabble-rouser who is prone to use disruptive tactics when others exercise their First Amendment rights. A person in this category may be taken before a judge to post a peace bond, and failure to do so results in imprisonment.

That is the way it has been done, but that does not mean that it is right. The practice is unconstitutional as a denial of due process says Hawaii's Third Circuit Court in *Santos v. Nahiwa* (8/31/70). "It is idle talk to argue," the Court says, "whether this is punishment, a fine or a preventive order. The substance of the results of the failure to put up the bond is that an indigent defendant is deprived of his liberty and the defendant with economic capacity may continue to be free by posting bond." The Supreme Court of Hawaii in *Santos v. Nahiwa*, 487 P. 2d 283 (7/6/71), reaches the same result.

Freedom of Assembly. What follows centers largely upon the fourth clause of the First Amendment that guaranteees "the right of the people peacefully to assemble, and to petition the Government for a redress of grievances." No attempt will be made in this section to discuss problems, except incidentally, that arise largely in civil disorder situations—either nonviolent or violent.

Often when people exercise either their right to speak, or their right to assemble, law enforcement officials may face challenges that tax both their ingenuity and their professional competency. And, it is in the way that they use the law, in such incidents, that their stature is measured on both

---

[3] Majority and concurring opinions, *Niemotko v. Maryland*, 340 U.S. 268 (1951), for a discussion of standards in regulating speech.

counts. How to apply the law impartially should pose no challenge, but a like assessment cannot be made on how to apply the law so that action taken in the name of law measures up to acceptable constitutional standards.

As has been observed in the section on freedom of speech, states may, constitutionally have laws to control the unbridled exercise of speech. The same is true as to the right of the people to assemble together. States and municipalities may take steps for the comfort and welfare of their inhabitants with respect to their right peaceably to assemble in public places. Such regulatory power takes in a number of situations. For example, in the regulation of streets for traffic and for parades and the use of public parks, reasonable controls may be imposed, constitutionally, without abridging people's rights.

When law enforcement officers engage in policing large or small gatherings, peaceful or nonpeaceful, most of the legal problems that come up are similar to those that come into play in free speech confrontations. In actuality, this is not entirely true, as in any demonstration—housewives obstructing a residential street to the free movement of traffic, or a massive protest march—such action is *conduct* more than speech.

It is accepted, generally now, in legal circles, that the protection of First Amendment rights against government action will depend on the First Amendment as to federal action and on the due process clause of the Fourteenth as to state action. Confusion exists in the minds of many people who believe that this is not the case.[4] They are bound to an illusion that the Fourteenth Amendment incorporates the First. Much of this thinking can be traced to opinions of the Supreme Court that followed in the wake of its 1925 *Gitlow* decision.

The decisions were so numerous and so strong that they lent weight to the erroneous contention that the Fourteenth Amendment incorporates the First. Put another way, it is one thing to say the right is so fundamental to an "orderly concept of liberty" that it is protected against arbitrary state action through due process of the Fourteenth Amendment, and quite another to say the right is incorporated whole under the Amendment's due process clause. States are not, therefore, held to identical federal standards. They do have more leeway under state laws to regulate assemblages. This seems to stand out in the Court's holding in *Adderly v. Florida,* 385 U.S. 39 (1966).

In *Adderly,* the Court (5-4) for the first time upheld convictions of

---

[4] It is the First Amendment that is discussed in this framework of reference and no other. The Fourth and parts of the Fifth and Sixth Amendments have been incorporated (since 1960) whole, and the states are bound to meet substantive federal standards with respect to them.

participants in a peaceful civil rights demonstration who had been convicted under Florida's state "malicious trespass statute." A group of 200 students had gone to the county jail to protest the arrest of fellow students and local policies of discrimination, including segregation in the county jail. The congestion caused by the demonstration would have made vehicular access to the service entry difficult, but no vehicles tried to enter or leave while the crowd was present. The sheriff told the demonstrators that they were trespassing upon jail property and gave them ten minutes to leave. Some left but others, including the petitioners, remained and were arrested.[5]

In another case, *Cameron v. Johnson*, 390 U.S. 611 (1968), the Court (7-2) held that while picketing cannot be made a crime, blocking the entrance to a public building can constitute a criminal act (and that a Mississippi law that prohibits pickets from obstructing or interfering with entrances of public buildings is sufficiently clear and unambiguous . . . to survive charges of vagueness).

Civil rights demonstrators in *Cameron* staged a large demonstration on the courthouse site where they had maintained picket lines for a period of nearly three months before the arrests were made. The arrests occurred a day after the enactment of the *Anti-Picketing Law* at which time the sheriff, accompanied by other officials, read the new law to the pickets at the "march route" and directed them to disperse, which they did. The next day, in large numbers, they appeared at the courthouse and resumed picketing along the then unmarked "march route." (The police barricades had been removed the day before.) They were arrested, and others arrested later, and formally charged with violation of the anti-picketing statute. (This case involved a review of a denial by the District Court for the Southern District of Mississippi of appellants' petition for declaratory and injunctive relief.)

In *Gregory v. Chicago*, 394 U.S. 111 (1969), bad legislation moved the Court to reverse comedian-civil rights leader Dick Gregory's disorderly conviction arising out of his refusal to disperse his peaceful and orderly march from Chicago's city hall to and around Mayor Daley's home. Gregory and some forty other fellow demonstrators were arrested. The Court held unanimously, through Chief Justice Warren, that the convictions were so unsupported by the evidence that they violated due process.

Concurring in the result, Mr. Justice Black says, with Justice Douglas agreeing, that the majority makes too short shrift of an important case. This opinion brings out the fact a local law can be drawn narrowly "forbidding disruptive picketing or demonstrations in a residential area." In

---

[5] See "Supreme Court," 81 *Harv. L. Rev.*, 138-144 for a good discussion of the inferences that can be drawn from the decision.

this case the petitioners were arrested for no more than a refusal to obey a police order, Justice Black points out. (Justice Douglas and Harlan wrote separate concurring opinions.)

It is evident from the cases discussed that police regulatory action, in relation to the many variables that are inherent in different kinds of demonstrations, requires a high degree of sensitivity on the part of law enforcement officers toward the rights of participants. Law enforcement officers sorely need guidelines to help them perform their duties intelligently and effectively while policing public assemblages. To try to outline these guidelines is not a task that can be undertaken, in any detail, in a book of this nature.

The authors would hope that legislative bodies will do more by way of intelligent lawmaking that will meet constitutional mandates, and that local government officials will do more by way of policy formulation that will reflect a balancing of interests to the end that the rights of all people will be accorded the protection that is their "due" under due process of law.

FOURTH AMENDMENT RIGHTS

Search and Seizure. The right of every person to enjoy personal freedom from unlawful restraint is firmly imbedded in the history and traditions of the Anglo-American legal system. The right of personal liberty is still the central force in our concept of free government and serves to distinguish our system from others in different parts of the world. Under our system of government our concept of personal liberty is inconsistent with unlawful arrest practices. An illegal arrest ordinarily will render inadmissible evidence obtained by search and seizure incident to such arrest, as having been taken in violation of the accused's constitutional rights under the Fourth Amendment to the Federal Constitution and corresponding provisions of state constitutions.

Few decisions of the United States Supreme Court between 1949 and 1968 have generated as much controversy—excepting the confession rulings of 1966 and 1967—as those dealing with issues raised under the Fourth Amendment. Since the provisions of the Amendment cover some of the most critical areas of criminal investigation—arrest, search and seizure, and even, in some circumstances interrogation, and lineup identification—the issues bring into sharp focus the dilemma of order versus liberty.[6] No area of the criminal law offers a richer variety of fact situations than searches and seizures, especially when Fourth Amendment problems are meshed with arrests.

---

[6] Landynski, Jacob W. (1960). *Search and Seizure and the Supreme Court,* p. 13. The Johns Hopkins Press, Baltimore.

A look at the work of the Court in 1966 and 1967 provides corroborative evidence. During the two terms, the Court delivered twenty full-blown opinions in search and seizure cases—including two in the area of administrative searches, two on "stop-and-frisk," two on wiretapping, and one on electronic surveillance. The seven decisions are classed as search and seizure cases as the Court brought the practices under the due process clause of the Fourteenth Amendment during the two terms.[7]

The Fourth Amendment commands that the right of the people to be secure in their persons, houses, papers, and effects, against UNREASONABLE searches and seizures, shall not be violated. In the same sentence, the amendment sets out the conditions under which warrants may issue, and prescribes what they must necessarily contain. In other words, inferentially, the amendment indicates that an arrest or a search or seizure of things is reasonable only when effected with a valid warrant. It seems that many persons are unaware of the fact that the amendment also protects *persons* from unreasonable seizures (arrests), as well as from unreasonable searches and seizures of *physical objects*. It is clear that the amendment does *not* prohibit *reasonable* searches and seizures. However, whether the action of a law enforcement officer in a search and seizure is reasonable or unreasonable is a question which cannot always be answered readily.

The word "reasonable" is an elastic term of doubtful value by way of definition. That word, and its bedfellow, "probable," when coupled with the word "cause," may pose many problems in law enforcement. Whenever an arrest is made, or an object seized, "reasonable" or "probable" cause must be considered in determining the legality of the action taken. "Probable cause" is an attempt to balance the requirements of order and liberty. It requires more than mere suspicion or "hunch," but less than absolute certainty.

The Fourth Amendment, by inference, therefore, states that all arrests or searches and seizures of things, without a valid warrant, are unreasonable. But the inference must be interpreted in the light of history. From that history, situations can be identified when arrests or searches and seizures without a valid warrant were considered as being reasonable. Law enforcement officers, from the earliest days of the English Common Law, as well as private persons, were empowered to arrest, without a warrant, for certain kinds of offenses. An arrest could be made for a felony com-

---

[7] *Camara v. Municipal Court*, 387 U.S. 523 (1967), *See v. Seattle*, 387 U.S. 541 (1967), *Berger v. New York*, 388 U.S. 41 (1967), *Katz v. United States*, 389 U.S. 347 (1967), *Terry v. Ohio*, 392 U.S. 1 (1968), *Sibron v. New York*, 392 U.S. 40 (1968), *Peters v. New York*, 392 U.S. 40 (1968)—one opinion was written for the two latter cases,—and *Lee v. Florida*, 392 U.S. 378 (1968).

mitted or attempted in their presence. Likewise, an arrest could be made for a breach of the peace in their presence. In both cases, arrests without a warrant were justified on the theory of *emergency* and *necessity*: in the case of a felony, in order to prevent escape; when a breach of the peace was in progress, in order to restore order, and only incidentally, if at all, to prevent escape. What must be borne in mind is that *the common law exceptions must be read into the Fourth Amendment.*

Actually, there is little distinction between the authority of a private person to make an arrest, and the authortiy of a law enforcement officer to do the same thing. Indeed, it was not until 1827 that the rule differentiating the legal authority of private persons from that of law enforcement officers originated. Around that time, law enforcement officers' authority was enlarged somewhat without lessening that of a private person.

Broadly speaking, when there is a felony, law enforcement officers can excuse the fact that they made an erroneous arrest by showing that they reasonably and honestly believed that the person arrested was involved in its commission. (In California and New York, when a police officer has reasonable cause for believing that a felony has been committed, and that the person arrested has committed it, he may lawfully arrest, even though it should afterward appear that no such felony was in fact committed. In some states, a felony in fact must have been committed, a ruling which is more restrictive than the common law. In states such as North Carolina and Texas, an arrest for a felony cannot be made without a warrant unless there can be shown a reasonable belief that the person might escape if not immediately arrested.)

A private person who makes an erroneous arrest for a felony, in order to excuse his mistake as to the identity of the person arrested, must show, according to the prevailing viewpoint, that so far as the mistake was concerned, he was honestly and reasonably mistaken, and that a felony had in fact been committed by someone.

As a principle of general law, well established in most jurisdictions, a public officer for a particular county or municipality has no official power to arrest offenders beyond the boundaries of the county or district for which he is appointed.[8]

An officer's power of arrest, when acting beyond the limits of the geographical unit to which he is appointed, becomes that which is conferred upon a private citizen in the same circumstances.[9]

It should be noted that when in "hot pursuit" or "immediate pursuit" of an offender, with probable cause to arrest, an officer has authority to

---

[8] *Brittain v. United States Fidelity and Guaranty Co.,* 219 Ky. 465, and *People v. Martin,* 36 Calif. Reporter 924.

[9] *People v. Alvarado,* 208 Cal. App. 2d, 629 and *People v. Ball,* 162 Cal. App. 2d, 465.

enter private property or to cross city, county or state boundaries. (In other words, when pursued by an officer, an offender cannot claim "sanctuary" by crossing the boundary of a political subdivision, or by stepping within his own property or abode.)

In many states, law enforcement officers and private persons can arrest a person committing, or attempting to commit, a misdemeanor in their presence. In some states, however, this authority is conferred only on law enforcement officers.

Perhaps the only general statement that can be safely made in regard to arrest without a warrant are: (1) Anyone, law enforcement officer or private citizen, in all states, may make an arrest to stop the commission of a felony or to apprehend one who has committed a felony; (2) Anyone, law enforcement officer or private citizen, in most states, may make an arrest when the offense is a breach of the peace actually being attempted or committed in the presence or view of the person making the arrest. It is not safe to generalize more than that.

Many pitfalls can be encountered by an officer when he deprives a person of liberty through the process of arrest. To perform this task properly, not only knowledge of the rules of law is required, but of equal importance, judgment becomes an asset of immeasurable value. And, as part of the general picture, the need for reform in arrest laws cannot be overlooked, such as consideration of a Uniform Arrest Act,[10] which would free law enforcement from much of the present conflict between protective responsibilities and legal requirements.

While there are variations among the states concerning arrest laws, a fairly common pattern exists, with the result that differences are not nearly as pronounced as many would believe. Law enforcement officers should know the arrest laws of their own jurisdictions, and know them well, since perhaps the most typical law enforcement task is the arrest of a person for criminal behavior. The law of arrest must be regarded as a basic tool of the law enforcement vocation.

A search and seizure of property is almost invariably effected when a person is taken into custody on a criminal charge. For that reason, and because searches and seizures often occur even when an arrest is not made, some review of the limitations of the Fourth Amendment is deemed proper.

The rules regulating search and seizure were unknown in early English Common Law. It has been noted that the current limitations have crept

---

[10] See Section 12 of the Model Arrest Act drafted under the auspices of the *Interstate Commission on Crime,* as well as an article by Warner, Sam Bass (1942). "The Uniform Arrest Act." *Virginia Law Review,* 28:315. Also see Articles 2 and 3, American Law Institute's "A Model Code of Pre-Arraignment Procedure," Tentative Draft No. 1, March 1, 1966, which was stillborn, however, as a result of *Miranda v. Arizona,* 384 U.S. 436 (1966).

slowly into the law. It would seem that the first time the question arose was during the trial of Bishop Atterbury in 1723.[11] Representatives of the Crown intercepted some letters which tended to support the charge of treason against the accused.

The accused contended that the letters had been seized illegally, and asked that the Crown be prohibited from using them as evidence. The Court did not agree with the arguments, presented on behalf of the accused Bishop, supporting the request that the letters be excluded as evidence, and admitted them as proper. The rule originated in this case held that if evidence was relevant and trustworthy, an inquiry would not be made as to how the evidence was obtained. The Court held that if the accused was indeed not guilty, as charged, his innocence could be established even though the letters were used as evidence, and, therefore, excluding the evidence was unnecessary to the prisoner's defense. The Court indicated its interest in but one goal: searching out the truth as to innocence or guilt.

The colonists brought the rule to this country. It survived challenges and remained the rule in the colonies. It continued as precedent after the Constitution's adoption. Its life span covered 307 years in United States history, from 1607 to 1914: from the day the first settlers arrived at Jamestown, Virginia, to the day in Washington, D.C., when the United States Supreme Court, in a unanimous decision, created the federal exclusionary rule of evidence, applicable to federal courts, in search and seizure cases.

Prior to 1914, with the exception of a couple of states where state courts modified the rule somewhat, the rule of the *Bishop Atterbury* case substantially reflected the law of the states, and the national government, its Territories and Possessions, on search and seizure. In 1914, a mounting fear of invasions of personal security by unreasonable searches and seizures caused the United States Supreme Court to qualify the ancient common law rule. In a momentous decision, the *Weeks Case*, the high court declared that if illegally seized evidence was held admissible, the Fourth Amendment would be of no value, and "might as well be stricken from the Constitution." [12] The court did not completely renounce the ancient common law rule, but qualified the rule by devising procedural methods to circumvent the rule. This is the decision which established the exclusionary rule, which, before 1961, was followed by the courts of about one-half of the states. This principle established in the *Weeks* case was merely an exception to the common law rule, an exception confined solely to the exclusion of evidence obtained in violation of a constitutional right.

The rule did not have much of a following in state courts until the adoption of the Eighteenth (Volstead) Amendment in 1919. Abuses were

---

[11] *Bishop Atterbury's Trial,* 16 How. St. Tr. 323 (1723).

[12] *Weeks v. United States,* 232 U.S. 882 (1914).

attributed to law enforcement officers in the securing of evidence while investigating "prohibition" violations, for this was a period when the manufacture, sale, transportation, or possession of intoxicating liquors was a federal offense.

State courts began to adopt the federal exclusionary rule of the *Weeks* case. One authority, in describing the situation, does so in these words:

> However, the Eighteenth Amendment, for a time, caused the Fourth Amendment, as it relates to proof of crime, to be, in the language of an eminent writer, "of interest to a wider circle, including many not ordinarily deemed undesirable citizens." The result was a tendency on the part of courts to exalt the latter (amendment) at the expense of the enforcement of the former.[13]

The eminent writer and scholar, Wigmore, in his inimitable way, characterizes the rule of the *Weeks* case as based on "misguided sentimentality."[14]

Whether the exclusionary rule which, under certain circumstances, bars the admission of evidence secured as a result of unreasonable search and seizure, is "misguided sentimentality," or not, the fact remains that as time passed, many states ranged themselves on the side of the exclusionary rule. When *Wolf v. Colorado*, 338 U.S. 25 (1949), was decided, only seventeen states followed the federal exclusionary rule. Then, steadily, the states began to adopt the federal exclusionary rule, until, by 1960, a majority of the fifty states were following the rule in whole or in part. The appendix to the *Elkins* case lists the states which followed the rule, and that particular decision, rendered June 27, 1960, is rich in history with respect to the growth of the law of search and seizure.[15]

However, in an historic decision of far-reaching effect on law enforcement, the United States Supreme Court, in *Mapp v. Ohio*, 367 U.S. 643 (6/19/61), held in a 5-4 decision, that all evidence obtained by searches and seizures in violation of the Constitution, is, under due process of the Fourteenth Amendment, inadmissible in a state court. The decision expressly overrules the *Wolf* case of 1949, and earlier decisions like it. Thus, in *Mapp*, the Court imposed the federal exclusionary rule on all states. (Mapp's conviction, however, was reversed, 6-3.)

Mr. Justice Harlan, in his dissent in *Mapp* summed up one view when he said, "But in the last analysis I think this Court can increase respect for the Constitution only if it rigidly respects the limitations which the Constitution places upon it, and respects as well the principle inherent in

---

[13] McKelvey, John J. (1944). *Law of Evidence,* 5th Edition, Section 127. West Publishing Company, St. Paul, Minnesota.

[14] Wigmore, John H. (1922). "Using Evidence Obtained by Illegal Search and Seizure." *American Bar Association Journal,* 8:482.

[15] *Elkins v. United States,* 364 U.S. 206 (1960).

its own processes. In the present case I think we exceed both, and that our voice becomes only a voice of power, not of reason."

Mr. Justice Clark, in delivering the majority opinion, summed up another view when he said, "There are those who say, as did Justice (then judge) Cardozo, that under our constitutional exclusionary doctrine 'the criminal is to go free because the constable has blundered.' . . . In some cases this will undoubtedly be the result. But, as was said in *Elkins*, 'there is another consideration—the imperative of judicial integrity.' . . . The criminal goes free, if he must, but it is the law that sets him free. Nothing can destroy a government more quickly than its failure to observe its own laws, or worse, its disregard of the charter of its own existence. . . . Our decision, founded on reason and truth, gives to the individual no more than that which the Constitution guarantees him, to the police officer no less than that which honest law enforcement is entitled, and, to the courts, that judicial integrity so necessary in the true administration of justice."

In its decision the Court laid to rest many doubts relative to the path that the law of search and seizure will follow in this country. Some questions still remain to be answered, however.

For example, the People of Michigan, by referendum in 1936 and 1952, amended the Michigan Constitution to give their police more authority in the search and seizure area. The amendments permit state courts to admit evidence on dangerous weapons and narcotic drugs, when seized outside the curtilage of a dwelling, and, excepting an unusual situation, takes out of issue any question on how the evidence was obtained. The amendments were the subject of heated debate in 1962 by the delegates to the Michigan Constitutional Convention of 1961-1962. The amendments were incorporated, with some improvement in phraseology, despite strong opposition, as Article I, Section 11, Michigan Constitution of 1963, effective January 1, 1964. There was a definite question, however as to the constitutionality of the provision due to the ruling in *Mapp*. Of local concern was the fact that the *Mapp* decision, and its effect, ran counter to the voted desires of a majority of the people of Michigan.

The validity of the provision had been argued in the Michigan Supreme Court one year before *Mapp*, in *People v. Winkle* (358 Mich. 551). The Court in this case upheld the proviso, stating that it was unnecessary to decide whether the search was reasonable or unreasonable. Three years later, the question as to whether *Mapp* superseded the Michigan constitutional provision was argued in *In re Winkle* (372 Mich. 292). The Court based its decision on the ground the search was reasonable. In 1966, the Court again held a search to be reasonable in *People v. Blessing* (378 Mich. 51, 142 N.W. 2d 709), but a majority could not be mustered to decide whether *Mapp* did or did not supersede the provision.

Finally, after nine years of avoiding the issue, the Court met it head-on in *People v. Pennington* (383 Mich. 611, 178 N.W. 2d 471). On July 11, 1970, the Court held, 6-1, that the provision of Article I, Section 11, was in conflict with the Fourth Amendment as applied to the states by *Mapp v. Ohio,* and in such conflicts the Supremacy Clause (United States Constitution, Article VI, Clause 2) requires that the federal provision shall prevail. Thus the Michigan court, in this decision, points up the fact that *Mapp,* like the school desegregation case, is a decision that the United States Supreme Court assumes, perhaps, speaks the voice of all citizens, rather than echoing the unique desires of any one state, or any one group. (See Dallin H. Oaks, "Studying the Exclusionary Rule in Search and Seizure." *University of Chicago L. Rev.,* Vol. 37, No. 4, Summer 1970, pp. 665-757.)

Audio-Surveillance. Audio-surveillance by mechanical devices has always been related to search and seizure issues. Electronic eavesdropping invariably constitutes an invasion of privacy of the person whose conversation is overheard even when it is conducted under legal sanction. It is, therefore, a practice that is not to be commended, except, perhaps, under unusual circumstances and, then, only under very carefully defined standards. The authors would urge the reader, whatever his personal views on eavesdropping, to keep in mind at all times that the right to privacy is the most precious right guaranteed to people under the law. Invasions of the right have been before the Supreme Court of the United States in a number of wiretapping and electronic-eavesdropping cases.

The term "privacy," or "right to privacy," has been used three times in the 120 words that make up the last paragraph. As there is more than an average amount of confusion as to what "right of privacy" means, a few words of explanation may throw some light on what it means. It is a term of comparatively recent origin in modern law although it has its roots in Roman law. No reference is made to the term by authoritative writers of the common law, nor is the term included in the Bill of Rights as such. While there has been considerable conflict of judicial opinion as to the nature of the right it is, in essence, a phase of security of the person, and is commonly defined as *the right to be left alone.*[16] The Supreme Court of the United States makes frequent reference to the term in its decisions on wiretapping, and in those that relate to its more sophisticated Big Brother—electronic eavesdropping.

The first case in which the United States Supreme Court considered the status of wiretapping was *Olmstead v. United States,* 277 U.S. 438 (1928). The first case in which the United States Supreme Court considered the

---

[16] Fisher, Edward C., Edited by Donigan, Robert L. (1967). *Laws of Arrest,* pp. 15-16. The Traffic Institute of Northwestern University, Evanston, Illinois.

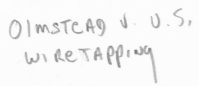

OlmsTEAd v. U.S.
wiReTApping

status of mechanical eavesdropping was *Goldman v. United States,* 316 U.S. 129 (1942).

In *Goldman,* the Court held that evidence procured by the use of a detectaphone attached to the wall of a room, in order to allow agents in the room to pick up conversations on the other side of the wall, was admissible. The agents' actions did not involve physical trespass. Supreme Court decisions on mechanical eavesdropping from *Goldman* to *Katz v. United States,* 389 U.S. 147 (1967), reflect an evolutionary pattern in weaving constitutional principles that has been markedly similar to that in wiretapping cases.

The Court, in *Olmstead,* held (5-4) that messages passing over telephone wires are not within the protection against unreasonable search and seizure. "The Amendment itself," said the majority, "shows that the search is to be of material things—the person, the house, his papers, or his effects. The description of the warrant necessary to make the proceeding lawful, is that it must specify the place to be searched and the person or *things* to be seized. . . ." Chief Justice Taft also noted that not only did the police fail to violate the amendment by tapping (a physical interference with a means of communication), as such, but neither did they do so at any point along the way, in the course of gaining access to the wiretap evidence. "The evidence was secured by the use of the sense of hearing and that only. There was no entry of the house or offices of the defendants . . . the intervening wires are not part of his house or office."

In a short dissent in *Olmstead,* Mr. Justice Holmes branded wiretapping a "dirty business" and declared, "We have to choose and for my part I think it a less evil that some criminals should escape than that the Government should play an ignoble part." Justice Brandeis wrote an exhaustive separate opinion in the course of which he pointed out that constitutional clauses conferring powers to government have been broadly interpreted to cover activities and objects "of which the Fathers could not have dreamed." Brandeis warned, "The progress of science in furnishing the Government with means of espionage is not likely to stop with wiretapping."

At the time the *Olmstead* case was decided there was no federal statute governing wiretapping. The *Federal Communication Act* was enacted in 1934. Section 605 provides that "no person not being authorized by the sender shall intercept any communication and divulge or publish the existence, contents, substance, purport, effect or meaning of such intercepted communication to any person. . . ." (47 U.S.C. 605).

Soon after the enactment of the *Federal Communications Act,* the Supreme Court held in *Nardone v. United States,* 302 U.S. 379 (1937), that evidence obtained by wiretapping in violation of section 605 was inadmissible in Federal courts. The decision was based not on constitutional grounds, but rather, on the Court's supervisory powers over Federal courts.

The Court passed on a variety of wiretapping questions following the 1937 *Nardone* decision. It would move toward further limitations, then, move a short step back, but, overall, the trend was to limit, more and more, the use of information, or things, obtained through wiretaps in both federal and state courts. The impact was marginal, however, with respect to state courts due to a 1952 decision of the Court.

In 1952, in the case of *Schwartz v. Texas*, 344 U.S. 199, the Supreme Court held that, although it was a Federal crime for state officers to *divulge* wiretapping evidence, section 605 did not render such evidence inadmissible.

Five years after *Schwartz*, the Court held in *Benanti v. United States*, 355 U.S. 96 (1957), that wiretap evidence obtained by state officers under sanction of state law, could not be admitted in Federal courts. The decision did not deter states with permissive wiretap statutes very much. These states took the position the decision did not bind state courts as it was based on a federal statute (Section 605 F.C.A.), and not the Federal Constitution.

The Court "seemingly" ended the impassé in *Berger v. New York*, 388 U.S. 41 (1967) when the Court held (5-4) the New York statute to be unconstitutional. Thus the Court did an about-face in *Berger* from its 1928 *Olmstead* decision without expressly overruling *Olmstead*. New York courts, nevertheless, continued to issue orders of interception by requiring an applicant for an order to build enough facts into a showing of probable cause "to meet" the constitutional standards suggested by *Berger*.

Berger left a great deal of confusion in its wake. Controversy ranged far and wide as to whether *Berger* outlawed wiretapping entirely—on its specificity requirements to obtain an order or warrant—or whether the decision was an invitation to legislatures to set standards so orders or warrants could issue that would meet constitutional standards. The Court's answer came sooner than expected by most observers.

Six months later in *Katz v. United States*, 389 U.S. 347 (1967)—with Mr. Justice Marshall taking no part in the decision—the Court held (7-1) that the Fourth Amendment protects persons, not things. The failure of agents to get a warrant (in placing an electronic listening device on a public telephone booth), "is fatal to a gambling conviction," declared the Court, expressly overruling both *Olmstead* and *Goldman*. The decision means that the constitutionality of electronic eavesdropping no longer hinges on trespass.

The rate of falling precedents continued as the Court held (6-3) in *Lee v. Florida*, 392 U.S. 378 (1968), that evidence obtained in violation of Section 605 of the *Federal Communications Act* cannot be used in a state criminal prosecution, expressly overruling *Schwartz*. Among other reasons, the majority deems its decision "counseled by experience." The Court made it clear that the hope expressed in *Schwartz* that enforcement of Section 605 could be achieved under the penal provisions of the *Communications Act* has proved vain.

On June 19, 1968, the President of the United States signed into law the *Omnibus Crime Control and Safe Streets Act of 1968*. Title II (confession admissibility) and Title III (permissive wiretapping) have generated more polemics than any legislation since the days of President Franklin D. Roosevelt's New Deal in the thirties. The provisions of Title III affect the law on wiretapping in a way that nullifies much of the case law the Supreme Court has mounted over the years. Whether the Court will sustain Title III, in whole or in part, remains to be seen.

Stop and Frisk: Stop and frisk legislation has become a topic of national concern and debate largely since the enactment of stop and frisk legislation by New York State on July 1, 1964. There is nothing very novel about the legislation. The practice, popularly called stop and frisk in modern times, has roots that go back more than 300 years. Detention and questioning were well known under English Common Law. Early case holdings and statutes empowered the night-watch of each town to detain "suspicious night-walkers" until the morning, at which time the watchman would either release the suspect or arrest him, if grounds for arrest were discovered.[17]

The word "frisk" has a well-understood meaning in police parlance. It is a slang term used to describe the precaution of running the hands quickly up and down and around a person's clothing to discover if he carries a weapon. Courts have justified the procedure, generally, as a precautionary measure for the purpose of discovering weapons which might pose a threat to the officer's safety while questioning a person under investigation.

Long before New York's law brought stop and frisk into sharp focus in the public eye, other states had adopted legislation allowing police officers more latitude in effecting detentions and questioning suspects than is permitted under New York's law. These states had modeled their legislation around Warner's proposed *Model Arrest Act of 1942* which had come as an aftermath of an *Interstate Crime Commission* investigation. A *Model Code of Pre-Arraignment Procedure,* Tentative Draft No. 1, released March 1, 1966, by the American Law Institute (prepared in collaboration with

---

[17] Stern, Loren G. (1967). "Stop and Frisk: An Historical Answer to a Modern Problem." *The Journal of Criminal Law, Criminology and Police Science,* 58:532. Also see Fisher, Edward C., *op. cit.,* especially pp. 69-78 and 290-94.

the American Bar Association's Advisory Committee on the Police Function), also contains more permissive provisions than those in New York's stop and frisk legislation. Furthermore, many state courts, like those of California and Ohio, had sanctioned stop and frisk procedures for a number of years.

Statutes and judicial sanction were predicated on the idea that the Fourth Amendment does not prohibit all searches and seizures, but only "unreasonable" searches and seizures. The Amendment's first clause clearly says that only unreasonable searches and seizures are forbidden. The perennial problem, then, has centered around what kind of police conduct, when an officer detains and questions a person, is reasonable or unreasonable.

Courts measure an officer's actions, as well as those of a private person, in such a situation, on the scales of an abstract concept the law calls "probable cause." In stop and frisk laws the term "reasonable suspicion" is used. This, of course, is an even more abstract term than probable cause. Critics of such legislation find fault, and properly so, with a term that does so little by way of setting a meaningful standard. However, proponents of the legislation say that just as the Constitution fails to define probable cause, so too, have the framers of stop and frisk laws failed to define reasonable suspicion.

Most courts have traditionally applied a lower standard in determining the legality or illegality of an officer's actions when it relates to a temporary stopping and questioning of a "suspicious" person for the purpose of establishing the identity of a suspect. Often, the stop is accompanied by a frisk. It was inevitable that these long-standing police practices would be subjected to scrutiny by the Supreme Court of the United States. It came as no surprise when the Court granted certiorari in 1967 to review two New York stop and frisk cases and an Ohio case.

The law made by the Supreme Court while writing on a clean slate in the *Terry v. Ohio,* 392 U.S. 1 (6/10/68) case—and the two companion cases of *Sibron v. New York,* 392 U.S. 40 (1968) and *Peters v. New York,* 392 U.S. 40 (1968)—though studded with ambiguity, when each of the four opinions in *Terry* is assessed, has been praised by proponents of stop and frisk and cursed by its opponents. Viewing the opinions, singly, beginning with Chief Justice Warren's majority opinion (8-1), differences show up in judicial philosophy and, to be sure, some questionable logic stands out.

In facing up to stop and frisk the Court points out that, "We would be less than candid if we did not acknowledge that this question thrusts to the fore difficult and troublesome issues regarding a sensitive area of police activity—issues which have never before been squarely presented to this Court." The main issue, as framed by the Court is "whether it is always unreasonable for a policeman to seize a person and subject him to a limited search for weapons unless there is probable cause to arrest."

To the People's suggestion that the use of such terms as "stop" and "frisk" is outside the protection of the Fourth Amendment, because neither action rises to the level of a "search" or "seizure" within the meaning of the Constitution, the Chief Justice said: "We emphatically reject this notion. It is quite plain that the Fourth Amendment governs 'seizures' of the person which do not eventuate in a trip to the station house and prosecution for crime—'arrests' in traditional terminology." The Court pinpoints its objection more specifically in saying that, "We, therefore, reject the notions that the Fourth Amendment does not come into play at all as a limitation upon police conduct if the officers stop short of something called a technical 'arrest' or a 'full-blown search.'"

It is difficult, after reading the opinion, to avoid the conclusion that the Court in *Terry* sets up a more fluid concept of what constitutes probable cause than it has ever recognized before in arrest cases.

Indicating a belief in a need for legislation on stop and frisk, Mr. Justice Harlan in his concurring opinion, states that, "If the State of Ohio were to provide that police officers could, on articulable suspicion less than probable cause, forcibly frisk and disarm persons thought to be carrying concealed weapons, I would have little doubt that action taken pursuant to such authority could be constitutionally reasonable." He did find, however, under common law-principles, sufficient grounds to sustain the officer's actions that led to Terry's arrest. It appears from his opinion that the real issue the Court should resolve is whether a police officer has a right to forcibly stop a person to investigate a suspected crime under circumstances similar to those in the *Terry* case.

Centering more on common law-principles, Mr. Justice White, in his concurring opinion, brought out that "There is nothing in the Constitution that prevents a policeman from addressing questions to anyone on the streets." And, further, that "it seems to me the person may be briefly detained aginst his will while pertinent questions are directed to him." The opinion also points up the fact that, "the person stopped is not obliged to answer, answers may not be compelled, and refusal to answer furnishes no basis for an arrest, although it may alert the officer to the need for continued observation. . . . In my view, it is temporary detention, warranted by the circumstances, which chiefly justifies the protective frisk for weapons."

The lone dissenter, Mr. Justice Douglas, says that the Court grants police officers a greater authority to make seizures and conduct searches than a judge has to authorize such actions. "To give the police officer greater power than a magistrate is to take a long step down the totalitarian path," he declares. If such a step is desirable, it should take the form of a constitutional amendment "only after a full debate by the people of the country."

On the other hand, there is a school of thought which regards the stop and frisk decisions as "the opening guns in a war against police misconduct." [18] They emphasize the Court's severe condemnation of state tribunals that take too broad-minded a view of what are and what are not acceptable standards of police conduct.

The lesson to be learned from *Terry* is that it is constitutionally permissible for an officer to detain an individual for investigation without probable cause to arrest if the officer has reasonable grounds, based on specific facts, clearly expressed, that the detention was necessary in the interests of crime detection and prevention. If the officer has reasonable grounds, based on specific facts, to believe that the individual detained is armed and dangerous, he may require the person to submit to a superficial frisk for weapons. If the frisk reveals an object which feels like a weapon, the officer may remove the object from the suspect's possession and examine it further. On the other hand, if the officer has no reason to detain the individual, the frisk is unreasonable. If he has no reason to frisk the individual, removing objects from the individual's possession is also unreasonable. If the officer conducts a search that goes beyond that necessary for the discovery of weapons, the search, although valid in the beginning, is unreasonable in scope. If the stop or the frisk or the scope of the frisk are held unreasonable, any evidence obtained by the officers as a result of these actions will be inadmissible in evidence.

The authors would urge that law enforcement administrators formulate policy on stop and frisk practices—and implement it with adequate supervision—to insure, as far as possible, that stop and frisk be used with circumspection, and, further, that they recognize the fact, as the Chief Justice points out in *Terry*, that stop and frisk is, indeed, "a serious intrusion upon the sanctity of the person, which may inflict great indignity and arouse strong resentment, and is not to be taken lightly." Any other course of action could mean that, ultimately, the Court will find a way to nullify the power it has granted to the police in *Terry v. Ohio*.

FIFTH AMENDMENT RIGHTS

Confessions. Another area of major concern to law enforcement, within the purview of constitutional guarantees, is the taking of statements from

---

[18] Silvek, Isidore (1968). "Eroding the Fourth Amendment: Stop and Frisk." *Commonweal*, July, pp. 455-56. Also see Schwartz, Herman (1967). "Stop and Frisk (A Case Study in Judicial Control of the Police." *The Journal of Criminal Law, Criminology and Police Science*, 58:433-64.

persons who are suspects in crimes, and, thereafter, using such a statement against an accused in a criminal trial. A useful purpose can be served at this point before taking up the evolution of the rules on confession admissibility—due to the wide sweep of Fifth Amendment rights—by resort to some preliminary comment.

The Fifth Amendment contains a bundle of rights, one of which is the privilege against self-incrimination, which, in essence, may be summed up, that no one should be required to betray himself out of his own mouth. This is a simple way to frame its legal application, but in the workaday world of reality, its application gives rise to a host of perplexing problems. Confession admissibility, as well as the use of both inculpatory and exculpatory statements—defined below—in both federal and state courts, now turns on whether or not such a statement was obtained in accordance with a number of very complex, and ambiguous rules that the Supreme Court of the United States has been spinning, beginning with its far-reaching pronouncements in *Escobedo v. Illinois*, 378 U.S. 478 (1964).[19]

Another observation which needs to be made is that, in the following material, no attempt will be made, except incidentally, to outline the Fifth Amendment's protection against self-incrimination beyond the limitations it sets on the use, by law enforcement officers, of a statement against a person who is a suspect in a crime or who stands accused of a crime. But, included under Fifth Amendment rights, hereunder, is a section entitled, "Lineup Identifications." The Sixth Amendment rights of a person accused of a crime to be confronted by his accusers, and to have the assistance of counsel, have been extended to lineup identifications, and beyond, during the course of the criminal law revolution of the nineteen sixties.

It is more logical to include lineup identifications, as part of a discussion on confessions, as is done by most legal commentators, than under Sixth Amendment rights. This is so for the reason that lineup identification procedures, and face-to-face confrontations, are inseparably entwined with the efforts of law enforcement officers to obtain statements during the overall course of criminal investigations.

The significance of statements of all kinds is perceived when one recognizes, as a fact, that more than 85 per cent of all police investigative time is expended in talking to people to obtain information that, more often

---

[19] A caveat must be included here. Much of what is said in this section—which covers the law through June 28, 1971, the last day of the 1970 term of the Supreme Court of the United States—*may* now be past history due to the federal Crime Control Bill that became law on June 19, 1968, as to which reference is made hereafter. Many persons question the constitutionality of the legislation while others take an opposite view. The text material looks at the law from both before and after the Escobedo decision of June 22, 1964. As a result of this approach, the reader can see the law, as it is, at the time the material is read, no matter how the constitutionality of Title II of the Crime Control Bill is ultimately resolved. It is the history behind the law which is important, more so, in many respects, than the rules.

than not, become parts of a written record. It is obvious, then, that law enforcement officers should be well informed on the law of confessions, as well as related problems such as those that are involved in conducting a lineup, if they are to discharge their duties intelligently and effectively. This is especially so now as a result of decisions by the Supreme Court of the United States that have brought both inculpatory and exculpatory admissions under the Fifth and Fourteenth Amendments due process' protective umbrellas.

A few words of explanation, illustrated by a couple of examples, may be helpful in pointing out the difference between the two types of admissions. An "inculpatory" admission is an oral or written statement from which an inference of guilt can be drawn—not a complete acknowledgment of guilt as in a confession—whereas, an "exculpatory" admission is an oral or written statement that tends to show nonguilt: one incriminates and the other exonerates. A suspect admits that he was present at the scene of a homicide, but denies that he was the perpetrator. The statement that he was present could tend to incriminate him. A suspect in a homicide gave the police information that another person committed the offense. The accusatory statement tends to exonerate the suspect who gave the statement. The role of such statements in developing evidence against a suspect cannot be underestimated.

Confessions have been considered as a primary source of information about crimes for as long as crimes have been committed.

Until the middle of the 1960's American law enforcement officers, attuned to the centuries-old emphasis upon confessions as evidence, relied far too much, as had their predecessors, on obtaining confessions from suspects in making cases against them. Some of them were not too judicious as to the techniques they used so long as the confession they sought would become a part of the case file, which, far too often, was the case against the accused. (This can be understood, partly, when one takes into account the volume of crime, and the impossible case loads that are assigned to detectives in a large urban area.)

The law tacitly condoned, for much too long a time, the methods that were used by some officers. During most of the twentieth century, the state courts, and, indeed, even the Supreme Court of the United States [20] showed little concern with practices used by law enforcement officers to obtain incriminating evidence on a suspect, providing that it met the voluntary-trustworthy test—to sustain the use of confessions, the test sometimes achieved incredibly elastic qualities.

It was not until 1936 that the Supreme Court of the United States

---

[20] The failure of the Court to take up cases of alleged coercive police practices was not due to any reluctance on the part of the Court to enter the arena. It can be attributed to the fact that such cases did not come up to the Court from the state courts.

heard its first state confession case, *Brown v. Mississippi,* 297 U.S. 278, in which the conduct of a sheriff was so reprehensible that it shocked the conscience of self-respecting law enforcement officers.

On a Sunday night on April 1, 1934, a Mississippi sheriff tied two naked Negro prisoners to jailhouse chairs and beat them with a metal-studded leather strap and a rope until they confessed to murder. Their conviction was reversed by the Supreme Court on the ground that the confession was not voluntary, and that the use by the state of an obviously compelled confession violated the petitioners' due process rights under the Fourteenth Amendment. The primary emphasis in the decision was not on the sheriff's misconduct, as such, but on the fact that the trial judge was aware of the circumstances under which the confession had been obtained, and the lack of any evidence in the case besides the confession, but admitted it anyway.

That decision was the trigger, however, which set off a long judicial struggle to insure the rights of criminal suspects that reached a climax in 1966, *Miranda v. Arizona,* 384 U.S. 436, when all pretense at relying on the voluntary-trustworthy test came to a crashing end.

One must keep in mind, however, that *Miranda* did not completely erase the test. For this reason, it is essential to understand the old rules.

Under *Jackson v. Denno,* 378 U.S. 368 (6/22/64), a defendant has a right to a hearing and a decision by a judge, outside the presence of the jury, on the admissibility of a confession. The judge must determine that the confession was given voluntarily before it can be offered as evidence. *Miranda* adds another dimension. The judge must also determine that a confession passes *Miranda* requirements. The hearing, therefore, is two-pronged, and *Miranda* applies the same rules to inculpatory and exculpatory admissions.

Hence it is quite possible for a statement to measure up to *Miranda* yet be excluded on the ground it is involuntary. For example, a person can waive the *Miranda* rights. Thereafter, an officer can proceed to undo his good work by doing something to cause a judge to hold that a statement was not a product of the person's free will.

A suspect is evasive consistently in his answers. The officer, getting impatient, tells the suspect, falsely, his buddy confessed, and asks, "Why are you hedging?" A few minutes later the officer says, "I've had it. You either come clean, or your arthritic wife will be arrested as an accomplice, and your three children will be put in an institution." The suspect then spills his story. (There are also other situations in which the voluntary-trustworthy test continues to play a role.)

Moreover, the voluntary-trustworthy test which was the polestar in

Brown is so important, historically, that its meaning and changing role must be well known to those who enforce the law. In time, the test may be, again, the test and the only test a court will use in ruling on the admissibility of statements in criminal cases. This could come in the wake of Title II, *Omnibus Crime Control and Safe Streets Act of 1968*, an enactment of the Congress of the United States.

The new rules written into law, to regulate the use of confessions, apply only to federal courts, but are expected to influence state courts. Voluntariness is the sole test under the act.

When this is taken into account, added to the fact that the test complements *Miranda*, no officer can afford to be unmindful of what can and what cannot be done, lawfully, to obtain a statement which will stand up under pre-*Miranda* rules. Some knowledge of the rules can be gained by taking a quick look at history to highlight the principal issues that arose as courts began to take ever-increasing interest in police practices which were designed to elicit a confession.

At the outset, a distinction needs to be drawn between "voluntary" and "trustworthy," as the words appear on each side of the hyphen, to make up the so-called voluntary-trustworthy test. A confession was said to be *voluntary* when it was obtained without the use of force. A confession was said to be *trustworthy* when it was obtained under circumstances which were unlikely to have induced a false confession. From a practical viewpoint, no matter which test a court might apply, the same result was applicable. That is, when a confession was held to be either involuntary or untrustworthy, it was rejected as evidence.[21]

Under the voluntary-trustworthy test, a delay in taking the accused before a committing magistrate did not void a confession obtained during the delay. A prisoner, likewise, could be questioned over a reasonable period of time, with due regard shown for his personal welfare, and the resulting confession would be regarded as voluntary and trustworthy.

Such practices may have contributed to efficient law enforcement because, frequently, more than one suspect or offender was involved in a case. Investigators had the opportunity to confront several suspects or offenders, or, when circumstances indicated the need, a prisoner was detained while additional information was gathered. The interplay of various funds of information may have strengthened cases and may have made

---

[21] McCormick, Charles T. (1954). *Law of Evidence*, Sections 109-119. West Publishing Company, St. Paul, Minnesota. To review the reasons behind the voluntary-trustworthy test, see Inbau, Fred E. and Reid, John E. (1962). *Criminal Interrogation and Confessions*, pp. 140-209. The Williams and Wilkins Co., Baltimore.

it possible to effect arrests. All this seemed to be in the public interest.

The conventional voluntary-trustworthy test was used in state and federal courts. It was the practice of the United States Supreme Court in both federal and state cases, to determine from the trial court record whether or not the trial court jury had acted reasonably in holding that a confession had been obtained according to the voluntary-trustworthy test. The Supreme Court would reverse the trial court and invoke the due process clause of the Fifth or Fourteenth Amendments, if the record indicated that "force" had been used in securing evidence.

Most American-law enforcement officers, over the years, were familiar with the fact that, from the earliest common law, threats or promises would invalidate a confession. And, when the Court handed down *Brown*, they were aware that the use of torture was anathema. But, whether the suspect was interrogated day and night, by five officers or one, whether he received food or rest, or whether he could have a lawyer, friend, or relative to advise him, was not at issue, and irrelevant to the officer.

However, in 1943 and 1944, the United States Supreme Court renounced, in part, the voluntary-trustworthy doctrine as a measure for determining the validity of a confession. The federal "civilized standards" rule was spelled out. This rule was applied in the federal courts through the decision of *McNabb v. United States*, 318 U.S. 332 (1943), and, in modified form, when "inherent coercion" was involved, in the state courts through the Court's decision in *Ashcraft v. Tennessee*, 332 U.S. 143 (1944). Later cases, decided after 1943-1944, placed further restrictions on both federal and state officers. As a result of these decisions, law enforcement officers were progressively restricted in the area of prisoner interrogation.

In 1953, and for a time thereafter, there were indications that the United States Supreme Court was reverting to the voluntary-trustworthy test relative to confessions obtained by state and local officers. The Court said, in *Stein v. New York*, 346 U.S. 156 (1953), "The people of the state are entitled to due process of law."

However, this more relaxed trend was relatively short-lived. More restrictions were applied by the United States Supreme Court, and, so carefully, that the question has often been raised as to whether law enforcement officers may have *any* proper opportunity to question a prisoner. Some observers have commented that the pendulum may have swung too far in the direction of personal liberties, to the point that the general security is jeopardized. The Court's decision in *Mallory v. United States*, 354 U.S. 449 (1957) is, perhaps, illustrative of the close restrictions set by the Court on federal law enforcement officers under its inherent supervisory powers to regulate the use of evidence in federal courts.

In this case, the Supreme Court barred a confession because the accused was held and questioned over a period of seven and one-half hours before he was taken before a committing magistrate.

The decision reaffirmed the "civilized standards" doctrine of the *Mc-Nabb* case, holding that a confession obtained from prisoners while they were illegally detained is not admissible in evidence. Some distinguished legal scholars have supported the wisdom of the decision; yet, many distinguished jurists and conscientious law enforcement officers have aligned themselves in opposition to the harshness of the decision.

The Court stated that:

> In every case where the police resort to interrogation of an arrested person and secure a confession, they may well claim, and quite sincerely, that they were merely trying to check on information given by him. . . . Nor is there an escape from the constraints laid down upon the police by the Rule (federal rule 5 (a) on arraignment), in that two other suspects were involved in the crime. Presumably, whomever the police arrest they must arrest on 'probable cause.' It is not the function of the police to arrest, as it were, at large and to use an interrogatory process at police headquarters in order to determine whom they should charge before a committing magistrate on 'probable cause.'

Until 1963, however, the Court's main concern in passing on confession cases coming out of state courts, was whether or not the confession met a test of voluntariness. The tidy little apple cart was upset, however, in *Haynes v. Washington,* 373 U.S. 503 (1963), when the Court, for the first time, focused more on police methods than the voluntariness of the confession. The facts show that the police officers refused to permit the prisoner, Haynes, to contact his wife unless he confessed, and kept him in a technically incommunicado status, even though there was very little to indicate that his statement was in fact unreliable.

The next milestone—as it would prove to be later in the evolution in the law of confessions—was reached in *Gideon v. Wainwright,* 372 U.S. 335 (1963), in which the Court held than an indigent defendant had the right to have the assistance of counsel to represent him in all felony cases tried in state courts.

Following closely on the heels of *Gideon,* came the Court's ultimatum in *Malloy v. Hogan,* 378 U.S. 1 (1964), which was the vehicle used by the Court to extend the Fifth Amendment's protection against self-incrimination to the States. The law established in the two cases was the bridge the Court constructed that, later, it would use to overrule some long-standing precedents. *Gideon* and *Malloy* came into play again, when the Court, in a decision of less impact than *Miranda,* in *United States v. Wade,* 388 U.S. 218 (1967) held that the Sixth Amendment mandates defense lawyers to be present whenever the police place a suspect in a lineup for the purpose of identification.

The shock waves from *Malloy* (June 15, 1964) were just beginning to diffuse when the Court launched another thunderbolt on June 22, 1964, when, in *Escobedo v. Illinois*, 378 U.S. 478, the Court held that once suspicion has focused on an accused, and the purpose of interrogating him is to obtain statements which would tend to be incriminating, the accused must be advised of his right to remain silent and of his right to see his *retained* counsel. *Escobedo* is bottomed on the Sixth Amendment's right of counsel proviso applicable to the states through due process of the Fourteenth Amendment. Two years later, in *Miranda*, the Court swung to the Fifth Amendment to limit, even more, the use of confessions.

On June 13, 1966—a decision that will go down in the Court's history as one of its bellwether decisions—the Court in *Miranda v. Arizona*, 384 U.S. 436, in a cataclysmic opinion (5-4) held that any police interrogation during a period of incommunicado is inherently coercive, that the right to remain silent exists at the moment police custody begins (not merely after a person is formally charged with a crime), that a "voluntary" statement requires not only the lack of overt coercion, but also full knowledge of all constitutional rights.

Under this decision, the prosecutor may not use statements, whether exculpatory or inculpatory, stemming from a custodial interrogation (questioning initiated by law enforcement officers after a person has been taken into custody or otherwise deprived of his freedom of action in any significant way) unless procedural safeguards are utilized which assure that the individual involved is accorded his privilege against self-incrimination.

The court held that if certain standards were met, an in-custody statement could be legally coercive, but that the coercive features could be overcome by following certain procedures:

> Immediately, upon any detention which curtails freedom of movement and which involves police custody, the person must, in the absence of a clear, intelligent waiver of the constitutional rights involved, be warned prior to any questioning that he has a right to remain silent, that any statement he does make may be used as evidence against him, and that he has a right to the presence of an attorney, either retained or assigned. Further, the government must be prepared to prove that the individual understood the advice and by voluntary affirmative act knowingly and intelligently waived his rights. If the individual indicates 'in any manner whatsoever' that he does not wish to talk, the interview must cease. Persuasion or trickery of any sort to induce a person to speak despite his reservations will invalidate any statement taken.

This decision, *not retroactive*, (applying to past cases) according to *Johnson v. New Jersey*, 384 U.S. 719 (1966), indicates that the Supreme Court is unhappy with any questioning in the absence of counsel. If, in the future, the Court concludes that the state courts are not fully supervising the police, or that the warning concerning rights should not be given by those who are pressing for a waiver of such rights, it may require that counsel always be present, or it may rule out all pretrial admissions and confessions.

Between 1961 and 1969, in particular, the Supreme Court, via the due process clause, has shaped state criminal procedure to minimal federal standards. In the process, it has imposed federal decisional law—evolved under the Bill of Rights—upon state criminal prosecutions, always leaving the door slightly ajar, however, for states to formulate their own procedures consistent with minimum federal standards—resulting in many persons, who are quite knowledgeable on local and state crime problems, taking exception to the Court's rulings that bind the states under a federal code of criminal procedure.

Whether or not a particular state law having constitutional dimensions, like the various substitutes for disclosure of an informant's identity (which limit the recently incorporated rights of confrontation and cross-examination), is qualitatively equal to the federal standard relating to the subject matter must await a Supreme Court decision in every case. This method results in much litigation and uncertainty as each state attempts to develop its own procedures. Law enforcement officers, prosecutors, and trial judges find themselves on the horns of many dilemmas in trying to "second guess" the Supreme Court.

However, on the basis of past experience in the area of search and seizure (e.g., *Ker v. California,* 374 U.S. 23, and *Henry v. Mississippi,* 379 U.S. 443), it is reasonable to assume that the "experimentation" thus permitted the state will, inevitably, soften the impact of *Miranda* on state criminal procedure.

Limited studies have been conducted on the "hows" and "whys" of confessions as a sequel to *Miranda* in an effort to measure the effects of the decision upon law enforcement agencies' role in the prevention of crime and disorder and the preservation of the public peace (for community security). The studies are far too inconclusive, however, to prove anything.[22] As yet, then, not enough reliable research has been assembled to determine if *Miranda* is *hampering* effective law enforcement, is *unrelated* to crime control, or is too *limited* in its reach. Law enforcement agencies, generally speaking, have been unresponsive to research needs.

---

[22] See Medalie, Leitz, and Alexander (1968). "Custodial Police Interrogation in Our Nation's Capital: The Attempt to Implement Miranda.'" *Michigan Law Review,* 66:1347; Seeburger and Wettick (1967). "Miranda in Pittsburgh—A Statistical Study." *University of Pittsburgh Law Review,* 29:1; and (1967). "Interrogations in New Haven: The Impact of Miranda." *Yale Law Review,* 76:1519.

Research could be conducted by them, or in cooperation with other agencies, much more productively than by an outside agency alone.

If judicially-imposed controls on the police have gone too far in the balancing process, as many police administrators and others argue rather persuasively, then police administrators are the ones who should do much more than most of them have done, so far, to provide the courts with current and valid statistical data. For too long a time, judges have had to try to fill the vacuum with whatever statistical data they could find, which reached them, generally, through the hands of defense lawyers. Both police and courts will make more meaningful decisions if productive research is provided.

Chief Justice Roger J. Traynor, California Supreme Court, put it well:

> Amid the vociferous and often irresponsible castigation of courts for their zealous watch on due process, we do well to remember what a void the United States Supreme Court's rules have filled. The fault lies with the public, and particularly the legal profession, that constitutional rules have so long remained the major script of criminal procedure. In a wilderness all too little regulated by statutes, the Court has been compelled to formulate such rules out of cases that have come before it at random.[23]

Lineup Identifications. The doors of appellate courts were pushed open as forums to determine the "fundamental fairness" of police conducted lineups in a trilogy of decisions handed down by the Supreme Court of the United States on June 12, 1967.

In a landmark case, *United States v. Wade*, 388 U.S. 218, the Court held (6-3) that a lineup is a "critical stage" of a criminal proceeding and therefore a step that may be taken only after an accused has been afforded counsel, as a Sixth Amendment right. (The Court blew hot and cold in a rash of five full-blown opinions in shoring up the majority opinion.)

In a second case, *Gilbert v. California*, 388 U.S. 263, the Court declared that neither the Fifth nor Sixth Amendments bar the use of handwriting samples secured in the absence of counsel and without warning that the sample may be used against him at trial.

In its third lineup decision of the day, *Stovall v. Denno*, 388 U.S. 293, the Court held (6-2) that *Wade* doesn't apply retroactively. The Court also legitimated a witness' face-to-face identification of a suspect when unusual circumstances exist.

The Court may have got off to a late start in making lineup identification history, but its history in law enforcement is as old as the days when people began to commit crimes. No matter who has used the technique in criminal investigations—high priest, tribal-witch doctor, or modern police

---

[23] New York City Bar Association, 23rd Annual Benjamin N. Cardozo Lecture (1966). *The Devils of Due Process in Criminal Detection,* p. 6.

officer—its method has remained substantially the same. The victim of the crime, the witness to a crime, or the witness who knew the suspect, often has been the only key available to law enforcers to lead to the perpetrators of crimes. *Wade, Gilbert,* and *Stovall,* provide three examples of the role of today's witnesses in making out-of-court identifications of suspects that later were used for in-court identifications of the defendants.

In *Wade,* two bank employees had viewed him in a lineup with five or six others following Wade's indictment and the appointment of counsel to safeguard his interests. Each person in the lineup wore a strip of tape on each side of his face—which had been the bank robber's modus operandi—and each person was required to say something like "put the money in the bag."

In *Gilbert,* the defendant was convicted by the Superior Court of California of the armed robbery of the Mutual Savings and Loan Association of Alhambra and the murder of a police officer who entered during the course of the robbery. Four issues were raised by Gilbert in the Supreme Court. Only the two that were relevant to lineups will be considered.

Eleven witnesses identified Gilbert in the courtroom. The identifications were based on different circumstances that involved both lineup identifications and the identification of photographs of the defendant. (The Supreme Court recognized the probable validity of some of the courtroom identification evidence, but had reservations on other parts of the identification testimony. For this reason—among others—the Court remanded the case to the California court to determine whether it is "able to declare a belief that it was harmless beyond a reasonable doubt.")

The admission of handwriting exemplars at Gilbert's California trial sprang out of his arrest in Philadelphia by an FBI agent and Gilbert's refusal to answer questions about the robbery in Alhambra, California, without the advice of counsel. He later did answer questions of another agent about some Philadelphia robberies in which the robber used a handwritten note demanding that money be handed over to him, and during the interrogation gave the agent handwriting exemplars. The agent did not tell Gilbert that the exemplars would be used in any other investigation. The handwriting samples were admitted in evidence at trial in California over objection that they were obtained in violation of Gilbert's Fifth and Sixth Amendment rights. To this, the Supreme Court said, "even if Gilbert believed that his exemplars would not be used in California, it does not appear that the authorities improperly induced such belief."

In *Stovall,* a woman was stabbed eleven times in her home after her assailant had fatally stabbed her husband. She was taken to the hospital in serious condition. The next day Stovall was arrested, and an arraignment was promptly held but was postponed until he could retain counsel. The following day, the police, without affording Stovall time to retain counsel, arranged with the victim's surgeon to permit them to bring Stovall to her hospital room. Stovall was handcuffed to one of five police officers who . . . brought him to the hospital room. Stovall was the only Negro in the room. The victim identified him from her hospital bed after being asked by an officer whether he "was the man" and after Stovall repeated at the direction of an officer a "few words for voice identification." The victim and the officers testified at the trial to her identification of Stovall in the hospital room, and she also made an in-court identification of Stovall.

The Court said, "The practice of showing suspects singly to persons, and not as a part of a lineup has been widely condemned. However, a claimed violation of due process of law in the conduct of a confrontation depends on the totality of the circumstances surrounding it, and the present case reveals that the showing of Stovall to Mrs. Behrendt in an immediate hospital confrontation was imperative."

In the quiet atmosphere of the courtroom, *Wade* should not be too troublesome to prosecutors. They usually can make a courtroom identification on a defendant without resort to a lineup identification. Normally, a witness is simply asked if he sees the accused in court. Generally, a witness is not asked a question on a lineup. However, if a witness did observe a lineup, it may be brought out on cross-examination by defense counsel— as he did in *Wade*. The prosecutor may be able to use the identification, under these circumstances, to corroborate an independent identification free of "taint." It would seem likely, then, that, with some few cases excepted, *Wade* can be hurdled by prosecutors rather easily because they can avoid the pitfalls that took *Wade* to the Supreme Court.

In achieving that "fundamental fairness," demanded by *Wade*, prosecutors can take the lead. They can join with police administrators to provide simple and easily understandable guidelines, on jurisdictional levels, so officers on the streets will know what they can and cannot do. Prosecutors and police chiefs, for example, could sit down together, and decide jointly upon the kind of detailed records police officers should make on witness identification transactions so that prosecutors will have the information that they will need to protect their witnesses from attack.

Law enforcement officers on the streets do not fare so well, as *Wade* demands more from them than from prosecutors, and police chiefs. Practically speaking, however, ideals forged in judicial opinions do not always find stable homes on the streets of big cities.

No court ruling can stop police officers from conducting lineups and setting up face-to-face meetings between victims and suspects. Lineup identification procedures are as essential to crime detection as adequate police training to effective enforcement. *Wade* certainly doesn't preclude the use of reasonable on-the-street and station house procedures to identify suspects. Wade's purpose is to assure "fundamental fairness" in the conduct of lineups. A suspect can demand the presence of counsel at a lineup, or the right can be freely waived. That is not too much to ask, many people of good will say.

SIXTH AMENDMENT RIGHTS

The Assistance of Counsel. The most revolutionary application of the Sixth Amendment right to the assistance of counsel—insofar as the right bears directly on law enforcement—is the one that brings the "critical stage" to a pre-trial stage. This is *Miranda's* major thrust. *Miranda*, while bound to the Fifth Amendment, does call for the presence of counsel at the time a suspect is taken into "custody." The net effect, then, is that *Escobedo's* right to counsel requirement is swallowed up in the *Miranda* requirements.

Neither *Escobedo*, nor *Miranda* could have been launched by the Supreme Court if the Court had not done some earlier homework. This was done when the Court found reasons to justify its overruling of a number of precedents in order to propound the constitutional rule that it formalized in *Gideon v. Wainwright*, 372 U.S. 335 (1963). More than any other event the *Gideon* decision was responsible for helping to create the climate of legal reform in the 1960s.

The road to *Gideon* was a long one.[24] It began in Alabama on March 25, 1931, when nine Negro youths were taken off an open gondola railroad car by a sheriff's posse. Shortly afterwards they were charged with the rape of two white girls who were also riders on the car.

From then to *Gideon*, the need of an accused person to have the assistance of counsel was aired in the Supreme Court of the United States in a long line of cases. Among the cases heard by the Court was a number of confession-admissibility cases in which the right to counsel came up as a side issue. The cases are not regarded, however, as doctrinaire-producing decisions. They did provide some of the cement, however, to go into the making of the law that the court used, ultimately, when it applied the right to the assistance of counsel clause of the Sixth Amendment to the states through the Fourteenth Amendment's due process clause.

To try to telescope the confession cases—and others—into this short story on the right to counsel would do little more than throw just enough shadow to obscure the relevant legal history that has gone into the making of the law. Therefore, in this discussion, only four leading cases are considered in relation to the Sixth Amendment's right to counsel provision.

---

[24] Lewis, Anthony (1964). *Gideon's Trumpet*. Random House, New York.

The story has its beginning in 1931, in a Scottsboro, Alabama, courtroom. It drew near to its end in 1963, when the Supreme Court of the United States released its *Gideon* v. *Wainwright* bombshell. *Gideon* is not quite the end of the story, however, as some lines remain to be added to *Gideon's* script. Some comment will be made on this later.

How *Gideon* reached the *Supreme Court,* what happened after its arrival, where its teachings will end, are questions that can be put to one side for the present. A great deal can be learned about them by looking first at a history that had its inception in the Alabama courtroom. An interesting chain of events propelled nine young defendants into that courtroom.

On March 25, 1931, an undetermined number of Negro boys were riding a freight train moving south through Alabama. On the same train with them, were seven white boys and two white girls. The white boys ordered the Negroes to get off the overcrowded gondola car in which they found themselves inadvertently integrated. A fight followed. The white boys, outnumbered, were thrown off the train, except for one, who, in his rush to get off the train, fell between two cars and was pulled to safety by one of the Negro boys.

One of the white boys telephoned an account of the fight to the sheriff of Jackson County, Alabama. The sheriff and a posse met the train when it reached Paint Rock. Most of the Negroes had dropped off the train so that only nine were on the train to answer the sheriff's questions. They were arrested on a minor charge. Shortly thereafter, however, the two white girls who had been riding the train, each alleged she had been raped by six different Negroes, in turn.

The nine youngsters, ranging from thirteen to twenty-one years of age, were indicted for rape on March 31, six days after their arrest. They pleaded not guilty. And six days later these nine Negro boys—poor, ignorant and illiterate—went on trial for their lives in three groups. When the first case was called, the atmosphere in and around the courthouse was that of a Roman carnival. The Court's assignment of counsel (that included all the lawyers of the county) to represent the boys was a farce. The three groups were tried in a single day. All were found guilty in the one-day "trial," and sentenced to death.[25]

The Supreme Court of the United States, in reversing the convictions, *Powell v. Alabama,* 287 U.S. 45 (1932) said (8-1), "that in a capital case, where the defendant is unable to employ counsel, and is incapable adequately of making his own defense because of ignorance, feeble-mindedness, illiteracy, or the like, it is the duty of the court, whether requested or not, to assign counsel for him as a necessary requisite to due process of law."

---

[25] Barth, Alan (1961). *The Price of Liberty,* pp. 149-157. The Viking Press, New York.

The central part of the opinion is that the right to counsel in a criminal proceeding is "fundamental." *Powell's* message is that the duty to appoint counsel "is not discharged by an assignment at such a time and under such circumstances as to preclude the giving of effective aid in the preparation and trial of the case." It is important also, to note a limitation laid down by the majority in saying that state courts, "only have a duty to assign counsel, under special circumstances, in capital cases."

In another case, Johnson and Birdwell were arrested on November 21, 1934, and charged with feloniously uttering and passing twenty-one dollar Federal Reserve notes and possessing twenty-one such notes. Upon their arraignment on January 25, 1935, both pleaded not-guilty, and—in response to an inquiry of the court—stated that they were ready for trial. They were then tried, convicted, and sentenced to four and one-half years in the penitentiary, without the assistance of counsel.

Their convictions were reversed, *Johnson v. Zerbst*, 304 U.S. 458 (1938), in which the Court held that the Sixth Amendment included the right of federal indigent defendants to be assigned counsel. The clear and decisive language used by Mr. Justice Black leaves little question as to the importance of counsel to an accused person.

In a third case, one, Betts, was indicted for robbery. He was unable to employ counsel, and so informed the judge at his arraignment. He requested that counsel be appointed for him. The judge advised him that this could not be done as it was not the policy of the county to appoint counsel for indigent defendants, save for murder and rape. In a trial without a jury, Betts was found guilty and sentenced to eight years imprisonment.

The Supreme Court of the United States, *Betts v. Brady*, 316 U.S. 455 (1942) in affirming Betts' state court conviction, ruled (6-3) that an indigent defendant charged with a felony in a state court is entitled to appointed counsel only where special circumstances would make trial without counsel "offensive to the common and fundamental ideas of fairness."

In the fourth, and big case, Clarence Earl Gideon, a "used-up" man of fifty-one, who had been in and out of prison all his life, was arrested on June 3, 1961, for breaking and entering the Bar Harbor Pool Room in Panama City, Florida. Two months later almost to the day, his case was called for trial. Gideon said he was not ready for trial, because he had no counsel. He then requested the court to appoint counsel for him. The court refused, saying that the statutes of Florida provide for the appointment of counsel only in capital cases.

Gideon, according to the record, said, "The United States Supreme Court says I am entitled to counsel." When he made this statment he was clearly wrong, for the law, at this time, was as laid down in *Betts*.

Gideon was found guilty, and sentenced to serve five years in the state prison.

In reversing the Florida Supreme Court's denial of Gideon's petition for *habeas corpus,* the United States Supreme Court, in a unanimous opinion, expressly discarded *Betts'* special circumstance rule as a limitation on the right to appointed counsel. The Court held that the Fourteenth Amendment due process clause guarantees the assistance-of-counsel portions of the Sixth Amendment to defendants in state trials in both capital and non-capital felonies.

The road that ended with *Gideon* is now largely legal history. The gap in "fundamental fairness" for a poor man in a criminal court and the rich man who always has had the right to have *retained* counsel at his side, has been narrowed dramatically by the events of the 1960s. But the full story of the aftermath of *Gideon* remains to be written. The skirmishes on the front that *Gideon* opened are still being fiercely fought. One of them involved a fifteen-year-old boy, Gerald Francis Gault. Gault had been taken into custody for making lewd and indecent remarks over the telephone to a neighbor-woman.

That skirmish came to an end in the Court's epic decision (8-1) in *In re Gault,* 387 U.S. 1 (1967), that shook juvenile court personnel from stem to stern. Gault tells them that a young person, against whom a delinquency petition is filed, is entitled to having assigned counsel during the adjudicatory stage of a juvenile court proceeding.

The Burger Court moved a step ahead of its predecessor when on June 12, 1972 in *Argersinger v. Hamlin,* 407 U.S. 25, the court held 6-3, through Mr. Justice Douglas, that the right of an indigent defendant in a criminal trial to the assistance of counsel, which is guaranteed by the Sixth Amendment as made applicable to the States by the Fourteenth, *Gideon v. Wainwright,* 372 U.S. 335, is not governed by the classification of the offense or by whether or not a jury trial is required. No accused may be deprived of his liberty as the result of any criminal prosecution, whether felony or misdemeanor, in which he was denied the assistance of counsel. (Three justices filed concurring opinions agreeing the convictions should be reversed under the facts of the case.)

The major law enforcement problems, herein discussed, are but examples of a host of simliar problems confronting law enforcement daily. They are complex issues that must be solved within the fabric of the Constitution. And they are problems that must be solved by the mutual cooperation of law enforcement, prosecutors, courts, legislators, and executive officials.

There are some policemen who see the Constitution as a burden, as an obstruction to be overcome, as a technical barrier to be avoided when inconvenient, to be evaded where possible, and to be ignored if necessary. These policemen are pledged by oath to preserve, protect and defend the Constitution, but instead, due to ignorance or misguided zeal, they defile it, they dilute it, and they debase it. All of us have a responsibility to speak up, to "stand up and be counted."

Dwight J. Dalbey, in 1964, as a member of the F.B.I. Training Staff, addressed the California Peace Officers' Association.[26] His conclusions are pertinent:

> . . . as of this moment, the verdict of 2,000 years of the history of western civilization is that the courts are right. The exclusionary rule, and each of the other new concepts with which we are now so concerned, is nothing more than the continuation of a history of refinement in the processes of criminal justice which began at least 2,000 years ago.
>
> It is recorded in the Book of Acts (ch. 22) that when officers of the Roman Empire prepared to question the Apostle Paul concerning a riot with which he was believed connected, and brought out the cat-o'-nine tails as an instrument for speeding up the interrogation, Paul revealed to the officers that he was a citizen of Rome and, more than that, one of those classes of citizens which the Roman law prohibited the officers from whipping during the course of criminal interrogation. By successive stages and over successive centuries, our political ancestors gradually broadened the rights of the accused and laid increasing restrictions on the conduct of law enforcement officers. The accused was given a right to a speedy and public trial, rather than be forced to rot out his body and his years in a dungeon. He was given a right against double jeopardy rather than be required to stand trial again and again for the same offense until his mind, body, and purse were exhausted. He was given a right to have counsel to speak in his defense, a right to reasonable bail, and a right to be free from cruel and unusual punishments, and many other rights which we now take for granted.
>
> We have abolished the rack and the screw to make men talk, and the wheel on which men's limbs were broken in punishment. Each of these developments, and many more, was in its day a refinement in the processes of justice, just as the exclusionary rule and each of the other new concepts in the criminal law of today are further refinements. Each of them in its time was thought to be, no doubt, a radical departure and an onerous restriction on law enforcement. But what is the result to this hour of this constant refinement in the processes of criminal justice? The result is that each of us, you and I, your wife and my wife, your children and my children, and every other person in this Nation, eats, sleeps, works, plays, and has his being with a greater measure of human dignity than ever was enjoyed by the race of man in all the ages which have preceded us.
>
> Are we now, in the full enjoyment of these rights and privileges, to take

---

[26] Dalbey, Dwight J. (1964). "New Concepts in the Criminal Law." *The FBI Law Enforcement Bulletin*, 33:28-29.

the position that every refinement in the process of criminal justice over the past 2,000 years was right—that it was right to abolish the whip, the rack, and the screw, the rotting in the dungeon without trial, and all the other evils of the criminal law of centuries past, but that from this present moment forward each new refinement of the process is a mistake? Can we legally, logically, or morally take this position? I doubt it.

The future will have an answer, but I cannot read the future. The verdict of 2,000 years of history, which I can read today with my own eyes, calls for obedience to the mandates of the courts, acceptance of new refinements in the processes of justice, and more police training in the criminal law, so that we may understand the rules laid down by the courts, comply with them to the best of our ability, and give them a fair trial.

The law enforcement dilemma with respect to judicial restrictions is based upon a conflict between two major law enforcement responsibilities:

On the one hand, the law enforcement officer must protect the *individual citizen* in the exercise of freedom. The basic purpose of the *Bill of Rights and Constitutional guarantees* is to protect the personal rights of each individual citizen, innocent or guilty. The courts must be deeply sympathetic to this ideal when interpreting rules of procedure—or the law will not be respected.

On the other hand, the law enforcement officer must protect the *community* from the ravages of crime. The basic purpose of the *Criminal Law* is to protect society, *not* the criminal. The courts must be deeply sympathetic to the needs of the people when applying substantive law—or the law will not be respected.

Due process, according to one definition, means that "a person shall not be arbitrarily deprived of life, liberty, or property." Straight thinking on the part of lawyers, judges, and law enforcement officers must apply this concept with respect to the law-abiding citizen, and general public, as well as with respect to the anti-social person and criminal community.

Unrestrained application of substantive law can result in tyrannical action, with grave harm to the freedom of the citizenry; and, just as surely, unreasonable interpretation of procedural rules can result in stultification of the administration of criminal justice, with grave harm to the security of the community.

To achieve a wise balance is no easy task, but is an imperative necessity for the healthy growth and development of a democratic society.

TOPICS FOR DISCUSSION

1. How far should the people be allowed to go, in the exercise of free speech, or of free press, before restraints are imposed?
2. What reasons may be given to sustain the proposition that the people who adopted the Fourteenth Amendment in 1868 intended that it incorporate the Bill of Rights?

3. What remedial action might be undertaken, to bring about a proper balance between community security and personal liberty, in meeting law enforcement problems involved with the exclusionary rule?
4. Why would a judge suggest that "prompt inquiry into suspicious or unusual street action is an indispensable power in the orderly government of large urban communities"?
5. Are claims valid that allege that some crimes are unsolvable unless law enforcement officers are allowed some latitude in the interrogation of suspects?
6. When does the right to *requested* counsel begin? *Retained* counsel? *Assigned* counsel?
7. Is there a need, in some states, for a permanent governmental commission, to study and consider, on a long-term basis, the statutory and administrative changes which may be necessary in the administration of criminal justice, to supervise and insure the maintenance of proper standards, and to effect coordinated activities between law enforcement agencies?
8. Comment upon one of the five major sections of Appendix B.

Chapter X

CONSTITUTIONAL LIMITATIONS IN PERSPECTIVE

LAW ENFORCEMENT AND THE COURTS

A LARGE SEGMENT OF THE GENERAL PUBLIC, no doubt, is convinced that law enforcement officers are completely indifferent to the importance of civil liberties; another segment believes that law enforcement officers are almost totally ignorant of the substance of the Bill of Rights and constitutional guarantees; another segment is certain that law enforcement officers are highly suspicious of the principles of freedom, and another segment is of the opinion that law enforcement officers are apathetic in making sure that civil rights are observed.

Professional law enforcement officers are not indifferent, ignorant, suspicious, or apathetic relative to their responsibility. Significant proof of this is expressed by their day-to-day work. It can be said that law enforcement made good progress in the 1960-1969 period of rapid social and technological change, marked by unprecedented restlessness at home and abroad. Yet in this span of years, when the law should have risen to the task, it remained relatively static except for a molding influence the courts provided.

It has been generally recognized that state legislation and the legal profession did not keep abreast of alterations in society and government. The task of moving the law along a path designed to keep it in line with changing times fell, by defaults, to the courts, and largely to the Supreme Court of the United States. Between 1960 and 1969, the Court, in trying to fill a vacuum, showed an awareness of the social dynamics of the contemporary scene and a disregard for "judicial restraint" that was without parallel in the Court's history.

What this disregard of tradition and the accompanying changes in legal approaches demand is not a law and order that freezes man into predetermined patterns, but a law and order of change of movement, of options. Yesterday's order, if it is unresponsive, becomes tomorrow's oppression.[1] Little wonder, then, that many of the Court's decisions have drawn praise from social reformers, and condemnation from constitutional-law theoreticians. This is not new. Differences of opinion have marked the Court's work since its inception in 1789.

---

[1] Sullivan, Pearl S. (1968). "Justice for Whom?" *Saturday Review*, August, p. 16.

From an earlier day, Oliver Wendell Holmes, one of the most distinguished jurists and scholars to grace the Court's bench, in a speech at a meeting of The Harvard Law School Association, February 15, 1913, said: [2]

> The attacks upon the Court are merely an expression of the unrest that seems to wonder vaguely whether law and order pay. When the ignorant are taught to doubt they do not know what they safely may believe. And it seems to me at this time we need education in the obvious more than investigation of the obscure.
>
> I have no belief in panaceas and almost none in sudden ruin. I believe with Montesquieu that if the chance of battle—I may add, the passage of a law—has ruined a state, there was a general cause at work that made the state ready to perish by a single battle of law. Hence I am not much interested one way or the other in the nostrums now so strenuously urged. I do not think the United States would come to an end if we lost our power to declare an act of Congress void. I do not think the Union would be imperilled if we could not make that declaration as to the law of the several states. For one in my place sees how often a local policy prevails with those who are not trained to national views. . . .
>
> If I am right it will be a slow business for people to reach national views, asuming that we are allowed to work peaceably to that end.

Justice Hugo L. Black, speaking from the lecture platform instead of the Supreme Court bench, on May 20, 21 and 23, 1968, has given in detail his views on the Constitution—and the role of judges in interpreting it. The series of lectures could go down as landmarks in constitutional philosophy. Said Mr. Justice Black:

> Power corrupts, and unrestricted power will tempt Supreme Court justices just as history tells us it has tempted other judges. For, unfortunately, judges have not been immune to the seductive influence of power, and given absolute or near-absolute power, judges may exercise it to bring about changes that are inimical to freedom and good government. . . .
>
> I strongly believe that the basic purpose and plan of the Constitution is that the federal government should have no power except those that are expressly or impliedly granted and that no department of government—executive, legislative or judicial—has authority to add to or take away the powers granted or denied by the Constitution. . . .
>
> I deeply fear for our constitutional system when life appointed judges can strike down a law passed by Congress or a state legislature with no more justification than that the judges believe the law is "unreasonable." [3]

His fear mirrors that of divergent segments of the population. It is there because no Supreme Court of the United States, since its establish-

---

[2] (1913). Law and the Court. Reprinted from *Speeches by Oliver Wendell Holmes*, pp. 98-103. Little, Brown & Co., Boston.

[3] Columbia University Law School, New York. *Carpentier Lectures*. Also see Black, Hugo A. (1968). *A Constitutional Faith*, pp. 9, 12, and 24. Knopf, New York.

ment, has had to face the far-flung challenges that confront the present Court. Mr. Justice Holmes reflected on how to get people to see problems on a national level. Today's Court must reckon with issues that lie beneath the surface and may assume international dimensions. Its decision-making, in some measure, must take the "cold war" into account.

This international ideological struggle, with its beginnings in 1945, is reflected in the controversies enacted in the Supreme Court. Decisions that have touched on arrest, search and seizure, confessions, and the right to the assistance of counsel—to name only a few issues—have been the domestic counterparts of the worldwide conflict for the freedom of the human mind. In many decisions which have been made that affect criminal procedure, it would seem that "social utility" rather than "precedent" alone, has been the primary test employed by the Court in determining the balance between personal liberty and community security.

No doubt, the Court has had its eye on the image its decisions leave upon other nations of the world. To subordinate a due process model to a crime control model could have an impact upon the people of the uncommitted nations that could influence their political views. A nation that sets itself up as the show-case of democracy must do more than give lip service to the beliefs that it professes.

The fact that justices are individualists—like the rest of us—is bound to influence the makeup of their opinions. An opinion, therefore, is a reflection of the writer's philosophy on law—a product of his experiences and environment, past and present. When one justice says in *Miranda v. Arizona*, that "there can be no doubt that the Fifth Amendment privilege is available outside of criminal proceedings . . . ," and, another says, "I turn now to the Court's asserted reliance on the Fifth Amendment, an approach which I frankly regard as a *trompe l'oeil*" (an illusion). Such disparate views simply bring out the individualism of each justice.

Another reason why a majority of the Court has imposed its notions of what constitutes "fundamental fairness" upon state criminal law administration, can be summed up by a single word: defaults. The defaults cover a broad spectrum.

Many commentators point to law enforcement officers as the prime defaulters. Some officers, indeed, have used dubious or illegal practices. But to hold that their failures, more than others', required the Court to act, is disputable. The Supreme Court of the United States should not have been placed in a position in which *it* was forced to correct their defaults. Others should have done so.

The legal profession, from prosecutor to the states' highest appellate courts, and people in general, by their defaults, have been the prime offenders. No law enforcement officer alone ever brought about the conviction of any person accused of crime on evidence that was obtained in violation of the person's constitutional rights. Other persons played the leading roles. *Mapp* v. *Ohio* can be used to demonstrate this.

The actions of the officers in arresting Dollree Mapp, and in the search of her home, were clearly unreasonable under the dictum of *Wolf v. Colorado*. At the time, however, under the laws of the state of Ohio, the evidence taken from her home was admissible against her at her trial. But there was no reason why it should have been used against her.

The prosecutor could have refused to prosecute; the trial judge could have dismissed the charge; and the appellate court could have reversed the conviction. Thus, if at any one of these stages of the criminal proceedings, had some member of the legal profession done what should have been done, there would have been no case to review by the Supreme Court. The judicial machine was not stopped, however, and as a result, the Supreme Court of the United States was presented with an ideal factual situation to enable the Court, by a slim majority of one vote, to impose federal arrest and search standards upon the states.

Many individuals, besides lawyers, could have taken steps, long before Miss Mapp's arrest, which could have gone a long way toward protecting the due process rights of persons accused of crimes.

The citizenry of Miss Mapp's community could have demanded more competent police services: "In general, people receive the kind of law enforcement that they deserve," as this book's preface emphasizes. The city fathers could have taken enough interest in their police service to have initiated measures to upgrade the quality of police service that was rendered to their constituents. The lawmakers, both local and state, could have enacted laws that would have modernized archaic arrest and search laws under which, as far along as 1972, many law enforcement officers had to operate. And last, but certainly not least, the prosecutor could have taken action that would have kept many bad cases out of court, and probably, in addition, his action could have inhibited *Mapp*-type police practices.

The authors are not unmindful of police-prosecutor-judge relations—especially those that prevailed in the pre-*Mapp* era—in which teamwork often results in prosecutors and judges "playing the game," so to speak, in the spirit of promoting good working relations. *The sooner that this game comes to an end, the better! Now is the time* for prosecutors and judges to exercise more leadership in their relations with law enforcement personnel than most of them have done in the past.

Some of this has taken place in *Mapp's* wake. *Mapp*, then, can be viewed, in retrospect, as a *real blessing in disguise*. Police officers now are required to make better investigations. Prosecutors and judges have ceased relying too much upon the "ingenuity" of the police to develop a case.

Judges and prosecutors are tossed into the investigative picture and no longer have the case dished up to them on a silver platter. And more important, there are many signs that the police-prosecutor-judge team is joining together more and more to develop strategy, proper policy, and guidelines for law enforcement officers, and as a team, they provide impetus for both police education and training. All this bodes well for the future, as, in the long run, respect for civil rights and civil liberties is the surest avenue to police "professionalism."

A professional approach to police service encompasses a point of view that stresses due process over crime control. The line where due process comes to rest, at times, is a razor's edge. Jurists and legal scholars disagree, in many situations, on its location. So do justices of the Supreme Court of the United States. Over a seven-year period, 1961-1967, in criminal law cases in which major full blown opinions were written, dissents were registered in 62.65 per cent of the decisions.[4]

Such lack of consensus on the part of the Court tends to confuse most law enforcement officers. Most of them know that the Court is in no position to try to set precise guidelines. But pronounced ambiguities in decisions create tough legal problems for them to solve. Yet no one will tell them what to do in many situations. Police say that an opinion should be written to be understood, not misinterpreted. They do not stand alone in raising this kind of criticism. Many legal scholars have complained about poor legal draftsmanship in opinions like *Escobedo, Miranda* and *Terry*. Professor Henry M. Hart, Jr., of the Harvard Law School has remarked: "It has been said that too many of the Court's opinions are about what one would expect could be written in twenty-four hours. . . . Few of the Court's opinions—far too few—generally illuminate the area of law with which they deal."

A verse from *Through the Looking Glass* by Lewis Carroll, though facetious, carries a message that applies to some of the Court's open-ended opinions:

> "When I use a word," Humpty Dumpty said, in rather a scornful tone, "it means just what I choose it to mean—neither more or less."
> "The question is," said Alice, "whether you can make words mean so many different things."
> "The question is," said Humpty Dumpty, "which is to be master—that's all."

In a more concerned tone, the Chief Justice of the California Supreme Court, voicing his frustration in trying to interpret decisions of the Supreme Court of the United States, said:

> It falls regularly to the state judges and recurringly to federal judges to

---

[4] Source: *The Harvard Law Review*, Annual Volumes.

expound with common sense as well as constitutional sense the skywriting that at times dots just enough t's to cross the eyes, but trails off on the if's, and's, and but's. The loftier the message and the more removed from the local scene, the more difficult it is for the judges on the ground to work out the ground rules. . . . A rugged constitution, by definition, the law of the land, suffers a loss of vitality when it must circle in thin air indefinitely.[5]

The Justices of the Supreme Court of the United States are far enough removed from the local scene to be in need of this point of view from an outpost. Justices of the Supreme Court of the United States, and lower court judges, again and again, have asked for criticism. In July 1968, in an appearance before the Senate Judiciary Committee. Mr. Justice Fortas, in response to a question, said: "Senator, I believe firmly that the Supreme Court, in all its acts and deeds, should be the subject of open, full criticism."

Criticism of the Court should be of a texture, however, that recognizes the part the Court plays in safeguarding personal freedom. It could be much safer to vest freedom of person in the hands of the Court—fallible though it may be—than to depend too much on legislators and other partisan politicians as guardians of liberty!

"Revered and abused as no other Court has ever been, least known of the great institutions of the United States, the Supreme Court holds a unique power in the American system of government—a unique place in the American story." [6] History alone will be competent to assess the decisions of the Warren Court and the contributions of the Chief Justice as a moving force that led to those decisions.

THE CONSTITUTION AND JUDICIAL PHILOSOPHY

May we say a few words first, to set the stage, on the philosophy of the people on the American legal system of the 1953-1969 period, as it was in this span of time that the philosophy of one group left its indelible imprint on the law. Two distinct schools of thought are identifiable, with a third interposed. They were: (1) the "activists," or "idealists," who believed the Constitution needed to be interpreted to meet the social needs of the times; (2) the "stabilizers," or "realists," who believed social change should have been initiated, for the most part, by people other than judges; and (3) the "moderates," who melded into both schools of thought, but who leaned more toward the "stabilizers." [7]

"Judicial activism" or "idealism" became the dominant theme of the

---

[5] Traynor, *op. cit.*, p. 122.

[6] The Foundation of the Federal Bar Association (1965). *Equal Justice Under Law*, p. 5.

[7] This is not to imply that only lawyers fit these categories, but the influence nonlawyers exercise on legal questions is negligible, excluding crises situations.

Supreme Court of the United States with the arrival of its fourteenth Chief Justice. When Earl Warren was sworn in on October 5, 1953, he described himself as a "progressive moderate." What this really meant soon became apparent. From that day to his retirement on June 23, 1969, Earl Warren fashioned the Court to create a majority whose decisions over the sixteen-year period, often by 5-4 votes, brought bold reforms and raging controversy, and shaped the destiny of a nation.

From the 1953-1954 term of the Court through its 1968-1969 term, anguished protests sprang from many quarters that the activists on the Court had set themselves up as the ultimate arbiters of the Constitution. Some of the most eloquent protests came from within the Court itself in dissenting opinions. The question is, "Why all the dissent?"

Much of it can be attributed to the way different justices look at the Constitution. Some of them have tried to divine the intent of the people who adopted the Constitution and the Bill of Rights. And to a lesser extent, crystal-ball gazing has been used in relation to the Fourteenth Amendment of 1868. Other justices, however, have refused to read into the documents what the people who lived in those periods intended or would do if they were here today. Both sides, then, see the Constitution through different colored glasses. The Constitution is either "fixed," or it is "fluid."

The "fixed" Constitution is what most people would call simply "the Constitution"; that is, the document adopted in 1789 with its subsequent amendments. Put another way, under a "fixed" Constitution, justices would exercise judicial restraint in order to promote federalism and separation of powers—as "stabilizers." A "fluid" Constitution, on the other hand, is a national consensus that gradually emerges as to important public issues, such as whether the American scene should be desegregated. Under a "fluid" Constitution, "activist" justices would disregard judicial restraint when to do otherwise would interfere with the implementation of desirable political or social goals. Neither point of view, "fixed" or "fluid," if carried to its logical conclusion, is wholly acceptable to moderates.

The Court's mixture of philosophy, like that of the man on the street, draws a mixed reaction to many of its decisions. More significant, perhaps, is that because of the nature of the Court's work, it cannot satisfy everyone. In general, prior to 1954, stabilizers were satisfied with the work of the Court, and the activists were displeased. In the 1960s, activists, in general, were satisfied with the work of the Court, but most of them were disappointed with some of the Court's decisions, for example, *Terry v. Ohio*. Ironically, this criminal law opinion by Chief Justice Warren—upholding the right of the police to stop and frisk for weapons—was criticized by Mr. Justice Douglas as "a long step down the totalitarian path."

The Court's application of the Fourteenth Amendment's due process and equal privileges and immunities clauses to state courts drew fire from many quarters. Obviously, due process in *Terry* meant one thing to Mr. Justice Douglas, but something different to his brethren. Much of the difference in opinion is anchored in the Court's application of the Fourteenth Amendment's due process and equal privileges and immunities clauses to its decisions which affect Bill of Rights protections.

Some justices have concluded that it was the intent of the people who adopted the Fourteenth Amendment that it would incorporate whole, the first eight amendments of the Bill of Rights. After the Court's 1925 decision in *Gitlow v. New York*, the incorporation theory has come more and more to the fore. The philosophy slowly gained a following in the Court. However, up to the close of the 1970-1971 term, no majority has ever held that the Fourteenth Amendment incorporates the first eight amendments of the Bill of Rights. Opponents of this philosophy emphasize the fact that if such had been the intention there would be two due process clauses applicable to the states: the Fifth and the Fourtenth, and both would extend their protection to "any person."

For the first time, however, in *Mapp*, a majority of the Court—with reference to a single amendment, the Fourth—held that "Since the Fourth Amendment's right of privacy has been declared enforceable against the States through the Due Process Clause of the Fourteenth, it is enforceable against them by the same sanctions of exclusion as is used against the Federal Government." Four members of the Court objected vehemently to the majority adopting this brand of incorporation. They would have adhered to the case-to-case approach, taking into account the totality of the circumstances in deciding alleged violations of due process.

Mr. Justice Harlan, whom two other justices join, dissenting, declare that the Court's "reasoning ultimately rests on the unusual premises that because *Wolf* carried into the States a part of the principle of 'privacy' underlying the Fourth Amendment, it must follow that whatever configurations of the Fourth Amendment have been developed in the particularized federal precedents are likewise to be deemed a part of 'ordered liberty,' and as such enforceable against the States. For me, this does not follow at all."

The most important question raised in the aftermath of the *Mapp* decision was only lightly touched upon in Mr. Justice Clark's opinion. Did the decision mean that the Court would continue to protect the "core" of the Fourth Amendment, or did it mean that the Fourth Amendment's standard was taken over intact into due process? The area of state discretion would, of course, be considerably narrowed if *Mapp* meant the latter. The answer came two years later in *Ker v. California*, 273 U.S. 23. The Court, speaking through Mr. Justice Clark, held (8-1) that " the standard of reasonableness is the same under the Fourth and Fourteenth Amendments. . . ." Only Justice Harlan disagreed.

In sum, then, the incorporation theory at the end of the 1970-1971 term simply means that the Fourteenth Amendment's due process clause does place restrictions on state action. The Court in turning to selective incorporation in *Mapp*, engineered a procedure that requires the states to meet, substantially, federal due process standards in relation to a person's substantive rights, but left to the states some latitude in the application of procedural rules. The process of selective incorporation has moved a long way since *Gitlow v. New York*, but, as yet, it has not swept in all of the guarantees enumerated in the first eight amendments.

At the beginning of 1972, of the 23 safeguards of the Bill of Rights that restrict government action, all are now binding upon the states except the Second Amendment's guarantee of the right to bear arms, the Third Amendment's prohibition against the quartering of troops in private homes, the Fifth Amendment's requirement of grand jury indictments for all capital or infamous crimes, and the Eighth Amendment's bar against excessive bail. There is one further provision that does not concern criminal law and which has not been applied to the states: the Seventh Amendment's requirement that jury trials be allowed in all civil suits involving twenty dollars or more.

What stands out more than anything else in the years of the Warren Court, insofar as criminal procedure is concerned, is that the exclusionary rule is the most creative single act of the Supreme Court's history. The brand of selective incorporation established in *Mapp* provided the leverage the Court needed to enable it to pioneer wide-ranging reforms in criminal law in the remaining years of the Warren Court.

The Chief Justice set a precedent on his own before he relinquished his stewardship of the Court. In was established when he held a news conference on July 5, 1968.[8] It marked the first time any Chief Justice had gone before the press in such a wide-open, give-and-take session.

Asked by a reporter to pick out three or four high points that stand out as key moments of his career as Chief Justice, he named and discussed three of the Court's many decisions: (1) *Brown v. Board of Education*, 347 U.S. 483 (1954), school desegregation, (2) *Baker v. Carr*, 369 U.S. 186 (1962), "one-person one-vote," and (3) *Gideon v. Wainwright*, 372 U.S. 335 (1963), appointed counsel for poor persons in the courts.

Responding to a question as to which one of the three he felt, in his opinion, to be the most important, he said, "*Baker v. Carr* is about the most

---

[8] "Earl Warren Talks about the Warren Court." (1968). *U.S. News & World Report*, July, pp. 62-64.

basic case that has been decided in our time." Asked why, he replied, "I think a great many of these other problems would have been solved long ago if everyone had the right to vote and his vote counted the same as anybody else's." (It is notable that the Chief Justice made reference to only one of the Court's landmark decisions in the criminal law field.)

On June 23, 1969, Chief Justice Earl Warren, at the age of 78, stepped down. His departure, after sixteen years, ended an era which will go down in the Court's history as one in which "judicial activism" reached for the stars.

Like so many of his predecessors Earl Warren gave his name to a Court even though Article III of the Constitution established "one Supreme Court." There is a good deal of unfairness in this practice. No one man puts his exclusive stamp on the Court; its decisions mirror the best thinking of each member of the Court, or a majority of it.

However, as a practice, good or bad, it is likely to continue if for no better reason than, traditionally, this has been the practice in some courts. The practice is, on the whole, harmless enough, and often achieves a certain aptness.

President Richard M. Nixon disclosed his aptness in rating the power of a Chief Justice on May 22, 1969 when he nominated Warren Earl Burger as Chief Justice of the United States. The nomination is, he said, "the most important nomination that a President makes. . . . Our Chief Justices probably had more profound and lasting influence on their times and on the direction of the nation than most Presidents have had."

On June 23, 1969, Warren E. Burger took the oath of office, and became the fifteenth Chief Justice of the United States. His judicial record labels him as a "moderate conservative" on law and order issues. On the other hand, it shows him to be a "moderate liberal" on civil rights issues. His moderate-to-liberal credentials date back to Minnesota, where he was a member of the Governor's Interracial Commission. The Chief Justice's opinions as a member of the United States Supreme Court square with this appraisal of his judicial philosophy.

Decisions handed down in the 1969-1970 and 1970-1971 terms contain scant evidence of any overpowering reach by the Court to undo much of the handiwork of the Warren Court. However, there is substantial evidence in a number of opinions that *Mapp v. Ohio* and *Ker. v. California* appear ripe for overruling.

During the Terms, four justices expressed deep dissatisfaction with the results of the search and seizure exclusionary rule. Persuasive reasons were advanced why the rule should be replaced by a viable alternative. For example, in *Coolidge v. New Hampshire*, 403 U.S. 443 (6/21/71), 5-4, with the Chief Justice dissenting, in a rare action for one in his position, he suggests the enactment of legislation to admit evidence now barred from trials. The law, he said, should (1) provide penalties against law enforcement officials who violate the law, and (2) also direct that "no evidence otherwise admissible shall be excluded from any criminal proceedings because of violation of the Fourth Amendment."

Other conscientious persons, however, take a contrary view. Representative Emanuel Celler (D.) (New York), Chairman of the House Judiciary Committee, commented that "my inclination is in opposition" to the Chief Justice's suggestion.

Nevertheless, the changes in the Court's makeup lend strong support to an assumption a good measure of the Chief Justice's philosophy is likely to show up in future decisions of the Court.

The first change on the "Burger Court" occurred when Harry A. Blackmun took his place on the Court filling a seat on the Court that had been vacant in the 1969-1970 term as a result of Justice Abe Fortas' resignation. Justice Blackmun's voting record is an indicator that he, like the Chief Justice, is a "moderate conservative" with, perhaps, a bit more leaning toward the conservative side.

The retirement of Justice Hugo L. Black on September 17, 1971, after a near-record of thirty-four years on the Court, gave President Nixon his third opportunity to appoint an associate justice to the Supreme Court. The retirement of Justice John M. Harlan, September 23, 1971, gave President Nixon a rare opportunity to make a fourth appointment, four in President Nixon's first three years in office.

On September 23, 1971, President Nixon said he was "frankly looking" for persons with "a similar judicial philosophy" to that of his first two Court appointees—strict constructionists and believers in judicial restraint. In a speech on October 21, 1971, announcing his nominations of Lewis F. Powell, Jr., of Virginia, and William H. Rehnquist of Arizona, to be justices of the Supreme Court, President Nixon said:

> As far as judicial philosophy is concerned, it is my belief that it is the duty of a judge to interpret the Constitution and not to place himself above the Constitution or outside the Constitution. He should not twist or bend the Constitution in order to perpetrate his personal and social views.

Lewis F. Powell, Jr., a Richmond lawyer and the seventh Supreme Court member from Virginia, was confirmed by the Senate December 6, 1971 by a vote of 89-1.

William H. Rehnquist, an assistant United States Attorney General and the first Arizonan to sit on the high Court, was confirmed 68-26 on December 10, 1971.

The new justices were sworn in at a special ceremony on January 7, 1972. They lost no time in embarking on their duties as they took part in the regular Friday morning conference of the justices following the 10 A.M. ceremony.

Justice Powell, who succeeds the late Hugo L. Black, became the 99th justice in the history of the Court. Justice Rehnquist, number 100, succeeded the late John M. Harlan, and became last in seniority among the justices.

The nineteenth and twentieth centuries are dotted with instances of appointments that had the appearance of having been made for the purpose of changing the Court's course. The policy leaves much to be desired. It excludes, for instance, outstanding candidates for no reason except that their judicial philosophy may be somewhat at odds with the President's. Moreover, as history shows, it is a policy that can backfire.

A nominee's alleged judicial philosophy is not always a sure sign the same philosophy will carry over to his work on the Court. A given judicial philosophy does not always produce a given result. President Dwight Eisenhower learned this lesson from Chief Justice Earl Warren.

However, under present conditions the "new majority" appointed by President Nixon appears likely to be composed of justices inclined to exercise judicial restraint instead of plowing fresh fields.

Only time will tell whether the Court headed by Chief Justice Warren Earl Burger will earn a reputation as a "conservative Burger Court." But it is not premature to say that the Court which has replaced the Warren Court is one whose overall judicial philosophy breaks sharply with that of its predecessor.

DUE PROCESS BUILDING BLOCKS

The selective incorporation theory proclaimed in *Mapp* was a springboard used by the Court to jump to decisions like *Gideon, Malloy, Escobedo, Miranda, Wade, Katz* and *Lee*: decisions in which precedent after precedent was shattered in the criminal law revolution of 1960-1968.

The Court laid a foundation some years before for later decisions. Its work was begun in 1932 in *Powell v. Alabama* in which the Court constructed a building-block that it would need later. The preparation was continued in a series of confession cases. Each block would be used in one way or another on the road to selective incorporation that ultimately brought state criminal procedure more in line with federal standards. The time was at hand in *Mapp*. Thereafter, the Court used its building blocks to effect dramatic changes in Fourth, Fifth and Sixth Amendment rights.

The construction of blocks in the Court's opinions has a history in search and seizure cases that precedes *Mapp* by a number of years. Only the more important decisions that were decided shortly before Mapp will be considered.

In *Irvine v. California,* (1954), Mr. Justice Clark, who would be the author of the *Mapp* opinion, had served notice that he would vote to overrule the *Wolf* decision as soon as "needed converts" were available. But more than converts would be needed to overrule *Wolf*. The Court would have to do some bridge-building to contrive new constitutionally-based rules. This was done on June 27, 1960, in *Elkins v. United States,* when the Court renounced its long-held "silver platter" doctrine.

Evidence against Elkins was uncovered by Oregon police officers who were searching the home of another person for obscene motion pictures. They did not find what they were looking for but in the course of their search came upon wiretapping paraphernalia. A state court prosecution on wiretapping charges failed when the Oregon courts ordered the evidence suppressed on the ground the warrant with which the searchers were armed was invalid. Federal officers, who had followed the proceedings through the newspapers, took the evidence from a safe deposit box where it had been placed by the local police for safekeeping. A federal indictment was returned and Elkins was tried, and convicted. The United States Supreme Court authorized a review of the case.

The Court (5-4) overturned the "silver platter" doctrine that permitted evidence of a federal crime which state police came upon in the course of an illegal search for a state crime to be turned over to federal authorities for use in a federal prosecution, so long as federal agents did not participate in the search but simply received the illegal evidence on a "silver platter." (The decision probably demonstrated the Court's majority dissatisfaction with a doctrine which in reality barred only evidence showing overt federal participation, of a covert nature, in an unlawful seizure.)

More to the point, as a building block, is that the cut of the cloth in *Elkins* shows forward movement in two directions. Not only did the Court repudiate the "silver platter" doctrine, but it also appeared to be expanding the Fourteenth Amendment's protection against unreasonable searches and seizures from *Wolf's* "core" of the Fourth Amendment position to one coextensive with the Fourth Amendment in its entirety. In so doing, the Court constructed the last building block that it would need to repudiate the *Wolf* doctrine. One year later, the landmark decision of *Mapp v. Ohio* completed the logic of *Elkins*, and its antecedents, and "brought the states into alignment" with federal standards. *Mapp* did not make this clear. *Ker v. California* (1963), discussed above, removed any doubt as to what *Mapp* required.

Quite a bit has been said in this text about *Mapp v. Ohio*. Nowhere have the facts been brought out that took her to the Supreme Court. The facts can serve to complement the chronology of *Wolf* and *Elkins*; and, also, to accord to *Mapp* the recognition that is its due in legal history.

On May 23, 1957, at about 1:30 P.M., three policemen made a visit to Miss Mapp's home. They knocked at the door and demanded to be admitted. They wished, they said, to question her, but they refused to give any further information. They did not tell her they had come in response to a tip that a suspect wanted in a bombing incident "was hiding in the house and that there was a large amount of policy paraphernalia being hidden in the home." Miss Mapp telephoned her attorney who advised her to deny entry to the officers unless they produced a search warrant.

Frustrated, they took up a vigil outside the house for about three hours, after which they were joined by at least four more officers. When Miss Mapp did not come to the door immediately in response to their knocks, at least one of the several doors to the house was forcibly opened and an entry was gained. Upon the arrival of Miss Mapp's attorney, he was denied permission to see her.

When Miss Mapp demanded that the police officers produce a search warrant, one of the officers waived a piece of paper in front of her, which apparently was not a warrant, for it was not produced at the trial. Miss Mapp seized the "warrant" and pushed it inside the bosom of her dress. The officers recovered it after a struggle and put handcuffs on her because she was "belligerent," and imprisoned her in the bedroom.

In the course of their subsequent search, during which they ransacked the house, and even went through Miss Mapp's personal papers and photograph album, they found neither the suspect nor the gambling equipment. They extended their search to the second floor which Miss Mapp occupied with her young daughter, and found nothing. Then going to the basement, they opened a trunk in which they found allegedly lewd and lascivious books, pictures, and photographs. Miss Mapp disclaimed ownership, saying the material had been left behind by a former boarder, but she was nevertheless arrested, tried, convicted on an obscenity charge, and sentenced to prison.

The Ohio Supreme Court agreed that the search was lawless but held that the conviction must stand because Ohio followed the common-law rule of admissibility.

Turning again to building blocks in the law of search and seizure, the Court continued its work, after *Ker*, by abrogating the "mere evidence" rule in *Warden v. Hayden*, 387 U.S. 294 (5/29/67).

The police had a description of an armed robbery suspect and the house he had entered afterward which two witnesses had furnished shortly after the robbery. Within minutes, police arrived at the house in a number of patrol cars. An officer knocked and announced their presence. Mrs. Hayden answered, and the officers told her they believed that a robber had entered the house, and asked to search the house. She offered no objection. Hayden was found in an upstairs room feigning sleep. He was arrested. A search of the house uncovered a number of objects similar to those used in the robbery, including a jacket and trousers of the type the fleeing man was said to have worn. At Hayden's non-jury trial an objection was made to the admission in evidence of the jacket and trousers on the ground that they were "mere evidence." The objection was overruled. Hayden was found guilty of armed robbery. The District Court of Maryland denied *habeas corpus* relief. A divided panel of the Court of Appeals for the Fourth Circuit reversed. The Supreme Court of the United States authorized a review of the case and reversed the Court of Appeals for the Fourth Circuit thus affirming Hayden's conviction.

Five justices joined in obliterating the distinction between merely evidentiary materials, on the one hand, which could not be seized either under the authority of a search warrant or during the course of a search incident to an arrest, and on the other hand, those objects that may validly be seized, including the instrumentalities and means by which a crime is committed, the fruits of crime (such as stolen property), weapons by which the escape of the person arrested might be effected, and property, the possession of which is a crime.

The emphasis, according to the majority, should not be upon who has a superior right in the property, but upon the protection of the right of privacy. The requirement of the Fourth Amendment, said the Court, "can secure the same protection of privacy whether the search is for 'mere evidence' or for fruits, instrumentalities, or contraband."

In *Camara v. Municipal Court*, 387 U.S. 523 (6/5/67), a new species of probable cause is designed by a majority of the United States Supreme Court to strike a balance between the need for area-wide health and fire inspections and the right to be secure from warrantless searches.

In *Camara*, an inspector of the Division of Housing Inspection of the San Francisco Department of Public Health was told by a building manager that Camara, a tenant, was uing his premises unlawfully. Camara denied an inspector admission without a search warrant on visits made on two different days. A citation was then mailed to Camara ordering him to appear at the district atorney's office. Camara failed to appear. Two inspectors returned to Camara's apartment, and informed him he was required by law to permit the inspection. Camara nevertheless refused to admit them. Thereafter a complaint was filed, and Camara was arrested later.

Overruling *Frank v. Maryland*, 359 U.S. 260 (1959), the majority in Camara holds that administrative area inspections are significant intrusions upon the private interests protected by the Fourth Amendment. Thus, no longer are health and fire inspectors (also see, *See v. Seattle*, 378 U.S. 260, 6/5/67) entitled to search a home or business without warrant or consent.

In *Katz v. United States*, 389 U.S. 347 (12/18/67), the Court held that the Fourth Amendment renders inadmissible any evidence obtained by electronic eavesdropping conducted without warrant, overruling both *Olmstead* (1928), and *Goldman* (1942). The Court said that the Fourth Amendment is not limited to "constitutionally protected areas," but rather applies to persons.

Lastly, insofar as Fourth Amendment building blocks are concerned (for the purpose of this discussion), the Court in *Lee v. Florida*, 392 U.S. 378 (6/17/68), held that evidence obtained by state officers in violation of Section 605 of the Federal Communications Act, cannot be used in a state criminal prosecution, overruling *Schwartz* (1952).

Lee ordered the installation of a private telephone in his home. No private lines were available so he was given a telephone on a four-party line instead. A week later, at the direction of the local police department, the company connected a telephone in a neighboring house to the same party line. The police attached to this telephone an automatic actuator, a tape recorder, and a set of earphones. Evidence was obtained which resulted in the conviction of Lee and two co-defendants for violating the state lottery laws. Lee's conviction was reversed by the United States Supreme Court.

From *Wolf* to *Lee*, building block after building block was put in place by the Supreme Court as it moved from decision to decision between 1960-1969. The constitutional underpinnings for the decisions were laid by the Court in the search and seizure cases that have been discussed—as well as others. The Court had to construct them, first, to create new constitutionally required rules of evidence. (A similar methodology was used by the Court in Fifth and Sixth Amendment cases that has pioneered dramatic extensions of certain provisions of those amendments.)

A number of the Court's search and seizure opinions, and a much larger number that relate to confession admissibility and the right to the assistance of counsel, have not been considered. They were not included for the reason that the purpose of this section is to center on a single concept: how the Supreme Court formulated a rule in one case that it would use to create another rule in a later case. The essence of what has been said is summarized in the next few paragraphs with some comment on two additional opinions that have a bearing upon the work of the Court in the changing world of search and seizure law.

In *Olmstead,* the Court held that a voice is not a thing that is entitled to the protection of the Fourth Amendment. (A conversation is no more than "mere evidence," that cannot be seized, with or without warrant.)

Before *Mapp,* the Supreme Court was bound by the *Wolf* ruling. *Wolf* left the Court powerless, in the average search and seizure violation, to bar the use of illegally seized evidence in state courts. Prior to *Elkins,* the Court, bound by *Burdeau v. McDowell* (1921), permitted a state officer to introduce illegally obtained evidence in a federal court.

The *Elkins* decision provided the rationale the Court needed to reach its decision in *Mapp.* The Court would have been precluded from making its later holding in eavesdropping cases without *Hayden's* authority. (Abolishing the "mere evidence" rule enabled the Court to hold, later, that a voice is equivalent to a thing, and entitled to the protection of the Fourth Amendment. *Hayden* also enabled the Court to hold that the Fourth Amendment protects persons, not things.)

In *Terry,* the Court held that a stop and frisk are the same, constitutionally speaking, as a seizure and a search. *Camara* and *See,* though not mentioned in *Terry,* establish a watered-down version of probable cause to support the issuance of a search warrant. In sustaining stop and frisk procedures, in *Terry,* as constitutionally permissible, the Court sanctions a diluted probable cause standard.

In *Benanti v. United States,* 355 U.S. 96 (1957), the Court barred the use in federal courts, of evidence obtained from intercepted communications by state officers, contrary to Section 605 of the Federal Communications Act. In *Lee,* the majority explains that after *Benanti,* the only remaining support for *Schwartz* was the holding in *Wolf* which was subsequently overruled by *Mapp.* (Invoking doctrinal symmetry, the majority in *Lee* concludes that *Schwartz* cannot survive the demise of *Wolf.* The majority in *Lee* also deems its decision "counseled by experience." The hope expressed in *Schwartz* that enforcement of Section 605 could be achieved under penal provisions of the Communications Act has proved vain. "Research has failed," the majority says, "to uncover a single reported prosecution of a law enforcement officer for violation of section 605. . . .")

Hardly any one would expect a law enforcement officer to know all the fine shadings of the law as pivotal rules that the Court designs to reach uncharted plateaus. But most people do expect him to provide them with even and effective enforcement of the law. This requires more knowledge of the "whys" of law than of the "hows." The "whys" cannot be mastered easily. But today's law enforcement officer needs to recognize that "The history of what the law has been is necessary to the knowledge of what the law is."

CONGRESS AND THE COURT

At 6:30 P.M., February 18, 1967, a 312-page report which the President's Commission on Law Enforcement and Administration of Justice had adopted was released. The report ended with three reports expressing "Additional Views of Individual Commission Members."

One of these reports, signed by four members—three of whom are past Presidents of the American Bar Association— of the nineteen-member Commission, voices concern with trends in the criminal justice system. Three other Commission members, concurring, also signed this report.

This "minority" report agrees with the substance of the Commission report, but it emphasizes that its authors have doubts that

"relate to the difficult and perplexing problems arising from certain of the constitutional limitations upon our system of criminal justice. . . . The limitations with which we are primarily concerned arise from the Fifth and Sixth Amendments to the Constitution of the United States as they have been interpreted by the Supreme Court in recent years. . . . The question we raise is whether, even with the support of a deeply concerned President and implementation of the Commission's national strategy against crime, law enforcement can effectively discharge its vital role 'in controlling crime and violence' without changes in existing constitutional limitations. . . . Whatever can be done to right the present imbalance through legislation or rule of court should have high priority."

At 7:14 P.M., June 19, 1968, President Lyndon B. Johnson, signed the *Omnibus Crime Control and Safe Streets Act* of 1968 (Public Law 90-351, 90th Congress, H.R. 5037, June 19, 1968), popularly known as the Crime Control Act. He remarked at this time that he was far from satisfied with some provisions of the Act, but he said it contains "more good than bad." Both the good and the bad are spread out in four of the eleven Titles of the Act.

Money for Police. Title I authorizes billions of dollars through the Law Enforcement Assistance Administration to strengthen local police services— in such ways as the purchase of equipment, recruiting personnel, public education to prevent crime, construction of buildings and the organization of special police units. The law provides that 85 per cent of the money is to go to the states for subsequent allocation by governors.

Confessions. Title II of the Act purports to reverse various Supreme Court's holdings. The law applies only to federal courts, but it is expected to influence state courts. Voluntariness now becomes the sole test of admissibility of confessions. The law provides that a confession cannot be excluded simply because of a delay between arrest and arraignment. Police are given six hours to question a suspect. An eyewitness identification of a suspect is also admissible under the Act even though a lawyer may not have been present at the lineup.

Audio-Surveillances. Title III authorizes the issuance of wiretapping or "bugging" orders, by either state or federal courts, for the investigation of many crimes. At the same time, wiretapping and bugging are made federal crimes—if carried out privately. Penalty for a violation: $10,000, five years in prison, or both.

Gun Control. Title IV of the Act prohibits mail-order sale of firearms (other than rifles and shotguns) and prohibits the sale of pistols to persons under 21, or residents of another state. There is no requirement of registration of ownership of hand guns or any restrictions on mail-order traffic in rifles and shotguns.

No constitutional issue is raised by the provisions of Titles I and IV of the Act. (Title IV of the Act has been supplanted, however, by the gun control legislation signed into law by President Johnson on October 22, 1968.) Title II, by erasing the requirements set in *Miranda* and *Wade*, does raise constitutional questions. (The provision in Title II that voids *Mallory's* prompt arraignment rule is immune from constitutional attack as *Mallory's* requirement is a court-imposed rule of evidence.) Both Titles II and III, before and after the Act's adoption, have drawn a storm of criticism from numerous persons who hold that most of the Titles' provisions are unconstitutional. A contrary point of view has been voiced by others.

Issues of a different variety, in past years, have moved the people and Congress—and presidents as well—to defy the Court. The people amended the Constitution on one occasion as a rebuke to the Court. Congress has passed legislation to limit the Court, and presidents have used their power to restrain the Court.

The Constitution clearly says that the Supreme Court's appellate jurisdiction is subject to "such Exceptions and Regulations" as Congress may make (United States Constitution, Article III, Section 2, paragraph 2). Hence, Congress, in the use of its full power, if it should choose to employ it, could destroy judicial review. No such legislation has even been taken seriously but the people have used different powers delegated to them by the Constitution to limit the power of the Court.

The amendatory process has been used by the people to curb the Court's power as an aftermath of the Court's decision in *Chisholm v. Georgia*, 2 U.S. 419 (1793). This opinion originated out of an incident that aroused the emotions of the people of the 13 states of the new Union.

During the Revolution, Georgia had seized property from men loyal to the British Crown. With a pre-revolution claim on such an estate, two residents of South Carolina asked the Supreme Court to hear their suit against Georgia. It agreed, saying the Constitution gave it power to try such cases. The Court's *Chisholm* decision held in favor of the South Carolinians. The people of Georgia raged; other states took alarm. They were trying to untangle finances still snarled from the war. If they had to pay old debts to "Torries" they might be ruined. They adopted the Eleventh Amendment, forbidding any federal court to try a lawsuit against a state by a citizen of some other state. Thus the people overruled the Supreme Court for the first time, and established a far-reaching precedent of their own. They would give the ultimate decision on constitutional disputes.[9]

This has been the only time that the people have amended the Constitution to restrict the Court—at least as of this writing. However, the Court's reapportionment decisions, and its decisions imposing controls on law enforcement, have generated a great deal of concern in Congress. Many threats were made in Congress in the 1960s to limit the Court's power. Two such incidents stand out.

Spearheaded by Senator Everett Dirksen of Illinois, Congress called for a constitutional convention to upset the Supreme Court's reapportionment opinions. If 34 states had passed the resolution, this country would have had its first nationwide constitutional convention since the adoption of the Constitution. This would have brought into play a provision of Article V of the Constitution which says: "The Congress . . . on application of the legislatures of two thirds of the several states, shall call a convention for proposing amendments. . . ."

Congress provided that the amendment should remain before the states for a period of seven years. The seven-year period was contested, but the Supreme Court concluded that a seven-year period was not an unreasonable period to leave an amendment before the country for action.

By the end of 1968, the legislatures of 32 states had passed petitions asking Congress to call such a convention. The call for the convention failed, however, because at the end of 1970 the count fell short of the 34 required petitions.

Senator Sam J. Ervin, Jr., of North Carolina, a former justice of that State's Supreme Court, worked to put the admission of confessions out of reach of the Supreme Court of the United States. His proposed amendment to the United States Constitution, would have made the trial judge the sole arbiter of that, with the proviso that he must find the confession to be voluntary. This proposal failed to attract sufficient support in Congress.

Congress can also follow the legislative route to limit the power of the

---

[9] The Foundation of the Federal Bar Association (1965). *Equal Justice Under Law*, pp. 15-16.

Court. This leverage has been used. It was employed, for example, when an appeal was pending in the Supreme Court from a decision upholding the constitutionality of the Reconstruction règime in the South. Congress, fearing a reversal of the decision, stripped the Court of its power to hear appeals from habeas decisions in lower federal courts. The Court obeyed and dismissed the appeal, *Ex parte McArdle*, 7 Wallace Reports 506 (1869), without deciding the constitutional question. (Congress restored the Court's habeas jurisdiction almost 20 years later.)

On two well-known occasions in history, the Supreme Court has used its power over Congress to limit its authority. (The Court has declared a number of Acts of Congress to be unconstitutional, but, on balance, the Court has used its power sparingly.) The first occurred because of an act of omission by Secretary of States James Madison in 1801. This controversy between the Court and Congress was brought on by an unusual chain of events.

The *Federalist Congress* enacted two laws in February 1801. On February 13, a new Circuit Court law was enacted that reduced the number of Supreme Court justices from six to five, and authorized the appointment of 16 new federal judges. On February 27, a new law was enacted creating 42 new positions of Justice of the Peace.

President John Adams quickly selected nominees to fill the positions established by the two laws. They were confirmed by the Senate, and on March 3, Adams signed their commissions. John Marshall, doubling as Secretary of State and as Chief Justice of the Supreme Court, failed to deliver the commissions of the 42 persons appointed to be Justices of the Peace.

When Thomas Jefferson took office, as President, he directed his Secretary of State, James Madison, to withhold delivery of 17 of the commissions of the persons appointed to be Justices of the Peace, and to deliver the other 25.

Four of the 17 brought suit in the Supreme Court for a rule to show why a writ of mandamus should not be issued to compel Madison to deliver their commissions. The *Judiciary Act* of 1789 expressly granted the Court the authority to issue writs of mandamus in a case such as the one before it.

In *Marbury v. Madison*, 5 U.S. (1 Cr.) 137 (1803), Chief Justice Marshall, speaking for the Court, held that the Supreme Court has the power to declare unconstitutional an Act of Congress—the alleged basis of the doctrine of judicial supremacy. (The decision struck down as unconstitutional, Section 13 of the *Judiciary Act* of 1789, on the ground that Congress lacked the power under the Constitution to delegate original jurisdiction to the Court, i.e., the authority to issue writs of mandamus.)

The second encounter between Congress and the Court occurred 54 years later when the Court was faced with handing down a decision involving one Dred Scott, a slave.

Scott's action sought his freedom on the theory he had been taken from slave territory into free territory. As a result, he contended that he had become a free man under the *Northwest Territory Ordinance of 1787* and under the *Missouri Compromise Act of 1820*. Once having attained this status, he alleged, he could not be returned to slavery, despite his return to a slave state (Missouri).

In *Scott v. Sandford*, 19 Howard 383 (1857), Mr. Chief Justice Roger B. Taney, for the Court, held that parts of the *Missouri Compromise* violated the Fifth Amendment to the Constitution for it deprived slave owners of property without due process of law. (President Lincoln accused the Court of overstepping then and of helping bring on the Civil War through the decision. One should not overlook the fact that the people—not the Court—annulled the Dred Scott decision by waging war and by the adoption of the Thirteenth Amendment after the war. The nine Justices could only abide by the outcome.)

A third major occasion has arisen now that could precipitate a showdown between Congress and the Court—in relation to their respective powers—as a result of the enactment by Congress of the *Omnibus Crime Control and Safe Streets Act of 1968*. What the outcome may be cannot be foreseen clearly as this is written.

However, certain conclusions can be drawn about the Supreme Court that find adequate support in the record of the Court's past history, that disclose that (1) the Court has never been sacrosanct, (2) it is not supreme to the Constitution, and (3) it rules on the Constitution only with the consent of the people.

TOPICS FOR DISCUSSION

1. What conditions moved the Warren Court (1953-1969) to disregard a long line of legal precedents that had previously regulated law enforcement practices?
2. Why did the Supreme Court (1960-1969) hand down decisions that, in effect, supervised law enforcement activities?
3. How did some of the Court's criminal law decisions (1960-1969) which limited police activities turn out to be "blessings in disguise?"
4. What philosophy would distinguish a law enforcement agency that adheres more to a "due process" than a "crime control" model?
5. How do statistical data point up the fact that "due process" means different things to different people?
6. Why do Justices of the Supreme Court of the United States want to know how people, in general, react to the work of the Court?
7. What theories do different people—including Justices of the Supreme Court—

follow in order to make the Constitution of the United States a viable instrument of social control?

8. Why is there so much controversy relative to the power of the Supreme Court under the Fourteenth Amendment to regulate law enforcement?

9. What is the significance of the "selective incorporation theory" that the Supreme Court designed in *Mapp v. Ohio?*

10. Why was an agent of a state law enforcement agency, prior to *Elkins v. United States,* permitted to appear as a witness in a federal court, and allowed to introduce evidence that he had obtained during an unreasonable search?

11. Why was the exclusionary rule in *Mapp v. Ohio* the most creative rule announced by the Court in the 1960-1969 period?

12. What decisions did the Supreme Court of the United States hand down (1960-1969) to aid law enforcement agencies?

13. What powers could the people and Congress use to limit the power of the Supreme Court of the United States?

14. What power does the Supreme Court of the United States exercise to invalidate Acts of Congress?

15. Why does the Supreme Court of the United States rule on the Constitution only with the consent of the people?

16. What is the difference between a "how" and a "why" approach to criminal law instruction and study?

17. What are the philosophical differences between a (so-called) "liberal" and "conservative" court?

18. What philosophy does Chief Justice Burger allegedly follow to resolve a constitutional question?

19. What reasons can be given to sustain a conclusion that the United States Supreme Court which opened the 1971 term (October) has enough justices to constitute a "conservative" majority?

PART IV
AGENCIES OF CRIMINAL JUSTICE

Chapter XI

LOCAL AGENCIES

Since ancient times man has been subject to various regulations designed by the community to bring about socially desirable patterns of conduct. The objective of acceptable social behavior has been sought in many ways, but, in any period of time, some form of enforcement has characterized the quest. Such action has ranged from the sanctions and taboos of wily witch doctors to the relatively sophisticated operations of modern law enforcement agencies.

From early Anglo-Saxon development of even earlier traditions, crime has been regarded mainly as a local problem. Paralleling that concept has been a firm belief that, for the most part, enforcement should also be at the local level. Some modification of those concepts has been brought about by the birth and rapid development of organized crime, for its tentacles reach, not only across community lines, but also across state and international boundaries. Nonetheless, in general, crime always leaves its most scarring marks on the community in which it occurs.

Faced with such considerations, and regardless of the help available from outside law enforcement agencies, much of the burden of crime prevention and crime control must be borne at the local community level. *Enforcement of the law must be strengthened, more and more, where crime is spawned—in local communities.* That objective, far too often, is overlooked. But, that objective, in any community, can be achieved by farsighted police administrators and an enlightened citizenry working together for the common good.

Within the respective states, and excluding private police, state police, and federal police, there are several different types of law enforcement at the local level. These are not organized according to one common pattern, but perform a variety of functions depending on specifically assigned objectives.

There are approximately 46,000 units of criminal justice in state and local government.[1] (This figure does not include federal agencies, private agencies, or agencies operating where the population is less than 1,000). An interesting class project would be to list all agencies operating currently within the local county.

---

[1] See data, page 197.

The vast majority of these agencies consists of three men or less, working on a part-time basis, compensated by fees, selected or elected without regard for physical or mental qualifications, untrained, unsupervised, undisciplined, and poorly equipped. Yet, in a number of municipalities and counties, large numbers of officers are employed, work on a full-time career basis, are salaried, selected by civil service processes demanding high qualifications, given splendid training, good discipline, and provided with fine equipment and facilities.

In order to survey the vast panorama of local policing, we shall describe, first, policing in the cities, then policing in the counties, and finally, two irregular activities found in both.

POLICING IN THE CITIES

The core of the American police problem is centered in the cities. Numerically, the largest body of highly developed police is found in about four thousand cities, large and small.

The urban area of the United States, including all cities having over 2,500 population, contains more than 114,750,000 people who are protected by more than 233,500 policemen.[2]

The ratio of police personnel to population varies from 0.1 to 7.5 police per 1000 population; the national average is 2.0 per 1000.

The largest California police department is that of Los Angeles with 8,983 employees (6,806 officers and 2,177 civilians); the smallest is such a city as Etna with one employee.

The largest Michigan police department is that of Detroit with 5,590 employees (5,159 officers and 431 civilians); the smallest is such a city as Ahmeek with one employee.

The largest New York police department is that of the City of New York with 34,655 employees (31,671 officers and 2,984 civilians); the smallest is such a city as Clyde with one employee.

The percentage of civilian personnel varies between 10 and 14 per cent, with the national average about 13 per cent. This ratio has constantly been advancing, and is indicative of the substantial efforts being made to release highly trained police officers from mechanical and clerical tasks.

Although there are varying kinds of organizational structure, methods of control, available facilities, assigned functions, and levels of competency and integrity, the Chief of Police of Clyde must face many of the problems which are faced by the Commissioner of Police of the City of New York, albeit on a lesser scale.

---

[2] *Uniform Crime Reports.* Washington, D.C., United States Government Printing Office, 1971.

Both agencies will engage in *crime prevention* activities by working with juveniles, by cooperating with probation and parole personnel, by educating the public, and providing visible evidence of police ability and availability.

Both agencies will engage in *crime repression* activities by investigating crime, by identifying and apprehending offenders, by recovering stolen property, and by assisting in the prosecution and conviction of those who violate the law.

Both agencies will engage in the *regulation of noncriminal conduct,* by controlling the noncriminal citizen in such areas as traffic (vehicles, parking, pedestrians), public events (crowd control), and social relations (domestic disputes), in order to maintain community tranquility.

Both agencies will engage in the *provision of services* by rendering information, directions, advice, and general assistance, and through special services such as licensing and registration.

Both agencies will engage in the *protection of personal liberty* by protecting the individual citizen against unwarranted interferences on the part of the state, and by instructing the citizenry in terms of their duties, obligations, rights, and privileges in reference to the law.

In order to achieve their major objective, the prevention of crime and disorder and the preservation of the peace (for community security), and the protection of life and property and individual freedom (for individual security) both agencies will, to some degree, engage themselves in certain common functions.

All police tasks can be considered as line or staff. The line functions of policing can be designated as primary operational activities and special operational activities. The staff functions of policing can be desigated as primary staff services, auxiliary staff services, and inspectional services. These designations are arbitrary, and it must be said, there are varying opinions as to the nomenclature and placement of police functions and activities, and the most effective organizational structure.

Because there is a great public ignorance as to the work done by a municipal police agency, large or small, with many citizens assuming that the municipal police administrator, supervisor, and officer has a soft sinecure requiring only the muscle power to subdue a combative inebriate, only the intellectual capacity to sign a traffic ticket, and only the moral character necessary to avoid the commission of a public felony, the authors deem it wise and proper to familiarize all readers with the very demanding tasks and numerous responsibilities discharged by the local law enforcement agency. Perhaps after meditating on such imposing duties, the reader may better recognize the imperative need for careful selection and training of the municipal police officer, and the justification for salary levels commensurate with the assumption of so demanding a position.

I. **Line Functions** are those which accomplish, most immediately and directly, the objectives of the service.

　A. PRIMARY OPERATIONAL ACTIVITIES are those which are common to almost every municipal agency:

　　1. *Patrol activities*—the conduct of preliminary investigations; continuing surveillance of police hazards; provision of miscellaneous services to the public; crowd control; investigation of major and minor crime at the scene upon discovery or by request; enforcement of minor laws relating to vagrancy, begging, loitering, drunkenness, and other publicly offensive conduct; quelling disturbances of the peace; repressing disorderly conduct connected with personal, familial, and public disputes; attending minor injuries and emergencies; the interview and interrogation of those persons who have given reasonable cause for suspicion of their guilt; issuance of warnings and citations; arrest of offenders; and continual observation of the community to determine the need for police intervention or assistance.

　　2. *Investigatory (detective) activities*—the continued investigations of crime; recovery of stolen property; arrest of suspected and identified criminals; and case preparations for prosecution. Among the more frequent crimes handled by these officers are criminal homicide (murder, non-negligent manslaughter, manslaughter by negligence); forcible rape; robbery (stealing or taking anything of value from the person or his presence by force or violence or by putting in fear, such as strong-arm robbery, stickups); aggravated assault (assault with intent to kill, assault by shooting, cutting, stabbing, maiming, poisoning, scalding or by use of acids); burglary (breaking or entering, safe-cracking, or any unlawful entry to commit a felony or a theft); larceny (theft of bicycles, automobile accessories, shoplifting, pocket-picking, or any stealing of property or article of value which is not taken by force and violence or by fraud); auto theft (where a motor vehicle is stolen or driven away and abandoned); assault and battery; forgery (counterfeiting, or making, altering, uttering, or possessing, with intent to defraud, anything false which is made to appear true); embezzlement (fraud, con games, and obtaining money or property by false pretenses); stolen property offenses (buying, receiving, and possessing stolen

property); weapons violations (disregard of regulations or statutes controlling the carrying, using, possessing, furnishing, and manufacturing of deadly weapons or silencers); and offenses against the family and children (nonsupport, neglect, desertion, or abuse of family and children).

3. *Vice activities*—the represson and control of those offenses which tend to habituate, and through habituation, tend to corrupt and destroy the physical, mental, and moral health of the offender. Among the major vice areas are prostitution (sex offenses of a commercialized nature, such as keeping a bawdy house, procuring, transporting, or detaining women for immoral purposes); sex offenses (statutory rape, offenses against common decency, morals and chastity such as sex perversion); narcotics violations (offenses relating to unlawful possession, sale, or use of narcotic drugs); liquor law violations (unlawful possession, sale, use of intoxicating beverages, selling liquor to minors, sales after legal closing hours); gambling (promoting, permitting, or engaging in gambling).

4. *Traffic activities*—the promtion of safety on the streets and highways, with particular reference to drivers and pedestrians. The major traffic responsibilities of police agencies center around enforcement of the road and driving laws, including the drunk driving statutes; enforcement of parking ordinances; general enforcement of vehicle code requirements for vehicles and vehicle operators; pedestrian control; investigation of traffic accidents; traffic direction; traffic education; and, to a certain degree, traffic engineering.

5. *Juvenile activities*—the protection of dependent children, and the responsibility for handling juveniles who are the perpetrators of, or victims of, crime. Enforcement of the codes and statutes relating to juveniles; investigation, arrest, supervision or referral of juveniles who have been delinquent or criminal in behavior.

6. *Crime prevention activities*—involving the total community in a mutually supportive participatory effort to reduce and prevent crime. Working with all people and groups to curtail criminal opportunity and crime hazards (often mislabeled "Community Relations").

B. SPECIAL OPERATIONAL ACTIVITIES are those which are not common to all municipal agencies, but which have been assigned to the agency because it is the only executive arm of municipal government deployed on a twenty-four hour, city-wide basis, and are those activities which assist, in a peripheral manner, to accomplish the objectives of the agency.

1. *Ambulance and rescue activities*—consisting of special units for emergency services. Operation of ambulances for the rapid transportation of the injured, and operation of well-equipped emergency trucks are sometimes assigned to the police agency.
2. *Civil defense activities*—consisting of coordinating, training, and equipping departmental and auxiliary units for civil defense and disaster operations. Throughout the United States, the municipal police of the larger cities have been assigned major roles in this governmental activity.
3. *Animal regulation activities*—involving animal pound operations, licensing of dogs and cats, vaccination programs, and extermination of dangerous or stray animals.
4. *Youth service activities*—consisting, in communities, lacking adequate juvenile social, counseling, and recreational programs, in providing leadership for community youth. This activity varies from limited, voluntary, off-duty assistance to full-scale departmental units (often mislabeled "Community Relations").
5. *Guard service activities*—involving the assignment of police personnel to municipal government units handling large amounts of cash or valuable property.
6. *Licensing activities*—consisting, in some communities of registration, inspection, and enforcement of state and local licensing, ordinances, such as related to bicycles, certain businesses, and motor vehicles and their operators.
7. *Departmental reserve activities*—consisting of the deployment of a special unit whenever crime or traffic problems become excessive and tax the regular force beyond its capacity.
8. *Auxiliary volunteer reserve activities*—consisting in the recruitment, selection, training, and supervision of nonpaid, volunteer, citizen reserve or auxiliary units.

(It might be noted that this list of special operational activities could be greatly expanded, for in some areas, the police supervise probationers and parolees, register voters, assist in local census operations, examine prostitutes for venereal disease, give emergency relief or temporary lodging to the homeless or destitute, do sanitation inspections, or, in general, whatever odd tasks they are capable of performing.)

A somewhat humorous, albeit sad, example of such peripheral assignments is found in the following account:

Buren Grant, only policeman in Claremont, N.C., didn't mind too much when the town council required him to read water meters, check the town pumps, repair streets and haul gravel, but he called it quits when they wanted him to haul garbage and cut the town's grass in addition to his other jobs. Grant made $74.50 a week.[3]

II. **Staff Functions** are those which directly and primarily assist the administrative personnel in their tasks of organizing and managing the agency.

    A. PRIMARY STAFF SERVICES are those which most directly assist the administrators and supervisors, but which secondarily assist in making the work of line personnel more effective.

        1. *Personnel and training activities*—directed to the acquisition, preparation, motivation, and control of manpower needed to achieve departmental objectives. The selection of people is a primary task of this unit, and involves setting qualifications, recruiting candidates, screening and examining placement, probationary evaluation, and operating the promotional machinery. The determination of pay schedules and operation of position classification machinery often falls to this unit. Another primary task is the in-service training of recruit, senior officer, specialist, supervisor, and executive. The control of personnel through service rating processes, and by disciplinary activities, is also handled by such a unit. In general, that which relates to the safety, health, welfare and motivation of personnel, as well as to their competency and integrity, is the responsibility of such a unit.

        2. *Planning and research activities*—the conduct of advanced preparation for reorganization, for tactical problems, for general crime control strategy, for modernization of procedures, and for emergency operations. Evaluations of the legality and efficiency of current operations by systematic inquiry of a highly scientific nature is common to such units. The coordination of formalized policy and procedure, specific research into administrative and operational problem areas, and applications of statistical analysis and advanced public administration techniques are also assumed by such a unit.

        3. *Fiscal activities*—the processing of budget, payroll, accounting, and purchasing matters. In this unit, the budget estimates are coordinated, justified, and prepared for presentation. Audit of all funds, control of expenditures for personnel, equipment and

---

[3] *California Peace Officer*, March-April, 1963.

facilities, and the establishment of accountability are formalized and controlled.

4. *Public relations activities*—the planning of programs designed to gain and hold the good will and support of the general public. Such a unit often handles press relations, prepares announcements, bulletins and reports for the general public, conducts liaison with community organizations, sends representatives of the agency to address groups, prepares motion picture and photographic informational material, works with educational institutions, and, in general attempts to secure public support and co-operation (often mislabeled "Community Relations").

5. *Community relations activities*—that dialog and discussion which involves two-way communication with all individuals and groups in the community (popular, cooperative, supportive, and, as well, unpopular, negative, and rebellious) in order to develop meaningful public participation (at beat and precinct level) in police policy formulation, decision making, administration and operations (very rare).

6. *Civilian personnel activities*—directed to the utilization of non-sworn personnel within the agency. Recruits, screens, places, and supervises the clerks, typists, messengers, stenographers, secretaries and other civilian specialists.

B. Auxiliary Staff Services—are those which most directly assist the line personnel in the effective achievement of service objectives, but which secondarily assist the administrators and supervisors of the agency.

1. *Crime laboratory (criminalistics) activities*—the provision of scientific and technical personnel and facilities for the analysis, identification, and comparison of physical evidence. Ordinarily these services provide assistance in fingerprint operations (searching, developing, photographing, lifting, identifying, classifying, and filing); offer advanced photographic service (developing, printing, and processing crime scene photographs, assisting in identification photography; providing specialized photography by motion picture, press, stereoscopic, and miniature cameras); do metallurgical, ballistics, and explosive examinations (guns, bullets, bombs, restorations of serial numbers); provide ultra-violet identifications and surveillances; handle the polygraph (truth detector) examination of suspects; apply modern techniques of microscopy, spectroscopy, serology, and chemistry to minute evidence such as fibres, hairs, blood, poison, textiles, stains, dust, dirt, and debris; provide chemical tests for intoxication and nar-

cotic addiction (drunkometer, intoximeter, alcometer, breath-
alyzer, nalline testing); apply plaster of paris and moulage techniques (tool-marks, tire-tracks, foot-prints); examine questioned
documents (for hand writing, type-writing and ink identification); and, in general, apply the knowledges and skills of the
natural and physical sciences to the solution of crime.

2. *Detention (jail) activities*—to provide for the detention of arrestees pending completion of investigation or trial, and for the
incarceration of prisoners sentenced by the municipal courts in
areas where city prisoners are not placed within county facilities.
Common detention responsibilities include arrangements for
searching, booking, fingerprinting, photographing, feeding, do-
miciling, and medical care. Facilities for communication, bail,
attorneys, visits, and recreational, welfare, religious, and rehabilitative services vary from jurisdiction to jurisdiction depending
on both policy and statute. Many larger municipal jails maintain modern classification and treatment programs, jail farms,
and careful segregation of prisoners as to age, sex, crime, and
criminal history.

Many police officials feel that large-scale correctional operations are inconsistent and improper as police activities, as prisoners receive a distorted impression of policing if policemen act
as punitive, as well as investigative officers. Furthermore, few
police officers are trained in correctional techniques so as to be
able to work effectively with inmates in a rehabilitative type of
program. Nonetheless, most police agencies must provide, at the
very least, for the temporary detention of arrestees who are
awaiting trial or the completion of an investigation.

3. *Records and identification activities*—the administration, organization, and management of departmental record processes. Ordinarily, these activities include maintenance of the master name
index, records files for complaint, investigation, arrest, property,
identification, location and type of crime, and follow-up reports.
Identification activities center around the processing of fingerprints, photographs, criminal history records, and often include
files on aliases, monikers, tattoos, and deformities. Field investigation reports are collated, and the modus operandi procedures
which may utilize highly sophisticated mechanized records are
implemented. Information of interest to other agencies is processed, along with information required by state and federal
crime reporting units, and the data on warrants issued and criminals at large disseminated.

4. *Communications activities*—the maintenance of technical equip-

ment and machinery for rapid transmission of information throughout the agency. The police radio network, teletype system, departmental intercommunication system, and messenger service are supervised by this unit. In addition, the provision of field equipment of a highly specialized nature, such as walkie-talkie, miniaturized receivers and transmitters, wire and tape recorders, and emergency field communication equipment of a portable nature is managed by the communications experts.

5. *Property and maintenance activities*—the general quartermaster activities. Departmental property is inventoried, inspected, replaced, and maintained. Thousands of individual items for operational police activities are supervised, and, as well, the maintenance of departmental facilities and equipment, and the purchase and issuance of supplies needed for the police task.

6. *Transportation activities*—providing for the movement of men and materiel. Solo-motorcycles, three-wheeled motorcycles, motor scooters, bicycles, automobiles, trucks, buses, and other specialized rolling gear must be maintained if the agency is to work effectively. In some agencies, boats and ships are maintained for harbor, lake, and port patrol, and aircraft and helicopters for traffic and emergency purposes are available.

C. INSPECTIONAL SERVICES are those which assist, in a very special and sensitive fashion, the administration of the agency, and which are primarily dedicated to the elimination of graft, corruption, and organized crime.

1. *Inspection activities*—involving the routine examination of departmental personnel, facilities, and equipment. This unit follows-up on established policies and procedures to assure that there is full and complete compliance. It detects weaknesses in the organization in their early stages and recommends corrective action.

2. *Intelligence activities*—directed to the collection, collation, and application of information relating to those members of organized-crime who direct, finance, operate, and profit from large-scale gambling, narcotic, prostitution, extortion, liquor law violations, and other forms of racketeering. In many agencies, this unit also has the responsibility for the collection, collation, and referral of information relating to those individuals (and groups) that are continuously found to be in the center of labor-management disputes, minority group disturbances, and political picketing, and whose conception of the common good seems to be

manipulated by criteria other than the Constitution and Bill of Rights. The authors would not be surprised to see a substantial increase in intelligence energy directed to the area of "Upperworld" or "White Collar" Criminals.

3. *Internal affairs activities*—involving the special investigation of complaints relating to departmental services and individual personnel. Such a unit controls the investigation of all complaints, whether made in person, by telephone, or by letter, and whether identified or anonymous, and, when necessary, takes action leading to departmental discipline, or dismissal, arrest, prosecution and imprisonment of personnel guilty of misfeasance, malfeasance, or nonfeasance.

4. *Departmental vice activities*—consisting, in large agencies which have several geographical districts or divisions or precincts or stations, of a central vice unit empowered to investigate vice offenses throughout the jurisdiction. Such a unit, if energetic and incorruptible, makes it difficult, dangerous or impossible for the geographical district vice units, or their personnel, to offer immunity or protection to vice offenders.

Thus, one can easily conclude, the effective administration of a municipal police agency, whether it be one that employs 26 or 26,000 men, is no easy task, and requires the utmost of wisdom and learning from all its people in order to achieve its purposes.

In categorizing municipal police operations, some authorities have made a distinction between a "generalized" and a "specialized" operation. Such a distinction relates directly to the degree of specialization expected of the line officers—those who are immediately and directly performing the work of the agency.

It is highly recommended, where the capacities of the personnel are high, to operate in a generalized manner. The man of high capacity can be trained to do general patrol work, traffic work, preliminary and advanced investigation, vice and juvenile work, and can be assigned with great flexibility. But salaries must be increased, and training intensified, if the generalist officer is to be produced in any quantity.

Large agencies will, naturally enough, need a greater proportion of specialist personnel, for the amount of specialized work to be done is ample. Smaller agencies, for the most part, can utilize the generalist to a far greater degree, and with ultimate savings. A well-trained generalist can, in an eight-hour day, in many agencies, out-produce the specialist who limits his attention to one specific police activity. A well-selected generalist can, given the proper experience, prove to be the better police administrator, for his perspective is broad. Any overemphasis of specialization endangers development of a mutual interdependence which binds all personnel into one common effort.

POLICING IN THE COUNTIES

The County Sheriff. The duties of the county sheriff vary with the county. He may be sheriff, coroner, assessor, tax collector, public administrator, overseer of highways and bridges, custodian of the county treasury, keeper of the county jail, court attendant, executor of criminal and civil process, major law enforcement officer, or executioner.

There are 1,252 sheriff agencies with 49,484 employees serving a population of 37,178,000.

In most counties, he must be twenty-one years of age, a citizen, and a registered voter or on the tax rolls. No physical, educational, or moral qualifications are demanded. No knowledge of law or law enforcement is necessary.

In most counties, he is an elected official, and serves for two, three, or four years. The fact that he is elected, and for but a short period of time, greatly inhibits the development of this office. It has often been suggested that the office be made appointive, and career personnel installed, but the needed change has not yet been made.

His income, in most areas, depends upon fees, the bulk of which come from the service of court orders and from the management of the county jail. For every writ served, he receives a fee; for every prisoner in the county jail, he receives a stipulated amount of money per meal per prisoner, and often he is allowed to keep the difference between what he spends for food and what he receives. Very often, food and lodging for himself and his family, mileage allowances, and interest on cash balances entrusted to his care, are provided him.

Ordinarily, he can deputize anyone that he cares to as a regular deputy, special deputy, auxiliary deputy, or honorary deputy. Civil service for the sheriff's office is extremely rare, and the merit system is not often present.

He attends the superior court or circuit courts of the county (highest trial courts with general jurisdiction), acts as court crier, and enforces court orders.

He often provides law enforcement services to the county, and in the larger metropolitan areas, his police activities may be quite extensive with traffic, patrol, juvenile, vice, and investigative units providing general police service. In practice, he operates freely in the unincorporated territories of the county, sometimes works on a contract basis for smaller cities, and sometimes works in conjunction with municipal police agencies.

The role of the American Sheriff will become increasingly involved in any consideration of a solution to the complex crime problem facing local communities in these United States.

The growth of metropolitan areas has forced a reconsideration of the concept of "local control," and it is high time. As American frontiers opened up, our sheriff was called upon to perform yeoman service, for the "local community" encompassed many miles of jurisdiction. With urban development, little towns became little cities, and "local" reduced itself to city boundaries—and the sheriff-lawman was replaced by town marshal, constable or policeman in the incorporated areas. But today, those little towns and cities have multiplied themselves like growing cells, and any cluster of towns and cities must truly be considered as one local area. One would indeed be myopic not to understand that the problems of crime, congestion, and social disorganization affect wide areas and do not neatly confine themselves to municipal boundaries.

Many of these local areas have, today, a shamefully wasteful number of separate law enforcement units. In the State of New York, there are over 3,600 separate state and local units of criminal justice; in Cook County, Illinois, there are over 100 separate law enforcement units. Some form of consolidation, complete or partial, is well in order. The time has come— no, it has long been time—to reduce the number of units of law enforcement at the local level, for the American taxpayer has far too long borne the burden of overlapping and duplicated police services. We do not suggest a single national police, nor even a single state constabulary, for the strength of our democracy lies in healthy local government operations. We do suggest that dozens of crime labs, communications systems, records bureaus, training facilities, detention centers, purchasing systems, transportation operations, patrol, investigative, intelligence, juvenile, vice, ambulance, civil defense, animal regulation, licensing and reserve activities duplicate the work of like units within relatively small areas and are a frightful burden for our citizenry to maintain.

What will be the role of office of sheriff in the years to come? Some observers would point to those offices of sheriff in the United States which have withdrawn from the policing function—and suggest that the office of sheriff, in its present form, be abolished. They would have the sheriff turn over policing responsibilities to state police or county constabularies, and court and jail functions to clerks of the courts. Other observers would point to patterns, such as in Los Angeles County, and note that the office of sheriff not only services the courts, carries out civil process, maintains correctional facilities, and polices unincorporated areas—but also polices twenty-nine incorporated cities (40 per cent of all incorporated cities in the county) under contract, offers central training and technical services, and maintains central county-wide indexes of juveniles, bogus checks, and warrants. Which path will the American sheriff select? The path of withdrawal and abdication? Or the path of involvement and development? This is a key decision which must be made soon.

The American sheriff is in a unique position—if he is willing to accept the challenges of this day and age. The American sheriff does not have to be a "weak sister," surrendering his authority and power at the slightest challenge, but can well be an energetic force for good, strengthening his authority and power, developing his facilities, adding to his equipment, enlarging his personnel—*and offering his office as a locus for consolidation of area-wide law enforcement services.*

When we consider the three major operations in the administration of criminal justice—we find the office of sheriff with close ties to the policing function, to the judicial function, and to the correctional function.

Because he operates, not only in the policing area, but also with the courts, and in the correctional field, his attitudes and philosophy are apt to be more broad and balanced, and his actions more responsive and responsible than the attitudes and actions of more narrow, rigid, naive and unsophisticated specialists in crime repression or rehabilitation.

We are suggesting that the American sheriff has a unique opportunity —if he grasps it—to set the standards, mold the pace, and point the direction of motivated, intelligent, professional service in the administration of criminal justice. Because of his elected status, he will be far less likely to ignore the rights and privileges of the citizen (assuming that the citizens he serves have access to the ballot). Because of his close connection with the courts, he will be far less likely to sneer and scoff at the responsibility of the courts to enforce the Constitution and Bill of Rights. Because of his work in corrections, he will be far less likely to mock and deride the need for crime prevention and rehabilitation services. He can, if he wishes, set an example for all local law enforcement and for all the community in terms of cooperation, understanding, participation, communication and consultation—for he knows of the responsibilities of the police, prosecutor, courts, probation officers, correctional specialists, and parole officers. He will not become so emotionally involved in crime repression that he sees only arrest and conviction and punishment as important. He will not become so emotionally involved in criminal rehabilitation that he sees only counseling and treatment of anti-social individuals as important. His can be a balanced view.

If the sheriff is to rise to the moment, he must act in the following areas:

1. Selection procedures must be improved. The American sheriff is often criticized for lack of motivation and skillful personnel. Such criticism

is, in some cases, entirely unjustified—but, in some cases, ample evidence supports the charge. Men of character, capacity, and ability must be energetically recruited, and the screening program must allow entrance only to "the best."

2. Training programs must be upgraded. Recruit, refresher, supervisory, technical and executive programs must prepare the deputy for today's problems and utilize today's knowledge. Close relationships with colleges and universities must be developed—in order to tap their resources and challenge their capacity to assist. Training programs must be so bold and thorough and so effective that other law enforcement units beg room for their people, or copy the format.

3. Legal procedures must be strengthened. The sheriff must work with local and state legislators to revise statutes and prepare new law to provide for effective service. The sheriff must move for changes in the state constitution which will allow the sheriff to have a six-year term of office, with right to succession, while at the same time elevating the qualifications for sheriff—by requiring possession of a baccalaureate degree in police science or a law degree, coupled with law enforcement administrative experience of at least five years in a professional agency.

4. Effective planning and research must be undertaken. Administrative and operational policy and procedure must be audited to insure that the work of the sheriff's office is efficient, legal, moral, and compassionate. Study is needed to determine what kinds of consolidated services might be considered, agreed upon, and implemented. Total service under contract? Central services to be made available by the sheriff? Shared services between agencies?

5. Central records depositories must be developed. Centralized identification and intelligence data is a necessity today. Electronic Data Processing (EDP) may be needed for county-wide effectiveness. Massive central files or data banks, in the near future, will serve as repositories of facts from a variety of units to service all users who will interface with the system using simple transmission and receiving devices through existing phone lines. Today, we obtain fingerprint information and criminal histories, but tomorrow we will have facsimile transmission, rapid dissemination of operational data, and computerized tactical decisions. The sheriff is in an ideal position to service the country in this fashion, and to work closely with future tie-ins to state-wide and federal systems.

6. An example of professional dedication must be set. If changes are to come, they must come from the top—and that means that the top must do more than shuffle papers and scowl. Any law enforcement administrator "sets the tone" of the agency. If he is arrogant, narrow, rigid, insecure, frightened, and authoritarian—the agency will reflect his shortcomings by

poor morale, bad public relations, mechanical operations, high turnover, and continuing recruitment problems. If he is understanding, broad, open, confident, courageous, and democratic—the agency will reflect his strengths by high morale, good public relations, compassionate operations, long-term service, and excellent recruitment programs.

7. Public support and cooperation must be developed. This involves continuous communication and educational effort to eliminate public ignorance, apathy and hostility. The citizen must be helped to understand his stake in professional law enforcement and his personal responsibility to support—in dollars and in willing assistance—the sacred tasks of securing ordered liberty, community security, and personal liberty.

Other steps could be outlined, but these are the beginning steps to a new era in county law enforcement. Certainly sheriffs must eliminate all that is inefficient and wasteful; certainly sheriffs must wholeheartedly conduct the surgery to sever what is illegal and immoral; and certainly sheriffs must strive to rid their agencies of any cold and mechanical attitudes toward the citizen.

But, most important of all, the sheriff must accept his responsibility as chief law enforcement officer of the county—as he is designated in our state constitutions. If he does not assume his proper role, the office of sheriff will continue to diminish in importance and usefulness and will ultimately be replaced by state or district units of greater effectiveness.

The County Constable. There are many separate and distinct police units built around the office of constable. Like the sheriff, for the most part, he is elected and serves for a short period of time, one, two, three, or four years. Qualifications are minimal: in most counties he must be twenty-one years of age, a citizen, and a registered voter or on the tax rolls.

The duties of the constable, like those of the sheriff, vary with the county. He may be a minor law enforcement officer, executor of civil process for the local justice court, attendant to that court, tax collector, poundkeeper, or issuer of election notices.

His income, in most areas, depends upon fees, and because his duties are relatively limited, he usually has some other occupation, and is almost never found to be a full-time public officer. Like the sheriff, the elected constable can appoint deputies to assist him.

Whereas the sheriff may receive a basic salary, fees connected with the service of process, the difference between the actual cost and the lawful allowance for feeding prisoners, food and lodging for himself and his family, mileage allowances, and interest on cash balances entrusted to his care—income which may exceed that of the county judiciary, the compensation of the constable for occasional services is usually but a fraction of his private income, and makes it difficult to obtain career-minded people for the office.

Village, Town, Township and Borough Police. The county sheriff and county constable generally service the rural unincorporated areas of the county and occasionally, extend services to incorporated areas in the county through request or by contract.

The smaller communities—towns, villages, townships, and boroughs—have a variety of law enforcement personnel designated as constables, marshals, or policemen. With the rapid growth of the suburban areas, and the extension of highway facilities throughout the states, crime and traffic control problems of increasing intensity are faced by many small growing communities.

There are 2,076 suburban police agencies with 81,724 employees serving a population of 48,291,000.

Part-time, elected, short-term, nonprofessional police are often succeeded by full-time, selected career-minded progressive police who bring with them the advanced methods of crime and traffic control.

In some communities, the marshal has become the officer of the municipal justice courts, serving process and attending the court.

The fee system, utilized by the smaller, more quiet towns and villages, is often replaced by salary systems as the police service develops. In other areas, not willing to devote public moneys for the development of law enforcement services, the state police or county sheriff is utilized for any serious crime or traffic problem, while the local officer merely acts as watchman or traffic control officer for the local school.

The philosophy of local autonomy which asserts the independence of local governmental units very often inhibits the rapid development of effective police services in the smaller communities. Fearing prejudice or neglect by police who are not immediate neighbors, these communities often cling to obsolete law enforcement institutions and seem unwilling to pay the price for anything even remotely resembling a professional level of police service.

Special Function Units. In many counties of the United States, there appear units of law enforcement which have special functions—such as harbor police, bridge police, freeway police, tunnel police, park police—each assigned the responsibility of policing within a very limited jurisdictional area.

WOMEN POLICE

Most women working in law enforcement agencies are found at the local level—in municipal and county agencies of police, and probation, corrections, and parole assignments.

Anyone who enters a modern police building will observe many female employees. Some women are employed in a "civilian" category, doing clerical, typing, filing, dispatching, and other like tasks. If one looks about the detention area, he may see the police "matron" as she maintains custody of female prisoners and small children waiting for transfer to other facilities. In the operating divisions, particularly the juvenile and detective areas, the sworn "policewoman" can be found. She may be working in the detective bureau with missing persons or shoplifting details. She may be working in the juvenile bureau doing day investigations or evening patrol work. The sworn "policewoman" is an asset to the modern agency; she is skilled in the interview and interrogation of female victims and suspects; she is capable of dealing, with firm kindness, with the female arrestee—doing searches of the person, when probable cause justifies, that would be most difficult and embarrassing to the male officer. Whenever an undercover assignment necessitates the use of female personnel, the American policewoman is allowed to volunteer. Many a thief, or other type of molester, has been rudely surprised to find that the young woman he has approached is a police officer with full authority and power—and ability!

In the community, one can observe women working as crossing guards, or as "meter maids," attaching overtime parking tickets to vehicles whose owners do not obey the parking laws.

Women serve the courts by acting as probation officers, preparing presentence investigation reports, and supervising women and children who have been allowed the privilege of a suspended conditional sentence. Women serve in correctional institutions as security officers, counselors, therapists, teachers, assisting in the reform and rehabilitation of sentenced prisoners. As parole officers, women supervise the conduct of those who have been released prior to the expiration of their sentences, assisting them to adjust to community life, and enforcing the conditions of parole.

In many private enterprises, women work in the security departments, helping to reduce inventory shrinkage, discourage employee dishonesty, and eliminate shoplifting.

For the young woman who is considering a law enforcement career, there are many varieties of service. Turnover is relatively high, due to the fact that female employees often leave work to enter marriage, or if married, leave work to care for a new baby.

The five recent appointments of women to the United States Secret Service, and the two appointments of women to the Post Office Service as Postal Inspectors, indicate change. Women are now deployed on regular *patrol* beats in Peoria, Illinois, Indianapolis, Indiana, New York City and Miami, Florida. Washington, D.C., is recruiting an experimental patrol force of some one hundred women.

Women have always been in the forefront of the struggle to secure freedom and justice in this country. (History, for the most part, is written by men, so it is understandable, perhaps, that the role of women, in moving society from savagery to civilization, is under-reported!)

In the area of criminal justice, and particularly in the area of law enforcement, women have led in the fight to obtain fair play and due process. In the 1920's Jane Addams (of Hull House, Chicago) took an active advocate role in protecting and assisting Mexicans in dealing with over-aggressive police.[4]

The monumental expose of police deficiency that is popularly known as the Wickersham Report, was directed, in 1931, by a social worker— Edith Abbott, Dean of the Graduate School of Social Service Administration of the University of Chicago.[5]

You all know about the brave nuns of the Roman Catholic Church and their part following the explosion of Vatican II. The nuns were in the picket lines of Chicago and Selma far before the curates and pastors, and they were the first to speak up to pastors and bishops without fear, and they were the first to go to the streets with the poor and dispossessed and oppressed. Many a "fighting priest" got his first glimpse of a simple soul telling the king that he was naked in the example of an honest nun.[6]

The Los Angeles *Times* of April, 1972, tells us of a female security officer at Los Angeles Trade Technical College speaking the truth about the bugging and the dossiers of the campus police while the male officer involved was "taking the fifth" and refusing to testify.[7]

It would seem that the American policewoman, today, has a great opportunity to *lead* her male colleagues toward a more humane and compassionate policing, and away from an oppressive and mechanical mercenary role, by bravely speaking out when frightened men cower and tremble.

Fifty years ago, the woman in police work was a rarity. Today, as modern policing gives ever more attention to the relevancy of its efforts, the woman is much more in evidence. The authors of this text would not at all be surprised to see the number of women in criminal justice *quadruple* in the next decade, and receive appointments to *all* ranks and to *all* assignments.

---

[4] National Commission on Law Observance and Enforcement (1931). *Report on Crime and the Foreign Born*, p. 18. U.S. Government Printing Office, Washington, D.C.

[5] *Ibid.*

[6] Any perusal of the *National Catholic Reporter, America, Commonweal, Christianity and Crisis, The Critic*, during the years 1955-1970 will provide ample documentation for the role of the American nun in the Roman Catholic reform and renewal movement.

[7] *Los Angeles Times*, April 28, 1972.

UNORTHODOX LOCAL POLICE

Auxiliary, Reserve, Honorary Police or Deputies. In addition to the municipal, county, village, and special function police, there are a substantial number of persons who serve as auxiliary, reserve, or honorary policemen or deputy sheriffs.

These, usually, are non-paid volunteers, and are very often a "police headache." Civil defense activities, and manpower shortages, have brought many of these people into the periphery of the police service, yet, very often they may be poorly screened, poorly trained, and unreliable. Some join because of patriotism, but others join for "thrills," a "night out," to have an excuse for wearing a police uniform, or carrying a pistol, or for the "benefit" derived from carrying an identification card near their operator's license.

Most police administrators would prefer to rely upon regular, paid, full-time officers to accomplish the basic police tasks, yet, in grave emergencies involving natural or man-made disasters, the auxiliary or reserve or honorary police can be helpful.

Nonetheless, it is critically important that all such auxiliary, reserve, honorary non-paid police be carefully screened by any municipal or county agency capable of granting authority and power that accompanies a badge and identification card. Whether the holder is a patriotic citizen genuinely interested in civil defense, small-time politician with greedy interest in the honorary deputy position, or semi-neurotic police "buff," the requirements should be the same:

1. A thorough background investigation should be made, including fingerprinting and checks with local, state, and federal identification units, before the authority and power of a peace officer be granted.
2. Minimum training should be required, and should include weapons safety, laws of arrest, search and seizure, and pertinent federal, state, county, and municipal statutes, codes, and ordinances.
3. Hat pieces, badges, uniforms, identification cards, and vehicular equipment should be distinctively and conspicuously different from that of the regular full-time governmental units.

Integrated Police-Fire Services. There are, at present, seventy-three known municipalities in the United States and Canada which have complete or partial consolidation of police-fire activities. The Province of Quebec, Canada, has twenty-seven, the State of Michigan has fourteen, and the State of Illinois has eight.

This concept calls for the integration (or unification or consolidation) of duties. Some communities have a single Department of Public Safety, manned by public safety officers—PSOs—who perform both police and fire duties. Other cities have a *Director of Public Safety* with separate police and fire services under his direction. And other cities have separate agencies, with separate administration, but have *consolidated common services*.

The largest city with an integrated police-fire operation is Dearborn, Michigan (population 112,000). Ordinarily, population size runs between 10,000 and 25,000.

Because the term *"integration"* has become associated with the civil rights struggle, indicating interpersonal and intergroup activities of both colored and colorless persons, some agencies have found the term *"consolidated* police-fire services" less confusing.

The authors believe that the effectiveness of integrated or consolidated services depends, largely, upon the nature and extent of police and fire hazards, upon the quality and quantity of personnel, equipment, and facilities, and upon community demands upon police and fire services. Thus, they would neither universally recommend, nor categorically reject, the principle of integration or consolidation of police-fire services.

Experience seems to indicate that the operation works best in highly residential suburbs in large metropolitan areas, providing lower per unit costs, as well as better working conditions and higher pay.

We shall now consider policing in larger geographical areas.

TOPICS FOR DISCUSSION

1. Which are the largest and smallest police departments in this state?
2. What would seem to be the future role of the office of sheriff in this county?
3. What is the future for the woman who thinks of a career in law enforcement in this state?
4. What is the future role of the auxiliary, honorary, reserve police or deputies in this state? What is their present position?
5. Where is the location of the nearest example of "consolidated" police-fire services in this state?

Chapter XII

PRIVATE AGENCIES—STATE AGENCIES

Between the many agencies of law enforcement operating at the local level, and the many agencies operating at the federal level, are many private agencies and state agencies of law enforcement. They are considered in the same chapter because they resemble each other in one unique aspect: neither operates in such limited geographical jurisdictional areas as do the local agencies.

PRIVATE AGENCIES

There are thousands of people working in a variety of private (nongovernmental) law enforcement units. Some of these people perform very limited law enforcement duties—such as do doorkeepers and watchmen assigned to large scale housing and industrial facilities. Others operate in highly specialized fields—such as arson investigation. Nonetheless, these people are truly involved in the overall protective services of our nation and very often work closely with the formal governmental units of law enforcement.

Armored Car Agencies. Some of the private units of protection specialize in guarding cash, securities, and valuables, and offer armed escort for the shipment or transportation of gold, payrolls, and bank deposits, jewelry, and objets d'art. One of the oldest of such agencies is *Brinks, Inc.*, established in 1889.

Private Detective Agencies. Thousands of individuals (principals) and small firms offer private investigative services to private citizens, to attorneys, and to industrial and commercial enterprises. Private persons who desire personal service in the investigation of members of their family, family servants or potential family members, can hire investigations as extensive as time and purse will allow. Attorneys who desire information relative to clients, witnesses, suspects, jurors, or opponents to their cause, can and do utilize the private investigator to a great degree. Industrial and commercial leaders who desire information relative to competitors, potential executives and employees, manufacturing information which is not publicly available, or credit information, utilize the private investigative service to a larger extent than most people realize. One of the oldest of such agencies is the *Pinkerton Agency*, established in 1850.

Protective Alarm Agencies. Many homes and commercial facilities utilize a wide variety of alarm services. Burglar alarms, safe alarms, entrance alarms, boiler alarms, manufacturing process alarms, robbery alarms, fire alarms, and other specialized alarms, often technically sophisticated, are operated by many agencies throughout the United States. One of the best known is the *American District Telegraph Company*. Quite often, these alarm systems are connected to the police agency communication center, which allows prompt notice of robbery or burglary to field units. At times, a loud bell or siren is set to ring at the scene, while in many other cases, the notification is made silently.

Special Patrol Service Agencies. Some citizens desire more specialized protection, and more personalized attention, than the governmental agencies can provide. Private patrol agencies will provide special guards for weddings and parties, personnel for cafes and theatres and places of public recreation or entertainment, special motorcycle escorts for funeral corteges, and special patrol of house and grounds. Very often, they will run errands and do shopping favors for their clients as a regular part of their service.

Retail Security Units. Large merchandising establishments have found it beneficial to set up regular security units to lessen unnecessary inventory shrinkage, to screen employees, to investigate cases of shoplifting, to evaluate liability claims, and to maintain order and safety within the establishment.

Insurance Investigation Units. Most of the large insurance companies handling liability insurance have well-trained investigative personnel, who evaluate claims for possible fraud, establish facts in liability cases, and interview claimants. One of the best known private agencies of this nature is the *Mutual Loss Research Bureau* of Chicago, which specializes in arson investigation.

Plant Protection Units. Industrial concerns have found it necessary to provide for plant security and very often have formed individual plant forces rather than contracting for such services. The watchmen in many of these units are superannuated employees with very limited duties assigned to them—punching a time clock and watching for fires. In a substantial number of companies, however, plant protection services are highly sophisticated, and often include accident prevention and investigation, complicated control of traffic and pedestrian movement, escort of vendors and visitors, as well as basic law enforcement within the plant.

Industrial Security Units. Companies engaging in war contract work for the government are obliged to meet very stringent regulations relating to the security of the facility, its manufacturing processes, its personnel, and all classified material utilized. Physical security at these installations is extensive, including fences, lighting systems, alarm systems, isolation of restricted areas, and constant surveillance for security hazards and violations. Personnel security includes the processing and clearance of employees, pass and badge systems, lock and key systems, special procedures for handling of vehicles, visitors, vendors, incoming and outgoing packages and matériel, and searches for contraband. The security of classified information includes attention to the mechanics of record security, the transportation, utilization, and destruction of classified material, and investigations of violations. Some of the most advanced techniques of private law enforcement operations are found at this type of installation. (Note: There is some ambiguity in the use of the term "industrial security." Some use it to refer exclusively to the work involved in war-contract operations; others use it broadly to include fire protection, accident prevention, traffic control, personnel investigations, and the entire function of protecting life and property within a commercial enterprise.)

Polygraph Examiner Services. Private examiners, agencies made up of several examiners, and industry employed examiners, utilize the polygraph, or "truth detector." These examiners screen applicants for employment by reviewing their applications with the polygraph, often do regular and periodic examinations of employees who are in constant contact with cash or who are in a position to steal or embezzle with relative ease, and provide for special examinations for employees suspected of dishonesty.

Whether or not the polygraph technique is a valid procedure is a controversial question. Students who wish more information should obtain, from the Superintendent of Documents, U.S. Government Printing Office, Washington, D.C., copies of the 1964 hearings before a subcommittee of the Committee on Government Operations, House of Representatives, entitled, "Use of Polygraphs as 'Lie Detectors' by the Federal Government."

The Tenth Report of the Committee on Government Operations is rather negative in its conclusions:

> There is no "lie detector," neither machine nor human. People have been deceived by a myth that a metal box in the hands of an investigator can detect either truth or falsehood. . . .
>
> The polygraph machine is not a "lie detector," nor does the operator who interprets the graphs detect "lies." The machine records physical responses which may or may not be connected with emotional reaction—and that reaction may or may not be related to guilt or innocence. Many, many physical and psychological factors make it possible for an individual to "beat" the polygraph without detection by the machine or its operator. . . .

Polygraph testing is extensive and growing in the Federal Government. All too often it is used on trivial matters. This extensive reliance on the polygraph stems, partly, from lax administrative controls over investigators. . . .

The Department of Defense is the only Federal agency which has taken a small forward step to remove some of the objectionable procedures surrounding polygraph examinations. No other Government agency warns individuals about two-way mirrors and hidden microphones used while an individual's innermost secrets are disclosed in polygraph examinations. . . .

The polygraph technique forces an individual to incriminate himself and confess to past actions which are not pertinent to the current investigation. He must dredge up his past so he can approach the polygraph machine with an untroubled soul. The polygraph operator and his superiors then decide whether to refer derogatory information to other agencies or officials. . . .

As long as a notation is made in any official file that an individual refused to take a polygraph test, the examination is in no way "voluntary." The refusal too often is taken as a presumption of guilt; the file notation which follows an individual throughout his career often casts a dark shadow on his future. . . .

Federal investigators have given thousands upon thousands of polygraph tests, yet there has been no attempt to determine the validity of the procedure and no attempt to find out whether the polygraph operator really can detect falsehoods. No statistical proof has been compiled despite thousands of cases; no scientific proof has been produced despite thousands of opportunities. . . .

Students of law enforcement who are capable of conducting precise and thorough research, and who are interested in this field, could be of assistance to the vocation by assisting in a determination of the validity of the polygraph technique. (See Burkey, Lee M. (1965). "The Case Against the Polygraph." *American Bar Association Journal,* 51:855-857.)

Although the people who work in these private agencies of law enforcement are not members of governmental agencies, and are paid by private funds, they are, very often, given police authority and power. By deputizing as special deputy sheriffs, or by appointment as special officers of the municipal police agency, they receive the authority and power of a peace officer. Thus it is critically important for all such private law enforcement personnel to be rigidly screened by an agency of municipal or county law enforcement that can grant such authority and power.

As a matter of policy, just as in the case of auxiliary, reserve, or honorary non-paid police, it should be required of all private law enforcement personnel that:

1. A thorough background investigation be made before the authority and power of a special peace officer or special deputy be granted, including fingerprinting and checks with local, state, and federal identification units.
2. Minimum training be required, which includes weapons safety, laws of arrest, search, and seizure, and pertinent federal, state, county, and municipal statutes, codes, and ordinances.

3. Hat pieces, badges, uniforms, identification cards, and vehicular equipment be distinctively and conspicuously different from that of the regular governmental units of law enforcement.

STATE AGENCIES

The number and importance of law enforcement agencies at the state level are frequently overlooked. Some of these units have general police power, others are limited in function, and still others have but formalized regulatory duties. There are forty-nine states which employ some 54,754 persons in state police and highway patrol organizations.

The development of state law enforcement units has been spurred by such factors as technological advances, and recognition of the fact that a completely decentralized police operation is severely handicapped when dealing with crime and traffic problems that span hundreds of miles across scores of local jurisdictions.

Because many of these state agencies of law enforcement have been developed since the turn of the century, they have been able, very often, to avoid some of the less desirable customs and traditions of county and urban law enforcement.

State Police. State police agencies are of two types. Some, like the Michigan State Police, are clothed with general police powers, and enforce all state laws. Others, like the California Highway Patrol, specialize in the protection of the motorist, and direct most of their attention to enforcement of laws which govern the operation of vehicles upon the public highways.

The development of state police agencies has not resulted in a state central law enforcement unit which supplants the police of the counties, cities, towns and villages.

Each state police unit has developed in its own way, with no common assignment of duty. In some states, the state police are designated as fire, fish, and game wardens; in other states, they are required to execute civil process in actions to which the state is a party; in other states they are required to act as court attendants for Justices of the Peace on Indian Reservations; and in other states they conduct examinations for vehicle operator licenses.

Identification Units. State clearinghouses of identification are sometimes operated by the state police, as in Michigan, or are separate from the state police, as in California. These units, in varying degree, compile and analyze criminal statistics, maintain fingerprint files, and central records files, and cooperate with local law enforcement units in the dissemination of information of assistance to investigation and enforcement activity.

Criminalistics Units. The crime laboratory, at the state level, available to local law enforcement, is now a common device. Servicing state agencies, and cities and counties outside of the metropolitan areas (where many crime laboratories are usually available), the laboratory will examine, identify, and compare all types of physical evidence, provide expert testimony for prosecution, and scientifically examine crime scenes in major cases. Some state units are mobile, and travel throughout the state upon request.

Investigation Units. Various divisions, departments, or bureaus of investigation are found at the state level, conducting practically every type of civil and criminal investigation for the various state departments, commissions, agencies, and bureaus, the executive officers of the state, and often for local law enforcement agencies.

Specialized investigatory units are found at the state level, such as the narcotic units of some states, which not only cooperate and conduct mutual operations with local law enforcement units, but also with the Federal Bureau of Narcotics and Dangerous Drugs, the Bureau of Customs, the United Statees Coast Guard, and the FBI.

Liquor Control Boards and Commissions. Every state has some form of board or commission charged with licensing and regulating the alcoholic beverage industry, and assessing and collecting various revenues from the sale of alcoholic beverages. Investigative and enforcement work involves the investigation of persons who are applying for licenses, and enforcement of the liquor control acts of the state which prohibit or regulate the sale, use, possession, adulteration, dilution, misbranding or mislabeling of alcoholic beverages. These units work closely with the local law enforcement agencies, and with the Alcohol and Tobacco Tax Division of the Internal Revenue Service.

Conservation Agencies. Every state has some units of law enforcement to protect and conserve natural resources. State park systems often utilize their own law enforcement units to protect the parks, historical landmarks, beaches, hiking and riding trails, and recreational areas. State Foresters are often utilized to protect the timber and watershed areas of the state, to prevent and suppress fires, and to protect the forests from insects and diseases. State Fish and Game Wardens are utilized to conserve and protect birds, animals, and fish, to license anglers and hunters, and to enforce the fish and game codes of the state.

Health and Safety Units. The health and safety codes of the various states often provide for a state Fire Marshal, responsible for the elimination of fire hazards, investigation of fires, enforcement of fire and panic safety regulations, development of fire prevention programs, establishment of safety requirements, issuance of fire clearances and licenses to institutions. He and his deputies work closely with local fire officials in the enforcement of fire laws, ordinances and regulations.

Public Health units often have the responsibility of investigation and enforcement of state statutes relating to communicable diseases, licensing of hospitals, adulteration of food and drugs, pollution of public water, and public sanitation.

State Militia, or National Guard Units. No state has been content to remain without troops, even though well organized police organizations are available to the state. The second Amendment to the Constitution provides that "A well regulated militia, being necessary to the security of a free state, the right of the people to keep and bear arms, shall not be infringed."

If violent conditions arise—such as war, insurrection, rebellion, invasion, tumult, riot, breach of peace, public calamity, or major catastrophe, or resistance to the laws of the state or of the United States—and they are of such a nature that they cannot be contained by the ordinary governmental law enforcement units, the militia may be utilized.

The military unit is the initial force and ultimate power of government: initial, because it is the force that overcomes the enemy and establishes the government in the beginning; ultimate, as the governing authority when all other authority and power are ineffective to protect the state against disaster.

"Martial law," or "martial rule," is the exercise of the power which resides in the executive branch of the government to preserve order and insure the public safety in times of emergency, when other branches of the government are unable to function. Martial law is a law of necessity to be prescribed and administered by the executive power. Its object, the preservation of public safety and good order, defines its scope, which varies with the circumstances and necessities of the immediate situation.

Miscellaneous State Law Enforcement Agencies. Just as in the case of the federal law enforcement structure, which we will shortly examine, there exists a wide variety of peripheral law enforcement units.

Investigatory and enforcement units of state agricultural, finance, commerce, employment, insurance, investment, mental hygiene, motor vehicle, civil service, industrial relations, and marketing departments conduct a wide variety of enforcement functions of a civil and criminal nature.

Many states have turf commissions or horse racing boards which control horse racing and wagering at major and fair race tracks, and which inspect, investigate, and enforce state laws pertaining thereto.

All states have processes for the control, examination, licensing, inspection and investigation of members of various professions and occupations —such as accountants, architects, barbers, chiropractors, engineers, contractors, cosmetologists, dentists, detectives, doctors, lawyers, nurses, optometrists, osteopaths, pharmacists, shorthand reporters, social workers, teachers, veterinarians—*but*, as yet, do *not* examine, license, and investigate law enforcement officers working for state, county, and local governments, except in New York, where a beginning has been made. That is an interesting speculative matter for very thoughtful student of law enforcement and for every citizen.

One of the finest aspects of state law enforcement is the contribution made to the technical efficiency of state-wide law enforcement. The air patrols of state agencies are most helpful in the pursuit of fugitives, location of lost citizens, and in the study and control of traffic. The radio and teletype networks of state police not only assist them in terms of internal efficiency, but also the small local forces which often participate in their use. The criminalistics resources of state units have made it possible for many small local units of law enforcement to utilize the finest and most modern technical equipment in the solution of crime. The records and identification services of the state law enforcement agencies have provided a spur to improved reporting and records practices and to the utilization of *modus operandi* methods by local agencies.

Conclusions. The development of state police agencies is in the embryonic stage. Many are undermanned—with a shortage of trained personnel. Many are underequipped—with a shortage of necessary facilities and equipment. Many are underchallenged—with the capacity to provide many additional services, but legislatively delimited. And many are underdeveloped—with a leadership reluctant to assume additional functions or with a governmental environment that is unprogressive.

Nonetheless, the fact remains that some of the most progressive police administration in the United States is to be found at the state level. As the crime and traffic problems outgrow the capacity of the smaller local jurisdictions, there will be an increase in the responsibilities given to state law enforcement units. As these responsibilities increase, there is every indication that the enlightened professional leadership of state law enforcement agencies will accept the challenge, plan and develop programs of action, and obtain the necessary support to implement them.

There are many indications of a trend toward a substantial expansion of the scope and functions of state law enforcement agencies over the next couple of decades, and with that expansion, ever more effective containment of the police problems of crime and traffic.

TOPICS FOR DISCUSSION

1. What are the primary examples of private agencies of law enforcement in this locale?
2. What are the powers of the state police in this state?
3. What is the state "clearinghouse of identification" called in this state? Where is it located?
4. What are the chances of control, examination, licensing or certification, inspection and investigation of members of the law enforcement services of this state—by this state?

Chapter XIII

FEDERAL AGENCIES

MOST LAW ENFORCEMENT AGENCIES of the federal government exercise very wide territorial authority, although their specific functions are delimited. Because many of the federal agencies grew very slowly, their relative importance has been modified with the years; because they vary between very strong enforcement duties and relatively minor inspections and investigations, there is uncertainty as to scope; and because some deal primarily with security matters, others with criminal matters, others with regulatory matters of a quasi-criminal-civil nature, and others with military matters, there is a great diversity of objectives.

Nonetheless, there are thousands of people working in some twenty major, and scores of minor, law enforcement or investigatory units of the federal government. These units are located in the Executive Office of the President, in the major federal departments, in the independent agencies, and in various minor boards, committees, and commissions. Students of law enforcement should be familiar with the major units of federal law enforcement, their placement within the federal structure of government, their objectives and major functions.

EXECUTIVE OFFICE OF THE PRESIDENT

The National Security Council was established by the National Security Act of 1947. Its function is to advise the President with respect to the integration of domestic, foreign, and military policies relating to the national security. Under the direction of the Council is the *Central Intelligence Agency.* This unit advises the National Security Council in matters concerning intelligence activities of governmental departments and agencies as relate to national security; makes recommendations for the coordination of such intelligence activities; correlates and evaluates intelligence; disseminates such intelligence; performs, for the benefit of existing intelligence agencies, such additional services as can be more efficiently accomplished centrally, and performs any other functions and duties relating to intelligence as the National Security Council may direct.

The *Special Action Office for Drug Abuse Prevention,* established in 1971, is responsible for planning and policy and establishes objectives and priorities for all federal drug abuse prevention functions—education, training, treatment, rehabilitation, or research.

DEPARTMENT OF THE TREASURY

The Assistant Secretary serves as the U.S. representative to the *International Criminal Police Organization* (INTERPOL) and since 1962 has operated the National Central Bureau (NCB) linking our agencies with those of 114 foreign countries. (See discussion page 395.)

The *Bureau of Customs*, created in 1927, acts to collect and protect the revenue; to prevent fraud and smuggling; and to regulate people, carriers, cargo, and mail into and out of the United States. Customs Service Special Agents work with other agencies to safeguard agriculture, business, health and consumer interests.

The *Internal Revenue Service* (IRS), created in 1862, administers and enforces the internal revenue laws. Special Agents from Intelligence Division and Internal Security Inspectors act to insure maximum collection of taxes due the government.

The *United States Secret Service*, created in 1862, protects the person of the President, his family, the President-elect, government officers in order of succession, major Presidential and Vice-Presidential candidates, former Presidents and their families, and visiting heads of foreign states. It also enforces laws relating to coins, currency, and securities of the United States and foreign governments. It supervises the *Executive Protective Service* (White House, offices, grounds) and the *Treasury Security Force* (Treasury buildings and vaults).

The *Bureau of Alcohol, Tobacco and Firearms* (AT & F), created in 1972, enforces laws relating to alcohol, tobacco, firearms and explosives.

The *Consolidated Federal Law Enforcement Training Center* (CFLETC), established in 1970, is an interagency training center serving 23 federal law enforcement agencies.

DEPARTMENT OF DEFENSE

Army. The Deputy Chief of Staff supervises the *Provost Marshal General*, who provides, supervises, and controls the security clearances of facilities, projects and individuals in industry requiring access to classified information or contracts; supervises military police, prisoner-of-war activities, matters of good order and discipline, movement of refugees and traffic, prevention and investigation of crime within the army, and the apprehension of deserters and those absent without leave. The PMG also supervises and controls the Military Police Board, the Criminal Investigation Laboratory, the First Criminal Investigation Detachment, the Enemy Prisoner of War Information Bureau, and provides operational services for the correctional and custodial function.

The *Assistant Chief of Staff, Intelligence*, plans, coordinates, and supervises the collection and evaluation of information and the production, maintenance, and dissemination of intelligence, pertaining to the war potential, topography, military forces, and military activities of foreign countries; monitors the procurement, training, and assignment of military intelligence personnel; advises on counterintelligence activities; supervises military mapping; and performs the army cryptologic functions. The *Judge Advocate General* supervises the system of military justice throughout the army.

Navy. Within the purview of the Chief of Naval Operations is the *Assistant Chief of Naval Operations (Intelligence), Director of Naval Intelligence.* The *Bureau of Naval Personnel* acts on questions of naval discipline, rewards for return of deserters, and punishments; comments on and recommends relative to general courts-martial and courts of inquiry involving the personnel of the Navy; and supervises and controls naval places of confinement and prisoners. The office of the *Judge Advocate General* administers the program of military justice for the naval establishment.

Marine Corps. The *Assistant Chief of Staff, G-2,* formulates plans and policies pertaining to intelligence, counterintelligence, electronics warfare, and security. The *Inspector General* is responsible for the conduct of inspections and investigations.

Air Force. The *Inspector General* is responsible for investigations of major crimes, violations of public trust, personnel loyalty, and counterintelligence. He establishes policies concerning security and exercises staff supervision over the *Security Police*, the confinement and rehabilitation of prisoners, and the maintenance of discipline and censorship. The *Judge Advocate General* exercises general supervision over the administration of military justice pertaining to the Air Force. The *Assistant Chief of Staff, Intelligence*, develops and implements USAF intelligence plans and policies and coordinates the collection and production of air intelligence.

Thus, the student can see that each military establishment assumes responsibility for intelligence operations, investigation of crime, maintenance of security bases, posts, and installations, and provides for its internal administration of justice including the operation of courts and penal establishments.

"Uniformed" patrol duty is accomplished by the *Military Police* of the Army, by the *Shore Patrol* of the Navy, and by the *Security Police* of the Air Force. "Plainclothes" investigations and intelligence functions are accomplished by the *Office of Naval Intelligence* of the Navy, the *Office of Special Investigations* of the Air Force, and the *Military Police Criminal Investigation Division* of the Army. Thus the MP, SP, ONI, OSI, and CID.

Within the *Department of Defense* itself, the *Assistant to the Secretary of Defense (Special Operations)* is the principal staff assistant to the Secretary of Defense in the functional fields of intelligence, counterintelligence, communications security, Central Intelligence Agency relationship and special operations, and psychological warfare operations, and there are two units worthy of mention: The *National Security Agency*, established in 1952, performs highly specialized technical and coordinating functions relating to national security. The *Defense Intelligence Agency*, organized in 1961, has the responsibility of unifying effort in the intelligence activities of the separate services. The DIA works to eliminate duplication in the gathering, assessing, and distributing of intelligence of military value. The *Defense Investigative Service* (DIS), established in 1972, provides Personnel Security Investigations (PSIs) for Department of Defense components, including investigation of allegations of subversive affiliations.

DEPARTMENT OF JUSTICE

The *Law Enforcement Assistance Administration* (LEAA), established in 1968, assists state and local governments to reduce crime through its Office of Criminal Justice Assistance (grants), the National Institute of Law Enforcement and Criminal Justice (research and development), and the Office of Operations Support (evaluation, analysis, supportive services). (See discussion, page 399.)

The *Federal Bureau of Investigation* (FBI), created in 1908, is charged with investigating all violations of federal laws with the exception of those which have been assigned by legislative enactment or otherwise to some other federal agency. The FBI has jurisdiction over some 185 investigative matters. Among these are espionage, sabotage, and other subversive activities; kidnapping; extortion; bank robbery; interstate transportation of stolen property; civil rights matters; interstate gambling violations; fraud against the government; and assaulting or killing the President or a federal officer. Cooperative services of the FBI include fingerprint identification, laboratory services, police training, and the *National Crime Information Center* (NCIC).

The *Bureau of Prisons* supervises federal correctional institutions and community treatment facilities. The 48 programs consist of 3 for juveniles and youths; 6 for young adults; 6 for long term adults; 6 for intermediate term adults; 13 for short term adults; 4 for female offenders; 1 for intensive medical treatment; and 9 community treatment centers.

The *Immigration and Naturalization Service*, created in 1891, is responsible for administering the immigration and naturalization laws relating to the admission, exclusion, deportation, and naturalization of aliens. Through numerous enforcement activities, such as the *Border Patrol*, the service protects the national security of the United States and the welfare of those legally residing here.

The *United States Marshals Service*, was designated as a Bureau within the Department of Justice in 1973. Marshals responsibilities have greatly increased since the first U.S. Marshals were appointed in 1789. Today, they supervise the personal security of federal witnesses and their families, courtroom security, protection of federal property, and special assignments at the direction of the Attorney General.

The *Drug Enforcement Administration* (DEA) was established in 1973. The mission of DEA is to control narcotic and dangerous drug abuse through enforcement and prevention programs. The primary responsibility is to enforce the laws and statutes relating to narcotic drugs, marihuana, depressants, stimulants, and the hallucinogenic drugs.

DEA conducts domestic and international investigations of major drug traffickers concentrating efforts at the illicit supply or diversion. The DEA places particular emphasis on the immobilization of clandestine manufacturers, international traffickers and origins of diversion from legitimate channels. In addition, DEA works cooperatively with other agencies as well as independently to institute national drug abuse prevention programs.

The DEA regulates the legal trade in narcotic and dangerous drugs. This entails establishing import-export and manufacturing quotas for various controlled drugs; registering all authorized handlers of drugs; and inspecting the premises and records of legal handlers.

The DEA provides specialized training in narcotic and dangerous drug control to local, state, and federal law enforcement officers each year. Special training is also provided to forensic chemists, college deans, and security officers as well as industrial plant security personnel.

WATERGATE

The United States Department of Justice, and its principals—notably the offices of the Attorney General and the Director of the FBI—have been deeply involved in the national disgrace referred to as "Watergate" and related matters. The public eye is focused upon the investigation and prosecution of all officials involved in illegal activities and their coverup, and upon the development of law and policy to prevent future breaches of trust. The authors of this book are of the opinion that Watergate is the *beginning of a purge of governmental operations* that will effect many necessary changes throughout many levels of government—and that will be salutary for the nation, and for the goals of liberty and justice.

DEPARTMENT OF THE INTERIOR

The Department of the Interior includes the administration of over 500 million acres of Federal land, and trust responsibilities for about 50 million acres of land, mostly Indian reservations; the conservation and development of mineral and water resources; the promotion of mine safety and efficiency; the conservation, development and utilization of fish and wildlife resources; the coordination of federal and state recreation programs; the preservation of the nation's scenic and historic areas; the reclamation of arid lands through irrigation; and the management of hydroelectric power systems.

The *Bureau of Sport Fisheries and Wildlife* is responsible for the conservation of wild birds, mammals, and sport fisheries; its special agents and visitor protection specialists work to develop an environmental stewardship ethic for our society based on ecological principles, scientific knowledge of wildlife, and a sense of moral responsibility.

The *National Park Service*, established in 1916, administers the national parks, monuments, historic sites, and recreation areas. The Park Police and Park Rangers assist to administer these for the enjoyment and education of our citizens.

The *Bureau of Indian Affairs* was established in 1824. The Investigators and Indian Police assist the bureau in its efforts to encourage and train Indian and Alaska Native people to manage their own affairs under the trust relationship to the federal government.

The *Mining Enforcement and Safety Administration,* created in 1973, is responsible for the inspection of domestic mines and the enforcement of health and safety standards.

DEPARTMENT OF AGRICULTURE

The Department of Agriculture administers more than fifty regulatory laws designed to protect the farmer and the consuming public, and, as well, administers the national forests. The department administers national programs of animal disease eradication, animal quarantine, meat inspection, and enforces regulations to prevent harmful insects from entering and spreading in the United States. The *Forest Service* administers over 155 national forests located in 41 states and Puerto Rico, comprising over 187,000,000 acres. Its responsibility is to improve them, protect them from fire, insects, and disease, and to manage and control livestock grazing and watersheds.

The *Commodity Exchange Authority* conducts investigations to prevent price manipulation affecting agricultural commodities, to prevent false and misleading crop and market information, and to protect users of the commodity futures markets against cheating, fraud, and manipulative practices.

DEPARTMENT OF COMMERCE

The Department of Commerce is responsible for fostering, promoting, and developing the foreign and domestic commerce, the manufacturing and shipping industries, and the transportation facilities of the United States. The Assistant Secretary of Commerce for Administration has an *Office of Security Control,* which is responsible for developing policies and procedures for physical security and personnel security, and an *Agency Inspection Staff,* responsible for maintaining ethical conduct and practices of employees of the department.

DEPARTMENT OF LABOR

The Department of Labor is charged with promotion of the welfare of wage earners of the United States, improving their working conditions, and advancing their opportunities for profitable employment. Investigatory activities are coordinated by the *Office of the Solicitor.* Criminal cases under the Fair Labor Standards Act, and civil actions to recover damages under the Public Contracts Act, are handled by this office which enforces laws relating to manpower, minimum wages and maximum hours, child labor, employment security, the Mexican labor program, veterans' readjustment assistance program, workmen's compensation, veterans' reemployment rights, and apprenticeship training.

DEPARTMENT OF HEALTH, EDUCATION, AND WELFARE

The Department of Health, Education, and Welfare is charged with promoting the general welfare in the fields of health, education, and social security. The *Food and Drug Administration,* created in 1930, enforces the Federal Food, Drug, and Cosmetic Act, the Tea Importation Act, the Import Milk Act, the Caustic Poison Act, and the Filled Milk Act. Its activities are directed mainly toward promoting purity, standard potency, and truthful and informative labeling of the essential commodities covered by the provisions of these acts.

DEPARTMENT OF TRANSPORTATION

The *United States Coast Guard,* a military service and a branch of the Armed Forces of the United States, operates as a service in the Department of Transportation except when operating as a part of the Navy in time of war or when the President directs. Begun in 1790, it represents a united service made up of the old Revenue Cutter Service, the Lifesaving Service, the former Lighthouse Service, and the Bureau of Marine Inspection and Navigation. Part of its function is to carry out an effective port security program, and to enforce or assist in the enforcement of federal laws on the high seas or waters subject to the jurisdiction of the United States.

The *Federal Aviation Administration,* formerly the Federal Aviation Agency, promulgates and enforces safety regulations by inspecting, certifying, rating, and surveilling the activities of airmen; by enforcing the regulations relating to the manufacture, registration, safety and operation of aircraft; and by inspecting the air navigation facilities of the United States.

The *Federal Highway Administration* is a new agency, and has a sharp interest in highway safety. The National Highway Safety Bureau administers a national highway safety program to reduce deaths, injuries, and property damage resulting from highway traffic crashes.

INDEPENDENT AGENCIES

Many minor law enforcement units are located within the myriad of independent agencies of the federal government. Some of the more pertinent units are herewith listed:

In the *Atomic Energy Commission* is a *Division of Intelligence* and a *Division of Security.*

The *Civil Aeronautics Board* conducts special investigations to reduce aircraft accidents and prevent their recurrence.

The *Federal Communications Commission* has a *Field Engineering and Monitoring Bureau* which monitors, inspects, examines, and investigates to insure compliance with FCC rules and regulations.

The *Federal Trade Commission* has a *Bureau of Investigation* which inquires into monopolistic, unfair, or deceptive trade practices.

The General Services Administration utilizes the *Public Buildings Service* to protect federal buildings and their occupants. PBS employs more than 4,500 Federal Protective Officers, U.S. special policemen, and guards. This program has expanded rapidly as the threat from demonstrations, protests, thefts, bombings and other actions has increased.

The *Interstate Commerce Commission* has a *Bureau of Inquiry and Compliance* to assist in the regulation of common carriers engaged in transportation.

The *Tennessee Valley Authority* has a *Division of Reservoir Properties* which is responsible for providing services and facilities for property protection and law enforcement.

The *United States Civil Service Commission* has an *Investigation Division* within its Bureau of Departmental Operations. This unit conducts the Commission's investigative program which includes national agency checks and limited or full field investigations for non-sensitive or sensitive positions, enforcement of the civil service laws and rules, qualifications investigations of applicants for high-level administrative and professional positions, and evaluates the security programs of various governmental agencies for the President.

The *United States Information Agency* has an *Office of Security* which is responsible for personnel, physical, and document security.

The *Veterans Administration,* under the Assistant Administrator for Appraisal and Security, has an *Investigation Service* and a *Security Service,* and, under the Assistant Administrator for Construction, a *Safety and Fire Protection Division.*

In addition to these independent agencies within the federal structure, there are a few other units of particular interest to law enforcement people:

The *Commission on Civil Rights,* which is charged with the responsibility "to investigate allegations that certain citizens of the United States are being deprived of their right to vote and have that vote counted by reason of their color, race, religion, or national origin; to study and collect information concerning legal developments constituting a denial of equal protection of the laws under the Constitution; to appraise the laws and policies of the federal government with respect to equal protection of the laws under the Constitution. . . ."

The Smithsonian Institution utilizes the *National Zoological Park Police* to protect the mammals, birds, and reptiles in the National Zoological Park.

The U.S. Postal Service *Inspection Service* utilizes Postal Inspectors to protect the mails, postal funds, and property, to investigate internal needs which may affect security, to audit operations, and apprehend violators of postal laws.

CONCLUSIONS

Suggestions for the reorganization of federal law enforcement agencies have been proposed from time to time, but without a great deal of success. Some individuals have proposed a national police force which would *amalgamate* all agencies and functions within a central body—but this suggestion has always been strongly opposed by those who feel that a unitary national police might lead to the abuse of national power. Others have proposed that some of the functions be re-allocated more logically, such as moving the enforcement of the National Firearms act from the Alcohol and Tobacco Tax Division of the Internal Revenue Service to the Federal Bureau of Investigation. And yet others have suggested that certain functions be *consolidated,* such as bringing together the functions of the Bureau of Customs and the Border Patrol of the Immigration and Naturalization Service.

Some thought has been directed toward the installation of a *Central Law Enforcement Office* responsible for integrating and coordinating the work of the various federal units, and for channeling the attention of state, county, and municipal law enforcement units toward mutually troublesome areas.

The student of law enforcement must understand that not only are there many federal law enforcement units, but also, that it is difficult to compare them with law enforcement units operating at the state and local levels.

Nonetheless, some observers have pointed to the generally good public relations of the federal agencies, and to the generally consistent public support they receive, and on those premises, have made negative comparisons relative to law enforcement agencies of the state and local levels.

Certainly, the work of state and local law enforcement units is no less important to national stability and order than the work of federal agencies. And certainly, the work of professionally enlightened state and local agencies is no less effective than the work of federal agencies.

In the opinion of the authors, there are three basic reasons for the generally more benign public attitudes that federal units seem to induce:

1. The federal law enforcement officer is usually free of the troublesome duties of restoring a disturbed peace as quickly as possible at the disturbance or crime scene—a task which is difficult to achieve to the mutual satisfaction of all citizens concerned.
2. The federal law enforcement officer is usually free of the sensitive duties of enforcing the minor laws relating to parking, driving, noise, intoxication, and gambling—tasks demanded by the law, but which are accepted with very little grace by many citizens in the community.
3. The federal law enforcement officer is usually free of the gross attempts at political interference and pressure sometimes exerted upon local law enforcement—attempts that are often reflective of a grave lack of citizen responsibility, but which are made with arrogant presumption.

At any rate, the federal agencies, for the most part, have progressive personnel management policies, high standards of service, and operate, in general, with efficiency, integrity, and legality. Their personnel are, in the main, professional in attitude and habit, and exemplify the finest traditions of the American law enforcement vocation.

FORMAL AGENCIES OF LAW ENFORCEMENT: A COMMENT

In any given location in the United States, it is possible to find federal agents, state agents, county agents, municipal agents, auxiliary, honorary or reserve agents, and private agents of law enforcement.

Numerical estimates of the agencies and personnel involved in law enforcement are a tenuous undertaking. Nonetheless, the authors present the following *rough approximation* garnered from a variety of sources:

The number of personnel who are involved in full-time governmental criminal justice work, the number of agencies, and the amount of dollars expended involves mind-boggling data.

For example, expenditures for the years 1969-1970, for all governments in the nation for criminal justice, come to $8,571,000,000.00—over 8½ *billion* dollars! [1] The figures are most interesting to study:

EXPENDITURES

		Federal	State	Local
Police	$5,080,000,000.00 (59.3%)	$ 589M	$ 741M	$3,813M
Judicial	$1,190,000,000.00 (13.9%)	129M	293M	783M
Prosecution	$ 442,000,000.00 (5.2%)	102M	85M	257M
Indigent Defense	$ 102,000,000.00 (1.2%)	56M	10M	37M
Correction	$1,706,000,000.00 (19.9%)	92M	1,104M	609M
Other	$ 50,000,000.00 (0.6%)	65M	35M	6M
Total	$8,571,000,000.00 (100 %)	$1,032M	$2,268M	$5,505M

These figures do *not* include any data on expenditures involving part-time criminal justice personnel (auxiliary, honorary, reserve, voluntary, or special police), or expenditures in the private protection area (guards, watchmen, investigators, commercial and industrial security).

In our fifty states there are some 46,000 *units* of criminal justice in state and local government—without any consideration of the many units of federal criminal justice, or townships, boroughs and villages under 1000 population, or part-time criminal justice personnel, or the private protection area! These units are scattered as follows: [2]

AGENCIES

		State	County	Local
Police	14,806 (32 %)	203	4,800	9,803
Courts	13,235 (29 %)	1,690	6,248	5,297
Prosecution	8,501 (18.2%)	601	2,800	5,100
Defense	374 (0.8%)	108	239	27
Corrections, Adult	4,435 (9.5%)	398	3,022	1,015
Corrections, Juvenile	724 (1.5%)	369	312	43
Probation	2,445 (5.0%)	580	1,690	175
Miscellaneous (Academies, Administrative)	1,639 (4.0%)	?	?	?
Total	46,159 (100 %)	3,949	19,111	21,460

The number of people, in a nation of some 200 million, who are entitled to the possession of a criminal justice title, number well over one million, if we consider, in addition to full-time governmental personnel, all of those

[1] U.S. Department of Justice, Law Enforcement Assistance Administration, Criminal justice expenditure and employment 1969-1970, *Advance Report*, February, 1972, p. 5.

[2] These figures are extrapolated from an advance notice of the directory of criminal justice agencies being prepared under the direction of the Statistics Division of the Law Enforcement Assistance Administration's National Institute.

part-time, non-paid auxiliary, honorary, reserve, voluntary or special police, and all of those engaged in the private security area as guards, watchmen, investigators, and industrial security agents. The governmental area, alone, has more than three-quarters of a million: [3]

PERSONNEL

		Federal	State	Local
Police	489,367 (63.2%)	39,711	55,846	393,810
Judicial	95,524 (12.3%)	6,821	18,464	70,239
Prosecution	38,171 (4.9%)	6,776	6,780	24,615
Indigent Defense	3,063 (0.4%)		545	2,518
Correction	148,047 (19.1%)	5,737	90,334	51,976
Other	582 (0.1%)	310	272	
Total	774,754 (100 %)	59,355	172,241	543,158

It can be seen from even a cursory scanning of the above data that criminal justice is truly *big business* in the United States, and every state has many more units, people, and expenditures than is generally known. Take California, for example. Excluding the part-time, non-paid auxiliary, honorary, reserve, voluntary or special police, and excluding the 153 industrial security agencies with their guards, watchmen, and investigators, and excluding the 59 federal agencies and their personnel, there are still over a thousand units and some 60,000 people working full time with major criminal justice responsibilities! They are scattered in the following fashion.

CALIFORNIA CRIMINAL JUSTICE

Police (43,310)	*Number of Agencies*	*Number of Personne*
Municipal Police	346	23,590
Sheriff Departments	58	10,850
Marshal Offices	14	790
Constable Offices	220	220
California Highway Patrol	*	6,290
California State Police	*	198
Bureau of Criminal Identification and Investigation	*	37
Bureau of Narcotic Enforcement	*	113
Alcoholic Beverage Control	*	275
Department of Motor Vehicles	*	84
Department of Fish and Game	*	283
Department of Professional and Vocational Standards	*	62
Fire Marshal's Office	*	51
University of California Police	*	257
State College Police	*	210
Judicial (3,330)		
Courts (Superior, Municipal, Justice)	425	1,030
District Attorneys (and Investigators)	58	1,590
Public Defenders (and Investigators)	36	710
Correctional (13,930)		
Probation	60	5,520
Parole	58	1,260
Institutions	32	7,150
Totals	1,318	60,570

* (Operate out of geographically scattered offices)

---

[3] *Supra,* Note 1, p. 6.

Each student of criminal justice should carefully probe agencies, personnel, and expenditures for criminal justice activities in his own state, and, in addition, ascertain the number of non-paid, part-time, reserve, honorary, voluntary, special police, and the number of watchmen, guard, private investigator, industrial security police, in terms of dollars spent, units deployed, and personnel affiliated.

The cost, to the taxpayer, for governmental law enforcement services is high. Because of the formidable resistance to consolidation of law enforcement services in the great metropolitan areas, there is unnecessary duplication of records systems, communications facilities, detention centers, crime laboratories, and specialized activities, coupled with the problems of jurisdictional overlapping.

Because of the great resistance to county or district police in the rural areas, there are many tiny units of law enforcement which operate ineffectively due to limited budgets, or which operate effectively, but at a far greater cost than that of a general county or district police.

Our jurisdictional police scheme is based upon the concept of local autonomy, upon the philosophy of local control. Yet, when one studies the *metropolitan areas* of the United States from a police standpoint, and observes the urban, the suburban, and the rural area involved, often several counties, municipalities, townships and villages are found, and, as well, from fifty to one hundred police agencies.

Thus, local control, as relates to the metropolitan areas, results in many chiefs of police, police commissioners, city managers, councilmen, and consequently, many differing policies relating to police operations.

When one studies the *county and rural areas* of the United States from a police standpoint, and observes the generally haphazard provision of police services from available agencies, one arrives at a similar conclusion —that local control, as relates to the county and rural areas, results in many police administrators and many differing policies relating to police operations. Such a condition is often wasteful of the tax dollar, and often results in "patches" of poor policing.

The time may come when both citizens and police demand a more standardized and economical police service, with state or county forces providing uniform services in the rural and unincorporated areas, and with centralized metropolitan or district police providing uniform services throughout the metropolitan areas. Local control *can* be maintained by providing for community representation on the commissions controlling such units. Although some metropolitan area police departments have been organized (i.e., Miami, Toronto, Nassau County and Suffolk County, New York) such will not likely become the general rule until pyramiding police costs and skyrocketing crime problems mandate such extensive changes.

The authors are not in favor of a unitary, national police system, nor in a unitary state police system, for the dangers inherent in the abuse of such systems could well undermine the strength of our democracy which has a diffusion of governmental authority and power to the extent that government tyranny is always at a potential minimum.

The authors are in favor of changes in the scheme of law enforcement which would protect the autonomy of our communities, and yet, allow for a more efficient, less expensive, police operation.

The authors are in favor of changes in the scheme of law enforcement which would protect the vested career interests of our police practitioners, and yet, allow for a more uniformly competent, legal, and moral, less corruptible police operation.

The student who reads this text will either take up a professional career in government or private law enforcement, or remain outside of law enforcement as a citizen engaged in some other vocation.

If he takes up a professional career in law enforcement, the authors trust that he will be able to view the work of his chosen agency in relation to the total enterprise of law enforcement, and work to make that agency responsive and responsible to the community, to the state, and to the nation.

If he takes up some other vocation outside of the law enforcement area, the authors trust that he will work energetically, as a citizen, to promote law enforcement schemes of operation that are effective and edifying, and support, at all levels, the agencies that enforce the law in his stead.

TOPICS FOR DISCUSSION

1. What are the advantages and disadvantages of amalgamating all federal law enforcement units into one central unit? LEAD TO ABUSE OF POWER
2. What are the advantages and disadvantages of re-allocating law enforcement functions at the federal level?
3. What are the advantages and disadvantages of consolidating certain functions of law enforcement at the federal level?
4. What are the advantages and disadvantages of installing a central law enforcement coordinating office at the federal level?
5. Should the investigation of civil rights violations be handled by the FBI, or should a separate investigative unit be established under the United States Attorney General?
6. How extensive is overlapping and duplication of law enforcement services in this locale?

Chapter XIV

RELATED AGENCIES

IN ADDITION TO THE LARGE NUMBERS OF AMERICANS who are affiliated with agencies of law enforcement at the federal, state, county, municipal, or village level of government as full-time employees, and in addition to the many law enforcement functionaries associated with private protective agencies, and in addition to the thousands of part-time, non-paid auxiliary, reserve, or honorary law enforcement personnel, there are many other citizens engaged in criminal justice activities of a closely related nature.

COURTS

Courts which hear and determine criminal matters are found at the federal, state, municipal, and rural level.

Inferior courts, or courts of primary or limited jurisdiction, try minor matters, usually petty kinds of misdemeanors, and very often hold the preliminary hearing or examination of those accused of serious misdemeanors and felonies, thus acting as a committing agency for the higher courts.

Ordinarily, these courts are not courts of record, and the proceedings are generally informal, sometimes operating without prosecutor, defense counsel, or jury. Although they are permitted to set bail within certain limitations, they are often limited to the extent of punishment that they can impose.

In the federal system, the United States Commissioner or Magistrate may act as a committing official, set bail, and bind over for trial. In the larger municipalities are found the municipal, city, magistrate, or police courts. In the rural areas, the inferior court is that of the Justice of the Peace (J.P.). The J.P. is often an elected official, with limited knowledge of the law, operating part-time on a fee-basis.

Trial courts, or courts of original or general jurisdiction, try all cases brought before them, and often hear appeals from inferior courts. Cases come to them either directly through the complaint or information of the prosecutor, through the presentment or indictment of a grand jury, or indirectly, after commitment by the inferior courts after preliminary hearing or examination. Most of the cases are of major misdemeanors or felonies, and the court operates as a court of record—with proceedings transcribed—

in a formal manner, with prosecution and defense attorneys, and with juries if elected by the defendant.

In the federal system, the United States District Courts hear and determine cases based on criminal offenses that occur in the United States, in the territorial possessions of the United States, and on vessels of this nation. In the counties of the various states, or in districts made up of several counties, are found the county, state, district, superior, or circuit courts.

Some trial courts are courts of special jurisdiction, such as those dealing with juvenile, probate, or civil matters.

Appellate courts, or courts of appeal, are responsible for hearing and deciding appeals taken from decisions of the lower courts. If the case comes to them from an inferior court which is not of record, the case may be heard *de novo* (as new), with presentations of evidence, witnesses, and jury privileges; if the case comes from a court of record, however, the transcript of the trial court provides the material for the hearing. Appellate courts generally *affirm* the decision of the lower court, or *reverse* such decision and send the case back for retrial.

Supreme courts, or courts of last appeal, are found at the state and federal level. The name of this court differs in the several states, the most common name being either *Supreme Court* or *Court of Appeals* prefixed by the name of the state. Such courts are the final courts of appeal in the state system, and review cases on a variety of issues, such as interpretations involving the state Constitution, or mandated reviews of cases involving capital crimes. The United States Supreme Court is the final court of appeal in the federal court system, and hears appeals from state courts when issues involving the federal Constitution are involved.

These inferior, trial, appellate, and supreme courts have several kinds of court attendants, such as clerks, stenographers, and bailiffs. The court attendants of the inferior courts who keep order in the court, handle prisoners, serve orders of the court, and assist the court are often constables in the judicial districts, or deputy sheriffs or marshals in the municipal courts. The sheriff usually provides for court attendants in the courts of general jurisdiction, and in the federal system the United States Marshal has such responsibility.

PROSECUTION OFFICIALS

Prosecution is an American innovation. In 1704, in Connecticut, a statute provided that

> . . . Henceforth there shall be in every countie a sober, discreet and religious person appointed by the countie courts to be atturney for the Queen to prosecute and implead in the laws all criminals and to doe all other things necessary or convenient as an atturney to suppresse vice and immoralitie. . . .

The county is the jurisdictional level of government with the largest group of public prosecutors. Known as district atorney, county attorney, county solicitor, prosecuting attorney, or state's attorney, their powers are exercised within the county, or within districts composed of several counties.

In general, they are, within their jurisdictions, independent of each other, and relatively independent of state control.

Within many counties, there are found municipal prosecutors called city prosecutor, corporation counsel, or city attorney, and who conduct prosecutions independently of the district or county attorney, but who usually limit their authority to prosecutions for violations of municipal ordinances, misdemeanors, and the preliminary hearings of felony cases.

The prosecuting attorney, in the vast majority of jurisdictions, is a member of the bar. With rare exceptions, to qualify as a member of the bar, one must have completed an extensive course of study in an accredited law school, passed a comprehensive admission examination and have an unblemished record of acceptable conduct and moral behavior. Since the position does not offer great financial rewards, especially in the smaller jurisdictions, this elective position may be attractive to a young attorney in terms of furthering his future career—either through the acquisition of considerable trial experience, or by the publicity helpful to political potentials.

The prosecutor has almost unlimited discretion to initiate criminal proceedings, or to refuse to initiate them. In a majority of criminal cases, the police officer personally consults the prosecutor, or one of his assistants, before the formal accusation is prepared. The police officer, in applying for complaint or warrant, has an important responsibility to present all the pertinent facts of the case to the prosecutor, so that a complete evaluation can be made. The prosecutor has a powerful effect on the administration of criminal justice and greatly influences the efficiency of the police and the courts. His skill and integrity are of prime importance. Team-work between the police and the prosecutor is a must.

Canon 7 of the ABA's Code of Professional Responsibility imposes the primary duty on the prosecutor *not to convict, but to see that justice is done.* The prosecutor must "render to each his due." On occasion, an overzealous prosecutor, concerned about his conviction record, may engage in behind-the-scenes manipulation of charges in exchange for a "cop-out"—a plea of guilty. Thus, the prosecutor receives a guaranteed conviction for his record. An example of "reduced charge" would occur if a felony burglary charge, carrying a penalty of several years in state prison, was reduced to a misdemeanor theft or malicious mischief charge, with a penalty of several months in the county jail. There are many situations, however, when the acceptance of a lesser plea has a salutary effect, and can be considered quite proper. An extremely weak case, because of legal technicalities, with slim possibility of conviction, or a local community attitude relative to the offense which makes a fair trial virtually impossible, or where circumstances indicate that justice will be better served—are all valid reasons for a reduction of original charge.

As is unfortunately true, in some instances, the prosecutor may be more of a *politician* than an *attorney for the people*. When that is the case, his policies cause great harm to the police service, for he may be amenable to political pressures which demand the withholding of complaints, manipulation of charges, or an apathetic presentation of the people's case. These situations, however, are rare.

In larger cities, prosecutors often have a staff of investigators who have the responsibility of developing the case for trial, often by obtaining additional evidence, or by securing additional witnesses. The "small town D.A.," however, equipped only with the office space and secretary, finds that the ferreting out of facts falls upon his own shoulders.

DEFENSE OFFICIALS

Common to all jurisdictions is the right of the accused person to be represented by counsel. This is an effective right for those who are in a position to employ an attorney, but a somewhat theoretical protection for accused persons whose means are minimum.

Defendants may be represented by counsel of their own choosing, or by counsel provided for them. Theoretically, the court has the power to appoint counsel for an indigent defendant from any member of the bar, but most often, legal assistance for the poor comes from volunteer defenders within bar associations, from legal aid societies, or from the "Public Defender." This is changing rapidly. Procedures are being adopted, more and more, to provide for effective court-appointed counsel for indigent persons charged with crime.

The public defender system was devised to provide regular professional counsel for the poor defendant, and was originated in Los Angles County in 1913. Many communities now maintain public defenders through the use of public funds, and make their services available on request.

Two problems exist with reference to defense counsel. One has to do with public attitudes. It seems that the general public has a tendency to link the character of the offender with the character of his lawyer—thus ataching a stigma to those members of the bar who appear in defense of unpopular violators of the law. Some attorneys, consequently, tend to remain away from this field of law because they fear becoming known as a "mouthpiece" for unsavory characters.

Another problem has to do with the attitudes of fellow attorneys. It seems that some lawyers do not regard attorneys who engage in criminal law and defense work as having shown the best of judgment in selecting criminal law as a specialty. Such an attitude is not conducive to the development of a truly professional, highly motivated, altruistically inclined body of criminal law practitioners.

Public defenders often have a staff of investigators to assist in case development by obtaining additional evidence, or securing additional defense witnesses. Private defenders primarily rely upon private detectives and investigators to do such work.

JURIES

The application of the jury system to criminal cases first appeared, it is often said, in 1166 at the Assize of Clarendon, where jurors were obliged to denounce culprits in certain crimes.[1] Thus, in a sense, their responsibility was "accusatory." If the offender desired, as an alternative to ordeal or torture, to "put himself upon the country," a trial jury was selected from the body of denouncing jurors to determine the facts. Thus, in another sense, their responsibility became "adjudicative."

It was soon realized that the two functions of accusing and judging were incompatible and inequitable, and the juries were divided between the *grand inquest* or *grand jury*, and the *petit* or *trial jury*, membership in the grand jury becoming a disqualification for service on the trial jury.

Grand Jury. The grand jury has the function of serving as an initiating process by which one suspected of having committed a felony (or, in some states, a high misdemeanor) may be accused of crime and brought before a court of general jurisdiction. In some areas, the committing magistrates of lower courts may perform this function independently of the grand jury; in others, he serves only to detain or release the accused on bail pending action of the grand jury. In some areas, the prosecutor may perform this function independently of the grand jury by the filing of an information; in others, he must process his case through the grand jury.

In addition to its accusatory powers, the grand jury may be clothed with broad powers of investigation, either independently, or more often, with the participation of the prosecuting attorney. Very often, it is responsible for inspecting public institutions and auditing the accounts of public officials, as well as investigating the general criminal charges brought before

---

[1] The actual origin of the jury system is lost in history. However, for all practical purposes, most people accept 1166 as the year in which the present day jury system had its crude beginning.

it by the committing magistrates of the lower courts, by the prosecutor, or by the coroner.

The purpose of the grand jury is merely accusatory—that is, it decides whether or not there is enough evidence to hold an accused person for trial. As it meets in secret session, hearing one witness at a time, it can be utilized to preserve secrecy in the initial phases of an investigation, to by-pass the prosecutor or police if graft and corruption are suspected. Thus, it can act as a bulwark against tyranny by governmental officials. As it hears only the people's case and witnesses, and not that of the accused, the offender is better protected at a preliminary hearing for there he can be heard, represented by counsel, and afforded the opportunity to present his own witnesses.

If the grand jury acts on its own initiative, its accusation is in the form of a *presentment*; if it acts on the complaint of another source, its accusation is in the form of an *indictment*. If it decides that the allegations are correct, it issues a "true bill"; if not, "no bill."

Critics of the grand jury system indicate that its procedures are often inflexible and formal, with verbose accusations merely rubber-stamping the prosecutor's whim. Supporters of the system indicate that it is useful as an investigative body for probing into governmental corruption, and that until the preliminary hearing is made more effective, the grand jury serves as a useful indictive agency.

Grand juries range in size from one to twenty-three members, are selected each year by county supervisors, jury commissioners, or court officials, and generally come from the same list of eligible citizens used for trial jury selection.

Petit or Trial Jury. In the United States, where the ordinary trial jury is usually twelve persons (sometimes more if alternates are utilized), the jurors, drawn from voting registers or tax rolls, are not a particularly representative cross section of the American community. Even though qualifications are low, many citizens are either excluded from, or exempt from, jury duty.

Exclusions are understandable, and, *depending on the county*, persons can be excluded from jury duty who have been convicted of misdemeanors of moral turpitude, infamous crimes, felonies, violation of a public trust, bribery, or perjury. In addition, also excluded are persons of notorious bad character, and drunkards; idiots, lunatics, and those adjudged incompetent or of unsound mind. Also, persons not in full facility of hearing and sight, those disabled or infirm, those unable to read, write, and understand the English language, and persons not residing in the state for one year. Also, persons under twenty-five, over sixty-five; those not registered as voters, or who are ineligible to vote; those not owning property of a value of $150;

those who are not taxpayers; or those who are related to within the sixth degree of the litigants. Thus, some of the more common exclusions found within the fifty states.

Exemptions are almost endless, and, *depending on the county*, persons can be exempted from jury duty who are attorneys, doctors, teachers, druggists, clergymen, firemen, policemen, judges, members of the armed forces or militia, dentists, newspaper editors, school employees, ferrymen, road overseers, chiropodists, seamen, postal employees, state assemblymen, hospital employees, newspapermen, county treasurers, millers at corn, telegraph operators, express agents, nurses, osteopaths, veterinarians, registrars of deeds, engineers of sugar refineries, fish and game wardens, custodians of minors, constables, federal, state or county employees, radio broadcasters and announcers, armed forces reserve members, court clerks, women with minor children, naturopaths, guardians of the poor, veterans of the military service, faculty and students of colleges, women, millers at saw, accountants, grist and flour mill operators, gate keepers, telephone employees, train dispatchers, harvesters during season, cashiers of banks, factory foremen, and engineers, canal company employees, or, persons "exempt at the discretion of the Commissioner of Jurors." Thus, some of the more common exemptions found within the fifty states.

Because of the broad scope of exemptions from jury duty, with so many responsible members of the community literally unavailable, there is little wonder that the system is often subjected to criticism.

CORONER

The Coroner dates to approximately 1194 and his early duties were to see that taxes were collected, and to oversee criminal prosecution in order to direct the confiscation of the property of a convicted felon. From earliest times, he presided at inquests into deaths, recorded the facts, and reported to judicial authorities his findings.

Today, he is responsible for investigating violent deaths, or where there is reasonable suspicion of foul play. He may conduct a post-mortem examination of the deceased (autopsy) and may hold an inquest by summoning jurors to determine the cause of death.

He is frequently an elected official, with minimum qualifications for the office. Because he may be unqualified, and his jurors but laymen, there have been attempts made to abolish the office and substitute a *Medical Examiner* who is a qualified physician and surgeon. Massachusetts did so in 1877, and New York in 1915. The medical examiner is now used in many jurisdictions.

The coroner's inquest may result in issuance of arrest warrants by the coroner if homicide is determined. How many murders have been classified as natural or accidental deaths by coroners and their juries is conjectural; yet opinion is growing that scientific methods of crime detection should be accompanied by scientific operations of the coroner—thus, a continuing pressure for the qualified medical examiner.

PROBATION PROCESSES AND AGENCIES

The public usually thinks of a *probation officer* as one who supervises juvenile delinquents. Juvenile probation, however, is only a part of this important criminal justice process.

Probation is a condition imposed by a court upon an offender (after a plea or verdict of guilt) as an alternative to a *straight sentence*. The offender is turned over to a department that represents the courts. He is assigned to a probation officer (often called the "eyes and ears of the court"). The officer investigates the offender and reports his findings to the judge. In adult work, this is called a *pre-sentence investigation*. It is a *juvenile report* where minors are concerned. The idea is to make the punishment fit the offender as well as the crime. The probation officer hands the judge a written report which covers various points of information. Were the circumstances of the crime *aggravating* or *mitigating?* Did the defendant steal because he was desperately poor, or because he prefers stealing to honest work? Is he relatively reliable, or is stealing a habit? How many prior offenses has he committed? What do people say who know him? How do the police look at him?

On the basis of the probation report, the judge can do a more accurate job of sentencing the defendant, instead of "shooting from the hip" in ignorance of all the facts. His sentence can be straight probation (no jail time; report monthly); or, for example, probation for three years, the first six months to be served in the county jail, a fine of three hundred dollars, and restitution to the victim of four hundred dollars payable in monthly installments, or any variation or combination of these conditions.

There are certain crimes—high felonies—which do not allow probation. These are, for example, armed robbery, aggravated assault, first degree murder, rape, and in the federal courts, treason. Each state has its own laws, and these are changing as our society evolves.

Probation work is usually divided into felony and misdemeanor sections, servicing the superior and municipal courts, and into a large separate section to handle juvenile matters. As for the work of federal judges throughout the country, the federal courts have their own probation-parole officers.[2]

---

[2] *Federal Probation*, a quarterly published in Washington, D.C., is probably the most informative court and correctional journal. It is sent without cost to bona fide workers in the criminal justice process. Check it in the library, and if you wish to get it, write to Administrative Office of U.S. Courts, Supreme Court Building, Washington, D.C. 20544.

Here, as in less populated areas, probation and parole are often combined in one state-wide department which handles felonies. City courts often have their own probation officers for misdemeanants.

In routine minor cases and without written report, the judge may grant "summary probation," merely requiring the defendant to report periodically to the court clerk.

Because probation is rehabilitative, not degrading, it is seen as a positive form of punishment. It is far less expensive than prison or jail, costing generally one-fifth the cost. Further, the probationer is able to work and to support his family, keeping them from welfare. Through monthly payments, the offender can make restitution to the victim for damage he has caused. Probation is especially helpful in offenses concerning checks and property damage. Probationers repeat crime far less than people who spend time in prison.

Probation is essentially an American development. It began in 1841 with the work of John Augustus, a Boston shoemaker. He sat in court watching defendants, including children, sentenced to the House of Corrections for theft, drunkenness and other misdemeanors. One day Augustus asked the court to release to his custody a disheveled drunk named James Vayle. Instead of sentencing Vayle to the workhouse, the court complied, and three weeks later Vayle was not recognized by the court, due to his change in appearance and attitude. Between 1841 and 1852, the Boston shoemaker handled more than 1500 defendants, including women and children. He kept records which exist today. As a result of his work, the first probation law in the world was established in Boston in 1878.

Criticism of probation is often directed toward the courts for not allowing it in sufficient cases, or for granting the privilege too extensively to poorly calculated risks. Probation officers often are poorly screened, overloaded, ill-trained and underpaid. Nonetheless, probation officers stand high among the most dedicated, selfless and capable persons in the criminal justice process.

The largest probation department in the world is situated in Los Angeles County (due to the enormous size of the county). In the 1940s standards were elevated, requiring a college degree. As a result salaries rose, and officers there lead the field in professional operations.

Some observers have pointed to an alleged conflict between the values of law enforcement personnel and those of probation, guidance and parole officers. Such argument states that the police are primarily interested in protecting the community, whereas the officers of the court or paroling agency are primarily interested in the offender. This is a superficial analysis from a bygone era, and insults both the police and guidance officers. It is a false dichotomy.

Any professional law enforcement officer today is fully aware of his total responsibility "to prevent crime and disorder, preserve the peace, and protect life, freedom and property." He knows of the importance of crime prevention activities. For example, if he is a modern patrolman, he will sometimes work with a probation officer to implement a program for an alcoholic. If he is a modern parole officer, he may establish liaison with an arresting officer concerning a parolee and his family.

The professional officer today accepts this basic fact of human relations: all persons are much more alike than they are different. He has accepted his duties to those who live in skid row and ghetto areas, as well as his duties to those who live in the tract and plush areas. He has accepted his duties to the law-abiding, and to the law-breaker. Professional workers for the common good maintain respect for the activities of each other. All are part of the criminal justice system.

PENAL PROCESSES AND AGENCIES

Lockups, jails, juvenile halls, training schools, reformatories, work camps, chain gangs, honor farms, and prisons form an important part of our criminal justice system. Federal prisons account for some 30,000 offenders; state prisons care for some 200,000 persons ranging from first offenders to multiple felons. In addition, municipal and county detention facilities service 150,000 persons. Many of these, more than 50 per cent in some jurisdictions, are arrestees who are awaiting trial, or, in some felony cases, awaiting a preliminary hearing. Such persons are unadjudicated and therefore legally innocent. They may have served from a month to more than two years of dead time waiting for disposition in the congested and bulging court calendars of highly populated areas.

Many of the lockups, city jails and county institutions are a public disgrace. These make the police tasks doubly difficult. They thrust many first offenders into the world of crime. On the other hand, some are model institutions; many are starving for tax support to improve their facilities.

There are, in addition, over 100,000 juveniles in county juvenile homes, state training schools, and similar detention facilities. This figure has risen in recent years, due to the startling rise in teen-age crime.

In this country today, an estimated daily national average of persons under some form of detainment is about 1.5 million, with an expected 1.8 million by 1975.

The prison systems of this country, always a subject for discussion, have come in for violent criticism in recent years. A sharp increase in prison breaks and riots in 1971 culminated in the bloody debacle of the New York state prison in the rural town of Attica. Hostages were taken by prisoners and, after three days of futile negotiations, state troopers were ordered to attack. Forty-three persons, including nine correctional officers who had béen taken hostage, were killed in the attack—the largest death toll in this century. As a result, prisons and prison systems are under investigation and, as a part of our government, stand in the public eye in terms of their past and their future. Alleged brutality of guards and racial discrimination rank high in these inquiries. On the other hand, efforts of sincere penal officers become lost in the shuffle. Penal officers *live* in prisons and, in that sense, they are "serving time" as well as their charges. Many need training.

Dungeons and primitive lockups have existed from early times. Every large castle had its *donjon*. Historically, everyone knows of the Tower of London and the French Bastille. But modern prisons, constructed for punishment and reformation, are less than two hundred years old. They developed slowly here, beginning fifty years after our country was founded.

Prior to the American Revolution there were, of course, jails and workhouses. An abandoned copper mine at Simsbury, Connecticut, was used as a crude prison from 1773 to 1827. The first *penitentiary*, the Walnut Street Jail, was established in Philadelphia during President Washington's time. Operated by the Quakers, it was intended to change and improve criminals by keeping them alone in silence, where they could meditate, suffer remorse and repent. Handicraft work, any work done alone, was encouraged—shoemaking, weaving, dyeing, and the like. For this reason, the cells were comparatively large, and faced to the outside. The offender was brought to his cell blindfolded and saw virtually no one. The plan was to prevent "contamination" of one convict by association with another, and became widely known as the *Philadelphia System*. So impressed by it were European penologists that they adopted the system. Even today, there are vestiges of the system abroad.

Competing with the Philadelphia System was a prison built in a New York rural area near Syracuse. The famous *Auburn Plan* was begun in the prison of that name in 1824. This plan allowed convicts to work silently together during the day and returned them to solitary confinement at night. This old prison is still in operation behind its forty-foot wall, although the original buildings and the "silence plan" have vanished.

Since the Auburn Plan allowed prisoners to work together, it fitted better into the power machinery of the American industrial explosion which was getting under way. In the prison, there were power looms, jute mills, and primitive factories. The Auburn Plan over the next decades triumphed over the Philadelphia System.

One important change in the structure of prisons resulted from this triumph. Because the Auburn Plan required no handicraft work in the cells, these were built smaller and facing the inside, creating cell blocks.

The cells were seven feet long and three and a half feet wide, poorly ventilated, damp in summer and cold in winter. Later, cells were banked in stories and tiers, one over the other. The Auburn Plan served as the model for most state penitentiaries. Many of these outmoded piles of stone are still in use today.

Discipline was enforced by the lash. Prisoners wore stripes, and moved in groups under a slow shuffle known as the *lockstep*. Many torturous punishments came into being, some of which survive today. Gone, however, are the gag, the straightjacket, the douche, and the cat-o-nine-tails. Some punishments today are psychological rather than physical. Uncertainty concerning length of sentence is one of these.

After years of despair and decay in the prison system, a landmark event took place in 1870. Public officials, prison administrators and determined citizens formed the American Prison Association and put down a constitution and set of principles which were so enlightened and advanced that they have never been wholly implemented even today. The basic idea in the change was a repudiation of punishment *per se* in favor of the reform of the individual as a primary task of imprisonment. Trade training, parole and flexibility of sentence were set out as new methods.

Under these humane resolves, the first *reformatory* was established in Elmira, New York, in 1876 to handle youthful offenders. A rating system was begun, with marks given to the offender according to the gravity of his crime. These marks could be redeemed by good conduct. Emphasis fell on *training*, and productive labor. A direct result of the *Elmira System* was the building of some reformatories. The principle behind the Elmira System, however, soon gave way to the old-time punishment fixations. Unfortunately, these "junior prisons"—still called reformatories—are in operation in many states today.

At the turn of the century, following a study of the reformatory programs here, an improved method was installed at the Bedford Prison in Borstal, England. The *Borstal System* consists of a thorough study of the offender to determine his needs; minimum security; regular street clothing; and a fixed sentence of four years. The resident is given supervision and training from six to thirty-six months at an institution. He then spends the remainder of his four years on parole during a "license" period. Community sponsors interest themselves in the offender and help him in adjustment, employment and the responsibilities of citizenship.

PRISONS IN THE SEVENTIES

In the early 1970s the prisons of the United States erupted into violent breaks and mutinies, which intensified the prior wave of riots in the 1950s. The Attica riot, already discussed, was preceded and followed by others with less loss of life. In California's ancient San Quentin prison looking over San Francisco Bay, a revolutionary and talented black prisoner-writer named George Jackson was involved in a shooting scene in which three guards and three prisoners, including Jackson, lost their lives. In New Jersey, the state prison at Rahway erupted. Six hostages, including the warden, were taken by rebel prisoners. The governor came to the scene and dispatched two negotiators into the prison, who settled the break without loss of life.

Such events bring the prison system before the public eye. Prison systems tend to become corrupted with total power. Guard subcultures are showing a growing need for training and change. Penal authorities already largely agree that the old style huge prisons with their high walls and custody/warehouse emphasis are failures in today's society. Increasing emphasis is now placed upon the need for smaller, community-based programs and institutions which are accessible to community resources, and where everyone in the institution knows everyone else. (Sharp difference of opinion exists here between traditionalists and innovators. For example, Ramsey Clark, former United States Attorney General, states that "Community supervision is the future of corrections," while Edward M. Davis, Chief of Police of Los Angeles rejects the idea of "using our communities as a rehabilitation ground for dangerous, convicted felons," and states that it is "pretty obvious that home or community-based rehabilitation doesn't appear to be any more effective than institutional correction.")

It is now generally understood that poorly handled inmates are plunged into repeating crime as stigmatized and untrained competers in our society. Such repetitive crime—recidivism—is as high as 70 per cent. It turns the prison into a "revolving door" and quadruples the work of the police. It clogs the courts and increases the tax bills of property owners.

The public should soon come to understand that they own the prisons and that their business is failing—both the 70 per cent recidivism rate and the increasing severity of crimes committed by prison graduates are clear evidence that current prisons fail to rehabilitate in any positive way. Instead, they become breeding grounds for hatred of the establishment, a hatred that makes every citizen a target of violence. Prisons are a bad investment for citizen-taxpayers. Until recently, citizens have left the prisons to wardens, content that threatening people are kept out of sight. But prison administration has failed to rehabilitate, and instead, turns petty thieves into murderers. Either new management or operating procedure is the order of the day, but it must be one or the other. David Fogel, Head of the Minnesota Department of Corrections, is blunt: "Perhaps the best way to teach law-abiding behavior is to treat the non-law abider in a law-abiding manner inside our institutions," and he proposed an ombudsman to act as an advocate for inmates, protection of due process for inmates, protection against capricious administrators, the right to be represented and the presumption of innocence in institution disciplinary procedures, and the right to counsel when an inmate is behind bars and threatened with parole revocation.

Changes in society are reflected in the prisons. As this country's technology drives it toward equality, minorities thrust forward to claim a larger share of the "good life." The prisons usually lag behind such developments. The results are tragic and sometimes bloody. When social and economic justice "divides the pie" more equitably, we should have a better type of prisoner!

The Seventies are witnessing new types of inmates—the war resistor, the drug abuser, and especially, organized dissidents who are sometimes categorized as "political prisoners." Prisoners, predominantly black activists, who frequently unite with whites and chicanos, often are presenting demands for prisoner's rights rather than making escape attempts. They attack the system itself. Thoughtful prison officials admit that the old ways of repressive control are not working and must be changed. They are seeking more wide-open discussions and sharing of prison problems, treating the prisoners as mature people who have rights (instead of as five-year-old children) and who can be expected to act responsibly. There is discussion of changing the law to allow prisoners to retain their civil and personal rights, including due process and the right to vote. With votes at stake, politicians would take more interest in the problems of both prisoners and guards.

On the other hand, a blanket condemnation of all prisons overlooks the efforts made in recent years to accomplish reform of prisoners. A brief look at innovations, some tried and well integrated, and some too new to be assessed, is in order.

Classification has become a part of most prison systems in this country. As an in-prison process, classification decisions are usually made by a committee headed by the deputy superintendent and the departmental heads of Custody and of Treatment, the chaplain, and the sociologist or psychologist. Sometimes, but rarely, the issues are settled by vote, subject to the review and consent of the superintendent. After admittance, the offender is kept separate from the other inmates. He is studied, given physical, mental, educational and psychological tests. His background is reviewed, and a decision is made as to what security measures are required. He is then placed in terms of how the institution's resources can be coordinated with his needs. In practice, unfortunately, the needs of the institution often come first.

Prisoners, classified or not, are usually segregated in some way—certainly by sex; by race in many prisons, despite efforts outside to desegregate; by sexual background or inclination (lifelong homosexuals); by number of offenses (multiple felons from first offenders); by age (especially adults from juveniles); and by infirmity, illness, or crippling addiction.

The *indeterminate sentence*—the opposite of the flat-time sentence—has many forms. Although it is a hot subject for discussion today, it is as old as the 1840s, when it was expressed and effectively used by an English naval captain, Alexander Maconochie, who took over the Norfolk Penal Island, a dead-end prison one thousand miles from Australia. His first principle was that sentences for crime should not be for time served, but for labor performed and tasks accomplished.

Theoretically, the indeterminate sentence is one having neither a fixed minimum nor a fixed maximum. No such law has been adopted in the United States. One of the most elastic provisions of individual sentencing is found in California, where a judge may intone over an offender, "committed to the Department of Corrections, *one year to life*." Introduced with the most advanced and humane aims, this indeterminate sentence law was set up to reward prisoners with early release upon proof of rehabilitation. Instead of accomplishing this, it sometimes causes deepening anxiety and rage with each refusal of parole and the perspective of a possible *lifetime* in jail for a felony (robbery, for example) which might carry a flat-time sentence of *five years*. The average stay in prison per individual jumped to an average of three years—probably the longest overall *average* amount of time placed on offenders in the world. Prison officials are now studying legal changes.

In other jurisdictions as well, it was discovered that offenders were being kept in prison longer, rather than shorter, under the indeterminate sentence. Nevertheless, the usual indeterminate sentence as found in most states, tends to fit the penalty to the offender as well as to the crime. The usual elastic sentence is found in the words, "one to five years."

The first legislation in the United States empowering an indeterminate sentence was made in Michigan in 1869. They passed a law to allow early release of prostitutes under severe three year sentences, when evidence of reformation was provided. Other states soon began to allow parole eligibility in the latter part of the sentence. Most states now have fixed minimum and maximum limits to a sentence. "Good Time" laws, wiping out as much as one-third of a sentence for good behavior, were also adopted, as long-established measures in both Federal and state systems.

PAROLE PROCESSES AND AGENCIES

Parole is the conditional release of a prisoner, prior to the expiration of his sentence. Instead of prison controls, system controls occur. The parole board sets the time for release. Instructions follow as to the supervision, care, guidance and control of the parolee through monthly reports, interviews, budget scrutiny, visits and investigation of employment.

The parole process dates from 1840 through Sir Walter Crofton, an Irishman in England. It was also advocated by the French penologist deMarsangy in 1846. Prisoners came to be handled in a series of states; first, strict imprisonment; then labor on chain gangs; then freedom within a limited area; then a "ticket on leave" and finally, full restoration of liberty. Promotion from one stage to another was based on merit in labor and study, and on favorable conduct.

In the United States parole was utilized at the Elmira Reformatory in New York in 1876. It has since been adopted by all jurisdictions which utilize some flexibility of sentence. In less populated states, parole and probation are frequently combined in one officer. Usually, however, they are separate. Conditions imposed by parole can be light or heavy, rigid or flexible. Usually demands of parole supervision require permission to change residence, approved employment, submission of written reports, abstinence from liquor and drugs, and avoidance of companions with criminal records (the association rule). Permission is required to marry, to own an automobile, to contract debt, or to leave the state. If the conditions of parole are violated, the parolee may be reprimanded, penalized by more rigid rules, or returned to the prison to serve the remainder of his sentence. Severity of parole depends upon department policy, the parole officer himself, and the existing subculture in the community. Experienced parole officers are resourceful and flexible in their operations, and they nearly always carry staggering case loads.

Parole, like probation, has been criticized in its application. Many courts are reluctant to give up any of their sentencing power. Governors sometimes feel that parole infringes upon their power to pardon, although this is rare. Legislators are suspicious of seeming attempts to deprive them of their traditional power to "make the punishment fit the crime" rather than the individual. The general public tends to grow uneasy about the presence of the "ex-con" as there is a general feeling about inadequate retribution for a crime. This feeling breaks into active political concern after the commission of crime by anyone on parole, if the matter is publicized by the news media.

Parole authorities have a difficult task. They are saddled with the responsibility to determine, often after a quick study of a prisoner's background and a ten minute interview, whether to keep him in or let him out. Unfortunately "there is no conceivably relevant knowledge in existence to support either the decision to grant parole (to a given individual) or to deny it."[3] When prisons are overcrowded, pressure on parole officials rises; and when parole policy becomes too restrictive or capricious, the danger of prison riots increases. This relationship between parole practice and prison unrest is a little-investigated area. On the other hand, an image of leniency becomes politically embarrassing. There is no scientific basis for parole selection and we might as well flip a coin or draw straws.

Recently, parole has come into sharp criticism for alleged racial discrimination and over-reaction to reports of prison rule infractions. Because most parole boards are middle class, they tend to release prisoners who are exceptionally well-behaved in prison, although these are frequently persons who commit new offenses and are returned. Sometimes a difficult prisoner who refuses adjustment to prison may function better under freedom than the one who adjusts. Further, parole officers generally agree that "con men" get out first because they are most effective in first-impression short interviews.

Nonetheless, wise application of parole processes does result in an improved rehabilitation procedure. Pre-release training in prison and a discerning parole officer on the outside can make a crucial difference in the life of an offender and in the safety of the community. Perhaps any person who is deemed rehabilitated in the eyes of a parole board should become eligible for government insurance or bond. Any employer then hiring would have the government share responsibility for the conduct of the rehabilitated citizen.

The most recent innovation in parole policy is actually an attempt to embody the essential idea of Machonochie's 1840 system. Now called a contract system, the idea consists of having the new prisoner-candidate for parole sign a formal contract to accomplish certain things, different for each convict and arrived at only after careful study. Upon completion of these goals the prisoner is paroled. This is an attempt to create a positive incentive rather than a "do no evil" negative policy. If the prisoner accomplishes the goals, his disciplinary infractions are overlooked or seen as less important. In this system, the correctional authority can become a special unit authorized by the parole board to effect an offender's release upon completion of his contract.

Just as in the case of probation, criticism is often levelled because parole is either denied in too many cases, or allowed too frequently to bad choices. Just as in the case of probation, criticism is often directed toward the parole officer who may be poorly screened, underpaid, ill-

---

[3] American Friends Service Committee (1971). *The Struggle for Justice: A Report on Crime and Punishment in America.* Hill and Wang, New York.

trained and overloaded with cases. And just as in the case of the probation officer, we find parole officers who are dedicated, selfless, and highly motivated, extending themselves continuously, often in the face of great public apathy, indifference, ignorance and hostility toward the "ex-con."

Current developments inside the prison center around a better *departure adjustment* of the prisoner. This is accomplished through pre-release programs inside and trial leaves of various kinds outside.

A good pre-release program inside will consist of insight into oneself and others through group interaction and confrontation; discussions of community resources, and descriptions of the problems and feelings encountered during the shock of getting out.

Some prisoners are allowed to go out on a prison delivery truck for a day or week, or to buy clothing, or to apply for a job, to attend a funeral, or increasingly, to visit one's wife and family for a weekend or longer. These are *furloughs.*

When a prisoner is allowed to be with his wife under secluded circumstances on the prison grounds, it is called *conjugal visiting.* It has existed for years in Mexico, Scandinavian countries, and in some Southern prisons. Its purpose is to reduce sexual tension and consequent homosexuality in prison. Such an openly announced procedure is often resisted by both wives and prisoners. Married prisoners realize that their relief cannot be shared by single men, separated men, or men whose wives are unavailable. The morals of the community would not sanction extramarital arrangements. Therefore, allowing the prisoner to go home as in the furlough method is a more acceptable procedure.

Perhaps the most important pre-release developments are "work release" and "education release." Pioneered in North Carolina, *work release* is now a major thrust in many state prisons, and in the Federal system since new laws promulgated in 1966. Under work release, prisoners are allowed to work at an outside job during the day, and to return to the prison or to some other detention facility (e.g., Half-way House) at night. *Education release* allows the prisoner, subject to the same conditions, to go to school. However, the psychological makeup of some convicts finds these arrangements to be more trying than straight imprisonment. The majority, however, learn to prove themselves in the outside world, derive importance from earning a livelihood, and become stronger candidates for parole.

The last (and the oldest) but not least, prison improvement is *prison education.* When a wave of prison reform swept the country for a decade, beginning in 1912, libraries and some classes, but especially correspondence courses, were introduced. Many prisoners seized this chance to develop their minds and capabilities. In Kansas, for example, correspondence courses, with occasional visits by the instructors, were begun in Leavenworth Federal Prison and Kansas State Prison in 1913. Today, state laws require most prisons to provide a program to the sixth or eighth grade. Illiteracy becomes a special target. Most large northern prisons have a high school or high school equivalency program. College courses through extension divisions and special projects such as Project Newgate, and Rebound, are being developed to educate prisoners. Sadly, prison educators tend to become discouraged because of inadequate budgets and facilities. They frequently turn the job over to "inmate tutors" and assume supervisory roles. When teachers come in from the outside, however, this third force enlivens the program and multiplies the interest of prisoners and teachers inside.

Our country's judges are speaking out most forcefully. Chief Justice Warren Burger, in 1964, while a judge on the U.S. Court of Appeals in Washington, wrote strongly against the "warehouse" attitude. "It makes no more sense to keep people in prisons without treatment than to keep patients in hospitals without doctors; pure custody is both expensive and unproductive."[4] U.S. District Judge James E. Doyle, spoke very strongly about the inadequacy of prisons: "I am persuaded that the institution of prison probably must end. In many respects it is as intolerable as slavery, equally brutalizing to all involved, equally toxic to the social system, equally subversive of the brotherhood of men, even more costly by some standards, and probably less rational."[5]

It would seem that large changes are in store for all segments of the criminal justice system.

CONCLUSION

It should be obvious to the student that after the commission of a criminal offense, there are a great number of agencies and people who have a part to play in the investigation of the violation, the prosecution and trial, and the custody and treatment of the offender.

In addition, there are thousands of other people directly concerned with the administration of criminal justice—such as bail bondsmen, newspapermen, court clerks, organizations representing majority group members, such as the NAACP, organizations representing citizens interested in civil rights, such as the ACLU, and organizations representing citizens interested in governmental efficiency, such as the various taxpayers' associations and municipal leagues. These peripheral groups do much to mold public

---

[4] Burger, Chief Justice Warren E. (1971). "Treatment, not Punishment, is the Sensible Way." Los Angeles *Times*, November 11.

[5] Doyle, U.S. District Judge James E. (1972). Associated Press dispatch from Madison, Wisconsin. Los Angeles *Times*, April 7.

opinion, and exercise, in many communities, a great influence upon governmental operations.

When individuals and groups, peripheral to law enforcement, move to *assist* law enforcement in improving its policies and procedures to achieve more efficient, moral, and legal operations, they become welcome allies indeed; but when individuals and groups; peripheral to law enforcement, move to *obstruct* law enforcement in achieving its proper goals, they become grave impediments to the implementation of community tranquility and ordered liberty.

The authors are of the opinion that both formal law enforcement agencies, federal, state, local, and private, and related agencies, courts, prosecution, defense, juries, probation officers, penal officers, and parole officers, welcome the assistance of all individuals and groups interested in law enforcement processes, welcome their constructive criticism, welcome their interest and concern, and welcome their many avenues of communication with the general public.

The authors are of the opinion that both formal and related law enforcement agencies welcome the assistance, constructive criticism, interest and concern of every American—for every American is continually involved, in one way or another, with the protective, repressive, accusatory, judicial, custodial, and correctional operations involved in the administration of criminal justice.

Finally, the authors are of the opinion that the student of law enforcement must realize that his proposed career work is of concern, not only to the agency which may hire him, but to the other related agencies of law enforcement, to individuals and groups specifically interested in law enforcement processes, and to every American, in one way or another.

TOPICS FOR DISCUSSION

1. What is the relationship between the prosecutor's office and the law enforcement agencies (municipal and county) in this locale?
2. What is the availability of competent defense counsel in this locale?
3. What is the size of the Grand Jury; what are its duties; what is the selection process for Grand Jury service in this locale?
4. What kind of people serve on trial juries in this locale?
5. What technical background is required of the Coroner or Medical Examiner in this jurisdiction?
6. What is the relationship between probation and parole officers and the law enforcement agencies (municipal and county) in this locale?
7. What types of correctional institutions are located within 100 miles?
8. Is the "indeterminate sentence" effective in terms of treatment and rehabilitation?
9. Is the "classification system" effective in terms of treatment and rehabilitation?

PART V
PROCESSES OF CRIMINAL JUSTICE

Chapter XV

PROCESSES OF JUSTICE—INTRODUCTORY

Before discussing the pre-trial, trial, and post-trial processes involved in the administration of criminal justice, it might be wise to discuss several concepts related to our criminal law.

The source of our criminal and civil law system is the English Common Law—unwritten or traditional law—as modified and supplemented by statutes and decisions over the years.

A *Tort*, or civil wrong, is considered as a private offense committed against an individual. In civil actions, the victim institutes court action, may receive damages in a favorable judgment, and is primarily interested in *personal redress* for his injuries. Most tort actions are settled out of court by attorneys representing the parties at suit. Either the plaintiff or the defendant, consonant with procedural requirements, may appeal the judgment of the court.

A *Crime*, or public wrong, is considered a social offense against the State. In criminal actions, the people prosecute, damages, by ways of fines, go to the state rather than to the victim (or are otherwise allocated for some specific purpose), and *penalty* is an essential part of the process. Very few criminal cases are settled out of court, and the public prosecutor may or may not appeal an adverse decision of the court. (Whether an appeal can be taken depends on statutory provisions.)

Thus, an offense may be *simultaneously* a tort and a crime, and may be prosecuted by the victim *and* by the public. Thus, for the same offense, a person may be found guilty in a criminal action and sentenced to punishment, and, be found at fault in a civil action and required to pay damages.

The student of law enforcement will concern himself, primarily, with the criminal act and criminal law, rather than with the tort and the civil law.

A crime, simply defined, is an act, or omission to act, in violation of the law, to which is attached some form of punishment—disqualification to hold, or removal from, office; fine; imprisonment; or execution.

The criminal law, or law of crimes, consists mainly of formal statutes and ordinances which delineate offenses and their punishments. However, in a number of states, common law crimes remain in effect except as modified by statutes. Modification has been widespread in all jurisdictions, extending as far, in some states, as to completely abrogate common law criminal offenses.

At earlier common law, more so than today, felonies were somewhat precisely distinguished according *to their nature,* as "crimes *mala in se* and *mala prohibita;* the former class comprises those acts which are immoral or wrong in themselves, such as murder, rape, arson, burglary, larceny, breach of the peace, forgery, and the like, while the latter embraces those things which are prohibited by statute, because they infringe on the rights of others, although no moral turpitude may attach, and they are crimes only because they are prohibited by statute." [1]

The distinction is mainly academic today, as a number of misdemeanors are *mala in se,* and moreover, crimes called *mala prohibita,* currently infers that the mere doing of the forbidden act is the crime. In other words, a state of mind (intent) as an element, in such offenses, has been eliminated in such criminal statutes. Obviously, in dispensing with intent as an element, it becomes much easier to prove the crime. Violations of most traffic laws, curfew law violations, and restrictions against picking flowers in public parks are a few examples of many such offenses classed as *mala prohibita.*

Crimes may be distinguished according *to the penalties* attached to the offense. At common law, the *felony* was an offense that occasioned forfeiture of lands or goods, and to which capital or other punishment was added. The common law felonies were murder, manslaughter, rape, sodomy, robbery, burglary, larceny, and arson. In this country, at this time, there is no general forfeiture of lands or goods, nor any accepted test for felony offenses. In general, a felony may be said to be *an offense that is punishable by death or by imprisonment in a state prison.* Many of the common law felonies have been formalized by statute, and certain new felonies created. A capital offense is a felony that is punishable by death— the most common such offenses being treason, murder, kidnapping, and trainwrecking.

At common law, the *misdemeanor* was a minor offense with minor penalties attached. In general, a misdemeanor may be said to be *an offense that does not amount to a felony.* Most misdemeanors are punishable by fine or by imprisonment in the municipal or county jail. A few *high misdemeanors,* or *county court misdemeanors,* are punishable by large fines or by imprisonment in the state prison, and tried in courts of general jurisdiction, rather than in the inferior courts.

Finally, crimes may be distinguished according *to the method of recording and reporting offenses.* Thus, *major* crime in the United States

---

[1] See 22 *C.J.S.,* 8 Criminal Law.

consists of the following categories utilized in the Uniform Crime Reports: Murder and Non-negligent Manslaughter; Forcible Rape; Robbery; Aggravated Assault; Burglary-Breaking or Entering; Larceny-Theft over $50; and Auto Theft. (Also referred to as "Index Crime.")

OBJECTIVES OF CRIMINAL LAW

The body of criminal law, of interest to every citizen, protects several different interests; has several different objectives:

The Individual. Criminal law protects *each individual member of society* against *harm to his person* (laws such as refer to homicide, rape, mayhem, assault and battery); against *harm to his property* (laws such as refer to robbery, burglary, theft, and fraud); against *harm to his freedom of movement* (laws such as refer to kidnapping or false imprisonment); and against *harm to his domestic relations* (laws such as refer to adultery, abduction, neglect of dependents, or failure to provide).

The Government. Criminal law protects *governmental functions* against *disruption of public peace and order* (laws such as refer to treason, sedition, disorderly conduct, and disturbance of the peace); and against *harm to public administration* (laws such as refer to perjury or bribery).

The Common Good. Criminal law protects *public decency and the common good* against *corruptive influences and debilitating vices* (laws such as refer to bigamy, incest, perversion, prostitution, gambling, cruelty to animals, sale and possession of drugs and liquors).

Study of the criminal act, investigation and prosecution of the offense, and treatment of the offender are complex tasks, and will engage the student very deeply in his courses of criminal law, criminal evidence, criminal procedure, abnormal psychology, ethics, criminology, and correctional administration. Yet anyone who would aspire to the title of "professional" law enforcement careerist *must* gain such perspective.

TERMINOLOGY

There are certain terms utilized in discussions of criminal law and the processes of criminal justice which are often confusing to the uninitiated, and misused consistently by the general public. Some of the more pertinent concepts are as follows:

CORPUS DELICTI: An important rule of evidence in criminal cases requires proof of the *corpus delicti* (body of the offense). The term is defined in Black's Law Dictionary, 4th Edition, literally as "the substance or foundation of a crime; the substantive fact a crime has been committed."

Generally speaking, "The *corpus delicti* is a compound fact made up of two things: the existence of a certain act or result forming the basis of the criminal charge, as the occurrence of an injury or loss; and the existence of a criminal agency as the cause of this act or result. . . . As a general rule the connection of the accused with the crime, or the identity of the perpetrator, is not an element of the *corpus delicti*." [2]

(The word "element," as used above, does not refer to the essential elements of a crime such as "intent." Consequently, to avoid possible confusion, it might be better to view the *corpus delicti* of a crime as made up of two basic ingredients or parts, rather than as consisting of two elements.)

 ſ INTENT: Mere intent to commit a crime is never a violation, and never prosecuted. Every crime involves a criminal act or criminal omission to act, or criminal negligence. Intent or resolve to commit the act (excluding offenses mala prohibita) is an essential element in crimes, and usually indicated by the circumstances connected with the offense.

Some crimes require a *specific intent*—such as crimes of theft, where there must be an intent to deprive the owner of his property permanently.

Other crimes require a state of mind referred to as *general intent*. This means nothing more or less than conscious wrong doing (*mens rea*, mind of the thing), which, as far as proof is concerned, is inferred unless expressly denied. Moreover, there is a class of offenses wherein intent is immaterial, as discussed heretofore, when the mere doing of the forbidden act is the offense, regardless of the state of mind existing at the time of the act. The state of mind required in any given crime can be determined by reading the statute—though, at times, difficult to pinpoint.

Willed or intentional conduct is of the essence in criminal law. Yet, some acts are committed without the actual intent to bring about a particular result, but which seriously affect the public welfare. The law, resorting to expediency, manufactures intent to meet the traditional requirements of willed conduct, and, in so doing, prevents many wrongdoers from sidestepping justice on a technicality.

As an example, one might note that *culpable negligence*, in a very real sense, can be an equivalent for actual intent. (Doctor A, thinking of his golf game, prescribes 100 grams, rather than 10 grains, of a toxic drug, and the patient dies; Track Switchman B, watching a kite, pulls the wrong track lever at 3:00 p.m., and two trains collide with fatal injuries. The law, in such cases, will find Doctor A and Switchman B responsible.)

As another example, one might note that *constructive intent*, in a very real sense, denotes the transfer of actual intent. (Shooter C, intending to kill his friend D, hits Bystander E; Robber F, intending to rob store, kills owner G. The law, in such cases, will find that Shooter C actually intended to hit Bystander E, and that Robber F actually intended to kill Owner G.)

OMISSION TO ACT: Failure to act may be punishable. For example, failure to file an Income Tax Return, as required by law, is crime. (Or, as a further illustration, if Parent H wilfully fails to provide medical attention for Sick Child I, and, as a result thereof Sick Child I dies, Parent H will be criminally responsible for the death of the child.)

---

[2] *C.J.S.*, 916 Criminal Law.

ᶠ MOTIVE: The *reason* or *purpose* for the criminal act is never an element in any crime. Yet, the presence or absence of motive may be considered by the judge or jury, and may become very important in proving intent, and in cases involving circumstantial evidence.

ᶜ CONSPIRACY: The agreement to commit a crime, accompanied by some act toward the crime, is a criminal offense in some jurisdictions, even though the intended crime does not occur. In many jurisdictions, however, a conspiracy without an overt act toward carrying it out is enough to sustain a conspiracy charge, particularly as regards conspiracies to commit certain crimes.

ᶠ SOLICITATION: To counsel, induce, or entice another person to commit a crime is a criminal offense in some states, while in others, the common law concept of solicitation has been modified by statute, or, as in New York, expressly abrogated by statute. (Generally, in New York, the one who counseled, induced, or enticed another to commit a crime is deemed a principal and is charged with the basic crime itself.) The gist of the offense is soliciting another person to commit a criminal offense. There is no need to have an acceptance, agreement, or any other act on the part of the person solicited.

(*Entrapment*, that is, inducing a person to commit a criminal act not contemplated by him, for the purpose of prosecuting him, is a form of solicitation that renders prosecution improper or impossible. The entrapment, as commonly held, must be an inducement made by some type of government official.)

POSSESSION: It may be a criminal offense merely to possess prohibited articles. Such occurs in the case of narcotics in the possession of someone other than a doctor, pharmacist, or other authorized person; or possession of automatic weapons by someone other than, for example, police or military personnel on duty.

ATTEMPTS: The attempt to commit a felony or misdemeanor (usually of the *mala in se* types), which comes so close to success that public order is jeopardized, constitutes a misdemeanor offense in some jurisdictions, whereas in others, such attempts are designated as a felony or misdemeanor according to the nature of the attempt.

CONSENT: In crimes where lack of consent by the victim is an essential element of the offense—such as rape, robbery, theft and embezzlement—voluntary consent by the victim precludes successful prosecution.

PRINCIPAL: One who participates in a criminal act by committing the act, or by aiding, abetting, advising, or encouraging the offense, is called a *principal*. Some states (viz. Kentucky) refine such involvement by designating the participant as a principal in either the first or second degree. In many other states, an accessory before the fact is treated as a principal.

ACCESSORY: One who helps a felony offender escape or avoid arrest, or who harbors or conceals a felony offender, is called an *accessory*, or an *accessory after the fact*. Furthermore, in some states which lean more toward common law concepts, an *accessory before the fact* designates the mastermind, a person who engineers crime and protects criminals, but who is never at the scene when the crime is committed.

INCAPABLE: Certain persons are deemed incapable of committing a criminal act. Children under certain ages, idiots, morons, lunatics, insane persons, those who act in ignorance or mistake of fact, those who are unconscious, those who act under threat, and those whose act is by misfortune or accident cannot be successfully prosecuted if such incapacity can be shown.

JURISDICTION: The legal authority of an agency of government to deal with some matter is referred to as *jurisdiction*.

The jurisdiction of a police agency may apply to the specific laws it is responsible to enforce, or to the geographical area in which it operates. Thus, police jurisdiction deals with the *right* to enforce certain laws, or to operate in certain areas.

The jurisdiction of a court may apply to the person of the offender or to the subject matter of the offense. The jurisdiction of a court over the person of the offender applies only if he is physically present—that is, an offender cannot be tried *in absentia*. Some persons are exempt from the jurisdiction of our courts, such as foreign ambassadors. The jurisdiction of a court in relation to the offense is often complicated. Generally, the federal courts have jurisdiction relative to offenses which are violations of federal law committed within the United States, its territories, possessions, and on ships of the nation; state courts have jurisdiction relative to offenses which are violations of statutes, and which are committed within the state. Thus, court jurisdiction deals with the *right* to try a case.

VENUE: The geographical location of the offense often determines which court will hear or determine a case—which court has *venue*.

A criminal act or omission to act which is simultaneously a violation of both federal and state law *may* result in trials in *both* federal *and* state courts without violating the offender's constitutional right to protection from double jeopardy, for *two* sovereignties are involved, and *two* separate and distinct offenses. Because state statutes, county ordinances, and municipal ordinances are operative under the state constitution, under *one* sovereignty, offenders *cannot* be tried several times for offenses which are simultaneously violations of city, county, and state law. Thus, court venue deals with the *place* of trial.

COMPLAINT: A charge made by an individual, preferred before a magistrate with competent jurisdiction, that a specific person named in the complaint has committed an offense set forth in the complaint. The form is legal in nature and sets forth the facts to be laid before a magistrate in order to determine if a crime has been committed and whether or not there is probable or adequate cause to suspect the person accused of the offense.

INFORMATION: The form used to accuse a person of a criminal offense in the absence of an indictment. The information is differentiated from the indictment only by being presented by a competent legal officer (such as the District Attorney) rather than by a Grand Jury.

INDICTMENT: An accusation set down in writing which is found and presented by a legally assembled and sworn Grand Jury. If the Indictment is found to be a "True Bill" (evidence was presented establishing the fact that a crime has been committed, and that there is probable or adequate cause to suspect the person accused of the offense) then the accused is held to stand trial on the issue of guilt or innocence. The Indictment is returned to the court in which jurisdiction the Grand Jury is impaneled charging that the person named therein has committed some act which by law has been declared a public offense.

EXTRADITION: The process by which fugitives are returned by the government of the place to which they flee to the government of the place from which they fled is called *extradition*.

Between nations, extradition is provided by treaty. Between states, extradition (more correctly *rendition*) is provided by the Federal Constitution, and by interstate compacts. The Constitution provides for interstate rendition, stating that "a person charged in any state with treason, felony, or other crime, who shall flee from justice, and be found in another state shall, on demand of the executive authority of the state from which he fled, be delivered up to be removed to the state having jurisdiction of the crime." This provision has been interpreted by the Supreme Court as a moral obligation, and not as a mandatory requirement.

The processes of justice which take place after a crime has been committed involve many people other than the offender, victim, witnesses, and police. The prosecutor, grand jury, petit jury, court, probation office, penal institution, and parole office have significant roles.

In the following two chapters, the authors will attempt to delineate pre-trial, trial, and post-trial processes so that the student may gain an over-all perspective of the massive machinery which has been established to secure "equal justice under law."

(The reader may find it helpful to refer to Appendix C, Charts 1 and 2, while considering these chapters, for the authors have prepared flowcharts to illustrate the movement and interrelation of procedures and processes. In addition, flow charts inside book covers amplify the processes of criminal justice.)

TOPICS FOR DISCUSSION

1. According to the *Uniform Crime Reports*,[3] what are the most prevalent types of major crime in this locale?
2. Discuss the *forms* of complaint, information, and indictment utilized in this locale.

---

[3] For sale by the Superintendent of Documents, U.S. Government Printing Office, Washington, D.C. 20402.

Chapter XVI

PRE-TRIAL PROCESSES

AFTER A CRIME OCCURS, and is somehow made known (for many crimes are never observed or reported), the processes of justice may be started in motion in a wide variety of fashions.

The crime may be reported by the victim or offender to the police, to the prosecutor, to the grand jury, or to the coroner.

The crime may be observed by, or become known to, a member of the general public. He may, depending on the circumstances, make an immediate arrest of the offender; report the offense to the police department or prosecutor; or make information available to the grand jury or coroner.

The crime may be observed by, or become known to, a police officer. He may, depending on the circumstances, make an immediate arrest of the offender; issue a summons, citation, or notice of violation; begin an official investigation; report the offense for investigation by other officers or other agencies; request a complaint through the prosecutor's office; or make information available to the grand jury or coroner.

From the time that the crime is committed to the time that the offender is identified, there may be an interval of seconds or years. From the time the offender is identified to the time he is detained, there may be an interval of seconds or days. From the time the suspect is detained to the time of his arrest, there may be an interval of seconds or days. From the time of arrest to the time of booking, there may be an interval of minutes or days. From the time of booking to the time of arraignment there may be an interval of hours or days. From the time of arraignment to the time of trial there may be an interval of minutes or days. From the time of trial to the time of sentencing there may be an interval of minutes or weeks. In other words, depending on the type of offense and the circumstances surrounding it, the processes of justice may be swift or dilatory.

Often, after a crime occurs, there is ample time for a complete and thorough investigation which includes the search and recording of the crime scene, the collection and preservation of evidence, the application of modus operandi techniques, the uncovering of all sources of information, the surveillance of suspects, their interview and interrogation, the interview of witnesses and victims, and the obtaining of search and arrest warrants through the courts.

Often, after a crime occurs, if it is a minor offense, enforcement officers or magistrates may proceed by notice of violation, summons, or citation— that is, a written notice of the offense may be allowed as a privilege, in lieu of arrest. Traffic officers, fire, health, and building inspectors utilize this method to a great extent, and the offender generally has three choices open to him: (1) He can report to the specified place, place bail which has been set by schedule, forfeit it, and consider the matter ended (technically, not paying a "fine," but posting bail, automatically pleading guilty, and for-feiting bail); (2) He can report to the specified place, plead guilty, or innocent and request a trial and appear for arraignment at a specified time; (3) He can ignore the notice, summons, or citation, in which case one or two letters demanding his appearance will be sent to him, and if he ignores these, a warrant will be issued for his arrest.

And often, after a crime occurs, the police must act with immediacy, and make an on-the-scene arrest lest an offender escape justice.

ARREST

Arrest—the taking of a person into custody for the purpose of charging him with a crime—is a most sensitive area of police activity. Technically, in most jurisdictions, anyone, citizen or officer, can make an arrest for a misdemeanor or felony offense attempted or committed in his presence, for a felony offense committed, even though not in his presence, and on charges made by another that a felony offense has been committed. Practically, for the most part, the business of arrest is left to the law enforcement officer who is presumed to have the training and judgment necessary to make a good arrest.

An arrest is made by actual restraint of the subject, or by his submission to the custody of the person making an arrest. Generally, the subject is informed of the intention to arrest, the cause of arrest, and the authority for the arrest. (Obviously, this may be impossible when a subject is in the process of attempting or committing a crime, or being pursued after the commission of a crime, or after an escape from custody.) As much force as is necessary to make the arrest is allowable, but only the amount neces-sary to overcome resistance. Generally, if in the immediate pursuit of an offender, the officer may go outside the limits of his jurisdiction to make the arrest. Officers and citizens, in the case of a felony offense, but only officers in the case of a misdemeanor offense, may break in after demand-ing admission and explaining their purpose if they have reasonable cause to believe the offender to be inside.

Any person who willfully resists a lawful arrest, or interferes in the making of a lawful arrest, is guilty of a criminal offense. Yet, generally, any person may resist an unlawful arrest, and may meet force with force. (Some states take away that right if the person is being arrested by identified police officers.)

False arrest or false imprisonment is a dangerous situation for a police officer or citizen, for either may be liable for damages. Hence, whenever possible, a thorough investigation is made before the process of arrest, so that the probability that a crime was committed may be established, and so that facts may be developed as to the identity of the perpetrator. Whenever possible, an arrest warrant is obtained through the court—a legal order, in writing, commanding the arrest of the person named or described therein. When an officer says, "You're under arrest," this should always mark the commencement of an orderly procedure. It should *never* involve the crude application of massive power against a helpless victim; rather, it should involve the careful implementation of lawful authority in reference to a fellow citizen.

Some observers have made a distinction between an *arrest* and a *detention*. Other authorities, however, maintain that it is an illusion to draw any real distinction between an arrest and a detention.

When the police arrest someone, is that act also a detention? Of course, and the authors know of no position to the contrary. But, when police "stop," "field interview," "frisk," "field interrogate," "detain," or "hold" someone, is that detention also an arrest? Some people would say, "Certainly!"; others would state, "It could be"; and still others would say, "Of course not!" The issue is crucial, for if detention really means arrest, then the detention must meet the standards of probable cause.

To some people, *outside of law enforcement,* an arrest occurs whenever a person's freedom of movement is restricted by the authority and power of a police officer, whether or not liberty is curtailed for moments or hours, whether or not taken into custody, or whether or not charged with crime, whether or not booked, or prosecuted, or found guilty.

To most people, *in law enforcement,* an arrest occurs whenever a person is "taken into custody for the purpose of charging him with a crime." Thus, when a citizen is held, charged with a crime, and told, "You're under arrest," the arrest is a fact, formalized by booking, and the arrestee has a criminal record. Such arrest will appear in the statistical reports of the police agency whether or not a complaint is filed, whether or not a trial is held, and whether or not the accused is found guilty.

But, often, in some jurisdictions, in investigating crime, there are several suspects, and probable cause to arrest—but knowing that an arrest will result in a criminal record, officers request cooperation from such persons and "hold" them for questioning.

Often, while on patrol, an officer observes an individual in a compromising situation, so much so that an arrest on probable cause could be made—but the officer sometimes "detains" the person in order to get the facts. In such a case, if a person is not implicated, he is released—and spared the stigma of a criminal record.

There are other situations which may not constitute arrests in the eyes of the officer, such as "stopping" a vehicle for the purpose of identifying and verifying the title of the vehicle or the license to operate it. Similarly, when a person is abroad, late at night, under suspicious circumstances, he may be given a "field interview" or "field interrogation" and temporarily detained for the purpose of identification. Furthermore, a good citizen, in fulfilling his civic responsibility, may cooperate with the investigative agency and consent to a temporary, self-imposed restriction upon his freedom of movement. An example may be found in the situation where the officer says, "Would you mind coming down to the station for a while, so that we may check out this matter?" and the subject freely and voluntarily cooperates.

To most officers, the stopping, field interviewing, frisking, field interrogation, detention, or holding of a person for the purpose of identification, and the taking of a person to the precinct for questioning, do not constitute an arrest, for the party has not been formally accused of crime, nor booked. These *detentions*, regardless of their propriety, duration, extent of coercion, or whether or not the person is later arrested and booked, are *not* part of the agency's *arrest* records.

The Fourth Amendment, which bans "unreasonable searches and seizures," sets an arrest standard of "probable cause," meaning that there must be sufficient evidence to convince a prudent man that an offense has been or is being committed. In short, *arrest for mere suspicion is unconstitutional* (even though so widely practiced in some crime-ridden areas that around 100,000 such arrests a year are openly listed in the FBI's issue of *Uniform Crime Reports.*)

Some states have developed the concept of "pre-arrest detention" to permit police to act on "reasonable suspicion." Delaware, Rhode Island, and New Hampshire have adopted modified versions of the Uniform Arrest Act which allows the police to stop, question, detain and frisk any person "whom he has reasonable ground to suspect" of having committed a crime. Unless there is probable cause for *actual* arrest, the person must be released after two hours. This results in an "investigative arrest" and is now used, informally, in many states.

New York has a "Stop and Frisk" law which resembles the Uniform Arrest Act, except that suspects cannot be detained if the frisk or questioning fails to yield probable cause for *actual* arrest. The frisk is authorized when the officer reasonably believes his life might be endangered.

The reader must realize that there are fine distinctions and many legal niceties involved in this area, and a wide variety of procedures now in effect throughout the United States. Some jurisdictions are most careful and meticulous relative to their operations in this area; other jurisdictions are very lax and seem to rely upon the courts to draw the lines. The courts themselves issue a complicated array of interpretations, and the policeman, working in the field, has a difficult time in following the policies and procedures of his agency in such fashion that they will be satisfactory to prosecutor, trial and appellate courts of the state, and the United States Supreme Court.

Suffice it to say that both procedures, arrest and detention, can be abused, and are abused by unprofessional police.

With regard to arrests, statistical information can be helpful in pinpointing abuses, for wherever there are many arrests without the filing of complaints, or many filings without convictions, a grave problem may exist.

With regard to detentions, abuses are difficult to detect and identify. There is little statistical information relative to the numbers of "stops," "field interviews," "frisks," "field interrogations," "detentions," or holdings."

In some areas, not only are many people arrested and released each year without a complaint ever having been filed against them, but many more are detained and released without ever having been formally arrested and booked. *And herein lies one of the key causes of police-community conflict that will attract much attention in coming years.*

Both arrest and detention can certainly form a necessary and proper part of police operations. But clarification of the law is needed to provide for momentary "stops" based on reasonable suspicion, and temporary detention based on probable cause.

Although statistical records are kept relative to arrests which culminate in a booking, there is little information available as to the number of people who are "stopped," "field interviewed," "frisked," "field interrogated," "detained," or "held" for seconds, minutes, or hours. It may be necessary, as law enforcement becomes more sophisticated in its operations, to give greater attention to this area. In the absence of law enforcement attention, the courts may soon begin to inquire relative to this area of police activity, with the possibility of even greater restrictions being placed on the law enforcement officer. Rather than sweeping the question under the rug, or "running scared," American law enforcement must face up to the key question: *Is a detention an arrest?* Some policemen, motivated by zeal, would desire complete freedom in this area in order to strengthen their battle against crime. Such men should ponder the words of Justice Cardozo:

> Liberty in the most literal sense is the negation of law; for law is restraint, and the absence of restraint is anarchy. On the other hand, anarchy by destroying restraint would leave liberty the exclusive possession of the strong or the unscrupulous. . . .

Imprisonment is an involuntary situation where the personal liberty of a person is violated, where the person makes verbal or physical resistance, and where force, verbal or physical, is utilized to hold the person. Imprisonment may be privileged, as in the case of a legal arrest, or unprivileged, in which case false arrest and false imprisonment may be involved.

Searches of a person and the surrounding area may be made incidental to a lawful arrest. Whenever possible, a search warrant should be obtained through the court—a legal order, in writing, permitting the search of a specified person or place, and the seizure of the things named in the search warrant. Since the *Mapp* case, decided June 19, 1961, ". . . all evidence obtained by searches and seizures in violation of the Constitution, is, by that same authority, inadmissible in a state court."[1] Now *all* law enforcement officers, federal, state, and local, are bound by the exclusionary rule which provides that evidence obtained illegally shall not be admissible in court.

The area of arrest, search, and seizure is a complicated and delicate zone of police activity. Professional police education and training programs lay great stress on this sphere of activity, and attempt to inculcate a clear understanding of proper police authority and the limitations to that authority due to constitutional considerations and court interpretations.

BOOKING

After the arrest is made by officer or citizen, there occurs what is referred to as *booking*—the registering, formally, in the law enforcement records system, of the date, time, charge, name of arrestee, and name of arresting person. The arrestee now has a "police record" which will remain on file.

Ordinarily, the arrestee is booked on a specific charge for violation of a state statute, or county or municipal ordinance. Yet, in a few jurisdictions, the arrestee may be booked for "Suspicion of ....," or, in others, on an "Open Charge," or, in others, as "Held for Investigation." If the arrest is made legally, and according to reasonable belief, there is no reason why the suspect or offender should not be booked for the specific offense. No person should ever be booked unless there is reasonable cause for arrest. There are no *crimes* known as "Suspicion of.........," "Open Charge," or "Held for Investigation."

If the arrest is made *illegally*, as a form of attitude punishment, or as a form of extra-judicial sanction for police "problem cases," or as the result of department production demands, with the person being detained for the

---

[1] *Mapp v. Ohio*, 367 U.S. 643 (1961).

ordinary maximum allowable twenty-four or forty-eight hours and then released without being charged before a magistrate, and such detention considered as a "police department sentence," a mockery is made of due process, police authority violated, and police power tyrannically exercised. The same can be said for the departmental policy which requires that all persons found with a club or gun or other possible weapon in their automobile are to be booked "Suspicion of Robbery," checked out, and released without being charged. It is in this manner that some citizens have received a lengthy "police record"—so lengthy in some areas of some cities that it is said that ". . . there's no one in this area with a first-time robbery record; they all have two or three on their 'rap sheets'!"—a police record that, in fact, may not be indicative of anti-social behavior, but which, *on the record* appears to be highly derogatory. One recent report, 1961, of a State Assembly Interim Committee on Criminal Procedure stated, "The Committee finds that hundreds of persons are arrested and released . . . each year without a complaint ever having been filed against them. Each of these persons acquires a permanent arrest record which presents a serious handicap to his prospects for employment." If police records are to have genuine integrity and meaning, these policies must be completely eradicated whenever they are found to exist. (It is significant that a movement is growing to change the forms of application for employment so that the entry "List all *arrests*" is amended to read "List all *convictions*.")

At any rate, after booking, formal detention then ensues in city or county jail, and the case is prepared for court.

As to how long a period of time may elapse between the detention of a person and his arrest, or between the arrest of a suspect and his booking, or between his booking and his arraignment (being brought to court to be charged with an offense and answering to it) is a matter of policy and statutory law, and which varies widely between jurisdictions.

It has been suggested that a maximum of two hours detention be allowed before an arrest is made, and twenty-four hours between arrest and appearance before a magistrate. Some state laws provide that an arrestee must be charged "forthwith," and others "without unreasonable delay," and yet others impose strict statutory time limits. Policies and rules which are too strict may hamper legitimate police operations; those which are too loose may encourage abuses of the police power.

The use of the time between original detention or arrest and the preliminary hearing may be proper—in preparing evidence, interviewing witnesses, procuring the complaint—or, it may be improper—in the induction of admissions or confessions by force, threats, or promises of reward. When the "third degree" is used to obtain admissions or confessions, police operations are brutalized, false confessions made possible, and public confidence destroyed.

Interviews and interrogations at police headquarters should never be used as a method of finding probable cause for holding a person when, in fact, the person has been illegally detained on mere suspicion or "hunch."

Recourse from false arrest or third degree method is limited; often, the jurisdiction and its agents are deemed privileged or immune from suit; often, if judgment is obtained, the officer is too impecunious to pay damages; and often, such occurrences are thoroughly whitewashed or covered up. (If a violation of constitutional rights is involved, according to a 1961 United States Supreme Court decision, a suit for damages may be instituted in the federal courts.[2])

Some authorities have suggested that all police interviews and interrogations after detention be placed on tape or sound-film recording; others have suggested that jurisdictions be required to maintain liability insurance, or be required to make public compensation for illegal damages inflicted; and still others have suggested that an assault and battery illegally committed by police on a detained suspect be made a felony offense.

Recourse from overly prolonged detention is also difficult. Often, prolonged detentions are the result of inadequate arrest laws and rules of criminal procedure. To complete an investigation, to protect a victim or witness, or to prevent flight, a suspect, whose arrest was impossible to delay, is often held by devious means. He might be held for the maximum allowable time, and then instantly re-booked on another offense, in order to justify the extension of detention. If his friends and relatives have engaged an attorney, there is often the device of "the wheel" to avoid service of a *writ of habeas corpus*—the suspect is either booked "John Doe," or "Hold for Investigators—En Route County Jail," whereby the prisoner is transported from station house to station house in order to maintain his detention. Instances occur where official policy demands that whenever a telephone call is received inquiring as to the detention of a felony prisoner, the headquarters detective units be immediately notified, and the prisoner immediately removed to another detention facility. Such practices can be understood, even though difficult to justify, for the investigator labors, often, under grave handicaps.

One study, completed in 1959, indicated that in the *year* 1956, in a large police department in the United States, 20,000 defendants were held at least seventeen hours before they were booked; that 2,000 were illegally detained two days or longer; and that 350 were held for three days or more

---

[2] *Monroe v. Pape*, 365 U.S. 167 (1961).

without being charged, without being allowed bail, and without due process.

It would seem that early production before a magistrate is part of due process. Theoretically, in the United States, only a short time elapses between the recording of the arrest (booking) and production before court, but, practically, very often, too great a time elapses.

A large percentage of persons arrested, and entitled to be brought before a magistrate, are released without being charged. In some jurisdictions, as many as 40 per cent of those arrested are released without being charged before a magistrate—a rate which tends to indicate that many of those arrested persons should not have been placed under arrest in the first place, or tends to indicate the use of the "roust arrest" as a form of police punishment for certain anti-social members of society, or as a means of fulfilling production goals, or to "clean up" an area.

PRE-TRIAL DETENTION OR RELEASE

As has been previously stated, the booked prisoner is detained in city or county jail pending a hearing. During this time he may be released from custody through various devices available to him:

He may be released on a *waiver* or *discharge* by the arresting agency. Often, acting on a reasonable belief, officers arrest a suspect, but later, his innocence becomes manifest, and he is released—by a waiver or discharge— a free man. Often, military personnel are given a waiver or discharge on minor offenses, and released to the military police or shore patrol for military discipline. They are then free, as far the arresting agency is concerned, although they may undergo court-martial or company punishment by the military establishment.

He may be released on *bail*. Bail is the posting of cash or security, or a personal recognizance, as a guarantee of appearance in court. If the accused cannot post bail in the form of cash or security, the promise by a surety to pay money if the bailee does not appear is allowed—hence the existence of the bail *bondsman*. Not all offenses are bailable, and the court may deny bail, or raise the amount. If the bailee does not appear in court, bail may be forfeited, and a warrant for arrest issued. (Bail may be permitted after booking, pending preliminary examination; after preliminary examination, pending arraignment; after arraignment, pending trial; after trial, pending sentence; and after sentence, pending appeal.)

And, a detained person may be released on a *writ of habeas corpus*. This writ, meaning "you have the body," is a legal order of a court commanding that the person detaining another produce the prisoner. This procedure is designed to provide a means of evaluating the legality of a detention. If the court determines that there is no cause to detain the prisoner, it may order his release. If, however, it finds that the detention is proper, it will return the prisoner to custody.

If the arrestee who has been booked and detained cannot be given a waiver or discharge, cannot raise or obtain bail, and cannot obtain a *writ of habeas corpus*, he must remain in confinement until his preliminary hearing. During this time of detention, the formal accusation is being prepared.

During the detention of the defendant, the arresting officers, or the detectives assigned to the follow-up investigation, will contact the prosecuting attorney or one of his assistants. The officers will relate the facts of the case and present the evidence establishing the *corpus delicti*. On the basis of the interview with the officers, with an analysis of the reports available, and, in some cases, with citizen witnesses, the prosecutor will determine if there is sufficient evidence to undertake prosecution. If he finds that sufficient evidence exists, he will prepare a formal accusation and file it with the proper court. The court will issue a warrant on the basis of the formal accusation. The warrant gives the police authority to hold the defendant pending further hearings and examinations.

During this period, moreover, a law enforcement agency may continue to investigate the crime, because very often the arrest is only the beginning of an investigation. It is one thing to sustain a *prima facie* case in the preliminary hearings (showing a likelihood that the accused committed the crime charged), and quite another thing to prove in court *beyond a reasonable doubt* that the accused committed the crime for which the arrest was made.

If the prosecutor feels that there is insufficient evidence, he may refuse to issue a formal accusation. In most cases where such a refusal is made, the defendant immediately receives a waiver and is discharged from police custody.

ACCUSATIONS

The formal accusation may take the form of a *complaint*, a *presentment*, an *indictment*, or an *information*.

The *original complaint* may be made by a private person, a victim, the police, or the prosecutor, and is superseded by the formal complaint; the formal complaint is a charge, preferred before a magistrate, that the person named has committed a specific offense, with an offer to prove the facts, to the end that prosecution may be instituted.

A *presentment* differs from an indictment in that it is an accusation made by a grand jury upon their own motion, either upon their own observation and knowledge, or upon evidence before them; whereas an *indict-*

ment is preferred at the suit of the government and is usually framed by the prosecutor and laid by him before the grand jury to be found (true bill) or ignored (no bill).

An *information* resembles, in form and substance, an indictment, but is filed at the mere discretion of the prosecutor, without the intervention or approval of a grand jury. Some states, Michigan being an example, seldom use the traditional grand jury in bringing formal accusations against a person accused of a felony. The prosecutor, in lieu thereof, prepares the information which is presented in trial court. This is a practical system in busy areas, where there are hundreds of cases being processed each week.

These written documents are the foundation of the record in criminal cases. The formal complaint is issued by and signed by the prosecutor (even though the original complaint may have been signed by officer, citizen, or victim); the indictment is issued by the grand jury and signed by its foreman; the information is issued by and signed by the prosecutor.

The purposes of the written accusation are to:

1. Assist the *defendant* by protecting him against further prosecution for the same offense, and by informing him of the nature of the charge so that he may prepare his defense.
2. Assist the *prosecutor* by clearly delineating the confines of the case.
3. Assist the *court* in determining trial proprieties and proper sentence.

It must state the venue (location of offense and trial), the offense, the day committed, and the name of the accused. It may charge the accused in several different ways, and it may contain a joinder of offenses and parties.

It must be correct, for, if it is defective, the defense will move *to quash* and the judge may dismiss the case, or cause the prosecutor to amend the accusation before further action.

HEARINGS AND EXAMINATIONS

Following arrest, with or without an arrest warrant, the detained person must be taken before a committing magistrate without unnecessary delay. Magistrates have jurisdiction to try and dispose of *certain minor offenses*; in serious cases, a magistrate of a lower court (justice of the peace, judge of a municipal court, and like magistrates) conducts a *preliminary hearing*.

In some jurisdictions, at the time of the preliminary hearing, the government must make out a *prima facie* case (one good on its face) as to a serious misdemeanor or felony or the magistrate must dismiss the charge. When the charge is substantiated, that is, the evidence indicates probability of guilt, the magistrate, depending on the nature of the offense, binds the accused over to the grand jury or to a higher court for trial.

Various alternatives which may be available to an accused are briefly considered hereunder:

1. The accused may *waive* a preliminary hearing, or grand jury examination, and go directly for arraignment and trial to a court of general jurisdiction. In this case, the prosecutor may use his formal complaint as the basis for preparing an information.

2. The accused may be taken, on the basis of a presentment or indictment before the grand jury for *grand jury examination*. Here, an attempt will be made to show that the crime charged did occur, and that it is reasonable to believe that the accused may have committed it. The grand jury hearing or examination is a *closed* hearing (i.e., not open to the public); the prosecutor presents the people's case; the accused, generally, is neither heard, nor represented by counsel. If the grand jury's verdict is to hold the defendant for trial, it will issue a "true bill" and bind the defendant over for trial; if its verdict is to release the defendant, it will issue "no bill" and the defendant will be freed.

3. The accused may be held, on the basis of a formal complaint, before a magistrate for *preliminary hearing*. Here, an attempt will be made to show that the crime charged did occur and that it is reasonable to believe that the accused may have committed it.

The preliminary hearing is, in no sense, a trial for the determination of guilt or innocence, but a procedure to ascertain whether or not there is enough evidence to hold the accused for trial. It emerged in 1554 in England through a statute that required that all arrested persons were to be examined by a magistrate to make sure that the innocent were freed and the guilty prosecuted. Thus, it was a development of the earlier continental inquisition (still followed in certain areas of Western Europe) which had the same purpose.

The preliminary hearing is an open hearing; not only does the prosecutor present his case, but the accused, too, may put on a case, testify on his own behalf, present witnesses, and be represented by counsel.

The preliminary examination takes place in a court of limited jurisdiction, before an examining or committing magistrate, who must decide whether to discharge the accused for lack of *prima facie* evidence, or to commit him to jail pending arraignment and trial, or to admit him to bail during the intervening time.

If the accused is held to answer for the charge, the prosecutor will proceed to prepare an information for the trial court; however, if a *prima facie* case is not made out, the charge is dismissed and the accused is released from custody.

The proceedings that take place during a preliminary hearing or examination are informal. The arraignment that takes place before the trial is a formal proceeding that inaugurates the trial process.

We proceed now to the trial.

TOPICS FOR DISCUSSION

1. Is it possible to eliminate all abuses of the processes of detention and arrest?
2. Should application forms for employment be revised to call for information on "convictions," rather than for information on "arrests"?
3. Is it possible to enlarge the processes of "release on recognizance" so that more poor and indigent arrestees, who cannot raise bail, can be freed pending trial?
4. Will recent court decisions lead to a requirement that Grand Jury procedures be altered to provide accused with "assistance of counsel"?
5. In this locale, how long a period of time can ensue:
   a) Between "stop," "identification," "frisk," and "detention"?
   b) Between "detention" and "arrest"?
   c) Between arrest and booking?
   d) Between booking and arraignment?
   e) Between arraignment and preliminary hearing?
   f) Between preliminary hearing and trial?
   g) Between trial and sentencing?
   h) Between sentencing and execution of sentence?

Chapter XVII

TRIAL AND POST-TRIAL PROCESSES

IN THE CASE OF A MINOR OFFENSE, the accused person comes to trial on the basis of the informal complaint.

In the case of a serious misdemeanor or felony, the accused comes to trial on the basis of the formal complaint if he has elected to waive preliminary examination; on the basis of the presentment or indictment of a grand jury, if he is bound over for trial following a grand jury hearing or examination; or on the basis of the information, if he is bound over for trial following a preliminary hearing or examination.

ARRAIGNMENT

Arraignment—being brought before the court to be charged with an offense or offenses and answering to it or them—is the first step in the formal trial process. What happens at this time, particularly as to the form and name of certain procedural devices, varies somewhat among the jurisdictions, but, in general, follows a pattern.

The formal complaint, presentment, indictment, or information is read, (sometimes the defendant is given a copy of the accusation, a list of witnesses, and a list of jurors), and he is asked how he pleads. In some states, arraignment can be waived by the accused; in other states, the furnishing of the accused with a copy of the accusation takes the place of formal arraignment. The plea of the accused must be made in open court, and several alternatives are open to him.

Guilty. The accused may plead guilty to the offense charged, or, with the approval of court and prosecutor, to a lesser offense. The court may refuse to accept a plea of guilty and enter a not guilty plea.

Nolo Contendere. The accused, in federal courts and some state courts may plead *nolo contendere* which is not an admission of guilt, but an indication of readiness to accept conviction and sentence rather than go to trial. (If civil action against the defendant is forthcoming, he can thus avoid having the guilty plea to the criminal offense become a part of the trial for the civil offense.)

Stand Mute. The accused can stand mute, that is, say nothing. The court, in that event, will automatically enter a plea of not guilty. The legal effect is that the accused waives no irregularities which have occurred up to the time of arraignment.

Motions of Abatement, Demurrer, Quash, Dismiss, Continue. The accused may plead abatement, file a demurrer, move to quash or dismiss the accusation—in effect stating that the accusation is defective. This may be due to the fact that the court does not have jurisdiction over the offender or offense, or because of a former acquittal or conviction for the same offense, or due to a pardon, or because the statute of limitation has run out, or because of a misnomer of the defendant, or because of a misjoinder of defendants, or due to some other technical deficiencies in the accusation. The motion to continue is a request for more time prior to trial, or for a delay in beginning the trial.

Nolle Prosequi. The prosecutor may move *nolle prosequi,* and withdraw the accusation, due to the fact that he knows that he cannot prove the charges. Sometimes a "nol pros" is necessary if key evidence is lost or destroyed, or if a key witness is unavailable.

Not Guilty. The accused may plead not guilty. (Certain defenses may be raised under this plea, such as insanity, self-defense, alibi, intoxication, statute of limitations, or double jeopardy.)

Submission on Transcript. The accused may occasionally indicate his willingness to have the official transcript of the preliminary hearing or Grand Jury examination serve as the basis for a court decision.

The court decides whether or not to dismiss the accusation, or to allow its amendment; whether or not it will accept a guilty plea and set the time of sentencing; and whether or not the case will go to trial. The court will also decide whether or not to allow bail, the amount of bail, and whether or not to continue bail.

If a trial is indicated, the court will ask the accused whether he desires a *court* or *jury* trial.

If the defendant elects a *court* trial, the judge will assign his case to a court where a judge will hear and decide both the law and the facts of the case and make a judgment of guilt or innocence.

If the defendant elects a *jury* trial, the judge will assign his case to a court where a judge will hear and decide the law, and where the jury will hear and decide the facts of the case, and, as well, decide guilt or innocence. (In some jurisdictions, however, in an offense such as criminal libel, the jury determines the law and the facts.)

TRIAL

"In all criminal prosecutions, the accused shall enjoy the right to a speedy and public trial. . . ."

How soon the trial will begin after arraignment depends upon the court calendar. Ordinarily, the priority follows this pattern:

1. Criminal cases have precedence over civil cases.
2. Felony offenders—accused in custody.
3. Misdemeanor offenses—accused in custody.
4. Felony offenses—accused on bail.
5. Misdemeanor offenses—accused on bail.

Generally, the defendant may obtain time to prepare for trial, usually about five days; if he desires a postponement or continuance after arraignment, usually not over thirty days.

The defendant and the judges must be present throughout the trial.

Jury Trial. If the defendant has elected a jury trial, the jurors must be selected. Generally, jurors for trials are taken from lists of registered voters or taxpayers of the community, and a jury panel is drawn. (In some jurisdictions, one panel serves all judges; in other jurisdictions, there is a separate panel for each judge.)

From the jury panel (venire) veniremen are sent to the trial court for *voir dire* ("voir dire" means "to speak the truth" and comes from the ancient juror's oath) examination. Both the prosecutor and the defense counsel examine jurors for their suitability to serve on the trial jury. They can be challenged *for cause*, or on a *peremptory* basis. Peremptory challenges—arbitrary challenges for which no reason need be given—are generally limited to from five to thirty challenges. Challenges for cause have no limit, and can be general (prior conviction, failure to qualify, unsound mind) or particular (bias or prejudice). After jurors have been selected (and often one to four alternates in addition) the trial is ready to begin. (In some jurisdictions, in civil cases, the plaintiff and defendant agree to utilize less than twelve jurors.) The jurors are sworn, and they select one of their body to speak for them—a foreman.

In many jurisdictions, jeopardy for the accused begins at the time the jury is sworn. (In a court trial, jeopardy begins when the first witness is sworn.)

ORDER OF TRIAL

1. **Opening Statements by Prosecution and Defense.** Trial generally begins with the opening statements of the prosecutor and the defense counsel. This gives the prosecutor the opportunity to sketch out, broadly, the general facts of the case and his proposed course of action in the prosecution for the people. The opening statement by defense counsel gives him the opportunity to prepare the judge and jurors for his defense methodology.

2. Prosecutor's Case. The prosecutor will now begin his case, and brings on his first witness.

(Witnesses who will establish the elements of the offense will usually precede witnesses who will introduce physical evidence.)

He begins with a *direct examination* of his witness, confining himself to simple questions, and bringing forth facts in chronological order. After he has satisfied himself that the witness has made the necessary points as to information known to him about the crime, the prosecutor rests.

The defense counsel now begins *cross examination* of that same witness. In most states, defense counsel must restrict himself to the facts that were brought out in direct examination. After he has interrogated the witness to accomplish various purposes, such as, to test the truth of his statements, defense rests.

The prosecutor may now decide to engage in *redirect examination,* but must, generally speaking, limit himself to new material which was brought out in cross examination.

After redirect examination by the prosecutor, the defense counsel may elect to *recross-examine* the witness, but must confine himself to material brought out in redirect examination.

In this fashion, the prosecutor brings on his witnesses and his experts, and when he has done as much as possible in meeting the proof required in the particular crime, he rests his case.

3. Defense Case. After the prosecutor has put on his case, the defense counsel may move for a *dismissal,* on the basis that the state (prosecutor) has failed to prove guilt "beyond a reasonable doubt." If his motion is granted, the case is dismissed, and the defendant is released from custody. If his motion is denied, defense counsel must now put on his case.

He brings on his first witness for direct examination, and then the prosecutor has the option of cross examination; if cross examination by the prosecutor takes place, the defense may decide to engage in redirect examination; following that, the prosecutor may elect to recross examine. After defense counsel has brought forth his witnesses and experts, and has done as much as possible to prove the innocence of the defendant, the defense counsel rests his case.

4. Prosecutor's Rebuttal. The prosecutor may now engage in *rebuttal,* and bring forth previous or additional witnesses and experts, in order to bolster any parts of his case that may have been weakened by the defense case. He uses the same format of direct and redirect examination, in each case followed by defense counsel's elected cross and recross examination. When he is satisfied, the prosecutor rests his case.

5. Defense Surrebuttal. The defense counsel may now engage in *sur-*

rebuttal, and bring forth previous or additional witnesses and experts, using the same format explained before. When he is satisfied, defense counsel rests his case. If he did not move for dismissal at the conclusion of the prosecutor's case, he will certainly make that motion at this time, indicating that the prosecutor did not meet his proof.

6. Summations by Defense and Prosecutor. *Summations,* or closing arguments, by defense counsel and prosecutor, are now in order. Each attempts to review the law and the facts for the judge and jury, and to summarize the important facets of the case at bar.

7. Jury Instructed and Charged. After summation, the judge, in most jurisdictions, will read and give to jury certain written *instructions* as to the legal principles which should be applied to the facts of the case. The court's instructions will include many legal rules, for example, the meaning of "burden of proof" and "presumption of innocence." He will also *charge* the jury with their responsibility for rendering a "true and just verdict."

8. Deliberation and Verdict. The jury now will retire to the jury room where they will be given an adequate opportunity to deliberate upon the issues, away from everyone, including the judge himself. The *bailiff* (law enforcement officer attending the court) watches over the jury to secure their privacy, and, if they need many hours or days, he sees that they are fed and housed and transported without contamination by outside contacts. When the jury has reached a verdict, it returns to the court and the foreman announces the verdict. (In civil trials, the verdict does not have to be unanimous, merely a majority; in criminal trials, however, in most states, unanimity was mandatory. On May 22, 1972, the United States Supreme Court held, in two cases, that unanimous jury verdicts are *not* constitutionally required for convictions on criminal charges in State courts.[1] A *hung jury* is one which is unable to reach a majority or unanimous decision.) If the defense counsel desires, the jury may be *polled,* each member of the jury giving his verdict as his name is called.

If the jury brings forth a verdict of not guilty, the defendant is released from custody, with the charges dismissed by the court.

9. Motions. *Motions* are now in order. Defense may move for a new trial or for a mistrial if any error or irregularity prevented justice from being served. He may point out errors of the judge in admitting or excluding evidence, in directing or charging the jury, for a finding contrary to law or evidence, or for being absent during trial. He may point out mis-

---

[1] Also note that the Supreme Court in *Williams v. Florida,* 399 U.S. 78 (6/22/70) held that the 12-man jury is not a constitutional requirement in a criminal case. (There was a 6-man jury in the *Williams* case.)

conduct of the jury in casting lots to decide the verdict, in receiving evidence out of court, or in communicating with outsiders. He may point out that the defendant was absent during part of the trial, or he may point out that newly discovered evidence would serve to clear the accused.

If a mistrial is declared, or a new trial granted, the accused will be placed on bail or remanded to custody until the time of the new trial.

10. Judgment. The formal pronouncement which is entered on the record, and pronouncement of sentence usually follows within twenty days of the verdict. Defense counsel, at this time, may raise various motions, such as a *motion in arrest of judgment* because of defects in the accusation or in the record.

Presentence Investigation. Before the defendant appears for sentence, there occurs, in most jurisdictions, what is called a *presentence investigation.* The judge needs information to guide him in setting a proper sentence. The presentence investigation, conducted, ordinarily, by probation or parole officers, is a written report which contains the family history of the accused, his personal history—including his health, educational, and criminal background, evaluation of the crime and its ramifications, and recommendations for restitution, for probation, or for institutionalization.

Sentence. Generally, the maximum and minimum punishments are set by law. The commonly used *indeterminate* sentence allows the judge to set a *non-specific* sentence for the purpose of individualized punishment and treatment of the offender, often in the terms of "not less than . . . and not more than . . ." Because of the wide variance between judges in sentencing habits, there has been great insistence on the proposal for a "sentencing court," or a "sentencing authority." Many a judge believes that he actually sentences "by hunch," and all judges feel that they could utilize much more information in order to determine a proper sentence.

When the guilty offender appears for sentencing, the judge has a wide variety of punishments that are his to impose, depending upon the offense, the presentence investigation, and statutory demands.

The offender may be sentenced to a period of incarceration in a jail, reformatory, prison, or other correctional institution.

The offender may be required to pay a monetary fine.

The offender may be sentenced to make restitution or to pay damages to those whom he has injured.

The offender may be sentenced to a forfeiture of public office, or to a disqualification to hold office.

The offender may be sentenced to a forfeiture of property, through confiscation.

The offender may be placed on probation, and, often to a period of supervised conduct, either by suspending the sentence, or by suspending the execution of the sentence.

The offender may be sentenced to a *combination* of the above, or,

The offender may be sentenced to death by hanging, gas, electrocution, or firing squad.[2]

In some cases, the offender may be committed to a state hospital or medical correctional facility (cases of narcotic addiction, alcoholism, insanity, or involving the sexual psychopath).

APPEALS

After sentence has been pronounced, the defendant may appeal his conviction to a "reviewing court."

If he appeals from an inferior court, the case is heard *de novo* (as new) in a court of general jurisdiction, for the most part. (This is due to the fact that many inferior courts are not courts of record.)

If he appeals from a court of general jurisdiction, the case for appeal is made on the record (transcript) of the trial court, and is heard in a state *appellate court.*

If he appeals from a state appellate court, the case for appeal is made on the transcripts of the trial and appellate courts, and is heard in the state *supreme court.*

In nearly all instances, a decision of the highest state appellate court affirming a conviction is a final disposition of the case. In some instances, however, the convicted person may seek relief from the *Supreme Court of the United States.*

The appellate court may *affirm* the finding of the lower court; may *modify* or *reduce* the degree of offense or punishment imposed; may *reverse* the finding of the lower court; may *set aside, affirm,* or *modify* proceedings around judgment; or may authorize a *new trial.* The appellate court uses a *writ of certiorari,* an order to the trial court to send the transcript of trial.

PARDON

A *pardon* by the President of the United States, or by the Governor of a state, consists of an extraordinary power of a chief executive to *release a person convicted of crime.*

Usually, a pardon assumes the innocence of the person, or the discovery of circumstances or facts which mitigate his responsibility, and has the effect of returning the person to society free of blame.

A *commutation of sentence* (or partial pardon) by a chief executive

---

[2] In *Furman v. Georgia,* 408 U.S. 238, June 29, 1972, the United States Supreme Court does *not* outlaw capital punishment if strict standards are adhered to by judges and juries.

consists of an extraordinary power to *change a punishment to one less severe*. A *reprieve* consists of an ordered delay in the execution of sentence.

Very often, equity may justify the issuance of a pardon, commutation of sentence, or reprieve. They are very difficult to obtain, and generally the person applying must have exhausted all other possible remedies before the request will be taken under consideration.

CONCLUSIONS

From the time that an offender commits a crime, to his final disposition, there may be an interval of hours, days, weeks, or months, or in some cases, many years of varied criminal processes.

The student of law enforcement will need to spend many hours of intensive study of the criminal law of his state and jurisdiction, of the laws of evidence, of the rules of criminal procedure, and of the laws of arrest, search, and seizure and their constitutional aspects. He should also obtain some familiarity with the federal criminal statutes and procedures. And, even after years of study and law enforcement experience, he will need to constantly refresh himself relative to newly enacted statutes and ordinances, to new applications of the law, and to the changing court interpretations of the law.

Without a solid grasp and wise application of law, evidence, and procedure, the law enforcement practitioner might well become a "misguided engine of destruction."

With a solid grasp and wise application of law, evidence, and procedure, the law enforcement practitioner genuinely will be the most important and vital man in his community in preventing crime and disorder and preserving the peace, and the most important and vital man to the American citizen in protecting life and property and individual freedom.

TOPICS FOR DISCUSSION

1. What types of sentences, in this locale, are most often imposed for misdemeanor offenses? For felony offenses?
2. What conclusions can be drawn if lower courts are frequently reversed by appellate courts in a state? What conclusions can be drawn if appellate courts in a state are frequently reversed by the United States Supreme Court?
3. Do "judges" and "courts" free vicious criminals, or is it that the "Constitution" protects the rights of all citizens, good and bad?
4. What is the relationship between the courts and the law enforcement agencies (municipal and county) in this locale?

Chapter XVIII

TECHNOLOGY AND THE CRIMINAL JUSTICE SYSTEM

THE ADMINISTRATION OF CRIMINAL JUSTICE in the United States is being subjected to critical analysis and major overhaul. There is great emphasis on education and training; more and more attention is being paid to auditing and revising laws to provide for effective law enforcement while at the same time zealously protecting the rights of suspect and accused; planning and research operations have been amplified; and there has been some centralization of identification and intelligence data.

All that is to the good, but such action has been hampered by lack of information, duplications of effort, cumbersome methods of communication, and failures to collate data. Generally, education and training programs, in terms of field research, have been limited to information available through individual agencies, and in terms of raw data, have been limited to the *Uniform Crime Reports* and random compilations issued by operating agencies. Legal research has been limited to information available from case decisions, bar association journals, and law school reviews. Planning and research units usually limit themselves to the assessment of available local data. Central depositories at the federal and state level have been limited to manually maintained fingerprint files and compilations of criminal histories.

Until recently, law enforcement and the administration of justice have been by-passed by the cybernetic revolution—by the applications of modern scientific management analysis technology—and by utilizations of integrated information systems. However, current developments are encouraging, and a space-age leap forward may be anticipated if public support and agency involvement continue to accelerate.

Indeed, there are very strong indications that we are moving toward a true system of criminal justice with all of its implications for change and improvement. It is ironic that the thrust toward systematization of the processes of criminal justice should hinge upon the very recent renaissance of interest in the application of computers, system sciences, and technology to the social problems of crime and criminality in America.

The need for development of a *system* of criminal justice was emphasized by the National Crime Commission, has been repeatedly given implicit recognition by educators and writers in the field of police science who have adopted the term "criminal justice" in lieu of, or in addition to, "police science" or "law enforcement." Thus, this volume was renamed to reflect its broadened perspective. A most urgent and forthright statement of the need for a system of criminal justice in our nation, was issued by Milton S. Eisenhower, President Emeritus of Johns Hopkins University, in his capacity as Chairman of the National Commission on the Causes and Prevention of Violence. He deplores "the fragmentation of police, court and correctional agencies" and strongly confirms that "some catalyst is needed to bring them together."

The National Commission Report stated: [1]

> It is commonly assumed that these three components—law enforcement (police, sheriffs, marshals), the judicial process (judges, prosecutors, defense lawyers) and corrections (prison officials, probation and parole officers)—add up to a "system" of criminal justice.
>
> A system implies some unity of purpose and organized interrelationship among component parts. In the typical American city and state, and under Federal jurisdiction as well, no such relationship exists. There is, instead, a reasonable well-defined criminal process, a continuum through which each accused offender may pass. From the hands of the police, to the jurisdiction of the courts, behind the walls of a prison, then back onto the street, the inefficiency, fall-out and failure of purpose during this process is notorious.
>
> In the mosaic of discontent which pervades the criminal process, public officials and institutions, bound together with private persons in the cause of reducing crime, each sees his own special mission being undercut by the cross-purposes, frailties or malfunctions of others. As they find their places along the spectrum between the intense concern with victims at one end, and total preoccupation with reforming convicted lawbreakers at the other, so do they find their daily perceptions of justice varying or in conflict.
>
> Under such circumstances it is hardly surprising to find in most cities not a smooth functioning "system" of criminal justice but a fragmented and often hostile amalgamation of criminal justice agencies. Obvious mechanisms for introducing some sense of harmony into the system are not utilized.
>
> One might expect the field to be flooded with systems analysts, management consultants and publicly imposed measures of organization and administration in order to introduce order and coordination into this criminal justice chaos. It is not. A recognized profession of criminal justice system administrators does not exist today.
>
> Apart from lack of leadership, the process of crime control in most cities lacks any central collection and analysis of criminal justice information. It has no focal point for formulating a cohesive crime budget based on system needs rather than individual agency requests. It has no mechanism for planning, initiating or evaluating system-wide programs, or for setting priorities. It has no specialized staff to keep the mayor or other head of government regularly informed of the problems and progress of public safety and justice. Crime receives high-level attention only as a short-term reaction to crisis.

---

[1] National Commission on the Causes and Prevention of Violence (1969). *Report*. U.S. Government Printing Office, Washington, D.C.

The pervasive fragmentation of police, court and correctional agencies suggests that some catalyst is needed to bring them together. An assumption that parallel and overlapping public agencies will cooperate efficiently can no longer suffice as a substitute for deliberate action to make it happen in real life.

These excerpts from the report of the National Commission on the Causes and Prevention of Violence are reflective of a number of other statements issued by various commissions, boards and study groups before and after this Report.[2] Each stresses the urgent need to fashion a coherent, harmonious system of criminal justice which will "bring us together." It is significant that the National Commission specifically criticized the general lack of any central collection and analysis of criminal justice information. Although it is not explicitly stated in these excerpts, the National Commission recognizes that the necessary foundation upon which to structure a criminal justice system is an information system which serves all functional branches of criminal justice. If we would thrust toward the achievement of systemic relationships in criminal justice, therefore, we need to concern ourselves with the development of criminal justice information systems.

Perhaps the single greatest contribution of science and technology to crime control and the administration of criminal justice is in the area of computer and system sciences and related technology applied to information systems.

Reports and records have always been vital to the administration of criminal justice: information has been collected, reported, classified, processed, stored, retrieved and utilized in many ways—but never with high speed and wide scope. A review of current data systems demonstrates that, for the most part, they are built around traditional manual clerical tasks such as recording, filing, checking, retrieving and some use of electric or mechanical accounting machines. These systems are proving inadequate and fail to meet current requirements in several respects. Such systems lack capacity to receive and process large volumes of data; they do not provide for rapid, accurate access to stored information; they seldom permit direct random access to data; they are incapable of providing real-time (immediate, instantaneous) access to data; they do not permit adequate dissemination of information at remote locations; they do not furnish data in adequate form or content; they do not provide adequate feedback of

---

[2] See, for example, Report of the Advisory Commission on Intergovernmental Relations, August, 1971, U.S. Government Printing Office, Washington, D.C. Robert E. Merriam, ACIR Chairman stated: "A basic flaw in our criminal justice system is that it lacks 'system.' It is a loose collection of institutions and procedures, operating autonomously and frequently in isolation. The police, the judges, the prosecutors and the correction officials must recognize their work interdependence and work together to build a sound and workable system. And state government must face up to its responsibility to provide effective leadership."

information for decision-making purposes; they depend on overly large numbers of clerical personnel; they are highly fragmented, often over-extended and offer little potential for growth; they contain unnecessary cross-references and duplications; they are not suited for interface with systems in allied agencies, they are most difficult to change or reorganize because of manual limitations, and they are based upon assumptions which have rarely been reassessed.

Information contained in agency records has not been shared on a regular and routine basis with other agencies to an optimum extent. Much information sharing has been on a person-to-person basis. If we are to have a criminal justice system, it is imperative that facts should be available to all agencies involved in the administration of criminal justice—police, prosecutor, defense, courts, probation, corrections, parole—and should be available at the point of decision.

This *sine qua non* of a criminal justice information system is realizable today and, in fact, is already beginning to be brought into being through the special efforts of a number of states and the Law Enforcement Assistance Administration (LEAA) through its funding of Project SEARCH (System for Electronic Analysis and Retrieval of Criminal Histories.) It is impor-tant for the student of law enforcement and criminal justice to contem-plate the anomaly that in a field of social science, such as criminal justice, the most significant advances are presently being fashioned by other than the social sciences, the legal system, or even public administration, *per se.* Technology has advanced so rapidly that it has literally dragged criminal justice administration kicking and screaming into the '70s. This is not to say that the social sciences do not have a vital role to play in the de-velopment of a system of criminal justice and the refinement of that system as it is developed. The social sciences, law, and public administra-tion all have vast responsibilities in this crucial area of national interest. It is hoped that they will accept the challenge and attempt to do as much within their own disciplines and spheres of influence as the physical sci-ences and technology have done in the few short years since the New York State Identification and Intelligence System (NYSIIS), the FBI National Crime Information Center (NCIC), the Law Enforcement Assistance Ad-ministration (LEAA) and the California Criminal Justice Information Sys-tem (CJIS) began to blaze the trail toward a more rational and scientific system of criminal justice. Indeed, to the extent that efforts to develop vast computerized information sharing systems to serve all agencies of criminal justice are successful, to that extent may such systems be designed to serve not only the operating but also the research needs of criminal justice ad-ministration. Social scientists will have enormous resources of empirical data available for multivariable search, more data about more people, more readily accessible and manipulatable than ever before in the history of the world.

COMPUTER TECHNOLOGY

In the last ten years, electronic data processing equipment—in particular, the electronic computer—has stimulated revolutionary changes in information-handling techniques. Computer-based information-processing systems have been developed for the military (e.g., air defense), for industry (e.g., cybernated production) and for commerce (e.g., airline reservations). These systems provide for centralized and organized storage of data that can be drawn upon by geographically dispersed user units equipped with communication devices and provide users with access to the central store of information with a speed, accuracy and unfailing memory unrivaled by any manual method.

Such systems accept data (input), hold data (storage), evaluate and classify data (processing/computing) and disseminate data (output/communications). By means of punch cards or magnetic tape, disc or drum, data are accepted. (Teletype or telephone lines can be utilized for handling data on a "real-time" or "time current" basis so that information can be fed into, processed and returned in a matter of seconds or microseconds.) Data held in storage can be programmed to interact with incoming information. After current data are received and processed with stored data according to a prepared computer program, "answers" can be issued by punch card, tape, optical display, or printout device.

In the past, police agencies have used data processing equipment with keypunch operators recording specific information relative to crime and traffic on punch cards or mark-sense cards. Now, many agencies store data by using magnetic tape, disc or drum, in which far more data can be stored and retrieved more quickly. Simpler card-sort procedures previously used in *modus operandi* operations are being replaced by computer programs to provide more sophisticated predictions and decisions relative to operational tactics. High-speed printers present a visual record of required data, and display devices such as map images point up locations of occurrences. Such information is easily transferred by telephone, teletype, facsimile and direct line to all users.

Even though every agency might develop a good internal data processing system, it is obvious that statewide, regional or nationwide systems in appropriate cases provide greater flexibility and eliminate unnecessary cross-referencing and duplications of files and efforts.

Computer science and related technology provide, for police, help in identifying suspects, aid in crime solution, and eliminate much wasted effort in licensing, personal descriptions, master name-indexing, juvenile indexing, fingerprints, criminal histories, *modus operandi* methods, wanted criminal lists, warrants, bogus check listings, stolen automobile reports, motor vehicle registrations and the like. For *prosecutors* and *defenders*, such systems provide data on complaint information and indictment filings. For *judges*, the systems provide data relevant to personal recognizance releases, bail and sentencing. For *probation, corrections* and *parole* personnel, data is useful for presentence investigations, correctional classification, treatment and rehabilitation processes. For *researchers*, such systems provide ample sources of data which can be interpreted with greater precision and which will lead to more sophisticated predictions. Such systems provide all users with opportunity for patterned analysis of data with more speed, accuracy and scope than heretofore thought possible.[3]

CURRENT DEVELOPMENTS

Up to now, most electronic data processing systems relating to the administration of criminal justice in the United States have been located in law enforcement agencies and are designed for information storage and retrieval of police-oriented data. This typology is also apparent in Canada and the United Kingdom. (The Royal Canadian Mounted Police has established a long-distance facsimile network allowing rapid transmission of fingerprints, mug shots and reports, and has computerized files such as stolen motor vehicles and other identifiable property; wanteds; parolees; and gun registrations. The United Kingdom has established a Police National Computer Unit which is developing a Joint Automatic Data Processing Unit in conjunction with police forces in England, Scotland and Wales. This system will involve remote terminals with visual display units dispersed throughout the British Isles.[4])

Currently, however, the trend is away from unifunctional application of the computer and toward "total systems" concepts. At the municipal level this has often entailed joining police-based and solely law-enforcement-oriented computer operations with other relevant governmental data systems. At the state level the trend is toward centralized criminal justice information systems which are multidisciplinary but restricted to agencies concerned with criminal justice. This latter development began with the New York State Identification and Intelligence System (NYSIIS) and the California Criminal Justice Information System (CJIS) and is now spreading rapidly (with financial encouragement from the Law Enforcement Assistance Administration [LEAA] of the U.S. Department of Justice). At

---

[3] See Whisenand, Paul and Tamura, Tug (1970). *Automated Police Information Systems.* John Wiley & Sons, New York.

[4] British Home Office and Metropolitan Police Joint ADP Unit (1970). *ADP Report No. 114.* Tintagel House, London.

the federal level, the FBI National Crime Information Center (NCIC) is basically oriented toward police and law enforcement; however, the FBI's development of a new computerized criminal history program (NCIC CCH) may ultimately involve data from all branches of criminal justice administration. This new NCIC Computerized Criminal History Program was developed by a consortium of states working together in the federally-funded Project SEARCH and adopted by the FBI in 1971.

The SEARCH System (and the various spin-offs that it has provided) is probably one of the most significant advances in nation-wide criminal justice administration which has occurred in this century. Project SEARCH was a voluntary multi-state effort to demonstrate the value and feasibility of a criminal justice data file and statistics system which is based on automated files created and maintained by individual states and providing for the interstate transfer of data. Originally ten states participated in a demonstration project during 1970, which successfully established the on-line capability of a system allowing for the interstate exchange of criminal offender files among various states based on a compatible "criminal justice offender record," integrating police, prosecution, court and correctional offender data.

Likewise, these SEARCH states designed a computerized criminal justice statistics system containing offense and arrest statistics, court statistics, probation and parole statistics, etc., to serve all functional branches of the criminal justice system, both intra and interstate. The concept was that there would be created a set of transaction-based statistical data which would be analyzed and which would generate reports.

In the original SEARCH effort a number of important special projects were carried out which included the following:

Integrated Record Development. A special project was carried out in California to link information concerning individual offenses, the offenders involved and the criminal justice processes. The project involved approximately 10,000 record entries from twelve counties of the state.

Specialized probation and parole requirements. A detailed study in New York related to statistical data required for planning, management, and program evaluation of probation and parole.

Simultaneous Statistics/History Generation. Connecticut established a system of offender-based data collection which would permit nearly automatic and simultaneous generation of statistical data and criminal history files.

Transaction Utility in Status Maintenance. Texas established an offender-based file that reflected the history of each arrest and the current status of an offender while he was in the criminal justice process. At the offender's exit from the system, a summary record was created.

Facsimile Equipment Demonstration. A demonstration of interstate facsimile fingerprint transmission between the states of Maryland, Michigan, Minnesota, and New York was successful.

All fifty states are now participating in the SEACH consortium. Current efforts are centered about the conversion of criminal history records for entry into the NCIC Computerized Criminal History (NCIC CCH) Program and the development of computerized state-wide fingerprint identification systems. Additional projects include the following: development of security and privacy concepts and standards; feasibility of holographical fingerprint identification/verification; feasibility of satellite communication of fingerprints and criminal history records; upgrading and increasing automation of fingerprint identification bureaus; standardization of incident reporting; and developing an interstate organized crime intelligence system.

Ultimately, all fifty states will be included in the SEARCH effort and participate in the FBI/NCIC Computerized Criminal History Program. However, it is anticipated that the success of the planned NCIC CCH Program will depend upon the development of central fingerprint identification bureaus in each state. It will also depend, of course, upon continued federal financial support to the states for data conversion of their records to be supplied in computer readable form to the FBI. It is conceived, and recommended by many, that the role of the FBI be limited to serve primarily as an index or directory, while the various state data centers serve as the actual information sharing mechanisms for the exchange of criminal offender records between and among the nation's criminal justice agencies.

STATE OF THE ART

Identification and Intelligence Systems Technology. Today, some fingerprint identification bureaus are almost completely automated. Computerized fingerprint and name searches are well within the state of the art, as are computerized criminal history records. (The most resistant and elusive portion of the fingerprint identification process is the automatic scanning and classifying of the fingerprints themselves.) There have been a number of breakthroughs in the analytic identification field, including latent print, personal appearance, fraudulent check and various other modules. Organized crime and other intelligence systems have been successfully computerized.

Digital Communications Technology. Vast studies are being made to improve a number of television, radio, microwave and land-line communications techniques. Walkie-talkies are smaller, lighter, and more effective generally. Digital receivers for police vehicles are becoming commonplace. Surveillance communications devices have become more sophisticated and more versatile. Transmission of digital data from remote stations and computer-to-computer interfaces over long distances have been achieved and now satellite communications are being enlisted in the anti-crime effort.

Facsimile Technology. One rapidly developing advanced communication technique involves the transmission of graphic material by facsimile over specially conditioned telephone wires on a short, medium or long-distance basis. Fingerprints, mug shots, criminal histories and reports may be scanned, translated to electrical form, transmitted, received and re-translated back to graphic form without the necessity of moving the original material over a long distance.

For example, a set of fingerprints may be transmitted from any part of New York State to NYSIIS in Albany in fourteen minutes or less. There, a hard copy of the set of prints is printed out, and main files are searched by a combination automatic and semimanual sequence. When the criminal history record is retrieved from the computer it is transmitted back to the agency of origin. The originating agency now has a hard-copy facsimile of the criminal history record—and what used to take from seven to ten *days* is now done in a matter of *minutes*. Methods are now being developed which will greatly increase the speed of transmission.

Optical Technology. The science and technology of optics will be increasingly associated with computer systems. Two developments are worthy of mention.

The Automatic License Plate Scanner [5] is programmed for on-the-scene operation. The objective is instant and automatic transmission of license plate numbers of passing vehicles from the highway to a remote computer, for real-time processing. If a transmitted license plate number matches any one of the license plate numbers of wanted motor vehicles stored in the computer memory, an immediate signal is received back at the location of transmission providing for immediate apprehension. The entire process requires less than one minute and should effectively reduce the incidence of auto theft and other motor vehicle related offenses.

Another development relates to in-house scanning equipment being programmed to automatically read and code alphanumeric and fingerprint data for computer processing. Automatic reading equipment (scanners) that transfer alphanumeric data from a document and directly enter such data into a computer memory have been available for some time.

A similar capability relating to fingerprints presents special problems which have not as yet been resolved. The major need is development of a compatible classification technique. Active research into the problem is being conducted by the British Home Office, New Scotland Yard, the Prefec-

---

[5] The ALPS system (Automatic License Plate Scanning) is a research and development project of NYSIIS, partially funded by LEAA, Department of Justice.

ture de Police of Paris and the Italian National Police in Rome. In the United States, NYSIIS and a host of computer manufacturers who recognize the marketability of such a device are conducting extensive research. The FBI has mounted a major research effort to develop an automated fingerprint scanning and classification system.

A new classification system based upon the characteristics of *one* fingerprint, rather than upon the characteristics of an entire set of ten fingers, will open up a dazzling era of successful criminal identification through the use of scene-of-crime fingerprints. (At the present time, odd prints found at crime scenes cannot as a practical matter be searched against the major fingerprint files.) The development of automatic scanning techniques utilized in conjunction with a new computer-compatible classification system will make it possible to convert without excessive expense the many millions of fingerprints which are presently maintained in the files of identification bureaus throughout the country. (Conversion to machine readable form, using manual techniques, of fingerprints on file in our larger identification bureaus, would cost many millions of dollars.)

Criminalistics Techniques. Computerized methods of classifying, identifying, comparing and analyzing physical evidence are being developed, along with medium and long-range research not ordinarily considered the mission of the operational forensic laboratory.

Facsimile and optical techniques, coupled with programmed analytical procedures, will be applied to the areas of ballistics, handwriting, voice prints and trace identification, as well as to the fingerprint area.

Criminalistics research will become increasingly involved in the design and implementation of scientific modules to be incorporated within computer-based information-sharing systems.

Statistical Techniques. Not only will the computer sciences utilize new computer-compatible mathematical techniques for the analysis of detailed data developed by criminalistics testing and experimentation, but they will also place the statistical discipline into a variety of crucial roles in the criminal justice system.

The currently maintained law enforcement data of a statistical nature relates mostly to police actions (with some incomplete references to further dispositions of cases) and is grossly inadequate, even for analysis, evaluation and decision-making feedback within the police structure. There is a vital need for relevant data concerning prosecution, court dispositions, probation, correctional institution and parole.

The history of statistical research in the administration of criminal justice is one of frustration, for unmet needs have existed—the vast storage of a variety of data, rapid search for and retrieval of data, and depth analysis of many variables—needs now capable of being satisfied by computer science and technology.

In the monumental report of the Wickersham Commission in 1931,[6] it became obvious that data about detention, prosecution, bail, release, sentencing, probation, corrections, parole, grand and petit juries and police procedures, all necessary for analysis and evaluation, were unavailable. The ensuing thirty-six years evidenced no great amelioration of the situation, and the President's Commission on Law Enforcement and the Administration of Justice found that accurate, current and usable data were unavailable in many areas of their inquiry.

Computer science and technology will provide ultimately for more reliable, valid, standardized and consistent methods of statistical research in the administration of criminal justice—and perhaps even fantastic strides in crime pattern analysis, crime prediction, manpower deployment, treatment and rehabilitation methods, and a nationally coordinated approach in meeting the problems associated with crime and disorder.

Criminological Research. Undreamed-of-storehouses of empirical data will become readily available for criminological research by means of computerized data banks.

The Federal Bureau of Investigation has been conducting a continuous study of the careers in crime of more than 300,000 offenders whose criminal records have been computerized. In New York, NYSIIS has an extensive computer data base of criminal history relating to more than half a million persons who have been convicted of crimes for which criminal processing involves fingerprinting.

It may be anticipated that additional computer banks will be developed in other cities, states, regional areas and national centers which will have similar potential for expediting and optimizing the resources available for criminological research.

In order to utilize this vast reservoir of information, to evaluate the activities of agencies working in the administration of criminal justice and to perform basic research on system performance and agency effectiveness, a new host of research criminologists will be required. As the social sciences apply the powerful tools of computer science, greater scope will be provided for inquiry, and greater reliability will be achieved in predicting behavior. The great problems of interpersonal and intergroup conflict will be studied with a thoroughness heretofore thought impossible, and inquiry into the etiology, diagnosis and prognosis of antisocial deviant behavior will provide insight relative to effective methods of control.

HUMAN RIGHTS AND CIVIL LIBERTIES

There has been much concern about the impact of technology upon human rights and civil liberties. This has centered for the most part around

---

[6] The National Commission on Law Observance and Enforcement, popularly known as the *Wickersham Commission*, published its report in 1931.

computerized information systems containing "people files." Criminal justice data banks must be protected against misuse. Even though an information system containing data about individuals must be made secure and protected from compromise by criminals or others who might wish to subvert systems capabilities, the primary goal of a security commitment must be the preservation of human rights. Human rights, civil liberties and adherence to Constitutional guarantees are critical criteria of systems survival. The most critical human right involved is the right to privacy.

The system which is security engineered to guarantee the right to privacy will most likely meet all other security criteria. Protecting the right to privacy is the ultimate test of the viability of a criminal justice data bank. Any information storage and retrieval system which does not have the means and the will to preserve inviolate the right to privacy of all whose records it contains will not survive—nor should it survive.

Former President Johnson, in a Special Message to Congress on Crime in the United States,[7] stated:

> Justice Brandeis called the right of privacy the "right most valued by civilized men." It is the first right denied by a totalitarian system. It is associated in the minds of most Americans with the right to be free of unlawful searches and forced self-incrimination. It is a hallmark of a free society. . . . We would indeed be indifferent to the command of our heritage if we failed to take effective action to preserve the dignity and privacy of each among us.

The capability of the computer process to assist the agencies of criminal justice is a great boon, and one which must not be jeopardized by less than absolutely scrupulous and constantly rigorous adherence to all security methods which will effectively secure the right to privacy. The issue of privacy must be kept in the forefront in all planning, development, implementation, supervision and administration of criminal justice data banks, for the issue of privacy lies in the heart of our cherished concept of liberty. Provisions for confidentiality of information, restrictions on improper circulation, and sanctions against unauthorized uses must be written into the basic legislation and administrative rules which authorize and govern criminal justice information systems.[8]

The large-scale information bank compels us to consider the needs of security and, in particular, the doctrine of the right to privacy. We need to protect private personality as zealously as we protect private property, for insofar as we protect the right to privacy, we protect the right to share and communicate data. The protection of privacy implies parameters for a

---

[7] Johnson, President Lyndon (1967). *Special Message to Congress on Crime in the United States, Text.* New York *Times*, February 7.

[8] See Westin, Alan F. (1966). "Science, Privacy and Freedom: Issues and Proposals for the 1970's—Part 2." *Columbia Law Review*, 66:1205.

criminal justice data bank relating to when, where, with whom, what, how and why information should be shared or withheld. As with all rights, a paramount public interest accepted by the community and explicitly recognized should equate, in productive equilibrium, the claim of privacy with the need to share information.

It is the opinion of the authors that computerized criminal justice data banks will enhance rather than diminish human rights and civil liberties, if such data banks are properly developed and controlled.

If operated independently of any particular agency, its integrity can be better assured; it can provide a greater degree of isolation for confidential data and a greater guarantee of privacy than a manual locally based filing system; and when tested and effective methods of security are applied, access to data can be restricted only to those who have a right to know and a need to know.

DATA BANK SECURITY OPERATIONS

Only persons dedicated to the preservation of constitutional guarantees, committed to the integrity of system information, and alert to the nuances of property and proprietary rights should be entrusted with control of or access to the data base.[9]

The criminal justice data bank security program should assist both user and central facility personnel to maintain the highest standards of personal integrity in the face of potential threats from organized crime or attempts by any unauthorized persons to obtain information. Security measures must be developed (1) to safeguard and protect the assets and personnel of the central data facility; (2) to meet the expressed needs of participating agencies and supply security requirements implied by their current methods and rules of operation; (3) to protect the human rights and civil liberties of individuals whose records are stored in the data bank; (4) to protect the integrity of all information from subversion, compromise, misuse or abuse by criminal or other elements whose interests are inimical to the cause of justice; (5) to protect the central data facility against contamination of stored data by rejecting information which is improper in itself or tainted by the means by which it was acquired, or which is simply of no importance to the system; (6) to standardize concepts and procedures relating to the storage and security of confidential information.

---

[9] See testimony of Gallati, Dr. Robert R. J. (1966). "The Computer and Invasion of Privacy." *Hearings before a Subcommittee of the Committee on Government Operations, House of Representatives, Eighty-Ninth Congress, Second Session,* July, pp. 149-158. U.S. Government Printing Office, Washington, D.C. Also note testimony of Gallati, Dr. Robert R. J. at hearings before the Constitutional Rights Subcommittee of the Senate Judiciary Committee (so-called Ervin Committee), March 10, 1971.

Those who administer, supervise or utilize a criminal justice data bank assume a grave responsibility relative to security. A computer-based information system is an inanimate object, a neutral tool, and can be used against society or for society, depending on the motivations of the users. If the criminal justice data bank is to be a valuable tool to serve society, to serve the citizen, all those associated with its operation must be pledged to effective and edifying security operations.

Personnel Security. The security of a computer-based information-sharing system depends ultimately upon the people involved. Machines are, in themselves, neither good nor bad; only people are "good" or "bad." The security of any information system rests upon the persons who control it and upon the persons who operate it. It is essential, therefore, that the personnel who control or operate any part, no matter how insignificant, of the total system, be worthy of confidence. Background investigations, clearance levels, internal intelligence, training, bonding, procedural guides and close supervision may be used to assure service integrity.

Physical Security. Computer-based information systems need physical protection from fire, civil disaster, sabotage, subversion, penetration, unauthorized access and destruction of facilities. Because such systems involve remote communications links, the geographical scope of the physical security task is not limited to the location of the central data bank. To maintain physical security, classified areas may be designated, passes and badges issued to personnel, visitor controls installed, fire prevention devices and fireproofing built in, civil defense shelters and bombproof storage for irreplaceable records maintained, disaster and damage control planning required, along with frequent inspections of remote stations, and attention to locks, safes, fencing, alarm systems and guard services.

Transmission Security. The transfer of data may be by courier, telephone, teletype, mail, facsimile transmission, microwave, radio or television. The input/output device of remote locations must be compatible with the i/o device at the central facility; the signal or message will either go directly into the computer and obtain a response directly from the computer (as in time-sharing or "on-line" response time situations), or it will be processed by a semiautomated manual intercept, which depends upon a person to relay signals or messages. Transmission security uses devices to prevent electronic eavesdropping—such as "scramblers," coded messages, key devices, line checks, shielding—as well as methods of identification of sender and receiver, access control over i/o devices, classification of information, burning/shredding of waste paper, and security of stowage methods.

Data Bank Security. Protection against accidental, malicious or subversive contamination of the data base is essential. File separation and compartmentation, logic and legality tests to verify access controls and establish a record of transactions, internal monitoring of all changes of the master file, logging of errors, "zero" balance accounting and records of output can be built into the system. Computer manufacturers have an obligation to develop security controls to assure that societal value systems are not destroyed by this new tool which may be used to maintain our freedom—but which also has the potential for our subjugation.

Information Security. The end product of any computer-based information-sharing system is the data it inputs, processes, stores, retrieves and outputs, and the integrity of that data must be zealously guarded. Personnel security, physical security, transmission security and data bank security are useful only to the extent that they assure the security of the information contained within the system.

Certain types of information should be excluded from a criminal justice data bank—such as is contained in census, tax, election, social security, unemployment insurance, workmen's compensation and similar files. The names of confidential informants and information illegally obtained or derived from grand jury minutes would not be submitted for inclusion in the system, and it might be deemed desirable to exclude certain family court information.

At any rate, information will vary in sensitivity depending upon its source, its content and its relation to other information already stored. In voluntary systems which recognize the right of the originator of the information to restrict its dissemination, the information must be carefully controlled by the receiving facility. If the originator did not recognize the degree of sensitivity of data submitted (because he was not aware of the existence or relationship of other stored information) a greater or lesser security classification should be applied and the originator alerted.

It is necessary to consider who will qualify as a user and who may have access to data. The insertion of data must be monitored, for excess and irrelevant information can impair the efficiency of the data bank almost as much as deliberate sabotage; tainted information of course, must be excluded to prevent contamination of the data base. Only persons who have the right to know and the need to know should have access to information in the system.

A NEW CONCEPT OF DYNAMIC SECURITY

Because the concern for human rights and civil liberties is so closely related to data bank security operations, a new concept of *dynamic security* is being developed. A negative, or "Maginot Line," approach to computer security is inadequate for this space age. A positive, or "dynamic" link between liberty and security must be involved in the development of computerized information systems. Justice will be more effectively provided, human rights and civil liberties guaranteed, and agency operations made more efficient by the rapid and secure transfer of information. Under a dynamic security data exchange system a summons, notice of violation or citation may be utilized in place of physical arrest for minor crimes; more rapid arraignment may be possible; bail or release on recognizance may more easily be granted; sentencing may be based more on real information than on hunch; parole and probation evaluations may have greater predictive reliability; and correctional classification and treatment programs may be more closely tailored to individual needs.

The concept of dynamic security should stimulate the manufacturers of computers and associated equipment and the developers of software systems and programs to adopt a commitment to greater social consciousness relative to the impact of their products and services upon the totality of a democratic society. The horizons of the industry must be lifted so that security is regarded as more than just an incidental by-product of management controls—just as the automobile industry has finally come to regard safety as a larger consideration than an incidental part of the production of more powerful vehicles. Management controls must be optimized and made to serve the abiding social values of liberty and privacy as well as the needs of security and efficiency.

The administration of criminal justice must serve ordered liberty through an affirmative program which will not only enhance the integrity and effectiveness of the agencies involved, but which will also protect and guarantee human rights and civil liberties. Thus, the collection, storage, retrieval and dissemination of criminal justice information must be *positively* oriented toward protection for all citizens.

Dynamic security does not involve retreating into the hollow shell of an index system or directory. Criminal justice data banks contain "people information" and it is important to the best interests of society that such information be made available to the agencies involved in the administration of criminal justice so that proper decisions may be made. There is need for equilibrium in our balance between individual liberty and community security, and neither liberty nor security need be sacrificed for the other if the concept of dynamic security is applied to computer science and technology. We can have both personal freedom and an ordered society, but we cannot if we allow the scales to become unbalanced. Eternal vigilance is the price of liberty—and order.

PRIVACY PROBLEMS

The computer has compelled society to consider the potential threat to privacy occasioned by information data banks. Certainly, we need to protect personal privacy as zealously as we protect private property, for as we protect the right of privacy, we protect the right to share and communicate. There have already been a number of hearings conducted by the House of Representatives and the Senate, and the legislative bodies of some states, concerned with the threat that computer data banks may invade the privacy of our people.

Many very prominent and articulate citizens have expressed their fears of the potential of large data systems handling derogatory information about people.

At the Hearings Before A Subcommittee of the Committee On Government Operations, House of Representatives, Eighty-Ninth Congress, First and Second Sessions [10] (commonly known as the Gallagher Committee) many outstanding citizens expressed their alarm at the prospect of a National Data Center proposed by the Bureau of the Budget, and further development of the FBI National Crime Information Center, as follows:

Vance Packard: "Let us remember, 1984, is only 18 years away. My own hunch is that Big Brother—may turn out to be not a greedy power seeker, but rather a relentless bureaucrat obsessed with efficiency. As he, more than the simple power seeker could lead us to that ultimate of horrors, a humanity in chains of plastic tape."

Congressman Horton: "The argument is made that a central data bank would use only the type of information that now exists and since no new principle is involved, existing types of safeguards will be adequate. This is fallacious. Good computermen know that one of the most practical of our present safeguards of privacy is the fragmented nature of present information. It is scattered in little bits and pieces across the geography and years of our life. Retrieval is impractical and often impossible. A central data bank removes completely this safeguard."

John de J. Pemberton, Jr., then Executive Director, American Civil Liberties Union: "There are two dangers to civil liberties inherent in the existence of such an information center (FBI Crime Information Center). The first of these (is) the widespread use of incomplete and unexplained arrest records. These problems are even more grievous in the all-to-common case today of those arrested for the valid exercise of constitutionally protected rights. No reliable procedure exists for differentiating such arrests in present FBI records from arrests made for the normal incidents of criminal conduct—yet, the problem remains, and will be accentuated by the creation of a central pool of information. Such a pool will serve only to multiply the deprivation of the civil liberties of those who are wrongly

---

[10] See *The Computer and Invasion of Privacy*, pp. 2, 3, 6, 13, 35, 78, 79, 174, 175, 179, 182, and 183. (1966) and *Special Inquiry on Invasion of Privacy*, pp. 348, 385, and 386. (1966) U.S. Government Printing Office, Washington, D.C.

arrested and even convicted for merely exercising their rights. Inaccurate and prejudicial data will be made available to a greater number of police officials and through them to still greater numbers of unauthorized persons. Our second concern is that it will be the repository for not just crime. It is said that other Federal investigative agencies will be invited to feed whatever information they choose into the huge reservoir that the national network of computers will store and retrieve."

Likewise, at the Hearings Before The Subcommittee On Administrative Practice and Procedure of the Committee On The Judiciary of the United States Senate, Nineteenth Congress, Final Session [11] (commonly known as the Long Committee) prominent citizens articulated their fears for the future:

Professor Arthur R. Miller, University of Michigan Law School: "The ability of the Government to record and use information in the law enforcement area is particularly frightening: 'arrested, 1/1/40; convicted, 6/1/40; felony, served Leavenworth for 3 years.' What chance has that man got in society when anyone has access to his file. Yet, he may simply have been a conscientious objector, but the person inputting the data did not have the sensitivity or the judgment to record that fact. A massive computer installation containing extensive files on criminals and alleged criminals that can be reached simply by digital dialing and is available to governmental or private offices not involved in law enforcement poses a serious threat to the individual. A state official may direct an inquiry to the computer file of 'known' criminals, find an entry under the name of his subject, and rely on that entry to the subject's detriment without attempting to verify its accuracy or exploring the possibility that additional information might eliminate the innuendo of the computer record. I find that to be frightening, absolutely frightening, especially if those data banks are made available for non-law enforcement purposes."

Lawrence Speiser, Director, Washington Office, American Civil Liberties Union: "I would like to point to the announcement which was made last month of the establishment of a national crime information center by the FBI. This was established without, as far as I know, congressional approval or congressional knowledge. What it collects, how the information is safeguarded, how it is distributed, what agencies can get information, whether it relies on investigative reports that are never tested and whether this information is freely available, it seems to me, are matters that should be of concern to this subcommittee and of Congress.

"However, the stake here is large; the right of a free people to remain free, unencumbered by the knowledge that for each individual, Big Brother

---

[11] See *Computer Privacy* (1966). U.S. Government Printing Office, Washington, D.C.

has an electric file collecting every tidbit of information. There would be no escape. No mistakes would ever be undone. Skeletons in the closets would always be there, only they would be compactly and efficiently transformed into eternal electrical impulses on tape.

"Efficiency is not the only hallmark of good government. There are other values in a society dedicated to the most comprehensive right of its citizens, 'the right to be left alone.' "

The testimony quoted above, and additional testimony of people too numerous to list, effectively aborted the U.S. Bureau of the Budget plan for a National Data Bank. Professor Alan F. Westin, author of "Privacy and Freedom," [12] a standard text in this area, states that the princial reason the Bureau of the Budget ran into such grave difficulty was that their administrators had failed to plan carefully and incorporate safeguards in their proposed system. Project SEARCH, and the NCIC CCH Program derived from it, while at least as sensitive as the National Data Bank, may benefit from the insights generated by the proposal of the Bureau of the Budget. There is a need for rules, safeguards, penalties and remedies. This point of view was expressed by the National Crime Commission in its *Task Force Report: Science and Technology* [13] in these words:

> The most delicate part of any criminal justice information system is the record of previously arrested people and accompanying information about them —whenever government reports contain derogatory personal information, they create serious public policy problems.
>
> The record may contain incomplete or incorrect information.
>
> The information may fall into the wrong hands and be used to intimidate or embarrass.
>
> The information may be retained long after it has lost its usefulness and serves only to harass ex-offenders, or its mere existence may diminish an offender's belief in the possibility of redemption.
>
> As a check on the users and manager of the file, all inquiries should be kept in a permanent record and that record audited regularly to verify the validity and handling of the inquiries. Unauthorized disclosure should be subject to serious penalty.
>
> The audit should be by a different agency from the one operating the system. This group could also monitor the computer programs to insure that there are no unauthorized modes of access. They could also try by various means to penetrate the system as a running check upon its security.

As the SEARCH interstate exchange criminal offender record information developed and later became operational under the aegis of the FBI/NCIC, it was apparent that grave concern had to be accorded to security and privacy. After much soul searching the consortium of state represen-

---

[12] Westin, Alan F. (1967). *Privacy and Freedom.* Atheneum, New York.

[13] President's Commission on Law Enforcement and Administration of Justice (1967). *Task Force Report: Science and Technology.* U.S. Government Printing Office, Washington, D.C.

tatives who formed the Project Group—the policy-making body of Project SEARCH—issued Technical Report No. 2.[14] This landmark document served SEARCH as a valuable guide on these previously uncharted frontiers and became the basis for the FBI/NCIC Computerized Criminal History Program Security and Confidentiality doctrine. Among the valuable contributions of this report was the code of ethics which participants in Project SEARCH voluntarily pledged themselves to observe. It was the first such code adopted by criminal justice agencies for self-regulation of computerized information systems.

CODE OF ETHICS

One of the most meaningful ways in which dedication to security and commitment to privacy can be manifested is to adopt a *Code of Ethics*. The authors recommend the code contained in SEARCH Technical Report No. 2 to all who control or participate in criminal justice data banks. The code in Article I defines the Limitations of the System—including limitation to the criminal justice function, limitation of the category of users, limitation of functions and limitation of information contained in the system. In Article II the code addresses the Integrity of Information—which includes assurance of individual privacy, rules for the collection, maintenance and dissemination of data, providing for an advisory committee to provide policy direction for the system and to entertain complaints about alleged intrusions on individual privacy. Finally, Article III provides canons governing the Use of the Data Base for Research—requiring of researchers a commitment to privacy and the safeguarding of the anonymity of the individual subjects concerned.

Many of the privacy principles enunciated in Technical Report No. 2 and memorialized in the SEARCH Code of Ethics have been incorporated in the regulations for security and confidentiality of the FBI/NCIC Computerized Criminal History Program. This represents a giant step forward in terms of the general acceptance by law enforcement and criminal justice of the viability of privacy concern in computerized information systems. These regulations limit the data in the CCH System to that with the characteristics of public record and specifically reject social history data for the interstate system. Provision is made for purging/expunging of data. Direct access is strictly limited to criminal justice agencies in the discharge of their official, mandated responsibilities. It is provided that all computers interfaced or otherwise accessing the NCIC CCH System must be under the management control of an authorized criminal justice agency and the information must not be intermingled or centrally stored with non-criminal

---

[14] SEARCH (1970). *Security and Privacy Consideration in Criminal History Information Systems, Technical Report No. 2.* California Crime Technological Foundation, Sacramento.

social files, such as revenue, welfare and medical, etc. Users of the data, including researchers, are carefully circumscribed and provisions are made for monitoring and disciplinary action where indicated. Likewise, establishing of adequate state and federal criminal penalties for misuse of criminal history data is endorsed. The right of an individual to see and challenge the contents of his record is upheld and a permanent committee on security and confidentiality has been established within the FBI/NCIC Advisory Policy Board. Written use and dissemination agreements have been negotiated and the principle of auditing by the Security and Confidentiality Committee has been accepted. Furthermore, the development of model state statutes for protecting and controlling data is encouraged.

SECURITY AND PRIVACY LEGISLATION

The Security and Privacy Committee of Project SEARCH developed *A Model State Act For Criminal Offender Record Information.*[15] The primary purpose of the Model Act is to provide the basis for individual states to develop their own legislation regulating the security and privacy of computerized criminal offender record systems. To the extent that these legislative enactments in the various states are fundamentally uniform, or at least, not in conflict, the ends of justice will be enhanced.

The basic strategic approach adopted by the Security and Privacy Committee was a conscious affirmation that computerized criminal justice information systems are essential for the effective administration of criminal justice and that such systems can be developed and operated with adequate security against unreasonable invasions of individual privacy—indeed, that they can be so developed and operated as to provide new dimensions of personal freedom and protection for civil liberties and constitutional rights.

The tactical approach adopted by the Security and Privacy Committee was a deliberate effort to bring forth an "ideal" type of act—one that would reflect the highest possible standards, while at the same time retaining practical viability. If the statute were to err, it was intentionally designed to err on the side of privacy protection. There was no model of any kind to guide the committee, so every step was a first step. It was recognized that the present and future success of any nationwide computerized criminal offender record information system depends to a great extent upon the security and privacy protection capabilities of the various states and that these must be supported by appropriate legislation.

The committee seized the opportunity to face up to the problem of indirect access by non-criminal justice government agencies and by non-

---

[15] SEARCH (1971). *A Model State Act for Criminal Offender Record Information, Technical Memorandum No. 3.* California Crime Technological Foundation, Sacramento.

governmental agencies and individuals who are currently alleged to be putting to good use the criminal offender records they receive from federal, state and local criminal justice agencies. The "good use" is claimed to contribute to the prevention of crime and, therefore, presumably serves appropriate criminal justice purposes. In many jurisdictions there are currently valid statutes requiring state and municipal agencies to search fingerprints and report offender record information to a whole host of non-criminal justice agencies. It should be noted that *a substantial percentage* of the fingerprint submissions processed by some central state bureaus, and responded to with a summary case history record, are received from *other* than criminal justice agencies. The wise use of criminal offender information in the applicant/licensee area may help prevent crime, to that extent, it undoubtedly serves society as meaningfully as when such information is utilized in the post-criminal event sequence. The model statute was drafted to take into account the "need to know" of many fingerprint contributors who are not usually included in any list of criminal justice agencies. By the same token, the act contemplates very strong proscriptions against access where legitimate criminal justice purposes cannot be clearly spelled out.

The Model Act provides for both a Criminal Offender Records Control Committee and a Security and Privacy Council. The Committee is intended to set privacy and security standards, promulgate regulations, and generally to be responsible for controlling the operation of the record-keeping system. It is intended to be a coordinating body, drawing together criminal justice agencies which are already engaged in the collection, storage, dissemination and usage of criminal offender records. It is not intended as a heavy administrative structure, superimposed upon existing agencies, but instead as a working group of representatives of those agencies. The Council is chiefly an advisory body, designed to represent the interests of both the criminal justice community and the general public. Its members should be broadly representative both of the community and of the relevant interests. The Council is intended to be sensitive to problems that the public, or some portions of the public, may think exist in the record-keeping system, to identify and examine the system's deficiencies, and to offer prompt and appropriate recommendations for the correction of those deficiencies. The Council has also been given responsibility for the evaluation of individual complaints that criminal offender records are inaccurate or otherwise misleading.

The Model Act provides that regulations be issued relating to class access, expunging and purging, access and dissemination, research, rights of individual access and challenge and the application of civil and criminal penalties. Model regulations have been drawn up by the Project SEARCH

Privacy and Security Committee to complement the Model State Act. These recommended regulations are intended to offer guidance to states in carrying out the provisions of the act. The regulations are more specific than the act and are designed to supplement it.[16]

A rider (Section 7) was attached to the 1970 Omnibus Crime Control Act, the so-called "Mathias Amendment," requiring the administration of LEAA to submit "to the President and to the Congress recommendations for legislation to promote the integrity and accuracy of criminal justice data collection, processing and dissemination systems funded in whole or in part by the Federal Government, and to protect the constitutional rights of all persons covered or affected by such systems."

It should be noted that this mandate applied to intelligence as well as identification systems. Indeed, it applied to all criminal justice data systems at any level of government, wherever federally funded. On September 20, 1971, Attorney General Mitchell submitted to the Congress an historic legislative proposal entitled, "Criminal Justice Information Systems Security and Privacy Act of 1971," in response to the Congressional Mandate mentioned above. The Attorney General's letter of transmittal states:

> The draft bill provides for stringent controls over the security of and access to criminal justice information systems, contains appropriate provisions for updating of information in them, for purging of outdated information, and for allowing individuals to have access to criminal history records concerning them, in order to insure that they are accurate and complete.
>
> The draft bill also provides civil and criminal remedies against those who violate its provisions by unlawful dissemination or use of criminal justice information and authorizes the Attorney General to prescribe regulations to effectuate its provisions.
>
> The proposed legislation would, I believe, protect the constitutional rights of persons affected by the collection and dissemination of criminal justice information, while at the same time ensuring that the legitimate needs of law enforcement authorities for complete and accurate information may be satisfied.

Typical of widespread reaction to the proposed legislation are the following newspaper comments which appeared at the time the bill was introduced in the Senate: [17]

> The bill falls far short of proposals made earlier this year by legal experts, civil libertarians and members of Congress testifying before a Senate subcommittee on the threats posed to individual privacy by all types of federal data banks and by surveillance of lawful civilian political and social activity.
>
> It would not, for example, apply to files and data banks maintained by the Federal Bureau of Investigation or most other arms of the Justice Department,

---

[16] SEARCH (1972). *Model State Administrative Regulations for Criminal Offender Record Information, Technical Memorandum.* California Crime Technological Foundation, Sacramento.

[17] Angle, Martha (1971). *Column. The Washington Star,* September 22, Washington, D.C.

or to other federal law enforcement agencies like the Secret Service or U.S. Customs Bureau.

The measure gives sweeping power to the attorney general to promulgate rules and regulations to carry out its provisions.

It is not expected that the proposed legislation is likely to be passed in its present form; however, the very fact that such a bill was introduced with the support of the Nixon Administration is very significant in terms of security and privacy considerations and in terms of the future of state control over state and local criminal justice administration. On the one hand, it acknowledges the merit of many of those elements of privacy protection which have been demanded by persons sensitive to civil rights, civil liberties and constitutional guarantees. On the other hand, it attempts to establish a new theory of jurisdiction and control over state and local government, utilizing the concept of *federal power following federal funding*. This will undoubtedly raise very sensitive issues of constitutionality.

Some of the privacy provisions that are recognized are as follows:

1. The measure would establish for the first time at the federal level the right of an individual to access to his own criminal record for purposes of insuring its accuracy and completeness.

2. The bill would allow an individual who believes that criminal offender record information concerning him is inaccurate, incomplete or maintained in violation of the act, to challenge it and seek correction.

3. It also requires "procedures designed to assure that criminal offender record information concerning an individual is removed from the active records" after a "reasonable interval."

4. Any individual who believes criminal justice information concerning him has been illegally maintained, used or disseminated would be allowed by this bill to sue for damages.

5. Anyone willfully misusing, or illegally disseminating criminal justice information would be subject to criminal penalties of one year in prison and/or a $1,000 fine.

While these provisions represent enormous advances forward by the federal government, they fall far short of meeting the full range of concern of those who perceive a threat to individual freedoms in computerized data systems. This fear of "Big Brother" and "1984," is exacerbated by the bill's delegation of power to the Attorney General. Many fear that the act as introduced gives the Attorney General far too much authority to enact various unspecified rules, regulations and procedures controlling the conduct of state and local criminal information systems; and that although it appears to be an attempt to protect the security and privacy of criminal justice information systems, the delegation of authority is so broad as to wrest control of systems from the communities which have created and must support them. Many fear that, generally, this act is a somewhat weak attempt to establish specific security and privacy provisions. Yet, at the same time, it virtually gives a blank check to the Attorney General to impose his will upon *non-federal* operations, thus virtually negating the viability of any state and local statutes governing these systems which would now or hereafter conflict with the policy decisions of the Attorney General.

OTHER CONSIDERATIONS

The adoption of a code of ethics is one small step toward a total effort in this vital area, but an aggressive, positive attitude on our part requires far more than this alone. We must be willing to monitor Congressional hearings, testify before various governmental committees, and announce to all and sundry that we are, indeed, anxious, willing and ready to build into our systems all reasonable safeguards to protect individual privacy.

The authors strongly recommend that criminal justice systems developers affirmatively solicit the support of various groups that might be considered hostile if they were otherwise unaware of our intentions. Potential opponents can be made willing allies if they participate with us in our system development. We have nothing at all to hide; we want to build these systems in a climate of security and constant awareness of civil liberties. Let us bring in with us in our deliberations and our various developments the counsel and wisdom of those who have dedicated themselves to these propositions, and are more keenly aware than most, of all the dimensions of the right to privacy.

An article in "Computerworld" [18] states that Rep. Cornelius E. Gallagher (D., N.J.) has hailed a report which insists that studies for insuring privacy and confidentiality be completed before establishment of a National Data Bank. Gallagher said he was happy, "for once," to concur in the recommendations of an academically oriented group over the issue of the National Data Bank."

The report,[19] while tentatively approving the National Data Bank system, cautions that first a "high level continuing body, including nongovernmental members," must come forward with "positive, workable procedures."

It should also be noted that the Business Equipment Manufacturers Association (BEMA) has recently formed a privacy and security committee and the BEMA Board Chairman has suggested the establishment of a "rigid code of ethics"—and the development of technical means to safeguard stored data—to restore public faith by "positive action" in the area of privacy and security.

---

[18] *COMPUTERWORLD—The Newsweekly for the Computer Community,* November 19, 1969, Chicago, Ill.

[19] *The Behavioral and Social Sciences: Outlook and Needs*—released under the auspices of the National Academy and the Social Science Research Council.

It is submitted that criminal justice system developers have a great need to recognize the dimensions of the problems they face, and must take positive attitudes and affirmative action as a matter of top priority.

It is not the intent of the authors to suggest that increasing concern about the right of privacy and individual freedom should in any way be limited to computer technology, criminal justice information systems or technological developments generally. Criminal justice professionals should be aware of these concerns in reference to all of their activities. Many traditional practices and time-honored customs will have to be changed because of new social forces that will find their expression in judicial decisions and legislation at every level of government. The issues are more sharply drawn and more clearly perceived in certain areas of operations such as wiretaps and eavesdropping, psychological testing, physical surveillance, and, of course, information and intelligence systems; however, the issues are far more pervasive than these convenient categories. Every act, practice and procedure of every aspect of criminal justice administration needs to be carefully scrutinized to ascertain where privacy may be violated and sound the tocsin where necessary.

What we must be alert to in terms of privacy is the struggle for a particular human dimension in a highly structured society. While privacy problems exist everywhere, they are perhaps most acute in reference to the remarkable advances in electronic, optical, acoustic and other devices. The question that we must always ask ourselves is—if the new technology is on a collision course with the values of personal privacy and human dignity, can the collision be averted? The authors believe it can, provided, in timely fashion, that we recognize the danger and adjust the course accordingly.

COMPUTER INSTALLATIONS, CURRENT AND PLANNED

Computer installations are now operational at the federal, state, and local levels of government. Aside from matters of security and privacy, objections to criminal justice data banks have been voiced. Some have wondered if such information systems would threaten local agencies and weaken the American ideal of local autonomy, local control. But all evidence to date tends to indicate that information-sharing systems that are computer-based lessen inefficiencies and wasteful procedures without damage to jurisdictional boundaries. The data bank has become an available service that has relieved many costly pressures in record processing and storage, and the elimination of duplicated data files has provided savings in personnel, facilities, equipment, time and dollars for many users.

Installation at the Federal Level. In announcing the development of a nationwide information system, May 1, 1966, Mr. Hoover, the late Director of the Federal Bureau of Investigation, stated that "computer and communication technology has eliminated two major problems—burdensome volume and time lag—which make a manually operated national system impractical." [20] The philosophy underlying such a system was expressed in these words:

> The logical development of electronic information systems proceeds from local metropolitan systems to statewide systems and then to a national system. In effect, each succeeding system would afford greater geographical coverage. The information stored at each level will depend on actual need, with local metropolitan systems naturally having a data base much broader than that of either the statewide or national system. By the same token, state systems will store information of statewide interest which will not be stored within a national system. It is most important to avoid any concept that a national system eliminates the need for systems of lesser geographical scope—metropolitan and statewide systems must develop to serve local needs which could not possibly be met by any national system. The ultimate nationwide network will not be achieved until such systems develop in each state and the larger metropolitan population centers.[21]

Initial planning for the National Crime Information Center (NCIC) involved data relative to stolen automobiles unrecovered after a specified time, stolen property in certain categories, and some wanted persons. The National Crime Information Center began operation in January, 1967, with fifteen on-line state or metropolitan area terminals. Stored in NCIC computers from participating agencies were 40,000 records of stolen vehicles, 20,000 records of stolen plates, 20,000 records of stolen or missing guns, and 10,000 records of wanted persons. Also stored were records of 5,000 fugitives wanted on federal charges.

As of October 1, 1972, there were 4,059,120 active records in NCIC with the breakdown showing 122,556 wanted persons, 810,310 vehicles, 263,365 license plates, 801,031 articles, 526,198 guns, 1,305,988 securities, 6,515 boats, and 223,157 criminal offenders (computerized criminal histories). In September, 1972, NCIC network transactions totaled 2,943,115, averaging 98,104 daily. On September 26, 1972, a record number of 113,080 transactions were processed.[22]

This phenomenal growth of the NCIC operation is proof of the viability of law enforcement computer systems. It must be noted, however, that NCIC, until November, 1971, was currently dealing with "thing" files (i.e., stolen property and warrants) rather than the more sensitive type of files which contain derogatory data about people such as were being developed at the state level and stimulated by the LEAA funding of Project SEARCH. The LEAA computerized criminal history program that was being developed by a consortium of states was assigned to the jurisdiction of the

---

[20] Message from the Director. *FBI Law Enforcement Bulletin*, May, 1966.

[21] A national crime information center. *FBI Law Enforcement Bulletin*, May, 1966.

[22] See *NCIC Newsletter*, October, 1972.

FBI by the Attorney General, and the late Director Hoover announced that NCIC would be expanded in November, 1971 to include computerized criminal histories, stating:

> This month, the computerized criminal history information system becomes operational through the expanded services of the FBI National Crime Information Center (NCIC). For many years, the FBI, through a manual system, has exchanged criminal history information with local, state and federal agencies by mail. Now, working with state and local authorities, the FBI will accept criminal identification records for computer storage and make the computerized records immediately available to federal, state and local police, prosecutors, courts and correctional agencies for day-to-day use. In view of the ever-increasing interstate criminal mobility, this is a significant advancement for law enforcement and the administration of justice.
>
> Speculation, on the part of some, that the computerization of criminal history will lead to the wholesale misuse of such data is completely unfounded. Detailed security procedures have been established throughout the NCIC to insure that criminal information is used for only those purposes approved by law. Under Federal Statute, the FBI is authorized to exchange criminal identification, crime, and other records with "authorized officials of the Federal Government, the states, cities and penal and other institutions."
>
> The data to be included in criminal history records are documented information furnished by police, courts, and correctional agencies to accurately depict the individual's formal contacts with the criminal justice system from arrest until final disposition.
>
> As in the past, persons and agencies that misuse the computerized identification records will be immediately denied the services of the system. I am in full agreement with pending proposals to have Federal penalties established for the unlawful use of information obtained from the system. Further, individuals or agencies responsible for the unauthorized use of identification records can be sued in civil courts by persons who feel they have been wronged.[23]

Installation at the State Level. To a very large extent information-sharing computer installations relating to criminal justice are, at every level of government, law enforcement oriented. They are typically owned and operated by police agencies for their special purposes and do not purport to service the entire gamut of criminal justice administration. (This is equally true of similar systems found in the United Kingdom and on the Continent.) Yet, every informed observer has called for comprehensive approaches which take into account the interrelationship among all aspects of law enforcement, courts and corrections.

In view of the fact that the New York State Identification and Intelligence System (NYSIIS) is the only currently operating system that takes a total systems approach, involving all agencies involved in the administration of criminal justice, and because such approach may well set the pattern of future state-level systems, it deserves special consideration.

---

[23] Message from the Director. *FBI Law Enforcement Bulletin,* November, 1971.

NYSIIS was created as an agency in 1965.

The concept of NYSIIS rests upon the following basic principles of the unitary nature of criminal justice: all criminal justice agencies need to participate in and share a joint data bank; the submission of information thereto should be primarily voluntary; NYSIIS is to be a service agency only, with no powers, duties or facilities to arrest, prosecute, confine or supervise; security and privacy considerations must permeate the system and involve central and remote NYSIIS operations; new dimensions of science and computer technology can be applied to provide greater effectiveness in filing methodology and the utility of processed data; and that criminological research will be supported by a vast resource of computerized empirical data available for variable searching to test theses, hypotheses, theories and pilot projects, thereby enabling criminal justice administration to evaluate its own procedures, practices and operations.

NYSIIS is now bringing to some 3600 agencies of criminal justice—police, prosecutors, courts, probation, correction and parole—the advantages of computer science and related technology. The independence and integrity of contributing agencies are preserved, for no agency is required to participate unless it so desires and then only to the extent it desires. With the exception of fingerprints and criminal case dispositions mandated by prior law, the nature and degree of information submitted is voluntary, and dissemination of information is strictly in accord with the desire of the contributor. Thus, NYSIIS holds information as the trusted custodian of the criminal justice community. Security engineering prevents contamination of the data base by excluding tainted data, by establishment of personnel, physical, transmission, data bank and information security measures, and by guarding against improper disclosures which would jeopardize human rights or civil liberties. The integrity of the system and the confidentiality of the data are considered prime concerns of NYSIIS, and all responses to user requests for information are within specific right-to-know and need-to-know requirements. The system's dual objectives of effective law enforcement and protection of individual rights have received endorsements from the Vera Institute, the New York Civil Liberties Union, and from the New York State Combined Council of Law Enforcement Officials.

Many advantages have accrued to criminal justice agencies from the establishment of NYSIIS. Among the more significant improvements are included: initiation of the nation's first statewide criminal justice facsimile transceiver network for rapid transmission of arrest fingerprints to NYSIIS and the rapid return of summary criminal history responses; initiation of a twenty-four hour daily service in the Bureau of Identification to assist criminal justice agencies on a round-the-clock basis; and reorganization, realignment and streamlining of internal procedures and work flow. Through the establishment of the state-funded facsimile system, and computerization of several components of the identification function in the Bureau of Identification, criminal justice agencies in New York State now have, for the first time, the capability of transmitting fingerprints to NYSIIS and receiving a detailed summary case history in less than three hours (a process which formerly required seven to ten days).

The criminal records of more than 600,000 persons have been converted to computer readable form so that these records, enriched with additional relevant data, may now be produced directly from the NYSIIS Burroughs B-6700 computer and transmitted by facsimile device to the police, sheriffs, prosecutors, criminal courts, probation, correction and parole authorities as requested. Among many significant breakthroughs achieved by NYSIIS research and systems studies is the fantastic capability of searching incoming sets of fingerprints by computer against a base file of 2.5 million fingerprint classifications in no more than thirty seconds. Likewise, NYSIIS has developed an operational wanted system which enables criminal justice agencies anywhere in the state to check rapidly on suspects, missing persons, amnesiacs, etc., against both the statewide NYSIIS file and the nationwide files of the FBI's computerized National Crime Information Center (NCIC). Concomitantly, after extensive research and study of personal privacy considerations, NYSIIS initiated a pilot organized crime intelligence capability which is being used as a model by the United States Department of Justice for its own computerized organized crime files. Indeed, LEAA is currently using the NYSIIS intelligence system as the keystone in an attempt to inaugurate a nationwide computerized intelligence-sharing network.[24] The innovative thrust of the NYSIIS commitment has guided the conceptualization of many facets of federal involvement toward a more scientific and rational system of criminal justice administration. Funding from the Law Enforcement Assistance Administration (LEAA) has been received by NYSIIS for original research in automatic license plate scanning to apprehend automobile thieves, for psychological and anthropometrical studies to define the elements of an effective computerized personal appearance data base, for in-depth evaluation of the economic impact of organized crime, for latent print identification, for the development of new methods of taking fingerprints and a host of other vital analytical, criminalistic and criminological research studies.

Until the current stimulus caused by Project SEARCH, California was the only other state that had made significant progress toward a criminal

---

[24] Gallati, Robert R. J.: *State Criminal Justice Information Systems,* American Federation of Information Processing Societies, 1971 Fall Joint Computer Conference Proceedings, Montvale, N.J.

justice information system, although it like many other states, had already developed effective law enforcement systems to serve police purposes.

California State Programs. The Department of Justice (DOJ), with the Lockheed Missiles and Space Company, designed a statewide criminal justice information system which will involve police, prosecutors, courts, probation, corrections and parole agencies.

The California information system has been developed as a federation of organizational computer centers tied together by the information that the user needs and will operate within a framework of compatibility rules. The system will utilize computers belonging to the various agencies involved in the administration of criminal justice; coordination will emanate from the state's central information center which will serve as a central electronic index or directory of information stored in the files of the participating computer centers, and which will function as a switching facility. The center will be supported by charges for services rendered based on size and population of the jurisdiction, number of transactions requested, or number of items stored or involved in the processing data. Benefits to local law enforcement will be twofold: (1) reduction of duplication in collection, storage and processing; (2) increase in accessibility and application of data. The Department of Justice is the principal coordinating agency for local law enforcement and supports the concept of an automated statewide law enforcement information system.

The *Bureau of Criminal Identification and Investigation* (CII), within the Department of Justice, utilizes an RCA computer and current operations include a firearms file (over 2.6 million records of concealable weapons; 100 daily inquiries), law enforcement arrest statistics (arrests and dispositions, 4,000 inquiries per week), narcotic prescriptions (by doctor, quantity, patient, type; 30,000 per month) and charitable trust reports. Planned new applications involve miscellaneous property files (600,000 records), modus operandi-crime pattern recognition data, statistical reports, sex registrant file, narcotic registrant file (64,000 drug offenders), name cross-reference master file (8.5 million), criminal history file (2.3 million) and fingerprint file (200,000 file searches).

The *California Highway Patrol* operates a rapid communications system for recording and disseminating information on stolen and wanted motor vehicles called *Autostatis* (Automatic Statewide Auto Theft Inquiry System).

CLETS (*California Law Enforcement Telecommunications System*) is a high-speed message system which will allow any urban or local law enforcement agency within the state to transmit a message to any similar agency and obtain instant information concerning stolen property and wanted persons. CLETS is currently operational and will continue to expand its capabilities to link more than 450 California law enforcement agencies to Sacramento and the NCIC in Washington. The *Department of Motor Vehicles* has completed a real-time system for vehicle and driver registration.

Florida State Program. The Florida Crime Information Center (FCIC) is a computer-based law enforcement criminal justice information system which includes over 261 computer teleprocessing terminals in city, state and federal law enforcement agencies.

The Department of Law Enforcement is continuing the research necessary for the development of FCIC into a complete criminal justice information system. This includes the design of Florida's Uniform Crime Reporting Program (UCR) to interface with and utilize the FCIC network and computers for data collection and analysis. Also included is the development of a fingerprint processing technique which utilizes microfilm and computer technology for the rapid identification of persons fingerprinted for criminal and non-criminal reasons. In criminal matters this identification becomes an input to the person's criminal history or "rap sheet" for return to the fingerprint contributor. This "file" is also maintained on-line for inquiry by law enforcement and criminal justice officers in the performance of their official duties.

New York, California and Florida have recognized that *central direction* of computer development is necessary if a state is to harness this important tool and obtain maximum benefit from its use.

A score of other states have been developing centralized capabilities and, with the encouragement provided by the FBI, NCIC Computerized Criminal History Program, by LEAA through Project SEARCH and by other funded innovations, it is certain that more central direction at the state level will be the rule in the future. Indeed, it is safe to predict that by 1975, virtually every state will have a state wide criminal justice information system. These states, now members of the SEARCH consortium, are likely to be among the first to have fully developed systems—Arizona, Arkansas, California, Colorado, Connecticut, Florida, Georgia, Illinois, Maryland, Massachusetts, Michigan, Minnesota, Nebraska, New Jersey, New York, Ohio, Pennsylvania, Texas, Utah, and Washington.

This is not to say that many other states do not now have sophisticated computer potential. Delaware, Kansas, Kentucky, Louisiana, Mississippi, Missouri, and Oklahoma are but a few of the other states which have joined the SEARCH consortium as it has expanded to include additional states working toward statewide criminal justice information systems.

Installation at the Local Level. There is a hierarchy of responsibility in the administration of criminal justice, and even though the federal government and the states have a broad role due to geography, the largest responsibility rests at the local level. Most local criminal justice data bank systems are oriented to local operations, are most often owned and operated by police agencies, and currently are not designed to satisfy the requirements of prosecutors, courts, probation, corrections and parole units.

Some local systems involve application of development programs to assign manpower in response to changing patterns of crime or to meet emergency needs. Most systems are concerned with some form of pattern analysis of criminal activity within the jurisdictional area. Virtually all local systems record and tabulate statistical information as to crimes reported, arrests made and cases cleared in order to assemble data for state and federal crime reports, and to provide guidance to administrators. Where no state system is operational, these local systems concern themselves with identification files, stolen motor vehicles, identifiable stolen property and warrants-wanted listings. Some local systems have developed modus operandi programs and pattern analyses which attempt to predict the possible location and time of criminal activity.

Programs at the federal or state level do not diminish the need for local programs. As stated by the National Crime Commission, "the overall program must be geared to the circumstances and requirements of local and state agencies; and, wherever practical, the files located at these levels. Even the specifications and procedures of the national system must conform to local needs, and should be developed by people familiar with them." [25]

Local programs exist at the county level, in the county-metropolitan context and at the metropolitan level.

County Programs. *Alameda County, California.* Thirteen communities around Alameda County, in the San Francisco Bay Area, have developed a computerized Police Information Network (PIN) which provides for real-time dissemination of warrant data and plans have been drawn up to incorporate modus operandi, traffic control and message switching.

Los Angeles County, California. The Los Angeles Sheriff's Office has embarked upon a very ambitious system called ORACLE (Optimum Record Automation for Court and Law Enforcement) utilizing a combination of videofile and computer capabilities. This countywide television information system will tie together the fourteen sheriff's stations throughout the county to speed and automate the handling of 18,000,000 Sheriff's Department law enforcement documents.

Dade County, Florida. The Information Network and File Organization

---

[25] The President's Commission on Law Enforcement and Administration of Justice (1967). *The Challenge of Crime in a Free Society*, p. 268. U.S. Government Printing Office, Washington, D.C.

(INFO) utilizes a computer system for motor vehicles and license plates, wanted persons and summons control applications.

Brevard County, Florida. The Sheriff's office has implemented a system covering crime history, traffic control and accident statistics, arrests and jail applications.

Nassau and Suffolk Counties, New York. Computer interface with the State Police and NCIC has been established and additional capabilities are being implemented.

County-Metropolitan Program. Wales (Washington Area Law Enforcement System) involves the participation of the Washington Metropolitan Police as well as the law enforcement agencies of Montgomery, and Prince Georges Counties of Maryland and Alexandria, Arlington and Fairfax Counties in Virginia.[26]

It is interesting to note that WALES is operating effectively in the very home base of NCIC which underscores the separate roles of local, state and federal computer systems. Even though NCIC maintains a directory of wanted persons and stolen vehicles, the need for a local program is not diminished.

One of the most significant and potentially far reaching aspects of WALES is the fact that the system is being used to monitor the progress of offenders through the arresting process. Thus there will be greater protection of the individual offender's rights as he passes through the system and at the same time statistical and research data will become readily available to enable administrators to adjust the various operations which are not functioning in proper fashion to the detriment of civil liberties and compromise of constitutional guarantees.

CLEAR (County Law Enforcement Applied Regionally) is a system servicing 38 local police agencies in Cincinnati and Hamilton Counties, Ohio, with police records and it is tied in with NCIC and the Ohio Highway Patrol LEADS.

Metropolitan. *Los Angeles, California.* The Los Angeles Police Department has participated in the planning of a metropolitan group similar to the Police Information Network (PIN) in Alameda County. The Southern Police Information Network (SPIN) will first deal with warrants and eventually tie in with the Northern California PIN. Los Angeles Police Department has done experimental work with a natural language *modus operandi* system which feeds the complete crime report into the computer which then does an analysis of key words and phrases.

A design study was conducted with the goal of automating all informa-

---

[26] Ross, Charles U. (1969). "WALES in Washington, D.C." *Output—The Monthly Feature of Public Automation,* December.

tion-processing tasks. Phase I was directed to achievement of more economical processing of crime reports, wants-and-warrants and field interviews, to the minimization of time required to process and communicate relevant information and to developing the greatest possible accuracy, relevancy, availability and utilization of such data. Phase II will computerize arrest reports, field activity reports, traffic accident reports, traffic enforcement selective deployment, patrol officer deployment and car plan generation. Phase III will include fingerprint identification, property reports and pawnbroker files in a real-time storage and retrieval program. Phase IV will deal with personnel, training, motor transport, supply and equipment records processing by the automated system.[27] It is to be noted that the Los Angeles Police Department recently announced that their computerized warrant/wanted file is successfully operational.

New York City Police Department, New York. The New York City Police Department has utilized since 1961, a computer for the batch processing of crime statistics, taxicab operator files, traffic accident information and data for administrative studies. An annual hazard report is issued which lists the police hazards for each beat, precinct, district and borough and which has been found useful to both tactical and patrol forces. The department has computerized the storage of part of its criminal fingerprint files and has experimented with conversion of the Henry system to a single fingerprint system which also involves ridge counts, sex, race and age. Operation "Corral" proved that bulk processing of motor vehicle license numbers at random into a real-time computer would facilitate the apprehension of auto thieves.

It is anticipated that the City of New York will embark on a total criminal justice data bank system to supplement the NYSIIS program. This planned project, supported by the Vera Institute, will be the first municipal undertaking to provide information-sharing capabilities for all the agencies of criminal justice within the locality.

The New York City Police Department recently announced the successful implementation of its advanced computerized communications system SPRINT (Special Police Radio Inquiry Network). This is a command and control system which enables dispatchers to determine from among the more than 1000 department vehicles the available radio motor patrol car nearest the scene of any call for assistance, while at the same time it provides essential data that may be required, such as location of nearest hospital or other municipal facility. It has reduced significantly the average dispatch time; at the present time the average elapsed time is less than twenty seconds.

---

[27] System Development Corporation (1966). *An Information System for Law Enforcement,* Technology Series. SDC, Santa Monica, California.

St. Louis, Missouri. The City Police Department has pioneered in the field of computer technology. Development work for this highly sophisticated system began as early as 1963. This system has implemented an extensive number of applications, such as message switching for the St. Louis Department and eighteen other departments in the St. Louis metropolitan area, as well as the Missouri Highway Patrol pending arrival of their own computer which is on order.

The most outstanding accomplishment to date, however, and noteworthy in the entire field of metropolitan law enforcement is St. Louis' accomplishment in developing a computer assisted resource allocation program. This system allows the department to make peak utilization of every man and patrol car by being able to accurately predict manpower needs. Personnel can then be scheduled and beat structures designed to fit the particular need for a given period of time. In addition, the analytical ability of the system permits rescheduling in minimal amounts of time based on changing conditions. Further, the computer system helps reflect changes in crime density or patterns. This allows commanders to be sensitive to probabilities of crime occurring in certain areas. Arrests have already increased in areas where computerized allocation has been used.[28] It is anticipated that a system will be developed so that maps can be produced for the use of patrol and tactical forces through a computer-plotter technique.

Chicago, Illinois. The Chicago Police Department utilizes many computer programs for producing reports relating to crime statistics, manpower allocation, assignment and workload, and for administrative control. The computer inquiry system can speed "hot desk" information via ultramodern communications facilities, to the field forces in seconds. Vital information is on-line concerning stolen cars, wanted persons and stolen property and is immediately available by radio or telephone. Facsimile transmission of fingerprints to the identification division has speeded up the arraignment process and saved thousands of police manhours. The computer provides daily evaluations of crime which identify high crime rate areas and predict the location and time of expected criminal activity.

The department is conducting research relative to a case reporting system on a real-time basis which will allow the immediate updating of all related files and eliminate a great deal of typing, duplicating and filing. The Chicago Police Department is also exploring the substitution of a video system in lieu of the existing teletype and facsimile network. In addition, squad cars are now being dispatched by computer, reducing arrival time by some three minutes.

San Diego, California. This city's computer system became operational

---

[28] Videtti, Joseph A., Jr. (1969). "Application of Computers in Law Enforcement." *Police,* July-August.

in June, 1967, with a computerized traffic enforcement program and an initial vehicle information file containing traffic contact data from the previous two months. The initial design of the system was to have a capability that would enable a search to be made on a partial vehicle description as well as on a complete license number and also to be able to build a file from available traffic data with a minimum of coding. This is especially critical because of San Diego's geographical location on the Mexican border.[29]

Kansas City, Missouri. The police department recently commissioned the Automated Law Enforcement Response Team (ALERT) system.

The ALERT network centers on a computer in police headquarters. Its electronic files contain information and processing power for the following major data analysis functions:

1. Stolen vehicle records and data about the car and its owner. About 1,500 inquiries are processed monthly.

2. Lists of wanted persons, including reasons for current pickup orders, nature of the arrest warrant, the authorizing agency, the individual's arrest and conviction records, fingerprint code, last known residence, and history of resisting arrest, carrying concealed weapons, or attempting suicide. About 11,000 inquiries are processed monthly.

3. Alias checking to analyze all names received and insure aliases and names similar in spelling to the one received are checked before officers complete actions in the field.

4. Identification of habitual criminals and persons believed to be involved in organized crime.

5. Daily wanted-persons location analysis producing printed lists for each officer assigned a beat, noting the names of wanted persons known to frequent the beat.

6. Uniform crime reporting procedures to insure local data is compatible with data gathered by other law enforcement agencies nationwide.

7. Information on each department employee, including his blood type and persons to be contacted in the event of an emergency.

Other Cities. Some of the larger cities that have sophisticated computer capabilities available for law enforcement and criminal justice include the following: Phoenix, Tucson, Denver, Honolulu, Indianapolis, Baltimore, Boston, Detroit, Rochester, N.Y., Cleveland, Portland, Oregon, Philadelphia, Dallas and Buffalo.

These examples of states, counties, county-metropolitan and metropolitan systems are by no means a complete listing, but it does give some idea of the proliferation of computer installations in the law enforcement and

---

[29] *Ibid.*

criminal justice sector. There are many more states, counties, and cities that have made important advances, but they are too numerous to be recounted here. Indeed, any attempt to catalogue existing installations and on-going systems is likely to obsolesce almost before it appears in print—so rapidly is this area of development expanding. With additional support from LEAA for these vital adjuncts of modern criminal justice operations we may expect to see the number of installations and applications of computers and related technology increase factorially.

Installation Problems. Installation of criminal justice data bank systems at the federal, state and local levels is an ongoing process that is most complex and conditioned by a host of factors involving politics, budget, personnel, equipment, facilities, policies, procedures and fundamental philosophy.

Whether or not the system will be a limited or total agency process is conditioned by both philosophy and availability of resources. The authors of this text support the concept of a total criminal justice data bank system which provides for information sharing by police, prosecutor, courts, probation, corrections and parole units, and suggest that anything short of such approach truncates the criminal justice information process and suboptimizes computer science and technology capability.

Whether or not the interchange of information between criminal justice agencies and noncriminal justice agencies is proper must be settled. Some design concepts assert that information within state welfare files, motor vehicle files, employment office and educational institutions is pertinent to cases handled in the administration of criminal justice. Other design concepts tend to assert an independent integrity for criminal justice data bank processes and flatly exclude exchanges of information with noncriminal justice agencies.

A very strong position was taken by the late Director Hoover and the FBI NCIC Computerized Criminal History Program Advisory Policy Board on this subject. The NCIC CCH Security and Confidentiality document of the NCIC Advisory Policy Board, dated August 31, 1971, states:

> The Board endorses the following statement by the Director of the FBI before the Subcommittee on Constitutional Rights on March 17, 1971. If law enforcement or other criminal justice agencies are to be responsible for the confidentiality of the information in computerized systems, then they must have complete management control of the hardware and the people who use and operate the system. These information systems should be limited to the function of serving the criminal justice community at all levels of government—local, state and federal.
>
> All computers interfaced directly with the NCIC computer for the interstate exchange of criminal history information must be under the management control of a criminal justice agency authorized as a control terminal agency.

Similarly, satellite computers accessing NCIC through a control terminal agency computer must be under the management control of a criminal justice agency. Management control is defined as that applied by a criminal justice agency with the authority to employ and discharge personnel, as well as to set and enforce policy concerning computer operations. Management control includes, but is not limited to, the direct supervision of equipment, systems design, programming and operating procedures necessary for the development and implementation of the computerized criminal history program. Management control must remain fully independent of non-criminal justice data systems and shall be primarily dedicated to the service of the criminal justice community.

CONCLUSIONS

There is a national, indeed, an international,[30] trend toward the utilization of computer science and technology in the administration of criminal justice at every level of government.

Perhaps the degree to which the cybernetic revolution has involved itself is illustrated in the presentations of the First, Second, and Third National Symposiums on Law Enforcement Science and Technology, at the Illinois Institute of Technology. These three-day professional forums addressed themselves to new and improved means of crime control and criminal justice administration by use of computer and electronic technology. Papers on information storage and retrieval, simulation studies, criminalistics applications, criminological research, operations and communications processes, crime prediction, and administrative utilization were presented. Virtually every computer hardware (equipment) and software (analysis, design, and mathematical paperwork) vendor in the United States was represented, along with the British and Canadian representatives.

The National Crime Commission noted that there has been surprisingly little impact by science and technology upon the criminal justice system. (As recently as 1965, the United States Department of Justice was the only Cabinet department with *no* share of the fifteen billion dollar federal research and development budget!)

However, today it would be safe to say that there is ample evidence that the agencies of criminal justice are interested in computers, and that the computer industry is avidly wooing the agencies of criminal justice. There has been a large commitment of the private funds of computer hardware and software vendors to the research and development of sophisticated methods within the administration of criminal justice. Even though the great foundations have had limited past involvement, the publication of

---

[30] An international conference on the application of computers to law enforcement was held in Paris, France in November, 1971, under the auspices of INTERPOL. More than forty nations were represented and reported varying applications from merely record keeping to on-line real-time operational capabilities.

the Report by the President's Commission on Law Enforcement and Administration of Justice (National Crime Commission) is stimulating their more active participation, and they presumably now see the potential for use of "seed" money to stimulate innovation and imaginative cybernetics to combat and control crime and disorder. Some smaller foundations are now giving encouragement and financial support for computer experimentation—the Vera Institute, for example, sees great possibilities in computer science and technology for improvement of arrest, bail and sentencing process, and the enhancement of civil liberties. The Civil Liberties Union has recognized that more sophisticated cybernetic procedures should enable the agencies of criminal justice to be effective in serving society and, at the same time, in protecting human rights and civil liberties.

System Analysis. There will probably be an unprecedented increase in the utilization of computers in the administration of criminal justice. There are pitfalls, however, in proceeding too rapidly; "keeping up with the Joneses" can be perilous in the computer "stampede." Demands upon criminal justice agencies are overwhelming, and frustration may lead to undue haste in acquiring computer hardware, particularly where high-pressure salesmanship carries the day. Potential purchasers of computer systems must avoid precipitous implementation before making a thorough analysis of the system's requirements. The method of a system analysis is to study the operations of an agency, along with its goals and purposes, in order to understand current procedures and inherent problems.

The objective of system analysis is to improve system performance by designing an operation that optimizes the integrity and timeliness of decision-making information required at each point within the decision network supported by the information system. The sequence of systems analysis and design must incorporate the application of advanced information-processing techniques in use or under development—it must, in other words, be oriented toward the future, as far as that future can be determined. Many an agency with a second-generation computer is hard pressed to implement real-time applications because these latest capabilities were not properly planned for in the system design. Such comment is not intended to minimize the desirability and need for computer systems in the administration of criminal justice—it is intended to point up the indispensability and mandatory use of system analysis.

Standardization. There is always a tendency for people who have failed to do proper system analysis to re-invent the wheel. While every system is necessarily unique in some respects, likewise, every criminal justice system is similar in other respects.

There seems, for some inexplicable reason, to be a tendency by most agencies to spend large sums of money developing applications or systems which have already been implemented by other agencies. This does not mean to say that one organization's solutions can always be lent to another's problems, but where computerization is concerned there are many areas of universality.

One way of solving this problem would be to arrive at some area of standardization concerning computer systems. This concept has already been inaugurated by the Federal Bureau of Investigation with NCIC, but this standard is only mandatory toward those who participate in the NCIC system. There is much more that can be done that will significantly reduce developmental costs. Perhaps the Research Committee of the International Association of Chiefs of Police could appropriately act as a clearinghouse for application programs that are re-usable by different jurisdictions with minor or no adjustments required.

Impact of LEAA. With the recent reorganization of the Law Enforcement Assistance Administration there will undoubtedly develop new dimensions to the war on crime. There will be an emphasis upon high impact grantsmanship and general modernization of the criminal justice system to reduce crime.

The LEAA, by the end of 1973, will have been given $2,409,000,000 to spend. If the monies are expended in 1973 as in 1969, 1970, 1971 and 1972, the American criminal justice system will be the most extravagantly equipped in the history of the world, and the criminal justice/industrial complex a major economic entity. But, if crime rates continue to panic the nation, if clearance rates continue to indicate the impossibility of police miracles, and if recidivistic rates continue to demonstrate the impotency of corrections, we might well suspect that the monies were allocated by traditionalists in anachronistic patterns guaranteed to perpetuate the heavy-handed ineffective practices of past decades.

Because technology can be the handmaiden of freedom or tyranny, the student of criminal justice might well look into the constitution of the commission which has been allocating LEAA monies in his state. Are they largely men of limited vision who see answers to the problems of the 70's in firepower, repressive law, and massive force? Or are they men with the broad vision to see that the problems of the 70's will never be solved by repeating the mistakes of the 40's, 50's and 60's, and who are more interested in criminal justice philosophy, and role and policy than in gadgets and gear and guns? Tomorrow's criminal justice system will give the definitive answer!

A New Era. Computer science and related technology have helped to stimulate a new interest, involvement and commitment to research in all the dark alleys of criminal justice administration. There is now general recognition that it is imperative to end the historic non-involvement of federal resources in crime research.

We may look forward to a new plateau of crime prevention and control—freedom from crime and fear of crime. All of our citizens have the right to protection of their persons, property and neighborhoods from anti-social attacks, and, as innocent, suspect or guilty, all citizens have the right to just and proper treatment by those who are engaged in the administration of criminal justice. Computer science and related technology will form a potent strategic and logistic force as all of our communities at all levels join efforts to achieve ordered liberty. Fortunate indeed are those who now enter the agencies of criminal justice for career service in this challenging, exciting and revolutionary era.

TOPICS FOR DISCUSSION

1. What is the current state of computer sciences and related technology relative to the administration of criminal justice in this city? county? state?
2. What relationship does the concept of "dynamic security" have to police-community relations?
3. What is meant by the term "people files"—as opposed to "thing files" and how does it relate to criminal justice records?
4. Discuss the distinction between "system analysis" and "system design."
5. What are some of the long-range implications of the LEAA-funded project to computerize offender records in all states of the nation (Project SEARCH)?

PART VI
EVALUATING CRIMINAL JUSTICE TODAY

Chapter XIX

ORGANIZED CRIME AND CORRUPTION

ORGANIZED CRIME is a cancerous growth on American society with ill effects which reach everyone in one degree or another. Its corrosive effects present a most serious threat to the community in all aspects of life. An essentially subversive force, organized crime strikes at the very heart of democracy itself.

The National Crime Commission expressed it in this manner:

> Organized crime—is dedicated to subverting not only American institutions, but the very decency and integrity that are the most cherished attributes of a free society. As the leaders and their racketeering allies pursue their conspiracy unmolested, in open and continuous defiance of the law, they preach a sermon that all too many Americans heed: The government is for sale; lawlessness is the road to wealth; honesty is a pitfall and morality a trap for suckers.
>
> The extraordinary thing about organized crime is that America has tolerated it for so long.[1]

It is extraordinary indeed that the most powerful nation on earth in this enlightened era should have permitted itself to be placed at the mercy of a Sixth Column of lawless pirates.

President Nixon in his message to Congress on April 23, 1969, affirmed the reality of this threat to our very survival as a nation:

> Today, organized crime has deeply penetrated broad segments of American life. In our great cities, it is operating prosperous criminal cartels. In our suburban areas and smaller cities, it is expanding its corrosive influence. Its economic base is principally derived from its virtual monopoly of illegal gambling, the numbers racket, and the importation of narcotics. To a large degree, it underwrites the loan sharking business in the United States and actively participates in fraudulent bankruptcies. It encourages street crime by inducing narcotic addicts to mug and rob. It encourages housebreaking and burglary by providing efficient disposal methods for stolen goods. It quietly continues to infiltrate and corrupt organized labor. It is increasing its enormous holdings and influence in the world of legitimate business. To achieve his end, the organized criminal relies on physical terror and psychological intimidation, on economic retaliation and political bribery, on citizen indifference and governmental acquiescence. He corrupts our governing institutions and subverts our democratic processes.

---

[1] The President's Commission on Law Enforcement and Administration of Justice (1967). *The Challenge of Crime in a Free Society*. U.S. Government Printing Office, Washington, D.C.

For him, the moral and legal subversion of our society is a lifelong and lucrative profession.

The situation has deteriorated to the degree that highly respected scholars who have dedicated years of their lives to exhaustive study of this terrifying phenomenon speak of appeasement, accommodation, negotiation, treaties and diplomatic relations with the fourth branch of the government.[2]

THE CONFEDERATION

One may well ask the question: If it is certain that there is truly this grave threat to our country and its people, why have we failed before now to prevent its development into such monstrous proportions? The answer, like the problem, is very complex; however, some reasons for the extreme predicament with which we now find ourselves confronted include the following:

- The difficulty of achieving a precise definition, or even an agreed upon label, for the phenomenon.
- The fact that the "enemy" has not been precisely identified and acknowledged as an organization.[3]
- Public understanding is limited and public support is wavering and ambivalent.
- Our system of justice with its Constitutional guarantees was not designed to deal with this kind of problem.
- Organized crime has many well-intentioned and unwitting allies among our most distinguished citizens.

Problems of Definition. The very existence of so many varied names for the structure of the organization that controls organized crime is evidence of the difficulty of defining its essence. In an attempt to select a single label that would best describe the organization of organized crime, the nation's top experts, during their meetings at the Conferences on Combating Organized Crime in 1965, in Oyster Bay, New York, took cognizance of the proliferation of commonly used names and rejected them as providing poor terms for designating this conspiracy. The term *Mafia*, for example, was rejected because its origin is Sicilian and refers to a Sicilian-based organization, whereas this conspiracy is based in the United States and has many non-Sicilian members. The term *Cosa Nostra* is also limited, because it implies incorrectly that all members of the conspiracy are Italian,

---

[2] Cressey, Donald R. (1969). *The Theft of the Nation*, pp. 323-324. Harper & Row, New York.

[3] *Ibid.*, p. 323.

and because the term is not known to be used in any place other than the New York City area.[4] In Chicago, members of the conspiracy refer to themselves alternately as the *Syndicate* or as the *Outfit*, terms which were also rejected as local. In New York City, English-speaking members prefer to refer to themselves as the *Organization*, but this term was rejected because it is both local and not very descriptive. The term *Confederation* was accepted as the best term to describe the character of an overall arrangement that now dominates organized crime in the United States.

Some of the conferees asserted that this conspiracy consists of twenty-four well-organized member units, known as *families*, loosely bound together into a single, national confederation. The families have defined rackets and geographical territory.[5]

While the term *Confederation* was agreed upon by the group, we still find many of those same experts currently utilizing the terms *Mafia* and *Cosa Nostra* in their writings, so the confusion continues. This kind of unscientific and sensationalized approach has created a credibility gap with the public and alienated many who would otherwise give strong support to the thrust against organized crime.

Problems of Identification. Merely deciding upon a descriptive label or satisfactory definition, even if it were universally accepted, does not solve the problem of precise identification of the phenomenon. At the present time the very invisibility of organized crime and criminals (except those relatively few who may be indicted) tends to create the aura of a myth and an unrealistic appraisal of the threat. As long as we treat organized crime as though it were a myth, a journalistic exercise in hyperboles, a diverting and intriguing "other" group who kill each other off and do not really bother us too much, we are in real trouble as a nation. As long as our society has a vague, ambivalent, disorganized concept of the threat of organized crime, *qua* organization, it will thrive. Just so long as the response of society is intermittent, apathetic and disorganized, the organization of organized crime will continue to prosper and the threat will become more sinister.

Despite the weight of evidence and the unanimity of the authorities, there are many profound thinkers, even some among criminal justice professionals, who are not intellectually convinced that a conspiracy commonly

---

[4] Messick, Hank: *Lansky.* New York, G. P. Putnam's Sons, 1967. Hank Messick uses the term "National Crime Syndicate" and flatly asserts that "organized crime is not the province of any one ethnic group or secret society." He further states, ". . . if every member of the Mafia (or La Cosa Nostra) were jailed tomorrow, organized crime would be just as powerful as ever."

[5] *Combatting Organized Crime,* a report of the 1965 Oyster Bay, New York, Conferences, Executive Chamber, State Capitol, Albany, N.Y., 1966.

referred to as "organized crime" really exists. This incredulous attitude of many people who perhaps should know better exasperates the true believers who are driven by frustration to evermore flamboyant warnings of the extreme peril we face. This polarization of opinion concerning the reality of organized crime tends to sustain those who find it more comfortable to consider it all a myth, thereby assuaging their guilt feelings, tranquilizing their neurons and reaffirming their faith in the always victorious good guys. Unfortunately, it is no myth, no ghost-like wraith; organized crime is not dead. In fact, it is very much alive and lives in Brooklyn as well as in Newark, Chicago, Philadelphia, New Orleans, Detroit, Tucson, San Francisco, Miami, Los Angeles, and in hundreds of villages and little hamlets no bigger than Apalachin.

Some city fathers like to deny that they have organized crime. Indeed, until recently, there were high officials in the New York City Police Department who contended that organized crime was an illusion.[6] That this is no longer an accepted viewpoint in the New York Department is evidenced by the fact that the Police Commissioner has appointed a Deputy Commissioner for Organized Crime, who will devote his full attention and whatever resources he requires for the single purpose of combating organized crime.

The Law Enforcement Assistance Administration has taken a very strong position concerning the threat of organized crime and has published a handbook designed to help police officers throughout the nation recognize and combat organized crime.[7] Likewise, there can be no doubt that Attorney General John N. Mitchell was convinced of the reality of organized crime. In an address to the Associated Press Managing Editors Convention he stated that organized crime is the most dangerous of all.[8] Finally, President Nixon has deplored the failure to clearly identify the enemy:

> It is vitally important that Americans see this alien organization for what it really is—a totalitarian and closed society operating within an open and democratic one. It has succeeded so far because an apathetic public is not aware of the threat it poses to American life. This public apathy has permitted most organized criminals to escape prosecution by corrupting officials, by intimidating witnesses and by terrorizing victims into silence.[9]

---

[6] Deputy Commissioner for Organized Crime, William P. McCarthy, New York City Police Department, speaking at a meeting of the Legislative Action Committee of the United States Conference on Mayors in Wilmington, Delaware, on December 15, 1971, said, "I can remember a meeting in 1963, of the chief officers of the New York Police Department, when the vast majority of those present decided the concept of organized crime was absurd."

[7] LEAA, Technical Assistance Division (1971). *Police Guide on Organized Crime.* Law Enforcement Assistance Administration, Washington, D.C.

[8] See LEAA (1971). *Newsletter,* December. Law Enforcement Assistance Administration, Washington, D.C.

[9] Message of the President to the Congress of the United States, April 23, 1969.

Problems of Public Support. It is certainly understandable that public support in the past has never been sustained and zealous when one realizes that less than a dozen years ago the existence of a nationwide organized crime conspiracy was denied by some of our most respected law enforcement officials. Most of these have since been converted. There is probably more latent skepticism among intellectuals today than among those on the firing line. However, some of the most persistent doubters are now being converted into true apostles. Professor Donald R. Cressey was not at all certain that a nationwide organization of criminals existed when he was invited to work for the National Crime Commission. Today the author of *Theft Of The Nation* deplores the continued skepticism of his friends and colleagues and is almost evangelical in his fervor.[10]

Aside from the inherent confusion among some leaders of our society and the public generally, concerning the existence of this somewhat elusive phenomenon, we must recognize the will-o-the-wisp character of the threat, the cultivated invisibility of its action and the difficulty experienced by so many who seek to understand this "thing" in a meaningful way. Today, the average member of the public understands war as never before because the stark reality of war is brought into his living room via television news. Organized crime, on the other hand, comes to him in fictional guise, competing with other sensationalized entertainment programs. How do you realistically depict a concept like "organization" in audio-visual form? The other primary sources of public education concerning organized crime are the Sunday supplements and some of the more grubby periodicals, where there is strong competition from sex, scandal, and more conventional types of blood-letting. Most recently there has been a rash of books which have become best sellers, such as *The Godfather, Honor Thy Father, The Valachi Papers, The Gang That Couldn't Shoot Straight, Lansky*, etc. While some of these books should help to convince at least some segments of the better-read public of the reality of the organized crime threat, there have been similar exposés in the past which generated very little lasting or residual public support.

Obviously, the public is generally not too much predisposed to conversion, since so many enjoy the services of their friendly corner cigar store bookmaker, who, of course, is a "nice local chap not connected with those gangsters you hear about." Some members of the public are indulged by the minions of organized crime in various other ways less socially acceptable, such as prostitution, narcotics, illegal booze, untaxed cigarettes, smuggling, labor racketeering, and loan sharking. The Confederation offers goods and services that millions of Americans desire even though declared illegal by their legislatures.

---

[10] Cressey, *op. cit.*

A very special problem of public support arises from the ethnic tie of some of the core groups of the Confederation. Use of the terms *Mafia* and *Cosa Nostra* are violently objected to by Italo-Americans and their sympathetic friends. Representative Mario Biaggi in a dramatic speech on the floor of the House of Representatives on May 1, 1969, attacked President Nixon's message on organized crime in these words:

> I had hoped that the new Administration's fight against organized crime would not be steeped in the disgraceful tradition of the past. But now I know better. I know that the era of untruths, distortion and fantasy for the benefit of the public image is still with us.
>
> Once again, it has been clearly implied that organized crime is the exclusive preserve of Americans of Italian origin. In that context, President Nixon's crime message last week was disappointing, sad, misleading, unfair—and I regret to say—insulting to our nation's 22 million law-abiding Americans of Italian ancestry.

Regardless of the merits of the controversy, it is apparent that public support for an all-out, united front against organized crime and the Confederation is jeopardized by the failure of many protagonists to respond sensitively to objections concerning their stigmatization of law abiding Italo-Americans. Just as many blacks were alienated by demands for "law and order" and saw that term as a racist signal, so many Italo-Americans interpret the use of the terms *Mafia* and *Cosa Nostra* as implications of group guilt.

Problems of Our System of Justice. There is an inherent dichotomy between those at one end of the spectrum, who see crime control as paramount and those at the other extreme, who deem due process the overriding priority. It is the role of criminal jurisprudence in a democracy to maintain a delicate balance between these two extremes. We can, indeed, we must, seek to maintain both due process and a viable system of crime control; the two are not incompatible, and ways must be found to reconcile both in dynamic equilibrium.

The long-term immunity from legal accountability that the major figures in organized crime have enjoyed constitutes a black record in the administration of justice in this country. It can truly be said all of us are being denied "due process of law." [11] More, however, is involved than the symbolic meaning of the failure here of justice. The motivation of the major organized crime figure is not that of the typical offender. Passion, poverty, ignorance, or mental disease play a very small part. Whatever the validity of the concept of deterrence elsewhere, in this area it seems to have a valid, if inverse, meaning. These professional criminals calculate how low the risks of

---

[11] Lumbard, E. (1962). "The Lawyer's Responsibility for Due Process and Law Enforcement." *Syracuse Law Review,* 12:430.

conviction are and how high the rewards of success go. Change that balance and one can reasonably expect to change their behavior patterns. Today the young man in organized crime knows all he has to do is to run the risk of conviction for a few years as he works his way up. When he arrives at a certain point, wealth, power and immunity from legal accountability are his. This success story of the top man can be, and has been, repeated *ad nauseam.*[12]

Some say that Constitutional guarantees were drawn up at a time when the nation did not have to deal with so sinister and evil an underworld government. They say that the protections in the Constitution were designed for honest citizens only, and, in any event, were not created to permit internal subversion of our government by an "alien" enemy. There is general agreement that our penal laws are probably adequate to deal with the problem of attacking organized crime, but that our criminal procedures for enforcing, prosecuting and adjudicating these criminal sanctions simply are not designed for the nature of the threat, for they are designed to deal with incident crime and individual criminals acting separately or with accomplices, but not in an organized, cartelized, well-financed and directed fashion.

Some of the additional legal weapons and tools, which appear to be essential to achieve convictions and provide an effective legal response to the challenge, may include the liberalization of pre-trial discovery, witness immunity statutes, special protection for witnesses who fear to testify due to intimidation, use of the injunction, evidentiary rules that do not require accomplice testimony to be corroborated, revised search and seizure laws, the right to appeal a pretrial order to suppress evidence, and allowance of judicially supervised electronic surveillance.

Of course, another very relevant area of concern is the validity of the plethora of sumptuary laws that abound in all our states. Many say we should re-evaluate the so-called victimless crimes, the outlawing of gambling, prostitution, narcotics and other matters regulating personal conduct which it is often said harms only the individual himself rather than society. In Quebec, Canada, a provincial crime commission has recommended legalizing prostitution and gambling to break up the power of organized crime which has been imported from New York City and Buffalo, New York, and has spawned a rash of gangland slayings and public corruption.[13] As President Nixon has stated, new legal approaches are needed. Perhaps an entire revision of our structure of criminal jurisprudence is in order.

---

[12] The President's Commission on Law Enforcement and Administration of Justice (1967). *Task Force Report on Organized Crime*, p. 105. U.S. Government Printing Office, Washington, D.C.

[13] See *Chicago Tribune*, Sunday, November 16, 1969.

Problems of Unwitting Allies. There are at least two kinds of respectable and even distinguished allies that are most cherished by the Confederation since they are their most sincere, effective and impeccable guardian angels. The first are those who stoutly maintain that there is no such thing as a Confederation, or if there is some kind of organized crime, it is in the nature of gangs of pick-pockets, confidence men, burglars, gypsies and their ilk. They find it incredible that there could be an invisible nationwide organization larger than the largest conglomerate, and in terms of profits, as big as U.S. Steel, AT&T, General Motors, Standard Oil of New Jersey, G.E., Ford Motor Co., IBM, Chrysler and RCA put together. Meyer Lansky, the gang's leading financial wizard, may have been overly modest when he chortled in 1966: "We're bigger than U.S. Steel." [14] President Nixon has estimated the total annual "take" from illegal gambling alone at $20 to $50 billion—larger than the entire Federal Administrative budget in 1951. [15]

These kinds of fantastic figures tend to boggle the mind and create skepticism among people who are unwilling to pursue the facts further. They prefer to dismiss the whole thing from their minds. The thought of Meyer Lansky as an international financier *par excellance* is unsettling and threatens their comfortable smug stereo-type of gun-toting racketeers— who probably only exist in the movies, anyway.

The second type of unwitting ally is the crusader for law and order who raises such a hue and cry about violence and street crime (a substantial portion of which has its root causes in Confederation activity such as narcotics) in order to assure that the priorities are ordered in that direction, instead of toward nonviolent organized crime.

These are the kinds of allies that can't be bought for money, although indirectly and discreetly their causes may be partially supported by some Confederation cash. And it is cash well spent if attention is diverted away from the Confederation itself.

In any event, many people in the pursuit of their own goals, which may be entirely honorable, unwittingly assist the Confederation in its preoccupation for low visibility and keeping things on an even keel.

CORRUPTION

Perhaps the most pervasive problem of all that is created by organized crime is the nullification of government at the law enforcement and administration of criminal justice level and also at the legislative level, where members of federal and state legislatures as well as city councils and county

---

[14] "Cosa Nostra—the Poison in our Society." (1969) *Time* Magazine, August 22.

[15] Message of the President to the Congress of the United States, April 23, 1969.

supervisors are "bought." It is now recognized that organized crime cannot exist without the corrupters and the corrupted, and that this corruption itself is the worst evil of all among the by-products of organized crime. People know when crime pays. Kids in the slums see the cop on the beat take money. They know the pusher seldom gets caught, and his wholesaler is virtually never touched. They learn this lesson better than any middle-class values taught in the schools from which they drop out. The implication of the failure of our legal system to hold accountable those who openly flaunt our laws undermines the entire system. Not only is crime not deterred, it is indirectly promoted. No society can call itself civilized and allow this situation to continue.[16]

Police Corruption. Until very recently there was almost no public recognition given by the police themselves to the ever-present problem of endemic corruption within their ranks. With the growth of professionalism and the adoption of new value systems as expressed in codes of ethics and a heightening self-respect, the police profession has as last come to grips with the monster. At the 76th Annual Conference of the International Association of Chiefs of Police (IACP) on October 1, 1969, former New York City Police Commissioner Howard R. Leary, as Chairman of the Organized Crime Committee of the Association, recommended for the first time in IACP history, that the IACP publicly acknowledge the problem of corruption in law enforcement. He reported:

> Considering the relationship among syndicated crime, politics, and public officials, the committee asked that police recognize more fully the corrosive effects of organized crime on law enforcement, and the relationship between organized crime and street crime. The committee recommended that IACP publicly acknowledge the problem of corruption in law enforcement.

Horror stories of police corruption abound in the media and the literature and have been affirmed by every investigation of any consequence from the Wickersham Commission, to the Kefauver Committee to the McClellan Committee to the De Cavalcante and De Carlo revelations to the most recent utterances of the President and the Attorney General, down to the explosive Knapp Hearings in New York City.

The Knapp Commission. While the New York City Police Department has had its share of major scandals and corruption investigations over the years—the Lexow and Seabury Investigations, the Harry Gross scandal, etc.—there has never before been an investigation like that conducted in 1970 and 1971, by a Commission under the chairmanship of Whitman Knapp, Wall Street lawyer and former Assistant District Attorney under

---

[16] See footnote 12.

both Frank Hogan and Thomas E. Dewey. There are several unique aspects to this investigation which make it enormously significant in the annals of American police:

1. The investigation was initiated in response to the demands of two very frustrated and persistent members of the force.

2. The most revealing testimony was elicited from policemen who were themselves involved in corruption and who related sordid details implicating themselves as well as other police officers.

3. It revealed widespread graft in connection with narcotics. (Prior scandals for the most part, involved gambling which had been rationalized by rogue cops as "clean graft," as opposed to the "dirty money" from prostitution or narcotic bribery. It had been assumed by many in the police department that gambling, rather than narcotics, was its achilles heel.)

4. The investigation disclosed the incredible reluctance of highly placed political officials and ranking police officials to take any action on the disclosures of the police officer informants.

5. The investigation has generated an entirely new concept in the Department of the cancer of corruption; that the problem cannot be solved merely by focusing on individual acts of wrongdoing—that it arises out of an endemic and systemic condition which must be attacked on all fronts. Thus, First Deputy Commissioner William H. T. Smith deplored the breakdown in public confidence and said the people "are sick of bobbing for rotten apples in the police barrel. They want an entirely new barrel that will never again become contaminated." [17]

6. Finally, the revelations of the Commission have strengthened the reform campaign of Police Commissioner Patrick V. Murphy. He has an opportunity to construct out of the ashes a truly professional edifice that will endure and provide a beacon for police everywhere.

Whatever happens, for better or worse, in the 32,000 uniformed member Police Department of New York City has a ripple effect upon municipal police departments everywhere. Corruption investigations, stimulated in many cases by the events in New York City, have sprung up in numerous other cities here and abroad—in Chicago, Philadelphia, Newark, Albany, Jersey City, Tijuana, Mexico and even in London, England. "Bent copper" —underworld argot for corrupt police—has tarnished the shining facade of famed Scotland Yard. Anthony Judge, ranking staff member of the Police Federation, which is both a collective bargaining instrument and professional organization for police throughout Britain, expressed the widespread dismay concerning the large number of "Bobbies" arrested for robbery, theft, extortion and other offenses:

---

[17] Smith, First Deputy Police Commissioner William H. T. (1971). Lecture at the Maxwell School, Syracuse University, October 28. He further stated: "There is a long tradition of police thought regarding the control of police corruption. It centers around the belief that corruptibility is ingrained in human nature; and in coping with his behavioral manifestations we have only to devise suitable punishment for the overt offenders—that is, for those who get caught— and, as a way of controlling corruption, it has failed."

We have at the moment a serious problem of corruption among the metropolitan police. There have always been individuals who have gone wrong. But now what's worrying is that some policemen are acting in a criminal manner in concert." [18]

The story of the Knapp Commission will be told and retold and undoubtedly be the subject of a book and possibly a movie. It is difficult to assess the long term effect it will have upon the police profession. The short-term effect upon the police in New York City has been devastating to morale. The Civil Service Leader [19] reported on January 4, 1972, that there had been 359 voluntary retirements in the Department since July of 1971. The *entire* top echelon of police commanders at the time of Commissioner Murphy's appointment, less than a year and one-half before, had by January, 1972, "put in their papers" for retirement. The long-term effect may well be a positive one based upon salutary changes that are likely to be effected in the way the police police themselves. The New York Department, by accepting the concept of amnesty, is beginning to turn bad cops around—something they never did before—and getting them to work within the force to expose other corrupt policemen. Chief Counsel to the Knapp Commission, Michael Armstrong, says:

> Honest cops are starting to turn corrupt ones in. And, of course, the creation of an outside agency which would consist of people whose entire careers and promotion ladders were based on investigation alone (a concept Commissioner Murphy has already supported), goes a long way to helping the police stay in line.
> Finally, with all this, we have to instill pride in the force. But I firmly believe that pride has been there all the time. It just hasn't come through. Look at the reasons Droge and Logan and even Phillips (the policemen who testified against other policemen at the Public Hearings) gave for joining. Each one noted that he wanted respect. But a cop, even an honest one, couldn't have that respect when everyone down to the grass roots knew where police corruption was. By changing the system I think we can get rid of the kind of cynicism among the cops that has caused young and basically honest cops to start taking graft and, instead, let their pride in themselves and their own honesty counteract the corruption. And then we'll have real morale in the New York City Police Department.[20]

What Chief Counsel Armstrong is suggesting is the equivalent of a civilian review board for dealing with the problem of corruption, similar to the more familiar civilian review boards of the past whose primary emphasis was upon brutality. This is bound to be a controversial issue for

---

[18] *Washington Post*, November 30, 1971.

[19] *Civil Service Leader*, a weekly newspaper for public employees. New York, N.Y.

[20] Davidson, Barbara (1971). "The Knapp Commission Didn't Know it Couldn't be Done." The New York *Times* Magazine, January 9.

many years to come. Many people are convinced that brutality and corruption are endemic,[21] and this new concept of a civilian review board for corruption will undoubtedly be attractive to them as was the prior concept of a civilian review.

More and more people have become aroused about the problem of police corruption, particularly as it relates to drug traffic.[22] The Knapp Hearings have confirmed suspicions that already existed and have struck a responsive chord in the people's consciousness, perhaps because of the tremendous frustration our American public is experiencing as it observes with horror the proliferation of addiction. It is not likely that extensive narcotic corruption will be met with apathy by our society. It is recognized that more police corruption originates today from narcotics involvement than from any other source.[23]

The Knapp Commission has spotlighted police corruption in its efforts to focus on police reform. This is not to say that corruption does not exist in large measure in other branches of criminal justice administration. Indeed, it is futile to attempt to convince the police to be honest if all about them they find graft, bribery, pay-offs and corruption among better educated, better paid and more honored members of the criminal justice community. Any attempt to wipe out police corruption that overlooks the need for strict observance of ethical practices throughout the entire criminal justice system is foredoomed to repeat the failures of the past.

Corruption of Prosecutors. The corruption of the police is fairly simple and straight-forward bribery and it is a reasonably visible phenomenon. As a result, policemen are often indicted and convicted; however, it is rare that one finds a prosecutor being arrested and brought to trial for corruption in office. Yet Professor G. Robert Blakey, Notre Dame Law School,

[21] Sayre, Wallace S., and Kaufman, Herbert (1965). *Governing New York City*. Norton Publishers, New York.

[22] Brown, William P.: The golden arm of the law, *Nation*, October 25, 1971. Doctor Brown, a professor at the School of Criminal Justice, State University of New York, a former New York City police inspector, sounds the tocsin. "The nature of narcotics adds another element to the ethical problems that always arise where there is a continuing association between the police and a criminal group. A certain corrosion comes from all such 'business' contacts, but while other criminals have only a professional interest in their dealings with the police, police pressure or tolerance literally means the difference between what the addict accepts as a good life and the hell of drug deprivation. The investigator—with a tradition and with possibilities for taking criminal advantage is prone to, and possibly eager for, seduction. That, then, is the challenge: either police administration accepts the responsibility for the reasoned, sophisticated control of narcotics law enforcement, or it accepts responsibility for continued inefficiency with regard to the important criminals, continued overstress on nonprofessional criminals, and corruption on a scale that no body of public servants can endure."

[23] Cawley, Donald F., Chief of Patrol, New York City Police Department, in testimony before the New York State Investigation Commission, April, 1971.

the nation's leading expert on the legal aspects of organized crime prosecution, has said:

> Useful as corrupt police may be, no dollar of corruption buys as much real protection as the dollar which directly or indirectly influences the public prosecutor or one of his trusted assistants. After all, the prosecutor makes the crucial decision as to whether the suspect shall be prosecuted or not.

Corruption in the Courts. Unlike the situation of the prosecutors, it seems that there is an open season on the judiciary. Several judges have recently been indicted, convicted and disbarred in New York, Massachusetts, and New Jersey in connection with Confederation-sponsored briberies, shakedowns and conspiracies to defraud. It is essential that organized crime nullify not only the processes of the administrative branch of government, but the bench as well.

Retired Chief Justice of the United States, Earl Warren, in answer to a news correspondent's question about organized crime, stated:

> I will say that that kind of crime cannot exist and flourish in any community unless there is corruption in some form, in some segment of law enforcement. It might be the police, it might be the prosecutor, it might even be contributed to by the courts.[24]

This is a most salutary admission despite its obvious naiveté. As any police officer who has ever served on a vice detail will affirm, the good Chief Justice is being most charitable. There are many who are convinced that the focus of the infection is right in the black-robed laps of the judiciary.

Corruption in Rehabilitation. The long arm of the Confederation easily reaches into the very heart of our penal institutions. While maximum security prisons may keep offenders from escaping to the outside world, they seem totally unable to keep the outside underworld from maintaining its power within. The Valachi revelations, and innumerable other investigations throughout the nation have revealed the role that organized crime plays in the corruption of rehabilitative efforts. U.S. Senator Dodd states:

> Today our training schools and prisons are hotbeds of criminality. It is in the institutions where new knowledge in the methods and techniques of crime is passed on to the younger inmates.[25]

These are the training camps for the "soldati" of the Confederation who all too often successfully corrupt the institutions and sheriffs, probation, correction and parole officials.

---

[24] Lewis, Anthony (1969). "A Talk with Warren on Crime, the Court, the Country." The New York *Times* Magazine, October 19.

[25] Dodd, Thomas J. (1969). "Corrections do not Correct." *Trial—The National Legal Magazine*, October-November.

We observe the pall of corruption casting its noxious spell over the entire criminal justice process. The Confederation has managed to penetrate every facet to some degree. Recently, Ralph F. Salerno, renowned organized crime consultant, spoke of reports that an Ohio governor received $200,000 for a pardon; that a candidate for attorney general in "one of the New England States" had been offered $100,000 by the Confederation—and had been defeated when he rejected it. The same $100,000, Salerno reported, had been used against the candidate "to teach him a lesson." He also pointed out the fact that three federal judges in New Jersey were linked with organized crime in the notorious De Cavalcante bugged conversations which were taped by the FBI and later made public.[26]

One may conjecture that the dreary mess that serves us as a criminal justice process is kept in its incoherent, irrational, nonsystemic status by the pressure of Confederation concern that a more efficient system would be a grave threat to organized crime. If criminal justice administration can become better organized through systems analysis, and a true system of criminal justice begins to develop, organized crime will not easily survive. Criminal justice *systems* are a challenge to organized crime. According to Ralph F. Salerno, even a national criminal justice *information* system could really hurt the Confederation.[27]

ORGANIZED CRIME INTELLIGENCE

Aside from the degree of immunity and protection that is achieved by corruption and fear, success in combating organized crime is made more difficult by the insularity of the leadership from day-to-day criminal acts. The top men of the organized crime conspiracy do not ordinarily engage in specific crimes which are the business of their rackets. Chains of intermediaries insulate leaders from the rackets they control and the criminality they direct, so that they are not normally subject to substantive criminal charges. Yet the organization itself has permanency and form with well-defined organizational structures in which lines of authority are clearly drawn. It is possible, therefore, through intelligence efforts, to determine the identity and the status of the leaders, even if prosecution is not possible. Very little can be accomplished toward even understanding the nature of organized crime without a viable intelligence operation.

In general terms, the nature of organized crime *intelligence* is *information* gathered, analyzed and utilized for suppression of crime and corruption, and, most often, for investigation and prosecution of individuals and

---

[26] See *The Sunday Star Ledger*, Newark, N.J., November 23, 1969.

[27] Salerno, Ralph, and Tompkins, John S. (1969). *The Crime Confederation*, pp. 302, 303. Doubleday & Co., New York.

groups engaged in organized crime. Six general categories of information are normally collected:

1. Evidence of offenses, both substantive and conspiratorial.
2. Information that will aid in criminal prosecution.
3. Information that will help uncover specific areas of organized criminal activity.
4. Information which will help identify criminals active in organized crime.
5. Information which will help identify criminal associates.
6. Information concerning backgrounds and personal histories of known members of organized crime.

There are no clear distinctions among these categories; the distinction is primarily in terms of the purpose for which information is being gathered. To gain sufficient evidence concerning a specific crime, for example, it may be necessary to collect some information under all six headings. An intelligence operation will attempt to gather as much relevant information as possible. Since it has limited manpower, it will seek a balance between its efforts to collect information directly related to evidence and prosecution, and its efforts to compile complete dossiers on all suspected members of organized crime within its jurisdiction.

In determining what information is significant for describing organized crime and for supporting action against it, the criminal justice community keeps in mind several underlying assumptions.

First, organized crime is a way of life for its members; any information gathered on their actions may bear on illegal pursuits.

Second, intelligence cannot be limited to particular areas of criminal endeavor; organized crime will move in wherever a profitable gap exists.

Third, the process of gathering and applying organized crime intelligence may be aimed at destroying organized crime; but there must be a balance between the use of criminal intelligence (and the identification of information sources) in the prosecution of organized crime cases and the deferment of prosecution (with consequent protection of sources), so that a flow of information may be continued.

Fourth, because of the continuing efforts of organized crime to subvert a legitimate government for its own protection, a significant intelligence effort must be devoted to uncovering and breaking any possible links—whether existing through ignorance or malfeasance, and they could be either—between government and organized crime.

Finally, there is no clear-cut distinction between intelligence relevant to prosecution, and intelligence relevant to suppression of organized crime.

Information gathered for one purpose, and the methods used to obtain it, may apply partially or wholly to the other. The point of any such distinction is that intelligence is not only prosecution-oriented, but is also directed at minimizing corruption and at keeping the criminal organization off balance.

The "way of life" nature of organized crime, and the conspiratorial atmosphere in which it thrives, make identification of the criminal act extremely difficult. For this reason, it is generally considered useful to collect and organize intelligence information on the basis of criminals rather than criminal events (an approach colloquially known in some areas as "head hunting"). Consequently, the individual dossier is the primary file in the intelligence unit.

Information by itself, however, is not intelligence. After information has been collected, it must be analyzed and evaluated, including an estimation of its validity. To be meaningfully performed, this process requires skilled and knowledgeable people. Information gaps and areas for future investigative activity must thus be identified. An important consideration is when to cease collection, either because sufficient information has been obtained or because no criminal activity has been indicated. Other major functions include recommendations for prosecution in particular instances, and determination of how and with whom to share the results of analysis.

The Need for Intelligence Sharing. The need to share intelligence information is unmistakable. Organized crime knows no geographic boundaries; the key event in a conspiracy may occur in one jurisdiction, but its reflection in a criminal act may occur elsewhere. High mobility in and out of different jurisdictions is commonplace; thus old-style files based solely on local knowledge no longer are adequate. The relationship of the conspiracy and the criminal act must be shared by the investigative agencies of both jurisdictions if an effective assault is to be mounted against organized crime.

Through information-sharing, it is possible to identify more substantial offenses; to substantiate the relationship of suspects to a criminal organization; to provide more complete information about persons, organizations and suspected criminal acts.

With established cooperation, persons or areas of information are flagged in one agency so that relevant new information is transmitted automatically to another agency that has expressed a need for the data.

The result of such sharing is invariably more effective prosecution or suppression of organized crime.

The optimum pooling of intelligence information should include both vertical and horizontal dissemination—vertical as between local, state and federal levels of government, and horizontal as between separate jurisdictions at the same level of government.

Information should be shared not only among police agencies but with other criminal justice agencies—parole, probation, correction, the courts, district attorneys and crime commissioners—whose responsibilities may bring them into direct contact with some aspect of organized crime.

A primary consideration for information-sharing is security. Intelligence information generally is considered to be the property of the agency that obtains it; that agency has the right to control later dissemination to other agencies who need the information.

Each agency must protect its information sources and the information itself; in the process, it will demonstrate to other agencies that it will not misuse information entrusted to it.

The primary barriers to information-sharing are lack of trust, lack of cooperation, lack of information, and consequent ignorance of the existence of organized crime, and lack of official lines of communication. Additional restraints arise from the potentially harmful consequences of improper use of information, including slander or libel suits, and the undesirable disclosure of confidential sources of information as the result of the subpoena of intelligence files. All these barriers can be overcome, and information shared, by careful planning and application of basic security procedures.

Techniques to Share Intelligence. Until the last few years there were only four significant identifiable attempts to improve the sharing of organized crime intelligence:

1. The Law Enforcement Intelligence Unit (LEIU).[28] Any law enforcement agency which has one or more individuals engaged in full-time intelligence work can apply on a voluntary basis for full membership. Employees of governmental agencies which require criminal intelligence in their work, including agencies engaged in approving licenses and employment in areas of public trust, can apply for affiliate or associate memberships.

The LEIU was founded by a number of California intelligence units in 1956. Its coverage today includes the United States and Canada, and consists of 238 full members organized into four zones—eastern, central, western, and southern. The continuing business of the LEIU is transacted by an executive committee, composed of the zone chairmen and the national officers. The LEIU holds an annual meeting; the zones also have annual meetings.

The principal mechanism for facilitating information sharing is the index card. Each index card contains the name of a subject of interest, a list of criminal activities which he is known to engage in, and a set of identifying characteristics. The information on the card is selected to have

---

[28] Bishop, Wayne H. (1971). "L.E.I.U.—an Early System." *The Police Chief,* September.

a minimum sensitivity. The cards are reproduced and distributed to all the full members, except when a subject is judged to be of interest only within the zone and then only members within the zone receive it.

When a member wishes to obtain additional information concerning a subject, he can contact the source agency which submitted the index card. The source agency can be expected to have one of the richest intelligence files on that subject. The source agency can provide the answer to the query from its own files, do field work to obtain the answer to the query, or refer the requesting agency to alternate source agencies which also have extensive intelligence files on the subject. It is expected that the source agency will be aware of all the major alternate intelligence files which have significant quantities of information on each of the subjects for which they submit cards.

2. The New England Organized Crime Intelligence System (NEOCIS). The New England Organized Crime Intelligence System is essentially an interstate system designed exclusively to fulfill an intelligence function within the six-state region of New England. It is built upon the foundations established by the New England State Police Compact (NESPAC) consisting of the commissioners of the state police of the six New England States, who, several years ago, had recognized the need for greater cooperation between the state police forces in their region. They were cognizant of the need for information exchange in the area of organized crime.

The formation of NEOCIS began in 1968, when the New England State Police Administrators Conference and the New England Association of Attorneys General decided to pool their original cooperative efforts and seek a grant from the Law Enforcement Administration. The proposal called for the establishment of a regional center which would receive, process and store information regarding organized crime in New England. Additionally, as information was refined into intelligence, it would be disseminated in an appropriate fashion. The applicants also proposed that the establishment of such a center would permit research for the development of new strategies to combat organized crime and the coordination of these strategies throughout New England.

NEOCIS is operated by an executive director who is responsible to a steering committee composed of each member of the New England State Police Administrators Conference and the New England Association of Attorneys General. Two deputy directors—one for intelligence and one for strategy—provide functional control of each major segment of the system. The intelligence function directly concerns the collection of intelligence information, the analysis of this information, the production of intelligence reports on organized crime groups and individuals and the dissemination of this intelligence to appropriate agencies. The collection process embodies a number of intelligence agents deployed throughout the New England area under the supervision of the deputy director. The function of strategy is designed to develop plans of ways and means to suppress organized crime activity in this six-state area. This function is also responsible for the coordination and carrying out of whatever plans are developed.[29]

3. *The New York Metropolitan Regional Council (MRC).* The Council was established in order to promote cooperative efforts to solve the common problems of the communities located in the tri-state metropolitan area of New York City. In 1962, the Law Enforcement Committee of the Council was established with 250 police chiefs attending. The Committee is voluntary and has financial support from the member jurisdictions.

The most valuable outcome of the Law Enforcement Committee was establishment of an organized crime sub-committee. That sub-committee has substantially increased the sharing of organized crime intelligence by member departments. The principal result, however, has been to make the resources of the New York City Police Department more readily available to a great many of the smaller surrounding member departments.

MRC, with the assistance of LEAA funds, recently set up an interstate closed circuit television network between New York City and fourteen terminals in the New York-Connecticut-New Jersey tri-state metropolitan area. It is anticipated that organized crime intelligence information will be exchanged in this advanced and sophisticated manner.

4. *The New York State Identification and Intelligence System (NYSIIS).* The mission of the NYSIIS Organized Crime Intelligence module, in the broadest sense, has been to advance the state-of-the-art in methods of intelligence sharing and combating organized crime. The research and development conducted in developing the NYSIIS computer intelligence capability has also been shared with the criminal justice community. Will Wilson, former Assistant Attorney General of the United States, utilized this information and wrote in a letter to the director of NYSIIS dated March 7, 1969:

> Your making available to us the product of your three and one-half years of effort has unquestionably saved the Organized Crime and Racketeering Section (of the Justice Department) at least a like amount of time in research and development.

Thus NYSIIS has not only been designed to provide a computerized organized crime intelligence sharing mechanism for qualified agencies who wish to participate on a voluntary basis, but is also dedicated to promoting new concepts for a fresh approach and novel and innovative methods to combat this menace. The establishment of state organized crime preven-

---

[29] Zunno, Frank A. (1971). "NYSIIS and NEOCIS." *The Police Chief*, September.

tion councils, as provided for under Title 1, Part C of the Omnibus Crime Control and Safe Streets Act of 1968, stems from the conceptual work on strategies done by the NYSIIS staff and reported in "A Theory of Organized Crime Control: A Preliminary Statement," published in 1966.

The most unique aspect of NYSIIS is that it combines the first computerized organized crime intelligence module with a vast computerized identification system. Although the intelligence system and identification functions are maintained separately, with individual integrity for security and privacy purposes, whenever a person of interest to the organized crime section is arrested or otherwise inquired about, the computer discreetly alerts the organized crime section so that it may update its files accordingly. By the same token, other NYSIIS capabilities, such as the Automatic License Plate Scanner, which enables the organized crime intelligence section to maintain automatic surveillance of all vehicles known to be used by persons engaged in organized crime, will continuously contribute to the data base and enhance analytic evaluation to the benefit of the Organized Crime Prevention Council.

Aside from the dissemination of individual items or capsules of information upon the request of qualified agencies of criminal justice, NYSIIS produces the following:

1. For local agencies upon request:
    * Biographies of major figures
    * Photo file
    * Situation appraisals
    * Nickname or alias identification
    * License plate identification
    * Organizational charts with family links
    * Statistical data
    * Synopses of pertinent information on major activities and operations
    * Information on technology and techniques

2. For local agencies as appropriate:
    * Alerts to potentially dangerous situations
    * Current license plate reports
    * Activity and jurisdiction reports on major figures

3. For use at the state level:
    * Total picture of organized crime within state
    * Assessments of socio-economic impact
    * Suggest statewide strategies

- Support implementation of statewide strategies
- Coordinate efforts with adjoining states

4. For internal use by NYSIIS Intelligence Analysts:

   - Complete criminal biography (including weaknesses, problems, peculiarities, etc.)
   - Criminal specialty file
   - Incarceration report (including important fellow inmates and visitors)
   - Surveillance report listing
   - Alias or nickname file
   - License plate file
   - Photograph file
   - Infiltrated business file
   - Activities in adjoining states
   - Associates file
   - Conviction file
   - Family vacancy report
   - Organizational charts
   - Hangout file
   - Operating jurisdictional file

It is readily apparent that a vast computerized data base with the capability of multi-variable searching will enable experienced analysts to make predictions and evaluations that should help to combat organized crime whenever and wherever it may surface.

Aside from NYSIIS, some of the more significant statewide intelligence centers are being developed by the Pennsylvania Crime Commission, the California Department of Justice, and by the New Jersey, Illinois and Michigan State Police. It is not at all unlikely that during the 1970's a score of states will develop state-wide computerized data centers to service the criminal justice agencies in their respective sovereignties. This development of NYSIIS-type capabilities, added to the powerful thrust of the Department of Justice's commitment against organized crime, should result in the organization of necessary government resources to a degree which will match the organization of organized crime.

Federal Efforts. In 1968, the *Omnibus Crime Control and Safe Streets Act* became operative, and since that time there has been considerable activity devoted to establishing organized crime capabilities, including intelligence data banks at all levels of government.

The *Safe Streets Act* pointed to organized crime as one of the problem areas of law enforcement deserving special attention. In fiscal 1970, LEAA spent approximately $10.5 million funding programs to combat organized crime.

In line with the act, LEAA has strongly encouraged the formation of interstate intelligence centers to help state and local agencies monitor and combat organized crime. One example of this type of aid was an LEAA grant of $100,000 to the Florida Department of Law Enforcement for an intelligence group consisting of law enforcement agencies in Florida, Puerto Rico and the Virgin Islands. A key objective is to assimilate tactical and strategic intelligence information to prevent organized crime from developing in areas served by the new intelligence network.

In 1970, LEAA awarded $600,000 in discretionary funds to help finance a New England Organized Crime Intelligence System.

LEAA is also vitally interested in the organization and development of state-wide intelligence units. Statewide networks are able to coordinate the intelligence gathering functions of local agencies as well as cooperate in regional programs.[30]

On June 4, 1970, the President issued an executive order creating the *National Council on Organized Crime.*

The purpose of the council is to formulate a national strategy against organized crime and to coordinate carefully federal enforcement. The council is composed of the Attorney General, who serves as chairman; the Secretary of the Treasury; the Secretary of Labor; the Postmaster General; the Chairman of the Securities and Exchange Commission; the Assistant Attorney General, Tax Division; the Assistant Secretary of the Treasury for Enforcement and Operations; the Assistant Secretary of the Treasury for Tax Policy; the Administrator of the Law Enforcement Assistance Administration; the Director of the Federal Bureau of Investigation; the Director of the Bureau of Narcotics and Dangerous Drugs; the Director of the United States Secret Service; the Commissioner of Customs; the Commissioner of Immigration and Naturalization; the Commissioner of the Internal Revenue Service; the Chief Counsel of the Internal Revenue Service; and the Chief of the Organized Crime and Racketeering Section of the Criminal Division of the Department of Justice.

The mutual planning and combined intelligence of these many federal agencies have had a profound effect upon the war on organized crime.

Perhaps the most noteworthy of all recent information sharing developments in the area of organized crime has been undertaken by the *Organized Crime Task Force of Project SEARCH*. This is an effort to mount a prototype National Organized Crime Computerized Central Index. The

---

[30] Kleindienst, Richard G. (1971). "The Proper Function of the United States Government in the Fight Against Organized Crime." *The Police Chief*, September.

Task Force is composed of seven LEIU Executive Board members, seven Project SEARCH participants and LEAA observers.

The prototype system concept is based on the creation of a computerized index of public record data concerning organized crime and criminals. The records would be provided by LEIU member agencies (through the Organized Crime and Criminal Intelligence Branch of the California Department of Justice) and selected states. Each file in the index would contain only a subject's name, his personal identifiers, and other limited information about the subject and the name of the contributing agency. Each terminal would be provided with physical and electronic safeguards. The system would have a capability for retrieval of information by on-line file search by name as well as by other descriptors and identifying numbers, such as FBI number, driver's license number, etc.

Response to a query of the index by any of the terminals may take several forms. Generally, a query will result in receipt of the basic index information, which would include the name(s) of the agency that maintains additional information on the individual. The contributing agency could then be contacted by phone or mail to request desired information not in the computer. The agency contributing the record could have the option of requiring that the computer be programmed to *not* respond to a query by a requesting agency, and instead, inform the contributing agency that a query by Agency X had been made regarding one of the contributing agency's subjects. The contributing agency could then, at its discretion, contact the requesting agency to see why a query was made. In other cases a contributing agency may want to make only certain information contained in the index available to other agencies, or all information to some agencies and only some information to others.

The purpose of developing this prototype is to evaluate the desirability of an operational system that could gradually increase its data base and number of participants to function as an effective system with thorough nationwide coverage. A nationwide system utilizing a computer and storing basic summary information on individuals and acting as a pointer system to agencies having more detailed information, has many advantages over a manual card system.

Speed: Inquiries (name checks, etc.) can be answered in seconds, even with complete identifiers. New subjects entered are immediately available to all users, without waiting for manual card update.

Consistency: Common definitions and data terms will be developed for all subjects, so that users can expect the same information on all subjects, when available.

Correlation: The index data can be used in any agency's analysis programs to correlate subjects with activities. The index data itself can be analyzed to reveal patterns and trends in business areas or associate relationships.

Accessibility: The file can be accessed for any data element; for example, corporate owners, crime specialty, suspect physical descriptions, etc. The nationwide organized crime index could monitor conventional police information systems, and when inquiries are made on organized crime subjects, the contributing agency would be automatically notified.

Added Security: A system of passwords and checks will be developed so that only cleared persons can obtain data from the terminal.

It is anticipated that the prototype development will be successful and ultimately all fifty states will be on-line. It will encourage the creation of organized crime intelligence files at the state and local levels, where in many cases, such do not exist. Where such files now exist, they are often disorganized and data elements not standardized. Problems associated with security and privacy are minimized by utilizing only public record data in the system. Studies by NYSIIS had revealed that, even in the best organized crime intelligence files, 75 per cent or more of the information was, in the legal sense, public record data.

To achieve success in coping with organized crime information sharing is critical, but it is also absolutely necessary that law enforcement be organized and coordinated. It is essential that the available intelligence be carefully analyzed for effective direction of resources. The struggle with the Confederation in the past has been a very uneven one, since criminal justice was disorganized and governmental efforts were fragmented and uncoordinated. Matched against the superb, smoothly functioning organization of the Confederation, government agencies at every level were totally frustrated and pathetically ineffective.

The Need For Analysis. A recent survey of the nation's major organized crime intelligence units at the federal, state and municipal levels indicated that there is very little on-going analysis of Confederation data in the files of criminal justice agencies. Although some lip service is paid to analysis, it is most frequently neglected, except as it may be required for purposes of a pending prosecution. All too often the organized crime data lies buried and unmined, fallow and untilled in information files which are called upon only for regurgitative responses related to particular persons or incidents. There is a desperate need for intelligence analysts who can manipulate the data in order to study and develop assessments, strategies, estimates, evaluations, and thereby generate imaginative and meaningful intelligence. The utilization of a computer in such a process will help to assimilate, correlate, retrieve and analyze the available data. It will provide a powerful tool toward a more rational methodology and it will point out gaps in the collection of data which require attention in a renewed effort to supplement the information input.

Information by itself can never be intelligence. Analysis, to be meaningfully performed, requires skilled and knowledgeable people who can identify areas for future investigative activity. Other major functions include recommendations for prosecution or other strategy in particular instances, and determination of how and when to share the results of analysis.

The very heart of every intelligence process is analysis. Reappraisals and revisions to keep the studies current are required on a constant and continuous basis. The intelligence analyst must be able to withstand strong pressures to support conventional prejudices, demonstrate both imagination and articulation while maintaining vigilant attention to detail. The analytic process is a complex one, even though its application may appear deceptively simple when the problem is to evaluate the significance of a restricted piece of evidence. The analyst must be able to assess the reliability of the information source and the credibility of the information provided and take into account the inherent and vital element of feedback. The analyst must maintain a lively functional relationship with both the collector of raw data and the decision maker who relies upon his hypotheses. There should be dynamic interchange of communication and guidance as the channels among collectors, coordinators and consumers are kept constantly open.

There is truly a limitless need for analysis and for expertise among analysts. All of the professional disciplines have a role to play in the most sophisticated analyses. Economists may be required to assess the infiltration of legitimate business. Anthropologists may be needed to evaluate data in terms of cultural values and mores. Sociologists may be needed to help perceive the significance of societal and socioeconomic factors in the spread of the Confederation's operations. Social psychologists may be required to interpret the roles of the Confederation in terms of its impact upon behavior patterns and cultural norms. Lawyers are needed to provide the dimension of jurisprudence. There is an almost unlimited need for the broadest possible perspective in organized crime intelligence analysis. Indeed, every analyst should ideally be versed in all the disciplines and in every profession. The most successful analyst is truly a renaissance man!

STRATEGIES AGAINST THE CONFEDERATION

Before discussing specific strategies it may be fruitful to put the entire matter into perspective by providing the background for the modern concept of strategic warfare against the Confederation. It all began with the New York State Identification and Intelligence System (NYSIIS).

The need for criminal justice information sharing was dramatized by the laborious and almost fruitless investigation of the more than 100 members of organized crime who attended the infamous "Apalachin Meeting" in Apalachin, New York, November, 1957. The revelation of this meeting and its apparent purpose spurred the activities of the New York State Temporary Commission of Investigation which in 1958, was given the enormous and time-consuming task of conducting an all-out inquiry. After two years, all of the relevant official files in local and state agencies still had not been assembled. The majority of those agencies maintaining separate files about any of the Apalachin figures actually possessed only such items as newspaper clippings, copied files and scattered notes. In most instances, their accuracy was questionable, they were long out of date, and their value was virtually insignificant.

In terms of the origin of NYSIIS, the Apalachin meeting was important because it focused attention on the inadequacies of the existing criminal justice information system, and in a very real sense it marked a turning point in the administration of criminal justice in New York State. As a result of the lessons learned from the debacle of Apalachin, the State of New York took a major step towards the control of crime, both organized and unorganized, with the creation of the Identification and Intelligence System (NYSIIS).[81]

In carrying out the statutory mandate [82] "to establish, through electronic data processing and related procedures, a central data facility with a communications network which shall include organized crime intelligence," NYSIIS' first step was to identify the nature of organized crime, the significant elements of an effective governmental control program, and the general role NYSIIS might play in organized crime intelligence. NYSIIS stimulated the convening of a "think tank" on organized crime and was enabled to rely heavily on information collected from the discussions and program papers of the experts who attended the 1965 to 1967 Oyster Bay Conferences on Organized Crime. The second step toward the definition of the NYSIIS organized crime intelligence program began in the fall of 1966. With the consulting assistance of private intelligence specialists NYSIIS then established what was believed to be the elements of an effective intelligence program. These included the determination of the following:

1. That NYSIIS would develop an active and sophisticated intelligence

---

[81] New York State Identification and Intelligence System (1967). *NYSIIS Against Crime.* NYSIIS, Albany, New York.

[82] Article 21, Chapter 353 of the Laws of 1965, Amending the New York State Executive Law.

capability—using computerized files—to serve state and local agencies concerned with organized crime. These agencies would be voluntary participants.

2. That the NYSIIS organized crime intelligence capability should function within the strategy policies of an independent "board" responsible for coordinating statewide and regional efforts to combat organized crime.

State Strategy Board. This concept of a state strategy coordinating board or panel was further delineated through subsequent studies, all of which reinforced the recognized need for such a mechanism. Operating agencies contributing to the NYSIIS System would have available to them data collected from multiple sources throughout the state and, in addition, they would receive the analysis of that data as it interrelates with other data in the system, correlated by NYSIIS analysts. What became readily apparent was the need for a coordinating mechanism to formulate broad strategy based on intelligence estimates of the status and activity of organized crime within the state and to recommend priorities of action by operating agencies. Its primary tasks would be to encourage concerted, broad area attacks on organized crime, to formulate necessary strategies, and to aid in coordinating the resultant efforts of local and state law enforcement agencies.

Likewise, it was recognized at that time that to realize optimum benefits from its organized crime intelligence capability, NYSIIS should have a strong thrust toward maintaining cognizance of the scope and nature of organized crime activity and making estimates thereof available for strategic disruption of the organization rather than solely for the purpose of obtaining evidence for prosecution of individuals (attrition).

Strategies Old and New. It was accepted that the concept of intelligence at NYSIIS was properly directed toward a constellation of strategies and, therefore, should be expanded to include support for the needs of many and varied strategies, in addition to needs of attrition. NYSIIS studies indicated that the major prevailing strategies in 1966—and there has been little development of additional strategies at the operating level since that time —were:

1. *Attrition*—the most commonly employed strategy, in which individual suspects are apprehended and prosecuted for specific alleged crimes under due process of law. Except for the increased business overhead, it appears the organization is not harmed by attrition.

2. *Exposure*—the sensational hearings employed by commissions are the most ubiquitous examples of this strategy; however, in some instances they can be self-defeating. A notorious public reputation may aid

coercive activities and serve the purposes of putting victims of the Confederation in fear.

3. *Harassment*—this involves the employment of vagrancy arrests and other police techniques, such as frequent arrests for relatively minor charges. For general purposes this strategy costs more than it is worth in law enforcement resources, produces undesirable public relations side effects, and demeans the process of justice.

4. *The Ostrich Practice*—ignore organized crime and stoutly maintain that it is nonexistent in a given jurisdiction. This practice is widespread. Indeed some of the delegate attendees at the Oyster Bay Conferences denied that organized crime existed in their own cities. Unfortunately this practice, whatever the reasons for its use, operates in most instances to give aid and comfort to the enemy. It can also be very risky for the practitioner as ex-Governor Hughes of New Jersey so recently has been reminded.[33]

Aside from any very profound analysis of the merits, or demerits of any and/or all of these strategies, the plain fact of the matter is that, despite the application of these strategies over the years, organized crime is thriving today as never before. It is viable even in those jurisdictions (such as New York County) where there exist dedicated prosecutors at the federal, state and local levels, supported by superior law enforcement capabilities. In New York County attrition has been carried to the point of being a fine art; there are many arrests at all levels with successful prosecutions, even of the "higher ups," yet the underworld, as Judge Grumet[34] has indicated, is doing very nicely, thank you. It was quite obvious to the NYSIIS staff that new strategies had to be conceived and developed, new approaches that attack the organization, as well as those that are concerned primarily with individuals, were essential.

After considerable reflection, brainstorming, soul-searching and expenditure of consultant funds, NYSIIS brought forth for consideration additional strategies to provide a broader variety of techniques and strategies designed not only to increase the prosecution rate, but to disrupt the equilibrium of the organization sufficiently to reduce its strength.[35]

---

[33] See *West Long Branch, N.J., Outlook*, November 14, 1968—". . . ex-Governor Richard J. Hughes of this State recently announced there is to his knowledge 'no organized crime in New Jersey'." Very shortly after this statement the entire state was rocked with allegations of corruption and the infiltration of the Confederation in high places in the government of New Jersey.

[34] See *New York Times*, January 14, 1968. Judge Jacob Grumet of the New York State Supreme Court, a prosecutor for 37 years, said: "Organized Crime is bigger and more powerful than it was back in the thirties."

[35] *Combating Organized Crime, A Report of The 1965 Oyster Bay Conferences on Combating Organized Crime*. Albany, New York, Office of the Counsel to the Governor, Executive Chamber, State Capitol, April, 1966.

The process of defining new strategies is complex. There are several levels at which strategies may be identified, and there is a wide range of strategies which can be combined in different measures for different circumstances. Also, strategies depend upon the state of available knowledge of organized crime; as our knowledge increases, strategies will change. Thus, a dynamic element must be present in all strategic planning, an element that is reinforced by the dynamic nature of the adversary itself.

Strategies to control organized crime are limited by public policy. They must be consistent with an ultimate goal which could be either total elimination of organized crime or its control at some given level of activity. In addition, strategies are governed by moral and legal limits on the powers of law enforcement. They are also governed in a practical sense by the mechanisms available to support them, including intelligence resources, subsequent action mechanisms, public support, and governmental resistance to corruption.

Given these limitations to the process of defining strategies, it is possible to identify five potential strategies for dealing with organized crime:

1. *Subversion*—tactical actions calculated to breed internal dissension, to capitalize on existing dissension or to create distrust and suspicion.
2. *Alienation*—a wide variety of means devised to demonstrate and emphasize the disadvantages of membership in organized crime, and to alienate aspirant members from recruiters.
3. *Disruption*—concentrated efforts to disrupt or dislocate organized crime activities, thus reducing the return on investments or, alternatively, increasing the cost of the enterprise.
4. *Penetration*—efforts to buy information or informants, or to penetrate organized crime with law enforcement representatives.
5. *Blocking*—the use of public education to assist concerned persons to confine or eliminate further organized crime activities in their fields of interest.

The importance of these strategies lies in the fact that when they are properly implemented within the existing framework of law and in terms of the immediate organized crime situation, they may enable law enforcement to gain the initiative over organized crime.

It is obvious that further, more intensive and continuous research and analysis into the nature and problems of organized crime and its control are required. Further, that organized crime control will ultimately depend upon a *multi-strategy* approach that properly identifies problems and their solutions and is capable of a flexible, imaginative attack based upon an entire repertoire of possible strategies.

National Crime Commission Task Force. Stimulated by the 1965 and

1966 NYSIIS conducted Oyster Bay Conferences of organized crime experts, and similar stirrings among many intellectuals who were beginning to focus their attention upon the phenomenon of organized crime, there existed a cadre of exceptionally aware and concerned individuals who were dedicated to the defeat of organized crime in America. The creation of *The President's Commission On Law Enforcement And Administration Of Justice in 1965*, opened the floodgates to a confluence of many of our best minds just spoiling for a "no-holds barred" battle against the Confederation.

As a result of the cogitations of the experts at Oyster Bay and the concomitant development of new doctrines at NYSIIS, the National Crime Commission Task Force on Organized Crime (composed almost entirely of Oyster Bay participants) was well prepared to tackle the problem of analyzing the state of the nation in reference to organized crime and to propose recommendations to the President. That these recommendations were more than just pious pronouncements is evidenced by the fact that the Confederation was dismayed by the report. At the same time, efforts to eliminate sections justifying wiretapping and bugging came within a hair's breadth of succeeding and were frustrated largely by the conviction of the staff members who ultimately won their point despite Attorney General Clark's opposition. A major portion of that report, indeed the very life-blood of the entire document, is the detailed proposal for a National Strategy Against Organized Crime, and we may conclude that there is very real concern among the members of the Confederation that these concepts may cripple the organization of organized crime. Likewise, we must recognize that sincere civil libertarians take serious issue with the emphasis upon eavesdropping. The Report recommends among many other critically important things:

1. Other states should develop statewide intelligence systems such as exists at NYSIIS.
2. Interdisciplinary research should be conducted regarding the nature, development, activities and organization of these special criminal groups.
3. Groups should be created within the Federal and State Departments of Justice to develop strategies and enlist regulatory action against business infiltrated by organized crime.
4. Private business associations should develop strategies to prevent and uncover organized crime's illegal and unfair business tactics.

The seeds were sown at NYSIIS, cultivated at Oyster Bay, harvested by the National Crime Commission and brought to market in the Omnibus

Crime Control and Safe Streets Act of 1968.[36] Included in Title 1 of the Act is the promise of federal funding of up to $1 million for a "State organized crime prevention council." [37] The development of effective intelligence activities such as special organized crime intelligence units and information sharing are associated by propinquity in the language of the Act with the concept of the council. This has led some observers to couple these together.[38] Of course, this is precisely the thrust of the thinking at Oyster Bay and it was anticipated in the staff papers prepared by NYSIIS for the participants.[39] It may be said that the concept of a state organized crime prevention council sprang from the fertile imagination of the Honorable Eliot H. Lumbard, then Governor Nelson A. Rockefeller's Special Assistant Counsel for Law Enforcement, and was suggested by him to the conferees for the first time during the sessions at Oyster Bay. The larger concept of a National Organized Crime Intelligence Board was also discussed by Mr. Lumbard and memorialized in an unpublished manuscript.[40] Both concepts were allied with recognition of the need for three separate but interrelated mechanisms at whatever level of government the scheme is implemented, namely:

1. An interjurisdictional group to coordinate strategic planning.
2. A channel through which strategic estimates concerning organized crime—a prime requisite for proper strategic planning and interjurisdictional coordination—can be coordinated and reviewed.
3. The means for sharing pertinent data across the organizational and jurisdictional lines.

Toward Strategy Implementation. New and additional strategies will, of necessity, require new methods, new processes, new functions and even new agencies to put them into operation. As new agencies adopt new techniques, the empirical results will undoubtedly suggest additional strategies outside the circle of our "more-of-the-same" thinking about weaponry in this neglected area of governmental responsibility.

---

[36] Omnibus Crime Control and Safe Streets Act of 1968, Public Law 90-351, 90th Congress, June 19, 1968.

[37] *Ibid.*, Section 301 (b) (5), 82 Stat. 200.

[38] Smith, Dwight C., Jr. (1970). "Cooperative Action in Organized Crime Control." *The Journal of Criminal Law, Criminology and Police Science,* 59:492.

[39] See New York State Identification and Intelligence System (1966). *A Theory of Organized Crime Control: A Preliminary Statement* (Prepared by technical staff and consultants of NYSIIS as background material for the Third Oyster Bay Conference). NYSIIS, Albany, New York.

[40] Lumbard, E., and Smith, D. (1967). "A Proposal for a National Organized Crime Intelligence Board." NYSIIS, Albany, New York.

It may be taken for granted that many states will rise to the "carrot" of federal funding for the *prevention* of organized crime. Since attempts to prevent do not necessarily imply that the particular states requesting the funds need confess that they harbor within their boundaries any organized crime activity, those who have cherished the ostrich technique can accept federal money for this purpose in good conscience. The immediate problem to be faced by many, however, will be how to go about spending the funds in an acceptable fashion.

It would appear that the NYSIIS experience is relevant to the solution of such problems as bringing new and sophisticated organized crime intelligence strategies into a viable operational mode. It is not suggested that every state should attempt to duplicate the development of NYSIIS, but there are many lessons to be learned from the experience of NYSIIS and a better model does not presently exist, to the knowledge of the authors. What then has been the experience of the NYSIIS organized crime intelligence capability? How has NYSIIS progressed toward the goal of strategy implementation?

Proposed NYSIIS organized crime intelligence capabilities call for a selective analytical capability based upon a voluntary information sharing system; its concern is solely limited to information concerning those persons intimately associated with criminal organizations and their activities. The NYSIIS role is basically the following:

1. Process and disseminate organized crime intelligence and intelligence analyses to support qualified state and local agencies.
2. Provide assistance to other agencies in fostering the development of organized crime intelligence both within and outside of the state.
3. Coordinate with the organized crime intelligence activities of other states, regional groups, and national organized crime intelligence mechanisms.
4. Recommend areas that require collection, research, and studies useful in combating or suppressing organized crime within the state.
5. Maintain cognizance of the scope and nature of organized crime activity within the state and make estimates thereof available to responsible officials of government.

As strategies are identified and developed, NYSIIS is in a position to provide coordinated data, analytical estimates and even rational prognostication. Each of the techniques and strategies which are developed require intelligence support. *Since many of the strategies and techniques are directed toward disrupting the organization rather than obtaining evidence for prosecution of individuals (attrition), it is understood that the concept*

*of intelligence has to be expanded to include the needs of other strategies
in addition to the needs of attrition.*

Some of the specific additional strategies which have been identified by
NYSIIS as potential means of attacking the organization of organized crime
include the following:

1. The publication of a "Hood's Who" for the information of all officials.
2. Economic pressures to take the profit out of Confederation activities.
3. Utilization of the licensing and regulatory powers of government to
   assure that organized crime does not get a foot in the door.
4. Taxation of gamblers, gambling and other illegal activities to obtain
   revenue and provide leverage for enforcement and prosecution.
5. Study of details of criminal organizations to determine the vulnerable
   organizational spots to be concentrated upon in order to undermine
   the structure of the organized group.
6. Application of interdisciplinary knowledge specifically applied to
   the organization of organized crime.
7. Alert officials and appropriate members of the public to the places
   members of the Confederation frequent and the locations where
   they reside.
8. Identify and disclose, as appropriate, the businesses in which members of the Confederation engage or which intelligence indicates
   they intend to penetrate.
9. Predict the persons or groups whom organized crime will attempt to
   corrupt and recommend special precautions, as appropriate, frustrating their efforts.

Preliminary computer printouts have indicated that the correlation of
data with even rudimentary programming has disclosed some very startling
facts hitherto unknown to the individual agencies, each of whom had contributed his own data to the system. It appears that further, more sophisticated analysis will reveal circumstances which will cry out for specific
strategies, many of which would not otherwise have been conceived.

The authors would like to reaffirm that the NYSIIS concept of large-
scale computerized information sharing among all the agencies of criminal
justice is the soundest foundation for both the development of strategies
and the technical and logistic support required to carry out the strategies
devised. If the central data bank is located in an independent agency,
separated from enforcement, capable of stimulating voluntary submission
of organized crime intelligence, girdled with a firm commitment to research
and to the preservation of security and privacy, then you have all the neces-

sary ingredients to develop a true overall design to defeat organized crime through the relentless imposition of specific techniques and strategies as they are indicated in each set of circumstances.

There will be attempts to undermine these types of endeavors, but you may be sure that this is the hallmark of potential success. It is going to be a heartrending struggle to stay afloat, but the prize is worth the battle. The U.S. is at last ready to show that it will no longer tolerate organized crime—that the government is *not* for sale, that lawlessness is *not* the road to wealth, that honesty is *not* a pitfall, and morality is *not* a trap for suckers. It is worth all the travail to be counted among those who are helping the government show who is really going to run the country from now on— you may count on it, it will *not* be the Confederation!

ALLIES AGAINST THE CONFEDERATION

There are many vocations, professions and occupational groups who have contributed a great deal and are continuing to contribute to the struggle against organized crime. Many of these are non-governmental and function outside the usual community of official criminal justice agencies. Crime commissions such as those in Chicago, Baltimore, Miami and New Orleans have provided continuity of concern about organized crime during the lean years when it seemed impossible to get effective official action, or even attention to the ravages being wrought by organized crime.

It is to the everlasting credit of the media that crusading investigative reporters have fought the good fight, with the understanding support of their editors even though fighting organized crime was not in the past considered a popular endeavor. All the experts agree it is essential that the truth about the Confederation be told to the American public, but this is not a simple matter.

Effective communication to the public about organized crime is limited by several factors including the following:

- Legal inhibitions on investigative reporting
- Civil liberties problems
- The extent of media, corporate and editorial level understanding of the problems of their reporters and the support they need
- Timeliness and pressure of deadlines

These factors provide formidable barriers to media portrayal of organized crime; they reveal why such stories, even the best of them, are sometimes never told. Television, magazines and newspapers are faced with numerous legal and practical problems in their attempts to portray organized crime activities. Awareness by the media of the nature and activities of organized crime elements is not enough. Hard data competent to stand the test of judicial proceedings are as difficult for the media to gather as they are for the police. Hopefully, the media and the police working with their own resources could complement each other, lead to greater public awareness of the problems, and, eventually achieve significant inroads against organized crime.

Of course, there are risks in this type of joint effort. If the reporter works in combination with enforcement authorities, the dilemma is that his story may be frozen until any court trials that may result are concluded; by that time his story is stale. Indeed, his total effort here may be no more than having volunteered to be an unpaid police informant, which is not what a free press is all about. On the other hand, if he works independently of enforcement authorities, he runs risks of being accused of not reporting to the authorities evidence of crime as soon as it is obtained.

Aside from legal problems that arise, such as libel, right to privacy, and the propriety of various investigative methods, there are also the problems of being called as a witness and the reporter thereby being lost to his regular job for long periods of time, and also of having to disclose informants under penalty of contempt. Despite these formidable obstacles many outstanding investigative reporters have persevered in TV, radio, and the press and are only now coming into their own with the revitalized national commitment against organized crime.

Application of Administrative Sanctions. As we have seen, prosecution and adjudication are by no means the only, or indeed, even the most effective methods of combating the Confederation. Various governmental agencies are charged with making administrative decisions involving matters such as granting permits, licenses, franchises, investigating applicants for civil service positions, letting state funded contracts, etc. These regulatory functions normally require that the agency decide whether individuals are suitably qualified to assume a specific responsibility which is regulated by the state.

Government agencies should use administrative sanctions to supplement prosecutive actions against organized crime. To assure both success in combating organized crime and fairness to individuals not involved in any questionable activities, two principles should prevail. First, recognizing that evidence not formally admissible in a criminal proceeding may be used in administrative hearings and deliberations, a proper balance is required between the level of credibility of evidence and the seriousness of the sanctions implied by the administrative proceedings. Second, recourse should be provided to the affected person to appeal from the administrative action to assure that the action is not arbitrary or capricious, but does follow specific guidelines required of the administrative agency. There may be situations in which information (or its source) that would disqualify an applicant or bidder cannot be disclosed. The danger here is that, by disqualifying without disclosure, the administrative agency can establish an environment for bribery and the buying of contracts. There has to be a middle course in which the administrator has an opportunity to interrogate a bidder concerning the source of his capital without disclosing the information which has led it to ask the question. But, by and large, public agencies do not now have the machinery by which to inquire into a contractor's fitness. If the burden of proof is left on the bidder or applicant to demonstrate his financial and professional fitness, and if an appeal procedure exists by which an adverse decision can be questioned, the requirements of due process would seem to be met. *Thus, as a tactic to be used in fighting organized crime, governmental relationships such as licenses, contracts or loans can and should be denied to organized crime figures and their agents or business entities.*

Interjurisdictional Mechanisms. The very nature of the organization of the Confederation suggests the need for coordination among various agencies both in the operational as well as in the intelligence area. This coordination must be at all levels of government and among all relevant functional branches at each level. There are informal associations such as the previously described LEIU, and more formal associations based upon interstate compacts such as NEOCIS. In addition, we need to encourage expansion of the concept of interjurisdictional compacts ranging from local to regional, to national compacts dealing with organized crime. (Such compacts already exist providing cooperative action in the areas of probation, parole and juvenile affairs.) The success of the Federal Task Forces and the National Council on Organized Crime is proof of the efficacy of coherent and cooperative approaches to the problem of organized crime.

Government Leadership. The following very significant statement of consensus was arrived at by the conferees at Oyster Bay on May 7, 1966.[41]

> There are important values to be realized from having adequate communication between major elected or appointed government officials and those in government who learn of significant information concerning organized crime.
>
> There should be a routine, institutionalized procedure by which such intelligence is transmitted in writing to responsible officials. Such a procedure will be beneficial, both to those with responsibilities to collect intelligence and to those officials responsible for general policy and for effective administration of criminal justice in a democratic society. It will help eliminate the possibility of a "trust gap" growing between these two groups.
>
> A routine reporting procedure will minimize attacks that intelligence report-

---

[41] *Notes on the Third Oyster Bay Conference on Combating Organized Crime,* Executive Chamber, State of New York, pp. 32, 33, May, 1966.

ing is politically motivated, since intelligence will be given to an individual in his capacity as the responsible incumbent of a governmental office, rather than as the representative of a private political group. That procedure will support the constitutional and legal role of the elected or appointed official, rather than negate it through the absence of information.

A risk of abuse will be present, as in any reporting procedure. For example, reports could be used as the basis of reprisals against the source; it might also be used for improper political advantage. But that risk is not justification for withholding significant information about organized crime from the leaders of government. On balance, a greater abuse to society as a whole will result if the lack of information nullifies important goals of society, such as an effective program to control organized crime. Moreover, the duty to report is paramount in a democratic society; secrecy is the antithesis of our society.

Thus we have come full circle. We have many allies and techniques to help us in our struggle against organized crime. Public spirited citizens, crime commissions, investigative reporters, interjurisdictional mechanisms, administrative sanctions, but ultimately we must return to the fundamental of government leadership. Of course, if the government is corrupted by the Confederation or apathetic, this does not excuse civil servants and citizens from carrying on the struggle to fight the corruptors and purge the corruptees. Indeed, it makes it far more a matter of conscience to rise to the challenge and change the government leadership.

ORGANIZED CRIME TRENDS

There is very little on the horizon to give cheer, with the possible exception of the belated recognition of the problem by many officials and members of the public. One of the most disturbing trends is that reported by Ralph F. Salerno.[42]

Gang wars reminiscent of the roaring twenties—but this time with the white crime establishment on one side, and black and Spanish-speaking criminal elements on the other—could soon scourge the United States.

Police intelligence analysts in such cities as New York, Chicago, Cleveland, Detroit, Newark, Buffalo, and Philadelphia have already noticed and recorded the telltale signs of the beginning of a "new Mafia" in the major cities of the nation.

. . . we run the risk of gang warfare and the growth of a black and Spanish-speaking Mafia, which would be more difficult to combat than the one we have now. It would be better protected and indigenous to the community it cruelly exploits.

The doctrine of "equal rights" and "community control" applied to organized crime is a chilling thought and one which should stimulate even greater concern and determination to overcome the power of the Confederation now.

---

[42] Salerno, Ralph F. (1970). "New Crime Threat: The Black Mafia." *Coronet*, January.

There are some favorable signs in the increased attention being given to the problem at all levels of government. The continuous upgrading of the police service and the application of scientific method to the law enforcement profession should bring about a less corruptible, better educated, more efficient front line force against the Confederation. Federal funding of studies, planning, research and development to combat organized crime should help society ultimately to prevail against the Confederation.

Organized crime affects us all. The human pollution that it spews forth affects us more drastically than air or water pollution, yet we see comparatively very little involvement by the citizenry itself. There is still a long road ahead until we reach the kind of undertsanding of organized crime which will make its defeat a matter of prime relevance for every man, woman and child. The danger is that it may be too late before we turn the tide and we will have succumbed—a nation destroyed from within.

How much longer will we in America continue to tolerate this poison in our bowels? It must be assumed that the new directions being taken to fight air pollution and water pollution will stimulate an awakening and new recognition of the greatest polluter of them all. It is most encouraging to note the emphasis placed on organized crime research by the National Institute of Law Enforcement and Criminal Justice in the program and project plan.[43]

These research programs will not be limited to law enforcement responses and will include:

1. Ecological studies in depth in one or more neighborhoods.
2. Development of effectiveness measures.
3. Model state plans for coordinating attack by all relevant groups, including government, business, labor and citizens.
4. Development of course materials for colleges and universities.
5. Studies of the systems organization and operation of the provision of voluntarily sought illegal services such as in gambling and loan sharking.
6. Improved systems for gathering, analyzing and using intelligence concerning organized crime.
7. Studies of the methods of governmental and nongovernmental corruption.

CONCLUSIONS

It would appear from all that has been discussed that, even though we may have little consolation in the present situation, something is being

---

[43] National Institute of Law Enforcement and Criminal Justice (1970). *Fiscal Year 1970 Program and Project Plan.* NILE&CJ, Washington, D.C.

attempted at every level of government to seek victory over organized crime. Attempts are also being made to arouse the citizenry to the lateness of the hour and the time dimensions of the peril. However, one of the less obvious threats that should not be ignored is the potential of a popular revulsion so strong, so revolutionary, so conclusive that it may sweep away our democratic institutions. As the Confederation, unchecked, can destroy our nation from within; likewise, the continued growth of the Confederation may trigger a reaction more violent, more cruel and more destructive than the stimulus itself. We are fast approaching the point of imminent crisis.

It would seem that the National Crime Commission Report may not be relegated to dust gathering as were the many prior early warnings such as the Wickersham, Kefauver, and McClellan reports of other years. If something is done now and action is wise and sustained, we may escape the ultimate breakdown of democratic society. The authors are hopeful that this will be the case. A grave danger exists in increasing governmental activity at the national level which inevitably will result in a greater centralization of law enforcement authority and a concomitant loss of local autonomy. We are probably far from the day when this nation will accept the concept of a national police force, but every failure or inadequacy of our police on the local level brings us one step closer to such a possibility. Thus, the preservation of our heritage of democratic law enforcement operating largely at the local level depends to a significant degree upon the capability of local criminal justice to cope successfully with the machinations of evilly-adroit criminal syndicates and their odious minions.

It is essential that all readers of this chapter clearly understand that the various techniques, strategies and tactics outlined herein can be applied, just as methodically, in the fight against "white-collar" or "upperworld" crime, as soon as our citizenry, together with the ethical business and commercial community, decide to mount the attack.

The authors firmly believe in the principle of *subsidiarity* which posits that no higher unit of society should perform that which a lower unit of society is capable of accomplishing. If the local law enforcement *cannot* contain the disease of organized crime, then county agencies might rightfully be called upon to assist; if county agencies *cannot* achieve adequate control, then state law enforcement units might well be needed; and if the local, county, and state agencies find the problem *impossible* to handle, there is little choice but to cry out for federal leadership—or federal takeover. We must rededicate ourselves to more effective responses at every level, but most particularly at local levels where the actual criminal activity takes place and where the beginnings of the cycle of corruption provide the firm foundations for the entire structure of the Confederation.

TOPICS FOR DISCUSSION

1. What is the present status of the recommendations of the National Crime Commission Task Force on Organized Crime in this city? county? state?
2. Discuss some of the social and ethnic factors which are involved in organized crime.
3. What is meant by the use of the term "strategies" in reference to combating organized crime? How does organized crime intelligence support both tactics and strategies?
4. Discuss the involvement of the National Institute of Law Enforcement and Criminal Justice in research in the field of organized crime. What contributions were made by LEIU, MRC, NYSIIS, and the Oyster Bay Conferences?

Chapter XX

HUMAN RELATIONS

How does one evaluate a police agency in terms of its "human relations program"? Or, perhaps more fundamentally, what do we mean by "a human relations program"? Do we mean it to consist of public relations and publicity and all the "gimmicks" that go into a campaign of "selling" the public? Or, as one newspaper captioned a report of a human relations training program for police, does it imply that "police are being humanized"?

Although courtesy, cheerfulness, and consideration, as well as efficiency of operation, are of the essence in a good *public relations* program, and although these goals are sought to be developed in a *human relations* program, the differences between such programs lie in the "reason why."

Conceivably, the most "Scroogian" individual might have no peer in the extension of charity and human kindness if it were "good business." And the most dictatorial tyrant is often the very personification of democratic concepts, to all outward appearances, because to be otherwise would be to jeopardize his position of power and wealth.

If policing were nothing more than "big business," or if it were merely a "power structure" imposed on the people, a veneer of courtesy and good will would be sufficient. The veneer or "window dressing" would be necessary because without it the public would not long "buy" the service or "tolerate" the oppressive and unrelenting burden.

Policing is "big business" only in that it is "big budget," and it is a "power structure" only insofar as it must exert the "power of the state" to assure a peaceful and wholesome community life. *Essentially law enforcement in a democracy is one of the most humane services a human being can render to his fellows.* It is a sign of the cynicism of our times that law enforcement is not universally accepted as a humane service either by police officers themselves or by the public.

The trend in recent years, however, especially in police training schools, has been to give wider recognition to the human nature of police work and accordingly, to emphasize the dynamics of inter-personal and inter-group relations. It is significant to note that this attention is not an apathetic deference to the demand of pressure groups and merely a presentation of watered-down concepts of democracy in action, but rather a conscious policy of the forward-looking councils of progressive police administrators who are seeking to make our police officers as competent in dealing with people as they are in working with "things."

No one will deny that our law enforcement agencies have reached a high degree of competence in working with "things," for even a cursory glance would indicate great attention to crime laboratories, equipped with sophisticated technical equipment, communications apparatus, skillfully designed for the tasks required, and records and identification equipment of the most modern mechanized type.

INTERPERSONAL AND INTERGROUP RELATIONS

Until comparatively recently, however, it was not considered important whether or not a police officer could get along with people, command their respect, and secure their cooperation. He did not have to know what motivated people to act, nor how they were likely to react in various situations. Still less need he concern himself with how well people in the community got along with one another. Are not the police, the argument ran, strictly a law *enforcement* agency required impartially and impersonally to *enforce the law*, including anti-discrimination laws, if any exist, within the jurisdiction? Are not good intergroup relations solely the concern of educators, clergy, semipublic, and private agencies interested in such matters? Does it matter to police whether citizens dislike—or even hate—other citizens as a group as long as they do not get caught depriving members of the despised group of certain rights under law?

There were those who contended that good intergroup relations were not the business of police agencies, and that training that was not strictly "public relations" training was a waste of time, and ought to give way to "more important" training in the area of scientific crime detection and investigation, law, evidence, and procedure, police defense tactics, and first-aid.

Admittedly, these are highly important areas of police training, and no police training school worth the name would do otherwise than to stress such subject matters in its curriculum. But to say that the police have no role in bettering intergroup relations is to say that the police have no *crime prevention function*. To say that there is no room in the training curriculum for intergroup relations material is to say that the officer ought not to be trained in traffic accident prevention, nor indeed, in good patrol procedures, since the function of proper patrol is to prevent crime and disorder or reduce the number of favorable opportunities for their occurrence.

The main function of the police is to prevent crime and disorder, and most of our training is oriented along that line. If good community relations between different racial or other groups will tend to establish an atmosphere in which there is a reduction of such crime and disorder as grows out of intergroup conflict, then the police have a vital interest in considering the police role in intergroup relations in order to help bring and maintain harmony and peace in the community.

If deprivations of civil rights, assaults, teen-age gang wars, bombings, malicious mischief, and rioting, as related to intergroup tensions, can be prevented, then, as a very practical matter, the law enforcement task is the more easily and efficiently accomplished.

Thus, a modern police agency will use every means at hand to prepare itself for whatever role it can fill in the improvement of relations between people, if for none but the very practical consideration of providing better law enforcement to the community.

However, there are other than the very practical considerations. (Otherwise, it might be considered very "practical" to eject the "different" groups from the community or to prevent new citizens from joining the community, in the interest of peace and harmony.) One must consider the fact that the police agency is an important arm of a government which is dedicated to the preservation of human dignity and individual rights, and to the concept of a government of laws. No other agency is more intimately involved in the safeguarding of these rights and the guaranteeing of this dignity than the police force.

PREJUDICE AND MINORITY GROUP TENSIONS

While the average citizen looks to the police officer to protect his person and property and freedom from those who would do injury to them, the minority group member, too, having perhaps some vague idea that his rights are protected by law and that there is legal machinery for a redress of his grievances, seeks the officer to assist him against those who would deprive him of these rights.

The officer must be as well qualified to take necessary actions in these cases as he is in cases of assault and robbery or burglary or arson. He may not be selective in his enforcement duties either as to persons or as to laws. *All* laws must be enforced in behalf of *all* people.

To insure, within limitations, that this philosophy will prevail, modern professional police administrators have begun to rely upon intensive recruit training, as well as repeated inservice training, in human relations.

The recruit training is logically the most intensive. Our young men and women are recruited from among persons of all races and creeds and national origins, all economic groups, and have varying social and educational backgrounds. They are, perhaps, more intelligent than the average member of the community, but otherwise, they might be called "typical" of the local citizenry. As such, they are "typically" unconcerned—especially in the larger cities—with the affairs of others not in their family, religious, economic, or social group; and they entertain "typical" prejudices and preconceptions about people not of their own ethnic groups.

It becomes imperative then, that these young people "take inventory" of their personalities as it were, to discover whether it is possible for them to render fair and impartial police service to all members of the community, irrespective of accidental differences of race and national origin. Are they ready, they must ask themselves, to risk their lives in defense of the person, property, and liberty of total strangers against some of whom they may entertain typical community prejudices? Is the young Negro officer willing to jeopardize his life to protect the resented—or perhaps hated—white citizen in "the white man's world"? Will the officer, established in the tradition of his community, resolutely defend the rights of the migrant or immigrant newly arrived in his town from another state or nation and generally unwelcome?

These are serious questions for any person entering law enforcement to consider, and decide. Very often, upon his ability and willingness to change attitudes, if change is needed, will depend his success, not only as a police officer, but as a force for good in his community. *And the modern police officer is a force for good precisely because he is in a position, as one who represents the authority of the state, to influence attitudes in his community.* The officer who is obviously prejudiced will help to perpetuate prejudices in the community, and conversely, the officer "who plays no favorites," but, instead, renders professional service in the traditionally "color-blind" manner of doctors and lawyers and clergymen, will be playing his proper role in the life drama of building a healthier and more wholesome community—a community in which efficient law enforcement can thrive. He will, by example, teach the community, in a very real sense, the fundamentals of democratic life.

Thus, the student and the recruit should examine the phenomenon of ethnic prejudices in all its aspects—what it is, whence it comes, and how it is manifested in everyday life. He should examine the virus under the microscope of scientific reasoning and he will find that many of his favorite little preconceptions concerning racial superiority and inferiority in terms of intelligence, purity of blood, and physical strength are mythical. He will find that the obvious differences of skin color, texture of the hair, and facial features are quite superficial and accidental, and that, basically, he is much more like than unlike anyone else.

The student then should consider prejudice in the light of religious teaching—his own religious teaching—whatever his denomination. Any young man or woman aspiring to the law enforcement vocation can be challenged to reconcile his prejudices with the basic religious concept of the Brotherhood of Man under the Fatherhood of God. He is doomed, of course, to failure in attempting any reconciliation between racism and Godly conduct. He will find, at every turn, that Charity is the Creator's rule of life.

Finally, prejudice and discrimination should be considered in terms of their inconsistency with our fundamental legal concepts, our dedication to equality under the law, and our national jealousy of individual rights and human dignity. Possibly there is no personal characteristic which more clearly distinguishes us as a nation from much of the rest of the world than our deference to the human dignity of man. This concept is the foundation stone of our Declaration of Independence, and pervades most of our law from the Constitution, down through the decades, to most of our state, county, and village statutes and ordinances. Our courts are apt to halt the practices of millions of people, or the traditions and customs of decades, if they find that these practices, traditions, and customs are not consonant with the concept of the dignity of the individual human being. Nor, is this dignity conferred upon or possessed only by some—by the law-abiding, the educated, the white, the well-to-do, the intelligent, the clean, the healthy; rather, it is possessed by all men—the black, the weak, the poor, the confused, the addict, the immigrant, the alcoholic, the subversive, the ignorant, the prostitute, the hippie, the demonstrator, the young, and the infirm.

Thus, the tyro police officer should discover that neither in science, nor in religion, nor in law can a justification be found for whatever prejudices may be entertained, but rather, that these things have grown out of fear, a sense of insecurity, selfishness, and ignorance.

As police officers, we have done our part to alleviate the burden of racial tension in the community when we have disabused ourselves of wrongful attitudes, but as citizens and participants in community life, we should be aware of the social and political causes of tensions as well. Thus, we must be made cognizant, even in our training schools, of the part that slums and lack of recreation facilities play in intergroup and interpersonal conflict. As law enforcement officers, we must patrol those areas where masses of people are crowded together sometimes in the most inadequate of housing. As citizens, we should participate in those activities of the community which have as their goal the riddance of slums and the building of recreation areas in order to relieve the neighborhood of the human pressures that ultimately spell crime and conflict. Our activities as citizens can help us in our capacity as law enforcement officers. We should concern ourselves with unemployment, segregation, hunger, disease, and poor educational facilities, as well, since all of these are manifestly causative factors in interpersonal and intergroup conflict.

It must be recognized, too, that the exploitation of minority groups and the pandering to their sensitivities by venal and unscrupulous politicians and subversives tend to perpetuate cleavages and dissension in the community. It is a blind officer-citizen who fails to see the danger to his community in the activities of such self-serving persons, and who is not alert to his civic duty to rid, through democratic processes, such influences from the community. Nor can we, either as police officers or citizens, afford to permit to go unchallenged the disseminators of discord who preach and publish their racist theories on street corners and in "hate sheets." To support such persons, for an American citizen, is deplorable, for a police officer to do so is intolerable.

Norman L. Clowers, writing in the January-February, 1964, issue of *Police*, discusses prejudice and discrimination in law enforcement. This experienced policeman writes:

> Just as a child can learn prejudices from its parents, so too can a new officer learn prejudices from the older men. Many generations of experience enter into the teaching of a recruit by the older men. . . . When he works and associates socially with prejudiced, older men, the new man will acquire those same prejudices because of his desire for acceptance and recognition.
>
> When a large number of the members are prejudiced (the percentage may not have to be too large, a human being remembers a humiliating experience much longer than a pleasant one), the police prestige will be low. The officer will be discriminated against by the public; and the more he is discriminated against, the more he will hit back at those too weak to defend themselves. His frustration is released in many forms of aggression. A positive form of aggression may be used, such as a display of violence toward those he arrests or the indiscriminate issuance of traffic citations; or a negative aggression may be used by his refusal to do his job properly; such as stalling while on a call to a place he doesn't like or refusing to shake the doors of the store of a known "cop-hater." This in turn irritates the public, and the public strikes back in the only way they can—through the polls and by showing their disrespect of the police. The cycle is then complete. The officer is denied an adequate salary and status because he is rude or brutal, dishonest, and doing work that any laborer could do with an equal amount of success; and he is rude or brutal, dishonest, and doing a poor job because he is denied an adequate salary and a reasonable amount of prestige.
>
> In this continuing cycle it appears as though the police are the greater offenders. The few facts available indicate that the police are using their power in many ways to strike back. Many of those ways are subtle; others are not so subtle.
>
> One of the more subtle ways used to hit back is the placing of a heavier charge against a minority group member than the one placed against someone more able to fight back—even when the crimes committed by the two are identical. . . . One of the less subtle ways of hitting back is through the use of illegal searches to provide evidence for an arrest. . . .
>
> It is an easy matter for an aggressively prejudiced officer to discriminate against anyone by the simple expedient of either enforcing or failing to enforce the laws. . . .

The writer has observed that in those communities where the police live up to their oath of office by enforcing the laws fairly and justly, without letting their prejudices show and are not forced into nor allowed to practice discrimination, the police have the most agreeable working conditions and the highest pay and prestige. It appears as though it is only in those communities where the police are permitted to practice discrimination that discrimination is, in turn, practiced against them.

The words of Chief Clowers are certainly frank; but to call "a spade a spade" is often the beginning of wisdom. It is to the credit of the vocation that words such as these are now coming from within the police field, and being voiced by highly regarded practitioners.

Perhaps this appears to be a disproportionate amount of emphasis to place upon prejudice and minority group tensions as human relations problems. The fact is, however, these are probably the most serious of the human relations problems facing the American policeman today. Herein lie the dangers to the peace and harmony of the community. Out of such tensions grow the clashes between individuals, the conflict between youth gangs, and the violence and destruction of race riots.

Yet, there are other human relations problems which constitute formidable obstacles to good police-community relations, and consequently, to efficient and edifying law enforcement.

KERNER AND EISENHOWER COMMISSIONS

The Report of the *National Advisory Commission on Civil Disorders* was issued in March, 1968. In examining the patterns of disorder, the Kerner Commission concluded that of twelve deeply held grievances "police practices" was of the highest intensity. In probing for basic causes of riots, the Commission noted that the police are not merely a "spark" factor:

To some Negroes police have come to symbolize white power, white racism, and white repression. And the fact is that many police do reflect and express these white attitudes. The atmosphere of hostility and cynicism is reinforced by a widespread belief among Negroes in the existence of police brutality and in a "double standard" of justice and protection—one for Negroes and one for whites.

In discussing "What Can Be Done?" the Commission noted that

The abrasive relationship between the police and minority communities has been a major—and explosive—source of grievance, tension, and disorder. The blame must be shared by the total society.

The police are faced with demands for increased protection and service in the ghetto. Yet the aggressive patrol practices thought necessary to meet these demands themselves create tension and hostility. The resulting grievances have been further aggravated by the lack of effective mechanisms for handling complaints against the police. Special programs for bettering police-community relations have been instituted but these alone are not enough. Police administrators, with the guidance of public officials, and the support of the entire community, must take vigorous action to improve law enforcement and to decrease the potential for disorder.

The Commission recommends that city governments and police authorities:

- Review police operations in the ghetto to ensure proper conduct by police officers, and eliminate abrasive practices.
- Provide more adequate police protection to ghetto residents to eliminate their high sense of insecurity and the belief in the existence of a dual standard of law enforcement.
- Establish fair and effective mechanisms for the redress of grievances against the police and other municipal employees.
- Develop and adopt policy guidelines to assist officers in making critical decisions in areas where police conduct can cause tension.
- Develop and use innovative programs to insure widespread community support for law enforcement.
- Recruit more Negroes into the regular police force, and review promotion policies to insure fair promotion for Negro officers.
- Establish a "Community Services Officer" program to attract ghetto youths between the ages of 17 and 21 to police work. These junior officers would perform duties in ghetto neighborhoods, but would not have full police authority. The Federal Government should provide support equal to 90 per cent of employing CSO's on the basis of one for every 10 regular officers.

The Report of the *National Commission on the Prevention and Control of Violence* was issued in 1969. Students of the criminal justice system should examine both the Kerner and Eisenhower Commission Reports with care, and compare the programs of their local agencies with the commission recommendations. Chief Joseph Kimble, Beverly Hills, California, pinpointed the problem:

> The ways in which individual police officers interact with the public has largely been left to chance. There is a wide disparity between what the Chief *says* at the Kiwanis luncheon, and what the patrolman *does* in a dark street at midnight. It appears true that there are more police-community relations programs existing on paper than exist in the community. More concern for civil rights is contained in press releases than is demonstrated in toe-to-toe contacts with the reality of the situation. The policeman demands respect and his ethnic neighbor challenges, "Earn it!" (Italics in original)

PRESS RELATIONS

A "good press" is perhaps the goal of a public relations officer, but a consistently bad press has so many implications for poor police-community relations that it must be considered here at least briefly. People "know" their law enforcement agencies in large part through the medium of the press. Respect for, and confidence in, their law enforcement agency—or the lack of it—is based, to a great extent, upon what the public reads daily of law enforcement work. Indeed, loyal readers of a newspaper which is inclined to be unfriendly or hypercritical of the police are likely to be so inclined themselves.

On the other hand, a press that fails to inform its readers of the wrongful activities, the inefficiency or corruption of their public officers is shortchanging the reader, indeed worse, it is shirking its traditional duty to keep the community enlightened and alert. A community—a nation—is free in proportion to the freedom and courage of its press, and a police officer should be the last to insist upon a controlled or silent press lest he become the servant of slaves, or worse, the tool of tyrants.

The press, however, must act from a sense of responsibility. Too often is the commercial yardstick used in the determination of *what* is news and *how* it should be reported. Too infrequently, in the haste to "scoop" the competition, to compose the sensational headline, and to sell newspapers, is there sober investigation of what appear to be the facts. Half-truths and innuendoes, couched in slick language, which will permit the editor to get "off the hook" next week, may startle the people into buying newspapers today, but it is an injustice, not only to the public officers involved, but to the community confused thereby. Police officers are particularly resentful of press abuses where an officer, suspected or accused of wrongdoing and therefore the subject of "page one copy," is later exonerated completely. His exoneration, *if reported at all*, is usually buried with the advice to the love-lorn, or the hunting and fishing news. The tendency of readers is to remember the headline, to prejudge the case, and to draw broad conclusions irrespective of subsequently-developed facts. Irreparable harm has been done to the reputation of the policeman involved, certainly among his neighbors and acquaintances, but even more important, from the community point of view, the reputation of the department has been seriously compromised because, unfortunately, the entire department is judged on the basis of the wrongful activities of individual members. It is difficult enough for the agency to recover from the damages done by an individual officer who is in fact faithless to his trust; where there is no substance for the allegation, the damage becomes trebly difficult to bear.

There is a danger, however, and even perhaps a general tendency, of police to be *hypersensitive* concerning the reports of their activities in newspapers. Some officers and administrators would like nothing but heroic accomplishments reported. It is not headline news, they will argue, if the milkman absconds with the daily receipts; why then should a comparable crime committed by a police officer be the subject of such consternation on the part of the press? Those who would so argue have simply failed to comprehend the position of the police officer in the community. As important a man as the milkman is, he is not invested by society with the authority and power to suspend or withhold from people their most cherished possession—their freedom; he is not expected to be especially strong in resisting evil temptations; he is not held up to the youth of the community to be emulated; he is not, in a word, what the community puts forward as a representative of community virtue and strength.

Perhaps this sensitivity has given rise to a condition often complained of by the press: that police, too often, withhold information that is derogatory to the agency, attempt to hide the wrongdoing of an individual officer, or whitewash unsavory activities. This is unquestionably true, and to argue that newspapers themselves do the same thing, or that all other governmental agencies hide their dirty linen, or that the practice is common in business and industry, does not excuse the practice. The Chief of Police should be the first person to denounce a faithless police officer, and the department should be grateful for his dismissal and prosecution, *but*, only after it is clearly established that he is guilty of wrong. The department, and every member of it, should be constantly aware that they will be exposed to the merciless glare of public eyes when they have so conducted themselves as to be unworthy of confidence and respect.

The Chief of Police and the publishers of the community newspapers should be aware of the privileges and rights, as well as the limitations and responsibilities of both the police and the press in a free society. Cooperation for the common good should replace mutual suspicion and distrust in the affairs of both.

POLICE BRUTALITY

"Police brutality" is a term that is subject to a variety of definitions. The police Neanderthal would be inclined to react in a paranoid fashion:

> Police brutality is a nonexistent, vicious allegation, without basis in observed or proved fact, that has been brought to bear against police as a pressure weapon on the part of known liberal-radical-homosexual-left-leaning-pot-smoking-peace-demonstrator-hippie-nigger-lover types as a part of their continuing massive program to discredit regular police agencies so they can take over and invite the Russians in to loot and burn our homes, violate our daughters, and desecrate our churches.

The professional policeman would make key distinctions:

> Police brutality may be psychological, verbal, or physical, and consists of subtle, overt, or brutal misuse of police authority. Ranging from an indifferent or contemptuous glance to sadistic application of illegal violence, from cold silence to obscene vituperation, from unwillingness to take proper police action to delight in taking unnecessary action, from failure to consider any alternative to repressive action to selection of the most punitive possible sanction, police brutality reflects an insensitive and coarse attitude, or mode of operation, that ignores human dignity.

Many of us fail to understand the concept of "police brutality." It does not always result in blood and bruises—physical harm. It often is manifested in hurt feelings—when minorities or those with unorthodox life styles are not treated with the same respect by the police as are the majority or those with conformist life styles. Our police often talk differently to the non-conforming minority than they do to the conforming majority—and the former is treated as a suspicious character until it is proved otherwise, whereas the latter is treated as a decent citizen until it is proved otherwise.

It is true that the police are much less brutal today than they were a decade or so ago, but it is also true that the non-conforming minorities are much more aware of their rights than they were a decade or so ago, and they are beginning to demand the same civility that is shown to the conforming majority.

Police brutality is largely a semantic question, and its solution is more a matter of attitude than anything else. To treat anyone meanly, without any reason, may hurt him much more than striking him, and it may, indeed, encourage physical violence. The authors are pleased to note that more and more police are waking up to this fact.

There is little, if any, police brutality prevalent in an enlightened police agency today. The technique of the third-degree has disappeared as a routine tool of professional investigators. Those who depended upon it have been replaced by intelligent men who prefer to outwit and out think the criminal. The rubber hose of a bygone era has given way to the scientific laboratory, psychological interrogation, careful surveillance, and the precise collection of evidence. The "short-cut artist" has lost ground to the police investigator who is willing to work harder, wait longer, and present an "air-tight" case, rather than to come to court with a case resting solely upon a confession feloniously extracted, evidence illegally seized, or worse, to come in with the wrong man. Industry and courage have replaced indolence and cowardice.

This is not to say that there is not any police brutality today, nor that it is not a problem because there is so little of it. One case of police brutality a year is more than the department can stand. *Brutality is the prerogative of the police state. To tolerate any of it is to differ from the police state only in degree.*

Law and order is meaningful only if the laws are equitable and the order is just. If social and economic justice is missing in any area, the enforcement of law and order is the prolongation of injustice—and more and more of our people, including more and more of our police, understand that point.

The dinosaur became extinct because it depended on strength and ferocity, power and aggressiveness. But in the survival of the fittest, it was the versatile and the prudent which survived. Thus, in the course of time, the brutal police "Neanderthal" will be replaced with the sensitive and aware police professional.

The police "Neanderthal" wants more than *civility* from the public—he wants *deference*—a genuflection to his awesome authority and power. And if it is not given he feels a challenge to his authority, he feels very threatened, and he thereby immediately asserts his authority. Because, in the past policemen were to a large extent exempt from law enforcement and could rely upon the police subculture to protect them, the citizen was at the mercy of the "Neanderthal" policeman. He always met any real or imagined threat, insult, or attack with immediate and massive force, hoping that inspired fear would create *respect*. He lived in ignorance of the fact that inspired fear only creates hatred.

It is a sad fact that some police, enjoying their absolute control over people, became tyrannical in their arbitrary application of power. They became corrupted by the authority inherent in a police role, and inventive in the many techniques of breaking the spirit of any non-deferential people, thus making them feel helpless. Many policemen do their work as tough but fair men, and many are friendly and do a variety of favors for the public—but in the past no policeman dared to intervene on the side of a suspect, or dared to sound the tocsin relative to police corruption.

We all see ourselves as fair, just, humane and understanding, but many people, even most people, can be made to do almost anything when put into compelling environments, regardless of heredity, education, religious and ethical values. Any reader can observe a brutal policeman or a hateful offender and believe that he himself would never act in such fashion, but it is highly possible and even probable that he would be moved by the same subtle psychological/social forces and environmental situations to behave similarly. Any one of us can become a Calley at My Lai or a George Jackson at San Quentin!

Some readers may yawn at any discussion of police brutality just as some citizens yawned at My Lai abroad, and Kent State University here at home. The attitude is often expressed in the simultaneously expressed opinions that (1) It didn't happen, and, (2) "They" deserved it. We yawn because the activities are directed at "them" and not at "us." Such attitudes result in a situation wherein some people are vulnerable (the "torturables"), and some are not. Such attitudes result in a situation wherein the nonconforming minorities do not expect fair treatment, and do not receive it. If any status quo is unjust, people have but two options, to rebel or to conform. That is the reason why sensitive and aware police professionals are forcing much internal change in American policing.

The single most powerful *answer* to police brutality is a police leadership that will not tolerate it. The single most potent *reason* for police brutality is a police leadership that assumes a permissive attitude toward it.

Though most policemen today are repelled by the thought of beating a defenseless suspect in the backroom of a station house, or whipping a handcuffed prisoner, some, carried away by the reprehensive nature of the crime, or in retaliation against resistance to arrest, or because of a citizen's disrespectful attitude, may use unlawful or unnecessary force. Though this be understandable in terms of the heat and passion of the immediate situation, it is nonetheless intolerable. The officer must be so self-disciplined as not to permit his personal feelings to become involved. It may be difficult, and very nearly impossible, to dispassionately effect the arrest of one who has seriously offended, or who has seriously threatened the officer's life. But, the near impossible must be done. Police work is a difficult and trying vocation. Unless as little force as is necessary to effect an arrest is used, and unless this is universally and constantly demanded by the police administrator and supervisor, our system of jurisprudence and our laws of criminal procedure are empty and meaningless.

One commentator has said that "The policeman uses violence illegally because such usage is seen as just, acceptable, and, at times, expected by his colleague group. . . ."[1] The authors categorically state that the *professional* law enforcement officer rejects illegal violence as unjust, unacceptable, and abhorrent to the professional development of the vocation.

Occasionally, one is faced with the repellent experience of having a member of the law enforcement service tell crude jokes about the use of his choke hold, come-a-long, fist, sap, or baton. Such joking must be regarded as a protective device for the emotionally unstable.

Many people, when considering the question of physical force, suggest a simple choice: passive inaction, or unrestrained bellicosity. Such people do not give sufficient consideration to *the reasoned use of force.*

Reasoned use of force means that, at all times, pain inflicted on another, even if for the proper accomplishment of the police task, will never be a source of satisfaction or self-preening. The solemn duty of each officer is to measure the amount of force required, never to rejoice in the superfluity of applied force. The professional officer will regard the presence of violence as a hateful concomitant of reality and fallen nature, but never anything to glorify, to take pride in, to grow used to, or to take for granted. If one grows used to force, or takes it for granted, he will become calloused, his sensibilities will become blunted, his moral sense will be corrupted, and his spirit will be gross and crude. Such a spirit is like poison gas—invisible, odorless, and not readily detectable—but working quietly and

---

[1] Westley, William A. (1953). "Violence and the Police." *American Journal of Sociology,* 59:41. See also, Westley, William A. (1971). *Violence and the Police.* M.I.T. Press, Cambridge, for updated material.

leaving behind a kind of deadening of the soul. Such a spirit wreaks havoc within the police service. Such a spirit must always be openly rejected by all police leaders and supervisors.

No one expects a law enforcement officer unnecessarily to place his life in jeopardy, nor to take physical abuse without both defending himself and using the minimal degree of force necessary to halt the attack and place the attacker under control. This could require the taking of a human life; it often enough requires the use of the baton; but the officer will have a clear conscience if he can honestly say, "I did no more than was necessary."

Unfortunately, whatever he does, even necessarily and in minimum degree, will be called "police brutality" by some. All too frequently, unscrupulous defense attorneys will charge police brutality, especially where there is a confession or an admission against interest. Where a little artificial smoke can be generated, it is hoped that it will be believed that there must be a fire. There is a question here of professional ethics. At what point does an attorney's duty to his client give way to his responsibility to the welfare of the community? May the attorney use any device, any gimmick, to mitigate the plight of the accused, irrespective of the harm that ensues to the department and to the general good of the community?

Perhaps the test should be the attorney's firm conviction that what his client says is the truth—if buttressed by some other evidence to support it. Surely, if his client is guiltless of the charge, as he now claims, and his confession to the contrary has been extracted in fact only through mental or physical brutality, then the charge *should* be made and the officer should be punished. This should be done even though the community may suffer a loss of confidence in and respect for its police, one of whose agents has committed a criminal act. But, if the allegation of brutality is *specious* and is made merely for the purpose of creating a doubt, a grave disservice is done to the community, to say nothing of the mutilation of professional ethics. To put it another way, the rights of a single individual are more important than the right of a community to a feeling of assured confidence in the competence and integrity of its police, which is not so insignificant that it can be jeopardized by capricious and unfounded charges of police brutality.

CIVIL LIABILITY

The United States Supreme Court ruled, on June 21, 1971,[3] that a search or arrest without probable cause creates a cause of action against the officers. One month later, the U.S. Court of Appeals in Washington,

---

[3] *Bivens v. Six Unknown Named Agents,* 403 U.S. 388. (1971).

D.C. ruled that a local police chief may be sued personally for the misconduct of an arresting patrolman, even though the chief was unaware of the arrest when it was made. In both of these cases the officers had claimed that they had a traditional "immunity" from the law suits which involved their "official actions." (This immunity claim is based on the old argument that police cannot perform effectively if they are constantly under the threat of private damage actions for being too aggressive, especially when they must make immediate field decisions under pressure.) In the Supreme Court case, the decision stated, "Of course the Fourth Amendment does not in so many words provide for its enforcement by an award of money damages for the consequences of its violation. But it is well settled that where legal rights have been invaded and a federal statute provides for a general right to sue for such invasion, federal courts may use any available remedy to make good the wrong done." It cited the famous 1803 decision of *Marbury v. Madison* that "the very essence of civil liberty certainly consists in the right of every individual to claim the protection of the laws whenever he receives an injury." Further, the Court held that ". . . federal courts do have the power to award damages for violation of constitutionally protected interests. . . . For people in [the claimant's] shoes, it is damages or nothing." In the Court of Appeals Case, the court decisions relied on the 1866 Civil Rights Act which authorizes damage suits against officials "acting under color of law" for violations of constitutional rights. Heretofore that Act had been narrowly interpreted (authorizing suits for violations of particular federal rights, i.e. voting) but not for general misconduct by police.

The student of criminal justice can well ask himself the question: "Have you *ever* heard of a police department disciplining an officer for illegal search or illegal arrest?" One would suspect that the answer to the question provides the rationale for suggestions for establishing recourse by law.

One legislative proposal suggests that "Whenever the District Attorney declines to prosecute, or a judge dismisses charges, due to illegal search or arrest, the arrestee shall collect $500 from the police operating budget." The implication is that if the chief sees that one of his units is costing the agency $10,000 a week from the police budget, he will take immediate and forceful action to effect change of field conduct.

Another suggested form is as follows:

> Whenever a person is stopped by police or sheriff for field interview or field interrogation, or in any other way deprived of freedom of action to any significant degree, and such police or sheriff action results in an injury to person; damage to property; or detention longer than twenty minutes, and no arrest is made; or
> Whenever a person is arrested by police or sheriff, but discharged

from custody without the filing of a criminal complaint; or discharged after filing but before trial; or had charges dismissed at arraignment or preliminary hearing; or whenever a person is found not guilty at trial; or whenever a person is convicted of a criminal offense and has such conviction reversed on appeal; and no successful prosecution for the same offense occurs within 180 days,
The jurisdiction involved shall:

1. Expunge all notations of detention, arrest, prosecution, and/or conviction from the agency record system, and notify all other agencies which have been sent information on the matter, requesting like expungement; and
2. Reimburse such detained person, on the basis of regular take-home pay or minimum wage (whichever is larger) for any time held in custody longer than twenty minutes, or, if arrested, for any time held in custody from time of arrest; and
3. Pay all costs of medical care if personal injury occurs; and
4. Pay all costs of replacing or repairing damaged property; and
5. Pay all costs incurred by such person in securing his release, including reasonable attorney's fees; and
6. Vacate any stipulations as to probable cause, which were made as a condition of release.

Chief Justice Warren Burger, in the Supreme Court case referred to earlier, suggested remedial legislation and set forth a model. The Chief Justice noted that Congress or the states could enact legislation along the following lines:

(a) a waiver of sovereign immunity as to the illegal acts of law enforcement officials committed in the performance of assigned duties;

(b) *the creation of a cause of action for damages sustained by any person aggrieved by conduct of government agents in violation of the Fourth Amendment or statutes regulating official conduct;*

(c) *the creation of a tribunal, quasi-judicial in nature* or perhaps patterned after the United States Court of Claims, to adjudicate all claims under the statute;

(d) a provision that this statutory remedy is in lieu of the exclusion of evidence secured for use in criminal cases in violation of the Fourth Amendment; and

(e) a provision directing that no evidence, otherwise admissible, shall be excluded from any criminal proceeding because of violation of the Fourth Amendment. (italics added)

The *Law Enforcement Legal Review*, appearing in *The Police Chief* states that "Serious consideration of his proposal should be given in all jurisdictions."[3]

---

[3] "Law Enforcement Legal Review." (1971). *The Police Chief*, August.

POLICE REVIEW BOARDS

The people cannot afford to take lightly charges of incompetence, corruption, or brutality on the part of their police. They must be sufficiently alert and intelligent to detect these ills in their police force, and they must be courageous enough to expose them and to prosecute the wrongdoers. Freedom is a tenuous thing and will be retained only so long as the free man is willing, sometimes at considerable sacrifice and danger, to guard against its loss. The rise of the oppressive police state is directly proportionate to the spread of apathy in the community.

In the *Satires of Juvenal* appears the perennial question: *"Sed quis custodiet ipsos custodes?"*—"But who is to guard the guards themselves?"

Currently, the proposal to install "police review boards" as a method of control of police failure, is being debated, and the subject is of great interest to police administrators and practitioners, and to many interested citizens and civil libertarians.

The January, 1964, issue of the *Harvard Law Review* contains a *Note* relative to police review boards, and the February, 1964, issue of *The Police Chief* contains a critique of the Harvard Study. Concluding comments, from both articles, are as follows:

Harvard Law Review:

Any concluding preference between departmental and civilian review is impossible, since the various arguments and counterarguments deserve differing weight depending on differing local circumstances. The most important variable is the adequacy of existing departmental procedure. Where these procedures are intelligently designed and conscientiously followed, so that the community trusts their integrity, there is no need for an outside review system. Even where close analysis reveals procedural weaknesses in an internal system, but nevertheless the system satisfactorily performs the dual function of maintaining discipline and satisfying complainants, improvement of internal procedures will often be preferable to the adoption of a civilian system. The creation of an external disciplinary agency in such a case might generate unnecessary disruption and distrust and result in problems more grave than the procedural weaknesses in the original internal system. The less drastic and more profitable reform lies in correcting the weaknesses in the otherwise acceptable departmental procedure.

On the other hand, where an existing review procedure is basically faulty, or where a potentially adequate system has been abused or disregarded by police leaders, sometimes no internal reform can result in a complaint process that citizens will use with confidence. In these circumstances, a civilian board may be the only means through which the interest of aggrieved citizens in redressing violations of individual rights can be brought to bear on the discipline of police officers.[4]

---

[4] Note: "The Administration of Complaints by Civilians Against the Police." (1964) *Harvard Law Review*, 77:499. The above materials are restricted by copyright. Copyright © by The Harvard Law Review Association.

The Police Chief:

The review board, devoid of both responsibility and authority for the basic functions and administration, represents a superficial attempt to deal with more complex problems. Outside review boards represent a direct reflection upon inadequate police leadership, since they can exist only where police leaders fail, for whatever reason, to adequately discharge their responsibility to impartially investigate and deal with complaints by citizens against departmental personnel.

The assumptions upon which the review board concept rests, when examined carefully, provide a rather sweeping indictment of the law enforcement group. Where any group attempts to step forward and divest the police executive of the responsibility and the authority for disciplining his force, that group is saying:

1. Police administrators and commanders are not capable of rendering impartial judgments in cases involving complaints against officers due to the fact that all police officers are imbued with a "Pack Instinct" which makes them shield the wrongdoer rather than search for the truth.

2. Law enforcement cannot qualify as a profession because of the inability of its practitioners to establish and to enforce standards of conduct among themselves.

3. The courts of the community, because of their close daily working relationship with the police, tend to share the tendency to protect the accused officer, thus depriving the complaining citizen of an impartial hearing.

Enlightened citizens who share the professional police executives' desire to provide law enforcement services of the highest caliber are not likely to accept the politically expedient "solution" offered by review board advocates. The problems of law enforcement manifested by citizens' complaints will not be cured or even revealed by a rigid legalistic hearing procedure or by a panel of citizen-judges concerned only with the immediate aspects of the instant case. Those persons who share in the dreams of a police profession dedicated to public service recognize that the citizens of a community may see the fruits of those dreams if they are willing to insist upon the highest possible standards for selection and education. Failing in this, the community may indeed need an elaborate and intricate system for policing the police.[5]

There is, understandably, confusion relative to the concept of a "police review board." Some citizens, naïve as to governmental organization, confuse the review board concept with the concept of *lay administration,* through commissioners and commissions. Some police personnel, naïve as to alternatives in the format of review boards, assume that the review board, in *all* cases, would usurp the administrative prerogatives of the Chief.

The authors are unequivocally opposed to any review board format which would take the responsibility for personnel management, along with the authority and power to discipline, away from the law enforcement ad-

---

[5] "I.A.C.P. Critique of the Study." (1964) *The Police Chief,* February.

ministrator. But, these writers do not categorically reject the review board format which would allow scrutiny of police operations and personnel, and the transmission of advice and recommendations to the law enforcement administrator from a citizen body.

The Chief of Police should be, and must be, held responsible for the operations of his department and for the actions of every man in it. This means, if he is not to shift his responsibility, he must have authority and power to discharge it. In turn, this means that he must control the selection, promotion, transfer, and discipline of personnel.

The authors are in complete agreement with the statement of Chief Edward M. Davis of the Los Angeles Police Department, who, with great wisdom, stated:

> The right to discipline carries with it the power to control the conduct, actions, and attitude of the employees of an organization. When the right to discipline is vested with management, management has the essential tool with which to attain the desired behavior from employees. If, however, the ability to discipline employees is taken away from management, or if management must share this responsibility with some outside person or organization, management is then stripped of the most essential powers in the operation of any organization. When employees are subjected to disciplinary action from outside the organization, a fundamental rule of organization has been breached and the employee becomes confused, diffident, and inefficient.

(Cynics are quick to point out that self-scrutiny and self-discipline are worthy ideals, but it would seem a bit naïve to expect a Chief of Police to investigate or discipline himself or his men for violation of constitutional rights during operations which he and his commanders have ordered and supervised. Such cynicism must be answered by a police service that, *in fact*, holds itself and its people responsible for all its actions, and is willing and able to conduct such investigations and, where necessary, willing and able to discipline its members.)

In this regard, Arthur B. Caldwell of the Civil Rights Division of the United States Department of Justice, stated:

> Often times local officials contend that their own police trial board procedures are adequate for determining whether or not a particular complaint of police misconduct is justified. But with the very best of police trial board procedures, administered by objective and fair minded policemen, there will still persist a feeling that when policemen investigate complaints of their own wrong doing, and sit as judges of their own misconduct, they will continue to be accused of being something less than completely impartial judges.

It should be noted that when doctors engage in wrongdoing, it is the Medical Association that investigates unprofessional conduct; when lawyers engage in wrongdoing, it is members of the Bar who conduct inquiries, and when ministers engage in wrongdoing their clerical peers evaluate such evidence. (This, over and above any governmental investigations.) The authors of this text believe that the responsibility for control of professional conduct lies heavily upon the vocation itself.

For the most part, police discipline is currently handled by the Chief of Police, who, in many cases, is advised by an internal trial board, by the civil service commission, and by the city attorney. In addition to hearings conducted by such internal trial board, the charged employee may also be heard by the civil service commission, and may be tried in civil or criminal court. When the conduct of a law enforcement officer is questioned, a probe may be initiated by his supervisor or commanding officers, through regular departmental channels, or a probe may be initiated by a citizen, through many different channels.

The citizen may complain in person, by telephone, or in writing, identifying himself or remaining anonymous, to the police department: to supervisor, shift or watch commander, precinct or station commander, internal affairs unit, or to the Chief of Police. He may complain to the Police Commission, to the Mayor, to the City Manager, or to the City Attorney. He may complain to the City Council or to the Press. He may complain to the County Board of Supervisors, to the Grand Jury, or to the Attorney General or Governor of the state. He may complain to a Federal Grand Jury, to the United States Attorney in his district, to the United States Attorney General, to the FBI, local office or at Washington, D.C., or to the President. Indeed, the aggrieved citizen has many avenues of complaint open to him, even if there is very little effective recourse.

If the complaint of misfeasance, nonfeasance, or malfeasance can be sustained, personal redress may be forthcoming through civil suit, or retribution through internal departmental discipline, or through criminal prosecution. Civil suit may be instituted in local courts, or, if a violation of Constitutional Rights is involved (according to a recent United States Supreme Court decision) a suit for damages may be instituted in the federal courts.[6] In some states, legislation provides that the political subdivision may be sued, and found liable for damages. Chief Stanley Schrotel, past president of the International Association of Chiefs of Police, makes a statement that may be applicable:

> To be sure, police abuse of their authority must be eliminated, not by withdrawing essential authority, or by freeing the guilty, but by raising police standards to a level of trustworthiness *and by some means for holding a community responsible for any of its policemen found exploiting his authority.*[7] (Italics added)

[6] *Monroe v. Pape,* 365 U.S. 167 (1961).

[7] Schrotel, Stanley R. (1964). "Civil Liberties for All." *Police,* August.

At any rate, any citizen, cognizant of his duties and obligations, rights and privileges, should:

1. Report any and all abusive, immoral, or illegal conduct by police officers, or by the department.
2. Be prepared to document and prove his complaint with evidence (photographs, recordings, expert testimony) and with testimony of impartial third-party witnesses.
3. Follow-up to secure information as to action taken with respect to the specific complaint, and action taken to prevent similar occurrences.

And any professionally administered police department, with but even a minimum disciplinary and public relations program, should:

1. Publicly welcome, and thoroughly investigate any and all complaints relative to police services or conduct of department members, of whatever rank or assignment, whether such allegations are made in person, by telephone, or in writing, and whether made by an identified citizen or anonymously.
2. Require complete and accurate written reports from the officer involved, his immediate supervisor, his shift or watch commander, his precinct or station commander, with thorough interviews of victim, witnesses, or complainant, and with continuing follow-up to insure complete acquisition of all the facts.
3. Encourage public participation and observance of internal trial board hearings.
4. Present all substantiated facts to the press.
5. Seek complaints or indictments for criminal prosecution where clearly justified.
6. Follow-up relative to proved deficiencies to insure non-repetition by change of policies and procedures, and by clarifying or reassigning supervisory responsibilities.
7. Inform complainants of actions taken.

(Agencies with a greater sophistication will, generally, form minority-relations units or details to work closely with the minority press, with minority pressure groups, and with minority group leadership to improve communications and community cooperation; and they will be alert to all facets involved in the relationship between police discipline and police-community relations.)

Why, then, is there a current debate over the review board proposal? The debate is due to attitudes of police and public.

The attitude of *some citizens* is that law enforcement agencies will *always* cover up or whitewash deficiencies in police services or in individual members of the vocation. The essence of such community opinion lies in the fear that internal disciplinary machinery will not find an officer at fault because to do so would often be to find the policies or procedures of the agency at fault.

Such citizen fear, whether groundless or justified, can be eliminated in large part by:

1. Forming a Civilan Complaint Review Board within the department to review all complaints made by civilians against members of the department.[8]
2. Allowing distinguished citizens to serve as supplemental members, or non-voting guest members, of internal disciplinary boards in order to demonstrate police acceptance of the legitimacy of public scrutiny. The writers are fully confident that, in the vast majority of cases, such supplementary members, or non-voting guest members, could honestly report to the general public that internal disciplinary machinery was, in fact, honorably serving the police vocation *and* the public interest.[9]
3. Establishing police review boards, composed of Chiefs of Police of unquestioned integrity, on an *ad hoc* basis, empowered to *receive complaints* relative to the incompetence, illegality, or immorality of police agencies or policemen, *to conduct investigations, to make recommendations,* and, where necessary, *to issue public reports.*
4. Or instituting Advisory Boards, composed of respected citizens, who would receive complaints of deficiencies of service or conduct, receive and consider the results of agency investigation, and make recommendations to the Chief of Police.
5. Establish the position of *Ombudsman* to receive complaints from any citizen. In Sweden, the ombudsman, contrary to popular belief, is more interested in effecting changes of agency practice, to forestall future negative occurrences, than he is in adjudicating individual complaints.

The attitudes of some police is that community interest or recommendations relative to police deficiencies always represent ignorance, ill-will, or subversion. The essence of such police opinion lies in an extreme sensitivity, somewhat understandable in some areas, due to a history of unwarranted public attacks.

---

[8] Such a board has been most successful in New York City where the Deputy Commissioner for Community Relations, as Chairman, and two other Deputy Commissioners selected by the Police Commissioner comprised the entire personnel of the board.

[9] Trial Board hearings of the Los Angeles Police Department are open to the public.

Some loudly vocal self-styled police spokesmen have gone to radical extremes, hysterically describing all citizen interest and effort relative to Police Review Boards as "a scheme from the Communist handbook," or as "the work of Communist led or inspired groups." Such a reaction, to all citizen interest and effort relative to Police Review Boards, in the opinion of the authors, is, at best, pusillanimous nonsense, at worst, malicious subterfuge, and never serves the best interests of law enforcement.

Absolutely no allowance is made by such spokesmen for the possibility that the review board proposal could be made by highly intelligent, patriotic, highly motivated Americans. Absolutely no consideration is given to the possibility that the review board proposal, in some American communities, could be a legitimate reaction to deficiencies in policing.

In the opinion of the authors, such a position is fully as deplorable as the opinion of some citizens that all police and policing are crude, rude, and arrogant, abrasive, tyrannical, and completely indifferent to civil rights and the needs of minority groups. All sin, or all virtue, is not the exclusive possession of either police or public—yet, at times, spokesmen for either group seem unable to admit honesty and high motivation to the other.

And, the attitude of some citizens and some police is that any criticism of investigatory operations, any scrutiny of law enforcement operations, or any proposals of change in policy or procedure, whether made by fellow citizen, fellow police, courts, or civil libertarian, are to be regarded as the work of a subversive, un-American, Communist, fellow-traveler, or dupe of the Communist conspiracy.

J. Edgar Hoover, the late Director of the Federal Bureau of Investigation, often spoke very much to the point on the evils of Communism, and certain of his words are most applicable here, and worthy of serious consideration:

> Aggressive citizenship—participation in community affairs, exercising the right to vote, careful selection of those who represent us in government—is a vital factor in making the American system work.
>
> As a nation founded on the precepts of justice, equality, and freedom, we must always respect the dignity of the human being and the rights of the individual. Never must we permit bigotry and prejudice to sap our society of its strength. Unfortunately, the fear of Communism has sometimes led to unfair attacks on those whose views differ from the majority. Honest dissent must not be made the target of hysterical and reckless charges. Witch hunts, smears, and character assassinations have no place in this nation; such activities merely play into Communist hands and serve to confuse and divide our society.[10]

It seems dangerous to give Communism the credit for every impulse that scrutinizes or challenges investigatory operation. This harms, in our

---

[10] Hoover, J. Edgar (1961). "The Communist Party, U.S.A.." *Social Order, 11*:300-301.

opinion, the cause of American democracy and its institutions, and makes it appear that sensitivity to civil rights, or to the needs of minority groups, can only derive from the materialistic secularist tradition of Communism, rather than from the Judaeo-Christian tradition, and from our American democratic heritage. The authors would like to think that even though police agencies are often targets for the frustrated, intelligent criticism of investigatory or police operations, or interest in suggested improvements, are also the right of the patriotic American citizen, and not the sole possession of Communists, Communist dupes, or fellow-travelers.

Unfortunately, both citizens and police, in addressing the review board proposal, do not argue the issues and principles, confining themselves to the facts. Very often, both have tended to resort to the *ad hominem* form of argumentation that ends in labeling or name-calling, or to the *post hoc, ergo propter hoc* type of argumentation that ends in a complete confusion of causes and effects.

Every effort must be made to end the current tension whereby citizens pressing for review boards assume that police resistance is solely due to a desire to whitewash deficiencies, and whereby police resisting the review board proposal assume that citizen pressure is solely due to a Kremlin hatched plot. Americans owe much more than that to each other.

THE POLICE STEREOTYPE

Even though it is necessary for the public to be energetic in eliminating police deficiencies, it is only simple justice to demand that the people be no less energetic in manifesting their appreciation for competent police services by confidence, support, cooperation, and respect.

To stereotype all police as dull-witted and clumsy bunglers, or worse, as grafters, is to do the rankest injustice to a generally capable and intelligent group of dedicated citizens. Whatever may have been the shortcomings of our law enforcement people of half-a-century ago (and it is most unlikely that they were as stupid and incompetent as the gag writers have depicted them) it is offensive to the sensitivities of the modern, intelligent law enforcement agent to be so categorized. It is not that the police alone have suffered from unfair stereotyping; attorneys, doctors, and clergymen have long been the victims of anything but a fair, to say nothing of objective, appraisal. Nor is it that policemen are so thin-skinned as not to be able to take a bit of good natured "spoofing." This common stereotyping runs deeper than "spoofing," and too many people are influenced in their attitudes toward law enforcement by the Hollywood-spawned police stereotype. Too many people identify American police with police they have known in other parts of the world, and this identification is often tantamount to a condemnation depending upon the individual's unfortunate experiences with police in a less democratic atmosphere. Stereotyping of police by the public is no less harmful to good police-community relations than the stereotyping by police of certain groups in the community. Conflict rather than harmony, and mutual distrust rather than cooperation are the inevitable end products.

Dr. John J. Mirich, a specialist in police science education, and criminology scholar, has studied the police stereotype in our society and has made some very interesting comments. They are summarized as follows. Although it takes many years of education to become a district attorney, in order to deal with complex laws, we Americans naïvely believe that anyone is competent enough to enforce them with little education. While there are some city, county, and state police officers who are well qualified, they are a minority in terms of the national scene. A bachelor's degree in police science should be an absolute minimum academic requirement for those who are to enforce any municipal, county, state or federal law on a face-to-face basis, and such officers should be paid proportionately. While the district attorney may have hours, days, weeks, or even months to *research* legal interpretations, the police officer is expected to *apply* the law with split-second judgment. Sometimes the officer is supported by the court in his judgment; at other times he is not. No one can repair the social disgrace brought upon a person who is unjustly accused and arrested by an untrained policeman. No one can gauge the harm done to the community when legal sanctions are ignored or apathetically applied by an inept officer. Physical size, for far too many years, has been the primary emphasis in police selection. Contrary to popular opinion, ex-wrestlers and ex-boxers and ex-commandos do not make the best officers, if the only attribute they possess is physical prowess. Until local law enforcement does away with political favoritism in recruitment, establishes academic standards which require police science knowledge, and demands a high degree of emotional stability and moral character, police problems will be ignored by a disinterested public. In other words, law enforcement must change from vocation to profession. When this day arrives, crime will be better detected, citizens will be more adequately protected in terms of individual rights, criminal behavior will be better deterred, and the public will have more respect for the policeman. In turn, the policeman will receive the social, economic, and professional recognition he rightfully deserves, he will enjoy a healthy *esprit-de-corps*, and the whole nation will benefit. The old theory that "all citizens are qualified for all civil positions in our democracy," is not necessarily true of the law enforcement vocation. It requires specialists, and when law enforcement is nationally staffed with specialists, the public *will* develop a positive attitude toward the police officer and the police "stereotype" will then become affirmative and supportive.[11]

Every occupation and vocation has developed a stereotype of its practitioner. We may picture the lawyer as shrewd, calculating, articulate, tricky, and ready to inundate anyone through verbal pyrotechnics and written obfuscations—but we do *not* think of the individual lawyers that we know in those terms. We may picture the clergyman as pious, pompous, supercilious, prudish, smug, removed from the world and fanatically ascetic —but we do *not* think of the individual ministers, rabbis, and priests that we know in those terms. We may picture the doctor as grasping, selfish, indifferent, prissy, cold, curt and insensitive to suffering—but we do *not* think of the individual doctors that we know in those terms. We may picture the teacher as impractical, out-dated, sensitive, a dreamer out of contact with the world, isolated in an ivory tower—but we do *not* think of the individual teachers that we know in those terms. When we consider the policeman, we may picture him as brutal, visceral, arrogant, ignorant, lazy, prejudiced, and calloused—but we do *not* think of the individual officers that we know in those terms. There is a difference between the uncomplimentary stereotype and the individual practitioner, and we all can and do make the distinction.

Yet the policeman sometimes will, consciously or unconsciously, tend to imitate the uncomplimentary stereotype by his thoughts, words and deeds. Some policemen, contacting the public, present one face; contacting their fellow officers, another face; and in their contacts with their family and friends, yet another face. Personalities can and do change—and particularly so in the police service.

Contamination of the minds and warping the personalities of young policemen by some senior officers of poor motivation is one of the most damnable and horrifying situations encountered in law enforcement.

Carefully screened young men are often given fine training by police agencies, good education by collegiate institutions, and then subjected to "brain washing" by poorly motivated senior officers that would do credit to the most expert and fanatical totalitarian.

The recruit officer, given an environment where there are many poorly motivated men, becomes conscious of inept, immoral, and illegal habits which are unchallenged by his colleagues, and often supported by an agency consensus. He is first shocked by such attitudes and actions, but eventually learns to tolerate them. As time goes by, he begins to accept

---

[11] See Mirich, John J. (1958). "Certification of Local Law Enforcement: A Must." *The Journal of Criminal Law, Criminology and Police Science*, May-June.

them, and then begins to utilize them himself—and, if he is not of exceptional strength of character, soon resembles the others, eventually adapting to such personality change wholeheartedly, and then doing his part to "break in" other new officers, with the pattern continuing to perpetuate evil customs and shabby attitudes. Many a senior officer will admit that when he was a brand-new recruit, he was very often abashed, embarrassed, and shocked by the words and deeds of his colleagues.

Fortunately, for the future of the American police service, the past quarter century has seen a revolution in terms of acceptable attitudes and actions, and it is ever more common for the new officer to enter an environment where the professional senior officers set the prevailing tone. More and more, the poorly motivated officer is being ostracized by the vocation and by the public. Given another quarter century, the unfavorable stereotype of the policeman will be radically changed. More Serpico's?

POLICE-COMMUNITY PARTICIPATION

Perhaps the solution to many of these human relations problems lies in a closer and more meaningful participation by the police in community affairs, and by the public in working out solutions to police problems. In many departments, the leadership, the opportunity, and the organizational framework for such mutual cooperation exists. District and precinct citizen councils and youth councils afford an opportunity for the police and public to confer on community problems, but of equal importance, these councils serve as a vehicle for dispelling ignorance. Police will be made aware, especially in minority group neighborhoods, that all of the members of this or that minority group are not at all like those comparatively few who are in conflict with the law and with whom the police are more frequently in contact. The public, too, will find that their police are decent and God-fearing men coping daily with complicated problems, and often in a difficult and even hostile atmosphere. Sympathetic understanding and mutual good-will must spring from this kind of sharing in the community's law enforcement burden.

Perhaps in this way, too, the most difficult of all police problems—how to make more palatable the basically regulatory nature of police work—will be partially solved. Americans traditionally resist and resent the exercise of authority over them. This is true, even though they see the need for the exercise of such authority, and deliberately invest certain of their number with the power to exercise that authority. We are notorious, as a people, for selecting good and dedicated men as our President, our Governor, or our Mayor, paying them little in proportion to the burdens we expect them to carry, and then unmercifully criticizing them during their terms of office for all the ills of the community. In like manner, we criticize those to whom we have given the badge of police authority with the concomitant burdens of law enforcement. There is no question here of incompetence or malfeasance. Our elected and appointed public officials are fair game for criticism in season and out. The difference between the President's ordeal and that of the policemen lies in the fact that the President must leave office after eight years and give someone else the opportunity to be buffeted about. For the police officer it is a lifetime career.

However long we serve, and however well, we represent a potential threat to the freedom of the people. The people are inclined to guard jealously their heritage of freedom, and to suspect, even without concrete reason, those who are merely in a possible position to deprive them of it. This, in the final analysis, is a healthy circumstance. It makes police work extremely trying, but it is part of the price one pays for the privilege of being an American police officer.

TOPICS FOR DISCUSSION

1. How do interpersonal and intergroup relationships affect law enforcement operations in this locale?
2. How can a working policeman, "by example, teach the community, in a very real sense, the fundaments of democratic life"?
3. What effect can personal prejudice have upon the actions of a police officer? What effect can such actions have upon the status and stature of the law enforcement agency?
4. How does press coverage of the administration of criminal justice affect police-community relations in this locale?
5. How should the public pressure for police review boards be handled?
6. Is genuine recourse available today, to the nonconforming minority, with respect to criminal justice misfeasance, malfeasance, or nonfeasance?
7. Is it possible to alter a negative police "stereotype"?
8. What devices exist, in this locale, for the development of "police-community participation"?

Chapter XXI

EFFICIENCY, MORALITY, LEGALITY, COMPASSION

Oₙₑ should not attempt to evaluate law enforcement agencies and law enforcement officers by a cursory glance at their buildings, uniforms, vehicles, or press notices. Nor should one attempt to evaluate a law enforcement agency or officer merely because the community, *to all outward appearances*, seems to be infested with crime, or free from it.

Any objective and scientific measurement of a law enforcement agency or law enforcement officer should involve four considerations: efficiency, morality, legality, and compassion.

EFFICIENCY

The measurement of police efficiency is most difficult indeed. (Note: Readers should not confuse *efficiency* with *effectiveness*. An agency may be highly efficient, but most ineffective in accomplishing the goals of law enforcement.)

For one reason, units of work measurement that are standardized for the vocation are not yet available. How many juvenile cases should a juvenile investigator handle? How many traffic citations or summonses should a traffic unit issue in a day or week? How many reports should be handled by the patrol unit each night or month? How many cleared cases should the robbery squad produce each month or year? How many prostitutes should be arrested each month? *It all depends.*

It depends upon community support and cooperation. It depends upon the quality of police administration and supervision. It depends upon the competency and integrity of the individual police officer. It depends upon the quality of the prosecutor's office. It depends upon the quality of the local bench. It depends upon the effectiveness of the local correctional institutions. It depends upon the effectiveness of the local probation and parole officers. It depends upon the general quality of municipal, county, state and federal governmental units in the area.

Can we rely upon criminal statistics to determine if we are undermanned? If we have a satisfactory ratio of civilian employees? If we have crime rates proper to our jurisdiction and its environment? If we have a satisfactory clearance rate for major crime? If our arrests are sufficient? If the amount of property recovered is sufficient? If the trend of crime is abnormally high? No. We cannot rely upon criminal statistics to give us absolute determinations. Even though they have been collected for a relatively short period (beginning in the 1820s in France) they have an age-old deficiency: they are but averages, telling us what may be, but not telling us what should be.

Our Uniform Crime Reports (originated in 1930, and collected by the FBI under the aegis of the International Association of Chiefs of Police) are merely composites of local statistics, include many prorations, extrapolations and estimates, and are issued without rigid control over the local collection of data. There is good reason for the disclaimer "The FBI is not in a position to vouch for the validity of the reports received."

As we improve the selection process for law enforcement and get better personnel; as we improve our administrative and records processes; as we receive closer cooperation from the public; as we improve our methods of investigation—will we not have more arrests and successful prosecutions? Of course. And yet some will point to a *crime wave*, and, as is so common, rise up in righteous indignation and demand a "get tough" policy and the need for "cracking heads." Very few will think about the matter of statistical limitations, their objective veracity, and question every datum, frequency distribution, and interpretation.

The authors do believe in accomplishing the police task with the least amount of money, manpower, facilities, and equipment, and, at the same time, with the greatest success in achieving goals. But, the fact is that most police agencies are too undermanned, underpaid, undertrained, undersupervised, underequipped, and undersupported to be able to perform in a professionally efficient manner. Enrico Ferri, the Italian criminologist, pointed out that society has the criminality it deserves. The authors would point out that most communities have the level of police service that they deserve.

The greatest improvements in police efficiency will come about, not by applications of computers to police deployment, not because a more fleet patrol vehicle has been engineered, and not due to new buildings. The greatest improvements in police efficiency will ensue when attention is forcefully directed to obtaining the very best of talent available from the nation's manpower pool, educating and training it to the limit of its capacity, and moving it up through the ranks as quickly as it is able to accept and discharge its responsibility. This talent will bring undreamed of increases in efficiency—but with it, the greatest of headaches—for it will be merciless in eliminating archaic and Neanderthal attitudes and practices, demanding the utmost of dedication and production of all members of the vocation, and mandating professional example in all aspects of the service.

This is not to deprecate those few planning and research units now operating in our larger cities——they are doing yeoman service, and contributing substantially to agency improvement. But, the finest planning and research unit in the nation must still depend upon agency personnel for the implementation of its recommendations—and if that personnel is deficient, its work is largely in vain.

This is not to deprecate those highly motivated law enforcement professionals who are currently exemplifying the finest ideals of American law enforcement. This *is* to say that there is so great a need of them in the American law enforcement service today that we must make maximum efforts to recruit and enroll more and more men and women of the greatest capacity and character if we are to have impressive increases in efficiency.

To say that one police agency polices at a cost of $14.00 per capita population, and another at $6.00 per capita, and suggest that the latter is more efficient is as inane as to say that because one agency polices with 0.2 officers per 1000 population it is therefore more efficient than another that utilizes 6.0 officers per 1000. Such averages are meaningless without knowledge of the quantity of service provided, the quality of the service provided, and the amount of success achieved in accomplishing proper goals. And yet, such averages are helpful, to a degree, when comparing cities of approximately the same size, located around the same area.

Certainly, when we approach the area of efficiency, we can identify major police goals: the prevention of crime and disorder; the preservation of the peace; and the protection of life, property, and individual freedom. And, certainly, we can identify major police methods: crime prevention; crime repression; regulation of non-criminal conduct; provision of services; and protection of individual freedom. And, certainly, we can identify the major line, staff, auxiliary, and special activities. Yet, a variety of opinion exists that gives differing emphasis to such goals, functions, and activities. And that opinion differs according to the level of service—local, county, private, state, and federal; according to the region; and according to the community.

The fact is, there are no universally imposed or accepted standards for police administration and operations. For one reason, there does not exist a nationalized police in our nation; for another, the philosophy of local autonomy precludes the imposition of a single pattern of policing.

Certainly, we can identify major criteria of goal accomplishment: the absence of crime, disorder, congestion, accidents, and conflicts within the community; adequate (at least at some comparable average) rates of arrests, clearances, property recovered, and successful prosecutions; minimum employee ratios and minimum per capita costs consistent with adequate (at least at some comparable average) performance; and, the absence of community complaints regarding police services and personnel. Yet, here too, a variety of opinion exists that gives differing emphasis to such yardsticks, depending upon level of service, regional location, and community values.

Both the *goals* (with the implementing functions and activities) and the *criteria* or *measuring rods* for evaluating success are closely identified with the local environment, with the philosophy of the local police agency, with the force of community opinion, and with the value system of that particular region.

This is not to say that we have not developed *any* nationwide goals—for one can always turn to the formulation of nationally recognized police authorities and note their agreement in terms of very broad objectives. And this is not to say that we do not have *any* nationwide criteria—for one can now effectively use the ABA *Standards on the Urban Police Function*. It is important to carefully study Appendix D, starting on page 473.

Certainly, we can identify major factors which relate to successful goal accomplishment: adequacy of administrative talent to plan, organize, direct, coordinate, control, and evaluate agency activities; adequacy of management talent to ensure the propriety, effectiveness, morality, and legality of agency policies and procedures; adequacy of fiscal processes to ensure provision of necessary facilities, equipment, and manpower; adequacy of personnel processes to provide for the proper selection, training, regulation, and motivation of personnel; and adequacy of public relations and human relations processes to provide for the development and maintenance of public cooperation and good will. Yet, the proper identification of such factors, as far as a local police agency is concerned, must be done at the local level—not imposed from above—for such factors will vary with agency goals, criteria for goal accomplishment, and with the unique characteristics of the agency and community in question.

Finally, the authors wish to indicate their enthusiastic support for the movement to install planning and research units in law enforcement agencies. But, they must also indicate their strong belief that the finest planning and research unit will become frustrated and comatose if the top-level leadership does not proceed to implement the obviously necessary recommendations, and to install audit and follow-up processes to guarantee complete implementation and continuing support for the recommendations.

There is a heavy responsibility placed on the shoulders of the police executive who installs such a unit, for their studies may recommend, and adequately justify, changes which are radical and which may upset decades of unquestioned practices, and thus place the executive squarely upon the spot. If he makes an implementation of the recommendations, he upsets the equanimity of all personnel who are absolutely committed to the *status quo;* if he rejects, or tables, the recommendations, he may be tabbed as a bottleneck to progress. That is why it is most encouraging to note the development of such units in the police service, the implementation of their feasible and practicable recommendations, and their increased prestige—for that kind of development reflects great credit upon the law enforcement administrator and his commitment to the goal of ever increasing efficiency.

MORALITY

The evaluation of police morality is also most difficult.

Some people see the police as fundamentally amoral, as *mercenaries* who can and do make the transition from one regime to another without moral trauma.

Some police regard *obedience* more highly than truth, beauty or goodness, and seeing obedience as the highest good, come to believe that the police are the *only* truly moral force in society. Hence *moralistic* (not necessarily *moral*) police.

To become an increasingly moral person is to become an evermore mature personality. Maturity implies the capacity to confront complexities with the realistic perception and decisiveness demanded by each unique situation. Morality is implicit in this process of making choices because our choices will be, in varying degrees, good or evil (and sometimes evil in their mediocrity!).

Every choice, to some extent, is causative of a further humanizing or dehumanizing of self and/or others. To become *more* what we are meant to be (i.e., *men*) is good; whereas to act in such a way that we become *less* men is evil. To be moral is to be *realistic:* it is accepting the challenge of making what *is* to be, *be,* in fact. Men should be realists and treat men as men, relate to God as *God,* and to the *universe* as what it is—in itself, and as man's basis, environment, kingdom. Summarizing, we can say that the moral man lives and acts psychologically according to what is true ontologically (i.e., his gut-level decisions are consonant with the nature of being.)

Thus, the moral man does not let *things* dominate him. To the extent that he does, he is not what man is meant to be: the ruler/developer of all other creatures. Neither does the moral man sell his mind or his soul (his principles) to another. To the extent that he does, he is a *slave* and not a *man*—for to be a man, in essence, is to be free, to be capable of self-determination.

Much of what we experience in our current culture as "morality" is foreign to the Scriptural tradition in which our Judaeo-Christian culture is supposedly rooted.

Insofar as our culture is Christian, there is a logical presumption that we accept the principles, specifically the moral principles, of Christ. Christ's value judgments are to be, logically, our value judgments. And his morality was quite simple, albeit quite demanding: "This is my commandment: love one another as I have loved you" (John 15:12).

According to the dictates of Christ, *the moral man is to judge what is the most loving thing for him to do in any situation.* And the most loving thing for him to do is that which is most productive of dignity and honesty and goodness and humanness in the people involved in the decision. The Scriptural concept of "love" is far from the saccharine, impulsive, and characteristic notion which our current era often reflects.

Christ does not provide a catalogued morality of do's and don'ts. His morality is not one of categories, nor one of casuistry (e.g., "if such and such is the case, you then do such and such"). The actions of Christ well indicate his supreme recognition: *you cannot put people (or their actions) into boxes.* He teaches that we are not to judge or we shall be judged for judging (Matthew 7:1-2). And Christ does not say this because judging others is an impolite, "not-nice" thing to do, but because judging others is an *impossible* thing to do! There are too many mysteriously individual and environmental/historical determinants in the motivation of actions for us to ever know the degree of guilt of others—and, very often, of ourselves.

The Christ of our culture fulfills all commandments of the Old Law (and the laws of non-Judaeo-Christian cultures as well) by teaching that if we strive in *fact* to love all men, then we logically will not steal their goods, go to bed with their wives, destroy their property or their reputations or their persons. According to the Christ of Scripture, then, *to love is the whole law.*

Despite the apparent simplicity of having just one commandment, this value-judgment of Christ's, this morality, is *the* supreme challenge to man. Will men love? Will we accept the responsibility of making our own moral judgments in the mid-stream of life's complex demands, or in a situation of personal risk? Will men accept the awesome reality that no one else can exercise our freedom for us ?·(No one else can make our moral choices for each man is himself ultimately responsible for his own decision making.)

The history of Western culture presents evidence of man's grasping for the "Linus blanket" of false security. Again and again history shows that we complicate our lives by refusing to grow-up unto the potential of our human-beingness. We prefer someone else's ready-made answers to the risk of having to find and stand by our own. We have often found it easier to mind-spin innumerable pigeon-holes into which we can insert human beings than to grasp and deal with the mystery of individuality. We have often "objectified" all subjectivity out of operational existence. (Man exists in community, but the crux of moral judgments lies in balancing man's *communal* existence with his *ultimately individual* expression of existence.)

If criminal justice careerists dedicate themselves to the preservation and development of our culture's greatness, they dedicate themselves to the preservation and development of *human beings*. Incredible maturity is demanded of the criminal justice officer so that in being *"his own man"* he is, concomitantly, the *"best man"* for *others*.

(The authors fully realize that some readers will take grave exception to the ethical concepts and judgments just presented, and that other readers will share the reasoning. All readers will agree, we surely trust, that attention to this area is worthy of attention, study, and discussion—even though, in our current society, ethical understandings and motivations differ widely.)

Nonetheless, there is increasing interest in the subject of law enforcement behavior as related to the moral or ethical. The International Association of Chiefs of Police adopted a Law Enforcement Code of Ethics at their 1957 Conference. This Code was the subject of a study by a special committee of the IACP Executive Committee, which was made up of Past President Andrew J. Kavanaugh, Wilmington, Delaware; IACP Field Service and Traffic Director Quinn Tamm; and Franklin M. Kreml, Director of the Northwestern University Transportation Center. The Code was first developed, however, by the California Peace Officers' Association and the Peace Officers' Research Association of California in 1956. It has been adopted by the National Conference of Police Associations, and by many other law enforcement organizations. This Code of Ethics is well worth the attention of any student intending to enter law enforcement, as is also the Canons of Ethics which give practical extension to the Code.

* * *

Law Enforcement Code of Ethics

AS A LAW ENFORCEMENT OFFICER, my fundamental duty is to serve mankind; to safeguard lives and property; to protect the innocent against deception, the weak against oppression or intimidation, and the peaceful against violence or disorder; and to respect the Constitutional rights of all men to liberty, equality, and justice.

I WILL keep my private life unsullied as an example to all; maintain courageous calm in the face of danger, scorn, or ridicule; develop self-restraint; and be constantly mindful of the welfare of others. Honest in thought and deed in both my personal and official life, I will be exemplary in obeying the laws of the land and the regulations of my department. Whatever I see or hear of a confidential nature or that is confided to me in my official capacity will be kept ever secret unless revelation is necessary in the performance of my duty.

I WILL never act officiously or permit personal feelings, prejudices, animosities or friendship to influence my decisions. With no compromise for crime and with relentless prosecution of criminals, I will enforce the law courteously and appropriately without fear or favor, malice or ill will, never employing unnecessary force or violence and never accepting gratuities.

I RECOGNIZE the badge of my office as a symbol of public faith, and I accept it as a public trust to be held so long as I am true to the ethics of the police service. I will constantly strive to achieve these objectives and ideals, dedicating myself before God to my chosen profession . . . law enforcement.

* * *

The International Association of Chiefs of Police also adopted the Canons of Police Ethics at that same conference. They read as follows:

Canons of Police Ethics

Article 1. *Primary Responsibility of Job*

The primary responsibility of the police service, and of the individual officer, is the protection of the people of the United States through the upholding of their laws; chief among these is the Constitution of the United States and its amendments. The law enforcement officer always respects the whole of the community and its legally expressed will and is never the arm of any political party or clique.

Article 2. *Limitations of Authority*

The first duty of a law enforcement officer, as upholder of the law, is to know its bounds upon him in enforcing it. Because he represents the legal will of the community, be it local, state, or federal, he must be aware of the limitations and proscriptions which the people, through law, have placed upon him. He must recognize the genius of the American system of government which gives to no man, groups of men, or institutions, absolute power, and he must insure that he, as a prime defender of the system, does not pervert its character.

Article 3. *Duty to Be Familiar with the Law and with Responsibilities of Self and Other Public Officials*

The law enforcement officer shall assiduously apply himself to the study of the principles of the laws which he is sworn to uphold. He will make certain of his responsibilities in the particulars of their enforcement, seeking aid from his superiors in matters of technicality or principles when these are not clear to him; he will make special effort to fully understand his relationship to other public officials, including other law enforcement agencies, particularly on matters of jurisdiction, both geographically and substantively.

Article 4. *Utilization of Proper Means to Gain Proper Ends*

The law enforcement officer shall be mindful of his responsibility to pay strict heed to the selection of means in discharging the duties of his office. Violations of laws or disregard for public safety and property on the part of the officer are intrinsically wrong; they are self-defeating in that they instill in the public mind a like disposition. The employment of illegal means, no matter how worthy the end, is certain to encourage disrespect for the law and its officers. If the law is to be honored, it must first be honored by those who enforce it.

Article 5. *Cooperation with Public Officials in the Discharge of Their Authorized Duties*

The law enforcement officer shall cooperate fully with other public officials in the discharge of authorized duties, regardless of party affiliation or personal prejudice. He shall be meticulous, however, in assuring himself of the propriety, under the law, of such actions and shall guard against the use of his office or person, whether knowingly or unknowingly, in any improper or illegal action. In any situation open to question, he shall seek authority from his superior officer, giving him a full report of the proposed service or action.

Article 6. *Private Conduct*

The law enforcement officer shall be mindful of his special identification by the public as an upholder of the law. Laxity of conduct or manner in private life, expressing either disrespect for the law or seeking to gain special privilege, cannot but reflect upon the police officer and the police service. The community and the service require that the law enforcement officer lead the life of a decent and honorable man. Following the career of a policeman gives no man special perquisites. It does give the satisfaction and pride of following and furthering an unbroken tradition of safeguarding the American republic. The officer who reflects upon this tradition will not degrade it. Rather, he will so conduct his private life that the public will regard him as an example of stability, fidelity and morality.

Article 7. *Conduct Toward the Public*

The law enforcement officer, mindful of his responsibility to the whole community, shall deal with individuals of the community in a manner calculated to instill respect for its laws and its police service. The law enforcement officer shall conduct his official life in a manner such as will inspire confidence and trust. Thus, he will be neither overbearing nor subservient, as the individual citizen has neither an obligation to stand in awe of him nor a right to command him. The officer will give service where he can, and require compliance with the law. He will do neither from personal preference or prejudice but only as a duly appointed officer of the law discharging his sworn obligation.

Article 8. *Conduct in Arresting and Dealing with Law Violators*

The law enforcement officer shall use his powers of arrest strictly in accordance with the law and with due regard to the rights of the citizen concerned. His office gives him no right to prosecute the violator nor to mete out punishment for the offense. He shall, at all times, have a clear appreciation of his responsibilities and limitations regarding detention of the violator; he shall conduct himself in such a manner as will minimize the possibility of having to use force. To this end he shall cultivate a dedication to the service of the people and the equitable upholding of their laws whether in the handling of law violators or in dealing with the law-abiding.

Article 9. *Gifts and Favors*

The law enforcement officer, representing government, bears the heavy responsibility of maintaining, in his own conduct, the honor and integrity of all governmental institutions. He shall, therefore, guard against placing himself in a position in which any person can reasonably assume that special consideration is being given. Thus, he should be firm in refusing gifts, favors, or gratuities, large or small, which can, in the public mind, be interpreted as capable of influencing his judgment in the discharge of his duties.

Article 10. *Presentation of Evidence*

The law enforcement officer shall be concerned equally in the prosecution of the wrongdoer and the defense of the innocent. He shall ascertain what constitutes evidence and shall present such evidence impartially and without malice. In so doing, he will ignore social, political, and other distinctions among the persons involved, strengthening the tradition of the reliability and the integrity of an officer's word.

The law enforcement officer shall take special pains to increase his perception and skill of observation, mindful that in many situations his is the sole impartial testimony to the facts of a case.

Article 11. *Attitude Toward Profession*

The law enforcement officer shall regard the discharge of his duties as a public trust and recognize his responsibility as a public servant. By diligent study and sincere attention to self-improvement he shall strive to make the best possible application of science to the solution of crime and, in the field of human relationships, strive for effective leadership and public influence in matters affecting public safety. He shall appreciate the importance and responsibility of his office, hold police work to be an honorable profession rendering valuable service to his community and the country.

* * *

These Codes of Ethics have a strong tendency to become just so many words, pious and smug. To be of any real value, they must become understood and accepted by law enforcement personnel, and applied to the working environment. If they are understood, accepted, and applied, there should result a lessening of current moral abuses in the police service.

The late O. W. Wilson, former Superintendent of Police, Chicago, put the case clearly:

> Police administrators and supervisors must develop a high degree of "intestinal fortitude." We must have the strength within our agencies to run a "tight ship," and to detect and correct our own weaknesses. We should not have to wait for public pressures and newspaper exposés to call these matters to our attention. Too many of us—abiding by a false sense of camaraderie— conceive our function as being that of protecting our fellow officers. It is one thing to aid a man in combat; to cater to our sick; to care for the families of police officers; and to support a man in the rightful performance of his duties. It is another thing to cover up wrongdoing or the commission of a crime by one of our members. Friendship can be gained by being tolerant of such conditions, but friendship alone does not result in good administration or in the advancement of law enforcement. True leadership can be gained only by an intolerance

of wrongdoing by police officers. Unless we abide by the very highest standards among ourselves, we have no business enforcing the law upon others.[1]

Certainly, it must be clearly understood that the law enforcement officer is a human being, and subject to the frailties of human nature, never completely immune from temptation. Yet, it must be just as clearly understood that chronic or habitual moral lapses cannot be tolerated, cannot be minimized, cannot be rationalized, and cannot be blindly overlooked. *Eliminating such abuses is a primary goal of good leadership.*

LEGALITY

The assessment of police legality is, like the evaluation of efficiency and morality, a most difficult task.

For one reason, the determination of what is legal or illegal is often unclear, and dependent upon changing judicial interpretation. For another, the law enforcement officer must often act with dispatch, and without time for lengthy deliberation or legal research. Nonetheless, there is a heavy emphasis today placed upon scrupulous application of the law by those whose duty is to enforce it. This emphasis is continually reiterated by law enforcement executives and by the courts.

As an example of clear-cut *police* philosophy, we present a few of the statements of the late Mr. J. Edgar Hoover, Director, Federal Bureau of Investigation, and the late Mr. William H. Parker, Chief of Police, Los Angeles. They are taken, out of context, from their speeches and writings, but they are, nonetheless, very much to the point:

Mr. Hoover:

. . . one of the quickest ways for any law enforcement officer to bring public disrepute upon himself, his organization and the entire profession is to be found guilty of a violation of civil rights . . . Civil rights violations are all the more regrettable because they are so unnecessary. Professional standards in law enforcement provide for fighting crime with intelligence rather than force.

. . . law enforcement . . . in defeating the criminal, must maintain inviolate the historic liberties of the individual. To turn back the criminal, yet, by so doing, destroy the dignity of the individual, would be a hollow victory.

. . . it is in this area (violation of civil rights) that law enforcement must rise to prevent abuses, such as third-degree techniques, unlawful arrests, unreasonable detention, illegal searches and seizures. These practices are anathema to civil liberties, destroying the very heart of the American law enforcement system. They represent law enforcement at its worst.

Mr. Parker:

It has been suggested by some that police use drastic and extra-legal means in coping with . . . problems. Such tactics must be avoided, for it is the police

---

[1] Wilson, O. W., Address to the Annual Meeting of the International Association of Chiefs of Police, Montreal, Canada, October 3, 1961.

who must give meaning to those individual rights guaranteed to every person by the Constitution. Constitutional Rights are largely academic to the person who never gets into trouble. It is the person suspected of crime to whom these guarantees are translated into reality. . . .

In a perfect system of civil administration the function of the police is to curb the liberty of the individual only when it degenerates into license, and any material variation from this standard is to be deprecated as arbitrary and tyrannical. . . .

. . . I feel it mandatory that I declare myself on the matter of civil rights. I believe that we cannot pass lightly over those inalienable rights of individuals which are the greatest possession of a free people. I do not believe that the police service can afford either to ignore or to trample upon these priceless possessions, and I believe that history will indicate that every police organization which has assumed a tyrannical attitude has been doomed to oblivion. We still suffer today from the abuse of power by those who preceded us in the police profession. I believe that to avoid these fatal errors we must know and recognize the legal rights of individuals and be fully cognizant of when the law permits us to invade personal liberty. . . .

We do not argue a "fight fire with fire" philosophy—because such a premise could reduce the Bill of Rights to a heap of ashes. History shows that bad police methods breed disrespect for the law, shake the confidence of law-abiding citizens in the administration of justice and weaken the national morale. . . .

These comments by Mr. Hoover and Mr. Parker should be given great weight for they are not the idle remarks of amateur dabblers, but the eloquent words of two well-known crime fighters who are seasoned and mature police leaders, and practical law enforcement people.

It would be helpful if more American police executives were as direct and emphatic as Mr. Hoover and Mr. Parker. Too many of our citizenry believe that police thinking always stresses the expedient at the expense of the lawful. Too many of our citizenry believe that the words "civil liberties" are panic words to the police. Too many of our citizenry believe that police revert to "role playing" when discussing civil liberties. This is unhealthy. Every member of the law enforcement vocation must come to understand Constitutional Guarantees as positive and valued—and this should be so obvious that no citizen will ever be able to jump to the conclusion that the Bill of Rights is getting the "silent treatment" from American police leadership as a conscious plan.

As an example of clear-cut *court* philosophy, we present a comment by Mr. Justice Brandeis of the United States Supreme Court, who, in the case of *Olmstead v. United States,* spoke no less eloquently:

Decency, security and liberty alike demand that government officials shall be subjected to the same rules of conduct that are commands to the citizen. In a government of laws, existence of the government will be imperiled if it fails to observe the laws scrupulously. Our government is the potent, omnipresent teacher. For good or ill, it teaches the whole people by its example.

Crime is contagious. If the government becomes a law breaker, it breeds contempt for the law; it invites every man to become a law unto himself; it invites anarchy. To declare that in the administration of criminal laws the end justifies the means—to declare that the government may commit crimes in order to secure the conviction of a private criminal—would bring terrible retribution. Against that pernicious doctrine this Court should resolutely set its face.

And so should every law enforcement student, practitioner, supervisor and administrator.

All policemen must be knowledgeable and articulate defenders of the Constitution and Bill of Rights, fully as enthusiastic about constitutional guarantees as about crime clearances, fully as committed to safeguarding the civil rights of all as to safeguarding the property of all.

The Constitution and the Bill of Rights, as practical here-and-now matters, mean exactly what the police permit them to mean in the community. It is good to know that many American policemen are as fully committed to civil rights as any legislator, judge, or civil liberties attorney. The communities they serve have no doubts as to the commitments of their police. Such police set the pace for the entire law enforcement vocation—and stand as an example of professional dedication for the whole world to see.

COMPASSION

The consideration of police compassion—and by compassion, we mean the *principle of sympathetic effort*—is a new, but necessary, undertaking.

The day of the ruthless, inhumane, indifferent police officer has gone. The professional officer is sympathetic in that he can understand, share, and regard the problems of others. Sympathy does not at all imply that one must tolerate wrongdoing or accept anti-social behavior. The sympathetic officer does not avoid his duty, even when that duty will bring sorrow to some fellow citizen. But the sympathetic officer does not delight in anyone's misery, nor does he turn aside with cold indifference.

The policeman must deal with the burdened, grief-stricken and suffering citizen—whether that person be the victim of a crime, or the suspect involved.

A quarter-century ago, most members of the law enforcement vocation would have sneered at the idea of police compassion. Today, some members of the law enforcement fraternity would deride such a suggestion, but more would be inclined to define terms.

Some police have a view of their "job" that is as narrow as a laser beam, rigid as yesterday, and mechanical as a pair of handcuffs. "Our job," they say, "is to protect life and property and keep the peace." "We do this," they say, "by investigating crime, making arrests, and assisting in the prosecution of wrongdoers." Essentially, primarily, emphatically, they regard their work as *repressive*. Ordinarily, such officers do not see themselves as a *part* of the administration of criminal justice, as a link in the chain of police-prosecutor-court-probation-corrections-parole. Ordinarily, such officers would react to any suggestion of "compassion" as being the responsibility of "clergymen." Crime prevention? Let the churches, schools, parents and community organizations chew on that problem. Protecting personal liberty? Let the attorneys, courts, and civil rights organizations fight that battle.

Along with a rejection of anything not connected with crime repression, such police will demonstrate a good working vocabulary of labels—"do-gooders," "sob-sisters," "bleeding-hearts,"—to attach to any individual or group which does not give enthusiastic emphasis and priority attention to repressive methods of solving the problems of social disorganization. Some police leadership will give loud and vocal articulation of such set of mind. Some police supervisors will blindly accept such philosophy as that of a "real policeman," and play their part in brainwashing newly recruited members of the vocation. And some police officers will, sheep-like, adapt themselves to the majority opinion of their agency colleagues.

Many police, on the other hand, have a perception of their vocation that is broad, flexible, and compassionate. "Our job they say, "is to prevent crime and disorder and keep the peace——for the security of the community; and to protect life, property, and personal liberty—for the security of the individual." "We do this," they state, "by engaging in crime prevention activities, repressing crime, regulating non-criminal conduct, providing services, and insuring personal liberty." They see themselves as a strong link in the chain forming the administration of criminal justice. These officers work with juveniles, cooperate with probation, correctional and parole personnel, educate the public, investigate crime, identify and apprehend offenders, recover stolen property, assist in prosecution, control the non-criminal citizen, render advice and general assistance, provide special services, protect citizens against unwarranted interference on the part of the state, and instruct citizens relative to duties, obligations, rights and privileges in reference to the law. These officers welcome all individual and group assistance in solving interpersonal and intergroup conflict. Many police leaders, with wisdom and learning, infuse, by their example, good attitudes within their agencies, and by their example, instruct the total community in terms of responsible citizenship. These supervisors assist the newly accepted policeman to obtain a professional perspective relative to his work.

If you were to ask such officers about "police compassion," they would, in all probability, reply that all citizens, as responsible citizens, are truly compassionate, and that all police, as professional law enforcement officers are compassionate—if the compassionate person is one who has a feeling for the suffering of others as he assists his fellow man achieve his due. They would deny that law enforcement is committed to the interests of any one area or segment of the community, and indifferent to the rest; they would reject any view holding that policing was merely a ruthless and mechanical method of protecting the "haves" from the "have nots." They would articulate the humane police responsibility to all citizens—the good and the bad, the rich and the poor, the colored and the colorless, the intelligent and the stupid, the able and the inept.

In considering police methods, the specialist in repression might suggest that any method that gets the job done is acceptable. Such a view would indicate an indifference to the questions of efficiency vs. waste, legality vs. illegality, morality vs. immorality—there is but one task: remove the antisocial member of society by any means that will do the trick.

The professional officer, broad in perspective, would offer a different view: all methods must be directed toward efficiency, legality, morality, and compassion. This view rejects the amoral and pragmatic dogma that "the end justifies the means." It understands the importance of crime repression, but also understands the importance of crime prevention and the protection of personal liberty. In other words, this view sees more to the police role than the removal of the antisocial individual from circulation.

In considering police manpower, the specialist in repression might indicate that a good bicep, imposing height, and aggressiveness are at the heart of police qualifications. "Book learning," he would say, "is all right for the doctor or attorney, but is beside the point for the man with the badge." They would indicate that gentlemanly grace and virtuous behavior might be expected in the minister, but would be asinine to expect in terms of the man who wrestles drunks and cites speeders. And they might even infer the foul canard that "it takes one to catch one."

If you ask the officer of such narrow views to describe a "real policeman," his answers will indicate how he views his work, what his role expectations really are. If the man he describes is rough, tough, arrogant, abrasive, insensitive, abusive and visceral—you will understand why so many of the citizenry so regard the officer, for some officers so regard themselves!

The professional member of the vocation would state that character, learning, intellectual capacity, physical ability necessary for the tasks at hand, wisdom, and emotional stability are the *sine qua non* for modern police service. He would indicate that the problems faced by today's policeman are so complex that the personnel qualifications of a quarter-century ago are no longer realistic.

If you ask an officer of wide perspective to describe a professional policeman, you will find out how he views himself. If the man he details is intelligent, able, energetic, virtuous, stable, mature, and compassionate—you will understand how some citizens are now demanding better police service—for they have met some of these officers!

If we ask, now, "Is the American policeman compassionate? we can expect two different kinds of replies, with each dependent upon the concept of the police service held.

If one regards the police function as primarily repressive, if one is non-critical of methods used, if one expects little from the officer—one would not see the policeman as compassionate.

If one sees the American policeman as a professional, his goals broad, his methods proper, his qualifications high—one could understand the concept of police compassion.

In other words, if the concept of "gentleman cop" is a laughable idea, then so too will be the concept of "police compassion." If the idea of police having an interest in unemployment, segregation, hunger, disease, bad housing, deficient recreational facilities, and poor educational facilities is preposterous, then too will be any idea of policing other than that of wrestling drunks, writing traffic tickets, investigating crime, arresting offenders, and assisting in prosecution.

It would seem that any understanding of modern policing would include an understanding that human problems are police problems, that police problems are human problems, and that every policeman who is a professional is a compassionate officer in the true sense of the term. Time spent by police in improving relations between individual citizens and between groups of citizens will tend to establish an atmosphere in which there is a reduction of crime and disorder as grows out of interpersonal and inter-group conflict—and the police task will thus be made easier. Time spent by police in insuring the rights and privileges of citizenship will tend to establish a community attitude in which there is a lessening of fear, bitterness, frustration, hatred and misunderstanding as grows out of cold and mechanical application of the law—and the police task will thus be made easier.

Far too seldom does law enforcement ask the question, "Could *we* have done anything to prevent the last episode? Could *we* have done anything to insure personal liberty for that citizen?" It is always easier to blame the press, the home, the church, and the school—or the general public.

It is time that law enforcement accept the fact that today's problems must be met with today's solutions—that today's solutions involve today's knowledge of the law, police technology, psychology, sociology, ethics, anthropology, and human relations.

Whenever the vice officer handles an addict, bettor, prostitute, or pervert; whenever the traffic officer handles the speeder or pedestrian; whenever the juvenile officer handles the delinquent; whenever the patrol officer handles the family dispute; whenever the detective handles the disturbed person—*and arrests and prosecutions are NOT the sole and primary considerations*—then, those officers are compassionate in the finest sense of the term.

Admittedly, it is easier and cheaper to teach a policeman the mechanical techniques of his work—operating the radio, applying the police strangle, double-locking the cuffs, writing the ticket—than it is to teach an officer the psychological, sociological, anthropological, ethical and human relations aspects of his work. It is easier and cheaper to teach an officer a few sections of the penal and vehicle code than it is teach him how poor police work in the sensitive areas of arrest, search, and seizure will be rejected by the courts which assume their responsibility in enforcing the Constitution and Bill of Rights. It is easier and cheaper to teach an officer to "follow the book," than it is to teach him how to wisely utilize his discretion in performing his function.

Admittedly, it is easier to recruit the ham-fisted reject of the competitive world of commerce and industry than it is to recruit and enlist the "gentleman cop." If, in any police grouping, the majority of personnel represent the "rock-em, sock-em" specialists in crime repression, there will be monumental difficulties in changing traditional attitudes and habits.

The agency of Neanderthal philosophy, shabby methods, and inept personnel will merely exist, with continuing problems of recruitment and public relations, and with pay schedules that would insult any man of promise. But, in any police grouping that demonstrates, by leadership and actions, that it is dedicated to professional goals and standards, changes will take place, men of character, ability and capacity will be recruited, and, ultimately, working conditions and salaries will reflect the pride of the community in a truly progressive police service.

It may well be that the concept of police compassion is idealistic—but it is not a contradiction in terms. It all depends upon one's view of the American police service. A quarter-century ago, most members of the law enforcement vocation would have sneered at the idea of police compassion. Now, the concept may be better understood and better received.

Policing can never be at an optimum if the major interest is in efficiency and mechanical accomplishment—results, arrests, clearances. The police must always be interested, just as enthusiastically, in the legality and morality of these accomplishments.

Policing can never be at an optimum if police do not interest themselves in the human beings with whom they deal, for compassion is fully as necessary for the development of public support and cooperation as is attention to efficiency, legality, and morality. A few policemen have all the appeal of an IBM computer and are cold, compassionless automatons who seem to have forgotten long ago that all men are their brothers—whether the men are in the department, workers within the community, or subjects of the line-up. It is to the everlasting glory of American law enforcement that so many of its practitioners are truly efficient, legal, moral, and compassionate public servants, faithfully giving their lives to the best interests of their fellow citizens, their communities, and their nation.

CONCLUSIONS

The student of law enforcement must learn to distinguish between the areas of efficiency, morality, legality and compassion whenever he engages himself in any evaluations of a police agency or a police officer. He must diligently identify the principles which can be used to assess the activities of a law enforcement agency or the actions of a law enforcement officer.

He must learn to distinguish between "what is" and "what should be" and assume some responsibility in the task of bringing American law enforcement to the highest possible level of efficiency, an edifying level of morality, and an exemplary level of legality. It is a responsibility and task that will demand the utmost of his intelligence, moral character, motivation, and courage. It is a responsibility and task that cannot be overlooked in any approach to law enforcement. Those who accept the responsibility and set their minds and hands and hearts to the task might well ponder the words of Charles Sumner, once a United States Senator from Massachusetts:

> I honor any man who is the conscientious discharge of his duty dares to stand alone. The world, with ignorant intolerant judgment, may condemn; the countenances of relatives may be averted; and the hearts of friends grow cold—but the sense of duty done shall be sweeter than the applause of the world, the countenances of relatives, or the hearts of friends.

Ideals are like stars—one cannot easily touch or reach them—but, like the navigator, one can use them as guides, and, by following them, one can reach his chosen objectives.

Sometimes the person with high ideals is regarded as a bit odd, particularly, if his ideals are contrary to long-standing customs or prevailing opinions, necessitating great moral courage in order to maintain such ideals and corresponding conduct.

Chief Edward J. Allen, Santa Ana, California, poet laureate of the International Association of Chiefs of Police, puts it succinctly:

> All knowledge without action is stillborn;
> To put ideals into practice without fear
> May make you, for a moment, a thing of scorn—
> God soon will strike your hour—persevere!

TOPICS FOR DISCUSSION

1. Can there ever be, in this nation, "universally imposed or accepted standards for police administration and operations"?
2. Can *statements* of police ethics be actually translated into *everyday conduct?*
3. Is it fact or fancy to state that the words "civil liberties" are "panic" words to some police?
4. Is the concept of "gentleman cop" a dream when considering the many violent and sordid environments, and the many vicious and depraved individuals contacted in the course of a policeman's everyday work? Can "professional" law enforcement be done in the back alleys of high crime-incident areas? Do brutal and vicious people "understand" only a brutal and vicious language and response?
5. How do the words of Senator Sumner and Chief Allen apply to the working law enforcement officer in twentieth century policing?

Chapter XXII

RESEARCH AREAS AND CURRENT TRENDS

RESEARCH—EXHAUSTIVE INQUIRY—into the sphere of law enforcement is in the embryonic state, but is gaining momentum each year as more and more dedicated students, academicians, and practitioners interest themselves in planning for the future of the vocation. Careful perusal of key failures of the past, and a study of major accomplishments, are vital to any evaluation of police activity currently conducted, and to decisions determining what is to be done in the future.

RESEARCH AREAS

A few of the areas in need of continuing attention, in the opinion of the authors, are as follows:

OVERLAPPING, DUPLICATION. Studies of the overlapping or duplication of facilities, equipment, and activities which are wasteful of the tax dollar and law enforcement resources.

SIZE. Studies of the effect of size on police administration and operations to determine levels of adequacy, minimums, and maximums.

ACCOUNTABILITY. Studies of control devices to assure the properly responsive discharge of function necessary to the maintenance of local control. Studies of control devices to assure the properly responsible accomplishment of goals necessary to the maintenance of a professional quality of service.

CIVIL SERVICE—MERIT SYSTEM. Studies of civil service and merit system advantages and disadvantages, with recommendations for changes to assure protection from spoils operations; effective discipline and prompt discharge of inept and immoral members; recognition of, and incentives for, competent service; easy entrance and rapid advancement of qualified leadership potential; adequate salary and wage processes; mandatory education and training; and effective supervisory processes.

EDUCATION AND TRAINING. Studies of curricula for preservice and inservice education and training to determine proper substance and extension. Studies of potential areas of college-agency collaboration and mutual support.

WORK MEASUREMENT. Studies to determine extent of possible application of scientific management to the law enforcement service.

POLICE-COMMUNITY RELATIONS. Studies to assess police and public role expectations, value conflicts, conceptions of goals, areas of friction and hostility, the ecology of police-community issues, and the propriety of police functions in terms of community resources.

POLICY AND PROCEDURE. Studies to evaluate current and potential solutions to police problems, adequacy of operational methods, and the formalization of duties and responsibilities.

ORGANIZATION. Studies to evaluate current and potential structural arrangements of the organization. Studies to evaluate the effects of informal organization within the agency.

LEGISLATION. Studies to evaluate changes necessary in laws to provide for effective, legal, moral and compassionate police services, for better protection of the community, and for better protection of the individual citizen. Many suggestions have been made, from time to time, by various groups. Some types are those:

1. Providing grants-in-aid for training, contingent upon establishment of minimum selection standards and minimum training programs, or mandatory training programs as a condition precedent to appointment as law enforcement officer.
2. Providing for the examination and certification of law enforcement officers; basic, intermediate, and advanced credentials required for entry, supervisory, or administrative positions.
3. Providing for the planning, organization, and establishment of county, state, or national clearinghouses for information utilizing the latest techniques of electronic data processing.
4. Requiring the insurance or bonding of any person having the powers of a law enforcement officer applying to any injury or damages or intentional tort committed while acting within the scope of his office.
5. Making a political subdivision liable in money damages, for any injury attributable to an act or omission of a law enforcement employee when such act or omission was the proximate cause of injury.
6. Providing for "stopping for identification," "frisking," or "field interogation" based on probable cause, without arrest or booking, but with substantial damages for any willful and malicious abuse of the privilege.
7. Providing for up to a two-hour police detention, based on probable

cause, without arrest or booking, but with substantial damages for any willful and malicious abuse of the privilege.

8. Forbidding any person to resist arrest, even though it be unlawful arrest, when an officer is properly identified, but entitling any injured party to an award of substantial money damages in a civil action.

9. Regulating the use of electronic eavesdropping devices, polygraph instruments, and mail covers to instances specifically approved by court order after a showing of reasonable cause.

10. Requiring that a stopped, arrested, or booked person be given both oral and written statements of his rights to counsel, and to bail.

11. Providing for a wider use of citation, summons, or notice of violation to embrace a larger number of misdemeanors presently handled by physical arrest.

12. Requiring the release of an arrested person on a personal recognizance when certain conditions can be met.

13. Giving a prosecutor the right to appeal a court order to suppress evidence.

14. Providing costs or damages for injuries suffered by persons who assist in the prevention of crime or apprehension of offenders.

15. Providing governmental compensation to the victims of violent crime, as is done in Australia and Great Britain.

16. Requiring annual, quarterly, or monthly public reports relative to ratios of:

a) number and types of stops, frisks, field interviews and other detentions vs. number and type of arrests made;

b) number and type of arrests made vs. number and type of complaints filed;

c) number and type of complaints filed vs. number and type of convictions obtained;

d) number and type of traffic violations causing injury or death vs. number and type of traffic summonses or citations issued.

17. Establishing police review boards composed of Chiefs of Police empowered to receive complaints relative to incompetent or illegal or immoral police acts, to conduct investigations, to issue recommendations, and, where necessary, to issue reports.

18. Establishing processes for direct citizen participation in the formulation of criminal justice policy, procedure, rules and regulations so the taxpayer has a meaningful voice in determining priorities.

19. Decriminalizing victimless crimes—that is, removing criminal penalties for consenting adult behavior in such areas as gambling, use

and abuse of drugs, incest, bigamy, abortion, adultery, obscenity, pornography, prostitution and homosexuality.

The authors of this text neither arbitrarily endorse and support, nor arbitrarily reject and attack such legislative proposals. Each form of legislation must be considered in the light of national and community values, the current levels of efficiency, legality, morality and compassion in the law enforcement agency, alternatives available to achieve desired results, and the impact upon long-term police-community relationships.

The authors do suggest that the reader give serious consideration to all legislation which will improve American law enforcement, improve the safety of our communities, and guarantee the liberty of our citizens.

Certainly, many more possible areas of inquiry present themselves regularly to the law enforcement scholar. His is the task of establishing priorities consistent with the needs of his level of service, his region, and his community.

CURRENT TRENDS

As we look at law enforcement *today,* we see both positive and negative trends. Fortunately, for the future of the American police service, the positive and affirmative trends far outweigh the negative and deleterious.

Negative Trends. POPULATION MOBILITY. A key problem, and one increasing with the improvement in personal transportation, is the mobility of the population, both criminal and noncriminal, and the increasingly transient character of the urban community with thousands of people daily moving from state to state, from country to city, from city to suburb, and then re-moving as social and economic factors intervene. This trend makes for great difficulties in law enforcement operations as these thousands of moving citizens enter and then leave one law enforcement jurisdiction for another.

DOUBLE STANDARDS. In the area of gambling and prostitution, the law is most often applied against the bookmaker or prostitute, rarely against the customer. In some communities, when raids are made, it is the prostitutes, panderers, bartenders, bookmakers, and the like who are fined and jailed—not the client.

Some commentators have pointed out that this procedure is "futile, farcical, and hypocritical." As Sydney J. Harris, syndicated columnist, put it,

> The so-called "respectable" patrons of these joints are never fined or arrested; it is always the disreputable elements who take the rap, such as it is. Since they make their living out of this, they shrug it off stoically and charge it to "business expenses," as a kind of insurance premium they must pay to stay in business.

They provide the supply. The demand is generated by respectable and responsible members of society; by conventioneers from small towns, by suburban paragons of virtue sneaking into the city for a night of fun, by companies subsidizing the expense accounts of salesmen "entertaining" customers.

It is not riff-raff who patronize these girls and these places. It is the small-town vestryman, the suburban dentist, the loving husband and father who over-subscribes to the Girl Scout cookie drive back home. Ninety-nine per cent of the customers are what the milieu contemptuously refer to as "square Johns."

What if these square Johns were arrested in raids, fined or jailed for taking part in an illegal transaction? What if their names and addresses were publicized in the newspapers? How long do you imagine the business would continue to thrive. . . .[1]

Mr. Harris points out that he is not suggesting that we should engage in "this painful exposure of middle-class hypocrisy," but merely that "until we do, the raids are silly."

Other commentators have noted that "it takes two to tango," and suggested that the real attack on gambling and prostitution will commence when both gambler and client, prostitute and trick, are prosecuted. Cynics laugh at such suggestions, holding that any Chief of Police who undertook such measures would soon be out of a job—at the behest of the "good people" of the community. Such cynics speculate relative to crime rate expansion if income tax cheating, expense-account padding, price fixing, and usury were to be attacked as forcefully as drunkenness and petty theft.

WHITE-COLLAR OR UPPERWORLD CRIME. Students of criminal justice hear figures about the cost of street crime—the ordinary index crime—in terms of 10 to 20 billion dollars per year. They hear figures about the cost of syndicated or organized crime—the provision of goods and services falling generally into the "victimless crime" area—in terms of 20 to 50 billion dollars per year. But, according to Senator Philip Hart (D. Mich.), consumers are bilked out of 174 to 231 billion dollars each year. Senator Hart, Chairman of the Senate Subcommittee on Anti-Trust and Monopoly, estimates Americans are cheated out of 30 to 40 dollars of each 100 dollars they spend! His subcommittee found the extent of big business cheating annually was enormous:

> Monopolistic pricing above competitive levels—45 billion dollars;
> Food prices derived from deceptive packaging—14 billion dollars;
> Auto repair charges for work improperly done, unneeded, or charged, but not done—10 billion dollars;
> Costs above free market prices due to oil quotas—3 billion dollars;
> Auto and life insurance deceptive practices—17 billion dollars.

---

[1] Harris, Sydney J.: Strictly Personal (column). *Independent,* Long Beach, California, December 11, 1964. Reprinted by permission of Sydney J. Harris and Publishers Nswspaper Syndicate.

This cost of 94 billion dollars a year doesn't include additional cheating on medical care, housing, credit, defective products, and on useless drugs.

Past issues of this introductory text had a few paragraphs about the evils of syndicated crime, and now there is a full chapter. It would not be surprising, as more and more citizens and scholars probe into this area of consumer protection, that the revelations will make street crime and syndicated crime appear to be "small potatoes" in the "rip-off" stew.

It would not be surprising to see consumer fraud units developing at the federal, state, county, and municipal level, as criminal justice moves its attention away from the less harmful offenses to the more violent and avaracious types of antisocial conduct.

It would not be surprising to see criminal justice education and training programs devoting less time to pursuit driving, self-defense, and skill-oriented performance, and more time to people-oriented subject matter; less time to street crime-fighting methods, and more time to white-collar crime-fighting methods.

PARANOID TENDENCIES. Another negative current trend is in increasingly embarrassing police and public paranoid tendencies. Paranoia, as a neurosis, is characterized by delusional ideas which form a logically coherent system of thought, and which leave the rest of the personality relatively intact. A paranoiac type usually has an extraordinarily strong and unchangeable "set" of ideas about some subject, and until that subject is presented to his consideration, one would not notice his odd condition. And even if one might immediately intuit an "odd" attitude, if the paranoiac type is intelligent, unemotional, and articulate, one might conclude that, perhaps, he might be correct in his reasoning.

This paranoiac type holds on to his delusional ideas, with absolute conviction with "holy zeal," and cannot be swayed in the slightest. "Pet" themes involve *groups* of *"other people"*—such as the "dangerous liberals, soft on communism," "the Negroes," "the rigid authoritarian, soft on Fascism," the Freemasons, the Jews, the Communists, the NAACP, the Roman Catholics, the ADA, the juvenile delinquents, the Democrats, the integrationists, the hippies, the peaceniks, the traffic offenders, the Republicans, the sex deviates, the Mafia, the ACLU, the United Nations, the alcoholics, the unions, the welfare statists, the Socialists, the foreign aid supporters, the narcotic addicts, the "cops." (The student can test for the reaction syndrome by reading such a list, unexplained, to a subject.)

The paranoiac type will recognize things "behind" things, where others cannot. He will "read" his pet theme into daily events with ease. The seed of a paranoiac delusion is suspicion, distrust, and insecurity, and its brilliant flower is composed of personal vilification, hatred, and violence. This pitiable type of person will "see" all unsympathetic persons as minions or dupes of the despised adversary group.

The paranoiac type will often speak of the need for "common sense," and suggest simplistic solutions for complex problems. This type of common sense is uneducated, unreflective, and prejudiced, and often the possession of those who do not have the inclination to study or face unpleasant facts. The paranoiac type has a furor of criticism—loud, nasty, righteously indignant—even when he knows very little about the problem and is not qualified to have an opinion on the matter.

This is of great current significance to the law enforcement service for it has to do with the *climate of opinion* both in and out of the police agency. In times of stress—and these are years of agonizing stresses of all types— paranoiac personalities come to the fore, and they are "gifted" with a unique and clever ability to mobilize and energize the latent paranoid tendencies around them. Ordinary awareness turns to vigilance; vigilance turns to wide suspicion; wide suspicion turns to vilification; vilification turns to hatred— and it is *hatred* that handcuffs these types into a peculiarly destructive union.

Vigilance in the face of evil often causes a preoccupation with evil, and an extreme negativism, wherein the paranoiac type gives far greater attention to the things he is *against* than the things he is *for*. He finds that it is much easier to have suspicion and distrust than to have faith. And in keeping his energies ever alert for the adversaries something happens to him; he no longer keeps his mind on God and man with love, compassion and understanding. He is suspicious of almost everyone, except you and him, and secretly, he is suspicious of you.

In the opinion of the authors, the tendencies toward individual and mass paranoia have led to serious police abuses and to public witch hunts, and have often tended to separate rather than to join police and public.

Policemen and citizens who find the ACLU or the traffic offender, or the ADA, or the narcotic addict, or the Jews, or the NAACP, *as groups*, as objects of *hatred*, are disordered persons. A tendency toward paranoia, in policemen, and citizens, hampers police operations, destroys community stability, and debilitates the national morale.[2]

THE HIP SCENE. From coast to coast thousands of young people have joined hearts and seceded from the society of their elders. With "love-ins," "be-ins," and "happenings," they draw themselves together in amorphous groupings, patronizing coffee-houses, rock ballrooms, psychedelic boutiques, and public parks. Beneath the colors and sounds of this rapidly expanding

---

[2] Concepts adapted from Stern, Karl (1954). *The Third Revolution*, pp. 279-283. Harcourt, Brace, New York.

scene there lies deep disenchantment with the values of the over-30 generation. Perhaps our youth observe that greed and selfishness in our affluent society often results in almost total disregard of *human beings,* and almost total obsession with *things.* Perhaps our youth observe that almost every sincere interest in social or economic justice is put down as communistic by people who wish to avoid blame for their own bigotry or avarice. Some of the hippies and flower children seem to have a basic value system more in keeping with the mind of Hillel or Christ than with the mind of Madison Avenue, and the aura of a love-in may reflect more charity and good will than is to be found in the temples and parishes of our cities. Part of the growth of Christianity can be attributed to the fact that many instinctively decent people were nauseated by the excesses of Rome and its affluent empire. Could the revolt of many youngsters today be somewhat analogous? Is this a *negative* or *positive* trend?

While addictive, physically habituating drugs are less rare, the psychedelic or hallucinogenic mescaline, psilocybin, DMT and LSD are not uncommon, and the use of marihuana is widespread.

The problem is how to actualize the potentialities of the hippie for positive, productive and useful living without destroying personal integrity and valid values. Additional insight may come from a perusual of *the underground press.* Representative are the *Los Angeles Free Press,* the Chicago *Seed,* and the New York *East Village Other.*

ABUSE OF STATISTICS. In this era of the "scientific method," any statistical manipulation that is self-serving, rather than being most rigorously screened for careless interpretation, is also self-defeating, for when any agency "fiddles" with the data, or presents them in unverified fashion, or makes a misuse of a statistical correlation, or fails to reveal its completely limited application, that agency rightfully is the recipient of public scorn.

Veracity of data must always be given primary attention. To claim a high percentage of property recovered, when *in fact* much of it was recovered by other agencies, and *also* appears in *their* statistical presentations, is only productive of misleading information.

Correlation of data must always be properly used. Some law enforcement administrators point to the proper correlation between the number of traffic citations written and the reduction of accidents. And they point to splendid "selective enforcement programs" whereby all accidents are investigated to determine the violation involved, and bulletins issued after periodical analysis indicating the areas, hours, and violations involved as a guide to enforcement activity. And, as the accident rates go up, they ask for more manpower to enforce the traffic laws. No mention is made of a careful correlation between actual tickets written and the recommendations of the carefully prepared selective enforcement bulletins. Perhaps it is just as well, for if in fact, many of the monthly tickets were the result of pressure for production and easy trips to the "apple orchard" or "duck pond" (where, perhaps, no accident has occurred in years), a correlation study might tend to indicate that more attention should be paid to the quality of citations than to the number of personnel engaged in traffic enforcement, or the total number of citations written.

Utilization of data must always be honorable. Agencies with highly refined *modus operandi* processes (utilizing mechanized records to link crimes to those individuals who often offend according to a set pattern) are to be complimented. But, if in order to achieve a higher rate of crimes cleared by arrest, they arbitrarily close cases as cleared simply because they have arrested an offender with the same pattern, but no evidence or confession relative to complicity, or if they have offered a more lenient prosecution if the suspect will assist by admitting to prior offenses, even though he did not commit them, those agencies do a disservice to law enforcement.

Statistics are dangerous for police to mishandle. The authors, if deeply resentful of court decisions limiting police activity, *could* point out that the *Weeks* case, in 1914, was the first application of the exclusionary rule. They could point to the tremendous rise in crime since 1914, draw up impressive graphic devices to present the statistics, and then ask the reader to share their conclusion that the rise in crime since 1914 was a direct result of the *Weeks* decision. For most readers, our application of statistics would have been naïve.

Likewise, if the authors harbored a deep resentment toward the educated person in law enforcement, they *could* perhaps, assemble data to prove that the educated police officer made fewer arrests than the officer of limited education, and ask the reader to join their conclusion that the educated policeman was constitutionally incapable of becoming a "real policeman." Yet, in fact, the educated officer might be doing a better job in preventing crime and disorder, and in protecting personal liberties; in fact, his fewer arrests might all be good arrests with almost 100 per cent conviction. And, in fact, the "real policeman" of limited education might be making large numbers of arrests prematurely, or improperly, with a resultant low conviction rate, and, by illegal methods, breeding disrespect for the law and thus increasing ultimate crime rates. The probing mind would look behind the bare statistics.

Too, if the authors shared the old view that any "real policeman" should be of imposing physical stature, they *could* derive data indicating that the shorter law enforcement officer had many more contacts requiring the use of force than the giants of the agency, and ask the reader to join them in pressing for the continuation of high minimum height requirements. Although the data might be properly gathered and presented, there might be a failure to indicate that the short officer had more contacts of that nature because he worked in a certain area, or because he worked harder and had more overall contacts than his larger colleagues. Also, the presentation might fail to indicate that the training program for self-defense and subject control was inadequate. (The authors keep in mind a certain FBI zone school self-defense and subject-control instructor of formidable talents who must surely have stretched to meet the 5′ 7″ minimum height requirement of the Bureau.) Thus, too, would easy statistical manipulation in order to "make a point" do a great disservice to the vocation. Students should peruse the excellent article by Kamisar, Yale (1972). "How to Use, Abuse—And Fight Back With—Crime Statistics." *Oklahoma Law Review,* 25:239-258.

Emotional and Sensational Approaches to Data must be avoided. Statistics can be misused when considering crime rates, particularly if emotion replaces reason, and sensationalism confuses objectivity.

True enough, crime rates are increasing many times the rate of population increase. But should one conclude that police agencies are inept and helpless? That the nation is in deadly peril from the threat of criminal takeover? That teenagers are totally abandoned to wanton criminality? That violent crimes (murder, rape, robbery, aggravated assault) are so out of hand that panic is justifiable? That the Negro is responsible for the majority of crime increases? No. Distinctions must be made.

Police today are more efficient, crime reporting is more accurate, and data is more massive. Criminal behavior is a fact of history, and has been so throughout the life of this nation. Today, crime is pinpointed and recorded more precisely than ever before, publicized through a wide variety of media, and the subject of widespread argumentation and debate. But this does *not* mean that police are helpless and that the nation is in deadly peril.

Teenage crime has been a fact of history throughout the life of this nation. But today, there are more teenagers, and because juvenile criminality is sensational news, people are more conscious of teenage crime.

Violent crime has been a fact of history throughout the life of this nation. But even today, of total major crime, only about 14 per cent is in the area of murder, rape, robbery and aggravated assault—crimes against the *person*. About 86 per cent of the total major crime is in the area of larcenies, burglaries, and auto thefts—crimes against *property*.

Five times as many people are killed by automobiles as by murder, but murder seems to elicit more public concern. Yet, seven out of eight murders are committed by friends or relatives, not by strangers. Even though auto thefts indicate an amount of stolen property in excess of $360,000,000, three out of four auto thefts are cases of joy-riding by juveniles, with the vehicles returned to the owners within three or four hours.

Only about five per cent of the Negro population in any American community are involved in the commission of major crime. (And in 95 per cent of the cases of murder and rape, both victim and offender are of the same race.)

Crime by poor people, economically disadvantaged, educationally deficient, and socially rejected, has been a fact of history throughout the life of this nation. The Irish, Jewish, and Italian immigrant has been faced with the problem of ghetto crime, but with the American Negro, the problem today is more complex. The Irish, Jewish and Italian youth could get jobs with relatively little education and "learn on the job," but the American Negro today faces a labor market shrinking due to automation, and employment opportunities which require special skills and education acquired prior to hiring. The American Negro also faces more difficulties in integration and assimilation than did the Irish, Jewish and Italian resident of the earlier ghettos.

There *is* a sizeable amount of crime in the Negro ghetto, but the victim, ninety-nine times out of a hundred, is a Negro. Only by increasing opportunities for education, for employment, and for decent housing will this problem be abated—and such will entail the elimination of discrimination and ghettos from the American community.

Students of law enforcement, when discussing statistics of crime, whether they relate to the rates, types of offenses, age or race of the offender, must not allow emotion and popular apprehension to displace rational analysis.

This is not to say that the problem of crime is not serious, or in need of prompt and wholehearted efforts. It is to say that emotional and sensational judgments do not contribute to any effective solutions.

Students must learn statistical methods so that they can contribute to proper application of the scientific method, and so that they can make discerning interpretations of data. Perhaps Chesterton was right when he said that statistics should be used in the same way that an inebriate uses a lamp post—"for support, not illumination."

DISRESPECT FOR AUTHORITY. Finally, we would point out that most dangerous negative trend of all: the increasing disrespect for authority—God's or man's. Unfortunately (for the simplicity we'd like) this often means rejection of God's authority only as it is filtered through the institutions which claim monopoly on interpreting his will—and the rejection of societal authority as being a blind for the perverse imposition of the vested interests and security-insurance of the social class in power.

Thus, the truly objective law enforcement student must wrestle with a problem which is at least twofold—he must not only "psych out" and propose how to deal with the willful rebel, the truly self-centered, lawless solipsist who flouts laws because he will accept no law but his own, but he must also adjust to and treat in a totally different manner the mentality and person of the alienated minority rebel (who bears years of scarred experience which say the law is not for him), the conscientious objector (whose rejection of laws, albeit mistaken, is often out of an intense moral sense), or the campus rebel who feels that he has never experienced a country of which he can be proud (and therefore be moved to obey its laws).

Positive Trends. There are several trends in law enforcement *today* which give great promise for the future of the service.

MANPOWER IMROVEMENT. One very positive trend is in the area of manpower improvement. Most agencies are elevating the qualifications for career employment, eliminating unrealistic barriers such as the pre-entrance residence requirement, and the strict seniority system, and actively recruiting a "new breed" of personnel. And most enlightened agencies have paid increasingly emphatic attention to the elimination of the immoral and incompetent officer.

PRE-SERVICE EDUCATION. Pre-service educational programs are developing rapidly throughout the United States, with about 300 city colleges, junior colleges, colleges and universities offering short-courses, institute, and degree programs which lead to certificates and degrees from Associate of Arts to Doctorates. Ever growing are the academic institutions offering programs preparatory to careers in the administration of criminal justice: law enforcement—police science, police administration, public safety, criminalistics; criminal justice; criminology; corrections, and related studies. These programs enroll not only full-time students, but, in many cases, substantial numbers of practitioners working in the administration of criminal justice.

Some of these institutions have developed "field training" or "internship" programs in cooperation with criminal justice agencies, whereby students in their senior year attend the educational institution and, as well, spend time in criminal justice agencies in order to gain perspective.

Most of the academic programs require a thorough study of the organization, management, and operation of police services, the areas of specialized technique and procedure, together with a consideration of their legal and philosophical bases, and as well, require a well-balanced liberal arts regimen so that the graduates will not only be knowledgeable and informed, but also able to exercise authority wisely and maintain an absolute integrity of character in keeping with the goal of a professionalized police service.

Certainly, one can appreciate the fact that law enforcement vocations, during the past half-century, have evolved from simple jobs, requiring simple qualifications, to complex professional activities requiring great capacity for highly specialized knowledge and technique.

Traditionally, the police services have required their administrators to rise from the ranks. This policy, coupled with long outstanding low entrance requirements, has led to a shortage of professionally trained leaders. Until recently, college trained people have been reluctant to enter the lower echelons of the police service, but the trend has changed, and as more and more college trained people are proving themselves capable of rising to the top, they, in turn, are encouraging college graduates to enter the public service.

Today, as agencies engaged in law enforcement move toward a professional service, the colleges are becoming the training centers for tomorrow's administrators. Most of these pre-service programs are dedicated to the purpose of developing police leadership and are built around the future, rather than around the past. The studies comprise a balance between the "tool" or vocational type course, and the administrative type course, and students are expected to prepare themselves for supervisory and management roles, even though entrance to the police service is usually at the operational level.

IN-SERVICE TRAINING. Training programs are being expanded by almost every police agency at every level of government, such as the programs offered by the New York City Police Department, the Los Angeles County Sheriff's Department, the Michigan State Police, and the Immigration and Naturalization Service of the federal government. Recruit or threshold training, refresher or advanced officer training, specialty training, supervisory training, and executive development programs are no longer rare phenomena. Some agencies have developed cadet programs, in order to bring people of younger years into the service, and some of these cadet programs are carefully geared with local academic programs.[3]

---

[3] The New York City Police Academy conducts all its in-service courses at college level. In 1955, when the former Police Commissioner Michael J. Murphy was Commanding Officer of the Academy, he pioneered an undergraduate and graduate program conducted cooperatively between the City University of New York and the Academy. A number of other law enforcement agencies have since entered into active cooperation with local colleges and universities along these lines for their personnel. In most instances, the colleges and universities avail themselves of qualified instructors from the working practitioners of the local agencies for vocational courses, and use the instructional resources of the institution for background and general education courses necessary to a complete liberal arts curriculum. California State University, Long Beach, for example, utilizes as instructors active practitioners from Long Beach Police Department, Los Angeles County Sheriff's Department, Los Angeles Police Department, Long

INTERNATIONAL COOPERATION. The International Criminal Police Organization (INTERPOL) is an example of worldwide joint effort. Over 50 years old, INTERPOL is headquartered in Saint Cloud, France (a Paris suburb), in a modern seven-story building, with a staff of 120 police officers. On file are records of some two million name indexes, 100,000 fingerprint cards, and 6,000 photographs of specialized international criminals.

The 114 member countries exchange information and requests through their respective National Central Bureaus (NCBs). Since 1962, ours has been located in the Treasury Department—based on Treasury's efforts in the classic international offenses of counterfeiting, smuggling, financial frauds, and narcotics. In the United Kingdom, the NCB is in Scotland Yard; in Japan, the NCB is in the Japanese National Police; in Argentina it is in the Policia Federal; in Australia, in the Melbourne City Police Department; in West Germany, the NCB is located in the Bundeskriminalamt in Wiesbaden. Each NCB is linked with all police agencies in the country, and with the other 113 countries.

INTERPOL operates an international police radio network and utilizes international telex. Communications are rapid and the NCB in the United States can be connected with the NCB in Australia in ten seconds. Fugitive notices are disseminated by NCBs to immigration, customs, and police units and have accounted for thousands of locations of international fugitives. The operations are non political; no "political" cases are accepted. An example of *professional* police operation!

State Sponsored or Mandated Standards and Training. Although the FBI has done yeoman service in providing expertise for the training of local police through a "zone school" program, there is an increasing interest in standards and training at the state level. California, for example, has a Commission on Peace Officer Standards and Training, which, by subvention, offers assistance to local units of law enforcement in the training area. This group is engrossed in the development of a certification program which may eventually provide for the issuance of basic, intermediate, and advanced certificates or credentials, and which may eventually be required by local communities as a qualification for entrance or promotion. Thirty-eight States now have standards and/or training programs supervised by boards, commissions, or councils. These operations vary from the most minimal training sessions to very sophisticated programs involving liaison with educational institutions; minimum standards for recruitment, selection, and training; examination and certification; research; and extensive publications activity.

Beach City Prosecutor's Office, and the California Highway Patrol, as well as the full-time instructional staff of the college.

It is interesting and edifying, to note that the New York City Police Department sponsors a scholarship program to ensure that no police officer is denied the opportunity to obtain a college degree.

Criminal Justice Standards and Goals. Standards for police officer recruitment and training have long been accepted as desirable by the criminal justice profession. Recently, however, it has been recognized that the need for criminal justice standards and goals goes far beyond the limited scope of past endeavors. The authors note with approval a number of significant developments targeted toward system-wide standard setting.

One of the very first acts of LEAA Administrator Jerris Leonard after his appointment in 1971 was to announce the creation of the National Advisory Commission on Criminal Justice Standards and Goals. The Honorable Russell W. Peterson, Governor of Delaware, was named Chairman of the new Commission which will set national goals, performance standards, and priorities for improving the nation's criminal justice system. Governor Peterson is Chairman of the National Governors' Conference Committee on Crime Reduction and Public Safety. Sheriff Peter J. Pitchess of Los Angeles, California, was named Vice Chairman of the Standards and Goals Commission.

The 22-member Commission is composed of members of the criminal justice system, state and local officials, and representatives of citizens groups and businesses. Twelve task forces were originally set up to assist Commission members as they work with state and local governments and the criminal justice community to fashion meaningful yardsticks for measuring progress in the criminal justice field.

Governor Peterson said Commission members had studied the initial 12-task-force structure devised for the Commission and concluded that it would cause serious problems in coordination and duplication. The Commission has now been reorganized into four operational task forces, which will submit detailed staff reports in the areas of Police, Courts, Corrections and Community Crime Prevention.

Eight other task forces—Civil Disorders; Community Involvement; Drug Abuse; Education, Training and Manpower Development; Information Systems and Statistics; Juvenile Delinquency; Organized Crime, and Research and Development—will function in an advisory fashion, commenting upon the reports prepared by the four operational task forces.

Governor Peterson noted that the subject areas of the advisory task forces are topics of special concern which cut across the four operational areas.

"The contributions of these eight advisory groups is vital if our final reports are to address crime and delinquency effectively," he said.

The purpose of the Commission is to establish concrete standards and goals and to allow the dozens of state planning agencies and the hundreds of regional planning agencies to measure the problems in their own areas, and to see how and where they are ahead or behind these suggested standards, and by how much. They will then, presumably know exactly where they want to go, how to get there, how much it will cost and how long it will take. Basically, the task of the Commission is to provide a working blueprint for the reform of the entire criminal justice system—police, courts and corrections.

Very significant efforts at standard setting are also being undertaken by the American Law Institute (ALI), the International Association of Chiefs of Police (IACP), and the American Bar Association (ABA). The last-named Association has established a major project on Standards for Criminal Justice. In March, 1972, the twelve-member Advisory Committee on the Police Function issued a tentative draft of *Standards Relating to the Urban Police Function.* This important contribution to criminal justice professional literature will undoubtedly rank in importance with National Crime Commission's *Police Task Force Report.*

The Urban Police Function delineates and discusses ten approved standards which contain much food for thought, especially for practitioners and students of American law enforcement. Both groups need to become fully informed concerning them, and to recognize their significance: guidelines that merit the thoughtful consideration of all Americans who have concerns about the quality of their police services.

It is important to note, however, that the approved standards are in fact "standards" in the loosest sense of the term. The standards, for the most part, represent an approach for dealing with the critical problems and needs confronting virtually all police agencies. The use of the phrase "urban police function" is meant only to stress the fact that police problems in the large city are most critical and that some of the recommended solutions are not feasible in the very small police agency. However, the report does state that the basic principles advocated in the standards are applicable to all police.

Appendix D of this text (page 473) presents the final approved summary of these American Bar Association standards. They stress philosophy, role, policy formulation, public participation, accountability, due process, and are imaginative, creative, and innovative. They do *not* push for more repressive laws, gadgetry, firepower, or massive force. They do *not* perpetuate the heavy-handed priorities of traditional criminal justice processes. It will be very interesting to compare them with the LEAA goals, standards, and priorities to be issued by the LEAA Advisory Commission on Standards and Goals in early 1973, and all students are urged to do so.

The conclusion of the ABA Committee very well sums up its own standards and goals: "Greater understanding of the function of the police in a democratic society is necessary if there is to be needed improvement in the quality of police service."

To this the authors happily say "Amen!"

Governmental Study Commissions. Even though our people have perused reports of governmental commissions for 176 years, beginning with George Washington's 1794 Whiskey Rebellion commission, only recent commission reports have dealt heavily with criminal justice and its concerns.

On July 23, 1965, *The President's Commission on Law Enforcement and Administration of Justice* was established by President Johnson. Known as the *National Crime Commission,* this Presidential Commission divided its probe between five Task Forces: Assessment of the Crime Problem; Police and Public Safety; Administration of Justice; Corrections; and Science and Technology. On February 18, 1967, the Commission released its first report, "The Challenge of Crime in a Free Society," which embodies all the major findings drawn from its examination of every facet of crime and law enforcement in America.

Six principal themes run through the Crime Commission report: 1) Crime prevention is of paramount importance; 2) The system of criminal justice must itself be just and it must have the respect and cooperation of all citizens; 3) Throughout the criminal justice system, better-trained people are desperately needed and they must be used more effectively; 4) A far broader—and more profound—range of treatment is needed than the present correctional system provides; 5) Access to better information and to deeper and broader research is vital to police and correctional agencies; 6) Substantially greater resources must be devoted to improving the entire criminal justice system.

The authors of *Introduction to Law Enforcement and Criminal Justice* regard this report, the first significant national survey since *Wickersham* in 1931, as of great importance and recommend its study to all citizens, and, particularly, to all students of criminal justice.

Students should become familiar with the recent reports issued in the criminal justice area, and, at the very least, become thoroughly familiar with the following: [4]

1. *Commission on Law Enforcement and Administration of Justice* (Katzenbach), 1967, particularly: *Summary Report: The Challenge of Crime in a Free Society;* the *Task Force Reports* on *The Police,* on *Courts,* and on *Corrections.*
2. *Commission on Civil Disorders* (Kerner), 1968, *Report.*
3. *Commission on Causes and Prevention of Violence* (Eisenhower), 1969, *Report.*
4. *Commission on Campus Unrest* (Scranton), 1970, *Report.*
5. *Commission on Civil Rights* (Hesberg), 1970, *Report.*

---

[4] All available from U.S. Government Printing Office, Washington, D.C. 20402.

6. *Commission on Obscenity and Pornography* (Lockhart), 1970, *Report*.
7. *Commission on Marihuana and Drug Abuse* (Shafer), 1972, *Report*.

LEAA. In 1965, an *Office of Law Enforcement Assistance* (OLEA) was established within the U.S. Department of Justice, and the Attorney General was authorized to make grants to, or contract with, public or private nonprofit agencies to improve training of personnel, advance the capabilities of law enforcement bodies, and assist in the prevention and control of crime. The enabling act authorized the Attorney General to conduct studies, render technical assistance, evaluate the effectiveness of programs undertaken, and disseminate knowledge gained as a result of such projects. Police, courts, corrections, and other mechanisms for the prevention and control of crime were all within its scope.

Subsequent to the passage of the Omnibus Crime Control and Safe Streets Act in 1968, the program was retitled *Law Enforcement Assistance Administration* (LEAA) and today plays a key role in virtually all current developments in the criminal justice system, particularly those related to advanced technology.

During 1969, 1970, 1971, 1972 and 1973, the program received $63 million, $268 million, $529 million, $699 million, and $850 million. Appropriations now total more than $2,409,000,000!

Except for the Ford Foundation which has funded the *Police Foundation* to the comparatively modest tune of $75 million, no other major influence appears upon the horizon. It is essential, therefore, that we become aware of LEAA in all of its manifestations.

During 1971, LEAA was drastically reorganized to provide for additional regional offices with far greater authority. Also, three line offices were established in Washington, D.C.:

1. The *National Institute of Law Enforcement and Criminal Justice* which continues to have responsibility for LEAA research and development programs;
2. The *Office of Criminal Justice Assistance* which is responsible for actual grant operations, including supervising the 10 regional offices;
3. The *Office of Operations Support* which provides for administrative management of the Agency.

Jerris Leonard, the new Administrator of LEAA, in announcing the reorganization, stated:

A great deal has been accomplished by the LEAA program in less than three years. A nationwide crime control program is a reality; and it is a reality in every state, where the states are carrying out programs in cooperation with their cities and counties. . . .

But my candid feeling is that the LEAA program has not done enough; that it has weaknesses which have been a brake on progress; and that major changes must be undertaken now.[5]

Criticism of the LEAA has come from a number of sources and it is currently being carefully scrutinized by the General Accounting Office (GAO) which has taken several states to task for using LEAA funds to support social science oriented programs when funds were available from other sources. However, the most scathing criticism has come from Charles H. Rogavin who served as Administrator of LEAA from March 25, 1969, until June 1, 1970, and since his resignation has been President of the Ford-funded Police Foundation. His remarks to a House of Representatives Sub-committee are so revealing of the true nature of LEAA and the critical and enormous importance of this agency to the future of criminal justice that they are quoted at length.[6]

There is a tendency, in looking at the performance of LEAA during its three year life, to see its specific failures more clearly than its general, and far more significant failures. Questions about LEAA overlap with other federal programs and about such matters as inadequate auditing are important, and I do not minimize them. But what is far more important about LEAA, in my judgment, is that it has in the main failed to give policy leadership to the criminal justice agencies it supports, and has, therefore, become a giant subsidy program, making little contribution to the improvement of criminal justice administration in the nation.

That is not what Congress intended when it created the LEAA. As I understand it, Congress's interest in passing the Omnibus Safe Streets and Crime Control Act was to initiate a program of improvement and reform in the nonsystem of criminal justice throughout the nation.

The landmark report of the President's Commission on Law Enforcement and the Administration of Justice had documented deficiencies and provided a blueprint for remedial action. The Commission knew that a substantial investment would be required to improve the system but it also knew that money alone would not bring improvement. What was, and continues to be necessary is that people involved in criminal justice work enlist in the reform effort through planning and programs. It is easy to talk about creating systems. It is far more difficult to do it.

First, there must be agreement on definitions and second, agreement on issues. One cannot say that at the beginning of the LEAA or now, criminal justice administrators are on the same wavelength. And one cannot say that LEAA has made much of an effort to get them there. The best that one can say is that there is more commonality of interest and sophistication now than there was before 1967. The Congressional mandate that comprehensive planning be undertaken was a concept of good intention and good sense. But legislative declarations are not self-implementing. The mandate had to be implemented by people—some who had never been in criminal justice before, others who had

---

[5] LEAA (1971). *Newsletter*, July. LEAA, Washington, D.C.

[6] Reported in 1971, *Crime Control Digest*, October 7.

never engaged in planning, and practically none who were experienced in criminal justice planning.

It was easy to underestimate the complexity of what Congress asked for—comprehensive criminal justice planning. There was no precedent for coordinated planning in police, courts and correctional reform. And sadly, the lessons of other, successful federal programs, like the space program were ignored and we did not engage in a manpower development program to provide people for the complex tasks. Consequently, the planning has been of lesser quality and lesser value than Congress envisioned.

The second major problem in achieving Congress's objectives has been that too much money has become available too quickly for action projects. This program has grown from $63 million in 1969 to $529 million in 1971. Without effective planning, without development of people who can do the planning, without strong administration of the overall program, the LEAA has been compelled by the sheer availability of money to spend less than judiciously. The unavailability of sophisticated and experienced criminal justice planners, and the pressure on everyone to spend too much too quickly has been compounded by the public's simplistic notions about crime. I think that many people truly believed that the existence of LEAA and federal money would lead quickly to declines in crime. Those expectations have led criminal justice agencies to spend on things they hoped would lead to short-run statistical achievements, rather than on things which might lay the basis for real improvement. The public's lack of interest in improving just those parts of the criminal justice system in which real impact on crime might be made—for example, corrections—has discouraged the kind of investment in the correctional system which might, in the long run, make a real difference.

The third major problem is that the role of the LEAA has been murky since the beginning. The statute, as you are well aware, created a bloc grant program which places basic policy responsibility on the states. LEAA has no direct operational responsibility over the state's criminal justice elements, but in theory is given the authority to guide the reform of these elements. This would seem to require that LEAA establish objectives. But it has not been done. I cannot emphasize enough how significant this failure has been. It has, in my judgment, had a debilitating effect on everything LEAA has done. It has meant that although Congress has appropriated $860 million so far, there have been no priorities and no clear policies other than Congressional direction to emphasize organized crime and civil disturbance programs. There have been almost no directions or goals established by LEAA. Further there has been no attempt to measure what LEAA does. And indeed, most shocking of all, there is not even a knowledge of what LEAA funds are being spent on. But here is a program which has no goals, which does not measure, evaluate, or even inventory what it does; which has established no standards by which it can be measured, or by which the performance of the agencies it funds can be measured.

One other aspect of the LEAA program, the National Institute, was created to do highly directed, practical research on important issues in the criminal justice system . . . by this time, the Institute should have developed evaluation methods to be used by state planning agencies, and by LEAA itself. It has not, and so there is no evaluation of anybody's efforts—at the state, local or federal levels. The Institute should have been developing action designs to be funded by other parts of LEAA. For example, the Law Enforcement Education Program (LEEP) was to help educate criminal justice personnel. But LEEP has paid virtually no attention to curriculum development—consequently, its funds have been used simply to proliferate police science and criminal justice programs throughout the nation.

I would recommend that LEAA disperse no new funds through the bloc grant program until it has established goals and standards. I suggest that its plans and grant goals be more narrowly and realistically drawn, that funds be earmarked and directed at critical needs, that guidelines, yardsticks, and evaluation techniques be developed, and the states be made responsible for meeting goals.

Needless to say, Mr. Rogavin's recommendations have not been heeded and the LEAA program is proceeding merrily on its way. There are very few areas of criminal justice administration which will not be substantially impacted by the directions taken by LEAA in dispensing these monumental funds. Perhaps the one area that will be most directly affected is that of technological development, for this is one of the most obvious needs of criminal justice and it does not lend itself readily to the criticism of being just a subsidy program. The innovation required for such projects and their universal applicability commend themselves to the most scrupulous auditor of grants.

In April, 1972, the Associated Press reported that a branch of the Government Operations Committee, House of Representatives, headed by John Monagan (D. Conn.), had made an in-depth investigation of the bloc-grant program of the Law Enforcement Assistance Administration (LEAA), and that its report stated, of the monies now expended, that "too large a portion of those funds had been wasted on diversion for partisan political purposes, on exorbitant consultants' fees, on equipment and vehicles which are misused or not needed, on excessive payments to equipment suppliers resulting from widespread absence of competitive bidding and unethical relationships between state and local officials and suppliers' representatives," and that the report concludes that the LEAA programs "have been characterized by inefficiency, waste, maladministration, and, in some cases, corruption," and flatly states that the LEAA program has "had no visible impact on the incidence of crime in the United States."[7]

It would seem that police leadership often seems better prepared for comedy roles than serious administration. The emphasis on hardware, and the "smash 'em, bust 'em" philosophy of the police Neanderthal, is seen in many an LEAA proposal. Perhaps the interest of the nation would be better served if the millions of dollars had been utilized to retire the current police leadership and replace it with sensitive and aware people-oriented professionals!

---

[7] Los Angeles *Times*, April 10, 1972, p. 1.

VERA INSTITUTE OF JUSTICE.[8] The Vera Institute of Justice is a nonprofit research organization dedicated to the development of new techniques to improve the administration of criminal justice. Working in close cooperation with the police, courts, and many public and private agencies, the Institute's staff plans and operates demonstration projects which test new ways of safeguarding defendants' rights, saving money and man-hours for official agencies, and providing greater security and service to the public.

The Vera Institute of Justice had its beginning in October, 1961. Louis Schweitzer, a chemical engineer, learned that individuals were held in jail up to a year awaiting trial, not because they were considered unlikely to show in court but because they were unable to post bail. He concluded that these men, presumed innocent before trial, were in effect being penalized because they were poor. Determined to find a solution which would correct this injustice without endangering the public, he established the Vera Foundation which launched the *Manhattan Bail Project* in cooperation with New York University School of Law and the Institute of Judicial Administration; the *Manhattan Summons Project* followed.

MANHATTAN BAIL PROJECT. The project tested the hypothesis that defendants with sufficient "roots in the community" could be safely released on their own recognizance and be depended upon to return to court.

While awaiting arraignment in court detention pens, defendants (with the exception of those arrested for homicide, most narcotics offenses, and certain sex crimes) were interviewed by law students. The defendant was asked specific questions about his background; whether he was working, how long he had held his job, if he supported his family, if he had contacts with relatives in the city, how long he had lived in the city, and how long at his present address. The information was then verified by telephoning a friend, relative, or employer of the defendant. To insure objectivity and equal treatment for all prisoners, each item of information was evaluated by use of a point scale system. The maximum which could be obtained under this evaluation was twelve points. Defendants receiving five or more points were recommended to the court for release on their own recognizance.

The project, conducted for three years, demonstrated not only that judges would significantly increase their rate of releases when given verified information about the defendant, but also that this verified information was a good predictor of a defendant's reliability in returning to court. At the end of the action phase of the Manhattan Bail Project in August, 1964, 3,505 accused persons had been released on recognizance in New York City's Criminal Court. Of these 3,505 persons, 98.5 per cent re-

---

[8] New York Police Department (1966). "Vera Institute of Justice." *Police Management Review, Planning Bureau*, November-December, pp. 3-5.

turned to court when required. Only fifty-six persons—or 1.5 per cent—willfully failed to appear, as compared to a 3 per cent forfeiture rate on bail bonds.

Having developed this new technique, the Vera Foundation proceeded to the second stage of its plan—to implement the procedure on a broader scale. In January, 1964, the Office of Probation in New York City took over the work of the Manhattan Bail Project and extended the Release on Recognizance program.

MANHATTAN SUMMONS PROJECT. During the bail project the Vera staff focused its attention on an area of pre-trial detention not touched by bail reform—the detention in a police station following arrest, transportation to court in a van and the wait in the court pens.

The Vera staff reasoned that a defendant who could be safely released on his own recognizance after arraignment could also be depended upon to appear at arraignment without the necessity for police custody. To test this idea, the Vera Foundation, in close cooperation with the New York City Police Department, set up the Manhattan Summons Project in April, 1964. This experiment involved the issuance of summonses to persons charged with such minor crimes as petit larceny, simple assault, and malicious mischief.

Under the terms of the project, the defendant is brought to the local precinct station house where he is searched and questioned by the arresting officer. If he is possibly eligible for the issuance of a summons he is interviewed by law students using the same background questions and point-weight system as in the bail project. If the defendant has sufficient ties in the community and they are verified, a recommendation for his release on a summons is made to the desk officer. If the desk officer, whose decision is final, approves, the defendant is released immediately from the station house with a summons to appear in criminal court on a preselected date.

Of the first 2,676 cases recorded in the experimental phase of the Manhattan Summons Project, 1,014 cases were recommended for issuance of a summons. This recommendation was accepted in 987 or 96 per cent of the cases. As of June 1, 1966, only twenty-six persons—2.6 per cent—had failed to appear in court to answer summonses. Of the more than 900 persons appearing in court, the trial judge set bail in only twelve cases; the remaining were released to appear on their own recognizance for trial.

The second Vera project demonstrated that a technique which benefited both the defendant and society could be compatible with the aims of law enforcement. Summons release allows the defendant freedom pending trial to continue his employment, provide for his family, and retain counsel to prepare a proper defense. The police save many man-hours of custodial time and the cost of transporting prisoners to court. It also resulted in reducing the overcrowding in the Department of Corrections detention facilities.

Recognizing the benefit of the summons procedure in minor criminal cases, the administration of the Police Department announced a dramatic extension of the concept. Beginning December 1, 1966, all precincts in Manhattan instituted the summons procedure, with specially trained police officers interviewing and rating the defendants. Moreover, the Department made a further advance by extending this procedure from the few criminal charges originally considered to most non-fingerprintable misdemeanors or offenses.

In June 1966, a generous grant from the Ford Foundation enabled the Vera Foundation to reorganize and expand its activities as the Vera Institute of Justice. The goal of the Institute is to achieve innovative reform in the complete range of activities involved in the criminal process. The method of the Institute is the approach tested and proved successful in the Bail and Summons Projects, specifically: (a) the use of the small demonstration project to test new procedures, (b) the careful recording and evaluation of the project's results, and (c) the implementation of the proved technique on a broad scale as a regular, official procedure.

The authors of this text believe that such types of innovation, experimentation, demonstration, and creative change must become *everyday* occurrences in *all* police agencies if the goals of law enforcement are to be effectively accomplished.

CRIME PREVENTION UNITS. The city of Winston-Salem, North Carolina, assigned 10 per cent of police manpower to *crime prevention* duties, and achieved significant results in developing police-community cooperation, reducing crime and delinquency hazards, and providing professional police services to the community. Forty years ago, commenting on the Wickersham Report, August Vollmer said:

> No city can afford to be without a unit which will devote its whole time to Crime Prevention. Such a unit must receive official recognition in large enough measure to command respect from the members of the force and other community agencies. The workers must be scientifically trained for the task. No element of political influence should ever enter into their selection and a definite professional standard should be maintained. The crime prevention unit, by reason of its position in the city government, might initiate far-reaching plans for crime prevention through the medium of the school system. Such work, while in the nature of pre-delinquency activities, might in the long run be of broader value than any actual palliatives.[9]

---

[9] Vollmer, August (1932). "Abstract of the Wickersham Police Report." *The Journal of Criminal Law and Criminology,* 22:716.

Such units will probably become more common as police agencies take ever more interest in crime prevention as a legitimate police activity.

SINCERE POLICE DEDICATION. The most affirmative and positive trend of all today, is the *growing desire of law enforcement personnel to achieve, first, a more effective and edifying quality of service, and thence, greater public recognition in the forms of increased respect, cooperation, and support, both moral and economic.*

The authors believe that the following commentary (consisting of the *Conclusion* of the monograph *The Functions of the Police in Modern Society* by Egon Bittner, Ph.D., Brandeis University) is an example of brilliant analysis of the current police scene, and representative of the more motivated attitudes held by both academicians and practitioners.

The Psalmist spoke truly for all times when he said, "except the Lord keep the city, the watchman waketh but in vain." One of the greatest risks in all attempts to define the role of the police in society is to overestimate their significance. They are surely not the "thin blue line" that saves us from being inundated by depredation and chaos. Order and safety depend primarily on other factors and, in real peril, they could not be saved even if half of us took to policing the other half. In fact, it has been said that, "one might reasonably maintain that society would not go to pieces even if the state should exercise no coercion whatever." This opinion is probably as misleading in its implications as are the truculent and imperious voices which say that unless we let the police have their way they will refuse to play ball and leave us facing destruction. A more pragmatic view is forced to acknowledge that the availability of the police does make life safer and more orderly than it would be otherwise, but it refuses to accept that we are at their mercy.

The approach that avoids apocalyptic visions is called upon to give a practical interpretation to the belief that the police are of one cloth with the society they service. Certainly it does not compel the conclusion that whatever exists, exists for adequate reasons. The test of time, which a conservative view is apt to emphasize, is a tricky standard. It sometimes protects arrangements that have lasted merely because fear or neglect have prevented scrutiny. There is little doubt that many aspects of the modern police are just such survivals.

At an earlier time, when most of the people were illiterate or barely literate, when physicians knew less about diseases than a modern practical nurse, when lawyers barely knew how to use a few forms and were considered educated if they had a cursory acquaintance with Blackstone, policemen with a background of eight years of school were adequately prepared for the job. In any case, the definition of their tasks virtually never brought them into contact with people who were superior to them in any important respect. But all this has changed in the past two generations, and the police, by hewing to old standings, is falling back from year to year, increasingly becoming a field of opportunities for those who can do no better than join the simpler service occupations.

The failure of the police to keep up with the general upgrading of all occupations is augmented by the fact that, whereas at one time a certain degree of crudeness was acceptable, it can no longer be tolerated. In the first place, the policeman of the past had fewer matters to attend to. Under conditions where the vast majority of those official regulations of conduct we now take for granted were unheard of, keeping the peace and enforcing the law were relatively simple matters. This does not mean that social controls did not function, but only that they typically did not involve police interventions. Those problems that were beyond the scope of informal remedies and self-help, i.e., the problems that did require police attention, were ordinarily quite clear-cut and required no great subtleties of perception. Precisely the opposite is the case today. For a variety of reasons the number of problems people no longer feel competent to attend to themselves has multiplied enormously. Moreover, under conditions of anonymity prevailing in urban life, order in public life can be maintained only by formal means of control. Thus, while it once may have been sufficient if an officer knew the difference between a corpse and a live body, he must now, owing to the fact that he is inevitably involved in handling vast arrays of all sorts of human problems, be knowledgeable and judicious about virtually everything. In any case, crudeness on his part becomes quickly apparent, and it frustrates both him and the one who depends on his service.

In addition to the earlier grossness of the police task, the admissibility of crude police work in the past was connected with the then prevailing view that people on whom police attention centered deserved no better handling. Nothing the police could conceivably do to them would appreciably worsen their lot. People who were fair and considerate did not attract police interest, and those who did could not lay claim to being dealt with fairly and considerately. Nor did "those people" seem to object to the treatment they received; at least, the voice of their objections was not heard, let alone acknowledged. But this too is a thing of the past. Today policemen direct, control, and discipline persons from all walks of life, and crudeness on their part places them in a position of significant disadvantage. To be sure, crudeness can yet prevail but only at a cost sober judgment would find intolerable. Fear may prevent me from protesting the traffic patrolman's vulgarity but it will not inspire my trust in him as a public official. Nor will my feeling change by knowing that his manner was "provoked" by what he took to be uncooperativeness on my part. Waiters, psychiatrists, cab drivers, and teachers know that the handling of uncooperativeness is a necessary part of their occupational skill and it is not too much to expect the same of policemen. But it is not good manners that I expect. Instead, I should like, in my dealings with policemen, to be able to perceive them as qualified to do the serious and important work I know they have to do. To be sure, politeness does not indicate this, but the man who does not know that he should avoid offending me, or who works up more feeling than he can safely contain, is surely not the one to be trusted with anything more demanding than some simple service routine. But the sensitivity of the likes of me is the least important argument against police crudeness. Far louder than our voice sounds the voice of those who have until recently suffered the impositions of crudeness in silence. Here crudeness is not a simple mistake but specifically subversive. A policeman who appreciates the likely consequences of an approach that will cause resentment and indulges in it nevertheless contributes to what he is paid to prevent. It will not do to say that in police work the causing of resentment is often unavoidable. Precisely for that reason it must be avoided wherever possible.

It is sometimes said that the police must adopt as their work ethic the belief that no man's claim to dignity and civil rights is smaller than any other man's claim, and that neither age nor social status, nor race, nor even deviant conduct diminishes entitlement to decent treatment. Though this certainly appears desirable, it is possible that it matters less than the simple empirical fact that in degrading others they must stoop to the level of the degraded.

While civility and humaneness are desirable qualities in any person, and their possession may be indispensable for competent police work, they do not suffice. The opposite of the crude policeman is not one imbued with civic virtues and possessed of a polite manner; instead, he is the informed, deliberating, and technically efficient professional who knows that he must operate within the limits set by a moral and legal trust.

It has been urged in this study that the only way open toward the professionalization of the police leads through institutions of higher learning, more specifically, through professional schools of police work. This was urged not because academic scholarship has now much to offer that will make police work more methodical than it is but because in our society the university has become the sole home of every form of research, study, and exercise of critical reason. No occupation can hope to achieve dignity, seriousness, and importance that does not go this route. Of course, an occupation that has roots in the university can no longer encompass menial duties. But this will merely remove the incongruity of requiring that men who have the power and the duty to make decisions that affect permanently the welfare, prosperity, even the very existence of citizens, do work that can be safely entrusted to unskilled labor.

The public trust that authorizes and restricts police practices can be simply stated. A society committed to the achievement of peace by pacific means has created an institution with the monopoly to employ non-negotiably coercive force in situations where its use is unavoidably necessary. Procedures that go against the ideal may perhaps be excused occasionally, but they can never be defended. Above all, force may not be used for any other purpose but to effect restraint. To use it to teach someone a lesson is not only a violation of trust; it is also silly, for there are scarcely any other two things that are as completely opposed as violence and teaching.

It has been said that the creation of a highly trained, elite police force magnifies the danger of tyranny. This warning must not be taken lightly. It should be entered on the list of warnings against the other possible tyrannies of psychiatrists, engineers, and social workers. The simple fact is that we have become dependent on the availability of these professionals and we continually expect them to improve their methods, and thus become more powerful. Every power to do good is also a power to do harm and everything that can save life can also destroy it. This is the paradox of technique—the better it is perfected, the more neutral it becomes, and the more readily it is available for both good and evil. But in the last analysis this is not a peculiarly modern phenomenon. One of the greatest and one of the oldest themes of humanistic reflection concerns the tragic puzzle that men who seek to do right sometimes do wrong. Thus, having begun this section by invoking the Psalmist, it might perhaps be fitting to close it with an ancient Pythagorean prayer:

King Zeus, grant us good whether prayed for or unsought by us;
But that which we ask amiss, do thou avert.

* * *

This kind of exposition is becoming more frequent in the literature of criminal justice. Perhaps it is writings in this vein that influence the wondrous, inexplicable, extraordinary rebellions by idealistic practitioners—Wardens like Murton, Judges like Sirica, and Policemen like Serpico—often seen by colleagues as martyrs or holy fools.

Certainly, the time has arrived for sincere police dedication, sincere judicial dedication, sincere correctional dedication—and for quite some time this positive movement will be seen as offensively single-minded and uncharitable. For many people, the *professional* in criminal justice units will be seen as ridiculous, fanatical, freaky—not as a serious person adhering to an ideal of morality, or honor, or faith. But, perhaps, our professionals can educate our nation by their example, and give some hope to those who dispair of a really just and fair criminal justice system. And this can be the most significant positive trend of all! We must make it happen!

TOPICS FOR DISCUSSION

1. What types of research relating to law enforcement are now underway in this locale?
2. What kinds of legislation, in this locale, would provide for more effective and edifying law enforcement?
3. Will a "double standard" remain a "fact of life" for American police operations of the future?
4. Is it fact or fancy that some police tend to be defensive, hyper-sensitive, suspicious, distrustful, and insecure?
5. Are the statistics relating to law enforcement in this locale valid? Properly correlated? Honorably utilized? Objectively presented?
6. What amount of state sponsored, or state mandated, standards and training exist in this state?

Chapter XXIII

CAREER ORIENTATION—CONCLUSIONS

As LONG AS THERE ARE PEOPLE, there will be a need for criminal justice. Today, the demand far exceeds the supply of well-trained personnel. Such a need promises great opportunity for competent, dedicated young men and women of capacity and character.

CAREER ORIENTATION

The financial returns of a criminal justice career in an enlightened agency are usually adequate for dignified living—the necessities of life, plus a reasonable amount of comfort—and the current trend points to even more adequate compensation.

Entrance pay, at the lowest levels, varies widely throughout the nation, and according to the level of government, but usually ranges between $10,000 and $15,000. Supervisory and middle management personnel generally receive between $15,000 and $20,000 per year, and top administrators in the criminal justice vocation receive compensation that may vary from $20,000 to $40,000 annually. Size of the agency, regional area, compensation of other personnel in the governmental jurisdiction, and adjacent industrial and commercial organizations, will affect the remuneration of the law enforcement officer.

Salary is important, and cannot be minimized as an inducement for the recruitment of good personnel. However, the most important returns are in terms of service satisfactions—the knowledge that one is contributing to the well-being of society by protecting and assisting fellow-citizens, and by neutralizing or treating those fellow citizens whose actions are dangerous to life and property, peace and tranquility. Those who cannot appreciate this view—and who are primarily interested in material reward—should not think of criminal justice as a career field.

Physical Qualifications. The physical qualifications (height, weight, eyesight, etc.) vary from time to time, and from agency to agency. Those who are interested in a career appointment with a particular agency should investigate the physical requirements of that agency so that they might determine, in advance, their ability to meet those requirements.

A physical examination is usually required, to insure that the candidate is in a healthy condition, and, most often, any candidate with glandular disorders, diseases, deformities or any other condition which would limit or compromise career employment is rejected. Many police agencies require a physical agility examination, consisting of obstacle courses, and tests for muscular condition and coordination, in order to insure that candidates have the physical abilities necessary for the position.

Moral Qualifications. All candidates for criminal justice service in an enlightened agency must be of excellent moral character, and background investigations can be expected. These "B.I.'s" examine the past life of the applicant from birth to application date, and include contacts with friends, neighbors, relatives, references, teachers, employers, military commanders, and law enforcement agencies. Any pattern of chronically bad behavior will create a doubt about suitability for employment and that doubt will be resolved in favor of the agency, with the resultant rejection of the candidate. This is not to say that all candidates for criminal justice careers must have been "living saints," with a lifetime free of temptation and sin, but that any indication of habitual or chronic bad behavior, or any offense indicating moral turpitude and lack of moral responsibility, will result in elimination from consideration. Some agencies will require the candidate to submit to polygraph examination relative to the information submitted in making application for employment.

Educational Qualifications. The requirements in terms of formal education vary widely, but even in a mediocre agency a high school diploma or its equivalent is a minimal educational requirement. At the federal level of employment, and very often at the state level, the college degree is generally required. All candidates should have the mental capacity sufficient to master the skills, techniques, and scientific knowledge required for the job, as well as the ability to reason with minimum facility, and may expect to be examined for mental capacity and ability.

Emotional Qualifications. All candidates should possess the personality, adaptability and emotional stability necessary for the professional discharge of duty, and may expect to appear before an evaluation board for oral interview. Most of the enlightened agencies will require the candidate to complete paper and pencil psychological tests, and may require an interview with a clinical psychologist or psychiatrist. These evaluations make every effort to detect those persons who seek a criminal justice position in order to satisfy neurotic or psychotic needs. In a nutshell, what we are looking for, in progressive criminal justice institutions, is someone with a flexible mind, a sense of humor, a sense of life's complexities, a compassion for the lowly and humble, a love of the walking wounded, a refusal to be cowed by either power or the threat of violence, a capacity to live with the contradictions of life, and an ability to separate the permanent from the transient.

Aptitude for the Work. All candidates may expect to receive further evaluation after initial appointment during the period of probation, which, in most enlightened agencies, is for one or two years. This evaluation will seek to determine if the candidate for permanent career employment can actually assimilate the necessary information and technique, perform the duties and tasks, cooperate with fellow members of the agency, be amenable to discipline, work effectively with the criminal and noncriminal public, and demonstrate career potential. Those who are unsuited will be eliminated during this period of employment.

There is, no doubt, some basis for the statement of August Vollmer, who noted that a police officer is expected

> . . . to have the wisdom of Solomon, the courage of David, the strength of Samson, the patience of Job, the leadership of Moses, the kindness of the Good Samaritan, the strategy of Alexander, the faith of Daniel, the diplomacy of Lincoln, the tolerance of the Carpenter of Nazareth, and finally, an intimate knowledge of every branch of the natural, biological and social sciences. If he had all these he might be a good policeman.[1]

The demands upon the criminal justice personality are multiple: he must be courteous, but not servile or obsequious; he must be firm, but not rude or oppressive; he must be knowledgeable but not arrogant or supercilious; and he must be dignified, but not be pompous or snobbish.

The student of criminal justice can well understand, after meditating upon the screening process, why the demand for personnel far exceeds the supply—*increasing selectivity.*

One of the dangers of intense selectivity is that, if done by traditionalists and status-quo oriented people, we wind up with a candidate who is a walking example of internalized middle-class conformist attitudes and values and who has never come into open conflict with teachers, with parents, with legal authority—who has been carefully prepared to be obedient to all in authority, and to follow orders without question. Far too often, we end up with a conservative, conforming, somewhat frightened, well-meaning bewildered minor bureaucrat. And all the while we say we are looking for sensitive and aware personnel of great character who have the courage "to tell the king that he is naked."

ADVANTAGES AND DISADVANTAGES OF THE CAREER

No career orientation, no matter how brief, would be complete without some consideration of the current scene as it might affect those contemplating a career.

---

[1] Vollmer, August (1936). *The Police and Modern Society,* p. 222. University of California Press, Berkeley, California.

Disadvantages. Fortunately, the disadvantages are outweighed substantially by the advantages of a career, but, in all candor, they must be presented:

1. *Public Apathy, Indifference, Hostility and Ignorance.* Those who enter the service will find the great *apathy* and *indifference* on the part of the public to be frustrating phenomena. There exist many citizens who expect competent and edifying public services, and who are quite vocal in articulating their expectations, but who are unwilling to render the cooperation and support concomitantly required. The careerist may expect to find that he must expend great efforts to make clear the obvious, overwhelmingly justify the mere minimum, and reeducate the educated in terms of civic responsibilities.

Alexis de Tocqueville, commenting on American democracy over a hundred years ago, noted that "democracy" produces "individualism," and that individualism first weakens the virtue of public responsibility, and then ends up in pure selfishness; and that this type of individual is a defaulted citizen. But, he thought, the people of the United States would escape this fate because our Constitution would cause us to learn to seek the common good together. And he indicated his belief that we would be forced, by the need for cooperating in the management of our free institutions, and by our desire to exercise our political rights, into the habit of attending to the interests of the public. The criminal justice careerist, commenting on American democracy of this era, might be inclined to note that many of the people he contacts are more "individuals" interested in themselves, than "citizens" with a sense of responsibility to their community, state, and nation.

Recent events in the United States indicate that there is a great desire to remain free from involvement—even to the degree that citizens will stand by and watch crimes being committed without lifting a hand, without calling for help, without notifying the authorities. Such citizens must share the responsibility for such damage to the community.

Those who enter the service will find a certain *hostility* on the part of the public. There exist many citizens who desire protection, and tranquility in their community, but who feel that the laws were enacted for "the other guy," but not for them. Those who enter the service may expect to find that their very finest efforts for the community will often be misunderstood, resented, and sometimes bitterly opposed by otherwise good citizens, simply because they themselves are inconvenienced.

And, too, there exist, in almost every community, a certain number of citizens who resent authority in any form, delight in community disturbances, and do all that they can to obstruct the conduct of public business.

Those who enter the service may expect to find, in many situations, exhaustive testing of their patience, stability, and objectivity.

Those who enter the service will find a large-scale *ignorance* relative to the needs of the service, and its character. There exist many citizens who have a warped conception of criminal justice services, and who fail to appreciate that quality service demands quality material. The careerist may expect to contact many citizens who have little concern about the cramped, antiquated, ineffective facilities of their criminal justice agency, and who are indifferent to the obsolence of equipment that is so vital to their security.

Those who enter the service may expect to find that many of their close relatives and friends will not react with felicitations and pride, but will draw back in horror and disbelief, stating with great emotion, ". . . but *you* come from a *good* family!" or, ". . . but you are *too intelligent* a boy to be *wrestling drunks!*" or, ". . . but you have *too good an education to waste!*" or, ". . . but you are a girl of *too sensitive a nature to be searching female narcotic suspects!*" or, ". . . but *think* of the *people* you have to deal with." These reactions are quite illogical, but certainly common. Those same close relatives and friends would, most likely, react with pleasure and pride if the subject of such comments were to have selected, as a career, that of a proctologist, in medicine, or that of Sunday School or Catechism teacher or missionary to a leper colony or aboriginal tribe.

2. *Frustration Within the Agency.* There exist many agencies which are only in the embryonic stages of professional development, but nevertheless, earnestly recruit high quality personnel in terms of future goals.

Those who enter the service in such agencies may expect to find many frustrations due to the many changes taking place. Traditional beliefs, habits, attitudes, and customs must be recognized for what they are, and understood, even though not accepted. Very often, the new officer is given the most sophisticated training, but when he enters the field situation he finds that the gap between what is taught and what is done is immense— and that the highly motivated enunciations and instructions of his training supervisors are almost completely negated by the actual field practices he encounters. He must be able to recognize that conventional attitudes and habits have a tendency to stratify any organization and make changes more difficult. He must be able to observe and distinguish between the efficient and inefficient; between the moral and immoral; and between the legal and illegal—lending his talents and support wholeheartedly to the good, and withdrawing, with good grace and constructive attitude, from the bad. This is no easy task, and requires the utmost of energy, courage, tact, and charity.

Several instances in the United States reveal that there is, even among criminal justice personnel who deplore the apathy of the citizen, a certain tendency to remain silent in the face of wrong doing by fellow workers. Such people must share the responsibility for the damage that is done to the vocation.

Those who enter the service may expect to prove their merit before any progression in assignment of rank. Traditionally the services have required their supervisors, technicians, and administrators to rise from the ranks. Lateral entrance to specialized, supervisory, and managerial positions is extremely rare.[2] Very often, the new criminal justice careerist may become frustrated, because the merit system or civil service processes restrict rapid advancement, or because the agency may have fewer promotional avenues than he would desire. Here resides the need for patience, and trust that the development of a professional service will mandate more rapid and frequent promotion of qualified personnel, commensurate with the ability to assume increased authority and responsibility.

3. *Authoritarian and Anti-Intellectual Environments.* If the professional criminal justice practitioner asserts that he is the preventer of crime and disorder, the keeper of the peace, and the protector of life, property, and liberty he may expect some people to question this, demanding, from time to time some evidence that he means what he says. Such questioner will look for evidence in actions and, if actions do not correspond to words, the questioner will assume that the people are either fools, deceiving themselves, or liars, attempting to deceive others.

Some people would regard the American criminal justice worker as a passive, conforming, and unoriginal personality. It is certainly time that the American criminal justice agency be liberated from the "every day in every way we're getting better and better," school of thought, and given the freedom to engage in hard self-scrutiny, self-criticism, and self-reform so essential to progress.

But, many, particularly in leadership supervisory positions, are defensive about being studied. It is a fact that for the most part criminal justice workers represent a closed "in-group" isolated from society by the nature of their work—even though some members of the vocation would tend to deny this, or tend to brush it off as unimportant. (A few observers imply that the nature of criminal justice work produces an extraordinary proportion of leaders and supervisors whose behavior can be classified as bordering on a paranoid neurosis—but such conclusion may be questioned both in terms of charity and evidence.)

There is no question, however, that in the training of many careerists "unquestioning obedience" becomes a by-word synonymously with "good

---

[2] St. Louis, Missouri is one exception.

worker." The "good worker" seldom questions, rarely criticizes, hardly ever murmurs, usually accepts. Thus is often stifled the individuality that must mark the mature personality. While respect and submission to rightful authority are the duty of every worker, and are integral to the oath of office, some present training programs too often stress the negative. The positive duty of healthy questioning and honest criticism is seldom mentioned—rarely encouraged. Energetic temperaments rebel at such rigid confinement. But, either they submit (which usually means that they sincerely suppress their own insight and initiative because this has been presented as a "proper" thing to do), or else they leave the vocation. Potential leaders are lost to the service when the concept of obedience cannot embrace freedom of expression, differing views, and flexibility.

Thus, the question arises: *Can criminal justice work be made attractive to intelligent people if the internal pressures are both authoritarian and anti-intellectual?*

Because the criminal justice service has changed, in the past quarter century from the utilization of relatively uneducated men performing simple tasks under close supervision, to the utilization of well-educated men carrying out complicated tasks as individual experts relying heavily upon their own independent judgment, there is a question about the suitability of the traditional military type of organization in terms of modern and progressive operations and administration.

The authors of this text believe that there is a slowly developing authority-crisis within the system. Authority can no longer assume that unquestioning compliance which marked much of the past. What is involved is the very concept of authority. We must examine some of our long-held views on authority. We have all become aware that, the longer a view is held, very often, the less it has been thought about. Such may be the case relative to the exercise of authority.

We have a flaw which permits us to substitute, all but unknowingly, the symbol of a reality for the concept of that reality. We still tend to think in pictures. Thus, when we think of *structure*, of the hierarchical nature of organization, we tend to think of a pyramid, with the Chief as the apex, then the workers forming the broad base. And when we think of *authority* (the right to direct and command) we tend to think of it *also* as a pyramid in its implementation, moving downward vertically, from top to bottom.

True enough, almost every society or organization is, ultimately, hierarchical in its *structure*, and those which are not, are either unknown in recorded history, or are myths. *But*, there is nothing in the proper understanding of hierarchical *authority* which demands, for its protection, that we think of *it* as a pyramid, with the lines moving vertically downward.

The fact is that because we image authority as a pyramid, such simply reflects the *way* in which authority was exercised in society and organizations for centuries. This was the way in which king and emperor conceived and exercised their authority. History records, of course, what has happened to kings and emperors, but it also makes us aware that the only pyramidal structures of political authority to be found today are totalitarian and dictatorial. It is time that our thinking moved out of the deceptive cool shadow of the authority pyramid into the hot but honest sunlight.

Why should we not, for example, look now for a new thought-model of authority which would be offered, not by political systems crushed by the hands of time, but by sociological and psychological analyses of the most effective *mode* of exercising authority in the military and in business?

This is not, of course, to suggest that what is good for the U.S. Air Force or U.S. Steel is also the best for our local criminal justice department. Nor has any expert yet suggested that the commanding general of the U.S. Air Force or the president of U.S. Steel be elected by the airmen or employees. It is *not* a question of the source or nature of authority that is at issue here; it is merely a question of *how* authority is best exercised in order to accomplish the ends for which the authority was given in the first place.

Experts who have studied this question have come up with some very interesting observations. First, they point out, the person who holds authority has not even begun to exercise it when he has made a decision. He exercises authority only when he has enlisted the voluntary cooperation of those who must, in descending levels, make that decision work in the grubby, messy, concrete order in which executive decisions, live, languish, or die.

Second, experts point out that effective authority pulls as many people as it can into the process of decision making. To put it crudely, the person in power must have ears as well as a tongue.

Third, the better both ears and tongue are, the more effectively will authority be exercised, for experts have unearthed the fact that the top executives in every field are almost invariably those who command the widest working vocabulary. They can, in effect, communicate in the all-but-forgotten sense of that term; they can "get across"; they can be at one with those to whom they speak or write, since they expect an *answer* to what has been said or written. Language becomes a bridge, not a barrier; not a trumpet, but an instrument which two can play.

What the experts are saying, in effect, is that the executive who says LET IT BE DONE, has failed; he has succeeded only when those who are subject to his authority have first said LET US DO IT.

It is only the mature person who can both hold his tongue and open his ear, for each presupposes an authentic humility and yet a self-possession which knows what it knows, *but also knows that it does not know all.* The reverse face of maturity, of course, is to know when to close one's ears and to loosen one's tongue.

What the experts seem to be saying, then, is that every encounter between leader and led should be a creative moment. Good teachers are taught almost more than they teach, and unless the leader learns from the led that he too is foolish and ignorant, he is more likely to be a job holder than a leader when the crises arise.

The very suggestion that authority in the criminal justice vocation should resemble something other than a feudal kingdom will strike some, of course, as a dangerous democratization, or an invitation to anarchy. The fact is, however, that the most progressive agencies in the United States *stress* cooperation, participation, and communication, and *reject* the Neanderthal view that "authority does not have to give any reasons."

The experts point out one key fact: if there is to be any significant change (other than revolution) in any organization, *the change must come FROM THE TOP.* Where the pyramids remain, progress means more activity at the apex than that of shuffling papers. Calls for modernization and professionalization of services have been made for several decades—*but these calls will make no difference in those agencies where authority is authoritarian.*

Because the service has changed, in the past quarter century, from the utilization of relatively uneducated men performing simple tasks under close supervision, to the utilization of well-educated men carrying out complicated tasks as individual experts relying heavily upon their own independent judgment, there is a question about the suitability of the traditional forms of education and training in terms of modern and progressive operations and administration.

The authors of this text believe that there is a slowly developing education/training crisis within the criminal justice system. Education and training can no longer serve as a process by which outmoded attitudes and habits are transmitted to succeeding generations without audit, excision, and change. What is involved is the very concept of education and training for the system. We must reexamine some of our long-held views on education and training.

Sooner or later, in order to transmit an organized body of knowledge, standardized curricula must be developed on a nationwide scale. Sooner or later, agency training programs must be expanded to include a much wider variety of up-to-date materials, or curtailed in favor of college and university pre-entry programs.

The suggestion that education and training in the system should resemble something other than a helter-skelter conglomeration of subject matter areas taught by "rock 'em, sock 'em" practitioners will strike some, of course, as a call for dangerous centralization, or as an invitation to dictatorship by "egg-heads." The fact is, however, that the most progressive education and training programs in the United States stress thorough core training, up-dating of instructional material, close liaison with progressive agencies, and reject the archaic view that "educated men are not *real* men."

True enough, the educated person entering the criminal justice area will sometimes find that his erudition makes him suspect, and that he is feared and sometimes rejected by fellow workers who have not obtained an education, and who do not share his vision of a professional service. Such jealousy and resentment is particularly true of local agencies (county and municipal) where physical or political qualifications seem to be given exaggerated emphasis, and educational qualifications pegged at a low level.

True enough, the educated person entering a career in criminal justice will sometimes find that regardless of his capacity, ability, and documented performance, his opportunity for advancement is rigidly curtailed by civil service limitations and traditional promotional processes. Such barriers to rapid advancement of the qualified are particularly true of local agencies (county and municipal) where work experience and seniority seem to be given exaggerated emphasis, and capacity, ability, and demonstrated performance given a lesser weight.

If there are to be significant changes in education and training for criminal justice, those changes must involve nationwide cooperation and coordination to ease the entry and insure the progress of the educated and qualified candidate. The greatest evidence will be the development of programs which provide for lateral entrance, at supervisory and administrative rank, for graduates of educational programs who have completed a suitable internship, and the rapid promotion of such people in terms of capacity, ability, and demonstrated performance. The experience of the military and business would suggest that such programs would be both feasible and productive.

4. *Bureaucratic Environment.*[3] The bureaucracy has shown little capacity for radical innovations—for significant change—for the generation of, acceptance of, and implementation of new policies and procedures, methods and devices, which greatly differ from traditional approaches, although there is some movement in this direction.

Often, the bureaucracy is represented by the omniscient man at the top who gives the order that initiates all activity; and all authority and initiation is cascaded down by successive delegations, with complete dis-

---

[3] Concepts adapted from Thompson, Victor A. (1965). "Bureaucracy and Innovation." *Administrative Science Quarterly*, June, pp. 1-20.

cipline to assure that commands are literally obeyed. Responsibility is owed from bottom up; each position is narrowly defined; each person receives orders only from one person—there is but one source of legitimacy; and any conflict is deemed illegitimate. Thus conflict, which encourages innovation, is stifled, and creativity is depressed.

Often, the bureaucracy makes hierarchical position (rank) a reward for compliance. This creates competition for rank that is not based on professional competence but on conformity to agency criteria. Such competition creates psychological anxieties, and the only safe posture is conformity. Success is measured not by professional growth and esteem of professional peers, but by loyal commitment to the agency and its philosophy. The professional careerist finds that many of his colleagues are more concerned with the internal distribution of power and status (rank) than with professional goals. The first and primary reactions to new ideas and suggested changes are "How does that affect *us*?" not "How will this contribute to the goals of criminal justice?"

Often, the bureaucracy is represented by over-detailed task breakdowns when many specialized units contain many subspecialties, to the point that the members of some of these units know very little, and care very little, about what other units are doing. The agency becomes a number of small kingdoms with boundaries and frontiers, and when one unit completes its task and assigns the case to another unit, it drops all further interest. Specialized units are justified by the need to "pinpoint" responsibility, but actually, overspecialization results in irresponsibility in terms of large problem areas, for each specialized unit can dodge general responsibility as long as it discharges its limited function.

It would seem that if the bureaucracy is to become a vital and creative institution, professional people are necessary—people who are energetic, self-confident and, in a real sense, technical generalists. The agency with high entrance standards, open competitive examinations, and lateral entry will gain by the diversity of inputs, and the entire agency will be stimulated. Entering careerists will not give mechanical commitments to agency programs but to professional goals; they will see service not as just competition for rank, but as a means of professional growth and experience. Entering careerists cannot be expected to contribute constructively and creatively if the service continues to define "rank" as the principal indication of personal worth. In the progressive organization of the future, the assignment of the entering careerist will be less based on rigid and limited job slots and more based on extent and level of pre-entry professional preparation. The current signs of agency chauvinism will be replaced by interagency cooperation and demonstrated by exchange and movement of professional personnel.

It would seem that if the bureaucracy is to become a vital and creative institution, structural reorganization is necessary—so that there will be less emphasis on narrow, nonduplicating, nonoverlapping specifications of duties and responsibilities, and more decentralized and broad approaches developed. Narrowly designed job descriptions will be widened to emphasize professional and generalist abilities. The highly stratified organization with many "ranks" will be replaced with a structure that emphasizes professional capacity rather than rank status, and salary scales will be adjusted accordingly. Overspecialization will be eliminated and some overlapping and duplication, some vagueness, will make more communication necessary. Project teams with assignment during the life of the project will replace the current method of continuous specialized assignment. As Thompson says, "If formal structures could be sufficiently loosened, it might be possible for organizations and units to restructure themselves continually in the light of solving the problem at hand. Thus, for generating ideas, for planning and problem solving, the organization or unit would 'unstructure' itself into a freely communicating body of equals. When it came time for implementation, requiring a higher degree of coordination of action (as opposed to stimulation of novel or correct ideas), the organization could then restructure itself into the more usual hierarchical form, tightening up its lines somewhat." [4]

It would seem that if the bureaucracy is to become a vital and creative institution, administrative changes will become necessary. Rather than a single system of ranks with corresponding salaries, it may be necessary to devise many professional positions with corresponding salary scales. Professional status may be given higher pay and prestige than the managerial chain of command. Devices that restrict mobility, retirement systems, for example, will need to be altered.

Certainly suggestions of this nature will result in very strong resistance by workers who are oriented to traditional organizational patterns. Yet, if professionalization of the service is to occur, there must come some deemphasis upon *rank* as the measurement device for effective service, and more emphasis upon *professional performance*. The entering professional careerist will be less interested in the "bars and stars" incentives, and more interested in the incentives which promote professional growth and experience.

5. *The Failures of Leadership.* Although there are sensitive and aware leaders (Patrick V. Murphy, Commissioner of Police, New York City, or Tim Murphy, Superior Court, Washington, D.C., or David Fogel, Commissioner, Minnesota Department of Corrections, for example) there is a national crisis in terms of leadership.

---

[4] *Ibid.,* p. 16.

Current leadership is unable to achieve constructive solutions to such burning issues as racism, corruption, militaristic and mechanical excess, and is unable to develop a concept of the criminal justice role which balances due process and crime control, and which includes the idea of a mutually supportive criminal justice—public partnership in all sections of the community.

The criminal justice system has remained behind the times and still embodies numerous qualities of monarchial absolutism. Top administrators remain, for all practical purposes, the exclusive rulers of the criminal justice palace, and combine legislative, executive and judicial powers in one hand. Despite all sorts of boards and commissions, authority is most often exercised without being subject to effective accountability.

Top administrators are still chosen according to the criterion of conformity. The same complaints are voiced nationwide: decision-making without citizen participation; lack of openness; the repeated referral to the duty of obedience; insufficient motivation of criminal justice directives; an authoritarian style of administration that is patronizing toward any worker or citizen who is unable to have any recourse against leadership decisions.

Criminal justice leaders often place freedom at the head of the list of abstractions that they say they protect, but freedom often is not granted inside of the criminal justice establishment. Justice and equity are preached, but often ignored in practice. Secondary issues (equipment and facilities) are fought for, while the future oriented vision of criminal justice and clear priorities are neglected. Even the most cautious attempts of criminal justice academicians to help the practitioner in this situation are met with defensiveness and distrust. As a consequence, the criminal justice vocation grows more *passive* and the wider public grows more *apathetic*.

Whenever those in authority offer their personal opinions and concerns as divine commands and ordinances, whenever policy and procedure become ends in themselves, there the criminal justice mission is betrayed, and there the vocation distances itself from the public, and there the system enters into crisis.

It is asked: "Does not the superior strength and tenacity of the Neanderthal criminal justice leadership make any serious reform impossible? In this difficult hour of criminal justice, is there still a middle road between revolution and resignation?"

There *is* the possibility of serious reform, and there *is* a middle road between revolution and resignation!

Sensitive and aware leaders refuse to remain silent in the face of barbarity; they realize that silence out of opportunism, lack of courage, or superficiality makes one just as guilty as those responsible persons who were silent during the days of My Lai and Kent. Sensitive and aware leaders continually press for better service, for more appropriate forms of criminal justice-public relationships, and for more involvement in the quest for causes and solutions to problems of crime and disorder. Sensitive and aware leaders act together, for they know that a single person may not count for much, but five can make an impression and fifty can change the scene. Sensitive and aware leaders know that resistance to the *status quo* is not only permissible, but often required. Sensitive and aware leaders know that there can be no reform or renewal without a struggle, so they persevere with confidence and endurance, and they hold on to the hope for a criminal justice service that is responsive to American ideals, and more open, more humane, more credible and more professional.

Neanderthal criminal justice leadership trains its subordinates toward a juvenile dependence in an authoritarian framework wherein the top administrator decides what is to be thought and what is to be done. Even though he may reluctantly tolerate an expert, he prefers a carefully selected, safe, "yes" man. With this type of leadership the concealment of reality is endemic. In order to advance in his organization, the qualifications are servility, cowardice, lack of initiative, zealousness in carrying out orders, indifference to public opinion, and unconcern for the public welfare. (But even there, there will always be found some competent people of integrity who beat their heads persistently against the stone wall of institutionalized indifference.)

In our culture the violence of the respectable has become synonymous with American virtue. Our youngsters are taught from infancy to cultivate a manhood of strength, cunning and aggression, and the results are those grim men who find identity in the single-minded pursuit of authority and power. Many of our criminal justice leaders are criminological illiterates who do not yet understand the violence of those who strike out at dehumanizing tyrannies when no other course of action is possible. Non-violent methods are always to be preferred, but violent action in some circumstances may be the only way of upholding human dignity. There are times when the choice is not between violent and non-violent methods; it may be a choice between the crushing "legitimate" violence of the *status quo* or a purposeful violence leading to more just social structures. At least so thought our forefathers.

The problem of the seventies is not in the numbers of the dissenting and rebellious—it lies in the numbers of the apathetic and the docile! Emotional passivity is the problem: caring about nothing because it has become impossible to care about everything. Outrage is replaced by acceptance and numbed sensitivity. That is why the sensitive and aware leader, in pushing for change, is often forced to step so far out of line that it is he who looks odd, rather than the conforming leadership who continue to march in place, complacently, while the criminal justice institution remains irrelevant to the needs of the day.

The greatest failure of criminal justice leadership lies in a calloused ethical sensitivity. Some Neanderthal leaders see all criminal justice operations as an expression of the will of the people. They do not seem to realize that the will of the people may be the will of a wicked majority; they do not seem to realize that obedience to the will of the people is not sacred. Military and criminal justice leadership resemble each other whether they work for a monarchy, a dictatorship, or a republic: the government (which they identify as the will of the people) *is* their conscience, and if the government is wicked, their response is "love it or leave it." No tyranny can ever survive, for any length of time, without a subservient military and criminal justice system.

Docile submission to Neanderthal criminal justice leadership is *not* a virtue. Stone Age criminal justice leadership that does not permit moral examination of command decisions and operational policy by subordinate personnel is tyrannical and evil. As long as love and compassion are more sacred than is obedience (and the authors of this text so believe), insensitive leadership is the greatest disadvantage to the criminal justice career.

The authors strongly encourage readers of this text to consider a career in the criminal justice system, but they would be unfaithful to student trust if they were to paint an untruthful "rosy" picture. Come on in! *But come on in with your eyes wide open!*

Advantages. Certainly, many advantages present themselves for the consideration of anyone contemplating a career in law enforcement.

1. *Career Advancement.* If the qualified careerist finds that advancement is too dilatory or too infrequent in his agency, he will very often find that it is possible to qualify for and move to another agency, often at increased rank and pay. Many agencies hold "open" competitive examinations, allowing "outside" as well as agency personnel to compete. Thus, a worker in one agency may, after experience, move to another agency with higher pay; or a supervisor in one agency may receive appointment as an administrator in another; or a worker may receive appointment as head in another; or the worker may move from municipal employment to private employment. Even as a top administrator, he may move to state employment as head of a larger agency.

2. *Career Challenges.* The authors can think of no comparable vocation with greater challenge to the careerist of capacity and motivation. Every assignment, as agent, supervisor, or executive is an opportunity for personal development, increased perspective, and individual contribution. For the professionally oriented careerist, every minute, hour, day, month,

and year is stimulating, interesting, and rewarding; and every contact with colleague or citizen, child and adult, is filled with the potential for good.

3. *Service to Community, State, and Nation.* The criminal justice vocation is the bulwark of community and national stability and tranquility. Our nation is administered as a government of law, and criminal justice is the right arm of the executive function, the implementing agency of the legislative function, and the foundation builder of the judicial function.

For those who would heed the words of the late President Kennedy, who exhorted the nation: "Ask not what your Country can do for you but what you can do for your Country," the criminal justice career provides a worthy answer for qualified young men and women.

4. *Local Level Needs.* While it is true that there are many opportunities at the federal and state level of criminal justice, and in the private area, there are increasingly voiced pleas for qualified personnel by local agencies—those at the municipal and county level of government. More and more communities of this nation are awakening to the obvious necessity for improvements in selectivity, and are energetically seeking the young man or woman of potential. This is a great advantage to those deliberating a criminal justice career, and to those in college pre-service programs, for they can clearly sense the genuine opportunities to be found in career service at the local level.

5. *Affiliation with a Cause.* One of the greatest advantages of a criminal justice career lies in the potential for personal satisfaction that is derived from a dedication to the service of justice. Daniel Webster puts it well:

> Justice is the great interest of man on earth. It is the ligament which holds civilized beings and civilized nations together. Wherever her temple stands, and so long as it is duly honored, there is a foundation for social security, general happiness, and the improvement and progress of our race.
>
> And whoever labors on this edifice with usefulnes and distinction, whoever clears its foundations, strengthens its pillars, adorns its entablatures, or contributes to raise its august dome still higher in the skies, connects himself in name, and fame, and character, with that which is, and must be as durable as the frame of human society. . . .

CONCLUSIONS

The authors have attempted to sketch out a sound philosophy of law enforcement and criminal justice, brief its history, reflect on its legal limitations in a democratic republic, list its major agencies, delineate its basic processes, and evaluate its current position.

Certainly, such subject matter is worthy of great further consideration and study by any citizen, whether or not he contemplates a criminal justice career, and the authors would suggest that for any reader this forms but the beginning of a long acquaintance with criminal justice, its processes, its problems, its accomplishments, its needs, and its people.

To the man or woman who has decided upon a criminal justice career; to those members of the vocation who have dedicated themselves to assisting in its professional elevation; and to all who cooperate in the prevention of crime and disorder, the preservation of the peace, and the protection of life, property, and freedom in order to achieve ordered liberty in our beloved America—the authors extend their hand, their respectful salutations, their warm wishes for success, and their prayers for grace and guidance from the Source of All Law.

TOPICS FOR DISCUSSION

1. Where difficulties exist in recruiting sufficient number of personnel, should qualifications be lowered?
2. Can the external and internal disadvantages to criminal justice careers be minimized or overcome in the *near* future?
3. Are the advantages to careers in criminal justice sufficient to attract large numbers of people of high capacity and character?
4. Having read this *Introduction to Law Enforcement and Criminal Justice*, what *specific decisions* have you made in order to assist in the achievement of "ordered liberty?"

SELECTED BIBLIOGRAPHY

BOOKS

* Adler, Mortimer J. (1971). *The Common Sense of Politics*. Holt, Rinehart & Winston, New York.

* Ahern, James F. (1972). *Police in Trouble: Our Frightening Crisis in Law Enforcement*. Hawthorne Press, New York.

Alex, Nicholas (1970). *Black in Blue: A Study of the Negro Policeman*. Appleton-Century-Croft, New York.

* ABA Advisory Committee on the Police Function (1972) Approved Draft: *Standards Relating to the Urban Police Function*. American Bar Association, Chicago.

Asinof, Eliot (1970). *People v. Blutcher*. Viking, New York.

Banton, Michael (1964). *The Policeman in the Community*. Basic Books, New York.

Bennett, James V. (1970). *I Chose Prison*. Knopf, New York.

Berkeley, George (1969). *The Democratic Policeman*. Beacon Press, Boston.

Bickel, Alexander M. (1970). *The Supreme Court and the Idea of Progress*. Harper & Row, New York.

Black, Algernon D. (1968). *The People and the Police*. McGraw-Hill, New York.

Black, Hugo (1969). *A Constitutional Faith*. Knopf, New York.

Blumberg, Abraham (1970). *Law and Order: The Scales of Justice*. Aldine, New York.

Bordua, David (1967). *Police: Six Sociological Essays*. Wiley, New York.

* Brecher, Edward M. (1972). *Licit and Illicit Drugs*. Little, Brown & Co., New York.

Chapman, Brian (1970). *Police State*. Praeger, New York.

Chevigny, Paul (1972). *Cops and Rebels: A Study in Provocation*. Pantheon, New York.

Cipes, Robert M. (1968). *The Crime War*. New American Library, New York.

* Clark, Ramsey (1970). *Crime in America*. Simon & Schuster, New York.

Connery, Robert H. (1968). *Urban Riots*. Vintage, New York.

Conot, Robert (1967). *Rivers of Blood; Years of Darkness*. Bantam, New York.

Cramer, James (1964). *The World's Police*. Cassell, London.

* Cray, Ed (1972). *The Enemy in the Streets*. Anchor Books, New York.

Cressey, Donald (1969). *The Theft of the Nation*. Harper & Row, New York.

Dawson, Robert O. (1969). *Sentencing*. Little, Brown & Co., New York.

Douglas, William O. (1970). *Points of Rebellion*. Random House, New York.

Drinan, Robert (1969). *Democracy, Dissent, and Disorder*. Seabury, New York.

Fort, Joel (1970). *The Pleasure Seekers*. Bobbs-Merrill, New York.

Gaddis, Tom and Long, James (1970). *Killer*. Macmillan, New York.

Goodman, Mitchell (1970). *The Movement Toward a New America*. Knopf, New York.

Graham, Fred P. (1970). *The Self-Inflicted Wound*. Macmillan, New York.

* Grinspoon, Lester (1971). *Marihuana Reconsidered*. Bantam, New York.

Hacker, Andrew (1970). *The End of the American Era*. Antheneum, New York.

Harris, Richard (1970). *Justice*. Dutton, New York.

---

* Books which are particularly recommended for Criminal Justice Administrators, Supervisors, Senior Agents, Professors, Academy Instructors, Legislators, Governmental Executives, and seriously concerned students and citizens.

Hayden, Tom (1970). *The Trial.* Holt, Rinehart & Winston, New York.

Hersey, John (1968). *The Algiers Motel Incident.* Knopf, New York.

* Hunt, Morton (1972). *The Mugging.* Atheneum, New York.

Jacobs, Paul (1966). *Prelude to Riot.* Random House, New York.

Jones, Harry W. (1969). *The Efficacy of Law.* Northwestern University Press, Evanston, Illinois.

* Kaplan, John (1971). *Marihuana: The New Prohibition.* Pocket Books, New York.

* Kenney, John P. (1972). *Police Administration.* Charles C Thomas, Springfield, Illinois.

Klein, Herbert (1968). *The Police: Damned If They Do and Damned If They Don't.* Crown, New York.

LeFave, Wayne (1965). *Arrest.* Little, Brown & Co., New York.

Llewellyn, Karl N. (1960). *Common Law Tradition: Deciding Appeals.* Little, Brown & Co., New York.

Maas, Peter (1973). *Serpico.* Bantam, New York.

Menninger, Karl (1968). *The Crime of Punishment.* Viking, New York.

Methvin, Eugene (1970). *The Riot Makers.* Arlington, New York.

Miller, Frank W. (1969). *Prosecution.* Little, Brown & Co., New York.

Mitford, Jessica (1973). *Kind and Unusual Punishment: The Prison Business.* Knopf, New York.

* Morris, Norval and Hawkins, Gordon (1969). *The Honest Politicians' Guide to Crime Control.* University of Chicago Press, Chicago, Illinois.

Murton, Tom and Hyams, Joe (1970). *Accomplices to the Crime.* Grove Press, New York.

Navasky, Victor (1971). *Kennedy Justice.* Atheneum, New York.

Nelson, Jack and Bass, J. (1970). *The Orangeburg Massacre.* World Book, New York.

Newman, David (1966). *Conviction.* Little, Brown & Co., New York.

Niederhoffer, Arthur (1967). *Behind the Shield: The Police in Urban Society.* Doubleday, New York.

* Niederhoffer, Arthur, and Blumberg, Abraham (1970). *The Ambivalent Force: Perspectives on the Police.* Ginn and Co., New York.

* Packer, Herbert L. (1968). *The Limits of the Criminal Sanction.* Stanford University Press, Palo Alto, California.

Portola Institute (1971). *The Last Whole Earth Catalog.* Random House, New York.

Radano, Gene (1968). *Walking the Beat.* World, New York.

Reich, Charles A. (1970). *The Greening of America.* Random House, New York.

* Reiss, Albert J. (1971): *The Police and the Public.* Yale University Press, New Haven, Connecticut.

* Simmons, J. L. (1970). *Deviants.* Glendessary Press, Berkeley, California.

Skolnick, Jerome (1966). *Justice Without Trial: Law Enforcement in a Democratic Society.* John Wiley and Sons, New York.

* Skolnick, Jerome (1968). *The Politics of Protest.* Simon & Schuster, New York.

Tiffany, Lawrence P., McIntyre, D. M., and Rotenberg, D. L. (1968). *Detection of Crime.* Little, Brown & Co., New York.

Turner, William W. (1968). *The Police Establishment.* Putnam and Sons, New York.

Walker, Daniel (1968). *Rights in Conflict.* Bantam, New York.

Wambaugh, Joseph (1970). *The New Centurions.* Little, Brown & Co., New York.

* Westley, William A. (1971): *Violence and the Police.* M.I.T. Press, Cambridge, Mass.

Whittemore, L. H. (1973). *The Supercops.* Bantam, New York.

GOVERNMENT PUBLICATIONS

* Bittner, Egon (1970). *The Functions of Police in Modern Society*. Public Health Service Publication #2059.
* Commssion Reports:

1. President's Commission on Law Enforcement and Administration of Justice (Katzenbach):
   a. *Summary Report: The Challenge of Crime in a Free Society*
   b. *Task Force Report: The Police*
   c. *Task Force Report: The Courts*
   d. *Task Force Report: Corrections*
   e. *Task Force Report: Juvenile Delinquency and Youth Crime*
   f. *Task Force Report: Organized Crime*
   g. *Task Force Report: Science and Technology*
   h. *Task Force Report: Assessment of Crime*
   i. *Task Force Report: Narcotics and Drug Abuse*
   j. *Task Force Report: Drunkenness*

2. National Advisory Commission on Civil Disorders (Kerner): *Report*.
3. National Commission on the Causes and Prevention of Violence (Eisenhower): *Report*
4. National Commission on Campus Unrest (Scranton): *Report*
5. National Commission on Civil Rights (Hesberg): *Report*
6. National Commission on Obscenity and Pornography (Lockhart): *Report*
7. National Commission on Marihuana and Drug Abuse (Shafer): *Report*

(All of the above can be ordered from: Superintendent of Documents, U.S. Government Printing Office, Washington, D.C. 20402.)

APPENDIX A

PERTINENT SECTIONS OF THE UNITED STATES CONSTITUTION AND ITS AMENDMENTS

PREAMBLE:

We the People of the United States, in Order to form a more perfect Union, establish Justice, insure domestic Tranquility, provide for the common defence, promote the general Welfare, and secure the Blessings of Liberty to ourselves and our Posterity, do ordain and establish this Constitution for the United States of America.

ARTICLE I

Section 1. All legislative Powers herein granted shall be vested in a Congress of the United States, which shall consist of a Senate and House of Representatives.

Section 8. The Congress shall have Power To . . . constitute Tribunals inferior to the Supreme Court; . . .

Section 9. . . . The Privilege of the Writ of Habeas Corpus shall not be suspended, unless when in Cases of Rebellion or Invasion the public Safety may require it.

No Bill of Attainder or ex post facto Law shall be passed.

ARTICLE II

Section 1. Executive Power shall be vested in a President of the United States of America. . . .

ARTICLE III

Section 1. The judicial Power of the United States, shall be vested in one supreme Court, and in such inferior Courts as the Congress may from time to time ordain and establish. The Judges, both of the supreme and inferior Courts, shall hold their Offices during good Behaviour, and shall, at stated Times, receive for their Services, a Compensation, which shall not be diminished during their Continuance in Office. . . .

Section 2. . . . The Trial of all Crimes, except in Cases of Impeachment, shall be by Jury; and such Trial shall be held in the State where the said Crimes shall have been committed; but when not committed within any State, the Trial shall be at such Place or Places as the Congress may by Law have directed.

Section 3. Treason against the United States, shall consist only in levying War against them, or in adhering to their Enemies, giving them Aid and Comfort. No person shall be convicted of Treason unless on the Testimony of two Witnesses to the same overt Act, or on Confession in open Court. . . .

ARTICLE IV

Section 2. The Citizens of each State shall be entitled to all Privileges and Immunities of Citizens in the several States.

A Person charged in any State with Treason, Felony, or other Crime, who shall flee from Justice, and be found in another State, shall on Demand of the executive Authority of the State from which he fled, be delivered up, to be removed to the State having Jurisdiction of the Crime. . . .

ARTICLE VI

. . . This Constitution, and the Laws of the United States which shall be made in Pursuance thereof; and all Treaties made, or which shall be made, under the Authority of the United States, shall be the supreme Law of the Land; and the Judges in every State shall be bound thereby, anything in the Constitution or Laws of any State to the Contrary notwithstanding. . . .

BILL OF RIGHTS

AMENDMENT I

Congress shall make no law respecting an establishment of religion, or prohibiting the free exercise thereof; or abridging the freedom of speech, or of the press; or the right of the people peaceably to assemble, and to petition the Government for a redress of grievances.

AMENDMENT II

A well regulated Militia, being necessary to the security of a free State, the right of the people to keep and bear Arms, shall not be infringed.

AMENDMENT III

No Soldier shall, in time of peace be quartered in any house, without the consent of the Owner, nor in time of war, but in a manner to be prescribed by law.

AMENDMENT IV

The right of the people to be secure in their persons, houses, papers, and effects, against unreasonable searches and seizures, shall not be violated, and no Warrants shall issue, but upon probable cause, supported by Oath or affirmation, and particularly describing the place to be searched, and the persons or things to be seized.

AMENDMENT V

No person shall be held to answer for a capital, or otherwise infamous crime, unless on a presentment or indictment of a Grand Jury, except in cases arising in the land or naval forces, or in the Militia, when in actual service in time of War or public danger; nor shall any person be subject for the same offense to be twice put in jeopardy of life or limb, nor shall be compelled in any criminal case to be a witness against himself, nor be deprived of life, liberty, or property, without due process of law; nor shall private property be taken for public use, without just compensation.

AMENDMENT VI

In all criminal prosecutions, the accused shall enjoy the right to a speedy and public trial, by an impartial jury of the State and district wherein the crime shall have been committed, which district shall have been previously ascertained by law, and to be informed of the nature and cause of the accusation; to be confronted with the witnesses against him; to have compulsory process for obtaining Witnesses in his favor, and to have the Assistance of Counsel for his defence.

AMENDMENT VII

In Suits at common law, where the value in controversy shall exceed twenty dollars, the right of trial by jury shall be preserved, and no fact tried by a jury, shall be otherwise re-examined in any Court of the United States, than according to the rules of the common law.

AMENDMENT VIII

Excessive bail shall not be required, nor excessive fines imposed, nor cruel and unusual punishments inflicted.

AMENDMENT IX

The enumeration in the Constitution, of certain rights, shall not be construed to deny or disparage others retained by the people.

AMENDMENT X

The powers not delegated to the United States by the Constitution, nor prohibited by it to the States, are reserved to the States respectively, or to the people.

AMENDMENT XIV

Section 1. All persons born or naturalized in the United States, and subject to the jurisdiction thereof, are citizens of the United States and of the State wherein they reside. No State shall make or enforce any law which shall abridge the privileges or immunities of citizens of the United States; nor shall any State deprive any person of life, liberty, or property, without due process of law; nor deny to any person within its jurisdiction the equal protection of the laws. . . .

APPENDIX B

SELECTED CASE DIGEST

SELECTED CASE DIGEST

THE SELECTED CASES that are digested are not exhaustive. No attempt has been made to cite every case on a particular point, or even a majority of them. The cases that are digested deal mainly with federal-constitutional questions that have found their way up to the United States Supreme Court. It must be kept in mind, however, that state constitutions, statutes, and judicial decisions, as well as local laws, may impose further limitations upon the authority of law enforcement officers. Law enforcement officials should be familiar with them.

The material focuses primarily upon the principal rule of a decision without, generally, going into collateral issues that make up many opinions. Some of the cases are digested in more detail than others due to historical and philosophical implications that are bound up in them.

The case digests are listed *chronologically* within *topical areas* as this method tends to bring out in clearer perspective both the evolution and the revolution that have taken place in criminal law.

(To facilitate locating a case in the digest, an alphabetized list of cases is presented on page 467.

FIRST AMENDMENT RIGHTS*

FREEDOM OF SPEECH AND ASSEMBLY CASES

Schenck v. United States, 249 U.S. 47, 63 L. Ed. 470, 39 S. Ct. 247 (1919):

Mr. Justice Holmes in the Court's opinion enunciated his famous clear and present danger test. (The Court upheld a conviction under the *Federal Espionage Act of 1917*. The well-known words about shouting fire in a crowded theater are used to illustrate a situation in which free speech may be limited.)

Gitlow v. New York, 268 U.S. 652, 69 L. Ed. 1138, 45 S. Ct. 625 (1925):

The Court upheld the validity of New York's criminal anarchy act of 1902. (The left wing members of the *Socialist Party* met in convention in New York City, June 21-24, 1919. The convention delegates instructed its executive committee to draft and publish the *Left Wing Manifesto* and adopted *Revolutionary Age* as the left wing's official newspaper. The *Manifesto* appeared in the July 5, 1919 issue of the *Revolutionary Age* and furnished the basis for the conviction of its business manager, Benjamin Gitlow, of criminal anarchy in New York.)

Cox v. New Hampshire, 312 U.S. 569, 85 L. Ed. 1049, 61 S. Ct. 762 (1941):

The Court held unanimously that states may regulate parades as an incident to regulating streets for traffic purposes.

Chaplinsky v. New Hampshire, 315 U.S. 568, 86 L. Ed. 1031, 62 S. Ct. 766, (1942):

The Court held unanimously that states may "punish 'fighting words.'"

Kovacs v. Cooper, 336 U.S. 77, 93 L. Ed. 513, 69 S. Ct. 448 (1949):

The Court held that a state or municipality may prohibit on the streets the operation of sound trucks and loud speakers.

Feiner v. New York, 340 U.S. 315, 95 L. Ed. 276, 71 S. Ct. 303 (1951):

A conviction was affirmed under a New York statute which made it an offense to engage in disorderly conduct which might occasion a breach of the peace. (Feiner was making a soapbox speech at a street intersection. After a time the police demanded that he stop. When he kept talking they arrested him to keep the gathering from resulting in a fight.)

Dennis v. United States, 341 U.S. 494, 95 L. Ed. 1137, 71 S. Ct. 857 (1951):

The Court approved the trial judge's instructions to the jury that the charged teaching

---

* After the United States Supreme Court handed down its Gitlow opinion a long line of decisions have dealt with First Amendment rights and their applicability to the states through the Fourteenth Amendment. The cases raise many perplexing questions like whether picketing and demonstrations are embraced in speech. Only a few of the main cases are listed in this compilation.

and advocacy to overthrow the Government had to "be of a rule of principle to incite persons to such action, all with the intent to cause the overthrow or destruction of the Government of the United States by force and violence as speedily as circumstances will permit." (Chief Justice Vinson commented: "No important case involving free speech was decided by the Court prior to *Schenck v. United States.*" However, there are two great prior occasions when the scope of the First Amendment's proscription were debated: See *Ex parte Jackson* and *Abrams v. United States.*)

Beauharnais v. Illinois, 343 U.S. 250, 96 L. Ed. 919, 72 S. Ct. 725 (1952):

Justice Jackson's dissenting opinion makes it plain that the Fourteenth Amendment does not incorporate the First. (Later Court decisions seem to recognize this principle. The states under the due process clause of the Fourteenth Amendment still have more extensive powers over speech, press and assembly than the federal government.)

Poulas v. New Hampshire, 345 U.S. 395, 97 L. Ed. 1105, 73 S. Ct. 760 (1953):

The Court held that a state or municipality may by law require a permit to conduct a meeting in a public park.

Cox v. Louisiana, 379 U.S. 536, 13 L. Ed. 2d 471, 85 S. Ct. 453 (1965):

The Court said: "We emphatically reject the notion urged by the appellant that the First and Fourteenth Amendments afford the same kind of freedom to those who would communicate ideas by conduct such as patrolling, marching, and picketing on streets and highways, as these amendments afford to those who communicate ideas by pure speech. . . ."

Adderly v. Florida, 385 U.S. 39, 17 L. Ed. 2d 149, 87 S. Ct. 242 (1966):

The Supreme Court affirmed the convictions by a 5-4 vote in an opinion by Mr. Justice Black holding that the Florida trespass statute was sufficiently specific to sustain a conviction, that it was evenhandedly applied and that as applied it infringed no First Amendment rights since the state could "preserve the property under its control" for its lawfully dedicated use. (In this decision the Court for the first time upheld convictions of participants in a peaceable civil rights demonstration.)

Cameron v. Johnson, 390 U.S. 611, 20 L. Ed. 2d 182, 88 S. Ct. 1335 (1966):

The Court held 7-2 that while picketing cannot be made a crime, blocking the entrance to a public building can constitute a criminal act.

Gregory v. City of Chicago, 394 U.S. 111, 22 L. Ed. 2d 134, 89 S. Ct. 946 (1969):

Chief Justice Warren, in a short opinion, reversed Gregory's conviction. He said, "this is a simple case," concluding that since there was no evidence that the petitioner's conduct was disorderly, the march was protected by the First Amendment. (In effect, the petitioners were arrested for disobeying a law that did not exist until they were commanded to disperse. Justices Black and Douglas, concurring to reverse, thought the case to be of far greater importance than the majority's treatment of it indicated. There is a critical need, they contended, for some "narrowly drawn law" that can reconcile the rights of citizens to propagandize their views and protest through the medium of marches and demonstrations and the interest of government in regulating speech-connected conduct.)

Shuttleworth v. City of Birmingham, 394 U.S. 147, 22 L. Ed. 2d 162, 89 S. Ct. 935 (1969):

The Court, in an opinion by Mr. Justice Stewart, found a Birmingham, Alabama, ordinance to be unconstitutional on its face. (He observed that the ordinance conferred "virtually unbridled and absolute power to prohibit any 'parade, procession,' or 'demonstration' on the city's streets or public ways." Justice Stewart acknowledged that the conduct regulated was not "pure speech"—it did involve the use of public streets over which the municipality had a right to exercise considerable control. But previous decisions made it clear that picketing and parading may constitute methods of expression protected by the First Amendment.)

Brandenburg v. Ohio, 395 U.S. 444, 23 L. Ed. 2d 430, 89 S. Ct. 1827 (1969):

Chief Justice Warren in a per curiam opinion that overrules *Whitney v. California,* 274 U.S. 357 (1927), finds the *Ohio Criminal Syndicalism Act* (Ohio Rev. Code, section 2923.13) unconstitutional and unconstitutionally applied to the appellant, a leader of a Ku Klux Klan group. (The First Amendment bars laws prohibiting the "advocacy" of force or lawlessness that is not directed to inciting or producing imminent lawless action and not likely to incite or produce such action. Merely urging the moral propriety or even the moral necessity of a resort to force is distinguished from preparing a particular group for violent action. Justices Black and Douglas concur: the "clear and present danger" test should not be applied in First Amendment interpretations, they declare.)

Gooding v. Wilson, 405 U.S. 518, 31 L. Ed. 2d 408, 92 S. Ct. 1103 (1972):

In a 5-2 opinion by Mr. Justice Brennan, the Court holds unconstitutional a Georgia statute making it an offense to use "opprobrious words or abusive language, tending to cause a breach of the peace." Wilson was convicted on two counts of using abusive language to police during a demonstration at an Army headquarters. Justices Powell and Rehnquist did not participate. (The construction given the Georgia statute by the state courts had not limited it to "fighting words" that "have a direct tendency to cause acts of violence by the persons to whom, individually, the remark is addressed," and so it did not come under the narrow exception to the constitutional right of freedom of expression sanctioned by *Chaplinsky v. New Hampshire.*)

FOURTH AMENDMENT RIGHTS

SEARCH AND SEIZURE CASES

Boyd v. United States, 116 U.S. 616, 39 L. Ed. 746, 6 S. Ct. 524 (1886):

The Court, through Mr. Justice Bradley, held that there was a link between the Fourth and Fifth Amendments so that one became definitive of the other, and one test of the reasonableness of a search was whether or not its object was to uncover incriminating evidence. (The decision stands out as the Court's first authoritative utterance on searches. The *Boyd* holding created much confusion in lower courts until it was "virtually repudiated" eighteen years later in *Adams v. New York.*)

Adams v. New York, 192 U.S. 585, 48 L. Ed. 575, 24 S. Ct. 372 (1904):

The Court, in a unanimous opinion by Mr. Justice Day, refused to explicitly overrule the *Boyd* holding, but the Court limited that decision to the facts in the case. Hence, for all practical purposes the Court returned to the common-law rule of admissibility on search and seizure. (See *Bishop Atterbury's Trial* at page 104 of this text.)

Weeks v. United States, 232 U.S. 383, 58 L. Ed. 652, 341 S. Ct. 341 (1914):

The Court held unanimously, speaking through Mr. Justice Day, that in a federal prosecution the Fourth Amendment barred the use of evidence secured through an illegal search and seizure. (The Court unequivocally declared, moreover, that the Constitution did not protect against unreasonable searches by state officers. The decision's exclusionary rule has been viewed by most legal commentators as a judicially conceived rule of evidence without any basis in either the explicit requirements of the Constitution, or on legislation expressing Congressional policy in the enforcement of the Constitution.)

Burdeau v. McDowell, 256 U.S. 465, 65 L. Ed. 1048, 41 S. Ct. 574 (1921):

The federal rule of exclusion was held to be "a restraint upon the activities of sovereign authority and . . . not . . . a limitation upon other than governmental agencies." (This principle reflects the long-held historic-constitutional doctrine that the Bill of Rights bound only officers and agents of the federal government.)

Carroll v. United States, 267 U.S. 132, 69 L. Ed. 543, 45 S. Ct. 280 (1925):

In a 7-2 opinion Chief Justice Taft held that a moving vehicle can be stopped, and searched on probable cause that at the time it is carrying contraband or other illegally possessed goods. (The Chief Justice brought out that there "is a necessary difference between a search of a store, dwelling house or other structure in respect to which a proper official warrant readily may be obtained, and a search of a ship, motor boat, wagon or automobile, for contrabrand goods, where it is not practicable to secure a warrant because the vehicle can be quickly moved out of the locality or jurisdiction in which the warrant must be sought.")

People v. Defore, 242 N.Y. 13, 150 N.E. 585 (1926):

This decision by Mr. Justice Cardozo (prior to his appointment to the Supreme Court of the United States in 1932) is recognized as the leading case rejecting the *Week's* exclusionary rule.

Wolf v. Colorado, 338 U.S. 25, 93 L. Ed. 1782, 69 S. Ct. 1359 (1949):

With Mr. Justice Frankfurter writing for the majority (5-4) the Court subjected the states to the rule against arbitrary intrusions by the police—the essence of the Fourth Amendment. (The majority declined to take the step of enforcing this constitutional protection by banning the illegal evidence. In the 35 years between *Weeks* and *Wolf*, however, the due process clause of the Fourteenth Amendment had gradually acquired new potency, and when the Court considered *Wolf* the result was different. *Wolf* indicated clearly that the Court would reverse a state criminal conviction under due process when police action—in relation to persons suspected of crime—would offend the Court's sense of "fundamental fairness." This case-by-case approach came to an end in 1961 when the Court in its landmark decision in *Mapp v. Ohio* divested itself of major responsibility for the enforcement of the Fourth Amendment's right to privacy. *It is interesting to note Mr. Justice Black's concurring opinion in Wolf—in the light of the Omnibus Crime Control and Safe Streets Act of 1968—wherein he observes that "the Federal exclusionary rule is not a command of the Fourth Amendment, but is a judicially created rule of evidence which Congress might negate."*)

Rochin v. California, 342 U.S. 165, 96 L. Ed. 183, 72 S. Ct. 205 (1952):

That *Wolf* did not permit state courts to admit all unconstitutionally seized physical evidence, regardless of how outrageous or offensive the police methods employed was demonstrated in this famous "stomach-pumping" case. (The decision marks the real beginning of the Court's trek to discredit a case-by-case approach to search and seizure to the final step the Court took nine years later in *Mapp* when the Court incorporated the Fourth Amendment under the due process umbrella of the Fourteenth Amendment.)

Irvine v. California, 347 U.S. 128, 98 L. Ed. 561, 74 S. Ct. 381 (1954):

In this famous microphone-in-the-bedroom-case, the Court held (5-4), colored by five separate opinions, that the exclusion of illegally seized evidence from a state proceeding was not required by due process of law, no matter how shocking the violation, so long as there was no element of physical coercion. (This case limited the *Rochin* exception to *Wolf* to a situation involving coercion, violence or brutality to the person. Perhaps never has a court so castigated police misconduct while affirming a conviction based on such misconduct. What law enforcement officers, by large, neglected to take seriously, was the clear warning to them to put their house in order, or face judicially imposed controls. This opinion might well be required reading for all law enforcement officers, and young people who aspire to joining the ranks of law enforcement.)

People v. Cahan, 44 Cal. 2d 434, 282 P. 2d 905 (1955):

The California Supreme Court (4-3) adopted the federal exclusionary rule of the *Weeks* case. (The Court discusses warnings to law enforcement officers on illegal practices in earlier decisions, and, why, to try to deter such conduct, the Court felt impelled in *Cahan* to apply the exclusionary rule to California peace officers.)

Elkins v. United States, 364 U.S. 206, 4 L. Ed. 2d 1669, 80 S. Ct. 1437; *Rios v. United States,* 364 U.S. 253, 4 L. Ed. 2d 1688, 80 S. Ct. 1431 (1960):

The 5-4 *Elkins* decision overturned the so-called "silver platter" doctrine: the rule that evidence of a federal crime which state police come upon in the course of an illegal search for a state crime may be turned over to federal authorities so long as federal agents did not participate in the search but simply received the evidence on a "silver platter." (The Court used its inherent supervisory power to regulate the use of evidence in federal courts in reaching its decision with the result the decision does not turn on a constitutional question. *Elkins,* for the present, recognizes the principle laid down in *Burdeau v. McDowell* though there is a drift away from it as is manifested in a number of state court decisions since 1964).

Mapp v. Ohio, 367 U.S. 643, L. Ed. 2d 1081, 81 S. Ct. 1681 (1961):

Expressly overruling its 1949 *Wolf* decision, the Court dividing 5-4 (6-3 to reverse) in this bellwether opinion, held that the Fourth Amendment is applicable to the states through the due process clause of the Fourteenth Amendment. (In a concurring opinion, Mr. Justice Black agreed with five of his brethren to reverse Mapp's conviction —bottoming his views on the traditional due process approach—but refused to join with them to incorporate the Fourth under the Fourteenth Amendment.)

Ker v. California, 374 U.S. 23, 10 L. Ed. 2d 726, 83 S. Ct. 1623 (1963):

In the first state case to reach the Court after *Mapp,* dealing with *Mapp's* implication, the Court held (4-4) that searches by state police must conform to federal standards of reasonableness. Mr. Justice Harlan without passing on this question at all, cast the deciding vote to sustain the conviction on the ground the facts of the case showed no violation of "fundamental fairness" by the police. The Court held, further, that "States are not thereby precluded from developing workable rules governing arrests, searches and seizures to meet the practical demands of effective criminal investigation in the States . . ." (The lawfulness of petitioners' arrests by Los Angeles, California, police officers, was not vitiated by an unannounced entry. Compare *Miller v. United States,* 357 U.S. 301 [1958], wherein an opposite result was reached by the Court with respect to the admissibility in federal courts of evidence seized under similar circumstances.)

Preston v. United States, 376 U.S. 364, 11 L. Ed. 2d 777, 84 S. Ct. 881 (1963):

A unanimous Court held that an automobile must be searched at the time and place of arrest. (The search of the automobile at the police garage was too remote in time and place and was not, therefore, incidental to the lawful arrest. Later decisions have modified the *Preston* decision.

Stoner v. California, 376 U.S. 483, 11 L. Ed. 2d 856, 84 S. Ct. 889 (1964):

The Court held (with only Mr. Justice Black dissenting, in part, on other grounds), that the search of defendant's hotel room without his consent and with neither search nor arrest warrants, violated his constitutional rights, although with the consent of the hotel clerk. (Only the person, *as a general rule,* whose rights are being invaded can waive a constitutional right.)

Aguilar v. Texas, 378 U.S. 108, 13 L. Ed. 723, 84 S. Ct. 1509 (1964):

A divided Court applied the same standards for obtaining a search warrant to the states as those applicable to the federal government.

Cooper v. California, 386 U.S. 58, 17 L. Ed. 2d 730, 87 S. Ct. 788 (1967):

In this 5-4 opinion, the Court held that a search of an automobile is reasonable when by statute it is impounded for the purpose of forfeiture as it relates to the transportation of contraband, narcotics, alcohol and unregistered firearms. (Mr. Justice Douglas, in his dissent, said he felt the Court's opinion either "overrules *Preston* sub silentio," or "that when the Bill of Rights is applied to the states by reason of the Fourteenth Amendment, a watered-down version is used.")

McCray v. Illinois, 386 U.S. 300, 18 L. Ed. 2d 62, 87 S. Ct. 1056 (1967):

This 5-4 opinion is important in preserving the informer privilege. A reliable informant's identity generally need not be disclosed on a motion to suppress. (The dissenters in *McCray* center on another point that is extremely important: the question of arrest warrants and when and where they are essential. In earlier decisions—the *Hoffa, Lewis, Osborn* complex—the Court clarified the acceptable use of the informer.)

Warden v. Hayden, 387 U.S. 294, 18 L. Ed. 2d 782, 87 S. Ct. 1642 (1967):

In an 8-1 decision, the Supreme Court decided that officials may use as evidence in courts items such as clothing seized by the police in lawful searches of the residences of suspects. The Court, in short, abrogated the "mere evidence" rule. (This decision shows a "shift" in Fourth Amendment emphasis from property to privacy and redounds to the benefit of law enforcement officials as well as their quarry. The police can seize more things, but an accused can challenge more kinds of evil.)

Camara v. Municipal Court, 387 U.S. 523, 18 L. Ed. 2d 930, 87 S. Ct. 1727; *See v. Seattle,* 387 U.S. 541, 18 L. Ed. 2d 943, 87 S. Ct. 1737 (1967):

Speaking for a six-justice majority, Mr. Justice White's opinion held that health and fire inspectors are no longer entitled to search a home or business without warrant or consent. (*Frank v. Maryland,* 359 U.S. 360, was expressly overruled. The two cases establish a diluted-probable cause standards for such search warrants so it can be said that probable cause to issue a warrant exists if reasonable legislation or administration standards for conducting an inspection of the area are satisfied. Note should be taken, moreover, that the decisions hold that different official intrusions upon privacy not directed at obtaining criminal evidence constitute "searches" for Fourth Amendment purposes, but are not subject to the same probable cause standards as the ordinary search in criminal cases.)

Spinelli v. United States, 393 U.S. 410, 21 L. Ed. 2d 637, 89 S. Ct. 584 (1969):

A 5-3 opinion by Mr. Justice Harlan, in which four of the seven other members of the Court wrote opinions, wound up more or less announcing new probable cause standards for search warrant affidavits in which the affiant had relied upon an informer. (The majority projects a two-pronged test to determine what constitutes probable cause in an affidavit for a search warrant when an informer is used in a showing of probable cause. The Court sets up guidelines on how to show an informant's reliability and on how to show an informant's information is reliable. The Court held Spinelli's reputation to be immaterial in showing probable cause. See, however, *United States v. Harris* [1971] below, holding reputation evidence can be used.)

Davis v. Mississippi, 394 U.S. 721, 22 L. Ed. 2d 676, 89 S. Ct. 1394 (1969):

In a 6-2 opinion, by Mr. Justice Brennan, the majority held fingerprints to be within the range of items which may constitute illegally-obtained evidence. (The Court, by way of advice, suggests that it might approve a procedure whereby warrants would be issued for the limited purpose of bringing suspects to the station house for finger-printing even when the police lack reasonable grounds to make an arrest. This "sleeper" opinion could prove to be a blockbuster as it serves notice that the Fourth Amendment applies to the investigatory arrest stage of a prosecution, and that its proscription against unreasonable searches and seizures is violated by the "investigatory arrest"—detention without reasonable grounds to arrest.)

Frazier v. Cupp, 394 U.S. 731, 22 L. Ed. 2d 684, 89 S. Ct. 1420 (1969):

In a unanimous opinion by Mr. Justice Marshall the Court held that where there is an equal interest in property the consent of one user to search is good against both or all joint users. (The theory is not that one joint user can waive another's constitutional rights. However, a joint user can voluntarily waive his constitutional rights, and if evidence is found it is admissible against any joint user.)

Chimel v. California, 395 U.S. 752, 23 L. Ed. 2d 685, 89 S. Ct. 2034 (1969):

Mr. Justice Stewart held, 6-2, that a search incident to a lawful arrest in a home must be limited to "the area into which an arrestee might reach in order to grab a weapon or other evidentiary items." Such a search, the majority says, does not include drawers or other closed or concealed areas in the same room, nor does it include adjacent rooms. (*Chimel* expressly overrules *Harris* [1947], and *Rabinowitz* [1950] that permitted more latitude as to the permissible area of a search. *Chimel* also lends force to the view that *Cooper v. California* does not overrule *Preston* [1963]. *Chimel* speaks of "homes." But some courts apply the rule to other places such as automobiles. Consult the prosecutor, or local police legal advisor.)

Chambers v. Maroney, 399 U.S. 42, 26 L. Ed. 2d 419, 90 S. Ct. 1975 (1970):

In this opinion, Mr. Justice White, 7-1, softens limitations on automobile searches that followed in the wake of *Preston v. United States* (1963). (*Chambers* must be read with *Coolidge v. New Hampshire,* below, to devise a general rule on automobile searches.)

Whiteley v. Warden, 401 U.S. 560, 28 L. Ed. 2d 306, 91 S. Ct. 1031 (1971):

The Court through Mr. Justice Harlan held, 6-3, that a police radio broadcast based on an affidavit insufficient for issuance of an arrest warrant cannot furnish probable cause to arrest the suspect described in the broadcast. (Reasonable grounds requirements in a warrantless arrest are at least as stringent—if not more so—than need be recited in a complaint for issuance of an arrest warrant. See also *Beck v. Ohio, Hill v. California,* and *Chambers v. Maroney.*)

Williams v. United States (Elkanich v. United States), 401 U.S. 646, 28 L. Ed. 2d 388, 91 S. Ct. 1148 (1971):

Mr. Justice White in announcing the judgment for the Court, joined by J. J. Stewart and Blackmun, simply states that *Chimel* is not retroactive and is not applicable to searches conducted prior to the decision in that case.

Hill v. California, 401 U.S. 797, 28 L. Ed. 2d 484, 91 S. Ct. 1106 (1971):

The Court held, unanimously, through Mr. Justice White, that a mistaken pre-*Chimel* arrest of a man fitting the description of an accused whom the police had probable cause to arrest did not render unlawful a contemporaneous search of the accused's entire apartment where the arrestee was found.

Bivens v. Six Unknown Named Agents, 403 U.S. 388, 29 L. Ed. 2d 619, 91 S. Ct. 1999 (1971):

Mr. Justice Brennan for the Court, 6-3, held that an apartment dweller has a federal cause of action for damages against federal narcotics agents who allegedly violated the Fourth Amendment by entering his apartment without a warrant and arresting and searching his apartment without probable cause. (The various opinions contain a wide range of commentary why the search and seizure exclusionary rule has failed to effectively deter illegal police practices, and suggest possible alternatives to replace the rule.)

Coolidge v. New Hampshire, 403 U.S. 443, 29 L. Ed. 2d 564, 91 S. Ct. 2022 (1971):

This important decision, 5-4, by Mr. Justice Stewart raises four search and seizure issues, and the opinions are subject to several interpretations, and as an "explication" they leave much to be desired. Consult the prosecutor, or local police legal advisor, and act accordingly. The authors' interpretation is that (1) the only way of following *Coolidge* is to secure a warrant whenever possible, (2) if there is any question, *Coolidge* settles any controversy that when a warrant is issued it must be by "a neutral magistrate," (3) *Coolidge* limits *Chambers* on automobile searches, and (4) "plain view" is stated unequivocally, in at least the plurality part of the opinion, as restricting warrantless seizures. (Chief Justice Burger, dissenting, says that "This case graphically illustrates the monstrous price we pay for the Exclusionary Rule in which we seem to have imprisoned ourselves." Mr. Justice Black in his dissent declares that "there is no exclusionary rule in the Fourth Amendment, if it is properly construed. . . ." Mr. Justice Harlan concurs with Mr. Justice Stewart because he feels bound by *Mapp.* However, he begins his opinion by stating that both *Mapp* and *Ker* should be overruled.)

United States v. Harris, 403 U.S. 573, 29 L. Ed. 2d 723, 91 S. Ct. 2075 (1971):

The Court through Chief Justice Burger held, 5-4, that probable cause to search a suspected moonshiner's premises was established by an affidavit based largely on hearsay obtained by the affiant from a "prudent person" who had recent "personal knowledge" of the suspect's illegal whiskey sales and admitted having made several purchases of illegal whiskey from the suspect; magistrate who issued the warrant was entitled to consider, in determining whether probable cause existed, the affiant's knowledge of the suspect's reputation "as . . . a trafficker in non-taxpaid spirits." (Summed up, a policeman's knowledge of a suspect's reputation may be relied on in evaluating the reliability of an informant's tip. The decision, to this extent, modifies *Spinelli v. United States.*)

AUDIO-SURVEILLANCE CASES

Olmstead v. United States, 277 U.S. 438, 73 L. Ed. 944, 48 S. Ct. 564 (1928):

The Court held (5-4) through Chief Justice Taft, that messages passing over telephone wire were not within the protection of the Fourth Amendment, and, for this reason, the Amendment did not apply as there was no physical trespass on premises owned or under the control of the defendant. ("There was no searching . . . The evidence was obtained by the use of the sense of hearing and that only," said Taft. The ruling made it clear, at that time, that the Fourth Amendment protects material things—the person, the house, his papers or his effects.)

Nardone v. United States, 302 U.S. 379, 83 L. Ed. 314, 58 S. Ct. 275 (1937):

The Court held that wiretapping was within the "plain mandate" of Section 605 of the Federal Communications Act of 1934. (Justice Roberts asserted that the section prohibited interception and divulgence of telephone conversations.)

Schwartz v. Texas, 344 U.S. 199, 97 L. Ed. 231, 73 S. Ct. 732 (1952):

Speaking for the Court, and relying on *Wolf v. Colorado,* Justice Minton held that even though wiretapping was illegal (Section 605, Federal Communications Act), evidence so obtained, nevertheless, could be used in a state court.

Benanti v. United States, 355 U.S. 96, 2 L. Ed. 2d 126, 78 S. Ct. 155 (1957):

The Court through Chief Justice Warren held that Section 605 of the Federal Communications Act "contains an express, absolute prohibition against the divulgence of intercepted communications" in a federal prosecution. (States continued, nonetheless, to admit wiretap evidence despite the fact such evidnce was the fruits of a violation of federal law. In *Benanti* the Chief Justice cast doubt on the continued viability of the silver platter doctrine in search cases by referring to the matter as an "open question." This view was approvingly quoted three years later in *Elkins* when the Court overruled the silver platter doctrine.)

Lopez v. United States, 373 U.S. 427, 10 L. Ed. 2d 462, 83 S. Ct. 1381 (1963):

A majority of the Court held that the Fourth Amendment did not apply in the absence of a physical trespass when incriminating statements were obtained by an electronic listening device. (In this case an agent of the IRS had a recording device concealed on his person by means of which the defendant's incriminating statements were recorded.)

Berger v. New York, 388 U.S. 41, 18 L. Ed. 2d 1040, 87 S. Ct. 1873 (1967):

The Court (5-4), held New York State's permissive wiretap statute to be "too broad in its sweep resulting in a trespassory intrusion into a constitutionally protected area and is, therefore, violative of the Fourth and Fourteenth Amendments." (The Court pointed out that since *Mapp* [1961], "the Fourth Amendment's right of privacy has been declared enforceable against the States through the Due Process Clause of the Fourteenth Amendment." The decision did not outlaw wiretapping. It simply struck down New York's permissive wiretap statute as unconstitutional. There is an implication in the decision that a statute can be drafted that would meet constitutional requirements.)

Hoffa v. United States, 385 U.S. 293, 17 L. Ed. 2d 374, 87 S. Ct. 408 (1966); *Lewis v. United States,* 385 U.S. 206, 17 L. Ed. 2d 312, 87 S. Ct. 424 (1966); and, *Osborn v. United States,* 385 U.S. 323, 17 L. Ed. 2d 394, 87 S. Ct. 429 (1966):

This trilogy of decisions affirmed the legitimacy of using informers to gain evidence of criminality, either of the actual commission of the crime itself, or of incriminating statements, and in *Osborn,* the Court held that recordings can be made of the conversations. (The Court emphasized, in *Osborn,* that two federal district court judges had authorized [orally] the making of the recordings.)

Katz v. United States, 389 U.S. 347, 19 L. Ed. 2d 576, 88 S. Ct. 507 (1967):

The Court, with Mr. Justice Black dissenting, held that the Fourth Amendment "protects people, not places," and as a result, eavesdropping carried on by electronic means (equivalent to wiretapping) constitutes a "search" and "seizure" and is subject to the warrant requirements of the Fourth Amendment—overruling *Olmstead v. United States.* (This case involved the use of a nonpenetrating listening device to pick up a gambler's end of telephone calls he made from a public telephone booth.)

Lee v. Florida, 392 U.S. 378, 20 L. Ed. 2d 1166, 88 S. Ct. 2096 (1968):

Schwartz v. Texas was overruled in this 6-3 decision that held that evidence obtained by police officers in violation of Section 605, *Federal Communications Act,* is inadmissible in a state prosecution.

Fuller v. Alaska, 393 U.S. 80, 21 L. Ed. 2d 212, 89 S. Ct. 61 (1968):

The Court held in a per curiam opinion that *Lee v. Florida,* (1968), which overruled *Schwartz v. Texas,* (1952), is to apply prospectively: "(t)he exclusionary rule is to be applied only to trials in which the evidence is sought to be introduced after the date of our decision in *Lee.*" (Dissents were filed by Justices Black and Douglas.)

Desist v. United States, 394 U.S. 244, 22 L. Ed. 2d 248, 89 S. Ct. 1030 (1969):

The Court held, 5-3, through Mr. Justice Stewart, that *Katz* does not apply retroactively even to a case that was on direct appeal when *Katz* was announced. (The whole question of the "retroactivity of decisions of constitutional dimension should be rethought," Mr. Justice Black urged in his dissenting opinion.)

United States v. White, 401 U.S. 745, 28 L. Ed. 2d 453, 91 S. Ct. 1122 (1971):

Justice White's opinion approves of warrantless use of wired informant, and refuses to overrule *On Lee* (1952) and *Lopez* (1963). (The opinion was joined by the Chief Justice and Justices Stewart and Blackmun, and separate concurring opinions were filed by Justices Brennan and Black. Justice Brennan concurred solely on the separate ground that *Katz* should not be applied retroactively, while Justice Black concurred in the result on the grounds that the Fourth Amendment could not be expanded to protect against electronic surveillance. Federal Bureau of Investigation agents testified over objection to incriminating statements made by the defendant and transmitted by an electronic eavesdropping device worn by a government informer. The informer was not available at the trial to testify as to his conversation with the defendant.)

United States v. United States District Court, Eastern Michigan, 407 U.S. 297, 32 L. Ed. 2d 752, 92 S. Ct. 2125 (1972):

The Court, 6-2, in an opinion by Mr. Justice Powell, refuses to approve warrantless bugging of domestic "subversives." Chief Justice Burger and Justice White wrote concurring opinions. Mr. Justice Rehnquist did not participate. (The case was one involving Lawrence Plamondon, a member of the White Panthers who was accused of dynamiting a branch office of the Ceneral Intelligence Agency in Ann Arbor, Michigan. The Government acknowledged he had been the subject of wiretapping.)

STOP AND FRISK CASES

People v. Rivera, 14 N.Y. 2d 441, 201 N.E. 2d 32 (1964); *People v. Pugach*, 15 N.Y. 2d 65, 204 N.E. 2d 176 (1964):

The New York Court of Appeals, by a divided Court, held that "stop-and-frisk" procedures, as applied by the police officers in the two cases, both involving arrests that were made before the adoption of New York's "stop-and-frisk" legislation—could be sustained as constitutionally permissible. (The United States Supreme Court denied certiorari in both cases.) The Court said, in *Rivera*, that, "the evidence needed to make the inquiry is not of the same degree of conclusiveness as that required for an arrest. The stopping of an individual to inquire is not an arrest and the ground upon which the police may make the inquiry may be less incriminatng than the ground for an arrest for a crime known to have been committed." "[T]he right to stop and inquire," the Court continued, "is to be justified for a cause less conclusive than that which would sustain an arrest, so the right to frisk may be justified as an incident to inquiry upon grounds of elemental safety and precaution which might not initially sustain a search.")

People v. Peters, 18 N.Y. 2d 238, 273 N.Y.S. 217, 219 N.E. 2d 595 (1966):

For a third time, a majority of the Court upheld the constitutionality of "stop-and-frisk," this time, after New York's legislation had become effective. The United States Supreme Court granted certiorari, 386 U.S. 980 (1967).

(In several states law enforcement has been given so-called "stop-and-frisk" authority either by judicial fiat or statute. See, for example, *People v. Michelson*, 380 P. 2d 658 [Cal. 1963]; *State v. Dilley*, 231 A. 2d 533 [N.J. 1967]; legislation enacted in both *Massachusetts* and *Utah* in [1967]; and, local ordinance on "stop-and-frisk," enacted by the *Detroit [Michigan] Common Council*, effective July, 1968.)

Terry v. Ohio, 392 U.S. 1, 20 L. Ed. 2d 889, 88 S. Ct. 1868 (1968):

The Court, held 8-1, a "frisk" may be justified when its purpose is to "discover guns, knives, clubs, or other hidden instruments for assault of the police officer," when a reasonably prudent man in the circumstances would be warranted in the belief that his safety or that of others is in danger. (Thus, the essence of the holding is the self-protection of the officer. The Court said that a "pat-down for weapons" [i.e., a frisk] constitutes a "search" within the meaning of the Fourth Amendment. The Court side-stepped passing on the constitutionality of New York's "stop-and-frisk" legislation. Five opinions were written in the case.)

Morales v. New York, 396 U.S. 102, 24 L. Ed. 2d 299, 90 S. Ct. 291 (1969).

The Court, 7-1, remanded a murder conviction to the state courts for factual findings. (The New York Court of Appeals approved in principle an arrest that did not measure up to traditional reasonable grounds standards. So what was potentially one of the 1969 Term's most important rulings in the criminal law field results in no ruling at all. There has been a drift away from doctrinaire standards in search and seizure situations to a standard of reasonableness based on the totality of circumstances which is all to the good. This is the approach, seemingly, the New York Court followed in *Morales*. The Supreme Court's remand in *Morales* still leaves open the constitutionality of New York's stop and frisk legislation with the result that New York's stop and frisk decisions stand as good law in that State until such time as the United States Supreme Court may reach a contrary result.)

Adams v. Williams, 407 U.S. 143, 32 L. Ed. 2d 612, 92 S. Ct. 1921 (1972):

Mr. Justice Rehnquist's opinion holds, 6-3, a known informer's tip is sufficient to support a stop-and-frisk. (Acting on a tip supplied moments earlier—about 2:15 a.m., in a high crime area—by an informant known to him, a police officer asked Williams to open his car door. Williams lowered the window, and the officer reached into the car and found a loaded handgun—which had not been visible from the outside—in Williams' waistband, precisely where the informant said it would be. Williams was arrested for unlawful possession of the handgun. A search incident to the arrest disclosed heroin on Williams' person—as the informant had reported—as well as other contraband. That part of Mr. Justice Douglas' dissent should be noted, in particular, which says the officer made the arrest and search without first determining whether Williams had a permit to carry the handgun.)

FIFTH AMENDMENT RIGHTS

CONFESSION CASES

Brown v. Mississippi, 297 U.S. 278, 80 L. Ed. 682, 56 S. Ct. 461 (1936):

In this first state-confession case to go to the Supreme Court of the United States, the Court held that the use by the state of an obviously coerced confession violated the petitioner's due process rights under the Fourteenth Amendment. (The main emphasis was not on police misconduct—albeit that was shocking—but on an abuse of discretion by the trial judge in permitting the confession to be introduced.)

McNabb v. United States, 318 U.S. 332, 87 L. Ed. 819, 63 S. Ct. 708 (1943):

In a 7-1 opinion, in which Mr. Justice Reed did not take part, the Court held that a confession that had been obtained while the suspect was illegally detained under aggravated circumstances—failure to arraign promptly coupled with noncoercive police methods—was inadmissible in a federal court. (This rule became known as the federal "civilized standards" rule. The decision marked the beginning of a period in which the Court formulated new policy for federal criminal trials under the Court's inherent supervisory powers over lower federal courts.)

Ashcraft v. Tennessee, 322 U.S. 143, 88 L. Ed. 1192, 64 S. Ct. 921 (1944):

With Mr. Justice Jackson dissenting, the Court held that a confession obtained under *aggravating circumstances* (inherent coercion) coupled with unnecessary delays in arraignment, is involuntary, and inadmissible in a state court under due process of the Fourteenth Amendment. (Thus the Court coined the "inherently coercive" rule as a substantial equivalent of the "civilized standards" rule that had been created in *McNabb*.)

Mallory v. United States, 354 U.S. 449, 1 L. Ed. 2d 1479, 775 S. Ct. 1356 (1957):

The Court through Mr. Justice Frankfurter, in a unanimous decision, held that a confession could not be admitted in a federal court when it had been obtained during a period of detention in violation of prompt arraignment rules. (Because the *Mallory* rule was not bottomed on the federal constitution, it was not binding on the states through the Fourteenth Amendment due process clause.)

Haynes v. Washington, 373 U.S. 503, 10 L. Ed. 2d 513, 83 S. Ct. 1336 (1963):

The Court held (5-4) that when a confession is "obtained in an atmosphere of substantial coercion and inducements created by statements and actions of state authorities, "it is inadmissible under due process of the Fourteenth Amendment. (The police "coercion" in *Haynes* rested on their refusal to permit the prisoner to contact his wife unless he confessed, and kept him in a technically incommunicado status, even though there was very little to indicate that his statement in fact was unreliable. The Court expressly recognized, at that time, the need for custodial interrogation. "[C]ertainly, we do not mean to suggest that all interrogation of witnesses and suspects is impermissible," said Mr. Justice Goldberg.)

Massiah v. United States, 377 U.S. 201, 12 L. Ed. 2d 246, 84 S. Ct. 1199 (1964):

The Court held (6-3) that no indicted defendant can be interrogated under any circumstances in the absence of his attorney without having his Sixth Amendment right to counsel impaired. A brief *per curiam* opinion made the *Massiah* doctrine binding on the states under the Fourteenth Amendment. *McLeod v. Ohio*, 381 U.S. 356 (1965). (A government informer, in *Massiah*, concealed a radio transmitter under the front seat of his automobile. He and the petitioner had a lengthy conversation which, unknown to *Massiah*, was overheard by a government agent over his automobile radio while parked out of sight down the street. *Massiah* marked a turning point in the Court's philosophy of disposing of confession cases, on the basis, mainly, of the totality of circumstances. So long as the Court was concerned with the "totality of the circumstances" of a confession in deciding whether or not to reverse a state conviction, no single factor had conclusive impact. The Court shifted its position to a "single factor" rule in *Massiah*.)

Escobedo v. Illinois, 378 U.S. 478, 12 L. Ed. 2d 977, 84 S. Ct. 1758 (1964):

"We hold only," concluded the Court in its 5-4 opinion, "that when the process shifts from investigatory to accusatory and its purpose is to elicit a confession—our adversary system begins to operate, and, under the circumstances here, the accused must be permitted to consult with his lawyer." (The construction of the bridge that led to *Miranda v. Arizona*, was begun in *Gideon v. Wainwright*, 372 U.S. 335 [1963], and completed in *Escobedo*.)

Miranda v. Arizona, 384 U.S. 436, 16 L. Ed. 2d 694, 86 S. Ct. 1602 (1966):

A majority of the Court (5-4) in this epic decision, imposed upon law enforcement officers a scheme of preinterrogation warnings and advice as federal constitutional prerequisites to the admissibility of confessions and statements in state and federal prosecutions. The Court expressly held that the privilege against self-incrimination is available outside of criminal court proceedings and applies to police interrogations of persons "in custody." (It was in *Escobedo*, however, that a constitutional-rule was shaped as a springboard to *Miranda*. The main thrust of *Escobedo* is on the right of a suspect to consult with *retained counsel* in the pre-judicial stage of a criminal investigation. This was absorbed into *Miranda* as a very important ancillary rule. Neither the *Escobedo* nor the *Miranda* decisions could have come about, however, if the Court had neglected the homework that it finished in *Malloy v. Hogan*, 378 U.S. 1 [1964].)

Johnson v. New Jersey, 384 U.S. 719, 16 L. Ed. 2d 882, 86 S. Ct. 1772 (1966):

The Court held (7-2) that the *Miranda* rules apply only to cases in which the trial began after June 13, 1966, and, similarly, that the *Escobedo* rules affect only those cases in which the trial began after June 22, 1964—the respective dates of the two decisions.

Davis v. North Carolina, 384 U.S. 737, 16 L. Ed. 2d 895, 86 S. Ct. 1761 (1966):

In a 7-2 decision the Court held that the original "voluntariness" test will apply to cases arising before *Escobedo* was decided. (This decision is significant in that it shows the *Johnson* decision did not foreclose a person from seeking a reversal of a conviction on the grounds an involuntary confession had been used against him at the trial.)

Bruton v. United States, 391 U.S. 123, 20 L. Ed. 2d 476, 88 S. Ct. 1620 (1968):

Overruling *Delli Paoli v. United States*, 352 U.S. 232, Mr. Justice Brennan, writing for the majority, held that a confession of one defendant cannot be used at a joint trial in which it might prejudice a codefendant. ("Because of the substantial risk that the jury, despite instructions to the contrary, looked to the incriminating extrajudicial statements in determining petitioner's guilt, admission of Evans' confession in this joint trial violated petitioner's right to cross-examination secured by the Confrontation Clause of the Sixth Amendment," said the Court.)

Orozco v. Texas, 394 U.S. 324, 22 L. Ed. 2d 311, 89 S. Ct. 1095 (1969):

Mr. Justice Black, 6-2, states that once an accused is in custody, regardless of where he is in custody, *Miranda* warnings must be given, if a statement, or evidence derived therefrom, is to be admissible. (The State argued that *Miranda* is inapplicable to an interrogation of a suspect in his own bed, in familiar surroundings. The Court said questioning means more than station house questioning. The opinion makes it clear the gun found as a result of questioning the suspect could not be used on a retrial as it would be the fruit of the poisonous tree. *Miranda* does not contain an absolute mandate that its warnings must be given. It does no more than to say that non-compliance will result in the exclusion of a statement. There could well be circumstances when it would be imperative to get information in a hurry, for example, to save a person's life. The statement would be inadmissible, but a life would be saved.)

Frazier v. Cupp, 394 U.S. 731, 22 L. Ed. 2d 684, 89 S. Ct. 1420 (1969):

In this pre-*Miranda* decision (controlled by *Escobedo v. Illinois*), in a unanimous decision by Mr. Justice Marshall, for the first time since *Miranda*, the Court sanctions some trickery in obtaining a confession. (This opinion should be read very narrowly, however, as the Court clearly implies that the result might have been different if *Miranda* had been applicable. It is difficult to visualize how there could be a knowing and intelligent waiver of rights, after they have been given, when an investigator turns to deception to get a statement.)

Jenkins vs. Delaware, 395 U.S. 213, 23 L. Ed. 2d 253, 89 S. Ct. 1677 (1969):

The Court held, 7-1, that *Miranda's* standards do not apply to post-*Miranda* retrials of cases originally tried prior to that decision.

Harris v. New York, 401 U.S. 222, 28 L. Ed. 2d 1, 91 S. Ct. 643 (1971):

The Court, 5-4, in an opinion by Chief Justice Burger, held that a prosecutor may use illegally obtained confession to prove that a defendant who testifies is lying. (The Chief Justice said that an exception to the exclusionary rule of *Miranda* must be made to counter perjurious testimony by a defendant. It should be noted that the defendant's statement was voluntary and there had been some compliance with *Miranda*. The use of a confession for impeachment purposes should not be considered to extend to involuntary confessions which are inadmissible as being untrustworthy.)

LINE-UP IDENTIFICATION CASES *

United States v. Wade, 388 U.S. 218, 18 L. Ed. 2d 1149, 87 S. Ct. 1926 (1967):

In a decision marked by a galaxy of concurring in part and dissenting in part opinions, a majority of the Court held that police line-ups constitute a critical stage of the prose-

---

* Opinions, legally, fall under the Sixth Amendment Rights, but have been placed here due to obvious linkage with the Fifth Amendment Rights.

cutorial process, and the Sixth Amendment right to counsel attaches at that time, applicable to the states through due process of the Fourteenth Amendment.

Gilbert v. California, 388 U.S. 263, 18 L. Ed. 2d 1178, 87 S. Ct. 1951 (1967):

The Court, in a decision marked by similar divisiveness that characterized *Wade*, restated the basic principle announced in *Wade* and refined it with repect to testimony that is the "direct result of an illegal line-up." (The majority also stressed that only a *per se* exclusionary rule can be an effective sanction to assure that law enforcement authorities will respect the accused's constitutional right to the presence of counsel at the critical line-up. The majority also rejected the contention that the Fifth Amendment privilege was violated by placing the defendant in a line-up and having him repeat phrases used by the person who committed the crime at the time he committed it.)

Stovall v. Denno, 388 U.S. 293, 18 L. Ed. 2d 1199, 87 S. Ct. 1967 (1967):

A 6-2 majority of the Court in the last of the line-up cases handed down in the 1966-67 Term, limited the exclusionary rule to cases involving line-ups held after the June 12th announcement of the decision in *Wade*. (The Court changed its posture to a more fundamental fairness approach, in relation to law enforcement, in Stovall, than it exercised in *Johnson v. New Jersey* with respect to retroactivity. *Stovall*, moreover, by way of dictum, makes it clear that counsel at a line-up identification applies to pre-indictment stages. *Wade, Gilbert* and *Stovall* expand the *Schmerber* doctrine, *Schmerber v. California*, 384 U.S. 757 [1966], so that the net effect of the three cases is that one can be compelled against his will to appear in a line-up, to furnish a handwriting exemplar, to put on clothing or, as in *Wade*, to put strips of tape on one's face and, at least inferentially, to speak for voice identification. This latter act, along with possibly other performance such as walking or taking a particular stance, would seem to have some limitations.)

Simmons v. United States, 390 U.S. 377, 19 L. Ed. 2d 1247, 88 S. Ct. 967 (1968):

The Court, 6-2, shows its unwillingness to prohibit the use of photographs in apprehending offenders (which also spares the arrest of innocent suspects), either by its supervisory power or "still less" as a constitutional requirement. (An attorney need not be present at the viewing of photographs. Suggestions are offered on how photographs should be used to identify a suspect.)

Foster v. California, 394 U.S. 440, 22 L. Ed. 2d 402, 89 S. Ct. 1127 (1969):

The Court, 5-4, through Mr. Justice Fortas, in his pre-*Wade* line-up, held that what the police officers did in conducting the line-ups was "so unnecessarily suggestive and conducive to irreparable mistaken identification as to be a denial of due proces under the Fourteenth Amendment." (The opinion points up how not to conduct a line-up.)

Kirby v. Illinois, 406 U.S. 682, 32 L. Ed. 2d 411, 92 S. Ct. 1877 (1972):

In a 4-4 opinion by Mr. Justice Stewart (Mr. Justice Powell concurring in the result), the Court holds the formal charge—preliminary hearing, indictment, information, or arraignment—is the cutoff point when a person is entitled to have counsel present at a line-up. (The plurality opinion states the *per se* exclusionary rule of *Wade* and *Gilbert* doesn't apply to pre-indictment confrontations. However, wise prosecutors and law enforcement officers will continue to provide counsel at a line-up as very little weight can be given to a 4-4 decision.)

SELF-INCRIMINATION CASES

Adamson v. California, 353 U.S. 46, 91 L. Ed. 1903, 67 S. Ct. 1672 (1947):

Mr. Justice Reed, for the Court, held (in a 5-4 opinion) that a state constitutional provision, or statute, that allows the prosecutor or the court to comment on the failure of a defendant to testify is not unconstitutional as an abridgment of his privilege against self-incrimination under the Fifth and Fourteenth Amendments. (This decision is so rich in the history of the Constitution, the Bill of Rights, and the Fourteenth Amendment—especially Mr. Justice Frankfurter's concurring opinion—that it should be read to gain a better insight into the relationship between the Bill of Rights and the Fourteenth Amendment.)

Malloy v. Hogan, 378 U.S. 1, 12 L. Ed. 2d 653, 84 S. Ct. 1489 (1964):

The Court held (7-2) that the states, the same as the United States, cannot compel incriminating testimony—thus overruling *Adamson v. California*, 353 U.S. 46 (1947). (This decision makes the self-incrimination privilege of the Fifth Amendment applicable to the states through the due process clause of the Fourteenth Amendment.)

Murphy v. Waterfront Commission, 378 U.S. 52, 12 L. Ed. 2d 678, 84 S. Ct. 1594 (1964):

The Court held that the constitutional privilege against self-incrimination protects a state witness against incrimination under federal as well as state law and a federal witness against incrimination under state law—thus overruling *United States v. Murdock*, 284 U.S. 41.

Griffin v. California, 380 U.S. 609, 14 L. Ed. 2d 106, 85 S. Ct. 1229 (1965):

The Court held (6-2) that the Fifth Amendment forbids a state prosecutor's comment on failure of a defendant to explain evidence within his knowledge and bars an instruction from the court that such silence may be evidence of guilt. (This holding broadens the meaning of *Malloy v. Hogan*, 378 U.S. 1.)

Schmerber v. California, 384 U.S. 757, 16 L. Ed. 2d 908, 86 S. Ct. 1826 (1966):

With four justices dissenting, Mr. Justice Brennan, for the majority, held the prosecution can use as evidence in a drunken driving test the analysis of a blood sample taken without the consent of the accused without violating his Fifth, Sixth and Fourteenth Amendment rights against self-incrimination. (The Court distinguishes between the production of compelled physical evidence, and testimonial compulsion, i.e., words produced by someone's lips.)

Gardner v. Broderick, 392 U.S. 273, 20 L. Ed. 2d 1082, 88 S. Ct. 1913 (1968):

The Court held that a policeman who refuses to waive his Fifth Amendment privilege against self-incrimination (sign a waiver of immunity before testifying) cannot be dismissed from office solely because of his refusal. (Mr. Justice Fortas, speaking for the Court, notes that there is a difference between a police officer [a public officer] and a lawyer, stating that had the police officer refused to answer questions . . . without being required to waive his immunity . . . the privilege against self-incrimination would not have been a bar to his dismissal. It can be noted that the Court *may* eventually reject the Fortas' distinction as Mr. Justice Black, concurring in the result, said: "I find in these opinions [*Gardner* and *Uniformed Sanitation Men Association*] a procedural formula whereby, for example, public officials may now be discharged and lawyers disciplined for refusing to divulge to appropriate authority information pertinent to the faithful performance of their offices.")

Uniformed Sanitation Men Association v. Commissioner of Sanitation of the City of New York, 392 U.S. 280, 20 L. Ed. 2d 1089, 88 S. Ct. 1917 (1968):

The Court held substantially the same as in its *Gardner* opinion in regard to this class of city employees.

Benton v. Maryland, 395 U.S. 784, 23 L. Ed. 2d 707, 89 S. Ct. 2056 (1969):

In the Court's last decision of the 1969 Term, the Court through Mr. Justice Marshall, held, 6-2, that the Double Jeopardy Clause of the Fifth Amendment is applicable to the states through the Due Process Clause of the Fourteenth Amendment. (The decision overruled *Palko v. Connecticut,* (302 U.S. 319—1937), one of the Court's earlier landmark decisions. The Double Jeopardy prohibition "represents a fundamental idea in our constitutional heritage," Mr. Justice Marshall said. "*Palko,*" he continued, "represented an approach to basic constitutional rights which this Court's recent decisions have rejected.") *

California v. Byers, 402 U.S. 424, 29 L. Ed. 2d 9, 91 S. Ct. 1535 (1971):

In this 4-4 decision by Chief Justice Burger the Court held the Fifth Amendment's self-incrimination clause neither vitiates a California statute that requires a motorist involved in an accident to stop and identify himself nor requires a restriction on the prosecutorial use of the information that the statute compels a motorist to supply. (Mr. Justice Harlan finds that the statute in fact does involve self-incrimination. However, he is "constrained to hold that the presence of a 'real' and not 'imaginary' risk of self-incrimination is not a sufficient predicate for extending the privilege against self-incrimination to regulatory schemes of the character in this case." The *Marchetti-Grosso* line of cases—gamblers' wagering stamps—are distinguished from the present case.)

Kastigar et al. v. United States, 406 U.S. 441, 32 L. Ed. 2d 212, 92 S. Ct. 1653 (1972):

The Court, 5-2, in an opinion by Mr. Justice Powell, upholds the limited immunity the Organized Crime Control Act of 1970 gives witnesses who are compelled to testify before grand juries. "Transactional immunity would afford broader protection than the Fifth Amendment privilege, and is not constitutionally required," the Court declares. (Prosecutors had been waiting more than two years for the Court to settle the constitutional controversy. The federal law had been copied by several states.)

---

* This is not a self-incrimination decision. It is included in this section due to the close relationship between double jeopardy and self-incrimination.

SIXTH AMENDMENT RIGHTS

ASSISTANCE OF COUNSEL CASES

Powell v. Alabama, 287 U.S. 45, 77 L. Ed. 158, 53 S. Ct. 55 (1932):

In this early landmark case on the right to the assistance of counsel, Mr. Justice Sutherland, speaking for the Court, held that the right to counsel, guaranteed in federal prosecutions by the Sixth Amendment, is not binding on the states in noncapital cases, *providing the trial itself was fair*, through the due process clause of the Fourteenth Amendment.

Johnson v. Zerbst, 304 U.S. 458, 82 L. Ed. 1461, 58 S. Ct. 1019 (1938):

The Court held that the Sixth Amendment includes the right of federal indigent defendants to be furnished counsel.

Betts v. Brady, 316 U.S. 455, 86 L. Ed. 1595, 62 S. Ct. 1252 (1942):

In a 6-3 decision, the Court held that a state-court indigent defendant in a noncapital case, has no right to appointed counsel under the Amendment's due process clause. (During the reign of *Betts* the Court made it clear that denying a defendant the assistance of his own counsel in any case, at any stage, on any issue, constituted a per se violation of "fundamental fairness.")

Griffin v. Illinois, 351 U.S. 12, 100 L. Ed. 891, 76 S. Ct. 585 (1956):

The Court held 5-4 that the due process and equal protection clauses of the Fourteenth Amendment require that all indigent defendants be furnished a transcript for an appeal. (Strictly speaking, there was no opinion of the Court as Mr. Justice Black announced the Court's judgment in a four-man opinion.)

Gideon v. Wainwright, 372 U.S. 335, 9 L. Ed. 2d 799, 83 S. Ct. 792 (1963):

The Fourteenth Amendment, a unanimous Court held, requires a state to appoint counsel for indigent defendants in noncapital as well as capital cases—overruling *Betts v. Brady*, 316 U.S. 455 (1942).

Douglas v. California, 372 U.S. 353, 9 L. Ed. 2d 811, 83 S. Ct. 814 (1963):

The Court held 6-3 that there is an absolute right to the assistance of counsel to make a first appeal under the equal protection clause of the Fourteenth Amendment.

Mempa v. Rhay, 389 U.S. 128, 19 L. Ed. 2d 336, 88 S. Ct. 254 (1967):

The Court in a unanimous opinion held that the right to counsel attaches to a state probation revocation hearing at which a deferred sentence may be imposed.

Coleman v. Alabama, 399 U.S. 1, 26 L. Ed. 2d 387, 90 S. Ct. 1999 (1970):

Mr. Justice Brennan's principal opinion, in a case in which the defendant had been charged with assault with intent to murder, held that a preliminary hearing, if held, is a "critical stage," and an indigent defendant has a constitutional right to the appointment of counsel under the Sixth and Fourteenth Amendments. (Only Mr. Justice Marshall joined Mr. Justice Brennan. Six Justices wrote separate concurring and dissenting opinions. There was a vacancy on the Court at the time.)

Argersinger v. Hamlin, 407 U.S. 25, 32 L. Ed. 2d 530, 92 S. Ct. 2006 (1972):

The Court holds, 6-3, through Mr. Justice Douglas, that all defendants facing a possible jail sentence are entitled to be represented by legal counsel in their trial, and that the State must provide a lawyer if the defendant wants one and cannot afford the cost. (Three concurring opinions were filed.)

JUVENILE RIGHTS

DUE PROCESS FOR JUVENILE CASES

Kent v. United States, 383 U.S. 541, 16 L. Ed. 2d 84, 86 S. Ct. 1045 (1966):

The Court, dividing 5-4, held that a juvenile court must conduct a hearing prior to the entry of a waiver order transferring jurisdiction to a criminal court. (The opinion is decided on statutory grounds as an interpretation of the District of Columbia *Juvenile Court Act*. The constitutional mandates which emerged later in *Gault* were obviously close to the surface.)

In re Gault, 387 U.S. 1, 18 L. Ed. 2d 527, 87 S. Ct. 1428 (1967):

In this ground-breaking decision, with one justice dissenting, the Court held that the due process clause of the Fourteenth Amendment applies to proceedings in state juvenile courts to adjudicate a juvenile a delinquent. (The Court indicates that a juvenile is entitled, in the adjudicatory stage of a juvenile court proceeding, to substantially the same rights that are accorded to an adult in a criminal court. A wide divergence of views have been expressed by legal commentators and juvenile court personnel as to what *Gault* means, and its prospective reach on juvenile courts. One thing that does stand out is that *Gault* requires a complete alteration of the nation's juvenile court system.)

In re Winship, 397 U.S. 358, 25 L. Ed. 2d 368, 90 S. Ct. 1068 (1970):

The Court held, 5-3, through Mr. Justice Brennan, that the Due Process Clause requires that the conviction of a criminally accused be based upon proof of guilt beyond a reasonable doubt; the same standard applies to the adjudicatory stage of a juvenile delinquency proceedings in which a youth is charged with an act that would constitute a crime if committed by an adult. (Three standards of proof had been recognized in juvenile courts prior to *Winship*. They were (1) beyond a reasonable doubt, (2) by clear and convincing evidence, and (3) by a preponderance of the evidence.)

McKiever v. Pennsylvania (In re Barbara Burrus et al.), 403 U.S. 528, 29 L. Ed. 2d 647, 91 S.Ct. 1976 (1971):

Mr. Justice Blackmun for the Court, 6-3, held that the Sixth Amendment does not require trial by jury in state juvenile delinquency proceedings. (After examining past juvenile court decisions, Mr. Justice Blackmun established that the Court had only extended certain fundamental rights to the juvenile, and concluded that trial by jury was not an essential safeguard to assure procedural fairness. However, a state may adopt a higher standard than that prescribed. For example, Michigan, by statute, provides that a juvenile "may demand a jury of 6, or the judge . . . may order a jury of the same number to try the case.")

Ivan V. v. City of New York, 407 U.S. 203, 32 L. Ed. 2d 659, 92 S. Ct. 1951 (1972):

By way of a summary reversal of a New York Court of Appeals decision, the Court holds that *In re Winship* applies retroactively. (The reasonable doubt standard, because it is an essential of due process and fair treatment, applies to juvenile proceedings in which the youth is charged with an act that would be a crime if committed by an adult.)

ALPHABETIZED LIST OF CASES

APPENDIX C

PROCESSES OF JUSTICE: FLOW CHART

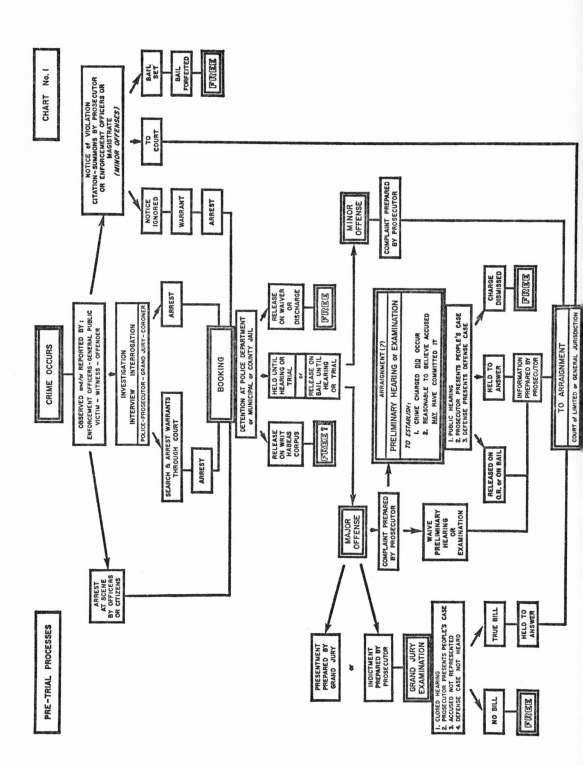

PRE-TRIAL PROCESSES

CHART No. I

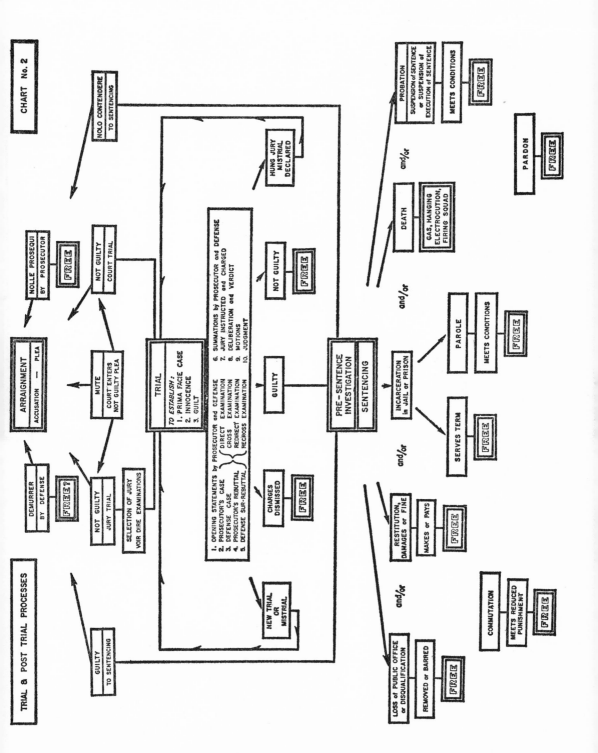

CHART No. 2

TRIAL & POST TRIAL PROCESSES

APPENDIX D
STANDARDS RELATING TO THE URBAN POLICE FUNCTION

Approved Draft

American Bar Association

Project on Standards for Criminal Justice

STANDARDS RELATING TO THE URBAN
POLICE FUNCTION*

PART I. GENERAL PRINCIPLES

1.1 Complexity of police task.

(a) Sincere police, as an agency of the criminal justice system, have a major responsibility for dealing with serious crime, efforts should continually be made to improve the capacity of police to discharge this responsibility effectively. It should also be recognized, however, that police effectiveness in dealing with crime is often largely dependent upon the effectiveness of other agencies both within and outside the criminal justice system. Those in the system must work together through liaison, cooperation, and constructive joint effort. This effort is vital to the effective operation of the police and the entire criminal justice system.

(b) To achieve optimum police effectiveness, the police should be recognized as having complex and multiple tasks to perform in addition to identifying and apprehending persons committing serious criminal offenses. Such other police tasks include protection of certain rights such as to speak and to assemble, participation either directly or in conjunction with other public and social agencies in the prevention of criminal and delinquent behavior, maintenance of order and control of pedestrian and vehicular traffic, resolution of conflict, and assistance to citizens in need of help such as the person who is mentally ill, the chronic alcoholic, or the drug addict.

(c) Recommendations made in these standards are based on the view that this diversity of responsibilities is likely to continue and, more importantly, that police authority and skills are needed to handle appropriately a wide variety of community problems.

1.2 Scope of standards.

To ensure that the police are responsive to all the special needs for police services in a democratic society, it is necessary to:

(i) identify clearly the principal objectives and responsibilities of police and establish priorities between the several and sometimes conflicting objectives;

(ii) provide for adequate methods and confer sufficient authority to discharge the responsibility given them;

(iii) provide adequate mechanisms and incentives to ensure that attention is given to the development of law enforcement policies to guide the exercise of administrative discretion by police;

(iv) ensure proper use of police authority;

(v) develop an appropriate professional role for and constraints upon individual police officers in policy-making and political activity;

(vi) provide police departments with human and other resources necessary for effective performance;

(vii) improve the criminal justice, juvenile justice, mental health, and public health systems of which the police are an important part;

(viii) gain the understanding and support of the community; and

(ix) provide adequate means for continually evaluating the effectiveness of police services.

1.3 Need for experimentation.

There is need for financial assistance from the federal government and from other sources to support experimental and evaluative programs designed to achieve the objectives set forth in these standards.

PART II. POLICE OBJECTIVES AND PRIORITIES

2.1 Factors accounting for responsibilities given police.

The wide range of government tasks currently assigned to police has been given, to a great degree, without any coherent planning by state or local governments of what the overriding objectives or priorities of the police should be. Instead, what police do is determined largely on an ad hoc basis by a number of factors which influence their involvement in responding to various government or community needs. These factors include:

(i) broad legislative mandates to the police;
(ii) the authority of the police to use force lawfully;
(iii) the investigative ability of the police;
(iv) the twenty-four-hour availability of the police; and
(v) community pressures on the police.

2.2 Major current responsibilities of police.

In assessing appropriate objectives and priorities for police service, local communities should initially recognize that most police agencies are currently given responsibility, by design or default:

(i) to identify criminal offenders and criminal activity and, where appropriate, to apprehend offenders and participate in subsequent court proceedings;
(ii) to reduce the opportunities for the commission of some crimes through preventive patrol and other measures;
(iii) to aid individuals who are in danger of physical harm;
(iv) to protect constitutional guarantees;
(v) to facilitate the movement of people and vehicles;
(vi) to assist those who cannot care for themselves;
(vii) to resolve conflict;
(viii) to identify problems that are potentially serious law enforcement or governmental problems;
(ix) to create and maintain a feeling of security in the community;
(x) to promote and preserve civil order; and
(xi) to provide other services on an emergency basis.

2.3 Need for local objectives and priorities.

While the scope and objectives of the exercise of the government's police power are properly determined in the first instance by state and local legislative bodies within the limits fixed by the Constitution and by court decisions, it should be recognized there is considerable latitude remaining with local government to develop an overall direction for police services. Within these limits, each local jurisdiction should decide upon objectives and priorities. Decisions regarding police resources, police personnel needs, police organization, and relations with other government agencies should then be made in a way which will best achieve the objectives and priorities of the particular locality.

2.4 General criteria for objectives and priorities.

In formulating an overall direction for police services and in selecting appropriate objectives and priorities for the police, communities should be guided by certain principles that should be inherent in a democratic society:

(i) The highest duties of government, and therefore the police, are to safeguard freedom, to preserve life and property, to protect the constitutional rights of citizens and maintain respect for the rule of law by proper enforcement thereof, and thereby, to preserve democratic processes;

(ii) Implicit within this duty, the police have the responsibility for maintaining that degree of public order which is consistent with freedom and which is essential if our urban and diverse society is to be maintained;

(iii) In implementing their varied responsibilities, police must provide maximum opportunity for achieving desired social change by freely-available, lawful, and orderly means; and

(iv) In order to maximize the use of the special authority and ability of the police, it is appropriate for government, in developing objectives and priorities for police services, to give emphasis to those social and behavioral problems which may require the use of force or the use of special investigative abilities which the police possess. Given the awesome authority of the police to use force and the priority that must be given to preserving life, however, government should firmly establish the principle that the police should be restricted to using the amount of force reasonably necessary in responding to any situation.

2.5 Role of local chief executive.

In general terms, the chief executive of a governmental subdivision should be recognized as having the ultimate responsibility for his police department and, in conjunction with his police administrator and the municipal legislative body, should formulate lawful policy relating to the nature of the police function, the objectives and priorities of the police in carrying out this function, and the relationship of these objectives and priorities to general municipal strategies. This will require that a chief executive, along with assuming new responsibilities for formulating overall directions for police services, must also:

(i) insulate the police department from inappropriate pressures including such pressures from his own office;

(ii) insulate the police department from pressures to deal with matters in an unlawful or unconstitutional manner; and

(iii) insulate the police administrator from inappropriate interference with the internal administration of his department.

PART III. METHODS AND AUTHORITY AVAILABLE TO THE POLICE FOR FULFILLING THE TASKS GIVEN THEM

3.1 Alternative methods used by police.

The process of investigation, arrest, and prosecution, commonly viewed as an end in itself, should be recognized as but one of the methods used by police in performing their overall function, even though it is the most important method of dealing with serious criminal activity. Among other methods police use are, for example, the process of informal resolution of conflict, referral, and warning. The alternative methods used by police should be recognized as important and warranting improvement in number and effectiveness; and the police should be given the necessary authority to use them under circumstances in which it is desirable to do so.

3.2 Avoiding overreliance upon the criminal law.

The assumption that the use of an arrest and the criminal process is the primary or even the exclusive method available to police should be recognized as causing unnecessary distortion of both the criminal law and the system of criminal justice.

3.3 Need for clarified, properly limited authority to use methods other than the criminal justice system.

There should be clarification of the authority of police to use methods other than arrest and prosecution to deal with the variety of behavioral and social problems which they confront. This should include careful consideration of the need for and problems created by providing police with recognized and properly-limited authority and protection while operating thereunder:

(i) to deal with interferences with the democratic process. Although it is assumed that police have a duty to protect free speech and the right of dissent, their authority to do so is unclear, particularly because of the questionable constitutionality of many statutes, such as the disorderly conduct statutes, upon which police have relied in the past;

(ii) to deal with self-destructive conduct such as that engaged in by persons who are helpless by reason of mental illness or persons who are incapacitated by alcohol or drugs. Such authority as exists is too often dependent upon criminal laws which commonly afford an inadequate basis to deal effectively and humanely with self-destructive behavior;

(iii) to engage in the resolution of conflict such as that which occurs so frequently between husband and wife or neighbor and neighbor in the highly-populated sections of the large city, without reliance upon criminal assault or disorderly conduct statutes;

(iv) to take appropriate action to prevent disorder such as by ordering crowds to disperse where there is adequate reason to believe that such action is required to prevent disorder and to deal properly and effectively with disorder when it occurs; and

(v) to require potential victims of crime to take preventive action such as by a legal requirement that building owners follow a burglary prevention program similar to common fire prevention programs.

3.4 Legislative concern for feasibility of criminal sanction.

Within the field of criminal justice administration, legislatures should, prior to defining conduct as criminal, carefully consider whether adequate authority and resources exist for police to enforce the prohibition by methods which the community is willing to tolerate and support. Criminal codes should be reevaluated to determine whether there are adequate ways of enforcing the prohibition. If not, noncriminal solutions to all or a portion of the problem should be considered.

PART IV. LAW ENFORCEMENT POLICY-MAKING

4.1 Exercise of discretion by police.

The nature of the responsibilities currently placed upon the police requires that the police exercise a great deal of discretion—a situation that has long existed, but is not always recognized.

4.2 Need for structure and control.

Since individual police officers may make important decisions affecting police operations without direction, with limited accountability, and without any uniformity within a department, police discretion should be structured and controlled.

4.3 Administrative rule-making.

Police discretion can best be structured and controlled through the process of administrative rule-making by police agencies. Police administrators should, therefore, give the highest priority to the formulation of administrative rules governing the exercise of discretion, particularly in the areas of selective enforcement, investigative techniques, and enforcement methods.

4.4 Contribution by legislatures and courts.

To stimulate the development of appropriate administrative guidance and control over police discretion, legislatures and courts should actively encourage police administrative rule-making.

(a) Legislatures can meet this need by delegating administrative rule-making responsibility to the police by statute.

(b) Courts can stimulate administrative development in several ways including the following:

(i) Properly-developed and published police administrative policies should be sustained unless demonstrated to be unconstitutional, arbitrary, or otherwise outside the authority of the police;

(ii) To stimulate timely and adequate administrative policy-making, a determination by a court of a violation of an administrative policy should not be a basis for excluding evidence in a criminal case unless the violation of administrative policy is of constitutional dimensions or is otherwise so serious as to call for the exercise of the superintending authority of the court. A violation *per se* should not result in civil liability; and

(iii) Where it appears to the court that an individual officer has acted in violation of administrative policy or that an administrative policy is unconstitutional, arbitrary, or otherwise outside the authority of the police, the court should arrange for the police administrator to be informed of this fact, in order to facilitate fulfillment by the police administrator of his responsibility in such circumstances to reexamine the relevant policy or policies and to review methods of training, communication of policy, and supervision and control.

4.5 Method of policy-making.

In its development of procedures to openly formulate, implement, and reevaluate police policy as necessary, each jurisdiction should be conscious of the need to effectively consult a representative cross-section of citizens in this process.

PART V. CONTROL OVER POLICE AUTHORITY

5.1 Need for accountability.

Since a principal function of police is the safeguarding of democratic processes, if police fail to conform their conduct to the requirements of law, they subvert the democratic process and frustrate the achievement of a principal police function. It is for this reason that high priority must be given for ensuring that the police are made fully accountable to their police administrator and to the public for their actions.

5.2 Need for positive approaches.

Control over police practice should, insofar as possible, be positive, creating inducements to perform properly rather than concentrating solely upon penalizing improper police conduct. Among the ways this can be accomplished are:

(i) Education and training oriented to the development of professional pride in conforming to the requirements of law and maximizing the values of a democratic society;

(ii) Inducements to police officers in terms of status, compensation, and promotion, on the basis of criteria that are related as directly as possible to the police function and police goals;

(iii) Elimination of responsibilities where there is a community expectation that police will "do something," but adequate lawful authority is not provided. Either the needed authority should be given or the police should be relieved of the responsibility;

(iv) Systematic efforts by prosecutors and judges to encourage conforming police behavior through: (a) a more careful review of applications for warrants and (b) formulation of new procedures to simplify and otherwise provide easy access for judicial review of applications for warrants, thereby encouraging maximum use of the formal warrant process;

(v) Requirements that police develop administrative policies controlling police actions which, if reasonable, would be sustained and utilized by the courts; and

(vi) Effective involvement of the community in the development of police programs.

5.3 Sanctions.

Current methods of review and control of police activities include the following sanctions:

(i) the exclusion of evidence obtained by unconstitutional means;

(ii) criminal and tort liability for knowingly engaging in unlawful conduct;

(iii) injunctive actions to terminate a pattern of unlawful conduct; and

(iv) local procedures for handling complaints against police officers, procedures which usually operate administratively within police departments.

Each of these should be continually reevaluated and changed when necessary to achieve both effective control over the exercise of police authority and the effective administration of criminal justice.

5.4 Need for administrative sanctions and procedures.

In order to strengthen administrative review and control, responsibility should formally be delegated to the police for developing comprehensive administrative policies and rules governing the duties and responsibilities of police officers together with procedures and sanctions for ensuring that these duties and responsibilities are met. Police administrative rules and procedures should establish effective investigative, hearing, and internal review procedures for alleged violations. Such procedures should include provisions for handling, monitoring, and reviewing citizen complaints in such a way as to ensure diligence, fairness, and public confidence. In developing such rules and procedures, recognition must be given to the need to conform procedures to administrative due process requirements, to develop means for ensuring impartial investigations, and to keep the public informed of all administrative actions as they are taken.

5.5 Tort liability.

In order to strengthen the effectiveness of the tort remedy for improper police activities, governmental immunity, where it still exists, should be eliminated, and legislation should be enacted providing that governmental subdivisions shall be fully liable for the actions of police officers who are acting within the scope of their employment. Neither tort liability nor costs attendant to the defense of a tort action should be imposed upon a police officer for wrongful conduct that has been ordered by a superior or is affirmatively authorized by police rules or regulations unless the conduct is a violation of the criminal law. Instead, liability and incidental costs and expenses in such cases should be borne by the governmental subdivision.

PART VI. POLICE UNIONS AND POLITICAL ACTIVITY

6.1 Collective interest of policemen and limitations thereon.

(a) Policemen have a proper collective interest in many aspects of their job such as wages, length of work week, and pension and other fringe benefits. To implement this interest, the right of collective bargaining should be recognized. However, due to the critical nature of the police function within government, legislation should provide that there shall be no right to strike. Effective alternatives to the right to strike should be made available as methods by which policemen can pursue their collective interest; and model procedures governing this important matter should be developed.

(b) The right of police to engage in collective action, however, should be subject to the following limitations:

(i) The preservation of governmental control over law enforcement policy-making requires that law enforcement policy not be the subject of collective bargaining.

(ii) The need to preserve local control over law enforcement and over the resolution of law enforcement policy issues requires that law enforcement policy not be determined by a police union or other police employee organization.

(iii) The maintenance of police in a position of objectivity in engaging in conflict resolution requires that police not belong to a union which also has non-police members who may become party to a labor dispute.

(iv) The maintenance of proper control by the police administrator over his department requires that collective action not interfere with the administrator's ability effectively to implement the policies and objectives of the agency.

6.2 Police officer contribution to police policy.

Policemen, as individuals and as a group, have a proper professional interest in and can make significant contributions to the formulation and continuing review of local law enforcement policies within individual communities. Methods should be developed by police administrators, therefore, to ensure effective participation in the policy-making process by all ranks including the patrolman who, because of his daily contact with operational problems and needs, has unique expertise to provide on law enforcement policy issues.

6.3   Political activity by policemen.

Policemen share the individual right to engage in political and other protected first amendment activity. However, police should not use their authority or the indicia of office, such as the uniform, for this purpose because of their possible coercive effect nor should they engage in collective political activity which compromises their ability to view objectively conflicts with which they may be called upon to deal.

PART VII.   ADEQUATE POLICE RESOURCES

7.1 Variety of police methods.

Police should be provided with effective methods for carrying out the full range of governmental responsibilities delegated to them. Adequate development of such methods requires:

(i) a variety of skills in individual police officers;

(ii) arrangements for police officers to make referrals to the various private and public services and resources available in the community, and the existence of sufficient resources to meet community needs; and

(iii) broad use of informal means of resolving conflict.

7.2 Important function of patrolmen.

The nature of police operations makes the patrolman a more important figure than is implied by his rank in the organization. He exercises broad discretion in a wide array of situations, each of which is potentially of great importance, under conditions that allow for little supervision and review. Even with the controls recommended in these standards, in the interest of developing a police profession as well as in the interest of improving the quality of police operations generally, the patrolman himself should understand the important and complex needs of policing in a free society and have a commitment to meeting those needs.

7.3 Recruitment.

In view of the broad diversity of the police role, experiments should be conducted which make use of different levels of entry for personnel and standards particularly relevant for the various levels. Such recruitment standards should be related directly to the requirements of various police tasks and should reflect a great degree of concern for such factors as judgmental ability, emotional stability, and sensitivity to the delicate and complicated nature of the police role in a democratic society.

7.4 Training.

Training programs should be designed, both in their content and in their format, so that the knowledge that is conveyed and the skills that are developed relate directly to the knowledge and skills that are required of a police officer on the job.

7.5 Recruitment of college graduates.

College graduates should be encouraged to apply for employment with police agencies. Individuals aspiring to careers in police agencies and those currently employed as police officers should be encouraged to advance their education at the college level. Communities should support further educational achievement on the part of police personnel by adopting such devices as educational incentive pay plans and by gradually instituting requirements for the completion of specified periods of college work as a prerequisite for initial appointment and for promotion. To increase the number of qualified personnel, police departments should initiate or expand police cadet or student intern programs which subsidize the education and training of potential police candidates.

7.6 Police education.

Educational programs that are developed primarily for police officers should be designed to provide an officer with a broad knowledge of human behavior, social problems, and the democratic process.

7.7 Importance of police administrator.

In addition to directing the day-to-day operations of his agency, the police administrator has the responsibility to exert leadership in seeking to improve the quality of police service and in seeking to solve community-wide problems of concern to the police. The position of police chief should be recognized as being among the most important and most demanding positions in the hierarchy of governmental officials.

7.8 Authority of police administrator.

A police administrator should be held fully responsible for the operations of his department. He should, therefore, be given full control over the management of the department; and legislatures, civil service commissions, and employee associations should not restrict the flexibility that is required for effective management.

7.9 Qualifications for police administrator.

In the screening of candidates to assume leadership roles in police agencies, special attention should be given to the sensitivity of the candidate to the peculiar needs of policing in a free society; to the degree to which the candidate is committed to meeting the challenge of achieving order within the restraints of the democratic process; to the capacity of the candidate to deal effectively with the complicated and important issues that police administrators must confront in the decision-making processes that affect police operations; and to the overall ability of the candidate to manage and direct the total resources of the agency. A community should employ the best qualified candidate without regard to his present location or departmental affiliation. Because of the fundamental importance of the objectives set forth in section 10.1, the police administrator should be given the necessary support, job security, and procedural safeguards to allow him to achieve these objectives.

7.10 Police department organization.

More flexible organizational arrangements should be substituted for the semi-military, monolithic form of organization of the police agency. Police administrators should experiment with a variety of organizational schemes, including those calling for substantial decentralization of police operations, the development of varying degrees of expertise in police officers so that specialized skills can be brought to bear on selected problems, and the substantial use of various forms of civilian professional assistance at the staff level.

7.11 Research.

A research capability should be developed within police agencies that will aid the police administrator in systematically formulating and evaluating police policies and procedures and that will equip the administrator to participate intelligently in the public discussion of important issues and problems involving the police.

7.12 Need for in-house police legal advisor.

Given the nature of the police function, police administrators should be provided with in-house police legal advisors who have the personal orientation and expertise necessary to equip them to play a major role in the planning and in the development and continual assessment of operating policies and training programs. The police legal advisor should be an attorney appointed by the police administrator or selected by him from an existing governmental unit.

7.13 Relationship of legal advisor to police administrator.

In view of the important and sensitive nature of his role, a police legal advisor or the head of a police legal unit should report directly to the police administrator. The relationship of a police legal advisor to a police department should be analogous to that of house counsel to a corporation. The police legal advisor should provide independent legal advice based upon his full understanding of the police function and his legal expertise, and should anticipate as well as react to legal problems and needs.

7.14 Priority tasks for legal advisor.

Among the range of tasks that may be performed by police legal advisors, priority should be given to assisting police administrators in:

(i) formulating the types of administrative policies that are recommended in these standards;

(ii) developing law-related training programs pertinent to increased understanding of the nature of the police function, of departmental policies, of judicial trends and their rationale, and of the significant role of the police in preserving democratic processes;

(iii) formulating legislative programs and participating in the legislative process;

(iv) maintaining liaison with other criminal justice and municipal agencies on matters primarily relating to policy formulation and policy review, and assessing the effectiveness of various agencies in responding to common legal problems; and

(v) developing liaison with members of the local bar and encouraging their participation in responding to legal problems and needs of the police agency.

PART VIII. POLICE PERFORMANCE IN THE CRIMINAL JUSTICE SYSTEM

8.1 Relationship of the criminal justice and other systems to the quality of police service.

(a) To the extent that police interact with other governmental systems such as the criminal justice, juvenile justice, and public and mental health systems, police effectiveness should be recognized as often largely dependent upon the performance of other agencies within these systems.

(b) For these standards to be of value in the criminal justice system, other parts of the system must operate, as a minimum, in such a manner that: (i) criminal cases are speedily processed; (ii) prosecutors and judges carefully review applications for warrants and use simplified procedures and otherwise provide easy access for impartial review of applications for warrants; (iii) the lower trial courts, especially in the larger cities, are conducted in a dignified and orderly manner, considerate of and respectful toward all the participants; and (iv) sentencing alternatives and correctional programs are as diversified and effective as possible.

PART IX. PUBLIC UNDERSTANDING AND SUPPORT

9.1 Contribution of legal profession.

Members of the legal profession should play an active role, individually and collectively, in developing local government policies relating to the police, in supporting needed changes in the form of police services, and in educating the total community on the importance and complexity of the police function. Among other things, each local bar association should appoint a special committee with which the police administrator can confer as to appropriate means of achieving objectives proposed in these standards.

9.2 Responsibility of educational institutions.

Educational institutions should undertake research and teaching programs which provide understanding of the complex social and behavioral problems which confront urban police.

9.3 The news media.

Public understanding of the police function is heavily dependent upon the coverage given by mass media to the newsworthy events in which the police are involved. Newspaper, radio, and television reporters assigned to reporting on police activities should have a sufficiently thorough understanding of the complexities of the police function to enable them to cover such events (as well as other matters that now go unreported) in a manner that promotes the public's understanding of the police role.

9.4 Openness by police.

Police should undertake to keep the community informed of the problems with which they must deal and the complexities that are involved in dealing with them effectively. Police agencies should cooperate with those who seek an understanding of police operations by affording opportunities for interested citizens to acquaint themselves with police operations and by providing access to the accumulation of knowledge and experience that the police possess.

PART X. EVALUATION

10.1 Measure of police effectiveness.

The effectiveness of the police should be measured generally in accordance with their ability to achieve the objectives and priorities selected for police service in individual communities. In addition, the effectiveness of police should be measured by their adherence to the principles set forth in section 2.4. This means that, among other things, police effectiveness should be measured in accordance with the extent to which they:

(i) safeguard freedom, preserve life and property, protect the constitutional rights of citizens and maintain respect for the rule of law by proper enforcement thereof, and, thereby, preserve democratic processes;

(ii) develop a reputation for fairness, civility, and integrity that wins the respect of all citizens, including minority or disadvantaged groups;

(iii) use only the amount of force reasonably necessary in responding to any given situation;

(iv) conform to rules of law and administrative rules and procedures, particularly those which specify proper standards of behavior in dealing with citizens;

(v) resolve individual and group conflict; and

(vi) refer those in need to community resources that have the capacity to provide needed assistance.

Traditional criteria such as the number of arrests that are made are inappropriate measures of the quality of performance of individual officers. Instead, police officers should be rewarded, in terms of status, compensation, and promotion, on the basis of criteria defined in this section which directly relate to the objectives, priorities, and essential principles of police service.

10.2 Responsibility of society and government generally.

The recommendations made in these standards require particular attention at the level of municipal government. Along with the recommendations relating specifically to police agencies, however, it should be recognized that police effectiveness is also dependent, in the long run, upon:

(i) the ability of government to maintain faith in democratic processes as the appropriate and effective means by which to achieve change and to redress individual grievances;

(ii) the willingness of society to devote resources to alleviating the despair of the culturally, socially, and economically deprived; and

(iii) the improvement of the criminal justice, juvenile justice, mental health, and public health systems as effective ways of dealing with a wide variety of social and behavioral problems, such as improvements in programs to provide assistance to citizens in need of help such as the person who is mentally ill, the chronic alcoholic, or the drug addict.

---

* The American Bar Association Project on Standards for Criminal Justice Approved Draft *Standards Relating to the Urban Police Function* is accompanied, in its full presentation, by substantial commentary. All readers are urged to obtain the full draft by writing to Circulation Department, American Bar Association, 1155 East 60th Street, Chicago, Illinois 60637.

INDEX

A general view of The Criminal Justice System

This chart seeks to present a simple yet comprehensive view
of the movement of cases through the criminal justice system.
Procedures in individual jurisdictions may vary from the pattern
shown here. The differing weights of line indicate the relative
volumes of cases disposed of at various points in the system,
but this is only suggestive since no nationwide data of this
sort exists.

Police   Prosecution   Courts

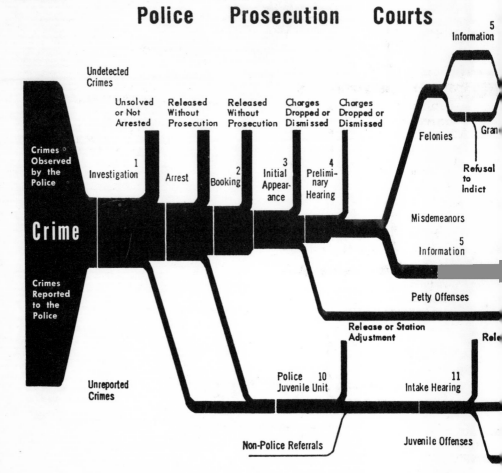

5
Information

Undetected
Crimes

Unsolved   Released   Released   Charges   Charges
or Not   Without   Without   Dropped or   Dropped or
Arrested   Prosecution   Prosecution   Dismissed   Dismissed

Felonies   Gran

Crimes
Observed   1   2   3   4   Refusal
by the   Investigation   Arrest   Booking   Initial   Prelimi-   to
Police   Appear-   nary   Indict
                                                  ance   Hearing

Crime   Misdemeanors

                                                             5
                                                             Information

Crimes   Petty Offenses
Reported
to the
Police   Release or Station
                                            Adjustment   Rele

                                            Police   10   11
Unreported   Juvenile Unit   Intake Hearing
Crimes

                        Non-Police Referrals   Juvenile Offenses

---

1 May continue until trial.

2 Administrative record of arrest. First
  step at which temporary release on
  bail may be available.

3 Before magistrate, commissioner, or
  justice of peace. Formal notice of
  charge, advice of rights. Bail set.
  Summary trials for petty offenses
  usually conducted here without
  further processing.

4 Preliminary testing of evidence
  against defendant. Charge may be
  reduced. No separate preliminary
  hearing for misdemeanors in some
  systems.

5 Charge filed by prosecutor on basis
  of information submitted by police c
  citizens. Alternative to grand jury
  indictment; often used in felonies,
  almost always in misdemeanors.

6 Reviews whether Government
  evidence sufficient to justify trial.
  Some States have no grand jury
  system; others seldom use it.